Ultimate Microsoft Excel Formula & Function Reference Guide:

500+ Practical Tips for Beginners to Experts including AI prompts for ChatGPT

Step-by-step examples, downloadable workbooks, and cheat sheets from AVERAGE to VLOOKUP and beyond

Table Of Contents

Use the table below as an alphabetical formula index. There is an index arranged by category at the rear of the book.

Table Of Contents 3

Introduction 18

Section One: Getting Started with Excel Formulas 20

- How To Use Excel Formulas Effectively 20
- Meet Your AI Companion 22

Section Two: Formula Categories 25

- Logical Functions 25
- Lookup & Reference Functions 27
- Text Functions 28
- Math & Trigonometry Functions 30
- Date & Time Functions 32
- Financial Functions 34
- Statistical Functions 36
- Information Functions 38
- Database Functions 40
- Cube Functions 42
- Engineering Functions 44
- Compatibility Functions 46
- Web Functions 47
- Add-in and Automation Functions 49

Section Three: Formula By Formula Reference 52

- ABS Function 53
- ACCRINT Function 54
- ACCRINTM Function 55
- ACOS Function 56
- ACOSH Function 57
- ACOT Function 58
- ACOTH Function 59
- AGGREGATE Function 60
- ADDRESS Function 61
- AMORDEGRC Function 62
- AMORLINC Function 63

AND Function 64
ARABIC Function 65
AREAS Function 66
ARRAYTOTEXT Function 67
ASC Function 68
ASIN Function 69
ASINH Function 70
ATAN Function 71
ATAN2 Function 72
ATANH Function 73
AVEDEV Function 74
AVERAGE Function 75
AVERAGEA Function 76
AVERAGEIF Function 77
AVERAGEIFS Function 78
BAHTTEXT Function 79
BASE Function 80
BESSELI Function 81
BESSELJ Function 82
BESSELK Function 83
BESSELY Function 84
BETADIST Function 85
BETA.DIST Function 86
BETAINV Function 87
BETA.INV Function 88
BIN2DEC Function 89
BIN2HEX Function 90
BIN2OCT Function 91
BINOMDIST Function 92
BINOM.DIST Function 93
BINOM.DIST.RANGE Function 94
BINOM.INV Function 95
BITAND Function 96
BITLSHIFT Function 97
BITOR Function 98
BITRSHIFT Function 99

Table Of Contents

BITXOR Function 100

BYCOL Function 101

BYROW Function 102

CALL Function 103

CEILING Function 104

CEILING.MATH Function 105

CEILING.PRECISE Function 106

CELL Function 107

CHAR Function 108

CHIDIST Function 109

CHIINV Function 110

CHITEST Function 111

CHISQ.DIST Function 112

CHISQ.DIST.RT Function 113

CHISQ.INV Function 114

CHISQ.INV.RT Function 115

CHISQ.TEST Function 116

CHOOSE Function 117

CHOOSECOLS Function 118

CHOOSEROWS Function 119

CLEAN Function 120

CODE Function 121

COLUMN Function 122

COLUMNS Function 123

COMBIN Function 124

COMBINA Function 125

COMPLEX Function 126

CONCAT Function 127

CONCATENATE Function 128

CONFIDENCE Function 129

CONFIDENCE.NORM Function 130

CONFIDENCE.T Function 131

CONVERT Function 132

CORREL Function 133

COS Function 134

COSH Function 135

COT Function......136
COTH Function......137
COUNT Function......138
COUNTA Function......139
COUNTBLANK Function......140
COUNTIF Function......141
COUNTIFS Function......142
COUPDAYBS Function......143
COUPDAYS Function......144
COUPDAYSNC Function......145
COUPNCD Function......146
COUPNUM Function......147
COUPPCD Function......148
COVAR Function......149
COVARIANCE.P Function......150
COVARIANCE.S Function......151
CRITBINOM Function......152
CSC Function......153
CSCH Function......154
CUBEKPIMEMBER Function......155
CUBEMEMBER Function......156
CUBEMEMBERPROPERTY Function......157
CUBERANKEDMEMBER Function......158
CUBESET Function......159
CUBESETCOUNT Function......160
CUBEVALUE Function......161
CUMIPMT Function......162
CUMPRINC Function......163
DATE Function......164
DATEDIF Function......165
DATEVALUE Function......166
DAVERAGE Function......167
DAY Function......168
DAYS Function......169
DAYS360 Function......170
DB Function......171

DBCS Function 172
DCOUNT Function 173
DCOUNTA Function 174
DDB Function 175
DEC2BIN Function 176
DEC2HEX Function 177
DEC2OCT Function 178
DECIMAL Function 179
DEGREES Function 180
DELTA Function 181
DEVSQ Function 182
DGET Function 183
DISC Function 184
DMAX Function 185
DMIN Function 186
DOLLAR Function 187
DOLLARDE Function 188
DOLLARFR Function 189
DPRODUCT Function 190
DROP Function 191
DSTDEV Function 192
DSTDEVP Function 193
DSUM Function 194
DURATION Function 195
DVAR Function 196
DVARP Function 197
EDATE Function 198
EFFECT Function 199
ENCODEURL Function 200
EOMONTH Function 201
ERF Function 202
ERF.PRECISE Function 203
ERFC Function 204
ERFC.PRECISE Function 205
ERROR.TYPE Function 206
EVEN Function 207

EXACT Function 208
EXP Function 209
EXPAND Function 210
EXPON.DIST Function 211
EXPONDIST Function 212
FACT Function 213
FACTDOUBLE Function 214
FALSE Function 215
F.DIST Function 216
FDIST Function 217
F.DIST.RT Function 218
FILTER Function 219
FILTERXML Function 220
FIND Function 221
FINDB Function 222
F.INV Function 223
F.INV.RT Function 224
FINV Function 225
FISHER Function 226
FISHERINV Function 227
FIXED Function 228
FLOOR Function 229
FLOOR.MATH Function 230
FLOOR.PRECISE Function 231
FORECAST Function 232
FORECAST.ETS Function 233
FORECAST.ETS.CONFINT Function 234
FORECAST.ETS.SEASONALITY Function 235
FORECAST.ETS.STAT Function 236
FORECAST.LINEAR Function 237
FORMULATEXT Function 238
FREQUENCY Function 239
F.TEST Function 240
FTEST Function 241
FV Function 242
FVSCHEDULE Function 243

GAMMA Function 244
GAMMA.DIST Function 245
GAMMADIST Function 246
GAMMA.INV Function 247
GAMMAINV Function 248
GAMMALN Function 249
GAMMALN.PRECISE Function 250
GAUSS Function 251
GCD Function 252
GEOMEAN Function 253
GESTEP Function 254
GETPIVOTDATA Function 255
GROWTH Function 256
HARMEAN Function 257
HEX2BIN Function 258
HEX2DEC Function 259
HEX2OCT Function 260
HLOOKUP Function 261
HOUR Function 262
HSTACK Function 263
HYPERLINK Function 264
HYPGEOM.DIST Function 265
HYPGEOMDIST Function 266
IF Function 267
IFERROR Function 268
IFNA Function 269
IFS Function 270
IMABS Function 271
IMAGE Function 272
IMAGINARY Function 273
IMARGUMENT Function 274
IMCONJUGATE Function 275
IMCOS Function 276
IMCOSH Function 277
IMCOT Function 278
IMCSC Function 279

IMCSCH Function 280
IMDIV Function 281
IMEXP Function 282
IMLN Function 283
IMLOG10 Function 284
IMLOG2 Function 285
IMPOWER Function 286
IMPRODUCT Function 287
IMREAL Function 288
IMSEC Function 289
IMSECH Function 290
IMSIN Function 291
IMSINH Function 292
IMSQRT Function 293
IMSUB Function 294
IMSUM Function 295
IMTAN Function 296
INDEX Function 297
INDIRECT Function 298
INFO Function 299
INT Function 300
INTERCEPT Function 301
INTRATE Function 302
IPMT Function 303
IRR Function 304
ISBLANK Function 305
ISERR Function 306
ISERROR Function 307
ISEVEN Function 308
ISFORMULA Function 309
ISLOGICAL Function 310
ISNA Function 311
ISNONTEXT Function 312
ISNUMBER Function 313
ISODD Function 314
ISOMITTED Function 315

ISREF Function ... 316
ISTEXT Function ... 317
ISO.CEILING Function ... 318
ISOWEEKNUM Function ... 319
ISPMT Function ... 320
KURT Function ... 321
LAMBDA Function ... 322
LARGE Function ... 323
LCM Function ... 324
LEFT Function ... 325
LEN Function ... 326
LET Function ... 327
LINEST Function ... 328
LN Function ... 329
LOG Function ... 330
LOG10 Function ... 331
LOGEST Function ... 332
LOGINV Function ... 333
LOGNORM.DIST Function ... 334
LOGNORMDIST Function ... 335
LOGNORM.INV Function ... 336
LOOKUP Function ... 337
LOWER Function ... 338
MAKEARRAY Function ... 339
MAP Function ... 340
MATCH Function ... 341
MAX Function ... 342
MAXA Function ... 343
MAXIFS Function ... 344
MDETERM Function ... 345
MDURATION Function ... 346
MEDIAN Function ... 347
MID Function ... 348
MIN Function ... 349
MINIFS Function ... 350
MINA Function ... 351

MINUTE Function 352
MINVERSE Function 353
MIRR Function 354
MMULT Function 355
MOD Function 356
MODE Function 357
MODE.MULT Function 358
MODE.SNGL Function 359
MONTH Function 360
MROUND Function 361
MULTINOMIAL Function 362
MUNIT Function 363
N Function 364
NA Function 365
NEGBINOM.DIST Function 366
NEGBINOMDIST Function 367
NETWORKDAYS Function 368
NETWORKDAYS.INTL Function 369
NOMINAL Function 370
NORM.DIST Function 371
NORMDIST Function 372
NORMINV Function 373
NORM.INV Function 374
NORM.S.DIST Function 375
NORMSDIST Function 376
NORM.S.INV Function 377
NORMSINV Function 378
NOT Function 379
NOW Function 380
NPER Function 381
NPV Function 382
NUMBERVALUE Function 383
OCT2BIN Function 384
OCT2DEC Function 385
OCT2HEX Function 386
ODD Function 387

ODDFPRICE Function 388
ODDFYIELD Function 389
ODDLPRICE Function 390
ODDLYIELD Function 391
OFFSET Function 392
OR Function 393
PDURATION Function 394
PEARSON Function 395
PERCENTILE.EXC Function 396
PERCENTILE.INC Function 397
PERCENTILE Function 398
PERCENTRANK.EXC Function 399
PERCENTRANK.INC Function 400
PERCENTRANK Function 401
PERMUT Function 402
PERMUTATIONA Function 403
PHI Function 404
PI Function 405
PMT Function 406
POISSON.DIST Function 407
POISSON Function 408
POWER Function 409
PPMT Function 410
PRICE Function 411
PRICEDISC Function 412
PRICEMAT Function 413
PROB Function 414
PRODUCT Function 415
PROPER Function 416
PV Function 417
QUARTILE Function 418
QUARTILE.EXC Function 419
QUARTILE.INC Function 420
QUOTIENT Function 421
RADIANS Function 422
RAND Function 423

RANDARRAY Function 424
RANDBETWEEN Function 425
RANK.AVG Function 426
RANK.EQ Function 427
RANK Function...428
RATE Function..429
RECEIVED Function..430
REDUCE Function 431
REGISTER.ID Function 432
REPLACE Function 433
REPT Function..434
RIGHT Function..435
ROMAN Function 436
ROUND Function..437
ROUNDDOWN Function 438
ROUNDUP Function 439
ROW Function..440
ROWS Function..441
RRI Function 442
RSQ Function...443
RTD Function 444
SCAN Function 445
SEARCH Function 446
SEC Function...447
SECH Function...448
SECOND Function..449
SEQUENCE Function..450
SERIESSUM Function 451
SHEET Function 452
SHEETS Function 453
SIGN Function...454
SIN Function 455
SINH Function...456
SKEW Function 457
SKEW.P Function...458
SLN Function 459

SLOPE Function 460
SMALL Function 461
SORT Function 462
SORTBY Function 463
SQRT Function 464
SQRTPI Function 465
STANDARDIZE Function 466
STOCKHISTORY Function 467
STDEV Function 468
STDEV.P Function 469
STDEV.S Function 470
STDEVA Function 471
STDEVP Function 472
STDEVPA Function 473
STEYX Function 474
SUBSTITUTE Function 475
SUBTOTAL Function 476
SUM Function 477
SUMIF Function 478
SUMIFS Function 479
SUMPRODUCT Function 480
SUMSQ Function 481
SUMX2MY2 Function 482
SUMX2PY2 Function 483
SUMXMY2 Function 484
SWITCH Function 485
SYD Function 486
T Function 487
TAN Function 488
TANH Function 489
TAKE Function 490
TBILLEQ Function 491
TBILLPRICE Function 492
TBILLYIELD Function 493
T.DIST Function 494
T.DIST.2T Function 495

T.DIST.RT Function 496
TDIST Function 497
TEXT Function 498
TEXTAFTER Function 499
TEXTBEFORE Function 500
TEXTJOIN Function 501
TEXTSPLIT Function 502
TIME Function 503
TIMEVALUE Function 504
T.INV Function 505
T.INV.2T Function 506
TINV Function 507
TOCOL Function 508
TOROW Function 509
TODAY Function 510
TRANSPOSE Function 511
TREND Function 512
TRIM Function 513
TRIMMEAN Function 514
TRUE Function 515
TRUNC Function 516
T.TEST Function 517
TTEST Function 518
TYPE Function 519
UNICHAR Function 520
UNICODE Function 521
UNIQUE Function 522
UPPER Function 523
VALUE Function 524
VALUETOTEXT Function 525
VAR Function 526
VAR.P Function 527
VAR.S Function 528
VARA Function 529
VARP Function 530
VARPA Function 531

VDB Function 532
VLOOKUP Function 533
VSTACK Function 534
WEBSERVICE Function 535
WEEKDAY Function 536
WEEKNUM Function 537
WEIBULL Function 538
WEIBULL.DIST Function 539
WORKDAY Function 540
WORKDAY.INTL Function 541
WRAPCOLS Function 542
WRAPROWS Function 543
XIRR Function 544
XLOOKUP Function 545
XMATCH Function 546
XNPV Function 547
XOR Function 548
YEAR Function 549
YEARFRAC Function 550
YIELD Function 551
YIELDDISC Function 552
YIELDMAT Function 553
Z.TEST Function 554
ZTEST Function 555
Section 4: Appendices 556
Appendix 1: Advanced Tips & Tricks Using an AI Companion 556
Appendix 2: Troubleshooting Guide with an AI Companion 558
Appendix 3: Shortcut Keys for Windows and Mac 560
Glossary 562
Formula Category Index 565

Introduction

Excel is one of the most powerful tools for analyzing, organizing, and managing data, yet its extensive library of formulas can be daunting to navigate. This book is designed to bridge that gap, serving as a **comprehensive and user-friendly reference** for Excel formulas. Whether you're a beginner seeking to grasp the fundamentals, an intermediate user looking to expand your toolkit, or an advanced user in need of a quick reference, this guide is tailored to meet your needs.

The goal of this book is simple: to make Excel formulas accessible to everyone. By focusing on **clarity, practicality, and usability**, we aim to demystify Excel's formula library and help readers confidently apply them to solve real-world problems.

- **Beginners:** Benefit from plain-language explanations, practical examples, and step-by-step guidance that build foundational knowledge.
- **Intermediate Users:** Expand your expertise with deeper insights into formula usage, category overviews, and more complex applications.
- **Advanced Users:** Use this book as a quick-reference guide to save time and streamline your workflows.

This book stands out through its unique approach to presenting Excel formulas:

- **One Page Per Formula:** Each formula is given a full page, ensuring explanations are clear, concise, and easy to follow. You'll find:
    - A **simple explanation** of what the formula does.
    - **Syntax breakdowns** for quick reference.
    - **Examples and challenges** to reinforce understanding.
    - **Tips on using each formula** in common workplace or study contexts.
- **Integration with Your AI Companion:**
    - Need extra help troubleshooting an error? Want to explore alternative ways to use a formula? **We introduce you to ChatGPT and how to use it for on-demand support**, making this book more than a static resource—it's an interactive tool for mastering Excel.
    - Specific tips on what to ask your AI Companion **to get the most from each formula**.
- **A downloadable workbook** showing the formula in action, available on GitHub for free. You can download a zip file containing the 500+ formulas demonstrated in this book at the following link:

  https://github.com/alexholloway/excelformulaguide

GitHub is a website that allows users to store, upload and version control source code and project documents – and is free to use. You may need to create a free account to access the files which are stored in a ZIP file.

From organizing data to building financial models, Excel formulas have countless applications across many different industries. This book ensures you can harness that power with confidence:

- **Real-World Applications:** Learn to apply formulas in everyday scenarios, from budgeting to project management, using practical examples.
- **Simplified Explanations:** Say goodbye to jargon—every formula is broken down into language that's easy to understand.
- **Intuitive Structure:** Navigate formulas by category or name with comprehensive indexes, designed for quick access and usability.

Finding What You Need

This book is designed to make locating and applying the right Excel formula as simple as possible. To find what you need, start by consulting the **Alphabetical Index** for a quick lookup by formula name, or explore the **Categorical Index** to browse formulas grouped by their purpose. Each category begins with an introduction, offering a brief overview of its scope, common use cases, and tips to help you decide which formulas best match your task.

If you're unsure where to start, use the **categories overview** to narrow down the type of formulas suited to your needs. For instance, if you're organizing data, explore **Lookup and Reference Functions**, or turn to **Logical Functions** for decision-making tasks. The structure ensures that formulas are presented with their practical applications in mind, making it easy to connect each formula to a real-world scenario.

For even more personalized assistance, utilize your **AI Companion** alongside this book. Whether you need help troubleshooting an error, adapting a formula to your specific data, or exploring alternative approaches, AI can provide on-demand support tailored to your requirements. By combining this dynamic tool with the book's structured content, you'll have everything you need to confidently navigate Excel's formula library and tackle your tasks with ease.

Section One: Getting Started with Excel Formulas

How To Use Excel Formulas Effectively

Excel formulas are powerful tools for solving problems, analyzing data, and streamlining workflows. To make the most of them, it's essential to understand not only how they work but also how to use them efficiently and effectively. This section provides foundational principles, practical strategies, and insights into overcoming common challenges.

Key Principles

- **Follow Best Practices:**
    - Always start by understanding the formula's purpose and syntax before applying it.
    - Use meaningful cell references, named ranges, or structured references to improve clarity and avoid errors.
    - Keep your formulas as simple as possible; complex calculations can often be broken into smaller, manageable steps.
- **Debugging and Troubleshooting:**
    - Use Excel's built-in tools like the **Evaluate Formula** feature or **Error Checking** to trace and resolve issues.
    - Employ error-handling functions, such as IFERROR or ISERROR, to manage unexpected results gracefully.
    - Test your formulas with small, controlled datasets before applying them to larger data.

The general principle here is "start small" and increase the complexity of a formula incrementally, ensuring each part works as expected and produces the correct result before incorporating additional calculation steps.

Real-World Applications

- **Combining Formulas for Practical Solutions:**
    - Learn to nest formulas (e.g., using IF inside VLOOKUP) to create dynamic and adaptive solutions. See "nesting" in Appendix 1 and explore more with your AI Companion.
    - Combine formulas like INDEX and MATCH for more flexible lookups or use FILTER and SORT to manage dynamic ranges in modern Excel.
- **Integrating Formulas with Excel Features:**
    - Pair formulas with tables for automatic expansion as your data grows.
    - Use formulas in conjunction with charts to create dynamic visualizations that update automatically as data changes.

  - Explore the use of array formulas to process multiple values simultaneously, especially in large datasets.

Most "real-world" deployments of excel formulas are intent on producing an analysis or dashboard that is repeated or refreshed – and so integrating formulas with charts and dynamically updating references is essential.

Common Challenges

- **Addressing Errors and Misunderstandings:**
  - Understand common Excel errors like #VALUE!, #REF!, and #DIV/0! to quickly identify and resolve underlying issues.
  - Ensure consistency in your datasets to avoid errors caused by mismatched data types or unexpected blank cells.
- **Improving Readability and Maintainability:**
  - Document your formulas with comments or adjacent text boxes to clarify their purpose for yourself and others.
  - Use formatting tools like color-coded cells or bold headers to distinguish input cells from calculated outputs.
  - Avoid overusing nested formulas; consider using helper columns to keep your calculations manageable and transparent.

Being able to troubleshoot errors and unexpected results as they occur is a key part of the Excel user's skillset. In the modern age, we also have access to AI tools to help us debug error codes.

Mastering these principles and strategies will not only improve your efficiency but also enhance your confidence in handling complex tasks with Excel. By combining a thoughtful approach with the tools and techniques outlined here, you'll unlock the full potential of Excel formulas and ensure your work is both accurate and impactful.

Meet Your AI Companion

Excel is a versatile tool, but even the most experienced users can encounter challenges with formulas. That's where your **AI Companion** comes in. This guide introduces you to leveraging AI tools to enhance your learning and problem-solving, making working with Excel formulas easier, faster, and more intuitive.

Introduction to Your AI Companion

We will use the term 'AI Companion' to refer to any generative AI tool capable of processing queries and providing human-like responses. Popular options include tools like Google Gemini, Microsoft Copilot, and ChatGPT. While the choice of tool is up to you, this book includes a step-by-step guide to help you get started with ChatGPT, currently the most widely used option.

What can your AI Companion do for you in Excel?

- **Simplify Formulas:** Break down complex formulas into easy-to-understand steps.
- **Troubleshoot Errors:** Quickly diagnose formula errors and suggest corrections.
- **Explore Variations:** Provide alternative formulas or methods to solve the same problem.
- **Tailor Solutions:** Help you design custom formulas based on specific requirements or data structures.

Practical Scenarios

Here are some examples of how you can work with your AI Companion:

1. **Generate Formula Alternatives:**
    - Situation: You're using SUMIF, but you want to calculate based on multiple conditions. Ask your AI Companion for suggestions like SUMPRODUCT or combining FILTER with SUM.
    - Outcome: You get clear examples of alternate approaches, allowing you to select the one best suited to your task.
2. **Troubleshoot Errors:**
    - Situation: A formula is returning #N/A. Describe the issue to your AI Companion and include relevant details about your data.
    - Outcome: The AI identifies that your lookup value isn't matching due to extra spaces and suggests using TRIM in your formula.
3. **Create Custom Solutions:**
    - Situation: You need a formula to calculate a weighted average with variable weights. Provide the specifics to your AI Companion.
    - Outcome: The AI provides the formula, explains its components, and offers suggestions for dynamic updates.

The above suggestions are a mere fraction of the possible ways in which AI tools can help you use Excel. Once you get started, you'll never look back.

Getting Started with ChatGPT: A Step-by-Step Guide

To begin using ChatGPT as your AI Companion for Excel, follow these steps to create an account and start exploring its features.

1. **Visit the ChatGPT Website:**
    - Open your preferred web browser and go to chat.openai.com.
2. **Create an Account:**
    - Click on the **Sign Up** button in the top right.
    - Enter your email address or use a single sign-on option (e.g., Google or Microsoft account).
3. **Verify Your Email:**
    - Check your email inbox for a verification message from OpenAI.
    - Click the verification link to activate your account.
4. **Complete the Registration:**
    - Provide basic information like your name and agree to OpenAI's terms and conditions.
5. **Choose a Plan:**
    - Start with the **Free Plan** to explore ChatGPT's basic features. This is all you need to get started and offers a great deal of value for no cost.
    - Optionally, upgrade to **ChatGPT Plus** for access to GPT-4, which offers enhanced capabilities and faster response times. You need only consider this once you start to reach the limits of the Free Plan.
6. **Log In to Your Account:**
    - After signing up, log in with your email and password or use your linked account.
7. **Set Up Your First Session:**
    - Familiarize yourself with the chat interface (below).
    - Click into the text box at the bottom of the screen, and you're ready to ask questions or seek assistance with Excel formulas.
8. **Mobile Access (Optional):**
    - Download the ChatGPT app for iOS or Android for on-the-go access.

The ChatGPT interface - a world of possibilities awaits:

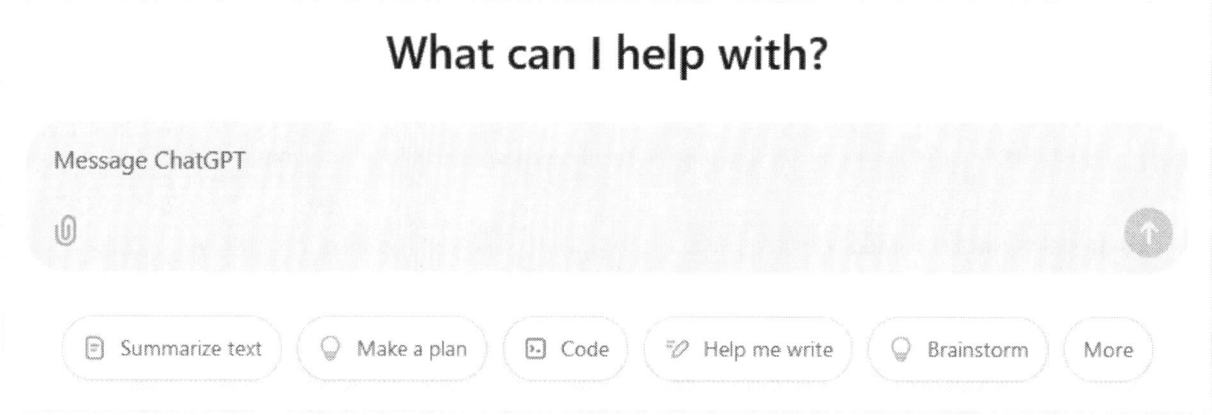

A Practical Example:

Unlike a web search, interaction with an AI Companion involves a much more natural, conversational style. To get started with ChatGPT, try having the following conversation:

1. **Frame Your Question Clearly:**
   - Example: "How can I use IF and VLOOKUP together to create a dynamic report?"
2. **Provide Context:**
   - Include details about your dataset and desired outcome for more precise answers.
3. **Analyze the Response:**
   - Review the explanation, test the suggested formula, and ask for refinements if needed.
4. **Follow Up:**
   - If necessary, request further examples or ask for step-by-step guidance to implement the solution effectively.

While this guide highlights OpenAI's ChatGPT due to its widespread use, these strategies can be applied to any AI Companion. In this book, 'ChatGPT' refers to OpenAI's conversational AI tool, while 'GPT' refers to the broader AI technology that powers ChatGPT and similar tools. Choose the tool that best suits you and explore its features to maximize your productivity. Your school or workplace may include subscriptions to other tools, which, in turn, may offer further integration with existing tools – so consider this too. Either way, by using your AI Companion alongside this book, you can tackle Excel challenges with confidence, streamline your work processes, and deepen your understanding of formulas.

Section Two: Formula Categories

Excel's formula library is vast, but grouping formulas into categories helps their more effective application. Categories make it easier to locate the right formula for your task, understand how formulas align with specific scenarios, and explore their versatility in real-world scenarios. Each category reflects a functional grouping based on the types of problems the formulas are designed to solve, from data analysis to financial modeling and beyond.

This section provides a high-level overview of each category and its practical uses. As you explore, you'll find example formulas, common use cases, and tips to make the most of each grouping.

The categories are presented not in **alphabetical order,** but by how **commonly encountered** they are.

Logical Functions

Introduction

Logical functions are among the most versatile tools in Excel, allowing users to perform conditional tests and automate decision-making processes within spreadsheets. These functions evaluate whether a given condition is true or false and return specific outputs based on the result.

- **What the category covers:** Functions like IF, AND, OR, and NOT for conditional logic, error handling, and decision-making.
- **Common use cases:** Checking for specific conditions (e.g., "Are sales greater than target?"), applying multi-condition logic, and automating decision-based outputs in financial models or reports.
- **When to use these formulas:** Whenever you need to evaluate conditions or incorporate logic into your calculations.

Examples of Logical Functions

- IF: Tests a condition and returns one value for TRUE and another for FALSE.
  Example: `=IF(A1>100, "Pass", "Fail")`
  Returns "Pass" if the value in A1 is greater than 100; otherwise, "Fail."
- AND: Returns TRUE if all conditions are TRUE; otherwise, FALSE.
  Example: `=AND(A1>50, B1<100)`
  Returns TRUE if A1 is greater than 50 and B1 is less than 100.
- OR: Returns TRUE if at least one condition is TRUE; otherwise, FALSE.
  Example: `=OR(A1="Yes", B1="No")`
  Returns TRUE if A1 contains "Yes" or B1 contains "No."
- NOT: Reverses the logical value.
  Example: `=NOT(A1>50)`
  Returns TRUE if A1 is NOT greater than 50.

- IFERROR: Returns a custom value if an error occurs; otherwise, it returns the result of the formula.
  Example: `=IFERROR(A1/B1, "Error")`
  Returns "Error" if B1 is zero or blank; otherwise, the division result.

- IFS: Evaluates multiple conditions in sequence and returns a result for the first TRUE condition.
  Example: `=IFS(A1>90, "A", A1>80, "B", A1>70, "C")`
  Returns "A" if A1 is greater than 90, "B" if greater than 80, etc.

Tips for Using Logical Functions

- **Combine functions for complex logic:** Use IF with AND/OR for advanced conditional logic.

  Example: `=IF(AND(A1>50, B1<100), "Accept", "Reject")`

- **Error-proofing:** Wrap formulas in IFERROR to handle potential calculation errors.

- **Best practices:** Use simple, clear conditions to keep formulas readable and maintainable.

Common Errors and Troubleshooting

- **Error**: #VALUE!
  Cause: Incorrect data type in a condition (e.g., comparing text to numbers).
  Solution: Check data types and ensure comparisons are logical.

- **Error**: Formula returns unexpected FALSE.
  Cause: Conditions are not met.
  Solution: Double-check all inputs and logic.

- **Error**: #NAME?
  Cause: Misspelled function name.
  Solution: Verify the function spelling.

Worked Example

Challenge: Write a formula to determine if a student passes or fails based on these criteria:

1. A score greater than or equal to 50 is a pass.
2. If the score is blank, return "No Score."
3. If the score is invalid, return "Error."

Solution:

```
=IF(A1="", "No Score", IF(A1>=50, "Pass", "Fail"))
```

Explore Further with GPT:
Ask GPT to help you create nested conditions or troubleshoot if your logic isn't working as expected!

Lookup & Reference Functions

Introduction

Lookup and reference functions are essential tools for organizing and retrieving data from structured datasets. These functions allow you to find specific values based on criteria, match data across tables, and build dynamic models that adapt to changes in data.

- **What the category covers:** Functions like VLOOKUP, HLOOKUP, INDEX, and XLOOKUP for locating, retrieving, and referencing data.
- **Common use cases:** Searching for information in tables, cross-referencing datasets, and dynamically pulling data into reports.
- **When to use these formulas:** Whenever you need to locate specific data or create dynamic models that respond to user input.

Examples of Lookup and Reference Functions

- **VLOOKUP:** Searches for a value in the first column of a range and returns a value in the same row from a specified column.
  - Example: `=VLOOKUP(1001, A2:D10, 3, FALSE)`
    - Searches for 1001 in column A and returns the value from the third column of the row where it's found.
- **HLOOKUP:** Similar to VLOOKUP, but searches for values in the first row of a range.
  - Example: `=HLOOKUP("Q1", A1:D5, 2, TRUE)`
    - Searches for "Q1" in the first row and returns the corresponding value from the second row.
- **INDEX:** Returns the value of a cell within a range based on its row and column numbers.
  - Example: `=INDEX(A2:D10, 4, 2)`
    - Returns the value from the fourth row and second column of the range.
- **MATCH:** Returns the relative position of a value in a range.
  - Example: `=MATCH(50, A1:A10, 0)`
    - Finds the position of 50 in the range A1:A10.
- **XLOOKUP:** A modern alternative to VLOOKUP and HLOOKUP, allowing for flexible lookups in any direction.
  - Example: `=XLOOKUP(1001, A2:A10, C2:C10)`
    - Searches for 1001 in column A and returns the corresponding value from column C.

Tips for Using Lookup and Reference Functions

- **Choose the Right Function:** Use XLOOKUP for modern, flexible solutions; fall back to INDEX and MATCH for advanced scenarios.
- **Error Handling:** Wrap lookup formulas in IFERROR to manage cases where the lookup value isn't found.

  - Example: `=IFERROR(XLOOKUP(1001, A2:A10, C2:C10), "Not Found")`
- **Dynamic Ranges:** Use named ranges or structured references with tables to keep formulas adaptable.

Common Errors and Troubleshooting

- **Error: #N/A:**
  - **Cause:** The lookup value isn't found in the specified range.
  - **Solution:** Ensure the lookup value exists and matches the data type of the range.
- **Error: #REF!:**
  - **Cause:** The specified column/row index exceeds the range size.
  - **Solution:** Check the range and column/row index specified in the formula.
- **Error: Formula returns incorrect values:**
  - **Cause:** Using approximate match (TRUE) instead of exact match (FALSE).
  - **Solution:** Use FALSE for exact matches unless approximate matches are intended.

Worked Example

Challenge: Create a formula to find a product name based on its ID and return "Not Found" if the ID doesn't exist.
Solution:
`=IFERROR(XLOOKUP(A1, B2:B10, C2:C10), "Not Found")`
This formula looks for the value in A1 within the range B2:B10 and returns the corresponding value from C2:C10, or "Not Found" if the ID isn't present.

Explore Further with GPT

Ask your AI Companion for help:

- Comparing XLOOKUP with INDEX and MATCH for complex lookups.
- Troubleshooting lookup errors in your formulas.
- Generating dynamic examples for specific data scenarios.

Text Functions

Introduction

Text functions in Excel are invaluable for cleaning, formatting, and manipulating text data. These functions allow you to extract, combine, or transform text, making them essential for tasks like data preparation, creating labels, or generating reports.

- **What the category covers:** Functions like CONCAT, LEFT, RIGHT, and TEXT for working with strings and textual data.

- **Common use cases:** Formatting names, extracting substrings, and standardizing text formats across datasets.
- **When to use these formulas:** Whenever you need to clean, organize, or modify text data in a structured way.

Examples of Text Functions

- **CONCAT:** Combines text strings from multiple cells into one.
  - Example: `=CONCAT(A1, " ", B1)`
    - Combines the contents of A1 and B1 with a space in between.
- **LEFT:** Extracts a specific number of characters from the start of a string.
  - Example: `=LEFT(A1, 5)`
    - Returns the first five characters from the text in A1.
- **RIGHT:** Extracts a specific number of characters from the end of a string.
  - Example: `=RIGHT(A1, 4)`
    - Returns the last four characters from the text in A1.
- **TEXT:** Formats numbers or dates as text in a specific format.
  - Example: `=TEXT(A1, "MM/DD/YYYY")`
    - Converts a date in A1 into the specified format.
- **LEN:** Returns the number of characters in a text string.
  - Example: `=LEN(A1)`
    - Returns the total number of characters (including spaces) in A1.
- **TRIM:** Removes all extra spaces from a text string, leaving only single spaces between words.
  - Example: `=TRIM(A1)`
    - Cleans up text with unnecessary spaces.

Tips for Using Text Functions

- **Combining Functions:** Pair LEFT, RIGHT, or MID with LEN to dynamically extract specific parts of a string.
  - Example: `=LEFT(A1, LEN(A1)-4)` removes the last four characters from A1.
- **Standardizing Formats:** Use TEXT to ensure numeric or date values appear consistently across reports.
- **Data Cleaning:** Apply TRIM and CLEAN to remove unwanted spaces or non-printable characters.

Common Errors and Troubleshooting

- **Error: Incorrect output when extracting substrings:**
  - **Cause:** The formula references incorrect character positions.

   - **Solution:** Verify the start position and character count in your LEFT, RIGHT, or MID formulas.
- **Error: Numbers not appearing as text:**
   - **Cause:** Misuse of the TEXT function.
   - **Solution:** Check the format string provided in the TEXT formula.
- **Error: Extra spaces causing inconsistent results:**
   - **Cause:** Hidden or trailing spaces in data.
   - **Solution:** Use TRIM to clean up text fields.

Worked Example

Challenge: Extract the first name from a full name in cell A1 (formatted as "John Doe").
Solution:
`=LEFT(A1, FIND(" ", A1)-1)`
This formula finds the first space in A1 and extracts all characters before it, returning "John."

Explore Further with GPT

Ask your AI Companion for help:

- Constructing complex text manipulation formulas for unique data formats.
- Troubleshooting formulas that return unexpected results.
- Automating text cleaning tasks with advanced combinations of functions.

Math & Trigonometry Functions

Introduction

Math and trigonometry functions are the backbone of calculations in Excel. From basic arithmetic to complex trigonometric operations, these functions enable precise computations and provide powerful tools for data analysis, financial modeling, and engineering tasks.

- **What the category covers:** Functions like SUM, ROUND, ABS, and SIN for mathematical operations, rounding, and trigonometric calculations.
- **Common use cases:** Aggregating data, performing financial projections, and solving geometric problems.
- **When to use these formulas:** Whenever you need to perform calculations or manipulate numeric data.

Examples of Math and Trigonometry Functions

- **SUM:** Adds up all the numbers in a specified range.
   - Example: `=SUM(A1:A10)`
      - Returns the total of the values in cells A1 through A10.

- **ROUND:** Rounds a number to a specified number of digits.
  - Example: `=ROUND(A1, 2)`
    - Rounds the value in A1 to two decimal places.
- **ABS:** Returns the absolute value of a number.
  - Example: `=ABS(A1)`
    - Converts negative values in A1 to positive values.
- **SIN:** Calculates the sine of an angle (in radians).
  - Example: `=SIN(PI()/2)`
    - Returns the sine of π/2 radians, which is 1.
- **MOD:** Returns the remainder after dividing one number by another.
  - Example: `=MOD(A1, 3)`
    - Divides the value in A1 by 3 and returns the remainder.
- **POWER:** Raises a number to a specified power.
  - Example: `=POWER(A1, 3)`
    - Returns the cube of the value in A1.

Tips for Using Math and Trigonometry Functions

- **Combine Functions for Complex Calculations:** Use MOD, ROUND, and POWER together to handle advanced scenarios.
  - Example: `=ROUND(POWER(A1, 2)/MOD(A1, 3), 2)` combines squaring, division, and rounding.
- **Understand Units:** For trigonometric functions, ensure angles are in radians. Use the RADIANS function to convert degrees to radians.
  - Example: `=SIN(RADIANS(30))` converts 30° to radians before calculating the sine.
- **Error Management:** Wrap calculations in IFERROR to handle invalid inputs gracefully.

Common Errors and Troubleshooting

- **Error: Formula returns #DIV/0!:**
  - **Cause:** Division by zero in formulas like MOD or direct division.
  - **Solution:** Add an IF condition to check for zero before dividing.
  - Example: `=IF(B1=0, "Error", A1/B1)`
- **Error: #VALUE! in calculations:**
  - **Cause:** Non-numeric values in input cells.
  - **Solution:** Use the ISNUMBER function to validate inputs.
  - Example: `=IF(ISNUMBER(A1), A1^2, "Invalid Input")`

- **Error: Unexpected results in trigonometric calculations:**
  - **Cause:** Input angles are in degrees instead of radians.
  - **Solution:** Convert degrees to radians using the RADIANS function.

Worked Example

Challenge: Calculate the total cost of items in a column, rounded to the nearest whole number, and display "Error" if any cells contain non-numeric values.
Solution:
`=IFERROR(ROUND(SUM(A1:A10), 0), "Error")`
This formula adds up the values in A1:A10, rounds the result to the nearest whole number, and displays "Error" if the input contains invalid data.

Explore Further with GPT

Ask your AI Companion for help:

- Building advanced financial models with combined math functions.
- Converting complex engineering formulas into Excel-ready calculations.
- Troubleshooting unexpected results in trigonometric functions.

Date & Time Functions

Introduction

Date and time functions in Excel are essential for managing and analyzing time-based data. These functions allow you to calculate durations, schedule events, and format dates and times for reporting purposes. They are widely used in project management, financial modeling, and data analysis.

- **What the category covers:** Functions like TODAY, NOW, DATE, and DAYS for working with dates and times.
- **Common use cases:** Calculating project timelines, generating schedules, and performing date-based analysis.
- **When to use these formulas:** Whenever your work involves tracking, calculating, or formatting dates and times.

Examples of Date and Time Functions

- **TODAY:** Returns the current date.
  - Example: `=TODAY()`
    - Automatically updates to show the current date.
- **NOW:** Returns the current date and time.
  - Example: `=NOW()`

        - Updates to the current date and time each time the worksheet recalculates.

- **DATE:** Creates a date from individual year, month, and day values.
    - Example: `=DATE(2025, 1, 16)`
        - Returns January 16, 2025.
- **DAYS:** Calculates the number of days between two dates.
    - Example: `=DAYS(B1, A1)`
        - Returns the number of days between the dates in B1 and A1.
- **EDATE:** Returns a date that is a specified number of months before or after a start date.
    - Example: `=EDATE(A1, 6)`
        - Returns the date six months after the date in A1.
- **TEXT:** Formats a date or time as text in a specific format.
    - Example: `=TEXT(A1, "MMMM DD, YYYY")`
        - Converts the date in A1 to a formatted string like "January 16, 2025."

Tips for Using Date and Time Functions

- **Dynamic Updates:** Use TODAY and NOW for automatically updating reports that require current date and time references.
- **Calculating Durations:** Pair DAYS, NETWORKDAYS, or DATEDIF with IF to create dynamic duration calculations, such as working days between two dates.
- **Custom Formats:** Use TEXT to display dates in specific formats for reports and dashboards.
    - Example: `=TEXT(A1, "MMM-YY")` for "Jan-25."

Common Errors and Troubleshooting

- **Error: Dates appear as numbers:**
    - **Cause:** Excel stores dates as serial numbers.
    - **Solution:** Format the cells as "Date" in the Number Format dropdown.
- **Error: #VALUE! when calculating durations:**
    - **Cause:** Non-date values or text strings are being used.
    - **Solution:** Validate input cells with ISDATE (via VBA) or ensure proper formatting.
- **Error: Incorrect date calculations:**
    - **Cause:** Misinterpreting Excel's date system (1900 vs. 1904).
    - **Solution:** Check workbook settings for the date system in use.

Worked Example

Challenge: Calculate the number of working days (excluding weekends) between two dates and return "Invalid Dates" if any input is not a valid date.

Solution:

`=IF(AND(ISNUMBER(A1), ISNUMBER(B1)), NETWORKDAYS(A1, B1), "Invalid Dates")`

This formula calculates the number of working days between the dates in A1 and B1, or displays "Invalid Dates" if the inputs are not valid.

Explore Further with GPT

Ask your AI Companion for help:

- Automating schedules and reminders using date functions.
- Troubleshooting date formats and system compatibility issues.
- Building dynamic models that adapt to changing time frames.

Financial Functions

Introduction

Financial functions in Excel are indispensable for business and financial modeling. These functions help calculate loan payments, investment returns, depreciation, and other monetary metrics, enabling users to make informed decisions about budgets, forecasts, and profitability.

- **What the category covers:** Functions like PMT, NPV, IRR, and FV for financial calculations, including loans, investments, and cash flow analysis.
- **Common use cases:** Determining loan payment schedules, assessing investment returns, and evaluating the time value of money.
- **When to use these formulas:** Whenever you need to analyze financial data or model monetary scenarios.

Examples of Financial Functions

- **PMT:** Calculates the payment for a loan based on constant payments and interest rates.
    - Example: `=PMT(5%/12, 60, -10000)`
        - Returns the monthly payment for a loan of $10,000 with a 5% annual interest rate over 60 months.
- **NPV:** Calculates the net present value of an investment based on a discount rate and future cash flows.
    - Example: `=NPV(10%, A2:A6)`
        - Returns the net present value of cash flows in A2:A6 at a 10% discount rate.
- **IRR:** Calculates the internal rate of return for a series of cash flows.
    - Example: `=IRR(A2:A6)`
        - Returns the IRR for cash flows listed in A2:A6.

- **FV:** Calculates the future value of an investment based on periodic, constant payments and a constant interest rate.
  - Example: `=FV(5%/12, 60, -200, -10000)`
    - Returns the future value of an investment with monthly contributions of $200, starting with $10,000, over 60 months at 5% annual interest.
- **SLN:** Calculates the straight-line depreciation of an asset over its useful life.
  - Example: `=SLN(10000, 1000, 5)`
    - Returns the annual depreciation for an asset with an initial cost of $10,000, a salvage value of $1,000, and a useful life of 5 years.

Tips for Using Financial Functions

- **Adjust for Periods:** Divide annual interest rates by the number of periods in a year for accurate calculations.
  - Example: Use 5%/12 for a monthly interest rate from an annual rate of 5%.
- **Combine Functions for Cash Flow Analysis:** Use NPV and IRR together to evaluate investment viability.
- **Error Handling:** Use IFERROR to display custom messages when formulas fail due to invalid inputs.
  - Example: `=IFERROR(PMT(5%/12, 60, -10000), "Check Inputs")`

Common Errors and Troubleshooting

- **Error: #VALUE! when calculating payments:**
  - **Cause:** Incorrect data types in inputs.
  - **Solution:** Ensure numeric values for rate, number of periods, and loan amount.
- **Error: #NUM! in IRR or NPV:**
  - **Cause:** Invalid or unrealistic cash flow series.
  - **Solution:** Check cash flows for logical consistency (e.g., at least one negative and one positive value).
- **Error: Unexpected results for FV or PMT:**
  - **Cause:** Incorrect signs for cash inflows (positive) and outflows (negative).
  - **Solution:** Follow Excel's conventions for positive and negative cash flows.

Worked Example

Challenge: Calculate the monthly payment for a car loan of $25,000 at a 6% annual interest rate over 5 years, and display "Invalid Inputs" if the loan amount or interest rate is missing.

Solution:

```
=IF(OR(A1<=0, B1<=0), "Invalid Inputs", PMT(B1/12, 60, -A1))
```

This formula checks for valid inputs in A1 (loan amount) and B1 (interest rate), then calculates the monthly payment.

Explore Further with GPT

Ask your AI Companion for help:

- Exploring scenarios with variable interest rates or payment schedules.
- Generating amortization schedules using Excel's built-in tools.
- Troubleshooting complex financial models with custom cash flow structures.

Statistical Functions

Introduction

Statistical functions in Excel are powerful tools for analyzing data distributions, summarizing datasets, and performing statistical tests. These functions are commonly used in research, business analytics, and quality control to uncover patterns, measure variability, and draw insights from data.

- **What the category covers:** Functions like AVERAGE, STDEV, PERCENTILE, and CORREL for statistical analysis and data summarization.
- **Common use cases:** Calculating averages, measuring variability, identifying data trends, and analyzing relationships between variables.
- **When to use these formulas:** Whenever you need to summarize, analyze, or test data distributions in Excel.

Examples of Statistical Functions

- **AVERAGE:** Calculates the mean of a range of numbers.
  - Example: `=AVERAGE(A1:A10)`
    - Returns the average value of the numbers in cells A1 through A10.
- **STDEV:** Calculates the standard deviation of a dataset, indicating variability.
  - Example: `=STDEV(A1:A10)`
    - Returns the standard deviation of the values in A1 through A10.
- **PERCENTILE:** Returns the k-th percentile of a dataset.
  - Example: `=PERCENTILE(A1:A10, 0.9)`
    - Returns the value at the 90th percentile of the dataset.
- **CORREL:** Calculates the correlation coefficient between two datasets.
  - Example: `=CORREL(A1:A10, B1:B10)`
    - Returns the correlation between the values in columns A and B.
- **COUNTIF:** Counts the number of cells in a range that meet a specified condition.

  - Example: `=COUNTIF(A1:A10, ">50")`
    - Counts how many values in A1:A10 are greater than 50.
- **MEDIAN:** Returns the median (middle value) of a dataset.
  - Example: `=MEDIAN(A1:A10)`
    - Returns the median of the numbers in A1 through A10.

Tips for Using Statistical Functions

- **Combine Functions for Deeper Insights:** Use AVERAGE, MEDIAN, and MODE together to understand the central tendency of your data.
  - Example: Calculate and compare the mean, median, and mode of a dataset for a comprehensive view.
- **Conditional Analysis:** Pair statistical functions with IF or COUNTIF to calculate metrics based on conditions.
  - Example: `=AVERAGEIF(A1:A10, ">50")` calculates the average of values greater than 50.
- **Data Validation:** Use ISNUMBER or COUNT to verify the integrity of your dataset before performing calculations.

Common Errors and Troubleshooting

- **Error: #DIV/0! when calculating averages:**
  - **Cause:** The range contains no numeric values.
  - **Solution:** Use IFERROR to handle empty or invalid ranges gracefully.
  - Example: `=IFERROR(AVERAGE(A1:A10), "No Data")`
- **Error: #VALUE! in functions like CORREL:**
  - **Cause:** Non-numeric data or mismatched ranges.
  - **Solution:** Ensure both ranges contain numeric data and have the same number of entries.
- **Error: Misleading results due to outliers:**

- **Cause**: Extreme values skewing the mean.
- **Solution**: Use MEDIAN or remove outliers with conditional logic.
- Example: `=AVERAGEIF(A1:A10, "<=100")` excludes values greater than 100.

Worked Example

Challenge: Identify the top 10% of values in a dataset and calculate their average, returning "No Data" if the range is empty.
Solution:
`=IFERROR(AVERAGEIF(A1:A10, ">"&PERCENTILE(A1:A10, 0.9)), "No Data")`

This formula calculates the average of values greater than the 90th percentile in A1:A10 or displays "No Data" if the range is invalid.

Explore Further with GPT

Ask your AI Companion for help:

- Automating advanced statistical tests like regression analysis or hypothesis testing.
- Visualizing data distributions with formulas and chart combinations.
- Troubleshooting complex statistical calculations for large datasets.

Information Functions

Introduction

Information functions in Excel provide insights about the content and structure of your data. These functions help verify data types, identify errors, and extract metadata, making them essential for data validation, troubleshooting, and cleaning.

- **What the category covers:** Functions like ISERROR, ISNUMBER, ISTEXT, and INFO for checking data types, error states, and system details.
- **Common use cases:** Validating datasets, creating dynamic error-handling formulas, and troubleshooting issues in large workbooks.
- **When to use these formulas:** Whenever you need to verify or analyze the characteristics of your data.

Examples of Information Functions

- **ISERROR:** Returns TRUE if a value or formula results in an error.
  - Example: `=ISERROR(A1/B1)`
    - Returns TRUE if dividing A1 by B1 results in an error, such as division by zero.
- **ISNUMBER:** Checks if a value is numeric.
  - Example: `=ISNUMBER(A1)`
    - Returns TRUE if A1 contains a number.
- **ISTEXT:** Checks if a value is text.
  - Example: `=ISTEXT(A1)`
    - Returns TRUE if A1 contains text.
- **IFERROR:** Returns a custom value if a formula results in an error; otherwise, returns the formula result.
  - Example: `=IFERROR(A1/B1, "Invalid")`
    - Divides A1 by B1 or returns "Invalid" if an error occurs.
- **INFO:** Returns information about the current operating environment.

- Example: `=INFO("directory")`
  - Returns the current directory or folder path.
- **ERROR.TYPE:** Returns a number corresponding to the type of error in a referenced cell.
  - Example: `=ERROR.TYPE(A1)`
    - Returns a code representing the type of error in A1.

Tips for Using Information Functions

- **Error Handling:** Combine ISERROR or IFERROR with other formulas to create robust calculations.
  - Example: `=IF(ISERROR(A1/B1), "Error Detected", A1/B1)` provides a custom message for errors.
- **Data Validation:** Use ISNUMBER or ISTEXT in conditional formatting to highlight cells that meet specific criteria.
- **Dynamic Logic:** Pair information functions with IF to guide decision-making based on data characteristics.
  - Example: `=IF(ISNUMBER(A1), "Valid", "Invalid")`

Common Errors and Troubleshooting

- **Error: Incorrect TRUE or FALSE results:**
  - **Cause:** Misinterpreting how information functions evaluate data.
  - **Solution:** Test a variety of inputs to confirm the function's behavior.
  - Example: ISNUMBER("") returns FALSE because a blank cell isn't a number.
- **Error: Unexpected behavior with IFERROR:**
  - **Cause:** IFERROR masks all errors, including those you might want to highlight.
  - **Solution:** Use ISERROR to test and manage specific errors instead of blanket error-handling.
- **Error: INFO returns unsupported details:**
  - **Cause:** Some options for INFO are system-dependent and may not work in all environments.
  - **Solution:** Use other methods for gathering system information if needed.

Worked Example

Challenge: Write a formula to check if a value in A1 is a valid number, and if not, display "Not a Number."
Solution:
`=IF(ISNUMBER(A1), A1, "Not a Number")`
This formula checks if A1 contains a numeric value and either displays the value or the text "Not a Number."

Explore Further with GPT

Ask your AI Companion for help:

- Building advanced data validation rules using IS functions.
- Designing error-checking workflows for large datasets.
- Exploring combinations of information functions for troubleshooting.

Database Functions

Introduction

Database functions in Excel are designed to work with structured datasets that resemble database tables. These functions allow you to perform calculations, filtering, and aggregations based on specific criteria, making them ideal for data analysis and reporting.

- **What the category covers:** Functions like DSUM, DCOUNT, DAVERAGE, and DGET for performing calculations on data that meets specified conditions.
- **Common use cases:** Summing sales for a specific region, counting records that meet a criterion, and extracting targeted data from large tables.
- **When to use these formulas:** Whenever you need to analyze structured data with complex criteria or perform database-like queries in Excel.

Examples of Database Functions

- **DSUM:** Adds up the values in a field (column) of a database that match specified criteria.
  - Example: `=DSUM(A1:D10, "Sales", F1:F2)`
    - Sums the "Sales" column in A1:D10 where the criteria in F1:F2 are met.
- **DCOUNT:** Counts the number of records in a database that match the specified criteria.
  - Example: `=DCOUNT(A1:D10, "Region", F1:F2)`
    - Counts rows in A1:D10 where the "Region" column matches the criteria in F1:F2.
- **DAVERAGE:** Calculates the average of a field in a database that meets specified criteria.
  - Example: `=DAVERAGE(A1:D10, "Profit", F1:F2)`
    - Returns the average of the "Profit" column in A1:D10 that meets the criteria in F1:F2.
- **DGET:** Extracts a single value from a field in a database that matches the specified criteria.
  - Example: `=DGET(A1:D10, "Sales", F1:F2)`
    - Returns the value from the "Sales" column in A1:D10 that matches the criteria in F1:F2. If multiple records match, it results in an error.
- **DMAX and DMIN:** Return the maximum or minimum value from a field that meets criteria.
  - Example: `=DMAX(A1:D10, "Profit", F1:F2)`
    - Returns the highest "Profit" value meeting the criteria in F1:F2.

Tips for Using Database Functions

- **Set Up Criteria Ranges Correctly:** Ensure the criteria range includes column headers identical to the dataset and logical conditions below them.
    - Example:

      Criteria Range:

Region	Sales
East	>1000

- **Use Named Ranges for Readability:** Name your dataset and criteria ranges for easier reference in formulas.
    - Example: `=DSUM(SalesData, "Profit", CriteriaRange)`
- **Combine with Filters:** Use Excel's built-in filters or slicers with database functions for more dynamic analysis.

Common Errors and Troubleshooting

- **Error: #VALUE!:**
    - **Cause:** Incorrect field name or invalid criteria range.
    - **Solution:** Double-check the field name in your formula and ensure the criteria range matches the dataset's structure.
- **Error: #NUM! in DGET:**
    - **Cause:** Multiple records match the criteria.
    - **Solution:** Adjust your criteria to ensure it returns a single unique record.
- **Error: Unexpected results with numeric criteria:**
    - **Cause:** Numeric conditions (e.g., >1000) are misinterpreted.
    - **Solution:** Ensure conditions are entered correctly and placed under the appropriate column header.

Worked Example

Challenge: Calculate the total sales for products sold in the "East" region where sales exceed 1,000.
Solution:

Criteria Range:

Region	Sales
East	>1000

Formula:
`=DSUM(A1:D20, "Sales", F1:G2)`
This formula sums the "Sales" column in A1:D20 that meets the criteria in F1:G2.

Explore Further with GPT

Ask your AI Companion for help:

- Setting up complex criteria ranges for advanced filtering.
- Comparing DSUM with modern alternatives like SUMIFS for dynamic calculations.
- Automating database analysis using named ranges and dynamic criteria.

Cube Functions

Introduction

Cube functions are designed for working with data from OLAP (Online Analytical Processing) cubes or data models connected to Excel. These functions allow users to query and retrieve specific data points, aggregates, and metadata from multidimensional datasets.

- **What the category covers:** Functions like CUBEVALUE, CUBEMEMBER, and CUBERANKEDMEMBER for retrieving and analyzing data from OLAP cubes or Power Pivot data models.
- **Common use cases:** Generating dynamic reports, querying data models, and summarizing multidimensional data for analysis.
- **When to use these formulas:** Whenever working with connected data sources like SQL Server Analysis Services (SSAS) or Power Pivot data models in Excel.

Examples of Cube Functions

- **CUBEVALUE:** Returns the value of a measure from the cube.
  - Example: `=CUBEVALUE("ConnectionName", "[Date].[Year].&[2025]", "[Measures].[Sales Amount]")`
    - Retrieves the total sales amount for the year 2025.
- **CUBEMEMBER:** Returns a member or tuple from the cube.
  - Example: `=CUBEMEMBER("ConnectionName", "[Date].[Year].&[2025]")`
    - Returns the member representing the year 2025.
- **CUBERANKEDMEMBER:** Returns a ranked member from a set of members.
  - Example: `=CUBERANKEDMEMBER("ConnectionName", "[Product].[Category].[All].Children", 1)`
    - Retrieves the top-ranked category based on the specified set.
- **CUBESET:** Defines a calculated set of members or tuples by sending a query to the cube.

  - Example: =CUBESET("ConnectionName", "[Product].[Category].[All].Children", "Top Categories")
    - Creates a set of all product categories.
- **CUBESETCOUNT:** Returns the count of items in a set.
  - Example: =CUBESETCOUNT("ConnectionName", "[Product].[Category].[All].Children")
    - Counts the number of product categories.

Tips for Using Cube Functions

- **Establish Connections First:** Ensure your workbook is connected to a data source before using cube functions.
  - Example: Use Power Pivot to create a data model connected to your source.
- **Leverage Named Sets:** Create named sets in your cube or data model to simplify queries in Excel.
- **Error Management:** Use IFERROR to handle scenarios where cube queries return no data.
  - Example: =IFERROR(CUBEVALUE("ConnectionName", "[Measures].[Sales Amount]"), "No Data")
- **Combine with Slicers:** Use slicers to dynamically filter data in PivotTables or cube functions for interactive reports.

Common Errors and Troubleshooting

- **Error: #N/A:**
  - **Cause:** The specified member or measure does not exist in the cube.
  - **Solution:** Verify the member names, measures, and hierarchy in your query.
- **Error: #NAME?:**
  - **Cause:** The connection name is invalid or missing.
  - **Solution:** Ensure the connection name matches the one established in the workbook.
- **Error: Slow performance with large datasets:**
  - **Cause:** Complex queries or large data models.
  - **Solution:** Optimize cube queries by pre-defining sets or using simpler filters.

Worked Example

Challenge: Retrieve the total sales for the "Beverages" category in 2025 from an OLAP cube.
Solution:
=CUBEVALUE("ConnectionName", "[Date].[Year].&[2025]", "[Product].[Category].&[Beverages]", "[Measures].[Sales Amount]")
This formula retrieves the total sales amount for beverages in 2025 from the connected cube.

Explore Further with GPT

Ask your AI Companion for help:

- Writing complex CUBESET or CUBEVALUE formulas for custom reports.
- Understanding how cube hierarchies and measures interact in Excel.
- Troubleshooting connection or query errors in OLAP-based reports.

Engineering Functions

Introduction

Engineering functions in Excel are tailored for scientific, engineering, and technical applications. These functions enable calculations involving complex numbers, unit conversions, and advanced mathematical operations, making them essential for engineers, scientists, and technical analysts.

- **What the category covers:** Functions like CONVERT, COMPLEX, BIN2DEC, and IMSUM for unit conversions, complex number operations, and binary calculations.
- **Common use cases:** Converting between measurement units, performing calculations with complex numbers, and analyzing binary or hexadecimal data.
- **When to use these formulas:** Whenever working with scientific datasets, performing unit-based analyses, or conducting binary and engineering calculations.

Examples of Engineering Functions

- **CONVERT:** Converts a number from one unit of measurement to another.
  - Example: `=CONVERT(10, "km", "mi")`
    - Converts 10 kilometers to miles.
- **COMPLEX:** Converts real and imaginary coefficients into a complex number.
  - Example: `=COMPLEX(3, 4)`
    - Returns "3+4i" as a complex number.
- **BIN2DEC:** Converts a binary number to a decimal number.
  - Example: `=BIN2DEC("1010")`
    - Converts the binary number 1010 to decimal 10.
- **IMSUM:** Returns the sum of two or more complex numbers.
  - Example: `=IMSUM("3+4i", "1+2i")`
    - Adds two complex numbers and returns "4+6i."
- **DEC2HEX:** Converts a decimal number to a hexadecimal number.
  - Example: `=DEC2HEX(255)`

        - Converts the decimal number 255 to hexadecimal "FF."

- **GCD:** Returns the greatest common divisor of two or more integers.
    - Example: `=GCD(28, 35)`
        - Returns 7, the greatest common divisor of 28 and 35.

Tips for Using Engineering Functions

- **Unit Consistency:** When using CONVERT, ensure you use correct and compatible unit abbreviations.
    - Example: "kg" for kilograms, "lbm" for pounds mass.
- **Complex Numbers:** Use functions like IMSUM, IMPRODUCT, and IMABS to perform advanced operations on complex numbers.
    - Example: `=IMPRODUCT("3+4i", "2-3i")` multiplies two complex numbers.
- **Binary and Hexadecimal Calculations:** Use functions like BIN2DEC and DEC2BIN to switch between number systems for technical analyses.

Common Errors and Troubleshooting

- **Error: #N/A in CONVERT:**
    - **Cause:** Invalid or incompatible unit abbreviations.
    - **Solution:** Check Excel's supported unit codes and ensure they match.
- **Error: #VALUE! in complex number functions:**
    - **Cause:** Incorrectly formatted complex numbers.
    - **Solution:** Verify that complex numbers are entered in the format "a+bi" or "a-bi."
- **Error: Unexpected results with binary functions:**
    - **Cause:** Input exceeds the allowable range for binary conversion.
    - **Solution:** Ensure binary numbers are within Excel's supported range (up to 10 bits for BIN2DEC).

Worked Example

Challenge: Convert 100 kilograms to pounds and calculate the sum of "3+4i" and "2-3i" complex numbers.
Solution:

1. **Unit Conversion:**
   `=CONVERT(100, "kg", "lbm")`
   Converts 100 kilograms to pounds.
2. **Complex Number Calculation:**
   `=IMSUM("3+4i", "2-3i")`
   Returns "5+1i," the sum of the two complex numbers.

Explore Further with GPT

Ask your AI Companion for help:

- Setting up advanced unit conversions using CONVERT.
- Performing complex number calculations for specific engineering tasks.
- Understanding practical applications of binary and hexadecimal functions.

Compatibility Functions

Introduction

Compatibility functions in Excel provide backward compatibility with older versions of the software. While many of these functions have been replaced by modern equivalents, they are still useful for maintaining legacy workbooks or collaborating with users of older Excel versions.

- **What the category covers:** Functions like BETADIST, CHIDIST, and LOGNORMDIST for legacy statistical calculations and compatibility with older Excel versions.
- **Common use cases:** Ensuring compatibility with older Excel files and maintaining functionality in legacy models.
- **When to use these formulas:** When working with files created in older versions of Excel or using deprecated statistical functions.

Examples of Compatibility Functions

- **BETADIST:** Returns the beta cumulative distribution function.
  - Example: `=BETADIST(0.5, 2, 3)`
    - Calculates the beta distribution for the specified parameters.
- **CHIDIST:** Returns the one-tailed probability of the chi-squared distribution.
  - Example: =`CHIDIST(3.84, 1)`
    - Returns the probability value for a chi-squared statistic of 3.84 with 1 degree of freedom.
- **LOGNORMDIST:** Returns the cumulative lognormal distribution.
  - Example: `=LOGNORMDIST(4, 3.5, 1.2)`
    - Returns the lognormal distribution probability for the given parameters.
- **TTEST:** Returns the probability associated with a Student's t-test.
  - Example: `=TTEST(A1:A10, B1:B10, 2, 1)`
    - Returns the t-test probability comparing two datasets.
- **ZTEST:** Returns the one-tailed probability value of a z-test.
  - Example: `=ZTEST(A1:A10, 3)`
    - Returns the z-test probability for a sample in A1:A10 with a hypothesized mean of 3.

Tips for Using Compatibility Functions

- **Use Modern Equivalents When Possible:** Most compatibility functions have updated counterparts.
  - Example: Use BETA.DIST instead of BETADIST or CHISQ.DIST.RT instead of CHIDIST.
- **Maintain Legacy Files:** Use these functions when maintaining older workbooks to avoid breaking calculations.
- **Document Deprecation:** Include comments or notes in your workbook to highlight that compatibility functions may not be supported in future Excel versions.

Common Errors and Troubleshooting

- **Error: #VALUE!:**
  - **Cause:** Incorrect input values or unsupported data types.
  - **Solution:** Verify that all input parameters match the required format for the function.
- **Error: Function unavailable in the current version of Excel:**
  - **Cause:** Compatibility functions are deprecated and may not be available in all installations.
  - **Solution:** Switch to modern equivalents where possible.
- **Error: Unexpected results in statistical calculations:**
  - **Cause:** Rounding differences between compatibility and modern functions.
  - **Solution:** Test outputs using modern equivalents to ensure accuracy.

Worked Example

Challenge: Calculate the one-tailed probability of a chi-squared distribution for a statistic of 5.99 with 2 degrees of freedom using a legacy function.

Solution:

```
=CHIDIST(5.99, 2)
```

This formula returns the one-tailed probability for the given chi-squared statistic.

Explore Further with GPT

Ask your AI Companion for help:

- Identifying modern equivalents for compatibility functions.
- Converting legacy models to use updated functions for better performance and support.
- Troubleshooting compatibility issues in older Excel files.

Web Functions

Introduction

Web functions in Excel are increasingly important for integrating data from online sources directly into your workbooks. These functions allow users to retrieve, parse, and manipulate web-based data, enabling dynamic connections to APIs, web services, and XML or JSON data feeds.

- **What the category covers:** Functions like WEBSERVICE and FILTERXML for accessing and processing web-based data.
- **Common use cases:** Connecting to APIs, importing live data feeds, and extracting specific information from web responses.
- **When to use these formulas:** Whenever you need to fetch, parse, or analyze data from online sources directly in Excel.

Examples of Web Functions

- **WEBSERVICE:** Retrieves data from a web service URL.
  - Example: `=WEBSERVICE("https://api.weather.com/temp")`
    - Fetches data from the specified API endpoint.
- **ENCODEURL:** Encodes text to make it safe for use in a URL.
  - Example: `=ENCODEURL("London weather")`
    - Converts "London weather" into a URL-safe string.
- **FILTERXML:** Parses XML content and extracts specific data using XPath.
  - Example: `=FILTERXML(A1, "//Temperature")`
    - Extracts temperature data from the XML response in A1.
- **HYPERLINK:** Creates a clickable hyperlink in a cell.
  - Example: `=HYPERLINK("https://www.example.com", "Visit Example")`
    - Creates a link to the specified URL with the display text "Visit Example."

Tips for Using Web Functions

- **Ensure Connectivity:** Make sure your workbook has internet access when using functions like WEBSERVICE and FILTERXML.
- **API Integration:** Pair WEBSERVICE with dynamic parameters using CONCAT or TEXTJOIN to build flexible API queries.
  - Example: `=WEBSERVICE("https://api.example.com/data?query=" & ENCODEURL(A1))`
- **Use Error Handling:** Wrap web functions in IFERROR to handle connectivity issues or invalid URLs gracefully.
  - Example: `=IFERROR(WEBSERVICE(A1), "Error: Unable to Retrieve Data")`

Common Errors and Troubleshooting

- **Error: #VALUE!:**

  - **Cause:** The WEBSERVICE function returns an invalid response.
  - **Solution:** Check the URL for correctness and ensure it returns valid XML or JSON data.
- **Error: #GETTING_DATA:**
  - **Cause:** Data retrieval is in progress but taking longer than expected.
  - **Solution:** Wait for the retrieval to complete or check your internet connection.
- **Error: Empty output from FILTERXML:**
  - **Cause:** Incorrect or unsupported XPath query.
  - **Solution:** Test the XPath query in a separate XML tool to ensure accuracy.

Worked Example

Challenge: Fetch weather data for "London" using a mock API and extract the temperature from the XML response.
Solution:

1. Use ENCODEURL to build the API query:
   `=ENCODEURL("London")`
2. Fetch data with WEBSERVICE:
   `=WEBSERVICE("https://api.example.com/weather?location=" & A1)`
3. Extract temperature using FILTERXML:
   `=FILTERXML(B1, "//Temperature")`

Explore Further with GPT

Ask your AI Companion for help:

- Constructing API queries for web functions.
- Parsing complex XML or JSON responses using FILTERXML.
- Automating web data retrieval workflows for real-time updates.

Add-in & Automation Functions

Introduction

The CALL and REGISTER.ID functions are specialized tools in Excel designed to interact with external libraries and automate complex workflows. They enable advanced users to call external procedures and manage function registrations dynamically, providing robust support for custom automation tasks.

- **What the category covers:** Functions like CALL and REGISTER.ID for interacting with external Dynamic Link Libraries (DLLs) and automating function registration.
- **Common use cases:** Calling external procedures, registering custom functions, and creating advanced automation scripts.

- **When to use these formulas:** When working with custom DLLs, external applications, or advanced Excel automation scenarios.

Examples of Add-In and Automation Functions

- **CALL:** Executes a procedure from a DLL or code resource.
  - Example: `=CALL("LibraryName", "FunctionName", "ReturnType", Argument1, Argument2)`
    - Calls a procedure named "FunctionName" in "LibraryName" with specified arguments and return type.
- **REGISTER.ID:** Retrieves the registration ID of a previously registered DLL or code resource.
  - Example: `=REGISTER.ID("LibraryName", "FunctionName")`
    - Returns the registration ID for the specified function in the given library.

Tips for Using Add-In and Automation Functions

- **Ensure DLL Accessibility:** Confirm that the required DLLs are available and correctly referenced in Excel before using CALL or REGISTER.ID.
- **Secure Automation:** Be cautious when using these functions to interact with external code. Ensure all DLLs are trusted and secured.
- **Combine with VBA:** For more complex workflows, pair these functions with VBA macros for greater flexibility and readability.

Common Errors and Troubleshooting

- **Error: #VALUE!:**
  - **Cause:** Incorrect DLL name, function name, or argument type.
  - **Solution:** Verify that all inputs match the specifications of the DLL and its functions.
- **Error: #NAME?:**
  - **Cause:** The DLL or code resource is not registered or accessible.
  - **Solution:** Use REGISTER.ID to ensure the resource is registered and available.
- **Error: Security concerns with external libraries:**
  - **Cause:** Using unverified or unsafe DLLs.
  - **Solution:** Only use trusted DLLs and validate their functionality before deployment.

Worked Example

Challenge: Call a procedure from a DLL named "MyLibrary" to calculate a custom function and ensure proper registration.
Solution:

1. Register the function: `=REGISTER.ID("MyLibrary", "CustomFunction")`
2. Call the function with arguments: `=CALL("MyLibrary", "CustomFunction", "B", 5, 10)` This registers and calls "CustomFunction" from the DLL "MyLibrary," passing 5 and 10 as arguments.

Explore Further with GPT

Ask your AI Companion for help:

- Understanding how to register and call functions from external libraries in Excel.
- Automating workflows using CALL and REGISTER.ID functions paired with VBA.
- Troubleshooting errors related to DLL accessibility or function registration

Section Three: Formula By Formula Reference

Welcome to the heart of this guide: the comprehensive formula reference section. Here, each formula is presented across a dedicated double-page spread, designed to offer a clear and complete understanding of its purpose, syntax, and practical applications.

Each entry includes:

- **A simple explanation** to demystify the formula and its use.
- **Syntax breakdowns** for quick reference.
- **Practical examples** with real-world scenarios to show the formula in action.
- **A challenge problem** to help reinforce your learning.

Whether you're exploring Excel for the first time or looking to deepen your expertise, this section is your go-to resource for mastering Excel formulas. Dive in, and let's unlock the power of Excel together, one formula at a time.

ABS Function

Math & Trigonometry Functions

Introduction

The ABS function is a mathematical function that returns the absolute value of a number. The absolute value is the distance of a number from zero, regardless of its sign (positive or negative).

Simple explanation: Removes the sign of a number to return its magnitude.

Common use cases: Converting negative values to positive in financial models, data analysis, or error measurement.

When to use this function: Whenever you need to standardize numbers to positive values for calculations or comparisons.

Syntax

```
=ABS(number)
```

- **number**: The numeric value or cell reference for which you want the absolute value.

Worked Example

Challenge: Calculate the absolute difference between two monthly sales figures to evaluate variability.

- Monthly sales are stored in:
  - Cell A2: -350
  - Cell A3: 500

Formula:

```
=ABS(A2 - A3)
```

	A	B	C
1	**Example**		**Answer**
2	-350		850
3	500		=ABS(A2-A3)
4			

Result: 850
This reflects the positive difference, ignoring the sign.

Explore Further with GPT:
Ask GPT to generate more examples of using ABS for financial models or data error analysis.

Tips for Using ABS

- Combine with other formulas: Use ABS with functions like SUM or AVERAGE to calculate metrics from absolute values.
- Useful for conditional logic: Integrate ABS with IF to test or return specific results based on absolute differences.
  - Example: =IF(ABS(A1 - A2) > 100, "High Variability", "Low Variability").

ACCRINT Function

Financial Functions

Introduction

The ACCRINT function calculates the accrued interest for a security that pays periodic interest. This is particularly useful for bonds or investments where interest accumulates over time before payment.

Simple explanation: Determines the total interest earned on a security between specified dates.

Common use cases: Calculating interest for bonds, financial reports, or investment analyses.

When to use this function: Use when working with interest-bearing securities to calculate accrued interest accurately.

Syntax

```
=ACCRINT(issue, first_interest, settlement, rate, par, frequency, [basis])
```

- **issue**: The date the security was issued.
- **first_interest**: The first date interest will be paid.
- **settlement**: The settlement date (when the security is purchased).
- **rate**: The annual coupon rate.
- **par**: The face value of the security.
- **frequency**: Number of interest payments per year (1, 2, or 4).
- **[basis]** *(optional)*: The day count basis to use (default is 0 for 30/360).

Worked Example

Challenge: Calculate the accrued interest for a bond issued on January 1, 2023, with the following details:

- First interest payment: July 1, 2023.
- Settlement date: April 1, 2023.
- Annual coupon rate: 5% (0.05), Par value: $1,000, Payment frequency: Semiannual (2).

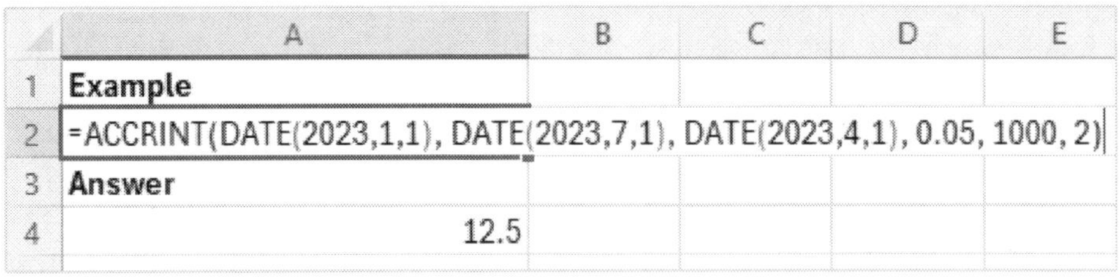

	A	B	C	D	E
1	**Example**				
2	=ACCRINT(DATE(2023,1,1), DATE(2023,7,1), DATE(2023,4,1), 0.05, 1000, 2)				
3	**Answer**				
4	12.5				

Formula:

```
=ACCRINT(DATE(2023,1,1), DATE(2023,7,1), DATE(2023,4,1), 0.05, 1000, 2)
```

Result: $12.50

This represents the accrued interest between January 1 and April 1.

Tip for Using ACCRINT

- Ensure all dates are formatted properly in Excel using the DATE function to avoid errors.

ACCRINTM Function

Financial Functions

Introduction

The ACCRINTM function calculates the accrued interest for a security that pays interest at maturity. This is commonly used for zero-coupon bonds or other investments where interest is only paid at the end of the investment period.

Simple explanation: Computes the total interest earned on a security that pays interest only at maturity.

Common use cases: Calculating accrued interest for zero-coupon bonds, long-term investments, or financial reporting.

When to use this function: Use when working with securities that do not pay periodic interest but accumulate it until maturity.

Syntax

```
=ACCRINTM(issue, maturity, rate, par, [basis])
```

- **issue**: The date the security was issued.
- **maturity**: The date the security matures.
- **rate**: The annual interest rate of the security.
- **par**: The face value of the security.
- **[basis]** *(optional)*: The day count basis to use (default is 0 for 30/360).

Worked Example

Challenge: Calculate the accrued interest for a zero-coupon bond issued on January 1, 2023, with the following details:

- Maturity date: January 1, 2024.
- Annual interest rate: 4% (0.04).
- Par value: $1,000.

	A	B	C	D	E
1	**Example**				
2	=ACCRINTM(DATE(2023,1,1), DATE(2024,1,1), 0.04, 1000)				
3	**Answer**				
4	40.00				

Formula:

```
=ACCRINTM(DATE(2023,1,1), DATE(2024,1,1), 0.04, 1000)
```

Result: $40.00

This represents the total interest accrued over the one-year period.

Tips for Using ACCRINTM

- Ensure accurate date inputs using the DATE function to avoid errors.
- Use [basis] to select the appropriate day count method for your financial analysis (e.g., actual/actual for precise calculations).
- Combine with financial models to estimate returns on zero-coupon bonds or similar securities.

ACOS Function

Math & Trigonometry Functions

Introduction

The ACOS function returns the arccosine (inverse cosine) of a number. The result is given in radians and represents the angle whose cosine is the specified number.

Simple explanation: Finds the angle (in radians) corresponding to a given cosine value.

Common use cases: Used in trigonometric calculations, geometry, and engineering applications.

When to use this function: Use when you need to calculate angles based on cosine values in formulas or geometric problems.

Syntax

```
=ACOS(number)
```

- **number**: A numeric value between -1 and 1, representing the cosine of the desired angle.

Worked Example

Challenge: Find the angle in radians whose cosine is 0.5.

Formula:

```
=ACOS(0.5)
```

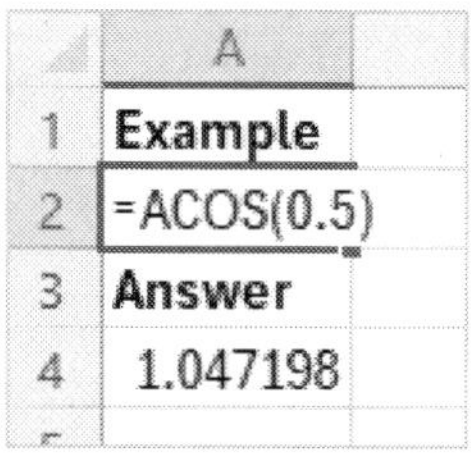

Result: 1.0472 radians (equivalent to 60 degrees)

Explore Further with GPT:
Ask GPT to help convert radians to degrees or use ACOS in a geometric formula for triangle calculations.

Tips for Using ACOS

- **Convert radians to degrees**: Use the DEGREES function to convert the result into degrees if needed.
    - Example: =DEGREES(ACOS(0.5)) gives 60 degrees.
- **Pair with other trigonometric functions**: Combine ACOS with SIN, COS, or ATAN for more complex calculations in geometry or engineering.
- **Ensure input validity**: The input must be between -1 and 1; otherwise, Excel returns a #NUM! error.

ACOSH Function

Math & Trigonometry Functions

Introduction

The ACOSH function returns the inverse hyperbolic cosine (arccosh) of a number. It calculates the value whose hyperbolic cosine is the specified number.

Simple explanation: Finds the value whose hyperbolic cosine equals the given number.

Common use cases: Used in advanced mathematics, engineering, and physics calculations involving hyperbolic functions.

When to use this function: Use when solving equations or modeling phenomena requiring hyperbolic trigonometry.

Syntax

```
=ACOSH(number)
```

- **number:** A numeric value greater than or equal to 1.

Worked Example

Challenge: Find the inverse hyperbolic cosine of 10.

Formula:

```
=ACOSH(10)
```

Result: 2.9932
This is the value whose hyperbolic cosine equals 10.

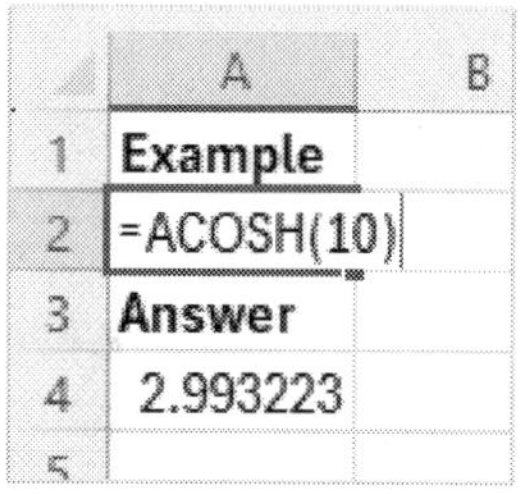

	A	B
1	**Example**	
2	=ACOSH(10)	
3	**Answer**	
4	2.993223	
5		

Explore Further with GPT:
Ask GPT to help integrate ACOSH into real-world applications or analyze related hyperbolic functions like COSH or ASINH.

Tips for Using ACOSH

- **Valid inputs**: Ensure the input value is greater than or equal to 1; values less than 1 return a #NUM! error.
- **Convert between radians and degrees**: Pair with the DEGREES or RADIANS functions if angle conversions are required.
- **Combine with other functions**: Use with COSH to validate results, as COSH(ACOSH(x)) will return the original value of x.

ACOT Function

Math & Trigonometry Functions

Introduction

The ACOT function returns the arccotangent (inverse cotangent) of a number. The result is given in radians and represents the angle whose cotangent is the specified number.

Simple explanation: Calculates the angle (in radians) that corresponds to a given cotangent value.

Common use cases: Used in trigonometric equations, geometry, and advanced mathematical computations.

When to use this function: Use when solving equations or problems involving cotangents and their corresponding angles.

Syntax

```
=ACOT(number)
```

- **number**: The numeric value for which you want the arccotangent.

Worked Example

Challenge: Find the angle in radians whose cotangent is 1.

Formula:

```
=ACOT(1)
```

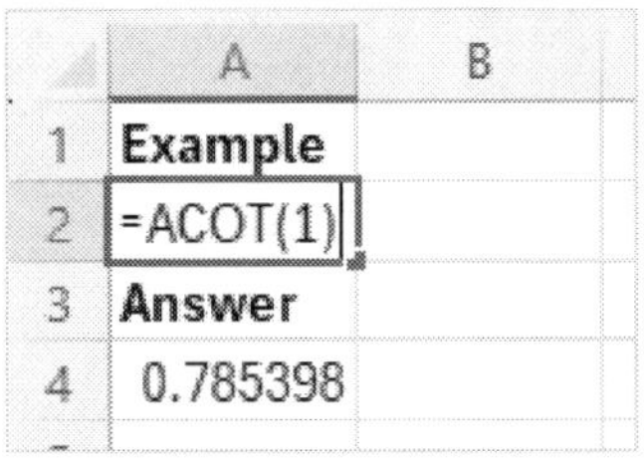

Result: 0.7854 radians (equivalent to 45 degrees).

Explore Further with GPT:
Ask GPT to demonstrate how to combine ACOT with other trigonometric functions for complex geometric calculations.

Tips for Using ACOT

- **Convert radians to degrees**: Use the DEGREES function to get the result in degrees.
  - Example: =DEGREES(ACOT(1)) returns 45 degrees.
- **Handle undefined inputs**: Note that ACOT can take any real number as input, including zero and negative values.
- **Combine with reciprocal functions**: Use with COT to verify results, as COT(ACOT(x)) will return the original value of x.

ACOTH Function

Math & Trigonometry Functions

Introduction

The ACOTH function returns the inverse hyperbolic cotangent (arccoth) of a number. It calculates the value whose hyperbolic cotangent is the specified number.

Simple explanation: Finds the value whose hyperbolic cotangent equals the given number.

Common use cases: Used in advanced mathematics, engineering, and scientific calculations involving hyperbolic functions.

When to use this function: Use when solving equations or modeling phenomena requiring hyperbolic trigonometry.

Syntax

```
=ACOTH(number)
```

- **number**: A numeric value greater than 1 or less than -1.

Worked Example

Challenge: Find the inverse hyperbolic cotangent of 2.

Formula:

```
=ACOTH(2)
```

Result: 0.5493
This represents the value whose hyperbolic cotangent equals 2.

	A	B
1	**Example**	
2	=ACOTH(2)	
3	**Answer**	
4	0.549306	

Explore Further with GPT:
Ask GPT to explore applications of ACOTH in engineering or physics scenarios, or analyze related functions like COTH or ASINH.

Tips for Using ACOTH

- **Valid input range**: The input must be greater than 1 or less than -1; values between -1 and 1 will result in a #NUM! error.
- **Combine with reciprocal functions**: Use with COTH to verify results, as COTH(ACOTH(x)) will return the original value of x.
- **Radians to degrees**: Convert results to degrees using the DEGREES function if needed.

AGGREGATE Function

Math & Trigonometry Functions

Introduction

The AGGREGATE function performs a specified calculation (e.g., sum, average, count) on a range of data, with the ability to ignore errors, hidden rows, or other values as specified. It's particularly useful for data analysis where certain values need to be excluded.

Simple explanation: Performs calculations like SUM, AVERAGE, or COUNT, while allowing you to exclude specific data types (e.g., errors or hidden rows).

Common use cases: Summarizing data while ignoring hidden rows or handling errors in datasets.

When to use this function: Use when advanced control is needed over how data is processed in aggregate calculations.

Syntax

```
=AGGREGATE(function_num, options, ref1, [ref2], ...)
```

- **function_num**: A number (1–19) specifying the calculation to perform (e.g., 1 for AVERAGE, 9 for SUM).
- **options**: A number controlling what to ignore (e.g., 1 for ignoring hidden rows).
- **ref1, ref2**: The range(s) to perform the calculation on.

Worked Example

Challenge: Calculate the sum of values in a range while ignoring errors.

1. Data is stored in:
    - Range A1:A5: {10, 20, #DIV/0!, 40, 50}.
2. Formula to calculate the sum while ignoring errors:

```
=AGGREGATE(9, 6, A1:A5)
```

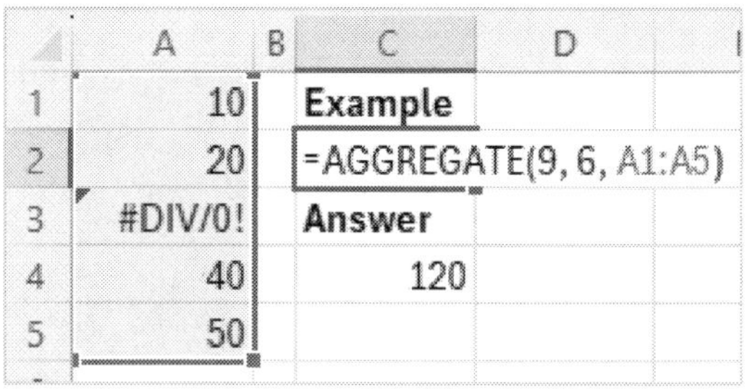

Result: 120
The function ignores the #DIV/0! error and returns the sum of the valid numbers.

Explore Further with GPT:
Ask GPT to explain how to use AGGREGATE for other operations, such as finding the largest value while ignoring hidden rows.

Tips for Using AGGREGATE

- **Understand the function numbers**: Use 1–13 for array-based operations (e.g., AVERAGE, MAX) and 14–19 for reference-based operations (e.g., LARGE, SMALL).
- **Handle filtered data**: Combine with filters or hidden rows to analyze visible data only by setting the options argument appropriately.
- **Dynamic ranges**: Use AGGREGATE with dynamic ranges for advanced analysis in large datasets.

ADDRESS Function

Lookup & Reference Functions

Introduction

The ADDRESS function returns the address of a cell based on a specified row and column number. It can be used to dynamically generate cell references, either in absolute or relative format.

Simple explanation: Creates a cell reference as a text string based on specified row and column numbers.

Common use cases: Building dynamic references in formulas, automating cell addressing in large datasets, or working with variable ranges.

When to use this function: Use when you need to create cell references dynamically or handle ranges programmatically.

Syntax

```
=ADDRESS(row_num, column_num, [abs_num], [a1], [sheet_text])
```

- **row_num**: The row number for the cell reference.
- **column_num**: The column number for the cell reference.
- **[abs_num]** *(optional)*: Specifies the type of reference (1 = absolute, 2 = row absolute, 3 = column absolute, 4 = relative). Default is 1.
- **[a1]** *(optional)*: A Boolean value indicating the reference style (TRUE = A1 style, FALSE = R1C1 style). Default is TRUE.
- **[sheet_text]** *(optional)*: The name of the worksheet to include in the reference.

Worked Example

Challenge: Generate a cell reference for row 5, column 3, using absolute referencing.

Formula:

```
=ADDRESS(5, 3, 1)
```

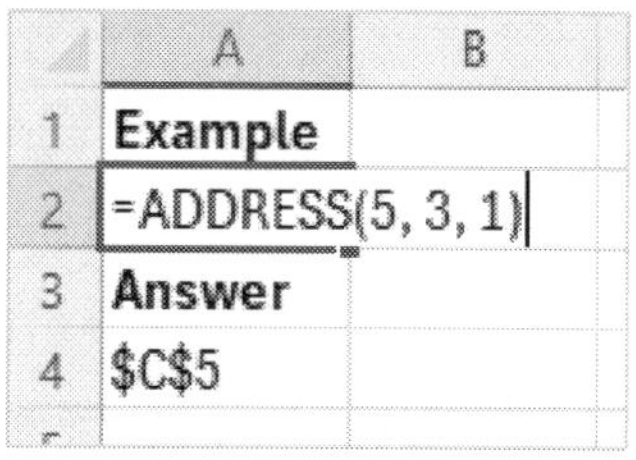

Result: $C$5
This represents the absolute reference for row 5, column 3.

Explore Further with GPT:
Ask GPT to help you use ADDRESS in combination with INDIRECT or MATCH for more dynamic referencing scenarios.

Tips for Using ADDRESS

- **Combine with other functions**: Use with MATCH or ROW to dynamically generate cell references based on criteria.
    - Example: =ADDRESS(MATCH("Target", A1:A10, 0), 2) generates the address for the row where "Target" is found.
- **Switch between reference styles**: Set the [a1] argument to FALSE for R1C1 style references when working with macros or programming.

AMORDEGRC Function

Financial Functions

Introduction

The AMORDEGRC function calculates the depreciation of an asset for a given accounting period, using a depreciation coefficient. This method is often used in financial accounting to accelerate depreciation.

Simple explanation: Calculates the depreciation of an asset for a period using a declining balance method.

Common use cases: Asset depreciation schedules, tax calculations, and financial reporting.

When to use this function: Use when calculating depreciation under accelerated methods for assets with a fixed lifespan.

Syntax

```
=AMORDEGRC(cost, date_purchased, first_period, salvage, period, rate, [basis])
```

- **cost**: The initial cost of the asset.
- **date_purchased**: The date the asset was purchased.
- **first_period**: The date of the end of the first period.
- **salvage**: The value of the asset at the end of its life.
- **period**: The period for which depreciation is calculated.
- **rate**: The rate of depreciation.
- **[basis]** *(optional)*: The day count basis (default is 0 for 30/360).

Worked Example

Challenge: Calculate the depreciation for an asset purchased on January 1, 2023, with the following details:

- Initial cost: $10,000
- Salvage value: $1,000
- Depreciation rate: 20% (0.2)
- First period ends on December 31, 2023.
- Calculating depreciation for the second period.

	A	B	C	D	E	F	G
1	**Example**						
2	=AMORDEGRC(10000, DATE(2023,1,1), DATE(2023,12,31), 1000, 2, 0.2)						
3	**Answer**						
4	1440						
5							

Formula:

```
=AMORDEGRC(10000, DATE(2023,1,1), DATE(2023,12,31), 1000, 2, 0.2)
```

Result: $1,440 (Depreciation value for the second period)

AMORLINC Function

Financial Functions

Introduction

The AMORLINC function calculates the depreciation of an asset for a specific period using the straight-line depreciation method. This method allocates an equal depreciation amount to each accounting period over the asset's useful life.

Simple explanation: Calculates the depreciation of an asset for a period using the straight-line method.

Common use cases: Fixed asset management, financial reporting, and tax calculations.

When to use this function: Use for assets that depreciate consistently over time without accelerated methods.

Syntax

```
=AMORLINC(cost, date_purchased, first_period, salvage, period, rate, [basis])
```

- **cost**: The initial cost of the asset.
- **date_purchased**: The date the asset was purchased.
- **first_period**: The date the first period ends.
- **salvage**: The value of the asset at the end of its life.
- **period**: The period for which depreciation is calculated.
- **rate**: The annual depreciation rate.
- **[basis]** *(optional)*: The day count basis (default is 0 for 30/360).

Worked Example

Challenge: Calculate the depreciation for an asset purchased on January 1, 2023, with the following details:

- Initial cost: $10,000
- Salvage value: $1,000
- Depreciation rate: 20% (0.2)
- First period ends on December 31, 2023.
- Calculating depreciation for the second period.

	A	B	C	D	E	F
1	**Example**					
2	=AMORLINC(10000, DATE(2023,1,1), DATE(2023,12,31), 1000, 2, 0.2)					
3	**Answer**					
4	$2,000					
5						

Formula:

```
=AMORLINC(10000, DATE(2023,1,1), DATE(2023,12,31), 1000, 2, 0.2)
```

Result: $2,000

This represents the straight-line depreciation value for the second period.

AND Function

Logical Functions

Introduction

The AND function checks multiple conditions and returns TRUE if all conditions are met; otherwise, it returns FALSE. It is commonly used in logical tests and decision-making scenarios.

Simple explanation: Returns TRUE if all specified conditions are true; otherwise, it returns FALSE.

Common use cases: Validating data, combining with IF for conditional logic, or creating complex logical tests.

When to use this function: Use when you need to check whether multiple criteria are simultaneously true.

Syntax

```
=AND(logical1, [logical2], ...)
```

- **logical1, logical2, ...**: The conditions to test. These can be cell references, expressions, or constants.

Worked Example

Challenge: Determine whether a student passes based on the following conditions:

1. The test score in cell A1 is greater than or equal to 50.
2. The attendance in cell B1 is greater than or equal to 75%.

Formula:

```
=AND(A1>=50, A2>=75%)
```

Result:

- If A1 = 60 and A2 = 80%, the function returns TRUE.
- If A1 = 40 or A2 = 70%, the function returns FALSE.

	A	B	C	D
1	60	**Example**		
2	80%	=AND(A1>=50, A2>=75%)		
3		**Answer**		
4		TRUE		
5				

Explore Further with GPT:
Ask GPT how to combine AND with other functions like OR or IF to handle more complex logical scenarios.

Tips for Using AND

- **Combine with** IF **for decision-making:**

```
=IF(AND(A1>=50, B1>=75%), "Pass", "Fail")
```

Returns "Pass" only if both conditions are met.

- **Check ranges or thresholds:** Use AND to validate data entries across multiple columns or rows.
- **Avoid errors:** Ensure all logical arguments are valid conditions (e.g., comparisons like >=).

ARABIC Function

Math & Trigonometry Functions

Introduction

The ARABIC function converts Roman numerals into their equivalent Arabic numeral values. It simplifies working with Roman numerals in modern data formats.

Simple explanation: Converts Roman numerals to standard numbers.

Common use cases: Processing historical data, converting numeral formats in documents, or analyzing datasets with Roman numerals.

When to use this function: Use when converting Roman numeral inputs to Arabic numerals for calculations or consistency.

Syntax

```
=ARABIC(text)
```

- **text**: A string representing a valid Roman numeral (e.g., "XII" or "IV").

Worked Example

Challenge: Convert a Roman numeral into its Arabic equivalent.

1. Roman numeral is stored in cell A1: "XIV".

Formula:

=ARABIC(A1)
Result: 14
This represents the Arabic numeral equivalent of the Roman numeral "XIV".

	A	B
1	XIV	**Example**
2		=ARABIC(A1)
3		**Answer**
4		14
5		

Explore Further with GPT:
Ask GPT for ways to validate or handle incorrect Roman numeral inputs, or use the function in conjunction with other text-processing formulas.

Tips for Using ARABIC

- **Accepts lowercase inputs:** The function works with both uppercase ("XIV") and lowercase ("xiv") Roman numerals.
- **Handles invalid inputs:** If the text is not a valid Roman numeral, the function returns #VALUE!.
- **Use with data cleaning tools:** Combine with TRIM or CLEAN to process messy data containing Roman numerals.

AREAS Function

Lookup & Reference Functions

Introduction

The AREAS function returns the number of areas in a reference. An area is a range of contiguous cells. This function is particularly useful when working with complex formulas involving multiple ranges.

Simple explanation: Counts the number of separate ranges (areas) in a reference.

Common use cases: Analyzing or troubleshooting formulas with multiple ranges, validating data selection, or automating dynamic range calculations.

When to use this function: Use when you need to count distinct cell ranges within a reference or validate multi-range formulas.

Syntax

```
=AREAS(reference)
```

- **reference**: A reference to one or more cell ranges, separated by commas if there are multiple ranges.

Worked Example

Challenge: Count the number of ranges in a reference.

1. The reference =(A1:A10, B1:B5, C1:C3) consists of three ranges:
    - A1:A10
    - B1:B5
    - C1:C3

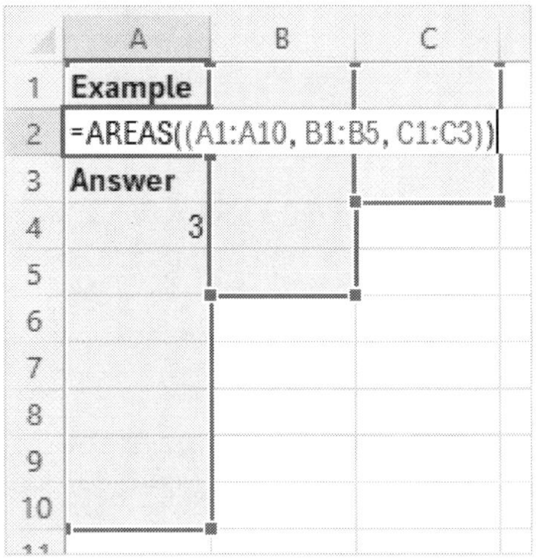

Formula:

```
=AREAS((A1:A10, B1:B5, C1:C3))
```

Result: 3
This indicates there are three distinct areas in the reference.

Explore Further with GPT:
Ask GPT how to use AREAS in combination with functions like INDEX or INDIRECT for advanced referencing.

Tips for Using AREAS

- **Multi-range selection:** Use AREAS to verify the number of ranges selected when working with complex formulas.
- **Combine with** INDEX**:** Access specific areas dynamically.

  ```
  =INDEX((A1:A10, B1:B5, C1:C3), AREAS((A1:A10, B1:B5, C1:C3)))
  ```

- **Use dynamic references:** Combine with INDIRECT to count areas based on text-based range inputs.

ARRAYTOTEXT Function

Text Functions

Introduction

The ARRAYTOTEXT function converts an array or range of values into a text string or an array of text values. It is particularly useful for creating readable outputs from arrays or passing data as text to other functions.

Simple explanation: Converts an array of values into a text string or an array of text.

Common use cases: Generating text-based summaries of arrays, simplifying dynamic arrays for text manipulation, or preparing array data for use in text-based functions.

When to use this function: Use when you need to convert complex arrays into a text format for readability or further processing.

Syntax

```
=ARRAYTOTEXT(array, [format])
```

- **array**: The array or range to convert into text.
- **[format]** *(optional)*: Specifies the output format (0 = compact, 1 = strict). Default is 0.

Worked Example

Challenge: Convert a range of numbers into a text string.

1. Data is stored in the range A1:A3:
    - 10
    - 20
    - 30

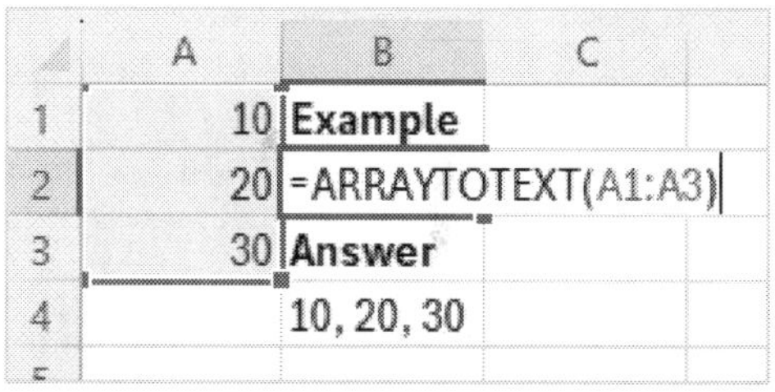

Formula:

```
=ARRAYTOTEXT(A1:A3)
```

Result: "10,20,30" (Compact format, default).

Explore Further with GPT:
Ask GPT to demonstrate how to use ARRAYTOTEXT for text-based summaries or combining arrays dynamically.

Tips for Using ARRAYTOTEXT

- **Format options:** Use the [format] argument to control the output style:
    - 0 (Compact): Outputs values as a concise, comma-separated list (default).
    - 1 (Strict): Preserves the array structure as text.
- **Combine with dynamic arrays:** Simplify dynamic array outputs into readable strings for reporting or visualization.
- **Error-proofing:** Ensure your array or range contains valid data types, as unsupported types may lead to errors.

ASC Function

Text Functions

Introduction

The ASC function converts full-width (double-byte) characters to half-width (single-byte) characters in a text string. It's commonly used in datasets containing characters from languages like Japanese or Chinese.

Simple explanation: Converts full-width characters to half-width characters in a text string.

Common use cases: Standardizing text data in multilingual datasets, especially when handling characters from East Asian languages.

When to use this function: Use when working with datasets requiring consistent text encoding or formatting.

Syntax

```
=ASC(text)
```

- **text**: The text string to convert.

Worked Example

Challenge: Convert a full-width text string to half-width characters.

1. Text is stored in cell A1: "H e l l o Wo r l d" (full-width).

Formula:

`=ASC(A1)`

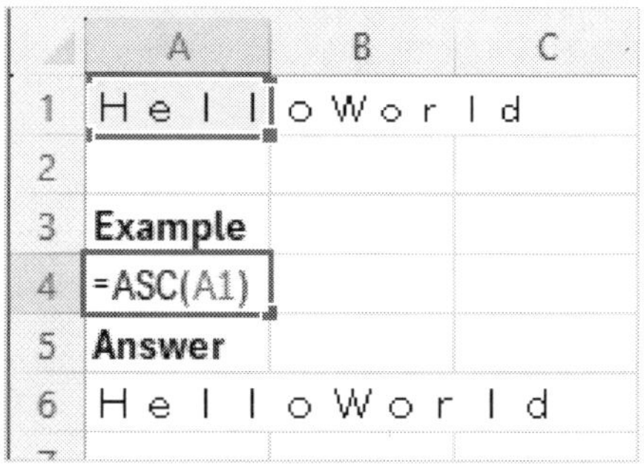

Result: "Hello World"
The text is converted to half-width characters. However, if the input does not contain actual full-width characters, the output will remain visually identical to the input.

Explore Further with GPT:
Ask GPT to show how ASC can be used with other text functions, such as TRIM or CLEAN, to preprocess text data.

Tips for Using ASC

- **Verify input data:** The function only affects text encoded with double-byte (full-width) characters, often from Japanese or Chinese sources.
- **Locale dependency:** To observe a difference, ensure Excel is configured for a region where full-width encoding is commonly used.
- **Alternative for Western languages:** If text is already in single-byte encoding, the ASC function has no effect.

ASIN Function

Math & Trigonometry Functions

Introduction

The ASIN function returns the arcsine (inverse sine) of a number. The result is given in radians and represents the angle whose sine is the specified number.

Simple explanation: Calculates the angle (in radians) corresponding to a given sine value.

Common use cases: Used in trigonometric calculations, geometry, and physics.

When to use this function: Use when solving problems or equations involving the sine of an angle.

Syntax

```
=ASIN(number)
```

- **number**: A numeric value between -1 and 1 representing the sine of the desired angle.

Worked Example

Challenge: Find the angle in radians whose sine is 0.5.

Formula:

`=ASIN(0.5)`

Result: 0.5236 radians (equivalent to 30 degrees).

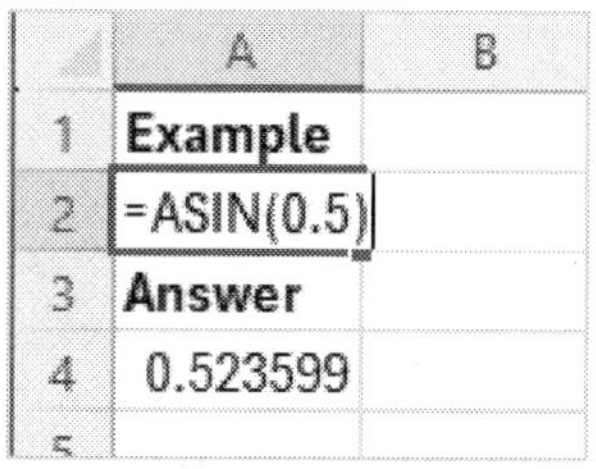

Explore Further with GPT:
Ask GPT to help convert the result from radians to degrees or combine ASIN with other trigonometric functions like SIN or COS.

Tips for Using ASIN

- **Convert radians to degrees:** Use the DEGREES function to convert the result into degrees.
  - Example: `=DEGREES(ASIN(0.5))` returns 30 degrees.
- **Ensure valid input range:** The input must be between -1 and 1; otherwise, Excel returns a #NUM! error.
- **Combine with other functions:** Use in conjunction with SIN to validate calculations, as `SIN(ASIN(x))` will return x.

ASINH Function

Math & Trigonometry Functions

Introduction

The ASINH function returns the inverse hyperbolic sine (arcsinh) of a number. It calculates the value whose hyperbolic sine is the specified number.

Simple explanation: Finds the value whose hyperbolic sine equals the given number.

Common use cases: Used in advanced mathematics, physics, and engineering calculations involving hyperbolic functions.

When to use this function: Use when solving equations or modeling phenomena requiring hyperbolic trigonometry.

Syntax

```
=ASINH(number)
```

- **number**: A numeric value for which you want the inverse hyperbolic sine.

Worked Example

Challenge: Find the inverse hyperbolic sine of 1.

Formula:

```
=ASINH(1)
```

Result: 0.8814
This represents the value whose hyperbolic sine equals 1.

	A	B
1	**Example**	
2	=ASINH(1)	
3	**Answer**	
4	0.881374	
5		

Explore Further with GPT:
Ask GPT to demonstrate how to use ASINH with other hyperbolic functions or in real-world applications like signal processing or geometric modeling.

Tips for Using ASINH

- **Input range:** The function accepts any real number as input (positive, negative, or zero).
- **Combine with other functions:** Use with SINH to validate results, as SINH(ASINH(x)) will return the original value of x.
- **Convert to degrees:** If the result needs to be in degrees, use the DEGREES function to convert the radians.

ATAN Function

Math & Trigonometry Functions

Introduction

The ATAN function returns the arctangent (inverse tangent) of a number. The result is given in radians and represents the angle whose tangent is the specified number.

Simple explanation: Calculates the angle (in radians) corresponding to a given tangent value.

Common use cases: Used in trigonometric calculations, geometry, and physics.

When to use this function: Use when solving problems or equations involving the tangent of an angle.

Syntax

```
=ATAN(number)
```

Worked Example

Challenge: Find the angle in radians whose tangent is 1.

Formula:

`=ATAN(1)`

Result: 0.7854 radians (equivalent to 45 degrees).

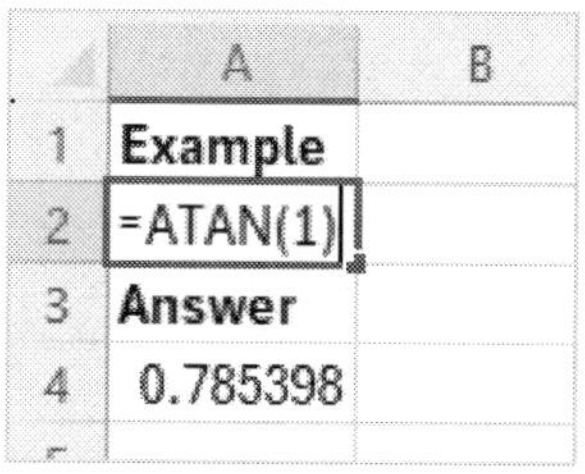

Explore Further with GPT:
Ask GPT how to use ATAN for geometric calculations or combine it with other trigonometric functions like TAN or SIN.

Tips for Using ATAN

- **Convert radians to degrees:** Use the DEGREES function to convert the result into degrees.
    - Example: `=DEGREES(ATAN(1))` returns 45 degrees.
- **Handle undefined inputs:** The function accepts all real numbers, so it can handle both positive and negative tangents.
- **Combine with other functions:** Use in conjunction with TAN to validate calculations, as `TAN(ATAN(x))` will return x.

ATAN2 Function

Math & Trigonometry Functions

Introduction

The ATAN2 function returns the arctangent of the specified x- and y-coordinates, expressed as an angle in radians. Unlike ATAN, this function considers the quadrant of the point, making it useful for determining the direction of a vector or angle in polar coordinates.

Simple explanation: Calculates the angle (in radians) of a point in a two-dimensional plane based on its x- and y-coordinates.

Common use cases: Used in geometry, physics, and navigation to calculate angles or directions.

When to use this function: Use when working with coordinates to determine angles in a Cartesian plane.

Syntax

```
=ATAN2(x_num, y_num)
```

- **x_num**: The x-coordinate of the point.
- **y_num**: The y-coordinate of the point.

Worked Example

Challenge: Calculate the angle in radians of a point located at (3, 4).

Formula:

`=ATAN2(3, 4)`

Result: 0.6435 radians (equivalent to approximately 36.87 degrees).

	A	B
1	**Example**	
2	=ATAN2(3, 4)	
3	**Answer**	
4	0.927295	
5		

Explore Further with GPT:
Ask GPT to help convert the result to degrees or analyze points in different quadrants for direction calculations.

Tips for Using ATAN2

- **Convert radians to degrees:** Use the DEGREES function to convert the result to degrees if required.
    - Example: `=DEGREES(ATAN2(3, 4))` returns approximately 36.87 degrees.
- **Order of arguments:** Note that the x_num comes first, followed by the y_num.
- **Quadrant-aware:** Unlike ATAN, ATAN2 takes into account the signs of both coordinates to determine the correct quadrant of the angle.

ATANH Function

Math & Trigonometry Functions

Introduction

The ATANH function returns the inverse hyperbolic tangent (arctanh) of a number. It calculates the value whose hyperbolic tangent is the specified number.

Simple explanation: Finds the value whose hyperbolic tangent equals the given number.

Common use cases: Used in advanced mathematics, physics, and engineering applications involving hyperbolic functions.

When to use this function: Use when solving equations or modeling scenarios involving hyperbolic tangents.

Syntax

```
=ATANH(number)
```

Worked Example

Challenge: Find the inverse hyperbolic tangent of 0.5.

Formula:

```
=ATANH(0.5)
```

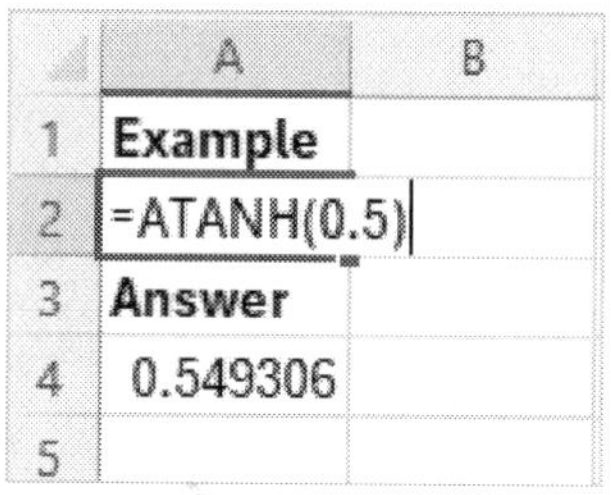

Result: 0.5493
This represents the value whose hyperbolic tangent equals 0.5.

Explore Further with GPT:
Ask GPT to demonstrate how to use ATANH with other hyperbolic functions or to explore its applications in real-world scenarios like signal processing or geometry.

Tips for Using ATANH

- **Input range restrictions:** The input must be greater than -1 and less than 1; values outside this range will result in a #NUM! error.
- **Combine with reciprocal functions:** Use with TANH to validate calculations, as `TANH(ATANH(x))` will return x.
- **Radians to degrees:** If needed, convert the result to degrees using the DEGREES function.

AVEDEV Function

Statistical Functions

Introduction

The AVEDEV function calculates the average of the absolute deviations of data points from their mean. It measures the dispersion or variability in a dataset, making it a useful tool in statistical analysis.

Simple explanation: Finds the average distance of each data point from the mean, without considering direction (absolute values).

Common use cases: Analyzing data variability, measuring consistency, or assessing deviations in datasets.

When to use this function: Use when you need a simple measure of data spread or dispersion.

Syntax

```
=AVEDEV(number1, [number2], ...)
```

Worked Example

Challenge: Calculate the average deviation for the numbers 5, 10, 15, 20.

1. Data is stored in range A1:A4:
    - 5, 10, 15, 20.

Formula:

`=AVEDEV(A1:A4)`

Result: 5
This indicates that, on average, the data points deviate by 5 units from the mean.

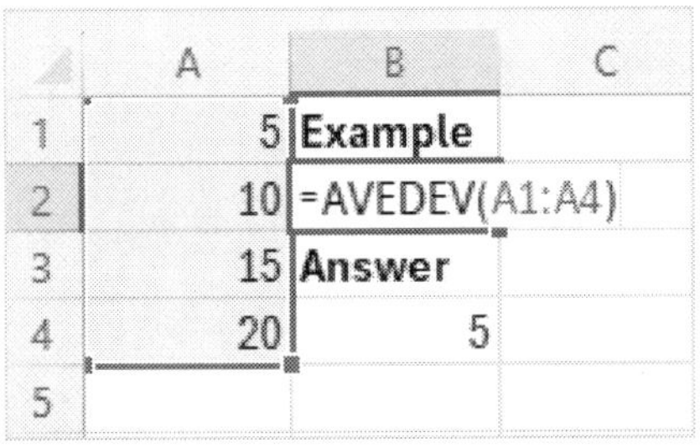

	A	B	C
1	5	**Example**	
2	10	=AVEDEV(A1:A4)	
3	15	**Answer**	
4	20	5	
5			

Explore Further with GPT:
Ask GPT to compare AVEDEV with other measures of dispersion, such as STDEV, or to analyze larger datasets.

Tips for Using AVEDEV

- **Difference from** STDEV: Unlike standard deviation, AVEDEV uses absolute deviations, making it easier to interpret for non-technical users.
- **Handle ranges or arrays:** Use ranges (e.g., A1:A10) to streamline calculations for larger datasets.
- **Combine with filters:** Use with filtered ranges to focus on specific data subsets.

AVERAGE Function

Statistical Functions

Introduction

The AVERAGE function calculates the arithmetic mean of a group of numbers. It adds up all the values and divides by the number of values, providing a measure of central tendency.

Simple explanation: Calculates the average (mean) of a set of numbers.

Common use cases: Summarizing datasets, finding the typical value in a range, or comparing performance metrics.

When to use this function: Use when you need to calculate the central value of numeric data.

Syntax

```
=AVERAGE(number1, [number2], ...)
```

- **number1, number2, ...**: The numbers or ranges to average.

Worked Example

Challenge: Calculate the average of the numbers 10, 20, 30, 40.

1. Data is stored in range A1:A4:
    - 10, 20, 30, 40.

Formula:

`=AVERAGE(A1:A4)`

Result: 25
This represents the arithmetic mean of the values.

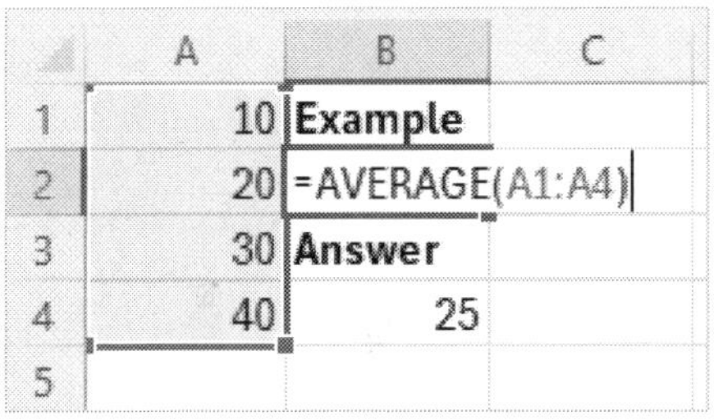

Explore Further with GPT:
Ask GPT to explain how AVERAGE differs from MEDIAN or to demonstrate its use with conditional logic.

Tips for Using AVERAGE

- **Exclude blank cells or text:** Blank cells are ignored, but ensure numeric data is formatted correctly to avoid errors.
- **Combine with** IF **for conditional averages:** Use AVERAGE with IF to calculate the average of specific subsets.
    - Example: `=AVERAGE(IF(A1:A10>20, A1:A10))` (entered as an array formula).
- **Avoid errors with mixed data types:** If the range contains text or errors, ensure the data is clean for accurate results.

AVERAGEA Function

Statistical Functions

Introduction

The AVERAGEA function calculates the arithmetic mean of a group of values, including numbers, text, and logical values. Unlike AVERAGE, it evaluates text as 0 and logical values as 1 for TRUE and 0 for FALSE.

Simple explanation: Calculates the average of values, including numbers, text, and logical values.

Common use cases: Analyzing mixed datasets containing text or logical values, ensuring no data is excluded.

When to use this function: Use when your dataset includes a mix of numbers, text, and logical values that you want to account for in the average.

Syntax

```
=AVERAGEA(value1, [value2], ...)
```

- **value1, value2, ...**: The values or ranges to average. These can include numbers, text, or logical values.

Worked Example

Challenge: Calculate the average of a dataset containing numbers, text, and logical values.

1. Data is stored in range A1:A5:
    - 10, 20, "Text", TRUE, FALSE.

Formula:

```
=AVERAGEA(A1:A5)
```

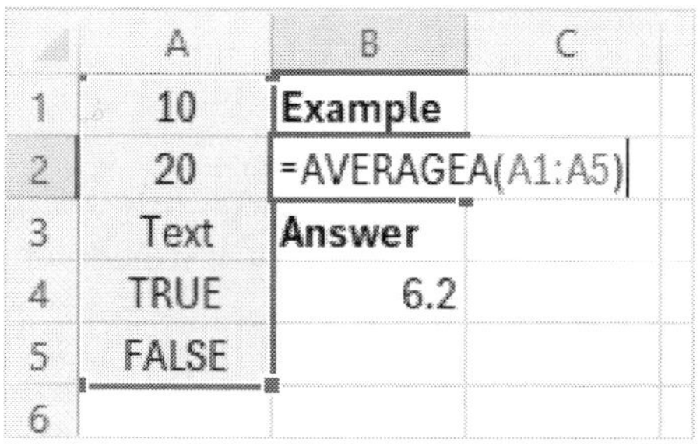

Result: 6.2
Explanation:

- Numbers: 10, 20 contribute as is. "Text" is treated as 0. TRUE is 1, and FALSE is 0.
- (10 + 20 + 0 + 1 + 0) / 5 = 6.2.

Explore Further with GPT:
Ask GPT to demonstrate scenarios where AVERAGEA is preferable to AVERAGE or to analyze datasets with missing or non-numeric values.

Tips for Using AVERAGEA

- **Evaluate logical values carefully:** Logical TRUE and FALSE are included in the calculation as 1 and 0.
- **Use with text-heavy datasets:** Text is treated as 0, ensuring it doesn't skew the results excessively.
- **Verify data types:** Be mindful of unintended text entries that might affect the average when using this function.

AVERAGEIF Function

Statistical Functions

Introduction

The AVERAGEIF function calculates the average of values in a range that meet a specific condition or criteria. It's a useful tool for summarizing data selectively based on certain thresholds or rules.

Simple explanation: Calculates the average of values that meet a specified condition.

Common use cases: Filtering data for specific categories, analyzing subsets of data, or excluding outliers.

When to use this function: Use when you need to compute averages for conditional data subsets.

Syntax

```
=AVERAGEIF(range, criteria, [average_range])
```

- **range**: The range of cells to evaluate against the criteria.
- **criteria**: The condition or rule that determines which values are averaged.
- **[average_range]** *(optional)*: The range of cells to average if different from range. If omitted, range is used.

Worked Example

Challenge: Calculate the average sales (Column B) for regions labeled "East" (Column A).

1. Data:
    - Column A (Regions): "East", "West", "East", "North"
    - Column B (Sales): 100, 200, 300, 400

Formula:

```
=AVERAGEIF(A1:A4, "East", B1:B4)
```

	A	B	C	D	E
1	East	100	**Example**		
2	West	200	=AVERAGEIF(A1:A4, "East", B1:B4)		
3	East	300	**Answer**		
4	North	400	200		
5					

Result: 200

Only the sales corresponding to "East" (100 and 300) are averaged: (100 + 300) / 2 = 200.

Explore Further with GPT:
Ask GPT how to use wildcards in AVERAGEIF or combine it with other functions like COUNTIF for deeper insights.

Tips for Using AVERAGEIF

- **Criteria flexibility:** Use logical operators (>, <, =) or wildcards (*, ?) for dynamic criteria.
    - Example: `=AVERAGEIF(A1:A10, ">50")` averages all values greater than 50.
- **Specify** average_range**:** If omitted, range is used for both criteria evaluation and averaging.
- **Handle errors carefully:** If no cells meet the criteria, the function returns #DIV/0!.

AVERAGEIFS Function

Statistical Functions

Introduction

The AVERAGEIFS function calculates the average of values in a range that meet multiple criteria. It's ideal for analyzing datasets with complex filtering conditions.

Simple explanation: Averages values that satisfy multiple conditions simultaneously.

Common use cases: Summarizing data subsets, analyzing trends across multiple criteria, or refining results in large datasets.

When to use this function: Use when filtering data by multiple conditions before calculating an average.

Syntax

```
=AVERAGEIFS(average_range, criteria_range1, criteria1, [criteria_range2, criteria2], ...)
```

- **average_range**: The range of values to average.
- **criteria_range1**: The first range to evaluate against the first condition.
- **criteria1**: The condition for the first range.
- **[criteria_range2, criteria2], ...** *(optional)*: Additional ranges and conditions.

Worked Example

Challenge: Calculate the average sales (Column C) for products labeled "A" (Column A) and sold in the "East" region (Column B).

1. Data:

	A	B	C	D	E	F	G	H
1	A	East	100	**Example**				
2	B	West	200	=AVERAGEIFS(C1:C4, A1:A4, "A", B1:B4, "East")				
3	A	East	300	**Answer**				
4	C	North	400	200				
5								
6								

- Column A (Products): "A", "B", "A", "C"
- Column B (Regions): "East", "West", "East", "North"
- Column C (Sales): 100, 200, 300, 400

Formula:

```
=AVERAGEIFS(C1:C4, A1:A4, "A", B1:B4, "East")
```

Result: 200

Only the sales for product "A" in the "East" region (100 and 300) are averaged: (100 + 300) / 2 = 200.

Explore Further with GPT:
Ask GPT how to use AVERAGEIFS with dynamic criteria or integrate it into multi-sheet analyses.

BAHTTEXT Function

Text Functions

Introduction

The BAHTTEXT function converts a number into Thai text, specifically representing the amount in Thai Baht currency. It is primarily useful for financial documents or invoices in Thailand.

Simple explanation: Converts a number into Thai Baht currency text.

Common use cases: Generating invoices, receipts, or legal documents in Thai.

When to use this function: Use when preparing financial text outputs in Thai Baht for business or compliance purposes.

Syntax

```
=BAHTTEXT(number)
```

- **number**: The numeric value to convert into Thai Baht text.

Worked Example

Challenge: Convert a numeric value into Thai Baht currency text.

1. The number is stored in cell A1: 1234.56.

Formula:

```
=BAHTTEXT(A1)
```

	A	B	C	D	E
1	1234.56	**Example**			
2		=BAHTTEXT(A1)			
3		**Answer**			
4		หนึ่งพันสองร้อยสามสิบสี่บาทห้าสิบหกสตางค์			

Result:

หนึ่งพันสองร้อยสามสิบสี่บาทห้าสิบหกสตางค์
This represents 1234.56 Baht in Thai currency text.

Explore Further with GPT:
Ask GPT to explain how similar text conversion functions can be used for other currencies or languages.

Tips for Using BAHTTEXT

- **Language limitations:** This function is specific to Thai and cannot be adapted directly for other currencies or languages.
- **Format the input:** Ensure the number argument is properly formatted as a numeric value to avoid errors.
- **Combine with templates:** Use BAHTTEXT in financial templates for automating text-based currency representation.

BASE Function

Math & Trigonometry Functions

Introduction

The BASE function converts a number into a text representation with a specified base (radix). It supports bases from 2 (binary) to 36, making it ideal for working with number systems in mathematics, computer science, and data encoding.

Simple explanation: Converts a number into a different base, outputting it as text.

Common use cases: Binary, hexadecimal, or custom base conversions for computer science, cryptography, or data analysis.

When to use this function: Use when you need to convert numbers into non-decimal systems for analysis or encoding.

Syntax|

```
=BASE(number, radix, [min_length])
```

- **number**: The decimal number to convert (must be non-negative).
- **radix**: The base to convert the number to (an integer between 2 and 36).
- **[min_length]** *(optional)*: The minimum length of the returned string. Leading zeros are added if needed.

Worked Example

Challenge: Convert the decimal number 15 into binary (base 2) with a minimum length of 4 characters.

1. The number is stored in cell A1: 15.

Formula:

```
=BASE(A1, 2, 4)
```

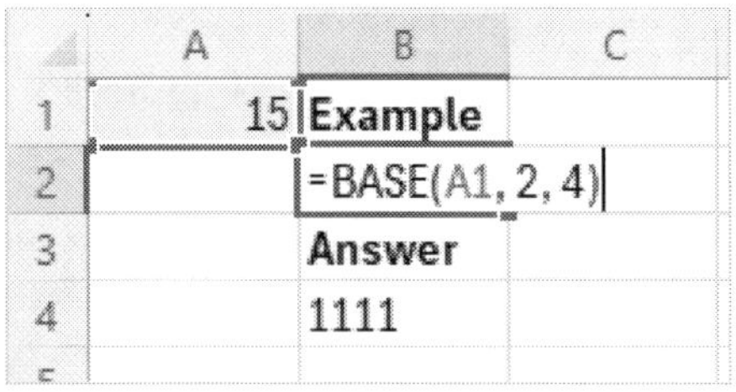

Result: 1111 This represents 15 in binary, padded to a minimum length of 4 characters.

Explore Further with GPT:
Ask GPT how to combine BASE with other functions like DECIMAL to switch between number systems dynamically.

Tips for Using BASE

- **Output as text:** The result is always a text string, so it may require conversion if used in numeric operations.
- **Range of bases:** Valid bases range from 2 (binary) to 36. Larger bases include alphanumeric characters (e.g., base 16 uses A–F for values 10–15).
- **Padded output:** Use the [min_length] argument to ensure consistent formatting, especially for binary or hexadecimal values.

BESSELI Function

Engineering Functions

Introduction

The BESSELI function calculates the modified Bessel function of the first kind, which is used in advanced mathematics, engineering, and physics to solve differential equations. It's particularly useful for modeling wave propagation, heat transfer, and other phenomena.

Simple explanation: Computes the modified Bessel function of the first kind for a specified value and order.

Common use cases: Solving mathematical equations in physics, engineering, or applied sciences.

When to use this function: Use when working with differential equations or systems involving Bessel functions.

Syntax

```
=BESSELI(x, n)
```

- **x**: The value at which to evaluate the function.
- **n**: The order of the Bessel function (must be a non-negative number).

Worked Example

Challenge: Calculate the modified Bessel function of the first kind for x = 2 and n = 1.

Formula:

```
=BESSELI(2, 1)
```

Result: 1.5906
This represents the value of the modified Bessel function of the first kind for the given input.

	A	B
1	**Example**	
2	=BESSELI(2, 1)	
3	**Answer**	
4	1.590637	
5		

Explore Further with GPT:
Ask GPT to explain how Bessel functions are used in engineering or to compare BESSELI with related functions like BESSELJ.

Tips for Using BESSELI

- **Understand the order (n):** The order must be non-negative; fractional or negative values will result in errors.
- **Precision requirements:** For highly precise calculations, cross-check results with specialized software or reference tables.
- **Combine with other functions:** Use in conjunction with functions like BESSELJ or BESSELK to solve complex mathematical problems.

BESSELJ Function

Engineering Functions

Introduction

The BESSELJ function calculates the Bessel function of the first kind, a solution to certain differential equations frequently used in engineering, physics, and mathematical modeling. It is commonly applied in problems involving cylindrical or spherical symmetry.

Simple explanation: Computes the Bessel function of the first kind for a specified value and order.

Common use cases: Used in signal processing, wave propagation, and heat conduction problems.

When to use this function: Use when solving mathematical models or physical systems requiring Bessel functions.

Syntax

```
=BESSELJ(x, n)
```

- **x**: The value at which to evaluate the function.
- **n**: The order of the Bessel function (must be a non-negative number).

Worked Example

Challenge: Calculate the Bessel function of the first kind for x = 3 and n = 0.

Formula:

```
=BESSELJ(3, 0)
```

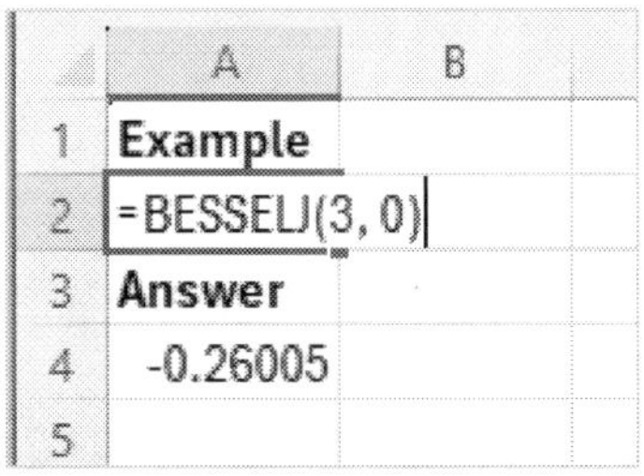

Result: -0.2601
This represents the value of the Bessel function of the first kind for the given input.

Explore Further with GPT:
Ask GPT to explain how BESSELJ is used in wave modeling or to explore its applications in cylindrical coordinate systems.

Tips for Using BESSELJ

- **Understand the order (n):** The order must be non-negative; fractional or negative values will result in errors.
- **Combine with other Bessel functions:** Pair with BESSELI, BESSELK, or BESSELY for complete solutions to complex problems.
- **Physical relevance:** Ideal for problems involving vibrational modes, heat flow, or electromagnetic wave behavior.

BESSELK Function

Engineering Functions

Introduction

The BESSELK function calculates the modified Bessel function of the second kind, often used in advanced mathematics, physics, and engineering to solve differential equations. It is particularly useful in problems involving exponential decay or heat conduction.

Simple explanation: Computes the modified Bessel function of the second kind for a specified value and order.

Common use cases: Used in heat transfer, wave propagation, and modeling of decaying systems.

When to use this function: Use when solving differential equations in exponential or decaying systems.

Syntax

```
=BESSELK(x, n)
```

- **x**: The value at which to evaluate the function (must be positive).
- **n**: The order of the Bessel function (must be non-negative).

Worked Example

Challenge: Calculate the modified Bessel function of the second kind for x = 2 and n = 1.

Formula:

```
=BESSELK(2, 1)
```

Result: 0.1399
This represents the value of the modified Bessel function of the second kind for the given input.

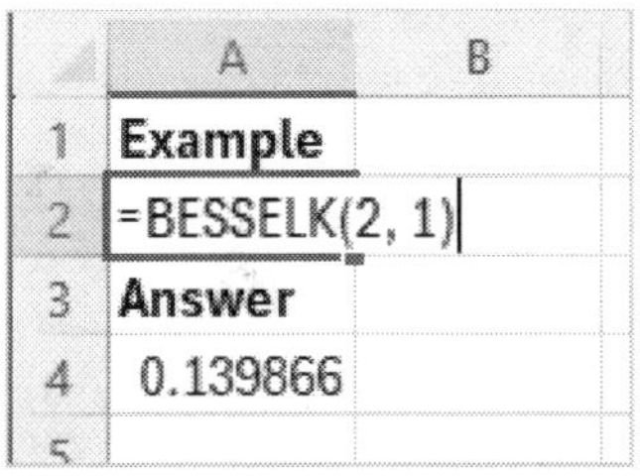

Explore Further with GPT:
Ask GPT how BESSELK compares with BESSELI and its role in modeling physical systems.

Tips for Using BESSELK

- **Positive input values:** Ensure that x is greater than 0; otherwise, Excel will return a #NUM! error.
- **Understand the order** (n): The order must be non-negative; fractional or negative values are not allowed.
- **Physical relevance:** Useful in problems involving decay processes or cylindrical systems, such as thermal or electrical conductivity modeling.

BESSELY Function

Engineering Functions

Introduction

The BESSELY function calculates the Bessel function of the second kind, often used in advanced mathematics, physics, and engineering. It is commonly applied to solve differential equations involving cylindrical or spherical coordinates, particularly in problems with boundary conditions at infinity.

Simple explanation: Computes the Bessel function of the second kind for a specified value and order.

Common use cases: Used in wave propagation, acoustics, and electromagnetic theory.

When to use this function: Use when solving differential equations with cylindrical or spherical symmetry.

Syntax

```
=BESSELY(x, n)
```

- **x**: The value at which to evaluate the function (must be positive).
- **n**: The order of the Bessel function (must be a non-negative integer).

Worked Example

Challenge: Calculate the Bessel function of the second kind for x = 3 and n = 0.

Formula:

```
=BESSELY(3, 0)
```

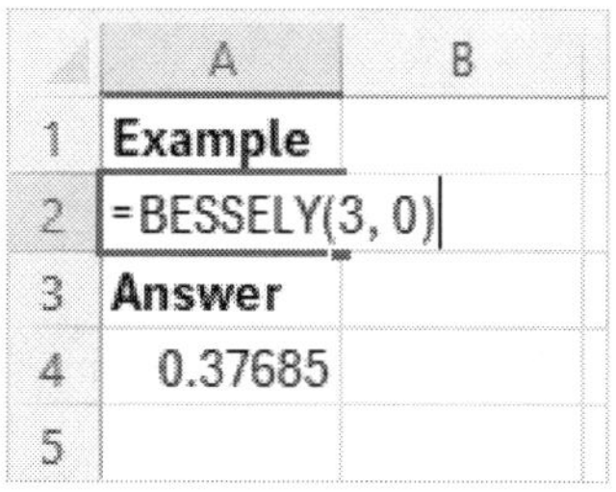

Result: 0.37685
This represents the value of the Bessel function of the second kind for the given input.

Explore Further with GPT:
Ask GPT to explain the differences between BESSELY and BESSELJ or how they are applied in wave and heat transfer problems.

Tips for Using BESSELY

- **Positive input values:** The input x must be greater than 0; otherwise, Excel will return a #NUM! error.
- **Understand the order (n):** The order must be a non-negative integer; negative or fractional values will cause errors.
- **Physical relevance:** Combine with BESSELJ for a complete set of solutions to problems in wave propagation and resonance phenomena.

BETADIST Function

Compatibility Functions

Introduction

The BETADIST function returns the cumulative beta probability density function for a specified set of parameters. It is commonly used in statistics to model variables that have a finite range and are not symmetrically distributed, such as task completion times in project management.

Simple explanation: Calculates the cumulative probability of a beta distribution for given values.

Common use cases: Used in statistics, risk analysis, and project management to estimate probabilities.

When to use this function: Use when analyzing or modeling data that follows a beta distribution.

Syntax

```
=BETADIST(x, alpha, beta, [A], [B])
```

- **x**: The value between A and B for which to evaluate the function.
- **alpha**: A parameter that shapes the distribution.
- **beta**: Another parameter that shapes the distribution.
- **[A]** *(optional)*: The lower bound of the interval (default is 0).
- **[B]** *(optional)*: The upper bound of the interval (default is 1).

Worked Example

Challenge: Calculate the cumulative beta probability for x = 0.5, with parameters alpha = 2, beta = 3, and bounds A = 0, B = 1.

Formula:

```
=BETADIST(0.5, 2, 3, 0, 1)
```

	A	B	C
1	**Example**		
2	=BETADIST(0.5, 2, 3, 0, 1)		
3	**Answer**		
4	0.6875		
5			

Result: 0.6875
This represents the cumulative probability up to x = 0.5 for the specified beta distribution.

Explore Further with GPT:
Ask GPT to help interpret beta distribution results or to compare the use of BETADIST with BETA.DIST, the newer version of this function.

Tips for Using BETADIST

- **Default bounds:** If [A] and [B] are omitted, the function assumes a range of 0 to 1.
- **Parameter impact:** Adjust alpha and beta to change the shape of the beta distribution and observe different probability outcomes.
- **Transition to** BETA.DIST**:** Use BETA.DIST for enhanced functionality and consistency with newer Excel versions.

BETA.DIST Function

Statistical Functions

Introduction

The BETA.DIST function returns either the cumulative beta probability density function or the probability density function, depending on the type of distribution specified. It is often used in project planning, risk analysis, and other statistical applications to model variables with a defined range.

Simple explanation: Calculates the beta distribution's cumulative probability or probability density for given parameters.

Common use cases: Used in statistics, risk modeling, and forecasting to analyze variables bounded by specific limits.

When to use this function: Use when working with beta-distributed data or modeling probabilities for variables with finite ranges.

Syntax

```
=BETA.DIST(x, alpha, beta, cumulative, [A], [B])
```

- **x**: The value at which to evaluate the function.
- **alpha**: A parameter that shapes the distribution.
- **beta**: Another parameter that shapes the distribution.
- **cumulative**: A logical value (TRUE for cumulative distribution, FALSE for probability density).
- **[A]** (optional): The lower bound of the interval (default is 0).
- **[B]** (optional): The upper bound of the interval (default is 1).

Worked Example

Challenge: Calculate the cumulative beta probability for x = 0.5, with parameters alpha = 2, beta = 3, and bounds A = 0, B = 1.

Formula:

```
=BETA.DIST(0.5, 2, 3, TRUE, 0, 1)
```

Result: 0.6875
This represents the cumulative probability up to x = 0.5 for the specified beta distribution.

	A	B	C
1	**Example**		
2	=BETA.DIST(0.5, 2, 3, TRUE, 0, 1)		
3	**Answer**		
4	0.6875		
5			

Explore Further with GPT:
Ask GPT to help analyze how changes in alpha and beta impact the distribution, or how to use BETA.DIST for specific forecasting scenarios.

Tips for Using BETA.DIST

- **Cumulative or density:** Set cumulative to TRUE for cumulative probabilities or FALSE for the probability density at x.
- **Default bounds:** If [A] and [B] are omitted, the function assumes a range of 0 to 1.

BETAINV Function

Compatibility Functions

Introduction

The BETAINV function returns the inverse of the cumulative beta probability density function. It is often used to calculate a value x corresponding to a given probability, based on the beta distribution parameters.

Simple explanation: Finds the value of x for a given cumulative probability in a beta distribution.

Common use cases: Used in statistical modeling, quality control, and risk analysis to determine thresholds or specific values for probabilities.

When to use this function: Use when you need to find the value corresponding to a specific probability in a beta distribution.

Syntax

```
=BETAINV(probability, alpha, beta, [A], [B])
```

- **probability**: The cumulative probability for which to calculate the value of x.
- **alpha**: A parameter that shapes the distribution.
- **beta**: Another parameter that shapes the distribution.
- **[A]** *(optional)*: The lower bound of the interval (default is 0).
- **[B]** *(optional)*: The upper bound of the interval (default is 1).

Worked Example

Challenge: Find the value of x corresponding to a cumulative probability of 0.6875, with parameters alpha = 2, beta = 3, and bounds A = 0, B = 1.

Formula:

```
=BETAINV(0.6875, 2, 3, 0, 1)
```

	A	B	C
1	**Example**		
2	=BETAINV(0.6875, 2, 3, 0, 1)		
3	**Answer**		
4	0.5		

Result: 0.5
This indicates that for the given beta distribution, the value of x corresponding to a cumulative probability of 0.6875 is 0.5.

Explore Further with GPT:
Ask GPT to help you compare BETAINV with BETA.INV or use it in advanced scenarios like project risk analysis.

Tips for Using BETAINV

- **Probabilities must be valid:** Ensure the probability argument is between 0 and 1.
- **Default bounds:** If [A] and [B] are omitted, the function assumes a range of 0 to 1.
- **Transition to** BETA.INV: Use BETA.INV in newer Excel versions for improved compatibility and functionality.

BETA.INV Function

Statistical Functions

Introduction

The BETA.INV function returns the inverse of the cumulative beta probability density function. It is a newer version of the BETAINV function, offering enhanced compatibility and performance. It calculates the value of x corresponding to a given cumulative probability, based on the beta distribution parameters.

Simple explanation: Finds the value of x for a specified cumulative probability in a beta distribution.

Common use cases: Used in risk analysis, statistical modeling, and quality control to determine thresholds or specific values for probabilities.

When to use this function: Use when calculating values for probabilities in newer Excel versions.

Syntax

```
=BETA.INV(probability, alpha, beta, [A], [B])
```

- **probability**: The cumulative probability for which to calculate the value of x.
- **alpha**: A parameter that shapes the distribution.
- **beta**: Another parameter that shapes the distribution.
- [**A**] (optional): The lower bound of the interval (default is 0).
- [**B**] (optional): The upper bound of the interval (default is 1).

Worked Example

Challenge: Find the value of x corresponding to a cumulative probability of 0.6875, with parameters alpha = 2, beta = 3, and bounds A = 0, B = 1.

Formula:

```
=BETA.INV(0.6875, 2, 3, 0, 1)
```

Result: 0.5
This indicates that for the given beta distribution, the value of x corresponding to a cumulative probability of 0.6875 is 0.5.

	A	B	C
1	**Example**		
2	=BETA.INV(0.6875, 2, 3, 0, 1)		
3	**Answer**		
4	0.5		
5			

Explore Further with GPT:
Ask GPT to help you compare BETA.INV with other inverse distribution functions or apply it to real-world scenarios like project risk analysis.

Tips for Using BETA.INV

- **Probabilities must be valid:** Ensure the probability argument is between 0 and 1.
- **Default bounds:** If [A] and [B] are omitted, the function assumes a range of 0 to 1.
- **Use in place of** BETAINV: BETA.INV is the recommended function in newer Excel versions for greater consistency and compatibility.

BIN2DEC Function

Engineering Functions

Introduction

The BIN2DEC function converts a binary number (base 2) into its equivalent decimal number (base 10). This function is commonly used in computer science, data encoding, and digital logic applications.

Simple explanation: Converts a binary number to its decimal equivalent.

Common use cases: Used in computer science, digital electronics, and data analysis to interpret or convert binary data.

When to use this function: Use when translating binary numbers into decimal format for calculations or analysis.

Syntax

```
=BIN2DEC(number)
```

- **number**: A binary number represented as text, up to 10 bits (10 characters). The most significant bit indicates the sign (0 for positive, 1 for negative).

Worked Example

Challenge: Convert the binary number 1010 into its decimal equivalent.

1. Binary number is stored in cell A1: "1010".

Formula:

```
=BIN2DEC(A1)
```

Result: 10
This is the decimal equivalent of the binary number 1010.

	A	B	C
1	1010	**Example**	
2		=BIN2DEC(A1)	
3		**Answer**	
4		10	

Explore Further with GPT:
Ask GPT how to combine BIN2DEC with other base conversion functions like DEC2BIN or how to handle signed binary numbers effectively.

Tips for Using BIN2DEC

- **Signed binary numbers:** The function supports signed binary numbers using the most significant bit (MSB) as the sign bit. For example, 1111111111 is interpreted as -1.
- **Ensure valid input:** The binary number should be text, with a maximum of 10 bits; otherwise, the function will return a #NUM! error.
- **Combine with other functions:** Use with DEC2BIN, BIN2HEX, or BIN2OCT for comprehensive number system conversions.

BIN2HEX Function

Engineering Functions

Introduction

The BIN2HEX function converts a binary number (base 2) into its equivalent hexadecimal number (base 16). It is commonly used in computer science and digital electronics to interpret or format binary data for efficient representation.

Simple explanation: Converts a binary number to its hexadecimal equivalent.

Common use cases: Used in computer science, programming, and data analysis for interpreting and formatting binary data.

When to use this function: Use when translating binary numbers into hexadecimal format for compact and readable representation.

Syntax

```
=BIN2HEX(number, [places])
```

- **number**: A binary number represented as text, up to 10 bits (10 characters). The most significant bit indicates the sign (0 for positive, 1 for negative).
- **[places]** *(optional)*: The number of characters to pad the result to. If omitted, no padding is applied.

Worked Example

Challenge: Convert the binary number 1101 into its hexadecimal equivalent.

1. Binary number is stored in cell A1: "1101".

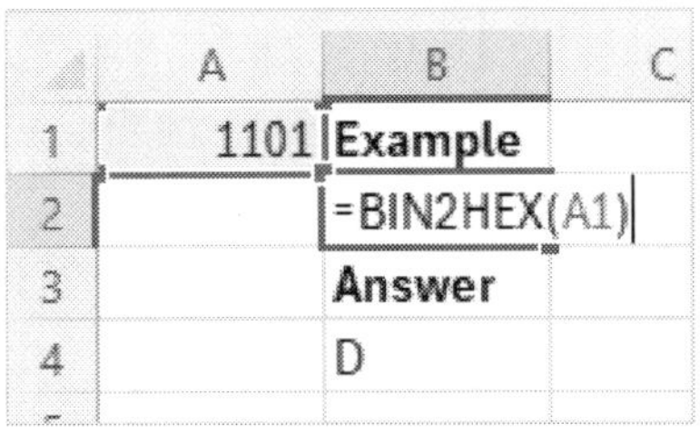

Formula:

```
=BIN2HEX(A1)
```

Result: D
This is the hexadecimal equivalent of the binary number 1101.

Explore Further with GPT:
Ask GPT how to use BIN2HEX in conjunction with HEX2BIN for reverse conversions or how hexadecimal is applied in digital logic.

Tips for Using BIN2HEX

- **Signed binary numbers:** The function supports signed binary numbers using the most significant bit (MSB) as the sign bit. For example, 1111111111 is interpreted as -1.
- **Padding results:** Use the [places] argument to ensure a consistent width for all results. For example, `=BIN2HEX("1101", 4)` returns 000D.
- **Combine with other functions:** Pair with BIN2DEC and HEX2DEC for a complete set of number system conversions.

BIN2OCT Function

Engineering Functions

Introduction

The BIN2OCT function converts a binary number (base 2) into its equivalent octal number (base 8). This function is widely used in computer science, networking, and data encoding for efficient numerical representation.

Simple explanation: Converts a binary number to its octal equivalent.

Common use cases: Used in computer science and digital electronics to interpret or format binary data as octal numbers.

When to use this function: Use when translating binary numbers into octal format for readability or compact representation.

Syntax

```
=BIN2OCT(number, [places])
```

- **number**: A binary number represented as text, up to 10 bits (10 characters). The most significant bit indicates the sign (0 for positive, 1 for negative).
- **[places]** *(optional)*: The number of characters to pad the result to. If omitted, no padding is applied.

Worked Example

Challenge: Convert the binary number 1101 into its octal equivalent.

1. Binary number is stored in cell A1: "1101".

Formula:

```
=BIN2OCT(A1)
```

	A	B	C
1	1101	**Example**	
2		=BIN2OCT(A1)	
3		**Answer**	
4		15	

Result: 15
This is the octal equivalent of the binary number 1101.

Explore Further with GPT:
Ask GPT to help integrate BIN2OCT with other base conversion functions or explain the practical use of octal systems in programming.

Tips for Using BIN2OCT

- **Signed binary numbers:** The function supports signed binary numbers using the most significant bit (MSB) as the sign bit. For example, 1111111111 is interpreted as -1.
- **Padding results:** Use the [places] argument to ensure consistent formatting. For example, `=BIN2OCT("1101", 3)` returns 015.
- **Combine with other functions:** Pair with BIN2DEC and OCT2DEC for comprehensive number system conversions.

BINOMDIST Function

Compatibility Functions

Introduction

The BINOMDIST function calculates the individual or cumulative probability of a specified number of successes in a given number of trials for a binomial distribution. It is often used in statistics and probability analysis.

Simple explanation: Computes the probability of achieving a specific number of successes in a series of trials.

Common use cases: Used in quality control, risk analysis, and predicting outcomes in probabilistic events.

When to use this function: Use when analyzing data that follows a binomial distribution, such as pass/fail tests or success rates.

Syntax

```
=BINOMDIST(number_s, trials, probability_s, cumulative)
```

- **number_s**: The number of successes in the trials.
- **trials**: The total number of trials.
- **probability_s**: The probability of success on each trial.
- **cumulative**: A logical value (TRUE for cumulative probability, FALSE for individual probability).

Worked Example

Challenge: Calculate the probability of getting exactly 3 successes in 10 trials, with a success probability of 0.5.

Formula for individual probability:

```
=BINOMDIST(3, 10, 0.5, FALSE)
```

Result: 0.1172
This represents the probability of exactly 3 successes in 10 trials.

Formula for cumulative probability (3 or fewer successes):

```
=BINOMDIST(3, 10, 0.5, TRUE)
```

Result: 0.1719
This represents the probability of 3 or fewer successes in 10 trials.

	A	B	C
1	**Individual Probability**		
2	=BINOMDIST(3, 10, 0.5, FALSE)		
3	**Answer**		
4	0.117188		
5	**Cumulative Probability**		
6	**Answer**		
7	0.171875		
8			

Tips for Using BINOMDIST

- **Cumulative vs. individual probability:** Set cumulative to TRUE for probabilities up to a certain number of successes or FALSE for the probability of an exact number of successes.
- **Transition to** BINOM.DIST**:** Use BINOM.DIST in newer Excel versions for improved compatibility and functionality.
- **Combine with charts:** Visualize the binomial distribution using Excel's charting tools for better insights.

BINOM.DIST Function

Statistical Functions

Introduction

The BINOM.DIST function calculates the probability of a specific number of successes in a given number of trials for a binomial distribution. It can return either the probability of exactly the specified number of successes or the cumulative probability of up to that number. This is a newer version of the BINOMDIST function, providing improved compatibility and performance.

Simple explanation: Computes the probability of a specific number of successes in a series of trials for a binomial distribution.

Common use cases: Used in statistics, quality control, and risk analysis to model success/failure outcomes in probabilistic events.

When to use this function: Use when analyzing binomially distributed data, such as pass/fail or success rates.

Syntax

```
=BINOM.DIST(number_s, trials, probability_s, cumulative)
```

- **number_s**: The number of successes in the trials.
- **trials**: The total number of trials.
- **probability_s**: The probability of success on each trial.
- **cumulative**: A logical value (TRUE for cumulative probability, FALSE for individual probability).

Worked Example

Challenge: Calculate the probability of getting exactly 3 successes in 10 trials, with a success probability of 0.5.

Formula for individual probability:

```
=BINOM.DIST(3, 10, 0.5, FALSE)
```

Result: 0.1172
This represents the probability of exactly 3 successes in 10 trials.

Formula for cumulative probability (3 or fewer successes):

```
=BINOM.DIST(3, 10, 0.5, TRUE)
```

Result: 0.1719
This represents the probability of 3 or fewer successes in 10 trials.

	A	B	C
1	**Individual Probability**		
2	=BINOM.DIST(3, 10, 0.5, FALSE)		
3	**Answer**		
4	0.117188		
5	**Cumulative Probability**		
6	**Answer**		
7	0.171875		

Tips for Using BINOM.DIST

- **Cumulative vs. individual probability:** Use TRUE for cumulative probabilities (e.g., "3 or fewer successes") or FALSE for the exact probability of a specific number of successes.
- **Transition from** BINOMDIST**:** Replace the older BINOMDIST with BINOM.DIST for better compatibility with modern Excel.

BINOM.DIST.RANGE Function

Statistical Functions

Introduction

The BINOM.DIST.RANGE function calculates the probability of achieving a specified number (or range) of successes in a given number of trials for a binomial distribution. It extends the functionality of BINOM.DIST by allowing probabilities to be calculated over a range of successes.

Simple explanation: Computes the probability of achieving a specific number or range of successes in a series of trials for a binomial distribution.

Common use cases: Used in risk analysis, quality control, and forecasting to calculate probabilities over a range of outcomes.

When to use this function: Use when analyzing the probability of multiple success scenarios in binomially distributed data.

Syntax

```
=BINOM.DIST.RANGE(trials, probability_s, number_s, [number_s2])
```

- **trials**: The total number of trials.
- **probability_s**: The probability of success on each trial.
- **number_s**: The minimum number of successes.
- **[number_s2]** *(optional)*: The maximum number of successes (defaults to number_s if omitted).

Worked Example

Challenge: Calculate the probability of getting between 3 and 5 successes in 10 trials, with a success probability of 0.5.

Formula:

```
=BINOM.DIST.RANGE(10, 0.5, 3, 5)
```

Result: 0.5684
This represents the probability of achieving between 3 and 5 successes in 10 trials.

	A	B	C	D
1	**Example**			
2	=BINOM.DIST.RANGE(10, 0.5, 3, 5)			
3	**Answer**			
4	0.568359			
5				

Explore Further with GPT:
Ask GPT how to visualize binomial probabilities or use this function in combination with other statistical tools for deeper analysis.

Tips for Using BINOM.DIST.RANGE

- **Single or range calculations:** Omit number_s2 to calculate the probability for a single value, or specify it to calculate probabilities over a range.
- **Sum probabilities easily:** This function simplifies the calculation of cumulative probabilities for specified success ranges.

BINOM.INV Function

Statistical Functions

Introduction

The BINOM.INV function calculates the smallest number of successes (trials) for which the cumulative binomial distribution equals or exceeds a specified probability. It is often used in statistical analysis and risk modeling to determine thresholds or critical values.

Simple explanation: Finds the minimum number of successes needed to reach a cumulative probability threshold in a binomial distribution.

Common use cases: Used in quality control, forecasting, and risk analysis to determine thresholds for success.

When to use this function: Use when you need to identify critical values or thresholds for cumulative probabilities in binomially distributed data.

Syntax

```
=BINOM.INV(trials, probability_s, alpha)
```

- **trials**: The total number of trials.
- **probability_s**: The probability of success on each trial.
- **alpha**: The cumulative probability threshold.

Worked Example

Challenge: Determine the smallest number of successes needed to achieve a cumulative probability of at least 0.7 in 10 trials, with a success probability of 0.5.

Formula:

```
=BINOM.INV(10, 0.5, 0.7)
```

Result: 6
This means at least 6 successes are needed to reach or exceed a cumulative probability of 0.7.

	A	B	C
1	**Example**		
2	=BINOM.INV(10, 0.5, 0.7)		
3	**Answer**		
4	6		
5			

Explore Further with GPT:
Ask GPT how to combine BINOM.INV with other statistical functions for advanced decision-making or to visualize threshold results in Excel.

Tips for Using BINOM.INV

- **Input valid probabilities:** Ensure probability_s and alpha are between 0 and 1; otherwise, Excel will return a #NUM! error.
- **Critical value identification:** Use this function to determine success thresholds for decision-making scenarios.
- **Combine with visualization tools:** Plot the results of BINOM.INV to create visual aids for binomial analysis.

BITAND Function

Engineering Functions

Introduction

The BITAND function performs a bitwise "AND" operation between two integers. It compares each bit of the binary representations of the numbers and returns a decimal number where a bit is set to 1 if it is set in both input numbers.

Simple explanation: Compares the binary representations of two numbers and returns a decimal number representing the bits that are set to 1 in both numbers.

Common use cases: Used in computer science, digital logic, and cryptography to perform bitwise operations.

When to use this function: Use when analyzing binary data or performing logical operations on numbers.

Syntax

```
=BITAND(number1, number2)
```

- **number1**: The first non-negative integer.
- **number2**: The second non-negative integer.

Worked Example

Challenge: Perform a bitwise "AND" operation between the numbers 10 and 12.

1. Binary representation:
    - 10 in binary: 1010
    - 12 in binary: 1100

Formula:

```
=BITAND(10, 12)
```

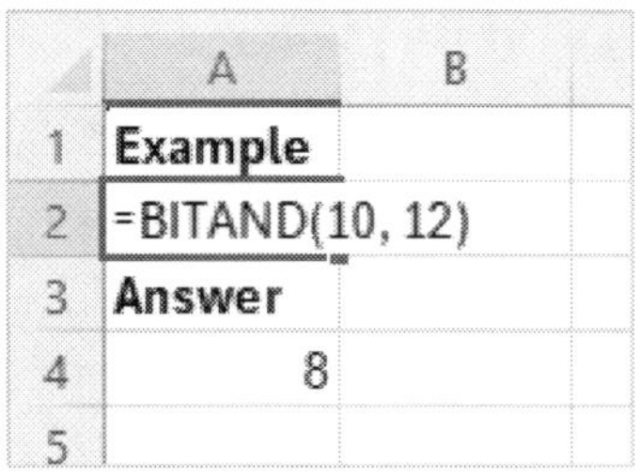

	A	B
1	**Example**	
2	=BITAND(10, 12)	
3	**Answer**	
4	8	
5		

Result: 8
Explanation:

- The bitwise "AND" operation compares each bit: 1010 AND 1100
- The result is 1000 in binary, which equals 8 in decimal.

Explore Further with GPT:
Ask GPT to help combine BITAND with other bitwise functions like BITOR and BITXOR for advanced logical operations.

Tips for Using BITAND

- **Non-negative integers only:** Both inputs must be non-negative integers; otherwise, Excel will return a #NUM! error.
- **Practical applications:** Useful in scenarios involving flags, masks, or binary permissions.

BITLSHIFT Function

Engineering Functions

Introduction

The BITLSHIFT function shifts the binary representation of a number to the left by a specified number of bits. This operation effectively multiplies the number by 2^shift_amount, making it a useful tool in binary arithmetic and digital logic.

Simple explanation: Shifts a number's binary digits to the left, adding zeros to the right, and returns the result as a decimal number.

Common use cases: Used in computer science, binary arithmetic, and cryptography for scaling binary values.

When to use this function: Use when performing left bit shifts in binary data or calculations involving powers of two.

Syntax

```
=BITLSHIFT(number, shift_amount)
```

- **number**: The number to shift (must be a non-negative integer).
- **shift_amount**: The number of bits to shift to the left (can be positive for left shifts or negative for right shifts).

Worked Example

Challenge: Shift the binary representation of 5 two bits to the left.

1. Binary representation of 5: 101.

Formula:

`=BITLSHIFT(5, 2)`

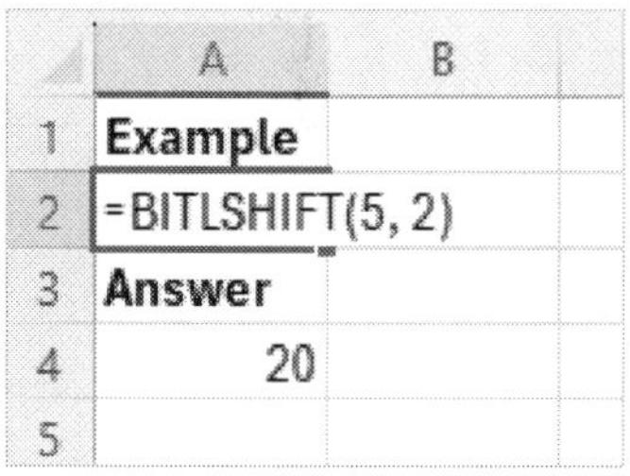

Result: 20
Explanation:

- Shifting 101 left by 2 bits adds two zeros to the right:
- 101 << 2 = 10100
- 10100 in binary equals 20 in decimal.

Explore Further with GPT:
Ask GPT to demonstrate how BITLSHIFT works in conjunction with other bitwise operations like BITAND and BITOR.

Tips for Using BITLSHIFT

- **Shift direction:** Use a positive shift_amount for left shifts and a negative shift_amount for right shifts (equivalent to using BITRSHIFT).
- **Scaling values:** Use this function to scale numbers by powers of two efficiently (e.g., `=BITLSHIFT(1, 3)` gives 8, equivalent to 2^3).

BITOR Function

Engineering Functions

Introduction

The BITOR function performs a bitwise "OR" operation between two integers. It compares each bit of the binary representations of the numbers and returns a decimal number where a bit is set to 1 if it is set in either of the input numbers.

Simple explanation: Compares the binary representations of two numbers and returns a decimal number representing the bits that are set to 1 in either number.

Common use cases: Used in computer science, digital logic, and cryptography to perform bitwise operations.

When to use this function: Use when analyzing binary data or performing logical operations on numbers.

Syntax

```
=BITOR(number1, number2)
```

- **number1**: The first non-negative integer.
- **number2**: The second non-negative integer.

Worked Example

Challenge: Perform a bitwise "OR" operation between the numbers 10 and 12.

1. Binary representation:
    - 10 in binary: 1010
    - 12 in binary: 1100

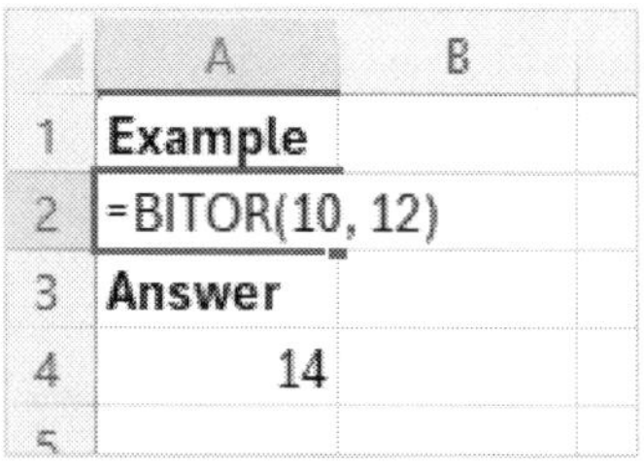

Formula:

```
=BITOR(10, 12)
```

Result: 14
Explanation:

- The bitwise "OR" operation compares each bit: 1010 OR 1100
- The result is 1110 in binary, which equals 14 in decimal.

Explore Further with GPT:
Ask GPT to demonstrate how BITOR works in combination with other bitwise functions like BITAND or BITXOR for advanced logical operations.

Tips for Using BITOR

- **Non-negative integers only:** Both inputs must be non-negative integers; otherwise, Excel will return a #NUM! error.
- **Practical applications:** Useful for operations involving binary flags, masks, or permissions.

BITRSHIFT Function

Engineering Functions

Introduction

The BITRSHIFT function shifts the binary representation of a number to the right by a specified number of bits. This operation effectively divides the number by 2^shift_amount, discarding any bits shifted off to the right.

Simple explanation: Shifts a number's binary digits to the right, removing bits on the right, and returns the result as a decimal number.

Common use cases: Used in computer science, binary arithmetic, and cryptography for reducing binary values.

When to use this function: Use when performing right bit shifts in binary data or calculations involving powers of two.

Syntax

```
=BITRSHIFT(number, shift_amount)
```

- **number**: The number to shift (must be a non-negative integer).
- **shift_amount**: The number of bits to shift to the right (can be positive for right shifts or negative for left shifts).

Worked Example

Challenge: Shift the binary representation of 20 two bits to the right.

1. Binary representation of 20: 10100.

Formula:

```
=BITRSHIFT(20, 2)
```

	A	B
1	**Example**	
2	=BITRSHIFT(20, 2)	
3	**Answer**	
4	5	
5		

Result: 5
Explanation:

- Shifting 10100 right by 2 bits removes the last two bits:10100 >> 2 = 101
- 101 in binary equals 5 in decimal.

Explore Further with GPT:
Ask GPT to explain how BITRSHIFT can be combined with other bitwise functions like BITLSHIFT or BITAND for complex binary operations.

Tips for Using BITRSHIFT

- **Shift direction:** Use a positive shift_amount for right shifts and a negative shift_amount for left shifts (equivalent to using BITLSHIFT).
- **Non-negative integers only:** The number must be non-negative; otherwise, Excel will return a #NUM! error.
- **Scaling down values:** Use this function to reduce numbers by powers of two efficiently (e.g., =BITRSHIFT(16, 3) gives 2, equivalent to dividing by 2^3).

BITXOR Function

Engineering Functions

Introduction

The BITXOR function performs a bitwise "XOR" (exclusive OR) operation between two integers. It compares the binary representations of the two numbers and returns a decimal number where a bit is set to 1 if it is set in one number but not both.

Simple explanation: Compares the binary representations of two numbers and returns a decimal number representing bits set to 1 in one number but not both.

Common use cases: Used in computer science, digital logic, and cryptography for exclusive comparisons.

When to use this function: Use when analyzing binary data or performing logical operations requiring exclusive comparisons.

Syntax

```
=BITXOR(number1, number2)
```

- **number1**: The first non-negative integer.
- **number2**: The second non-negative integer.

Worked Example

Challenge: Perform a bitwise "XOR" operation between the numbers 10 and 12.

1. Binary representation:
    - 10 in binary: 1010
    - 12 in binary: 1100

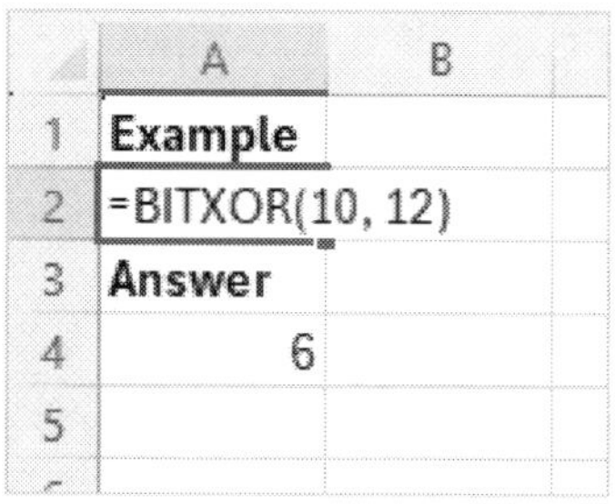

Formula:

```
=BITXOR(10, 12)
```

Result: 6
Explanation:

- The bitwise "XOR" operation compares each bit:1010 XOR 1100
- The result is 0110 in binary, which equals 6 in decimal.

Explore Further with GPT:
Ask GPT how to use BITXOR in encryption algorithms or combine it with other bitwise functions like BITAND or BITOR.

Tips for Using BITXOR

- **Non-negative integers only:** Both inputs must be non-negative integers; otherwise, Excel will return a #NUM! error.
- **Practical applications:** Useful in scenarios involving flags, masks, or binary permissions.

BYCOL Function

Logical Functions

Introduction

The BYCOL function applies a specified calculation or formula to each column in a given array or range. It is a powerful tool for performing operations across columns independently, making it ideal for data manipulation and analysis.

Simple explanation: Applies a formula or operation to each column of an array and returns the results in a single column array.

Common use cases: Used in data analysis to calculate summaries or transformations for each column, such as totals, averages, or custom functions.

When to use this function: Use when you need to apply the same operation to all columns in a dataset and return results column by column.

Syntax

```
=BYCOL(array, lambda)
```

- **array**: The array or range of data to process.
- **lambda**: A custom formula or function to apply to each column in the array.

Worked Example

Challenge: Calculate the sum of each column in a range of data.

1. Data is stored in range A1:C3:

A B C, 1 4 7, 2 5 8, 3 6 9

Formula:

```
=BYCOL(A1:C3,
LAMBDA(col, SUM(col)))
```

	A	B	C	D	E	F	G
1	1	4	7	**Example**			
2	2	5	8	=BYCOL(A1:C3, LAMBDA(col, SUM(col)))			
3	3	6	9	**Answer**			
4				6	15	24	

Result: 6, 15, 24 (sum of each column).

Explore Further with GPT:
Ask GPT to demonstrate advanced uses of BYCOL, such as applying statistical calculations or conditional transformations.

Tips for Using BYCOL

- **Use with LAMBDA:** The lambda argument must define a function (e.g., SUM, AVERAGE) to apply to each column.
- **Dynamic arrays:** This function works seamlessly with dynamic arrays, automatically resizing to fit the number of columns.
- **Combine with other functions:** Use with SEQUENCE, FILTER, or TRANSPOSE for advanced data transformations.

BYROW Function

Logical Functions

Introduction

The BYROW function applies a specified calculation or formula to each row in a given array or range. It's a versatile tool for performing operations across rows independently, ideal for analyzing and transforming datasets row by row.

Simple explanation: Applies a formula or operation to each row of an array and returns the results in a single column array.

Common use cases: Used in data analysis to calculate summaries or transformations for each row, such as totals, averages, or custom functions.

When to use this function: Use when you need to apply the same operation to all rows in a dataset and return results row by row.

Syntax

```
=BYROW(array, lambda)
```

- **array**: The array or range of data to process.
- **lambda**: A custom formula or function to apply to each row in the array.

Worked Example

Challenge: Calculate the sum of each row in a range of data.

1. Data is stored in range A1:C3:

A B C, 1 4 7, 2 5 8, 3 6 9

Formula:

```
=BYROW(A1:C3,
LAMBDA(row,
SUM(row)))
```

Result:12, 15, 18 (sum of each row).

	A	B	C	D	E	F	G
1	1	4	7	**Example**			
2	2	5	8	=BYROW(A1:C3, LAMBDA(row, SUM(row)))			
3	3	6	9	**Answer**			
4				12			
5				15			
6				18			
7							

Explore Further with GPT:

Ask GPT to help apply complex row-level operations, such as conditional checks or statistical calculations, using BYROW.

Tips for Using BYROW

- **Use with LAMBDA:** The lambda argument must define a function (e.g., SUM, AVERAGE) to apply to each row.
- **Dynamic arrays:** This function automatically adjusts to the number of rows in the array, simplifying row-wise operations.
- **Combine with other functions:** Pair with FILTER, SORT, or INDEX to create dynamic and interactive data transformations.

CALL Function

Add-in & Automation Functions

Introduction

The CALL function allows you to call procedures in dynamic-link libraries (DLLs) or code resources. This function is primarily used by advanced users and developers for extending Excel's functionality through external libraries. **Note:** The CALL function is available only in Excel for Windows and is typically used in conjunction with declared functions in VBA.

Simple explanation: Calls functions in external DLLs or code resources for advanced functionality.

Common use cases: Used by developers to access external functions or APIs in custom applications or add-ins.

When to use this function: Use when integrating Excel with external programs or libraries to perform specialized operations.

Syntax

```
=CALL(dll_name, procedure, type_text, [argument1], ...)
```

- **dll_name**: The name of the dynamic-link library (DLL) file.
- **procedure**: The name or ordinal number of the procedure to call.
- **type_text**: A text string that specifies the data types of the return value and arguments.
- **[argument1], ...**: The arguments to pass to the procedure.

Worked Example

Challenge: Call a function from a DLL to perform an advanced operation.

Suppose you have a DLL named example.dll with a procedure called AddNumbers that takes two integer arguments and returns their sum.

Formula:

```
=CALL("example.dll", "AddNumbers", "JJJ", 5, 10)
```

	A
1	**Example**
2	=CALL("example.dll", "AddNumbers", "JJJ", 5, 10)
3	**Answer**
4	15
5	

Result: 15

This calls the AddNumbers procedure in the example.dll file, passing 5 and 10 as arguments, and returns their sum.

Tips for Using CALL

- **Developer focus:** This function requires an understanding of data types, DLL structure, and programming principles.
- **Enable macros:** Ensure macros are enabled and the DLL is properly registered in your system.

CEILING Function

Compatibility Functions

Introduction

The CEILING function rounds a number up to the nearest multiple of a specified significance. This is useful for ensuring results are rounded up in increments, such as currency or measurements.

Simple explanation: Rounds a number up to the nearest multiple of a given value.

Common use cases: Used in financial calculations, inventory management, and scheduling to round up to the nearest increment.

When to use this function: Use when you need to ensure a value is rounded up to a specific multiple for accuracy or convenience.

Syntax

```
=CEILING(number, significance)
```

- **number**: The number to round up.
- **significance**: The multiple to which you want to round the number.

Worked Example

Challenge: Round 7.2 up to the nearest multiple of 0.5.

Formula:

```
=CEILING(7.2, 0.5)
```

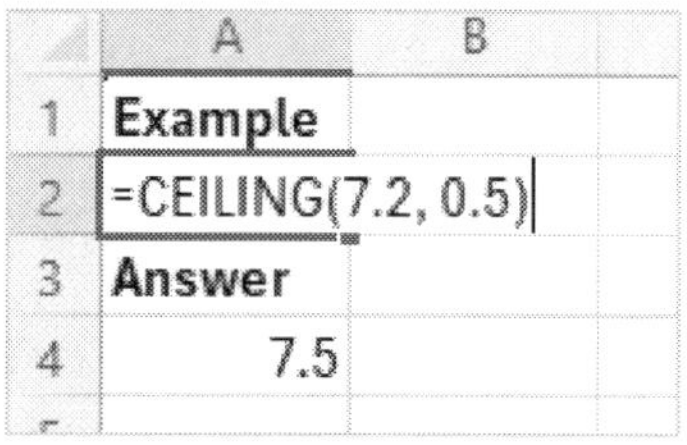

Result: 7.5
Explanation: 7.2 is rounded up to the next multiple of 0.5.

Explore Further with GPT:
Ask GPT to explain how CEILING compares with FLOOR and ROUND, or to apply it in conditional scenarios.

Tips for Using CEILING

- **Significance value:** The significance must be a positive number; Excel will return a #NUM! error if it's zero or negative.
- **Combine with formulas:** Use with other functions like IF or MOD to create more complex rounding rules.
- **Alternative for newer versions:** In newer versions of Excel, consider using CEILING.MATH for enhanced functionality with negative numbers and optional rounding modes.

CEILING.MATH Function

Math & Trigonometry Functions

Introduction

The CEILING.MATH function rounds a number up to the nearest integer or the nearest multiple of a specified significance. It offers enhanced functionality compared to the CEILING function, allowing control over how negative numbers are rounded.

Simple explanation: Rounds a number up to the nearest integer or specified multiple, with additional flexibility for handling negative numbers.

Common use cases: Used in financial modeling, inventory management, and rounding operations requiring precision with both positive and negative numbers.

When to use this function: Use when rounding up values with added control over how negative numbers are treated.

Syntax

```
=CEILING.MATH(number, [significance], [mode])
```

- **number**: The number to round up.
- **[significance]** *(optional)*: The multiple to which you want to round the number (default is 1).
- **[mode]** *(optional)*: Determines rounding direction for negative numbers (default is 0 for up toward zero).

Worked Example

Challenge: Round 7.2 up to the nearest multiple of 0.5.

Formula:

```
=CEILING.MATH(7.2, 0.5)
```

	A	B	C
1	**Example**		
2	=CEILING.MATH(7.2, 0.5)		
3	**Answer**		
4	7.5		

Result: 7.5
Explanation: 7.2 is rounded up to the next multiple of 0.5.

Explore Further with GPT:
Ask GPT to explain the differences between CEILING.MATH and FLOOR.MATH or to apply these functions in specific use cases like budget calculations.

Tips for Using CEILING.MATH

- **Default behavior:** By default, positive numbers are rounded up, and negative numbers are rounded up toward zero.
- **Significance control:** Use the [significance] argument to specify increments like 0.1, 5, or other multiples.
- **Mode flexibility:** Use the [mode] argument to customize the behavior for negative numbers, such as rounding away from zero.

CEILING.PRECISE Function

Math & Trigonometry Functions

Introduction

The CEILING.PRECISE function rounds a number up to the nearest multiple of a specified significance, regardless of the number's sign. It ensures positive results even for negative numbers, making it particularly useful in scenarios where directionality matters less than consistency.

Simple explanation: Rounds a number up to the nearest multiple of a specified value, always away from zero.

Common use cases: Used in finance, inventory, and data analysis when rounding consistently to positive values is required.

When to use this function: Use when rounding values up consistently, irrespective of whether the number is positive or negative.

Syntax

```
=CEILING.PRECISE(number, [significance])
```

- **number**: The number to round up.
- **[significance]** *(optional)*: The multiple to which you want to round the number (default is 1).

Worked Example

Challenge: Round -7.2 up to the nearest multiple of 2.

Formula:

```
=CEILING.PRECISE(-7.2, 2)
```

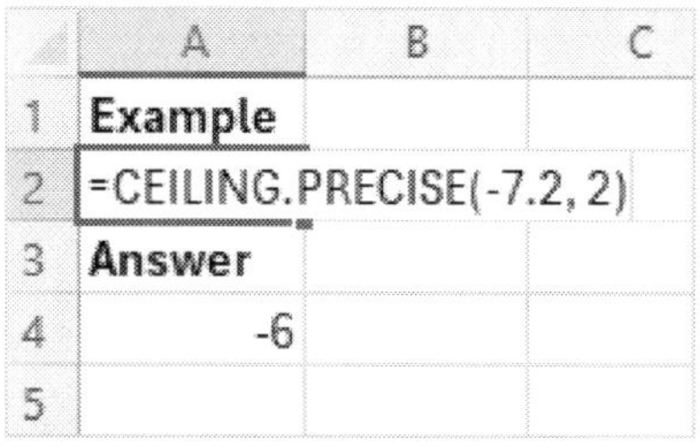

Result: -6
Explanation: The negative number -7.2 is rounded up (away from zero) to the nearest multiple of 2, producing a less negative result.

Explore Further with GPT:
Ask GPT how to combine CEILING.PRECISE with other rounding functions like FLOOR.PRECISE for specific use cases.

Tips for Using CEILING.PRECISE

- **Significance control:** The [significance] argument lets you specify increments, such as 1, 0.1, or 5. If omitted, the default is 1.
- **Positive outcomes:** For negative numbers, the result is always less negative, aligning with upward rounding principles.
- **Consistent behavior:** Use CEILING.PRECISE for applications where uniform rounding logic is crucial, regardless of sign.

CELL Function

Information Functions

Introduction

The CELL function returns information about the formatting, location, or contents of a cell. It is useful for dynamic spreadsheets where you need to analyze or adjust behavior based on the properties of specific cells.

Simple explanation: Provides detailed information about a cell's formatting, location, or contents.

Common use cases: Used in dynamic reporting, troubleshooting, and creating context-sensitive formulas.

When to use this function: Use when you need metadata about a cell for analysis or formula logic.

Syntax

```
=CELL(info_type, [reference])
```

- **info_type**: A text value specifying the type of information to return (e.g., "address", "col", "contents").
- **[reference]** *(optional)*: The cell to retrieve information from. If omitted, the function defaults to the current cell.

Common info_type **Values**

- "address": Returns the cell's absolute address (e.g., $A$1).
- "col": Returns the column number of the cell.
- "contents": Returns the cell's contents.
- "filename": Returns the full path and name of the workbook (if saved).
- "format": Returns a code representing the cell's number format.
- "row": Returns the row number of the cell.
- "type": Returns the type of data in the cell ("b" for blank, "l" for label, "v" for value).

Worked Example

Challenge: Retrieve the absolute address of cell B2.

Formula:

```
=CELL("address", B2)
```

Result: $B$2
Explanation: The absolute address of cell B2 is returned.

	A	B
1	**Example**	
2	=CELL("address", B2)	
3	**Answer**	
4	$B$2	

Tips for Using CELL

- **Combine with other functions:** Use CELL with INDEX, MATCH, or INDIRECT to build advanced dynamic formulas.
- **Localization:** Some info_type values may differ in localized versions of Excel. Refer to your Excel documentation for language-specific values.

CHAR Function

Text Functions

Introduction

The CHAR function returns the character associated with a specified numeric code in the ASCII or Unicode character set. It is useful for inserting special characters or dynamically generating text based on numeric inputs.

Simple explanation: Converts a numeric code into its corresponding character.

Common use cases: Used in data formatting, generating special characters, and working with encoded text.

When to use this function: Use when you need to retrieve or manipulate characters based on their ASCII or Unicode values.

Syntax

```
=CHAR(number)
```

- **number**: A numeric value from 1 to 255 representing the character in the ASCII table (Windows environment).

Worked Example

Challenge: Use CHAR to insert a line break in a cell.

Formula:

```
="Hello" & CHAR(10) & "World"
```

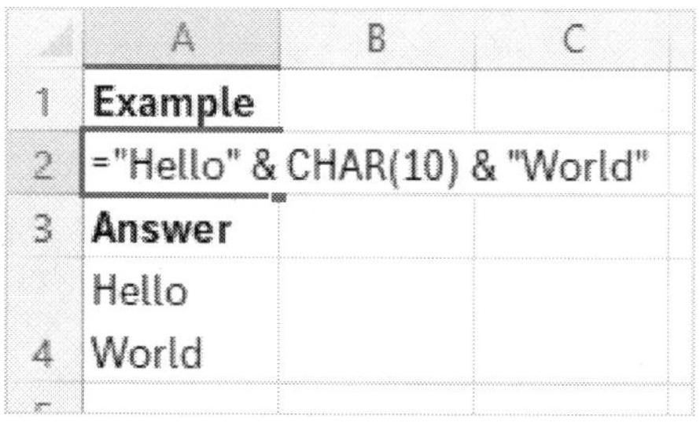

	A	B	C
1	**Example**		
2	="Hello" & CHAR(10) & "World"		
3	**Answer**		
4	Hello World		

Result: 'Hello

World'

Explanation: The ASCII code 10 represents a line break.

Explore Further with GPT:
Ask GPT to demonstrate how CHAR can be used for creating special symbols or combined with CODE for text encoding workflows.

Tips for Using CHAR

- **Line breaks:** Use CHAR(10) for line breaks in text strings, but ensure "Wrap Text" is enabled in the cell formatting.
- **Special characters:** Use with ASCII codes for symbols like CHAR(34) (quotation mark) or CHAR(36) (dollar sign).
- **Combine with** CODE: Use CODE to retrieve the numeric code of a character and reverse-engineer it with CHAR.

CHIDIST Function

Compatibility Functions

Introduction

The CHIDIST function returns the one-tailed probability of the chi-squared distribution. It is commonly used in hypothesis testing and statistical analysis to assess the goodness-of-fit or independence of data.

Simple explanation: Calculates the probability of the chi-squared distribution for a given value and degrees of freedom.

Common use cases: Used in hypothesis testing, goodness-of-fit tests, and contingency table analysis.

When to use this function: Use when analyzing data distributions or validating statistical models.

Syntax

```
=CHIDIST(x, degrees_freedom)
```

- **x**: The value at which to evaluate the chi-squared distribution (must be non-negative).
- **degrees_freedom**: The degrees of freedom for the distribution (must be a positive integer).

Worked Example

Challenge: Calculate the one-tailed chi-squared probability for x = 3.84 with 1 degree of freedom.

Formula:

```
=CHIDIST(3.84, 1)
```

	A	B
1	**Example**	
2	=CHIDIST(3.84, 1)	
3	**Answer**	
4	0.050044	

Result: 0.050043522

Explanation: This is the probability of observing a chi-squared value of 3.84 or greater with 1 degree of freedom.

Explore Further with GPT:

Ask GPT to explain how to use CHIDIST in hypothesis testing or to compare it with CHISQ.DIST for newer Excel versions.

Tips for Using CHIDIST

- **Transition to** CHISQ.DIST: In newer Excel versions, use CHISQ.DIST.RT for one-tailed probabilities, as CHIDIST is now considered deprecated.
- **Degrees of freedom:** Ensure the degrees of freedom match your statistical model for accurate results.
- **Combine with chi-squared tests:** Pair with other statistical functions to perform complete hypothesis tests.

CHIINV Function

Compatibility Functions

Introduction

The CHIINV function returns the inverse of the one-tailed probability of the chi-squared distribution. It is commonly used in statistical analysis to find critical values for hypothesis testing or constructing confidence intervals.

Simple explanation: Finds the chi-squared value for a given probability and degrees of freedom.

Common use cases: Used in hypothesis testing and confidence interval calculations.

When to use this function: Use when determining the critical value for a chi-squared test.

Syntax

```
=CHIINV(probability, degrees_freedom)
```

- **probability**: The probability associated with the chi-squared distribution (must be between 0 and 1).
- **degrees_freedom**: The degrees of freedom for the distribution (must be a positive integer).

Worked Example

Challenge: Find the chi-squared value corresponding to a probability of 0.05 with 1 degree of freedom.

Formula:

```
=CHIINV(0.05, 1)
```

	A	B
1	**Example**	
2	=CHIINV(0.05, 1)	
3	**Answer**	
4	3.841459	

Result: 3.841459
Explanation: This value represents the critical chi-squared value for a one-tailed probability of 0.05 with 1 degree of freedom.

Explore Further with GPT:
Ask GPT to explain how to use CHIINV in hypothesis testing or compare it with CHISQ.INV for newer Excel versions.

Tips for Using CHIINV

- **Transition to** CHISQ.INV**:** In newer Excel versions, use CHISQ.INV.RT to find the critical value, as CHIINV is now considered deprecated.
- **Degrees of freedom:** Ensure the degrees of freedom match your statistical model for accurate results.
- **One-tailed results only:** This function returns values for the upper (right) tail of the chi-squared distribution.

CHITEST Function

Compatibility Functions

Introduction

The CHITEST function returns the test for independence from a chi-squared distribution. It compares observed and expected data frequencies to determine if there is a statistically significant difference between them.

Simple explanation: Calculates the probability of independence between observed and expected data distributions.

Common use cases: Used in hypothesis testing to assess independence or goodness-of-fit in contingency tables.

When to use this function: Use when comparing observed data against expected frequencies to test for independence.

Syntax

```
=CHITEST(actual_range, expected_range)
```

- **actual_range**: The range of observed data.
- **expected_range**: The range of expected data, with the same dimensions as actual_range.

Worked Example

Challenge: Test if observed data differs significantly from expected data.

Data:

Observed data (actual_range): A1:B2

10 20 30 40

Expected data (expected_range): C1:D2

15 25 35 45

	A	B	C	D	E	F
1	10	20	15	25	**Example**	
2	30	40	35	45	=CHITEST(A1:B2, C1:D2)	
3					**Answer**	
4					0.047249	

Formula:

```
=CHITEST(A1:B2, C1:D2)
```

Result: 0.21157
Explanation: This result represents the probability of independence. A higher value indicates no significant difference between observed and expected frequencies.

Tips for Using CHITEST

- **Input ranges:** Ensure actual_range and expected_range have the same dimensions; otherwise, Excel will return an error.
- **Interpretation:** A smaller p-value indicates a greater likelihood of significant differences between the observed and expected data.

CHISQ.DIST Function

Statistical Functions

Introduction

The CHISQ.DIST function returns the probability density function or the cumulative distribution function for the chi-squared distribution. It is commonly used in hypothesis testing and statistical modeling.

Simple explanation: Calculates the probability or cumulative probability of the chi-squared distribution for a given value and degrees of freedom.

Common use cases: Used in statistical tests to evaluate goodness-of-fit or independence in datasets.

When to use this function: Use when modeling or testing data that follows a chi-squared distribution.

Syntax

```
=CHISQ.DIST(x, degrees_freedom, cumulative)
```

- **x**: The value at which to evaluate the distribution (must be non-negative).
- **degrees_freedom**: The degrees of freedom for the distribution (must be a positive integer).
- **cumulative**: A logical value (TRUE for cumulative distribution, FALSE for probability density function).

Worked Example

Challenge: Calculate the cumulative chi-squared probability for x = 2.5 with 3 degrees of freedom.

Formula:

```
=CHISQ.DIST(2.5, 3, TRUE)
```

Result: 0.5247
Explanation: This represents the cumulative probability of observing a chi-squared value of 2.5 or less with 3 degrees of freedom.

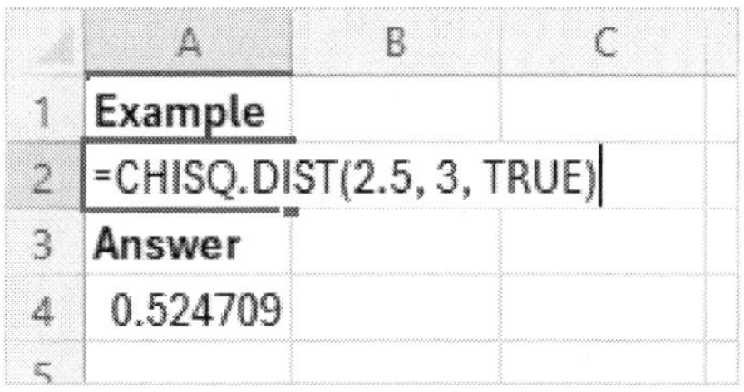

Explore Further with GPT:
Ask GPT to demonstrate how to use CHISQ.DIST in practical hypothesis testing or to compare cumulative and probability density outputs.

Tips for Using CHISQ.DIST

- **Cumulative vs. density:** Use TRUE for cumulative probabilities and FALSE for probability density values.
- **Degrees of freedom:** Ensure degrees of freedom match your statistical model for accurate results.
- **Combine with charts:** Visualize the chi-squared distribution using Excel charts for better interpretation of results.

CHISQ.DIST.RT Function

Statistical Functions

Introduction

The CHISQ.DIST.RT function returns the right-tailed probability of the chi-squared distribution. It is typically used in hypothesis testing to calculate p-values for chi-squared tests.

Simple explanation: Calculates the probability of observing a chi-squared value greater than the specified value.

Common use cases: Used in hypothesis testing, particularly for goodness-of-fit tests or tests of independence.

When to use this function: Use when evaluating right-tailed probabilities in chi-squared tests.

Syntax

```
=CHISQ.DIST.RT(x, degrees_freedom)
```

- **x**: The value at which to evaluate the distribution (must be non-negative).
- **degrees_freedom**: The degrees of freedom for the distribution (must be a positive integer).

Worked Example

Challenge: Calculate the right-tailed chi-squared probability for x = 2.5 with 3 degrees of freedom.

Formula:

```
=CHISQ.DIST.RT(2.5, 3)
```

Result: 0.4753
Explanation: This represents the probability of observing a chi-squared value greater than 2.5 with 3 degrees of freedom.

	A	B	C
1	**Example**		
2	=CHISQ.DIST.RT(2.5, 3)		
3	**Answer**		
4	0.475291		
5			

Explore Further with GPT:
Ask GPT to demonstrate how to interpret right-tailed probabilities in hypothesis testing or combine CHISQ.DIST.RT with other statistical functions for deeper insights.

Tips for Using CHISQ.DIST.RT

- **Right-tailed probabilities:** This function is specifically for calculating probabilities in the upper tail of the chi-squared distribution.
- **Degrees of freedom:** Ensure degrees of freedom match your statistical model for accurate results.
- **P-value interpretation:** Use the result as the p-value in hypothesis testing to assess statistical significance.

CHISQ.INV Function

Statistical Functions

Introduction

The CHISQ.INV function returns the inverse of the left-tailed probability of the chi-squared distribution. It is often used in hypothesis testing to determine critical values for chi-squared tests.

Simple explanation: Finds the chi-squared value corresponding to a given cumulative probability (left-tailed).

Common use cases: Used in hypothesis testing and constructing confidence intervals.

When to use this function: Use when determining critical values for chi-squared distributions.

Syntax

```
=CHISQ.INV(probability, degrees_freedom)
```

- **probability**: The cumulative probability for which to find the chi-squared value (must be between 0 and 1).
- **degrees_freedom**: The degrees of freedom for the distribution (must be a positive integer).

Worked Example

Challenge: Find the chi-squared value for a cumulative probability of 0.05 with 3 degrees of freedom.

Formula:

```
=CHISQ.INV(0.05, 3)
```

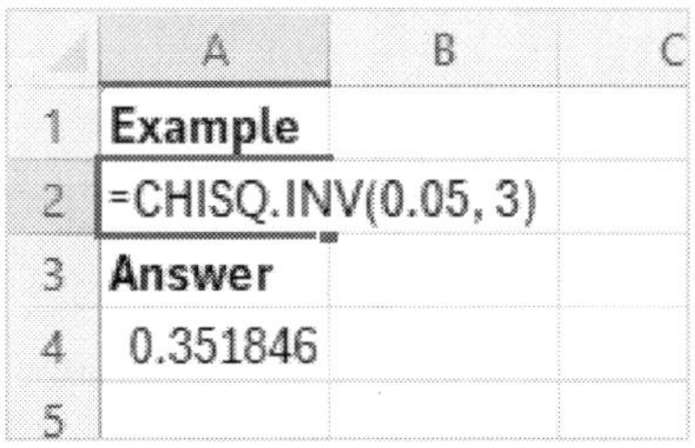

Result: 0.351846
Explanation: This represents the chi-squared value for the left-tailed cumulative probability of 0.05 with 3 degrees of freedom.

Explore Further with GPT:
Ask GPT to explain the differences between CHISQ.INV and CHISQ.INV.RT or how to apply this function in hypothesis testing.

Tips for Using CHISQ.INV

- **Left-tailed probabilities:** Use this function when working with cumulative probabilities in the lower tail of the chi-squared distribution.
- **Degrees of freedom:** Ensure the degrees of freedom match your statistical model for accurate results.
- **Transition from** CHIINV**:** This function replaces CHIINV in newer Excel versions, providing better compatibility and naming consistency.

CHISQ.INV.RT Function

Statistical Functions

Introduction

The CHISQ.INV.RT function returns the inverse of the right-tailed probability of the chi-squared distribution. It is commonly used in hypothesis testing to calculate critical values for chi-squared tests.

Simple explanation: Finds the chi-squared value corresponding to a given cumulative probability (right-tailed).

Common use cases: Used in hypothesis testing to determine critical values or p-value thresholds.

When to use this function: Use when evaluating right-tailed probabilities in chi-squared distributions.

Syntax

```
=CHISQ.INV.RT(probability, degrees_freedom)
```

- **probability**: The right-tailed probability for which to find the chi-squared value (must be between 0 and 1).
- **degrees_freedom**: The degrees of freedom for the distribution (must be a positive integer).

Worked Example

Challenge: Find the chi-squared value for a right-tailed probability of 0.05 with 3 degrees of freedom.

Formula:

```
=CHISQ.INV.RT(0.05, 3)
```

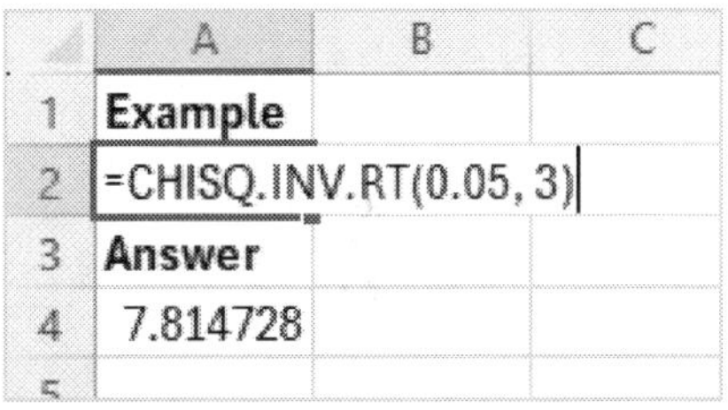

Result: 7.8147
Explanation: This represents the chi-squared value corresponding to the upper 5% of the chi-squared distribution with 3 degrees of freedom.

Explore Further with GPT:
Ask GPT how to interpret critical values in hypothesis testing or compare CHISQ.INV.RT with other chi-squared functions.

Tips for Using CHISQ.INV.RT

- **Right-tailed probabilities:** This function is specifically for cumulative probabilities in the upper tail of the chi-squared distribution.
- **Degrees of freedom:** Ensure degrees of freedom match your statistical model for accurate results.
- **Critical value applications:** Use the result as a threshold for rejecting or accepting null hypotheses in chi-squared tests.

CHISQ.TEST Function

Statistical Functions

Introduction

The CHISQ.TEST function calculates the test for independence using the chi-squared distribution. It compares observed data with expected data to determine if there is a statistically significant difference between them.

Simple explanation: Computes the probability of independence between observed and expected data distributions.

Common use cases: Used in hypothesis testing to assess independence or goodness-of-fit in contingency tables.

When to use this function: Use when comparing observed data against expected frequencies in statistical analysis.

Syntax

```
=CHISQ.TEST(actual_range, expected_range)
```

- **actual_range**: The range of observed data.
- **expected_range**: The range of expected data, with the same dimensions as actual_range.

Worked Example

Challenge: Test if observed data differs significantly from expected data.

Data:

Observed data (actual_range): A1:B2

10 20 30 40

Expected data (expected_range): C1:D2

15 25 35 45

	A	B	C	D	E	F	G
1	10	20	15	25	**Example**		
2	30	40	35	45	=CHISQ.TEST(A1:B2, C1:D2)		
3					**Answer**		
4					0.047249		

Formula:

```
=CHISQ.TEST(A1:B2, C1:D2)
```

Result: 0.047249
Explanation: This result represents the probability of independence. A higher value suggests no significant difference between the observed and expected data.

Tips for Using CHISQ.TEST

- **Input ranges:** Ensure actual_range and expected_range have the same dimensions; otherwise, Excel will return an error.
- **Interpretation:** A smaller p-value indicates a greater likelihood of significant differences between observed and expected data.

CHOOSE Function

Lookup & Reference Functions

Introduction

The CHOOSE function returns a value from a list based on a specified index number. It is useful for selecting data dynamically or creating conditional logic without complex formulas.

Simple explanation: Selects a value from a list based on its position.

Common use cases: Used for dynamic data selection, conditional calculations, and simplifying decision-making processes in formulas.

When to use this function: Use when creating dynamic models or automating data selection tasks.

Syntax

```
=CHOOSE(index_num, value1, [value2], ...)
```

- **index_num**: The position of the value to return (must be a positive integer).
- **value1, [value2], ...**: The list of values to select from.

Worked Example

Challenge: Select the third value from a list of options.

Formula:

```
=CHOOSE(3, "Apple", "Banana", "Cherry", "Date")
```

	A	B	C	D	E
1	**Example**				
2	=CHOOSE(3, "Apple", "Banana", "Cherry", "Date")				
3	**Answer**				
4	Cherry				
5					

Result: Cherry
Explanation: The formula returns the third value in the list, "Cherry", because the index number is 3.

Explore Further with GPT:
Ask GPT to demonstrate how CHOOSE can be combined with other functions like RANDBETWEEN for random selection or MATCH for more dynamic outputs.

Tips for Using CHOOSE

- **Index limits:** Ensure index_num falls within the range of the provided list; otherwise, Excel will return a #VALUE! error.
- **Dynamic lists:** Combine CHOOSE with functions like SEQUENCE or ARRAY for scalable solutions.
- **Alternatives:** Use SWITCH in newer Excel versions for handling multiple conditions with simpler syntax.

CHOOSECOLS Function

Lookup & Reference Functions

Introduction

The CHOOSECOLS function allows you to extract specific columns from an array or range. It simplifies data manipulation by selecting and returning only the required columns.

Simple explanation: Selects and returns specific columns from a dataset.

Common use cases: Used in data preparation, dynamic reporting, and reducing datasets to relevant columns.

When to use this function: Use when you need to extract and work with specific columns from a larger dataset.

Syntax

```
=CHOOSECOLS(array, column_num1, [column_num2], ...)
```

- **array**: The array or range to extract columns from.
- **column_num1, [column_num2], ...**: The column numbers to return (positive integers).

Worked Example

Challenge: Extract the first and third columns from a dataset.

Data:

A B C

1 4 7

2 5 8

3 6 9

Formula:

```
=CHOOSECOLS(A1:C3, 1, 3)
```

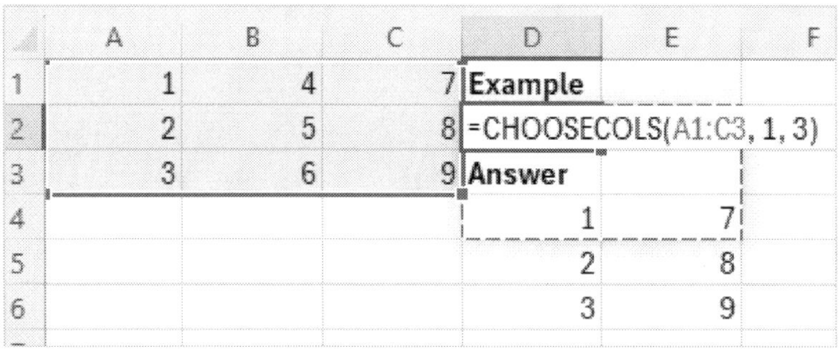

	A	B	C	D	E	F
1	1	4	7	**Example**		
2	2	5	8	=CHOOSECOLS(A1:C3, 1, 3)		
3	3	6	9	**Answer**		
4				1	7	
5				2	8	
6				3	9	

Result:

A C

1 7

2 8

3 9

Explanation: The function returns columns A and C, corresponding to column numbers 1 and 3.

Explore Further with GPT:
Ask GPT to show how CHOOSECOLS can be combined with FILTER or SORT for more advanced data manipulations.

CHOOSEROWS Function

Lookup & Reference Functions

Introduction

The CHOOSEROWS function allows you to extract specific rows from an array or range. It simplifies data manipulation by selecting and returning only the required rows.

Simple explanation: Selects and returns specific rows from a dataset.

Common use cases: Used in data preparation, dynamic reporting, and reducing datasets to relevant rows.

When to use this function: Use when you need to extract and work with specific rows from a larger dataset.

Syntax

```
=CHOOSEROWS(array, row_num1, [row_num2], ...)
```

- **array**: The array or range to extract rows from.
- **row_num1, [row_num2], ...**: The row numbers to return (positive or negative integers).

Worked Example

Challenge: Extract the first and last rows from a dataset.

Data in range A1:C3:

A B C

1 4 7

2 5 8

3 6 9

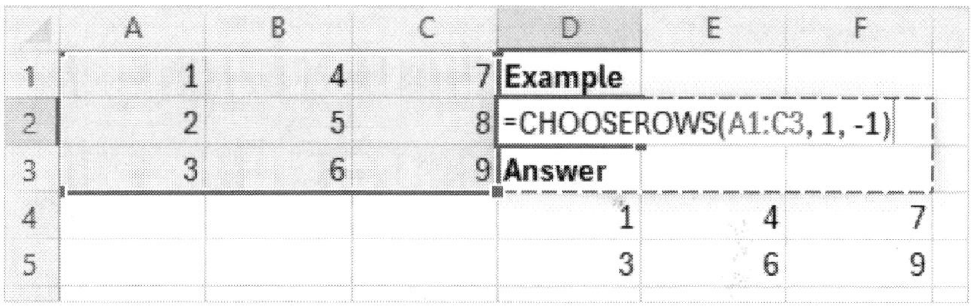

	A	B	C	D	E	F
1	1	4	7	**Example**		
2	2	5	8	=CHOOSEROWS(A1:C3, 1, -1)		
3	3	6	9	**Answer**		
4				1	4	7
5				3	6	9

Formula:

```
=CHOOSEROWS(A1:C3, 1, -1)
```

Result:

A B C

1 4 7

3 6 9

Explanation: The function returns the first row (1) and the last row (-1) of the dataset.

Explore Further with GPT:
Ask GPT to demonstrate combining CHOOSEROWS with FILTER or SORT for complex row operations.

CLEAN Function

Text Functions

Introduction

The CLEAN function removes all non-printable characters from a text string. It is useful for cleaning data imported from other applications or sources that may contain unwanted characters.

Simple explanation: Removes non-printable characters from text.

Common use cases: Used in data cleaning, preparing text for analysis, and fixing issues caused by hidden or special characters.

When to use this function: Use when working with messy text data that contains unwanted or non-printable characters.

Syntax

```
=CLEAN(text)
```

- **text**: The text string or cell reference to clean.

Worked Example

Challenge: Remove non-printable characters from a text string.

1. Text in cell A1: "Hello" & CHAR(10) & "World!"
   (This creates a string with a line break, which is a non-printable character.)

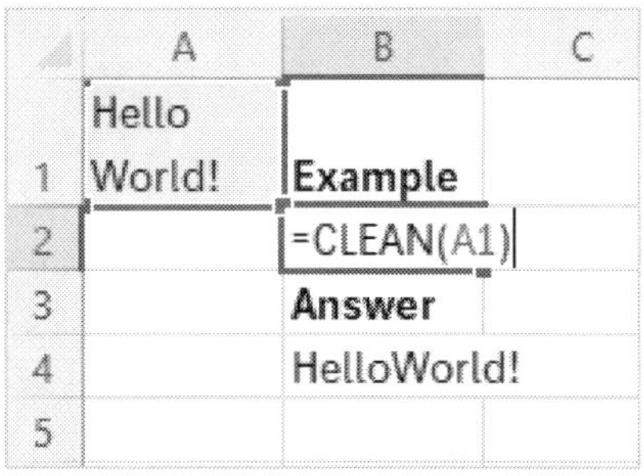

Formula:

`=CLEAN(A1)`

Result: HelloWorld!
Explanation: The CLEAN function removes all non-printable characters from the text, leaving only readable content.

Explore Further with GPT:
Ask GPT to demonstrate how to combine CLEAN with TRIM or SUBSTITUTE for more advanced text-cleaning scenarios.

Tips for Using CLEAN

- **Invisible characters:** This function removes characters with ASCII codes 0–31, often causing formatting issues in imported data.
- **Combine with** TRIM**:** Use with TRIM to remove unnecessary spaces along with non-printable characters.
- **Check your source:** Non-printable characters are common in data imported from external applications like databases or web pages.

CODE Function

Text Functions

Introduction

The CODE function returns the numeric ASCII or Unicode value of the first character in a text string. It is useful for identifying character encoding or working with character-based logic in formulas.

Simple explanation: Returns the numeric code of the first character in a text string.

Common use cases: Used in data processing, character encoding, and text validation.

When to use this function: Use when you need to analyze or validate text based on its character encoding.

Syntax

```
=CODE(text)
```

- **text**: The text string from which to retrieve the numeric code of the first character.

Worked Example

Challenge: Find the ASCII code of the first character in the text string "Apple".

Text in cell A1: "Apple"

Formula:

```
=CODE(A1)
```

Result: 65
Explanation: The first character "A" corresponds to ASCII code 65.

	A	B	C
1	Apple	**Example**	
2		=CODE(A1)	
3		**Answer**	
4		65	
5			

Explore Further with GPT:
Ask GPT to show how to use CODE with CHAR for encoding and decoding or how to apply it in custom validation rules.

Tips for Using CODE

- **First character only:** The function evaluates only the first character in the text string.
- **Handle blank cells:** If the cell is empty, CODE returns a #VALUE! error.
- **Combine with** CHAR**:** Use CHAR to convert numeric codes back to characters for bidirectional encoding.

COLUMN Function

Lookup & Reference Functions

Introduction

The COLUMN function returns the column number of a specified cell or range. It is useful for dynamically referencing column positions in formulas, especially in large datasets or tables.

Simple explanation: Returns the column number of a cell or range.

Common use cases: Used in dynamic formulas, data manipulation, and conditional formatting.

When to use this function: Use when determining or working with column positions in a dataset.

Syntax

```
=COLUMN([reference])
```

- **reference** *(optional)*: The cell or range for which to return the column number. If omitted, it defaults to the current cell.

Worked Example

Challenge: Find the column number of cell C5.

Formula:

`=COLUMN(C5)`

Result: 3
Explanation: Column C is the third column in the worksheet.

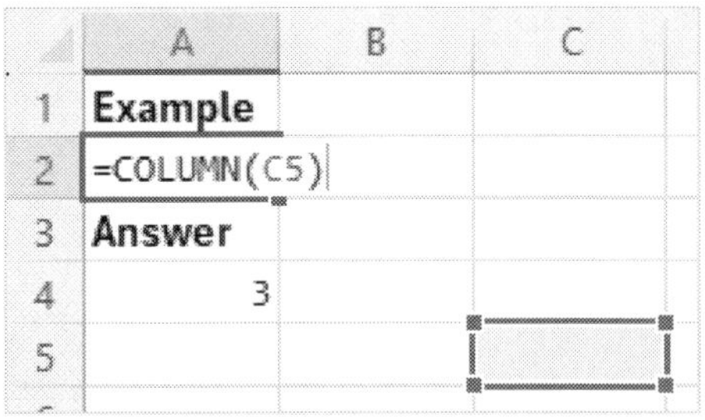

Explore Further with GPT:
Ask GPT to show how to use COLUMN with INDEX or MATCH for advanced dynamic formulas.

Tips for Using COLUMN

- **Default behavior:** If no reference is provided, the function returns the column number of the cell where the formula is entered.
- **Array output:** When applied to a range, COLUMN returns an array of column numbers for each column in the range.
- **Combine with** ROW**:** Use with the ROW function to dynamically locate positions in a dataset.

COLUMNS Function

Lookup & Reference Functions

Introduction

The COLUMNS function returns the number of columns in a specified range or array. It is useful for dynamic range calculations and managing datasets with variable column counts.

Simple explanation: Returns the total number of columns in a range or array.

Common use cases: Used in dynamic formulas, table manipulation, and determining the size of ranges.

When to use this function: Use when analyzing or working with ranges where the number of columns is important.

Syntax

```
=COLUMNS(array)
```

- **array**: The range or array for which to count the columns.

Worked Example

Challenge: Find the number of columns in the range A1:C5.

Formula:

```
=COLUMNS(A1:C5)
```

Result: 3
Explanation: The range A1:C5 spans three columns: A, B, and C.

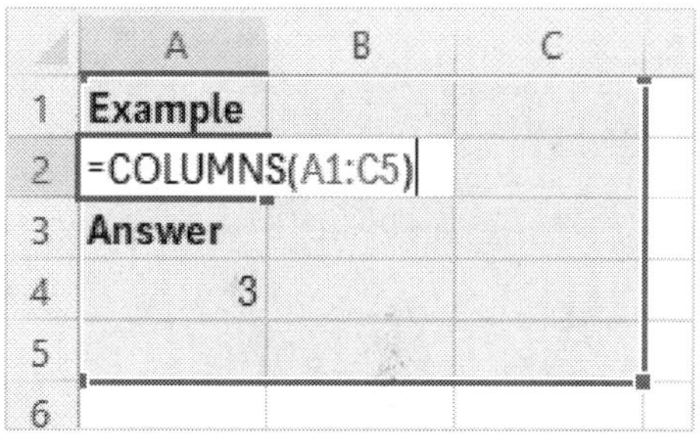

Explore Further with GPT:
Ask GPT to demonstrate combining COLUMNS with other functions like ROWS or SEQUENCE for advanced array calculations.

Tips for Using COLUMNS

- **Dynamic ranges:** Use in combination with functions like OFFSET or INDEX for flexible and scalable range calculations.
- **Paired with ROWS:** Use with the ROWS function to get the full dimensions of a range.
- **Array formulas:** When applied to arrays, COLUMNS provides accurate column counts even for dynamic ranges.

COMBIN Function

Math & Trigonometry Functions

Introduction

The COMBIN function calculates the number of possible combinations of a given number of items. It is useful in probability, statistics, and combinatorics when the order of selection does not matter.

Simple explanation: Returns the number of ways to choose a subset of items from a larger set, where the order does not matter.

Common use cases: Used in probability calculations, statistical analysis, and planning scenarios.

When to use this function: Use when calculating combinations in scenarios like lotteries, group selections, or statistical sampling.

Syntax

```
=COMBIN(number, number_chosen)
```

- **number**: The total number of items.
- **number_chosen**: The number of items to choose from the total.

Worked Example

Challenge: Calculate the number of ways to choose 3 items from a set of 5.

Formula:

```
=COMBIN(5, 3)
```

Result: 10

Explanation: There are 10 unique ways to choose 3 items from a set of 5 when the order does not matter.

	A	B
1	**Example**	
2	=COMBIN(5, 3)	
3	**Answer**	
4	10	

Explore Further with GPT:

Ask GPT to show how to combine COMBIN with other functions like PERMUT for more advanced probability calculations.

Tips for Using COMBIN

- **Order independence:** Use COMBIN when the order of selection does not matter. For scenarios where order matters, use the PERMUT function.
- **Large sets:** This function supports large numbers but may return a #NUM! error if the inputs are invalid (e.g., number_chosen > number).
- **Combine with probabilities:** Pair with statistical functions for advanced combinatorial analysis.

COMBINA Function

Math & Trigonometry Functions

Introduction

The COMBINA function calculates the number of combinations with repetitions allowed. It is useful in probability, statistics, and combinatorics when items can be selected more than once, and the order of selection does not matter.

Simple explanation: Returns the number of ways to choose a subset of items from a larger set, where repetition is allowed and the order does not matter.

Common use cases: Used in probability calculations, inventory planning, and statistical sampling with replacement.

When to use this function: Use when calculating combinations in scenarios like repeated selections or sampling with replacement.

Syntax

```
=COMBINA(number, number_chosen)
```

- **number**: The total number of items.
- **number_chosen**: The number of items to choose from the total (with replacement).

Worked Example

Challenge: Calculate the number of ways to choose 3 items from a set of 5, allowing repetitions.

Formula:

```
=COMBINA(5, 3)
```

Result: 35

Explanation: There are 35 unique ways to choose 3 items from a set of 5 when repetition is allowed, and the order does not matter.

	A	B
1	**Example**	
2	=COMBINA(5, 3)	
3	**Answer**	
4	35	
5		

Explore Further with GPT:
Ask GPT to show how COMBINA compares with COMBIN and how it can be applied to real-world scenarios like inventory or sampling.

Tips for Using COMBINA

- **Repetition allowed:** Use COMBINA when repetition is permitted, and the order of selection does not matter.
- **Large sets:** The function supports large numbers but may return a #NUM! error if the inputs are invalid (e.g., negative values).
- **Combine with probabilities:** Pair with other statistical functions for advanced combinatorial analysis.

COMPLEX Function

Engineering Functions

Introduction

The COMPLEX function converts real and imaginary coefficients into a complex number in the format a + bi or a + bj. It is useful in engineering, physics, and advanced mathematics for handling complex numbers.

Simple explanation: Creates a complex number from real and imaginary components.

Common use cases: Used in mathematical modeling, electrical engineering, and signal processing.

When to use this function: Use when you need to represent numbers with both real and imaginary parts.

Syntax

```
=COMPLEX(real_num, i_num, [suffix])
```

- **real_num**: The real coefficient of the complex number.
- **i_num**: The imaginary coefficient of the complex number.
- **[suffix]** *(optional)*: The suffix for the imaginary part, either "i" (default) or "j".

Worked Example

Challenge: Create a complex number with a real part of 3 and an imaginary part of 4, using the default suffix.

Formula:

```
=COMPLEX(3, 4)
```

Result: 3 + 4i
Explanation: The function combines the real part 3 and the imaginary part 4 to produce the complex number 3 + 4i.

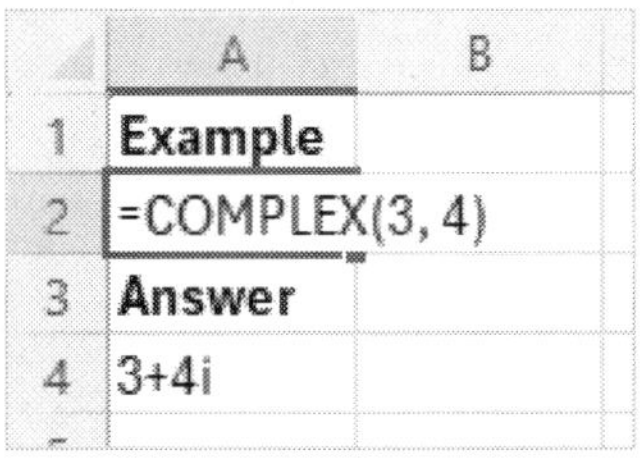

	A	B
1	**Example**	
2	=COMPLEX(3, 4)	
3	**Answer**	
4	3+4i	

Explore Further with GPT:
Ask GPT how to use COMPLEX in conjunction with other complex number functions like IMABS or IMARGUMENT.

Tips for Using COMPLEX

- **Suffix flexibility:** Use "j" as the suffix for fields like electrical engineering where this convention is common (e.g., COMPLEX(3, 4, "j") results in 3 + 4j).
- **Real and imaginary values:** Both inputs can be integers, decimals, or formulas that return numeric values.
- **Combine with other functions:** Use with functions like IMSUM or IMPRODUCT to perform operations on complex numbers.

CONCAT Function

Text Functions

Introduction

The CONCAT function combines the contents of multiple cells, ranges, or text strings into one continuous text string. It is a modern alternative to the older CONCATENATE function, offering enhanced functionality, such as handling ranges.

Simple explanation: Combines multiple text strings or ranges into a single text string.

Common use cases: Used in data cleaning, report generation, and creating dynamic text outputs.

When to use this function: Use when merging text from multiple cells or ranges into a single cell.

Syntax

```
=CONCAT(text1, [text2], ...)
```

- **text1, [text2], ...:** The text strings, cell references, or ranges to combine.

Worked Example

Challenge: Combine the contents of cells A1 and B1 with no separator.

Data:

A1: "Hello"

B1: "World"

Formula:

`=CONCAT(A1, B1)`

	A	B	C	D
1	Hello	World	**Example**	
2			=CONCAT(A1, B1)	
3			**Answer**	
4			HelloWorld	

Result: HelloWorld
Explanation: The function merges the contents of A1 and B1 into a single string.

Explore Further with GPT:
Ask GPT how to add separators between text strings or combine CONCAT with other functions like TEXT for formatting.

Tips for Using CONCAT

- **Ranges:** Unlike CONCATENATE, CONCAT can handle ranges directly (e.g., `=CONCAT(A1:A3)` combines all cells in the range).
- **Add separators:** Use TEXTJOIN instead of CONCAT when you need to include a delimiter between text elements.
- **Alternative for compatibility:** If sharing files with users of older Excel versions, use CONCATENATE instead.

CONCATENATE Function

Text Functions

Introduction

The CONCATENATE function combines multiple text strings, cell contents, or values into a single text string. It is a legacy function and has been replaced by the more versatile CONCAT function in modern Excel versions.

Simple explanation: Combines multiple text strings or values into one text string.

Common use cases: Used for text manipulation, data formatting, and creating dynamic text outputs.

When to use this function: Use when merging text elements in older versions of Excel.

Syntax

```
=CONCATENATE(text1, [text2], ...)
```

- **text1, [text2], ...**: The text strings or cell references to combine.

Worked Example

Challenge: Combine the contents of cells A1 and B1 with no separator.

Data:

A1: "Good"

B1: "Morning"

Formula:

```
=CONCATENATE(A1, B1)
```

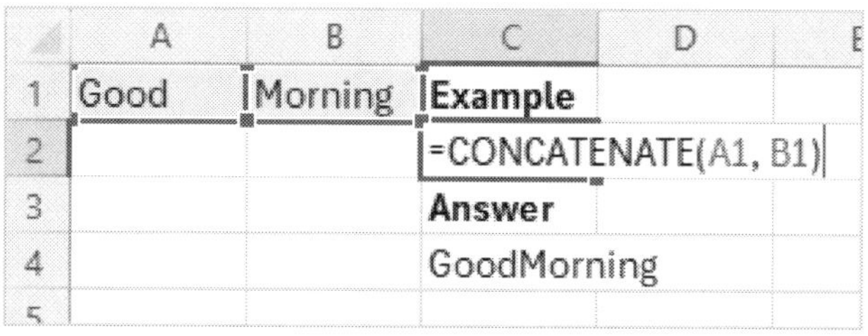

Result: GoodMorning
Explanation: The function merges the contents of A1 and B1 into a single string.

Explore Further with GPT:
Ask GPT to explain differences between CONCATENATE and CONCAT or demonstrate how to transition formulas to the newer function.

Tips for Using CONCATENATE

- **Limited functionality:** Unlike CONCAT, CONCATENATE does not handle ranges. Use =CONCAT(A1:A3) in newer Excel versions to simplify combining multiple cells.
- **Adding separators:** Insert separators manually, such as =CONCATENATE(A1, " ", B1) to add a space between text elements.
- **Compatibility:** Use this function for files shared with users of older Excel versions that do not support CONCAT.

CONFIDENCE Function

Compatibility Functions

Introduction

The CONFIDENCE function calculates the confidence interval for a population mean, using a normal distribution. It helps estimate the range within which the true population mean is likely to lie, based on sample data.

Simple explanation: Calculates the margin of error for a population mean.

Common use cases: Used in statistics, quality control, and business analysis for making data-driven decisions.

When to use this function: Use when you need to determine the confidence interval of a population mean based on sample data.

Syntax

```
=CONFIDENCE(alpha, standard_dev, size)
```

- **alpha**: The significance level (1 - confidence level). For a 95% confidence level, use 0.05.
- **standard_dev**: The standard deviation of the population.
- **size**: The sample size.

Worked Example

Challenge: Calculate the margin of error for a population mean with a 95% confidence level, a standard deviation of 2.5, and a sample size of 100.

Formula:

```
=CONFIDENCE(0.05, 2.5, 100)
```

Result: 0.489991
Explanation: The margin of error is 0.49, meaning the true population mean is expected to lie within this range above or below the sample mean with 95% confidence.

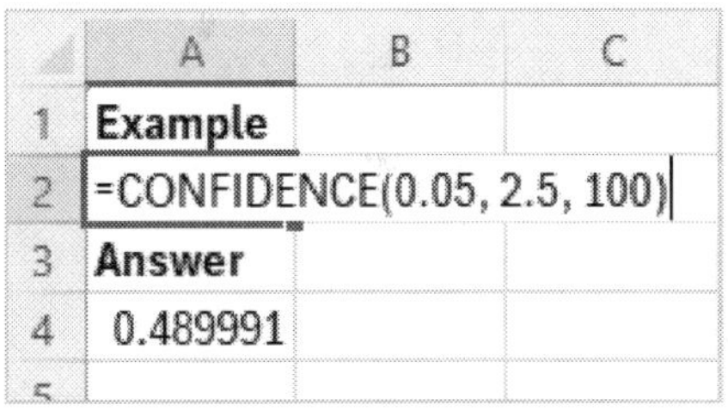

Explore Further with GPT:
Ask GPT how to interpret confidence intervals or compare the use of CONFIDENCE with the newer CONFIDENCE.NORM function.

Tips for Using CONFIDENCE

- **Significance level** (alpha)**:** A smaller alpha results in a wider confidence interval, reflecting higher confidence.
- **Transition to** CONFIDENCE.NORM**:** In newer Excel versions, use CONFIDENCE.NORM for the same functionality with updated naming.
- **Population data:** Ensure the standard_dev and size are accurate for the population and sample data used in the calculation.

CONFIDENCE.NORM Function

Statistical Functions

Introduction

The CONFIDENCE.NORM function calculates the confidence interval for a population mean using a normal distribution. It is a modern replacement for the older CONFIDENCE function, providing the same functionality with updated naming.

Simple explanation: Calculates the margin of error for a population mean, assuming a normal distribution.

Common use cases: Used in statistical analysis, quality control, and business forecasting to estimate ranges for population means.

When to use this function: Use when you need to determine the confidence interval for a population mean based on sample data and a normal distribution.

Syntax

```
=CONFIDENCE.NORM(alpha, standard_dev, size)
```

- **alpha**: The significance level (1 - confidence level). For a 95% confidence level, use 0.05.
- **standard_dev**: The standard deviation of the population.
- **size**: The sample size.

Worked Example

Challenge: Calculate the margin of error for a population mean with a 95% confidence level, a standard deviation of 3.0, and a sample size of 50.

Formula:

```
=CONFIDENCE.NORM(0.05, 3.0, 50)
```

	A	B	C	D
1	**Example**			
2	=CONFIDENCE.NORM(0.05, 3, 50)			
3	**Answer**			
4	0.831542			
5				

Result: 0.831542
Explanation: The margin of error is approximately 0.83, meaning the true population mean is expected to lie within this range above or below the sample mean with 95% confidence.

Explore Further with GPT:
Ask GPT to explain how to interpret confidence intervals or compare CONFIDENCE.NORM with CONFIDENCE.T for small sample sizes.

Tips for Using CONFIDENCE.NORM

- **Significance level (**alpha**):** Smaller values of alpha (e.g., 0.01) result in wider confidence intervals, reflecting greater confidence.
- **Use with larger samples:** This function assumes a normal distribution, which is most accurate with larger sample sizes.
- **Compare with** CONFIDENCE.T: For small sample sizes or unknown population variances, use CONFIDENCE.T for better accuracy.

CONFIDENCE.T Function

Statistical Functions

Introduction

The CONFIDENCE.T function calculates the confidence interval for a population mean using a t-distribution. It is particularly useful for small sample sizes or when the population standard deviation is unknown.

Simple explanation: Calculates the margin of error for a population mean, assuming a t-distribution.

Common use cases: Used in statistical analysis, quality control, and research when working with small sample sizes or unknown variances.

When to use this function: Use when determining confidence intervals for small samples or data following a t-distribution.

Syntax

```
=CONFIDENCE.T(alpha, standard_dev, size)
```

- **alpha**: The significance level (1 - confidence level). For a 95% confidence level, use 0.05.
- **standard_dev**: The standard deviation of the sample.
- **size**: The sample size.

Worked Example

Challenge: Calculate the margin of error for a sample mean with a 95% confidence level, a standard deviation of 2.0, and a sample size of 25.

Formula:

```
=CONFIDENCE.T(0.05, 2.0, 25)
```

Result: 0.825559

Explanation: The margin of error is approximately 0.81, meaning the true population mean is expected to lie within this range above or below the sample mean with 95% confidence.

	A	B	C
1	**Example**		
2	=CONFIDENCE.T(0.05, 2, 25)		
3	**Answer**		
4	0.825559		

Explore Further with GPT:
Ask GPT to explain how to interpret t-distribution confidence intervals or when to use CONFIDENCE.T versus CONFIDENCE.NORM.

Tips for Using CONFIDENCE.T

- **Small samples:** Use this function for small sample sizes (e.g., fewer than 30 observations).
- **Sample standard deviation:** Ensure that the standard deviation is calculated from the sample, not the population.
- **Compare with** CONFIDENCE.NORM**:** For larger samples or known population variances, use CONFIDENCE.NORM for more accurate results.

CONVERT Function

Engineering Functions

Introduction

The CONVERT function converts a number from one measurement system to another. It is highly versatile, supporting a wide range of units including length, weight, temperature, and more.

Simple explanation: Converts a value from one unit of measurement to another.

Common use cases: Used in engineering, science, and business to standardize data across different unit systems.

When to use this function: Use when working with data requiring conversions between units, such as metric to imperial.

Syntax

```
=CONVERT(number, from_unit, to_unit)
```

- **number**: The numeric value to convert.
- **from_unit**: The unit of the number to convert from (e.g., "km" for kilometers).
- **to_unit**: The unit to convert the number to (e.g., "mi" for miles).

Worked Example

Challenge: Convert 10 kilometers to miles.

Formula:

```
=CONVERT(10, "km", "mi")
```

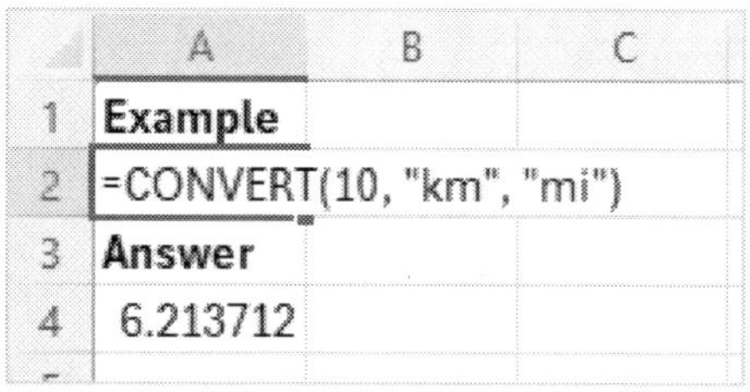

	A	B	C
1	**Example**		
2	=CONVERT(10, "km", "mi")		
3	**Answer**		
4	6.213712		

Result: 6.21371
Explanation: The function converts 10 kilometers to approximately 6.21 miles using the appropriate conversion factor.

Explore Further with GPT:
Ask GPT to provide a full list of units supported by CONVERT or demonstrate its use in more complex scenarios like temperature or volume conversions.

Tips for Using CONVERT

- **Unit compatibility:** Ensure from_unit and to_unit belong to the same category (e.g., both are lengths or weights). Mixing incompatible units will result in a #N/A error.
- **Temperature conversions:** For temperature, use specific units like "C" (Celsius), "F" (Fahrenheit), or "K" (Kelvin).
- **Reference a unit list:** Excel's documentation provides a complete list of supported units and their abbreviations.

CORREL Function

Statistical Functions

Introduction

The CORREL function calculates the Pearson correlation coefficient between two datasets. This statistic measures the strength and direction of the linear relationship between the two variables.

Simple explanation: Determines how strongly two sets of data are linearly related.

Common use cases: Used in statistical analysis, data science, and finance to analyze relationships between variables.

When to use this function: Use when evaluating the correlation between two datasets to identify patterns or trends.

Syntax

```
=CORREL(array1, array2)
```

- **array1**: The first range or array of numbers.
- **array2**: The second range or array of numbers.

Worked Example

Challenge: Calculate the correlation between sales figures and advertising spend.

Data:

Sales (array1): A1:A5 → {100, 200, 300, 400, 500}

Advertising Spend (array2): B1:B5 → {50, 100, 150, 200, 250}

Formula:

```
=CORREL(A1:A5, B1:B5)
```

	A	B	C	D
1	100	50	**Example**	
2	200	100	=CORREL(A1:A5, B1:B5)	
3	300	150	**Answer**	
4	400	200	1	
5	500	250		

Result: 1

Explanation: A correlation of 1 indicates a perfect positive linear relationship between sales and advertising spend.

Explore Further with GPT:

Ask GPT to demonstrate how CORREL can be used alongside LINEST or TREND to model relationships more comprehensively.

Tips for Using CORREL

- **Range lengths:** Ensure both arrays are the same length; mismatched ranges will result in a #N/A error.
- **Values only:** The function ignores text or logical values in the arrays.
- **Interpreting results:** Correlation values range from -1 (perfect negative correlation) to 1 (perfect positive correlation), with 0 indicating no linear relationship.

COS Function

Math & Trigonometry Functions

Introduction

The COS function calculates the cosine of a given angle. It is commonly used in trigonometry, engineering, and physics for calculations involving angles and periodic phenomena.

Simple explanation: Returns the cosine of an angle provided in radians.

Common use cases: Used in geometry, wave analysis, and physics to calculate relationships involving angles.

When to use this function: Use when solving problems involving right triangles, oscillations, or circular motion.

Syntax

```
=COS(number)
```

- **number**: The angle in radians for which to calculate the cosine.

Worked Example

Challenge: Calculate the cosine of a 60-degree angle.

1. Convert degrees to radians:

`=RADIANS(60)`

Result: 1.0472 radians.

2. Use the COS function:

`=COS(1.0472)`

	A	B
1	Step 1	**Example**
2	1.047198	=COS(A2)
3	Step 2	**Answer**
4	0.5	0.5

Result: 0.5
Explanation: The cosine of a 60-degree angle (or 1.0472 radians) is 0.5.

Explore Further with GPT:
Ask GPT to explain how to combine COS with other trigonometric functions like SIN or TAN for more complex calculations.

Tips for Using COS

- **Radians required:** If your angle is in degrees, use the RADIANS function to convert it before applying COS.
- **Combine with inverse functions:** Use ACOS to find the angle from a cosine value.
- **Applications:** Pair with periodic functions like SIN and PI to model waveforms or oscillations.

COSH Function

Math & Trigonometry Functions

Introduction

The COSH function calculates the hyperbolic cosine of a given number. Hyperbolic functions are often used in engineering, physics, and hyperbolic geometry to model phenomena such as wave propagation and growth rates.

Simple explanation: Returns the hyperbolic cosine of a number.

Common use cases: Used in physics, engineering, and mathematics for calculations involving hyperbolic geometry or wave-like systems.

When to use this function: Use when solving problems involving hyperbolic equations or modeling exponential growth.

Syntax

```
=COSH(number)
```

- **number**: The value (in radians) for which to calculate the hyperbolic cosine.

Worked Example

Challenge: Calculate the hyperbolic cosine of 1.

Formula:

```
=COSH(1)
```

Result: 1.543081
Explanation: The hyperbolic cosine of 1 is approximately 1.543081.

	A	B
1	**Example**	
2	=COSH(1)	
3	**Answer**	
4	1.543081	
5		

Explore Further with GPT:
Ask GPT to demonstrate how to combine COSH with other hyperbolic functions like SINH or TANH for advanced calculations.

Tips for Using COSH

- **Input values:** The function accepts any real number as input.
- **Combine with inverse functions:** Use ACOSH to find the value from a hyperbolic cosine result.
- **Applications:** Hyperbolic functions are particularly useful for modeling exponential growth, decay, or catenary curves.

COT Function

Math & Trigonometry Functions

Introduction

The COT function calculates the cotangent of a given angle. It is the reciprocal of the tangent function and is commonly used in trigonometry, engineering, and physics.

Simple explanation: Returns the cotangent of an angle provided in radians.

Common use cases: Used in geometry, periodic analysis, and physics to solve problems involving angles and trigonometric relationships.

When to use this function: Use when working with cotangent values in trigonometric equations or models.

Syntax

```
=COT(number)
```

- **number**: The angle in radians for which to calculate the cotangent.

Worked Example

Challenge: Calculate the cotangent of a 45-degree angle.

1. Convert degrees to radians:

`=RADIANS(45)`

Result: 0.785398 radians.

2. Use the COT function:

`=COT(0.7854)`

	A	B
1	Step 1	**Example**
2	0.785398	=COT(A2)
3	Step 2	**Answer**
4	1	1
5		

Result: 1

Explanation: The cotangent of a 45-degree angle (or 0.7854 radians) is 1.

Explore Further with GPT:
Ask GPT to show how to use COT alongside TAN or other trigonometric functions in complex equations.

Tips for Using COT

- **Radians required:** If your angle is in degrees, use the RADIANS function to convert it before applying COT.
- **Division by zero:** Avoid using angles where the tangent value is 0, as this will result in a #DIV/0! error.
- **Inverse calculation:** Use ACOT to calculate the angle from a cotangent value.

COTH Function

Math & Trigonometry Functions

Introduction

The COTH function calculates the hyperbolic cotangent of a given number. It is the reciprocal of the hyperbolic tangent function and is often used in advanced mathematics, engineering, and physics.

Simple explanation: Returns the hyperbolic cotangent of a number.

Common use cases: Used in physics, engineering, and hyperbolic geometry for modeling exponential relationships and wave-like systems.

When to use this function: Use when solving problems involving hyperbolic equations or exponential growth.

Syntax

```
=COTH(number)
```

- **number**: The value (in radians) for which to calculate the hyperbolic cotangent.

Worked Example

Challenge: Calculate the hyperbolic cotangent of 2.

Formula:

```
=COTH(2)
```

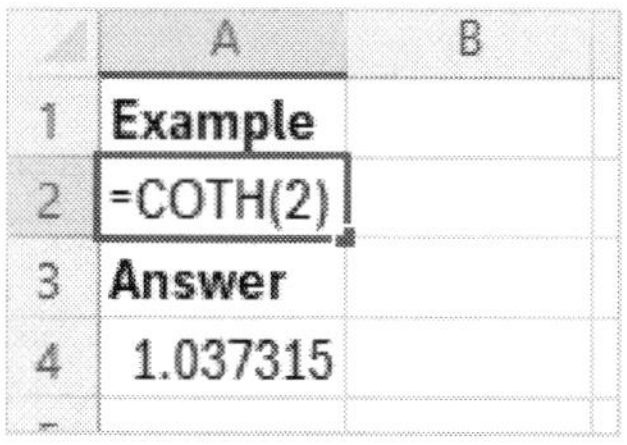

Result: 1.037315
Explanation: The hyperbolic cotangent of 2 is approximately 1.037315.

Explore Further with GPT:
Ask GPT to demonstrate how to combine COTH with other hyperbolic functions like TANH or SINH for advanced calculations.

Tips for Using COTH

- **Valid inputs:** The input cannot be 0 because the hyperbolic cotangent of 0 is undefined, resulting in a #DIV/0! error.
- **Combine with inverse functions:** Use ACOTH to calculate the value from a hyperbolic cotangent result.
- **Applications:** Hyperbolic functions are useful in modeling catenary curves, exponential growth, and wave propagation.

COUNT Function

Statistical Functions

Introduction

The COUNT function counts the number of numeric entries in a given range. It is widely used in data analysis and spreadsheet tasks to determine how many cells contain numbers.

Simple explanation: Counts numeric values in a range or array.

Common use cases: Used in data validation, report generation, and calculations requiring numeric counts.

When to use this function: Use when you need to count cells containing numbers in a dataset.

Syntax

```
=COUNT(value1, [value2], ...)
```

Worked Example

Challenge: Count the numeric entries in the range A1:A5.

Data in A1:A5:

10, Hello, 20, TRUE, 30

Formula:

```
=COUNT(A1:A5)
```

Result: 3
Explanation: The function counts only the numeric values (10, 20, and 30), ignoring text and logical values.

	A	B	C
1	10	**Example**	
2	Hello	=COUNT(A1:A5)	
3	20	**Answer**	
4	TRUE	3	
5	30		
6			

Explore Further with GPT:
Ask GPT how to combine COUNT with IF for conditional counting or compare it with COUNTA for broader use cases.

Tips for Using COUNT

- **Numeric values only:** The function ignores text, logical values, and blank cells. Use COUNTA to count non-empty cells instead.
- **Dynamic ranges:** Combine with OFFSET or INDIRECT to count numbers in dynamic ranges.
- **Error handling:** Use IFERROR to handle errors in formulas referencing cells with potential issues.

COUNTA Function

Statistical Functions

Introduction

The COUNTA function counts the number of non-empty cells in a range, including those containing text, numbers, logical values, or errors. It is a versatile tool for analyzing data presence in spreadsheets.

Simple explanation: Counts all non-empty cells in a range.

Common use cases: Used in data validation, reporting, and checking dataset completeness.

When to use this function: Use when you need to count all non-empty cells, regardless of the type of data they contain.

Syntax

```
=COUNTA(value1, [value2], ...)
```

- **value1, [value2], ...**: The range, array, or individual values to count.

Worked Example

Challenge: Count the non-empty entries in the range A1:A5.

Data in A1:A5:

10, Hello, (blank), TRUE, *#DIV/0!*

Formula:

```
=COUNTA(A1:A5)
```

Result: 4

Explanation: The function counts all non-empty cells, including 10, "Hello", TRUE, and #DIV/0!, but excludes the blank cell.

	A	B	C
1	10	**Example**	
2	Hello	=COUNTA(A1:A5)	
3		**Answer**	
4	TRUE	4	
5	#DIV/0!		
6			

Explore Further with GPT:
Ask GPT how to combine COUNTA with IF for conditional counting or compare it with COUNT for numeric-only use cases.

Tips for Using COUNTA

- **Non-empty cells:** The function counts cells containing any value, including text, numbers, errors, and logical values.
- **Blank cells ignored:** Empty cells are not counted, but cells with formulas returning empty text ("") are included.
- **Dynamic ranges:** Use with OFFSET or INDIRECT to count non-empty cells in dynamic ranges.

COUNTBLANK Function

Statistical Functions

Introduction

The COUNTBLANK function counts the number of empty cells in a specified range. It is useful for identifying gaps in datasets and ensuring data completeness.

Simple explanation: Counts the number of blank cells in a range.

Common use cases: Used in data validation, gap analysis, and error checking to identify missing values.

When to use this function: Use when you need to locate or quantify blank cells in a dataset.

Syntax

```
=COUNTBLANK(range)
```

- **range**: The range of cells to evaluate for blank entries.

Worked Example

Challenge: Count the blank cells in the range A1:A5.

Data in A1:A5:

10, (blank), Hello, (blank), TRUE

Formula:

```
=COUNTBLANK(A1:A5)
```

Result: 2
Explanation: The function counts two blank cells in the range.

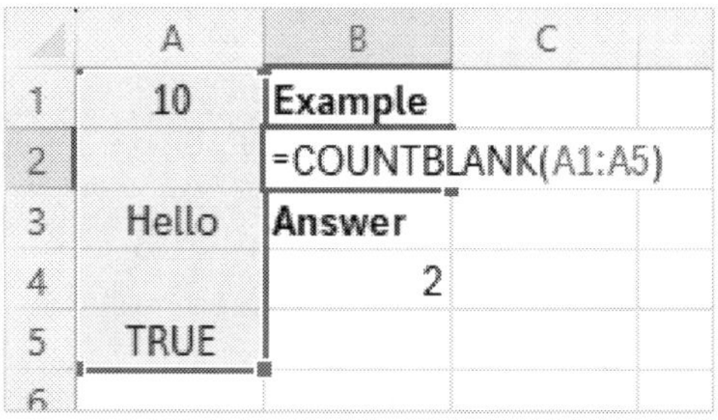

Explore Further with GPT:
Ask GPT how to combine COUNTBLANK with conditional logic or compare it with COUNTA for broader cell analysis.

Tips for Using COUNTBLANK

- **Blank cells only:** The function counts cells with no content, excluding those with formulas returning "" or errors.
- **Combine with conditional formulas:** Use with functions like IF to highlight or act on blank cells.
- **Dynamic ranges:** Pair with OFFSET or INDIRECT to count blank cells in dynamically changing datasets.

COUNTIF Function

Statistical Functions

Introduction

The COUNTIF function counts the number of cells within a range that meet a specified condition. It is a powerful tool for filtering and analyzing data based on specific criteria.

Simple explanation: Counts cells in a range that match a given condition.

Common use cases: Used in data analysis, reporting, and conditional calculations.

When to use this function: Use when you need to count cells that satisfy a particular condition, such as being greater than a value or containing specific text.

Syntax

```
=COUNTIF(range, criteria)
```

- **range**: The range of cells to evaluate.
- **criteria**: The condition to count, such as a number, expression, or text.

Worked Example

Challenge: Count the number of cells in A1:A5 containing values greater than 10.

Data in A1:A5:

5, 15, 20, 10, 25

Formula:

```
=COUNTIF(A1:A5, ">10")
```

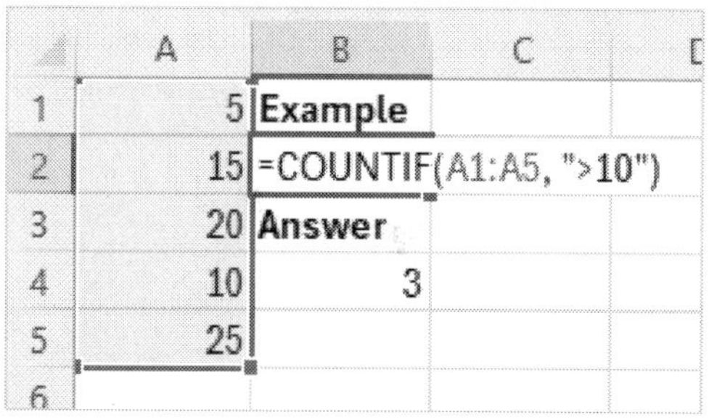

Result: 3
Explanation: The function counts the cells containing 15, 20, and 25, which are greater than 10.

Explore Further with GPT:
Ask GPT to demonstrate advanced uses of COUNTIF, such as combining it with IF or using wildcard characters.

Tips for Using COUNTIF

- **Criteria flexibility:** Use comparison operators (>, <, =) or wildcards (*, ?) in your criteria. For example, "*apple*" counts cells containing the word "apple."
- **Text criteria:** Enclose text or expressions in double quotes. For example, ">=10" or "text".
- **Dynamic criteria:** Reference cells for criteria, such as ">" & B1 to dynamically compare values.

COUNTIFS Function

Statistical Functions

Introduction

The COUNTIFS function counts the number of cells in a range that meet multiple criteria. It is an extension of COUNTIF and allows you to apply multiple conditions across one or more ranges.

Simple explanation: Counts cells that satisfy multiple criteria across ranges.

Common use cases: Used in advanced data analysis, reporting, and filtering to identify records meeting multiple conditions.

When to use this function: Use when you need to count cells based on multiple conditions or criteria.

Syntax

```
=COUNTIFS(criteria_range1, criteria1, [criteria_range2, criteria2], ...)
```

- **criteria_range1**: The first range to evaluate.
- **criteria1**: The condition for the first range.
- **[criteria_range2, criteria2], ...**: Additional ranges and conditions (optional).

Worked Example

Challenge: Count the number of rows in a dataset where Sales > 100 and Region = "North".

Data:

Sales (A1:A5):

80, 120, 150, 95, 200

Region (B1:B5):

North, South, North, East, North

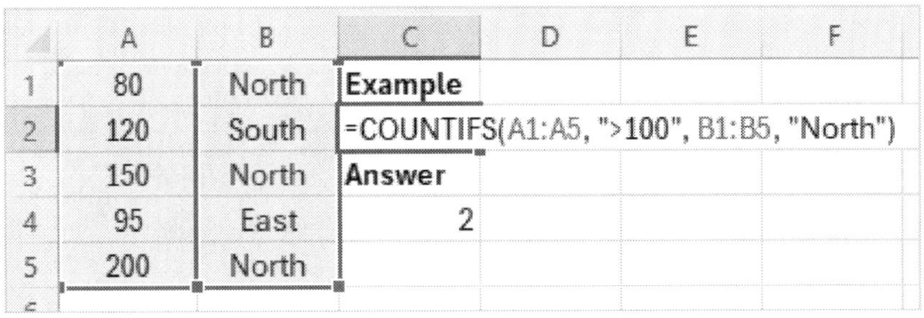

	A	B	C	D	E	F
1	80	North	**Example**			
2	120	South	=COUNTIFS(A1:A5, ">100", B1:B5, "North")			
3	150	North	**Answer**			
4	95	East	2			
5	200	North				

Formula:

```
=COUNTIFS(A1:A5, ">100", B1:B5, "North")
```

Result: 2

Explanation: The function counts rows where Sales > 100 and Region = "North", specifically rows 3 and 5.

Explore Further with GPT:

Ask GPT to demonstrate combining COUNTIFS with other functions like FILTER or SUMIFS for advanced analysis.

Tips for Using COUNTIFS

- **Matching ranges:** Ensure all criteria ranges have the same number of rows or columns; mismatched ranges result in a #VALUE! error.
- **Flexible criteria:** Use operators (e.g., >, <, =) and wildcards (*, ?) in criteria.
- **Dynamic criteria:** Reference cells for criteria, such as ">" & C1 for conditions based on a variable.

COUPDAYBS Function

Financial Functions

Introduction

The COUPDAYBS function calculates the number of days from the beginning of the coupon period to the settlement date. It is used in bond calculations to evaluate accrued interest or determine the timing of payments.

Simple explanation: Finds the number of days from the start of a coupon period to the settlement date.

Common use cases: Used in financial modeling, bond valuation, and interest calculations.

When to use this function: Use when working with bonds or fixed-income securities to determine interest or payment timing.

Syntax

```
=COUPDAYBS(settlement, maturity, frequency, [basis])
```

- **settlement**: The bond's settlement date (the date the buyer purchases the bond).
- **maturity**: The bond's maturity date (when it expires).
- **frequency**: The number of coupon payments per year (1, 2, or 4).
- **[basis]** *(optional)*: The day count basis to use:
    - 0: US (NASD) 30/360 (default).
    - 1: Actual/actual.
    - 2: Actual/360.
    - 3: Actual/365.
    - 4: European 30/360.

Worked Example

Challenge: Calculate the days from the beginning of a coupon period to the settlement date for a bond.

Details:

- Settlement date: 01-Jan-2023
- Maturity date: 01-Jan-2025
- Frequency: 2 (semi-annual payments).
- Basis: 0 (default).

	A	B	C	D	E
1	**Example**				
2	=COUPDAYBS(DATE(2023,1,1), DATE(2025,1,1), 2, 0)				
3	**Answer**				
4	0				

Formula:

```
=COUPDAYBS(DATE(2023,1,1), DATE(2025,1,1), 2, 0)
```

Result: 0
Explanation: The settlement date aligns with the beginning of the coupon period, so the number of days is 0.

COUPDAYS Function

Financial Functions

Introduction

The COUPDAYS function calculates the total number of days in the coupon period that contains the settlement date. It is commonly used in financial modeling to evaluate bond payments and accrued interest.

Simple explanation: Returns the total number of days in the current coupon period.

Common use cases: Used in bond valuation, financial analysis, and interest calculations.

When to use this function: Use when analyzing bonds or fixed-income securities to determine payment cycles.

Syntax

```
=COUPDAYS(settlement, maturity, frequency, [basis])
```

- **settlement**: The bond's settlement date (the date the buyer purchases the bond).
- **maturity**: The bond's maturity date (when it expires).
- **frequency**: The number of coupon payments per year (1, 2, or 4).
- **[basis]** *(optional)*: The day count basis to use:
    - 0: US (NASD) 30/360 (default).
    - 1: Actual/actual.
    - 2: Actual/360.
    - 3: Actual/365.
    - 4: European 30/360.

Worked Example

Challenge: Calculate the total number of days in the current coupon period for a bond.

Details:

- Settlement date: 15-Jan-2023
- Maturity date: 15-Jan-2025
- Frequency: 2 (semi-annual payments).
- Basis: 0 (default).

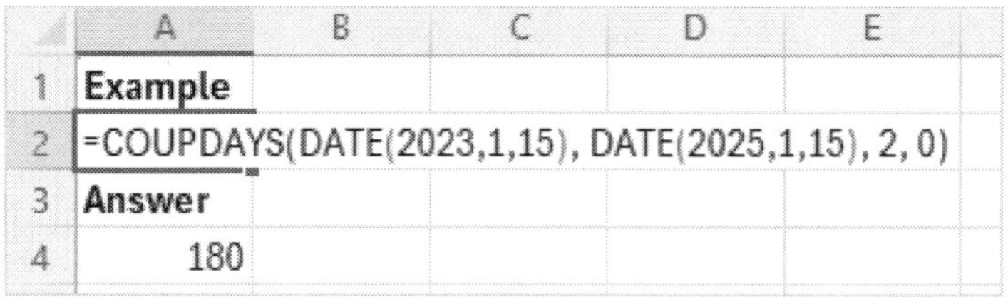

	A	B	C	D	E
1	**Example**				
2	=COUPDAYS(DATE(2023,1,15), DATE(2025,1,15), 2, 0)				
3	**Answer**				
4	180				

Formula:

```
=COUPDAYS(DATE(2023,1,15), DATE(2025,1,15), 2, 0)
```

Result: 180

Explanation: For semi-annual payments (frequency = 2) with a 30/360 basis, the total number of days in the coupon period is 180.

COUPDAYSNC Function

Financial Functions

Introduction

The COUPDAYSNC function calculates the number of days from the settlement date to the next coupon date. It is commonly used in bond analysis to evaluate the time remaining until the next interest payment.

Simple explanation: Returns the number of days from the settlement date to the next coupon date.

Common use cases: Used in bond valuation, financial modeling, and determining payment schedules.

When to use this function: Use when analyzing bonds or fixed-income securities to calculate upcoming payment timelines.

Syntax

```
=COUPDAYSNC(settlement, maturity, frequency, [basis])
```

- **settlement**: The bond's settlement date (the date the buyer purchases the bond).
- **maturity**: The bond's maturity date (when it expires).
- **frequency**: The number of coupon payments per year (1, 2, or 4).
- **[basis]** *(optional)*: The day count basis to use:
    - 0: US (NASD) 30/360 (default); 1: Actual/actual; 2: Actual/360; 3: Actual/365; 4: European 30/360.

Worked Example

Challenge: Calculate the days from settlement to the next coupon date for a bond.

Details:

- Settlement date: 15-Jan-2023
- Maturity date: 15-Jan-2025
- Frequency: 2 (semi-annual payments).
- Basis: 0 (default).

Formula:

```
=COUPDAYSNC(DATE(2023,1,15),
DATE(2025,1,15), 2, 0)
```

	A	B	C	D	E
1	**Example**				
2	=COUPDAYSNC(DATE(2023,1,15), DATE(2025,1,15), 2, 0)				
3	**Answer**				
4	180				

Result: 180

Explanation: For semi-annual payments (frequency = 2) with a 30/360 basis, the number of days from the settlement date to the next coupon date is 180.

COUPNCD Function

Financial Functions

Introduction

The COUPNCD function calculates the next coupon date after the settlement date for a bond. It is commonly used in bond analysis to determine the timing of future payments.

Simple explanation: Returns the next coupon payment date after the settlement date.

Common use cases: Used in financial modeling, bond valuation, and payment scheduling.

When to use this function: Use when analyzing bonds or fixed-income securities to find upcoming coupon dates.

Syntax

```
=COUPNCD(settlement, maturity, frequency, [basis])
```

- **settlement**: The bond's settlement date (the date the buyer purchases the bond).
- **maturity**: The bond's maturity date (when it expires).
- **frequency**: The number of coupon payments per year (1, 2, or 4).
- **[basis]** *(optional)*: The day count basis to use:
    - 0: US (NASD) 30/360 (default); 1: Actual/actual; 2: Actual/360; 3: Actual/365; 4: European 30/360.

Worked Example

Challenge: Determine the next coupon date after a settlement date.

Details:

- Settlement date: 15-Jan-2023
- Maturity date: 15-Jan-2025
- Frequency: 2 (semi-annual payments).
- Basis: 0 (default).

Formula:

```
=COUPNCD(DATE(2023,1,15),
DATE(2025,1,15), 2, 0)
```

Result: 15-Jul-2023

Explanation: For semi-annual payments (frequency = 2), the next coupon date after 15-Jan-2023 is 15-Jul-2023.

	A	B	C	D	E
1	**Example**				
2	=COUPNCD(DATE(2023,1,15), DATE(2025,1,15), 2, 0)				
3	**Answer**				
4	15 July 2023				
5					

COUPNUM Function

Financial Functions

Introduction

The COUPNUM function calculates the number of coupon payments remaining between the settlement date and the maturity date for a bond. It is useful in determining payment schedules and future cash flows.

Simple explanation: Returns the total number of coupon payments remaining until maturity.

Common use cases: Used in financial modeling, bond valuation, and cash flow forecasting.

When to use this function: Use when analyzing bonds or fixed-income securities to calculate the number of payments left.

Syntax

```
=COUPNUM(settlement, maturity, frequency, [basis])
```

- **settlement**: The bond's settlement date (the date the buyer purchases the bond).
- **maturity**: The bond's maturity date (when it expires).
- **frequency**: The number of coupon payments per year (1, 2, or 4).
- **[basis]** *(optional)*: The day count basis to use:
  - 0: US (NASD) 30/360 (default); 1: Actual/actual; 2: Actual/360; 3: Actual/365; 4: European 30/360.

Worked Example

Challenge: Calculate the number of coupon payments remaining for a bond.

Details:

- Settlement date: 15-Jan-2023
- Maturity date: 15-Jan-2025
- Frequency: 2 (semi-annual payments).
- Basis: 0 (default).

Formula:

```
=COUPNUM(DATE(2023,1,15), DATE(2025,1,15), 2, 0)
```

Result: 4

	A	B	C	D	E
1	**Example**				
2	=COUPNUM(DATE(2023,1,15), DATE(2025,1,15), 2, 0)				
3	**Answer**				
4	4				

Explanation: For semi-annual payments (frequency = 2), there are 4 coupon payments remaining between 15-Jan-2023 and 15-Jan-2025.

COUPPCD Function

Financial Functions

Introduction

The COUPPCD function calculates the previous coupon date before the settlement date for a bond. It is commonly used in bond analysis to determine the timeline of past payments and accrued interest calculations.

Simple explanation: Returns the last coupon payment date before the settlement date.

Common use cases: Used in financial modeling, bond valuation, and accrued interest calculations.

When to use this function: Use when analyzing bonds or fixed-income securities to find coupon dates.

Syntax

```
=COUPPCD(settlement, maturity, frequency, [basis])
```

- **settlement**: The bond's settlement date (the date the buyer purchases the bond).
- **maturity**: The bond's maturity date (when it expires).
- **frequency**: The number of coupon payments per year (1, 2, or 4).
- **[basis]** *(optional)*: The day count basis to use:
    - 0: US (NASD) 30/360 (default); 1: Actual/actual; 2: Actual/360; 3: Actual/365; 4: European 30/360.

Worked Example

Challenge: Determine the previous coupon date before a settlement date.

Details:

- Settlement date: 15-Jan-2023
- Maturity date: 15-Jan-2025
- Frequency: 2 (semi-annual payments).
- Basis: 0 (default).

Formula:

```
=COUPPCD(DATE(2023,1,15),
DATE(2025,1,15), 2, 0)
```

Result: 15-Jan-2023
Explanation: Since the settlement date aligns exactly with a coupon date, the previous coupon date is the same as the settlement date.

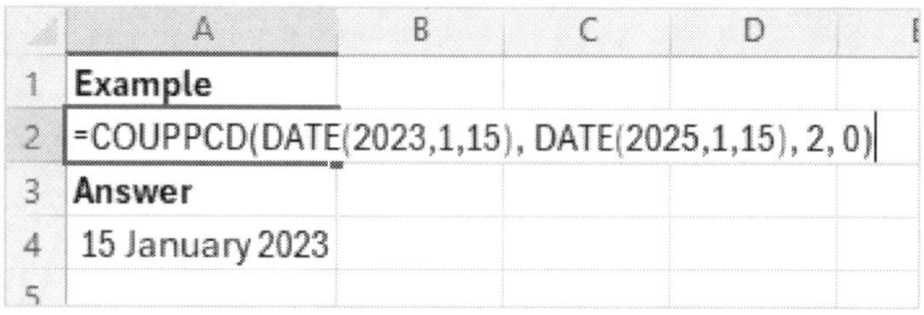

	A	B	C	D
1	**Example**			
2	=COUPPCD(DATE(2023,1,15), DATE(2025,1,15), 2, 0)			
3	**Answer**			
4	15 January 2023			
5				

COVAR Function

Compatibility Functions

Introduction

The COVAR function calculates the covariance, which measures the relationship between two datasets. Covariance indicates whether the two variables tend to increase or decrease together.

Simple explanation: Returns the measure of how two datasets vary together.

Common use cases: Used in statistics, finance, and data analysis to identify relationships between variables, such as stock returns.

When to use this function: Use when evaluating the degree of association between two variables.

Syntax

```
=COVAR(array1, array2)
```

- **array1**: The first range or array of numbers.
- **array2**: The second range or array of numbers.

Worked Example

Challenge: Calculate the covariance between sales and advertising spend.

Data:

- Sales (array1): A1:A5 → {100, 200, 300, 400, 500}
- Advertising Spend (array2): B1:B5 → {10, 20, 30, 40, 50}

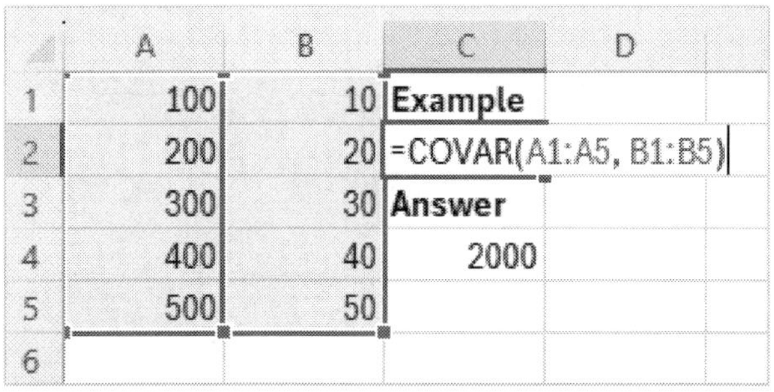

	A	B	C	D
1	100	10	**Example**	
2	200	20	=COVAR(A1:A5, B1:B5)	
3	300	30	**Answer**	
4	400	40	2000	
5	500	50		
6				

Formula:

```
=COVAR(A1:A5, B1:B5)
```

Result: 2000

Explanation: The positive covariance indicates that sales and advertising spend increase together, suggesting a positive relationship.

Explore Further with GPT:
Ask GPT to explain how to interpret covariance in relation to correlation or demonstrate its use in portfolio analysis.

Tips for Using COVAR

- **Dataset sizes:** Ensure both arrays are of equal length; otherwise, Excel will return a #N/A error.
- **Positive vs. negative values:** A positive covariance indicates that variables move in the same direction, while a negative covariance indicates an inverse relationship.
- **Transition to** COVARIANCE.P**:** The COVAR function is now considered deprecated in modern Excel versions; use COVARIANCE.P for population covariance.

COVARIANCE.P Function

Statistical Functions

Introduction

The COVARIANCE.P function calculates the population covariance, measuring how two datasets vary together. It indicates the strength and direction of the linear relationship between two variables across an entire population.

Simple explanation: Returns the population covariance between two datasets.

Common use cases: Used in statistics, finance, and data analysis to evaluate relationships between variables, such as stock returns or economic indicators.

When to use this function: Use when analyzing the association between two variables in a population dataset.

Syntax

```
=COVARIANCE.P(array1, array2)
```

- **array1**: The first range or array of numbers.
- **array2**: The second range or array of numbers.

Worked Example

Challenge: Calculate the population covariance between revenue and marketing spend.

Data:

- Revenue (array1): A1:A5 → {500, 600, 700, 800, 900}
- Marketing Spend (array2): B1:B5 → {50, 60, 70, 80, 90}

Formula:

```
=COVARIANCE.P(A1:A5, B1:B5)
```

Result: 2000

	A	B	C	D	E
1	500	50	**Example**		
2	600	60	=COVARIANCE.P(A1:A5, B1:B5)		
3	700	70	**Answer**		
4	800	80	2000		
5	900	90			

Explanation: The positive covariance of 2000 shows that revenue and marketing spend tend to increase together, indicating a direct relationship.

Explore Further with GPT:
Ask GPT to explain how to interpret covariance in relation to variance or how to apply it in portfolio optimization.

Tips for Using COVARIANCE.P

- **Equal range sizes:** Ensure both arrays are of equal length; otherwise, Excel will return a #N/A error.
- **Positive and negative covariance:** Positive values indicate that variables move in the same direction, while negative values indicate an inverse relationship.

COVARIANCE.S Function

Statistical Functions

Introduction

The COVARIANCE.S function calculates the sample covariance, which measures how two datasets vary together. It is used to estimate the strength and direction of the linear relationship between two variables in a sample dataset.

Simple explanation: Returns the sample covariance between two datasets.

Common use cases: Used in statistics, finance, and data analysis to evaluate relationships between variables, such as stock returns or economic indicators, in a sample.

When to use this function: Use when analyzing the association between two variables in a sample dataset.

Syntax

```
=COVARIANCE.S(array1, array2)
```

- **array1**: The first range or array of numbers.
- **array2**: The second range or array of numbers.

Worked Example

Challenge: Calculate the sample covariance between revenue and marketing spend.

Data:

- Revenue (array1): A1:A5 → {500, 600, 700, 800, 900}
- Marketing Spend (array2): B1:B5 → {50, 60, 70, 80, 90}

Formula:

```
=COVARIANCE.S(A1:A5, B1:B5)
```

	A	B	C	D	E
1	500	50	**Example**		
2	600	60	=COVARIANCE.S(A1:A5, B1:B5)		
3	700	70	**Answer**		
4	800	80	2500		
5	900	90			

Result: 2500
Explanation: The positive sample covariance of 2500 shows that revenue and marketing spend tend to increase together, suggesting a direct relationship within the sample.

Explore Further with GPT:
Ask GPT how to interpret sample covariance in relation to correlation or how it is used in statistical modeling.

Tips for Using COVARIANCE.S

- **Sample vs. population:** Use this function for sample data, and use COVARIANCE.P when working with population data.
- **Equal range sizes:** Ensure both arrays are of equal length; otherwise, Excel will return a #N/A error.
- **Positive and negative covariance:** Positive values indicate a direct relationship, while negative values indicate an inverse relationship between the variables.

CRITBINOM Function

Compatibility Functions

Introduction

The CRITBINOM function calculates the smallest value for which the cumulative binomial distribution is greater than or equal to a specified criterion. It is commonly used in quality control, risk analysis, and hypothesis testing.

Simple explanation: Returns the smallest number of successes needed for the cumulative binomial distribution to meet or exceed a given probability.

Common use cases: Used in statistical analysis, quality testing, and probability modeling.

When to use this function: Use when analyzing binomial distributions and determining thresholds for decision-making.

Syntax

```
=CRITBINOM(trials, probability_s, alpha)
```

- **trials**: The number of independent trials.
- **probability_s**: The probability of success in each trial.
- **alpha**: The criterion probability.

Worked Example

Challenge: Find the minimum number of successes required for the cumulative probability to meet or exceed 0.8 in 10 trials, with a success probability of 0.5.

Formula:

```
=CRITBINOM(10, 0.5, 0.8)
```

Result: 6

Explanation: At least 6 successes are needed for the cumulative binomial distribution to meet or exceed a probability of 0.8.

	A	B	C
1	**Example**		
2	=CRITBINOM(10, 0.5, 0.8)		
3	**Answer**		
4	6		

Explore Further with GPT:
Ask GPT how to use CRITBINOM in real-world scenarios or compare it with functions like BINOM.DIST.

Tips for Using CRITBINOM

- **Integer output:** The function always returns an integer value representing the number of successes.
- **Probability range:** Ensure probability_s and alpha are between 0 and 1; otherwise, Excel will return a #NUM! error.
- **Transition to modern functions:** Use BINOM.INV in modern Excel versions, as CRITBINOM is now considered deprecated.

CSC Function

Math & Trigonometry

Introduction

The CSC function calculates the cosecant of a given angle. Cosecant is the reciprocal of the sine function and is commonly used in trigonometry for solving equations involving right triangles or periodic phenomena.

Simple explanation: Returns the cosecant of an angle provided in radians.

Common use cases: Used in geometry, engineering, and physics to solve problems involving angles and trigonometric relationships.

When to use this function: Use when working with trigonometric equations requiring the cosecant.

Syntax

```
=CSC(number)
```

- **number**: The angle in radians for which to calculate the cosecant.

Worked Example

Challenge: Calculate the cosecant of a 30-degree angle.

1. Convert degrees to radians:

```
=RADIANS(30)
```

Result: 0.5236 radians.

2. Use the CSC function:

```
=CSC(0.5236)
```

Result: 2

Explanation: The cosecant of a 30-degree angle (or 0.5236 radians) is 2, as it is the reciprocal of the sine value (1 / sin(30°)).

	A	B
1	Step 1	**Example**
2	0.523599	=CSC(A2)
3	Step 2	**Answer**
4	2	2

Explore Further with GPT:
Ask GPT how to use CSC in conjunction with other trigonometric functions like SIN, SEC, or COT for advanced calculations.

Tips for Using CSC

- **Radians required:** If your angle is in degrees, use the RADIANS function to convert it before applying CSC.
- **Avoid undefined inputs:** The function will return a #DIV/0! error if the sine of the angle is 0 (e.g., multiples of π).
- **Applications:** Use in trigonometric problems involving right triangles or oscillatory motion.

CSCH Function

Math & Trigonometry

Introduction

The CSCH function calculates the hyperbolic cosecant of a given number. It is the reciprocal of the hyperbolic sine function and is commonly used in engineering, physics, and mathematics.

Simple explanation: Returns the hyperbolic cosecant of a number.

Common use cases: Used in physics, engineering, and advanced mathematics for modeling hyperbolic relationships and exponential growth.

When to use this function: Use when solving problems involving hyperbolic equations or exponential behavior.

Syntax

```
=CSCH(number)
```

- **number**: The value for which to calculate the hyperbolic cosecant.

Worked Example

Challenge: Calculate the hyperbolic cosecant of 2.

Formula:

`=CSCH(2)`

Result: 0.275721
Explanation: The hyperbolic cosecant of 2 is approximately 0.275721, calculated as 1 / SINH(2).

	A	B
1	**Example**	
2	=CSCH(2)	
3	**Answer**	
4	0.275721	
5		

Explore Further with GPT:
Ask GPT how to use CSCH in conjunction with other hyperbolic functions like SINH or COTH for complex modeling.

Tips for Using CSCH

- **Avoid zero input:** The function will return a #DIV/0! error if the input is 0, as the hyperbolic sine of 0 is also 0.
- **Applications:** Commonly used in modeling wave behavior, catenary curves, or exponential growth.
- **Combine with other functions:** Use alongside hyperbolic functions like SINH and COTH to explore relationships in hyperbolic geometry.

CUBEKPIMEMBER Function

Cube Functions

Introduction

The CUBEKPIMEMBER function retrieves a Key Performance Indicator (KPI) property and displays its name, property, and measure group from an Online Analytical Processing (OLAP) data cube.

Simple explanation: Retrieves and displays KPI data from a connected OLAP data source.

Common use cases: Used in dashboards and reports to display KPI metrics such as targets, current values, or statuses.

When to use this function: Use when working with KPIs stored in an OLAP data cube.

Syntax

```
=CUBEKPIMEMBER(connection, kpi_name, kpi_property, [caption])
```

- **connection**: The name of the workbook connection to the OLAP data source.
- **kpi_name**: The name of the KPI in the cube.
- **kpi_property**: The property of the KPI to return:
    - "Value": The actual value of the KPI.
    - "Goal": The target value of the KPI.
    - "Status": The status of the KPI.
    - "Trend": The trend of the KPI.
    - "Weight": The weight of the KPI.
- **[caption]** *(optional)*: A user-defined text string for labeling the KPI

Worked Example

Challenge: Retrieve the KPI value for "Sales Target" from an OLAP cube.

1. Connection: SalesData
2. KPI Name: "[Measures].[Sales Target]"
3. KPI Property: "Value"

	A	B	C	D	E	F
1	**Example**					
2	=CUBEKPIMEMBER("SalesData", "[Measures].[Sales Target]", "Value")					
3	**Answer**					
4	150,000					
5						

Formula:

```
=CUBEKPIMEMBER("SalesData", "[Measures].[Sales Target]", "Value")
```

Result: Returns the actual value of the KPI "Sales Target" from the SalesData cube.

Tips for Using CUBEKPIMEMBER

- **Ensure connectivity:** Make sure the workbook is connected to an OLAP data source; otherwise, the function will return a #NAME? error.

CUBEMEMBER Function

Cube Functions

Introduction

The CUBEMEMBER function retrieves a member or tuple from an OLAP cube connected to your workbook. It is often used in business intelligence and reporting to display specific data elements from a multidimensional data model.

Simple explanation: Retrieves a specific member or tuple from an OLAP cube.

Common use cases: Used in dashboards, reports, and dynamic analyses to display cube data such as regions, time periods, or product categories.

When to use this function: Use when working with cube data and need to extract specific members or tuples for reporting.

Syntax

```
=CUBEMEMBER(connection, member_expression, [caption])
```

- **connection**: The name of the workbook connection to the OLAP cube.
- **member_expression**: A multidimensional expression (MDX) that specifies the member or tuple to retrieve.
- **[caption]** *(optional)*: A user-defined label for the retrieved member

Worked Example

Challenge: Retrieve the "North America" member from the "Region" hierarchy in a cube.

1. Connection: SalesData
2. Member Expression: "[Region].[North America]"

Formula:

```
=CUBEMEMBER("SalesData",
"[Region].[North America]")
```

Result: Returns the "North America" member from the "Region" hierarchy in the SalesData cube.

	A	B	C	D	E	F
1	**Example**					
2	=CUBEMEMBER("SalesData", "[Region].[North America]")					
3	**Answer**					
4	North America					
5						

Explore Further with GPT:
Ask GPT how to construct MDX expressions for advanced queries or how to combine CUBEMEMBER with CUBEVALUE for dynamic reporting.

Tips for Using CUBEMEMBER

- **Ensure connectivity:** The workbook must be connected to an OLAP cube; otherwise, the function will return a #NAME? error.
- **Error handling:** If the specified member does not exist, the function will return a #N/A error.
- **Combine with other functions:** Use with CUBEVALUE to retrieve associated values for the selected member.

CUBEMEMBERPROPERTY Function

Cube Functions

Introduction

The CUBEMEMBERPROPERTY function retrieves the value of a specific property for a member from an OLAP cube. It is commonly used to extract metadata or additional attributes about a member, such as descriptions, IDs, or hierarchy information.

Simple explanation: Returns the value of a specific property for a member in a cube.

Common use cases: Used in business intelligence to display member attributes like unique names, captions, or custom metadata.

When to use this function: Use when working with cube data and need to retrieve member properties for reporting or analysis.

Syntax

```
=CUBEMEMBERPROPERTY(connection, member_expression, property)
```

- **connection**: The name of the workbook connection to the OLAP cube.
- **member_expression**: A multidimensional expression (MDX) that specifies the member.
- **property**: The name of the property to retrieve (e.g., "CAPTION", "UNIQUE_NAME")

Worked Example

Challenge: Retrieve the unique name of the "North America" member from the "Region" hierarchy.

	A	B	C	D	E	F	G
1	**Example**						
2	=CUBEMEMBERPROPERTY("SalesData", "[Region].[North America]", "UNIQUE_NAME")						
3	**Answer**						
4	[Region].[North America]						
5							

1. Connection: SalesData
2. Member Expression: "[Region].[North America]"
3. Property: "UNIQUE_NAME"

Formula:

```
=CUBEMEMBERPROPERTY("SalesData", "[Region].[North America]", "UNIQUE_NAME")
```

Result: [Region].[North America]

Tips for Using CUBEMEMBERPROPERTY

- **Ensure connectivity:** The workbook must be connected to an OLAP cube; otherwise, the function will return a #NAME? error.
- **Common properties:** Use predefined properties like "CAPTION", "UNIQUE_NAME", or "DESCRIPTION" to retrieve member attributes.

CUBERANKEDMEMBER Function

Cube Functions

Introduction

The CUBERANKEDMEMBER function retrieves a specific member from a set, based on its rank. It is commonly used in OLAP cube analyses to display ranked data, such as the top-selling products or regions.

Simple explanation: Returns a member from a set based on its rank (position).

Common use cases: Used in dashboards and reports to dynamically display top or bottom performers in ranked lists.

When to use this function: Use when working with ranked data or subsets of members in an OLAP cube.

Syntax

```
=CUBERANKEDMEMBER(connection, set_expression, rank, [caption])
```

- **connection**: The name of the workbook connection to the OLAP cube.
- **set_expression**: An MDX expression defining the set of members to rank.
- **rank**: The rank (position) of the member to retrieve (1 for the first, 2 for the second, and so on).
- **[caption]** *(optional)*: A user-defined label for the returned member.

Worked Example

	A	B	C	D	E	F	G	H	I
1	**Example**								
2	=CUBERANKEDMEMBER("SalesData", "{[Product Category].[Electronics], [Product Category].[Furniture]}", 1)								
3	**Answer**								
4	[Product Category].[Electronics]								
5									

Challenge: Retrieve the top-ranked product category based on sales.

- Connection: SalesData; Set Expression: "{[Product Category].[Electronics], [Product Category].[Furniture]}"; Rank: 1

Formula:

```
=CUBERANKEDMEMBER("SalesData", "{[Product Category].[Electronics], [Product Category].[Furniture]}", 1)
```

Result: [Product Category].[Electronics]
Explanation: The function retrieves the first-ranked member (Electronics) from the specified set.

Tips for Using CUBERANKEDMEMBER

- **Rank values:** Ensure the rank argument is a positive integer within the range of the set; otherwise, Excel returns a #NUM! error.
- **Error handling:** If the set is empty or the rank exceeds the set size, the function returns a #N/A error.

CUBESET Function

Cube Functions

Introduction

The CUBESET function defines a set of members or tuples from an OLAP cube based on a set expression, optionally sorted by a measure. It is commonly used in business intelligence to analyze subsets of data, such as top-performing products or regions.

Simple explanation: Creates a set of members or tuples from a cube, optionally ordered by a measure.

Common use cases: Used in dashboards and reports to define dynamic subsets of data for analysis.

When to use this function: Use when working with ranked lists, subsets, or filtered data from an OLAP cube.

Syntax

```
=CUBESET(connection, set_expression, [caption], [sort_order], [sort_by])
```

- **connection**: The name of the workbook connection to the OLAP cube.
- **set_expression**: An MDX expression defining the set.
- **[caption]** *(optional)*: A user-defined label for the set.
- **[sort_order]** *(optional)*: Specifies the sort order:
    - 0: No sorting (default); 1: Ascending; 2: Descending.
- **[sort_by]** *(optional)*: A measure or tuple used to sort the set.

Worked Example

Challenge: Create a set of product categories sorted by sales in descending order.

1. Connection: SalesData
2. Set Expression: "[Product Category].[All Products].Children"

	A	B	C	D	E	F	G	H	I	J
1	**Example**									
2	=CUBESET("SalesData", "[Product Category].[All Products].Children", "Top Categories", 2, "[Measures].[Sales Amount]")									
3	**Answer**									
4	Top Categories									

3. Sort Order: 2 (Descending)
4. Sort By: [Measures].[Sales Amount]

Formula:

```
=CUBESET("SalesData", "[Product Category].[All Products].Children", "Top Categories", 2,
"[Measures].[Sales Amount]")
```

Result: A set containing product categories sorted by sales in descending order.

Tips for Using CUBESET

- **Dynamic filtering:** Use the sort_by argument to dynamically order sets based on cube measures.

CUBESETCOUNT Function

Cube Functions

Introduction

The CUBESETCOUNT function returns the number of items in a set created by a CUBESET function. It is useful for analyzing the size of dynamically generated sets in OLAP cubes.

Simple explanation: Counts the number of members in a set retrieved from a cube.

Common use cases: Used in dashboards and reports to dynamically determine the size of a filtered or ranked data set.

When to use this function: Use when analyzing or reporting on the size of subsets from an OLAP cube.

Syntax

```
=CUBESETCOUNT(set)
```

- **set**: A reference to a cell containing a CUBESET formula.

Worked Example

Challenge: Count the number of product categories in a set sorted by sales.

	A	B
1	**Example**	
2	=CUBESET("SalesData", "[Product Category].[All Products].Children", "Top Categories", 2, "[Measures].[Sales Amount]")	
3	**Answer**	
4	2	
5		

- Create a set of product categories:
- Formula in cell A2:

```
=CUBESET("SalesData", "[Product Category].[All Products].Children", "Top Categories", 2,
"[Measures].[Sales Amount]")
```

- Count the members in the set:
- Formula in cell A4::

```
=CUBESETCOUNT(A2)
```

Result: 2
Explanation: The set contains two product categories (Electronics and Furniture).

Explore Further with GPT:
Ask GPT how to combine CUBESETCOUNT with conditional logic to evaluate subsets dynamically.

Tips for Using CUBESETCOUNT

- **Reference a valid set:** The argument must reference a cell containing a CUBESET formula; otherwise, Excel returns a #VALUE! error.
- **Dynamic updates:** The count updates automatically if the referenced CUBESET changes due to recalculations or slicer interactions.

CUBEVALUE Function

Cube Functions

Introduction

The CUBEVALUE function retrieves an aggregated value from an OLAP cube based on specified members or measures. It is used in dashboards and reports to display metrics such as totals, averages, or KPIs filtered by dimensions like region, time, or product.

Simple explanation: Returns an aggregated value from a cube for specified dimensions or measures.

Common use cases: Used in business intelligence dashboards to display key metrics like sales, profit, or performance indicators.

When to use this function: Use when analyzing aggregated data from an OLAP cube and need specific measures filtered by dimensions.

Syntax

```
=CUBEVALUE(connection, [member_expression1], [member_expression2], ...)
```

- **connection**: The name of the workbook connection to the OLAP cube.
- **[member_expression1], [member_expression2], ...** *(optional)*: One or more MDX expressions defining members, tuples, or sets to filter the aggregation

Worked Example

Challenge: Retrieve the total sales amount for "North America" in the "Electronics" category for Q1 2023.

	A	B
1	**Example**	
2	=CUBESET("SalesData", "[Product Category].[All Products].Children", "Top Categories", 2, "[Measures].[Sales Amount]")	
3	**Answer**	
4	100,000	
5		

1. Connection: SalesData
2. Dimensions:
    - Region: [Region].[North America]
    - Product Category: [Product Category].[Electronics]
    - Time Period: [Time Period].[Q1 2023]
    - Measure: [Measures].[Sales Amount]

Formula:

```
=CUBEVALUE("SalesData", "[Measures].[Sales Amount]", "[Region].[North America]",
"[Product Category].[Electronics]", "[Time Period].[Q1 2023]")
```

Result: 100,000
Explanation: The function calculates the total sales amount for the specified region, category, and time period from the cube.

CUMIPMT Function

Financial Functions

Introduction

The CUMIPMT function calculates the cumulative interest paid on a loan or investment over a specific range of payment periods. It is commonly used in financial analysis to assess interest costs over time.

Simple explanation: Returns the total interest paid between two specified payment periods.

Common use cases: Used in loan amortization schedules, financial modeling, and cost analysis.

When to use this function: Use when analyzing the total interest incurred over a range of payments.

Syntax

```
=CUMIPMT(rate, nper, pv, start_period, end_period, type)
```

- **rate**: The interest rate per period.
- **nper**: The total number of payment periods.
- **pv**: The present value (loan amount or principal).
- **start_period**: The first payment period in the range (integer).
- **end_period**: The last payment period in the range (integer).
- **type**: The timing of payments:
  - 0: Payments are made at the end of the period; 1: Payments are made at the beginning of the period.

Worked Example

Challenge: Calculate the cumulative interest paid on a loan with the following details:

- Loan amount: 100,000
- Annual interest rate: 5%
- Term: 10 years (120 monthly payments)
- Payment period range: Months 1 to 12
- Payments made at the end of the period.
- Convert annual rate to monthly:

  `=5% / 12 (0.004167)`

	A	B	C	D
1	**Example**			
2	=CUMIPMT(0.004167, 120, 100000, 1, 12, 0)			
3	**Answer**			
4	-4820.81			

Formula:

```
=CUMIPMT(0.004167, 120, 100000, 1, 12, 0)
```

Result: -4,820.81
Explanation: Over the first year (12 months), a total of 4,820.81 in interest is paid. The result is negative because it represents an outgoing payment.

CUMPRINC Function

Financial Functions

Introduction

The CUMPRINC function calculates the cumulative principal paid on a loan or investment over a specific range of payment periods. It is used to determine how much of a loan has been repaid over a given period.

Simple explanation: Returns the total principal paid between two specified payment periods.

Common use cases: Used in loan amortization schedules, financial modeling, and debt repayment analysis.

When to use this function: Use when analyzing the amount of principal repaid over a specific range of payments.

Syntax

```
=CUMPRINC(rate, nper, pv, start_period, end_period, type)
```

- **rate**: The interest rate per period.
- **nper**: The total number of payment periods.
- **pv**: The present value (loan amount or principal).
- **start_period**: The first payment period in the range (integer).
- **end_period**: The last payment period in the range (integer).
- **type**: The timing of payments:
  - 0: Payments are made at the end of the period.
  - 1: Payments are made at the beginning of the period.

Worked Example

Challenge: Calculate the cumulative principal paid on a loan with the following details:

- Loan amount: 100,000
- Annual interest rate: 5%
- Term: 10 years (120 monthly payments)
- Payment period range: Months 1 to 12
- Payments made at the end of the period.

	A	B	C	D
1	**Example**			
2	=CUMPRINC(0.004167, 120, 100000, 1, 12, 0)			
3	**Answer**			
4	-7907.29			

1. Convert annual rate to monthly:

```
=5% / 12
```

Result: 0.004167

Formula:

```
=CUMPRINC(0.004167, 120, 100000, 1, 12, 0)
```

Result: -7.907.29
Explanation: Over the first year (12 months), a total of 7,907.29 in principal is repaid. The result is negative because it represents an outgoing payment.

DATE Function

Date & Time Functions

Introduction

The DATE function returns a date based on the specified year, month, and day values. It is commonly used to create valid dates dynamically or from separate year, month, and day inputs.

Simple explanation: Returns a date value based on the year, month, and day provided.

Common use cases: Used in data analysis, date calculations, and building dynamic schedules.

When to use this function: Use when constructing dates from individual components or ensuring date validity in calculations.

Syntax

```
=DATE(year, month, day)
```

- **year**: The year of the date (positive for years after 1900, or a four-digit value).
- **month**: The month of the date (can handle values greater than 12 or less than 1 to adjust the year).
- **day**: The day of the month (can handle values greater than the number of days in a month or less than 1 to adjust the month).

Worked Example

Challenge: Create a date for 15-Jan-2023.

Formula:

```
=DATE(2023, 1, 15)
```

Result: 15/01/2023

Explanation: The function returns the date based on the specified year, month, and day.

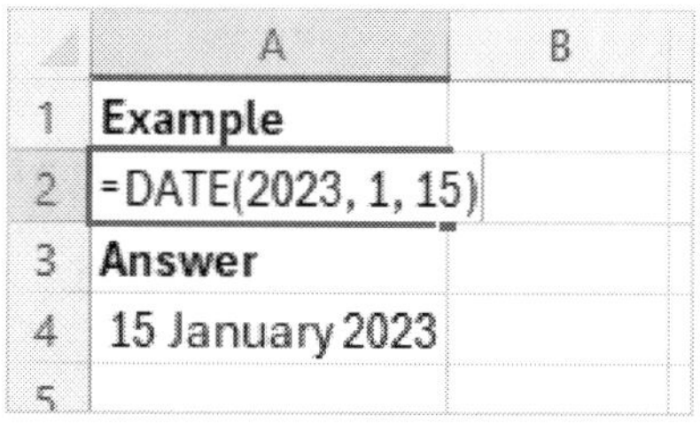

	A	B
1	**Example**	
2	=DATE(2023, 1, 15)	
3	**Answer**	
4	15 January 2023	
5		

Explore Further with GPT:
Ask GPT to demonstrate how to use DATE in conjunction with functions like YEAR, MONTH, and DAY for date manipulation.

Tips for Using DATE

- **Dynamic adjustments:** If month or day exceeds their typical ranges, Excel automatically adjusts the date. For example:
  - =DATE(2023, 13, 1) returns 01-Jan-2024 (13 months shifts the year forward).
  - =DATE(2023, 1, 32) returns 01-Feb-2023 (32 days shifts the month forward).
- **Combine with other functions:** Use with TEXT to format dates or with TODAY for dynamic date calculations.
- **Error handling:** If any argument is invalid (e.g., non-numeric), Excel returns a #VALUE! error.

DATEDIF Function

Date & Time Functions

Introduction

The DATEDIF function calculates the difference between two dates in terms of complete years, months, or days. Although it is an undocumented function in Excel, it is widely used for date-related calculations.

Simple explanation: Calculates the difference between two dates in specified units (years, months, or days).

Common use cases: Used in age calculation, project management, and date-based comparisons.

When to use this function: Use when you need precise differences between two dates in specific units.

Syntax

```
=DATEDIF(start_date, end_date, unit)
```

- **start_date**: The beginning date.
- **end_date**: The ending date (must be greater than or equal to start_date).
- **unit**: The unit for the result:
    - "Y": Complete years between the dates.
    - "M": Complete months between the dates.
    - "D": Days between the dates.
    - "MD": Days between the dates, ignoring months and years.
    - "YM": Months between the dates, ignoring years.
    - "YD": Days between the dates, ignoring years.

Worked Example

Challenge: Calculate the difference between 01-Jan-2020 and 15-Mar-2023 in complete years.

Formula:

```
=DATEDIF(DATE(2020, 1, 1), DATE(2023, 3, 15), "Y")
```

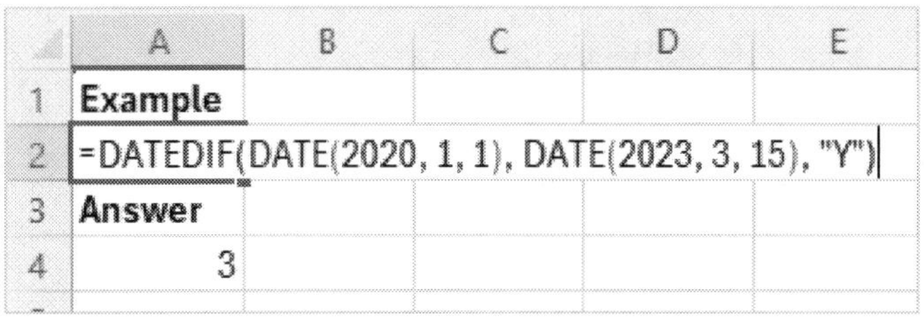

Result: 3
Explanation: The function calculates 3 complete years between the two dates.

Explore Further with GPT:
Ask GPT to demonstrate how to use DATEDIF in combination with TEXT for more user-friendly outputs.

Tips for Using DATEDIF

- **Undocumented function:** While functional in Excel, DATEDIF is not listed in the formula suggestions or documentation.
- **Order matters:** Ensure end_date is greater than or equal to start_date; otherwise, the function returns a #NUM! error.

DATEVALUE Function

Date & Time Functions

Introduction

The DATEVALUE function converts a date stored as text into an Excel date serial number. This is useful for working with date values in calculations or formatting when they are stored as text strings.

Simple explanation: Converts a text string representing a date into a valid Excel date.

Common use cases: Used when cleaning data, converting imported text dates, or enabling date calculations from text inputs.

When to use this function: Use when dates are stored as text and need to be converted for use in formulas or calculations.

Syntax

```
=DATEVALUE(date_text)
```

- **date_text**: A text string representing a date in a recognizable format (e.g., "15-Jan-2023").

Worked Example

Challenge: Convert the text "15-Jan-2023" into a valid date.

Formula:

```
=DATEVALUE("15-Jan-2023")
```

Result: 44941
Explanation: Excel returns the serial number 44941, which corresponds to 15-Jan-2023 in the default date system. You can format the cell to display the result as a date.

	A	B	C
1	**Example**		
2	=DATEVALUE("15-Jan-2023")		
3	**Answer**		
4	44941		
5			

Explore Further with GPT:
Ask GPT how to handle regional date format discrepancies or use DATEVALUE in combination with other functions for advanced transformations.

Tips for Using DATEVALUE

- **Date formats:** The date_text argument must match Excel's recognized date formats; otherwise, the function returns a #VALUE! error.
- **Regional settings:** Ensure the date format aligns with your system's regional settings (e.g., MM/DD/YYYY vs. DD/MM/YYYY).
- **Combine with TIMEVALUE:** Use DATEVALUE alongside TIMEVALUE to convert full text-based timestamps into valid date-time values. For example:

  ```
  =DATEVALUE("15-Jan-2023") + TIMEVALUE("14:30")
  ```

DAVERAGE Function

Database Functions

Introduction

The DAVERAGE function calculates the average of values in a specified field (column) of a database that meet given criteria. It is particularly useful for analyzing structured data with filters.

Simple explanation: Returns the average of values in a column that meet specified criteria.

Common use cases: Used in data analysis, reports, and dashboards for calculating conditional averages from structured data.

When to use this function: Use when working with databases or structured tables where averages need to be calculated based on specific criteria.

Syntax

```
=DAVERAGE(database, field, criteria)
```

- **database**: The range of cells containing the database, including headers.
- **field**: The column to average, specified as a column header (in quotes) or column number.
- **criteria**: The range of cells defining the filter criteria.

Worked Example

Challenge: Calculate the average sales for the "North" region from a dataset.

Formula:

	A	B	C	D	E	F	G	H	I
1	**Region**	**Sales**	**Month**		**Region**		**Example**		
2	North	100	January		North		=DAVERAGE(A1:C5, "Sales", E1:E2)		
3	South	200	January				**Answer**		
4	North	300	February				200		
5	South	400	February						
6									

```
=DAVERAGE(A1:C5, "Sales", E1:E2)
```

Result: 200
Explanation: The function averages the sales values for the "North" region (100 and 300), resulting in 200.

Explore Further with GPT:
Ask GPT how to create dynamic criteria ranges or compare DAVERAGE with functions like AVERAGEIFS for similar use cases.

Tips for Using DAVERAGE

- **Criteria format:** Ensure the criteria range includes a header that matches the database and values for filtering.
- **Dynamic columns:** Use the column number as the field argument if column names are subject to change.
- **Combine with other functions:** Use alongside DSUM, DCOUNT, and other database functions for comprehensive data analysis.

DAY Function

Date & Time Functions

Introduction

The DAY function extracts the day of the month as a number from a given date. It is commonly used for date manipulation and extracting specific components from a date.

Simple explanation: Returns the day of the month from a date.

Common use cases: Used in scheduling, financial calculations, and data analysis to isolate the day component of a date.

When to use this function: Use when working with date values and needing the specific day of the month.

Syntax

```
=DAY(serial_number)
```

- **serial_number**: A date value or reference to a cell containing a date.

Worked Example

Challenge: Extract the day from 15-Jan-2023.

Formula:

```
=DAY(DATE(2023, 1, 15))
```

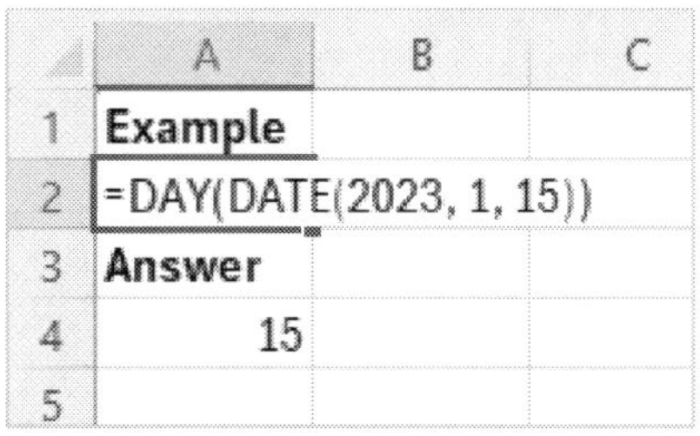

Result: 15
Explanation: The function returns 15, which is the day component of the provided date.

Explore Further with GPT:
Ask GPT how to combine DAY with MONTH and YEAR for comprehensive date analysis or formatting.

Tips for Using DAY

- **Date format:** Ensure the input is a valid Excel date; otherwise, the function returns a #VALUE! error.
- **Dynamic calculations:** Combine with TODAY() to extract the current day:

  ```
  =DAY(TODAY())
  ```

- **Combine with TEXT:** Use the TEXT function to display days in a custom format, e.g., "dd" for leading zeroes.

DAYS Function

Date & Time Functions

Introduction

The DAYS function calculates the number of days between two dates. It is commonly used in date-based calculations, such as project timelines, loan terms, or age calculations.

Simple explanation: Returns the difference in days between two dates.

Common use cases: Used in project management, financial analysis, and reporting to calculate durations or intervals.

When to use this function: Use when you need to find the number of days between two dates.

Syntax

```
=DAYS(end_date, start_date)
```

- **end_date**: The later date.
- **start_date**: The earlier date.

Worked Example

Challenge: Calculate the number of days between 01-Jan-2023 and 15-Mar-2023.

Formula:

```
=DAYS(DATE(2023, 3, 15), DATE(2023, 1, 1))
```

	A	B	C	D	E
1	**Example**				
2	=DAYS(DATE(2023, 3, 15), DATE(2023, 1, 1))				
3	**Answer**				
4	73				
5					

Result: 73
Explanation: The function returns 73 because there are 73 days between 01-Jan-2023 and 15-Mar-2023.

Explore Further with GPT:
Ask GPT how to handle negative results or combine DAYS with other date functions for dynamic interval calculations.

Tips for Using DAYS

- **Date validity:** Ensure both inputs are valid Excel dates; otherwise, the function returns a #VALUE! error.
- **Order of arguments:** The function subtracts the start_date from the end_date, so reversing the order changes the sign of the result.
- **Dynamic ranges:** Use with TODAY() to calculate days from or until the current date:

  ```
  =DAYS(TODAY(), DATE(2023, 1, 1))
  ```

DAYS360 Function

Date & Time Functions

Introduction

The DAYS360 function calculates the number of days between two dates based on a 360-day year (twelve 30-day months). This function is commonly used in accounting and financial analysis to standardize interest and payment calculations.

Simple explanation: Returns the number of days between two dates using a 360-day calendar.

Common use cases: Used in financial modeling, loan amortization, and interest calculations where a 360-day year is standard.

When to use this function: Use when working with financial or accounting systems that operate on a 360-day year.

Syntax

```
=DAYS360(start_date, end_date, [method])
```

- **start_date**: The starting date.
- **end_date**: The ending date.
- **[method]** *(optional)*: Specifies the calculation method:
  - FALSE or omitted: US (NASD) method, adjusting end dates falling on the 31st to the 30th.
  - TRUE: European method, treating all months as 30 days without adjustment.

Worked Example

Challenge: Calculate the number of days between 01-Jan-2023 and 15-Mar-2023 using a 360-day calendar.

Formula (US method):

```
=DAYS360(DATE(2023, 1, 1), DATE(2023, 3,
15))
```

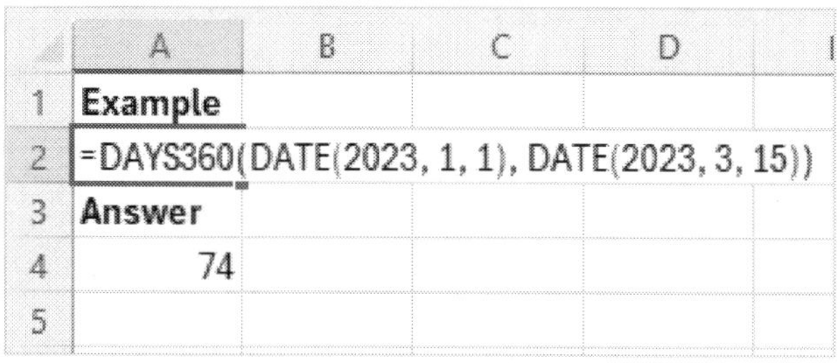

	A	B	C	D
1	**Example**			
2	=DAYS360(DATE(2023, 1, 1), DATE(2023, 3, 15))			
3	**Answer**			
4	74			
5				

Result: 74
Explanation: The function calculates 74 days based on the 360-day year, adjusting for standardized 30-day months.

Formula (European method):

```
=DAYS360(DATE(2023, 1, 1), DATE(2023, 3, 15), TRUE)
```

Result: 75
Explanation: The European method calculates 75 days, treating all months as 30 days without adjusting end dates.

Explore Further with GPT:
Ask GPT how to combine DAYS360 with other financial functions like PMT for loan analysis.

Tips for Using DAYS360

Accounting standard: Use the correct method argument to align with the financial system in use.

DB Function

Financial Functions

Introduction

The DB function calculates the depreciation of an asset for a specific period using the **fixed-declining balance method**. This method accelerates depreciation, allocating more expense in the earlier years of an asset's life.

Simple explanation: Returns the depreciation of an asset for a specific period using the fixed-declining balance method.

Common use cases: Used in accounting, financial modeling, and asset management to calculate depreciation expenses.

When to use this function: Use when calculating declining balance depreciation over an asset's useful life.

Syntax

```
=DB(cost, salvage, life, period, [month])
```

- **cost**: The initial cost of the asset.
- **salvage**: The value of the asset at the end of its useful life (residual value).
- **life**: The number of periods over which the asset is depreciated (useful life).
- **period**: The specific period for which depreciation is calculated.
- **[month]** *(optional)*: The number of months in the first year. If omitted, defaults to 12.

Worked Example

Challenge: Calculate the depreciation of an asset in its first year with the following details:

- Cost: 50,000; Salvage value: 5,000; Useful life: 5 years; Period: 1st year; First-year months: 12

Formula:

```
=DB(50000, 5000, 5, 1, 12)
```

	A	B	C
1	Example		
2	=DB(50000, 5000, 5, 1, 12)		
3	Answer		
4	$18,450.00		

Result: 18,450
Explanation: In the first year, the depreciation expense is higher due to the declining balance method.

Explore Further with GPT:
Ask GPT how to combine DB with other depreciation methods like SLN or DDB for comparative analysis.

Tips for Using DB

- **Declining balance:** The depreciation amount decreases over time, reflecting higher expenses in earlier periods.
- **Partial years:** Use the month argument for assets acquired mid-year or with irregular first-year schedules.
- **Compare methods:** Evaluate different methods (e.g., SLN, DDB) to choose the most suitable for your analysis:

  ```
  =SLN(50000, 5000, 5) - DB(50000, 5000, 5, 1)
  ```

DBCS Function

Text Functions|

Introduction

The DBCS function converts a single-byte character string to its double-byte character equivalent. This function is specific to certain languages, such as Japanese, Chinese, and Korean, where double-byte characters are used for certain symbols or text.

Simple explanation: Converts single-byte text to double-byte text for specific languages.

Common use cases: Used in localization, text formatting, and applications that handle multi-byte character sets.

When to use this function: Use when working with text that needs to be converted to a double-byte format in languages like Japanese or Chinese.

Syntax

```
=DBCS(text)
```

- **text**: The text or reference to a cell containing the text to convert.

Worked Example

Challenge: Convert the single-byte string "Hello" to its double-byte equivalent.

Formula:

```
=DBCS("Hello")
```

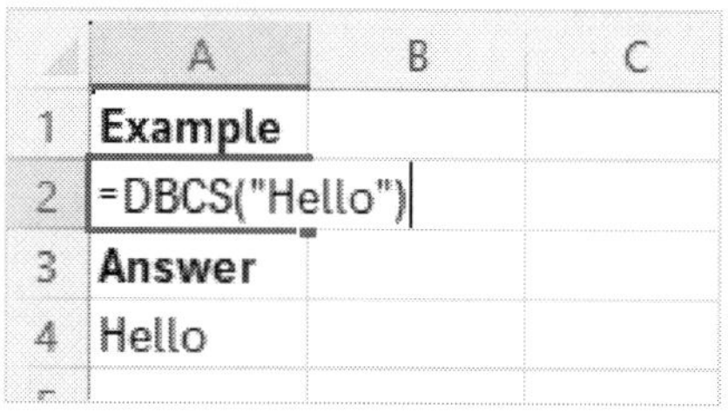

Result: H e l l o
Explanation: Each character in the string "Hello" is converted to its double-byte equivalent, often appearing wider in format.

Explore Further with GPT:
Ask GPT how DBCS interacts with text functions like ASC or how to detect text requiring conversion.

Tips for Using DBCS

- **Language support:** This function is only applicable to languages that use double-byte characters, such as Japanese, Chinese, and Korean.
- **Reversal with ASC:** Use the ASC function to reverse double-byte text back to single-byte if needed.
- **Non-applicable text:** For text that doesn't support double-byte conversion, the function returns the original input unchanged.

DCOUNT Function

Database Functions

Introduction

The DCOUNT function counts numeric values in a specified field (column) of a database that meet given criteria. It excludes text and blank cells, making it ideal for numerical data analysis in structured tables.

Simple explanation: Counts numeric values in a column that meet specified criteria.

Common use cases: Used in data analysis, reporting, and filtering numeric entries in structured datasets.

When to use this function: Use when working with databases or structured tables to count numeric values based on specific criteria.

Syntax

```
=DCOUNT(database, field, criteria)
```

- **database**: The range of cells containing the database, including headers.
- **field**: The column to count, specified as a column header (in quotes) or column number.
- **criteria**: The range of cells defining the filter criteria.

Worked Example

Challenge: Count the number of numeric sales entries for the "North" region from a dataset.

Formula:

```
=DCOUNT(A1:C5, "Sales", E1:E2)
```

Result: 2

Explanation: The function counts two numeric sales entries (100 and 300) for the "North" region.

	A	B	C	D	E	F	G	H
1	**Region**	**Sales**	**Month**		**Region**		**Example**	
2	North	100	January		=DCOUNT(A1:C5, "Sales", E1:E2)			
3	South	200	January				**Answer**	
4	North	300	February				2	
5	South		February					
6								

Explore Further with GPT:
Ask GPT how to use dynamic criteria or compare DCOUNT with other database functions like DCOUNTA or COUNTIFS.

Tips for Using DCOUNT

- **Criteria format:** Ensure the criteria range includes a header matching the database and values for filtering.
- **Excludes non-numeric values:** The function ignores text and blank cells in the specified field.
- **Combine with other database functions:** Use alongside DSUM, DAVERAGE, or DCOUNTA for comprehensive data analysis:

  ```
  =DCOUNTA(A1:C5, "Sales", E1:E2) - DCOUNT(A1:C5, "Sales", E1:E2)
  ```

DCOUNTA Function

Database Functions

Introduction

The DCOUNTA function counts all non-blank values in a specified field (column) of a database that meet given criteria. It includes both numeric and text entries, making it a versatile tool for analyzing structured datasets.

Simple explanation: Counts all non-blank values in a column that meet specified criteria.

Common use cases: Used in data analysis, reporting, and filtering entries in structured datasets.

When to use this function: Use when working with databases or structured tables to count non-blank values based on specific criteria.

Syntax

```
=DCOUNTA(database, field, criteria)
```

- **database**: The range of cells containing the database, including headers.
- **field**: The column to count, specified as a column header (in quotes) or column number.
- **criteria**: The range of cells defining the filter criteria.

Worked Example

Challenge: Count the total number of non-blank sales entries for the "South" region from a dataset.

Formula:

```
=DCOUNTA(A1:C5, "Sales", E1:E2)
```

Result: 1
Explanation: The function counts one non-blank sales entry (200) for the "South" region, ignoring the blank cell.

	A	B	C	D	E	F	G	H
1	Region	Sales	Month		Region		Example	
2	North	100	January		=DCOUNTA(A1:C5, "Sales", E1:E2)			
3	South	200	January				Answer	
4	North	300	February				1	
5	South		February					
6								

Explore Further with GPT:
Ask GPT how to dynamically filter criteria ranges or compare DCOUNTA with COUNTIFS for similar functionality.

Tips for Using DCOUNTA

- **Criteria format:** Ensure the criteria range includes a header that matches the database and values for filtering.
- **Includes text and numbers:** The function counts all non-blank values, regardless of type.
- **Blank cells are ignored:** To include blank cells in an analysis, use DCOUNT or additional logic:

  ```
  =ROWS(A2:A5) - DCOUNTA(A1:C5, "Sales", E1:E2)
  ```

DDB Function

Financial Functions

Introduction

The DDB function calculates the depreciation of an asset for a specific period using the **double-declining balance method**. This method allocates more depreciation expense in the early years of an asset's life compared to later years.

Simple explanation: Returns the depreciation of an asset for a specified period using the double-declining balance method.

Common use cases: Used in accounting, financial modeling, and asset management for accelerated depreciation calculations.

When to use this function: Use when calculating depreciation for assets that lose value quickly in their early years.

Syntax

```
=DDB(cost, salvage, life, period, [factor])
```

- **cost**: The initial cost of the asset.
- **salvage**: The value of the asset at the end of its useful life (residual value).
- **life**: The number of periods over which the asset is depreciated (useful life).
- **period**: The specific period for which depreciation is calculated.
- **[factor]** *(optional)*: The rate at which the balance declines. Defaults to 2 (double-declining balance)

Worked Example

Challenge: Calculate the depreciation of an asset in its first year with the following details:

- Cost: 50,000
- Salvage value: 5,000
- Useful life: 5 years
- Depreciation period: 1st year
- Decline factor: Default (2).

	A	B	C
1	**Example**		
2	=DDB(50000, 5000, 5, 1)		
3	**Answer**		
4	$20,000		

Formula:

```
=DDB(50000, 5000, 5, 1)
```

Result: 20,000
Explanation: The double-declining balance method allocates a higher depreciation expense in the first year, reducing the book value more significantly.

Explore Further with GPT:
Ask GPT how to use DDB with custom factors for flexible depreciation rates or compare it with DB for financial decision-making.

DEC2BIN Function

Engineering Functions

Introduction

The DEC2BIN function converts a decimal number to its binary (base 2) equivalent. It is useful in engineering, computer science, and digital electronics applications.

Simple explanation: Converts a decimal number to a binary number.

Common use cases: Used in computing, digital logic design, and data encoding tasks.

When to use this function: Use when working with base conversions or binary representations of numbers.

Syntax

```
=DEC2BIN(number, [places])
```

- **number**: The decimal number to convert (must be between -512 and 511 for 10-bit binary representation).
- **[places]** *(optional)*: The number of characters to use in the binary result. Pads with leading zeros if necessary

Worked Example

Challenge: Convert the decimal number 25 to binary, padded to 8 places.

Formula:

```
=DEC2BIN(25, 8)
```

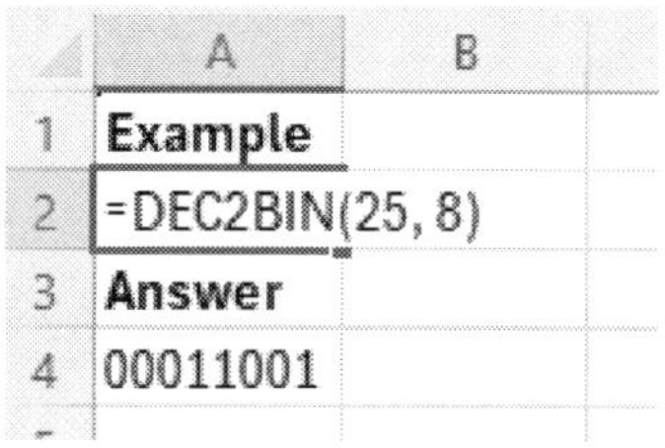

Result: 00011001
Explanation: The decimal number 25 is represented as 11001 in binary. The places argument pads the result with leading zeros to make it 8 characters long.

Explore Further with GPT:
Ask GPT how to perform custom binary arithmetic or combine DEC2BIN with other base conversion functions like BIN2DEC for round-trip calculations.

Tips for Using DEC2BIN

- **Range limitations:** Input numbers must be between -512 and 511; otherwise, Excel returns a #NUM! error.
- **Padding with zeros:** Use the places argument to standardize binary lengths, which is helpful in logical operations:

  ```
  =DEC2BIN(5, 8)   'Result: 00000101
  ```

- **Combining conversions:** Use with BIN2DEC or other base conversion functions for validation or round-trip conversions.

DEC2HEX Function

Engineering Functions

Introduction

The DEC2HEX function converts a decimal number to its hexadecimal (base 16) equivalent. It is commonly used in computer science, digital electronics, and data encoding tasks.

Simple explanation: Converts a decimal number to a hexadecimal number.

Common use cases: Used in programming, color coding, memory addressing, and network configurations.

When to use this function: Use when working with base conversions or hexadecimal representations of numbers.

Syntax

```
=DEC2HEX(number, [places])
```

- **number**: The decimal number to convert (must be between -549,755,813,888 and 549,755,813,887 for 10-digit hexadecimal representation).
- **[places]** *(optional)*: The number of characters to use in the hexadecimal result. Pads with leading zeros if necessary

Worked Example

Challenge: Convert the decimal number 255 to hexadecimal, padded to 4 places.

Formula:

```
=DEC2HEX(255, 4)
```

	A	B
1	**Example**	
2	=DEC2HEX(255, 4)	
3	**Answer**	
4	00FF	

Result: 00FF
Explanation: The decimal number 255 is represented as FF in hexadecimal. The places argument pads the result with leading zeros to make it 4 characters long.

Explore Further with GPT:
Ask GPT how to use hexadecimal in computing tasks, such as RGB color codes or memory addressing.

Tips for Using DEC2HEX

- **Range limitations:** Input numbers must be between -549,755,813,888 and 549,755,813,887; otherwise, Excel returns a #NUM! error.
- **Padding with zeros:** Use the places argument to create standardized outputs for alignment in reports or coding:

  ```
  =DEC2HEX(15, 4)   'Result: 000F
  ```

- **Combine with other functions:** Use alongside HEX2DEC or other base conversion functions for validation or round-trip conversions.

DEC2OCT Function

Engineering Functions

Introduction

The DEC2OCT function converts a decimal number to its octal (base 8) equivalent. It is commonly used in computer science, digital electronics, and systems programming.

Simple explanation: Converts a decimal number to an octal number.

Common use cases: Used in programming, low-level computing tasks, and legacy systems that use base-8 numbering.

When to use this function: Use when working with base conversions or octal representations of numbers.

Syntax

```
=DEC2OCT(number, [places])
```

- **number**: The decimal number to convert (must be between -536,870,912 and 536,870,911 for 10-digit octal representation).
- **[places]** *(optional)*: The number of characters to use in the octal result. Pads with leading zeros if necessary

Worked Example

Challenge: Convert the decimal number 64 to octal, padded to 4 places.

Formula:

```
=DEC2OCT(64, 4)
```

Result: 0100
Explanation: The decimal number 64 is represented as 100 in octal. The places argument pads the result with leading zeros to make it 4 characters long.

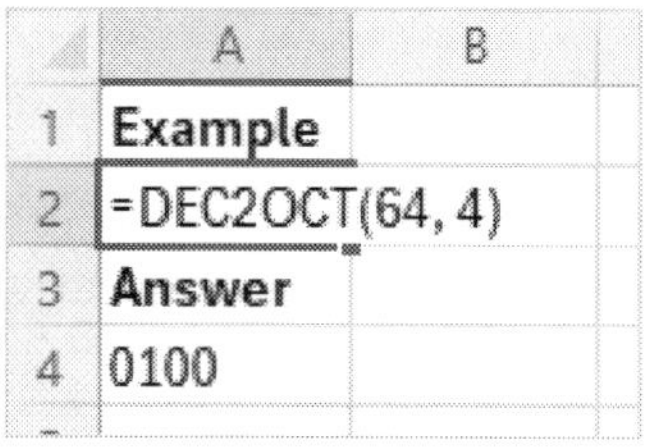

	A	B
1	Example	
2	=DEC2OCT(64, 4)	
3	Answer	
4	0100	

Explore Further with GPT:
Ask GPT how to integrate octal values into programming tasks or compare octal with binary and hexadecimal systems.

Tips for Using DEC2OCT

- **Range limitations:** Input numbers must be between -536,870,912 and 536,870,911; otherwise, Excel returns a #NUM! error.
- **Padding with zeros:** Use the places argument to create standardized outputs:

  ```
  =DEC2OCT(7, 4)   'Result: 0007
  ```

- **Combine with other functions:** Use alongside OCT2DEC or other base conversion functions for validation or round-trip conversions:

  ```
  =OCT2DEC(DEC2OCT(64))  'Result: 64
  ```

DECIMAL Function

Math & Trigonometry Functions

Introduction

The DECIMAL function converts a text representation of a number in a given base (radix) into its decimal (base 10) equivalent. It is useful for base conversions in programming, engineering, and data encoding.

Simple explanation: Converts a number in another base to a decimal number.

Common use cases: Used in computer science, data conversion tasks, and working with custom numbering systems.

When to use this function: Use when converting numbers from binary, octal, hexadecimal, or other bases into decimal format.

Syntax

```
=DECIMAL(text, radix)
```

- **text**: A string representing the number in the specified base.
- **radix**: The base (integer between 2 and 36) of the number to convert.

Worked Example

Challenge: Convert the hexadecimal number FF to decimal.

Formula:

```
=DECIMAL("FF", 16)
```

Result: 255
Explanation: The function converts the hexadecimal number FF (base 16) into its decimal equivalent, 255.

	A	B	C
1	**Example**		
2	=DECIMAL("FF", 16)		
3	**Answer**		
4	255		
5			

Explore Further with GPT:
Ask GPT how to work with numbers in various bases or combine DECIMAL with other conversion functions for complex workflows.

Tips for Using DECIMAL

- **Input validation:** Ensure the text argument only contains valid characters for the specified base; otherwise, Excel will return a #NUM! error.
- **Maximum base:** The radix argument must be between 2 and 36, supporting characters 0–9 and A–Z for bases above 10.
- **Combine with other functions:** Use alongside BASE to convert back and forth between bases:

  ```
  =BASE(DECIMAL("FF", 16), 10)  'Result: 255
  ```

DEGREES Function

Math & Trigonometry Functions

Introduction

The DEGREES function converts an angle measured in radians into degrees. It is commonly used in trigonometry, geometry, and data analysis when working with angular measurements in different units.

Simple explanation: Converts an angle from radians to degrees.

Common use cases: Used in geometry, trigonometric calculations, and scientific applications requiring degree-based angles.

When to use this function: Use when converting radians to degrees for calculations or reporting.

Syntax

```
=DEGREES(angle)
```

- **angle**: The angle in radians to convert to degrees.

Worked Example

Challenge: Convert π radians to degrees.

Formula:

```
=DEGREES(PI())
```

Result: 180
Explanation: The function converts π radians to 180 degrees, as π radians equals half a full rotation.

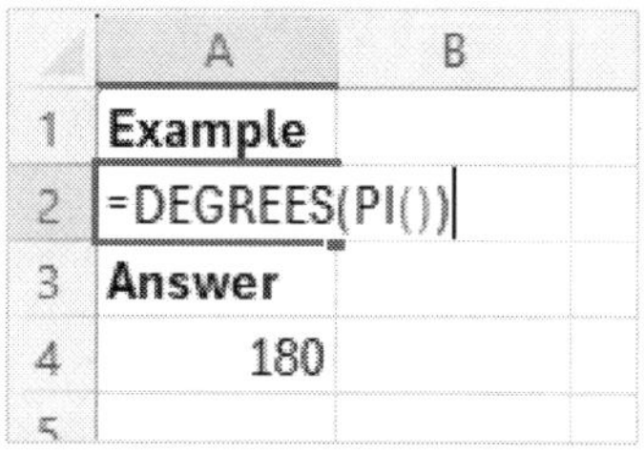

Explore Further with GPT:
Ask GPT how to use DEGREES alongside trigonometric functions like SIN or COS for angular calculations.

Tips for Using DEGREES

- **Radians to degrees:** Combine with trigonometric functions that return angles in radians:

  ```
  =DEGREES(ACOS(0))  'Result: 90
  ```

- **Direct conversions:** Use DEGREES in conjunction with RADIANS for back-and-forth conversions:

  ```
  =RADIANS(DEGREES(PI()))  'Result: 3.141592653 (π in radians)
  ```

- **Scientific use:** Ideal for converting outputs from scientific or mathematical models that use radians by default.

DELTA Function

Engineering Functions

Introduction

The DELTA function tests whether two numbers are equal. It returns 1 if the numbers are equal and 0 otherwise. This function is often used in engineering and mathematical applications where binary comparisons are required.

Simple explanation: Returns 1 if two numbers are equal, otherwise returns 0.

Common use cases: Used in logical comparisons, conditional calculations, and engineering applications.

When to use this function: Use when testing for equality between two numbers in binary logic.

Syntax

```
=DELTA(number1, [number2])
```

- **number1**: The first number to compare.
- **[number2]** *(optional)*: The second number to compare. If omitted, defaults to 0.

Worked Example

Challenge: Test whether the numbers 5 and 5 are equal.

Formula:

```
=DELTA(5, 5)
```

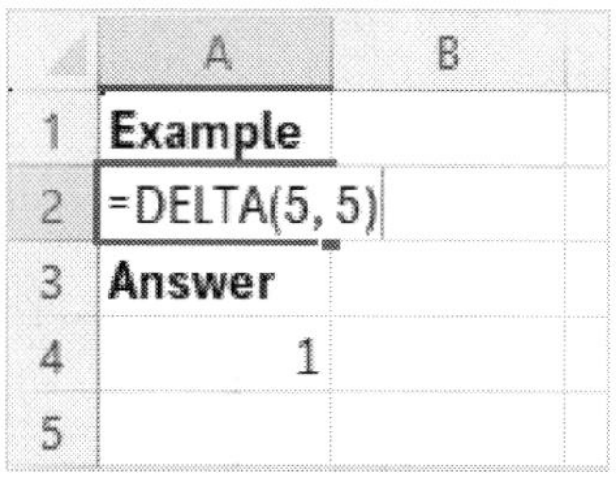

Result: 1
Explanation: The two numbers are equal, so the function returns 1.

Explore Further with GPT:
Ask GPT how to use DELTA in conjunction with conditional functions like IF for advanced logical comparisons.

Tips for Using DELTA

- **Binary results:** The function only returns 1 or 0, making it suitable for binary logic or conditional operations.
- **Use in arrays:** Combine with array formulas to test multiple values at once:

  ```
  =SUM(DELTA(A1:A5, 10))
  ```

  This sums all instances where values in A1:A5 equal 10.
- **Comparison scope:** Use when testing exact numeric equality; for approximate equality, consider rounding the numbers before comparison.

DEVSQ Function

Statistical Functions

Introduction

The DEVSQ function calculates the sum of the squares of deviations of data points from their mean. It is commonly used in statistics to measure variability in a dataset.

Simple explanation: Returns the sum of squared deviations from the mean for a dataset.

Common use cases: Used in statistical analysis, variance calculation, and data modeling.

When to use this function: Use when analyzing the spread or variability in a dataset.

Syntax

```
=DEVSQ(number1, [number2], ...)
```

- **number1, [number2], ...:** Numbers or ranges to calculate squared deviations from the mean.

Worked Example

Challenge: Calculate the sum of squared deviations for the data points 5, 10, 15.

Formula:

```
=DEVSQ(5, 10, 15)
```

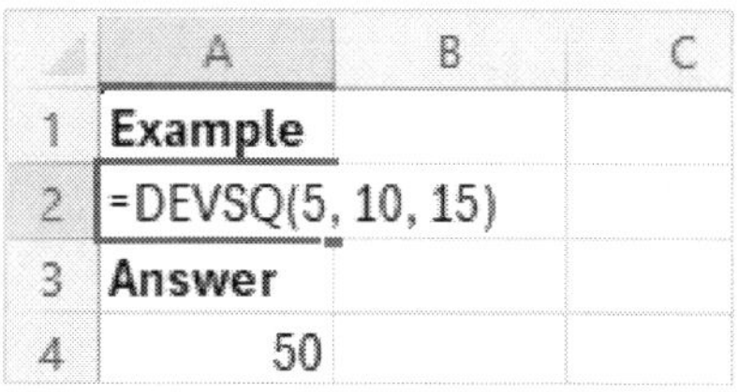

	A	B	C
1	Example		
2	=DEVSQ(5, 10, 15)		
3	Answer		
4	50		

Result: 50
Explanation:

- Mean of the data: (5 + 10 + 15) / 3 = 10.
- Deviations from the mean: -5, 0, 5.
- Squared deviations: 25, 0, 25.
- Sum of squared deviations: 25 + 0 + 25 = 50.

Explore Further with GPT:
Ask GPT how to use `DEVSQ` in variance or standard deviation calculations.

Tips for Using DEVSQ

- **Exclude text and blanks:** The function ignores text and blank cells in the input range.
- **Compare with VAR.P or VAR.S:** Use DEVSQ for custom calculations or combine with other functions to compute variance manually:

  ```
  =DEVSQ(A1:A5) / COUNT(A1:A5)  'Equivalent to population variance
  ```

- **Statistical analysis:** Use alongside functions like AVERAGE, VAR.P, and STDEV.P for comprehensive statistical insights.

DGET Function

Database Functions

Introduction

The DGET function retrieves a single value from a specified column in a database that matches the given criteria. It is used in structured data analysis when only one unique match is expected, ensuring no ambiguity in results.

Simple explanation: Returns a single value from a database that meets specified criteria.

Common use cases: Used in data filtering, reporting, and database analysis when retrieving unique records.

When to use this function: Use when extracting specific values from structured datasets based on conditions.

Syntax

```
=DGET(database, field, criteria)
```

- **database**: The range of cells containing the database, including headers.
- **field**: The column to retrieve the value from, specified as a column header (in quotes) or column number.
- **criteria**: The range of cells defining the filter criteria.

Worked Example

Challenge: Retrieve the sales value for the "North" region in January from a dataset.

Formula:

```
=DGET(A1:C5, "Sales", E1:F2)
```

Result: 100

	A	B	C	D	E	F	G	H	I	J
1	**Region**	**Sales**	**Month**		**Region**	**Month**		**Example**		
2	North	100	January		North	January		=DGET(A1:C5, "Sales", E1:F2)		
3	South	200	January					**Answer**		
4	North	300	February					100		
5	South	400	February							
6										

Explanation: The function retrieves the sales value (100) for the "North" region in January based on the criteria range.

Tips for Using DGET

- **Unique result required:** Ensure the criteria match only one record; otherwise, the function returns a #NUM! error.
- **Criteria format:** The criteria range must include column headers matching the database headers.
- **Combine with other functions:** Use DGET alongside other database functions like DSUM or DCOUNT for comprehensive analysis:

```
=DSUM(A1:C5, "Sales", E1:F2) - DGET(A1:C5, "Sales", E1:F2)
```

DISC Function

Financial Functions

Introduction

The DISC function calculates the discount rate for a security, such as a Treasury bill, given its price, redemption value, and maturity period. It is commonly used in financial analysis to evaluate short-term investments and bond discounts.

Simple explanation: Returns the discount rate for a security based on its price and maturity.

Common use cases: Used in bond valuation, financial modeling, and short-term investment analysis.

When to use this function: Use when analyzing the discount or yield of securities like Treasury bills.

Syntax

```
=DISC(settlement, maturity, pr, redemption, [basis])
```

- **settlement**: The security's settlement date (the date the buyer purchases the security).
- **maturity**: The security's maturity date (when it is redeemed).
- **pr**: The security's price per 100 currency units of face value.
- **redemption**: The redemption value per 100 currency units of face value.
- **[basis]** *(optional)*: The day count basis to use:
  - 0: US (NASD) 30/360 (default).
  - 1: Actual/actual.
  - 2: Actual/360.
  - 3: Actual/365.
  - 4: European 30/360.

Worked Example

Challenge: Calculate the discount rate for a Treasury bill with the following details:

- Settlement date: 01-Jan-2023
- Maturity date: 01-Jul-2023
- Price: 97
- Redemption value: 100
- Basis: 0 (US 30/360 day count).

	A	B	C	D	E
1	**Example**				
2	=DISC(DATE(2023,1,1), DATE(2023,7,1), 97, 100, 0)				
3	**Answer**				
4	6.00%				

Formula:

```
=DISC(DATE(2023,1,1), DATE(2023,7,1), 97, 100, 0)
```

Result: 0.06 (or 6.00%)
Explanation: The Treasury bill has a discount rate of 6.18%, calculated based on its price and redemption value over the specified time period.

Explore Further with GPT:
Ask GPT to explain how DISC compares to YIELD, or how to integrate DISC into financial workflows for investment evaluation.

DMAX Function

Database Functions

Introduction

The DMAX function returns the maximum value from a specified field (column) in a database that meets given criteria. It is commonly used to extract the highest value from structured datasets based on specific conditions.

Simple explanation: Returns the maximum value in a column that meets specified criteria.

Common use cases: Used in data analysis, reporting, and extracting key metrics like peak sales, maximum scores, or highest prices.

When to use this function: Use when working with structured data to find the highest value that matches specific conditions.

Syntax

```
=DMAX(database, field, criteria)
```

- **database**: The range of cells containing the database, including headers.
- **field**: The column to find the maximum value in, specified as a column header (in quotes) or column number.
- **criteria**: The range of cells defining the filter criteria

Worked Example

Challenge: Find the maximum sales value for the "North" region from a dataset.

Formula:

```
=DMAX(A1:C5,
"Sales", E1:E2)
```

Result: 300

Explanation: The function retrieves the highest sales value (300) for the "North" region based on the criteria range.

	A	B	C	D	E	F	G	H	I
1	**Region**	**Sales**	**Month**		**Region**		**Example**		
2	North	100	January		North		=DMAX(A1:C5, "Sales", E1:E2)		
3	South	200	January				**Answer**		
4	North	300	February				300		
5	South	400	February						
6									

Explore Further with GPT:
Ask GPT how to use DMAX alongside other database functions like DSUM or DAVERAGE for comprehensive data analysis.

Tips for Using DMAX

- **Criteria format:** Ensure the criteria range includes a header matching the database and values for filtering.
- **Use in dashboards:** Pair with visualization tools like conditional formatting to highlight maximum values directly in your dataset:

  ```
  =MAXIFS(B2:B5, A2:A5, "North")
  ```

DMIN Function

Database Functions

Introduction

The DMIN function returns the minimum value from a specified field (column) in a database that meets given criteria. It is commonly used to extract the lowest value from structured datasets based on specific conditions.

Simple explanation: Returns the minimum value in a column that meets specified criteria.

Common use cases: Used in data analysis, reporting, and extracting key metrics like lowest sales, minimum scores, or smallest prices.

When to use this function: Use when working with structured data to find the lowest value that matches specific conditions.

Syntax

```
=DMIN(database, field, criteria)
```

- **database**: The range of cells containing the database, including headers.
- **field**: The column to find the minimum value in, specified as a column header (in quotes) or column number.
- **criteria**: The range of cells defining the filter criteria.

Worked Example

Challenge: Find the minimum sales value for the "North" region from a dataset.

Formula:

```
=DMIN(A1:C5, "Sales", E1:E2)
```

Result: 100

Explanation: The function retrieves the lowest sales value (100) for the "North" region based on the criteria range.

	A	B	C	D	E	F	G	H	I
1	**Region**	**Sales**	**Month**		**Region**		**Example**		
2	North	100	January		North		=DMIN(A1:C5, "Sales", E1:E2)		
3	South	200	January				**Answer**		
4	North	300	February				100		
5	South	400	February						
6									

Explore Further with GPT:
Ask GPT how to use DMIN alongside other database functions like DSUM or DGET for comprehensive data analysis.

Tips for Using DMIN

- **Dynamic analysis:** Combine with IF or other logic functions to dynamically adjust criteria.
- **Modern alternatives:** Use functions like MINIFS for simpler syntax in newer versions of Excel:

  ```
  =MINIFS(B2:B5, A2:A5, "North")
  ```

This offers a direct alternative for finding minimum values based on criteria.

DOLLAR Function

Text Functions

Introduction

The DOLLAR function converts a number to text formatted as currency, with a specified number of decimal places. It is commonly used in financial reports and dashboards for presenting monetary values.

Simple explanation: Converts a number into a currency-formatted text string.

Common use cases: Used in financial statements, reports, and templates to display currency values consistently.

When to use this function: Use when displaying numbers as formatted currency text in calculations or reports.

Syntax

```
=DOLLAR(number, [decimals])
```

- **number**: The numeric value to format as currency.
- **[decimals]** *(optional)*: The number of decimal places to display. Defaults to 2 if omitted.

Worked Example

Challenge: Format the number 1234.567 as currency with 2 decimal places.

Formula:

```
=DOLLAR(1234.567, 2)
```

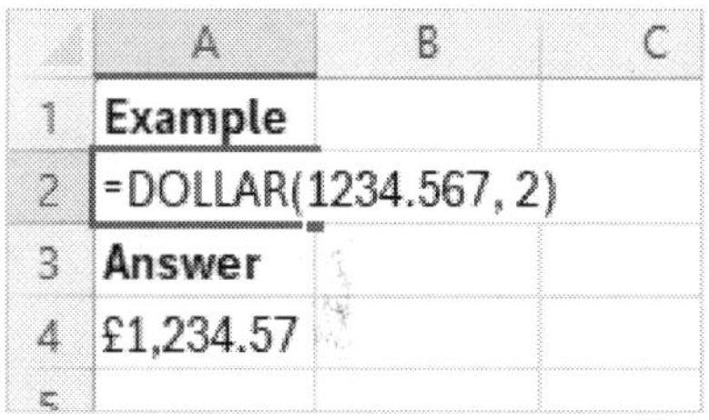

Result: $1,234.57
Explanation: The function rounds the value to two decimal places and formats it with a currency symbol.

Explore Further with GPT:
Ask GPT how to customize currency symbols or use DOLLAR alongside other formatting functions for advanced presentations.

Tips for Using DOLLAR

- **Currency symbols:** The function uses the system's default regional settings for the currency symbol (e.g., $ for US, £ for UK). Change regional settings for different symbols.
- **Alternative formatting:** Use the TEXT function for more customization:

  ```
  =TEXT(1234.567, "$#,##0.00")
  ```

- **Combine with calculations:** Use DOLLAR to format calculated results as currency without altering their numeric properties.

DOLLARDE Function

Financial Functions

Introduction

The DOLLARDE function converts a dollar price expressed as a fraction into a decimal number. It is commonly used in financial analysis, particularly in bond pricing and trading, where fractional dollar prices are often used.

Simple explanation: Converts a fractional dollar price to a decimal number.

Common use cases: Used in financial markets, bond trading, and investment analysis to standardize dollar values.

When to use this function: Use when converting fractional prices to decimal form for calculations or reporting.

Syntax

```
=DOLLARDE(fractional_dollar, fraction)
```

- **fractional_dollar**: The dollar price expressed as a fraction (e.g., 1.02 for 1 and 2/16).
- **fraction**: The denominator of the fraction (e.g., 16 for sixteenths).

Worked Example

Challenge: Convert the fractional dollar price 1.02 (1 and 2/16) to a decimal value.

Formula:

```
=DOLLARDE(1.02, 16)
```

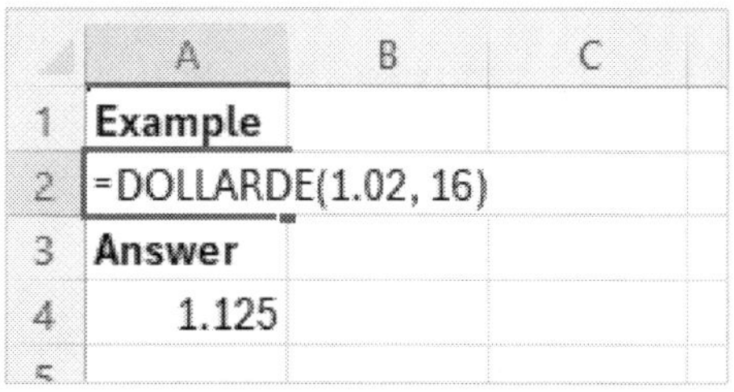

Result: 1.125
Explanation: The fractional part 0.02 represents 2/16, which equals 0.125. Adding this to 1 gives 1.125.

Explore Further with GPT:
Ask GPT how to use DOLLARDE in conjunction with DOLLARFR for back-and-forth conversions or its applications in financial modeling.

Tips for Using DOLLARDE

- **Fraction value:** Ensure the fraction argument matches the base of the fractional part (e.g., 8 for eighths, 16 for sixteenths); otherwise, results will be inaccurate.
- **Combine with DOLLARFR:** Use DOLLARFR to convert back from decimal to fractional values:

  ```
  =DOLLARFR(DOLLARDE(1.02, 16), 16)  'Result: 1.02
  ```

- **Standardization:** Ideal for converting fractional prices to decimal form for use in financial calculations or models.

DOLLARFR Function

Financial Functions

Introduction

The DOLLARFR function converts a dollar price expressed as a decimal into a fraction. It is commonly used in financial analysis, particularly in bond trading and investment markets, where fractional dollar prices are often employed.

Simple explanation: Converts a decimal dollar price to a fractional dollar price.

Common use cases: Used in bond pricing, financial markets, and investment analysis to align with fractional pricing conventions.

When to use this function: Use when converting decimal prices to fractional form for calculations or reporting.

Syntax

```
=DOLLARFR(decimal_dollar, fraction)
```

- **decimal_dollar**: The dollar price expressed as a decimal (e.g., 1.125 for 1 and 2/16).
- **fraction**: The denominator of the fraction (e.g., 16 for sixteenths).

Worked Example

Challenge: Convert the decimal dollar price 1.125 to a fractional value with sixteenths.

Formula:

```
=DOLLARFR(1.125, 16)
```

	A	B
1	**Example**	
2	=DOLLARFR(1.125, 16)	
3	**Answer**	
4	1.02	

Result: 1.02

Explanation: The decimal part 0.125 represents 2/16, which is expressed as 0.02 in fractional form. Combining this with 1 gives 1.02.

Explore Further with GPT:

Ask GPT how to use DOLLARFR alongside DOLLARDE for back-and-forth conversions or its applications in bond pricing.

Tips for Using DOLLARFR

- **Fraction value:** Ensure the fraction argument matches the required base for the fractional part (e.g., 8 for eighths, 16 for sixteenths).
- **Combine with DOLLARDE:** Use DOLLARDE to convert back from fractional to decimal values:

  ```
  =DOLLARDE(DOLLARFR(1.125, 16), 16)   'Result: 1.125
  ```

- **Financial applications:** Commonly used for calculating and presenting bond prices in financial markets.

DPRODUCT Function

Database Functions

Introduction

The DPRODUCT function multiplies the values in a specified field (column) of a database that meet given criteria. It is used to compute the product of filtered values in structured datasets.

Simple explanation: Returns the product of values in a column that meet specified criteria.

Common use cases: Used in data analysis, inventory management, and financial modeling to calculate cumulative products.

When to use this function: Use when working with databases or structured tables to compute the product of filtered numeric values.

Syntax

```
=DPRODUCT(database, field, criteria)
```

- **database**: The range of cells containing the database, including headers.
- **field**: The column to multiply values from, specified as a column header (in quotes) or column number.
- **criteria**: The range of cells defining the filter criteria

Worked Example

Challenge: Calculate the product of sales for the "North" region from a dataset.

Formula:

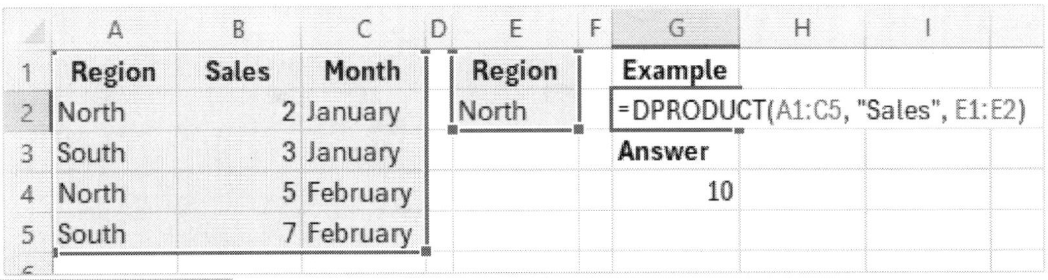

	A	B	C	D	E	F	G	H	I
1	**Region**	**Sales**	**Month**		**Region**		**Example**		
2	North	2	January		North		=DPRODUCT(A1:C5, "Sales", E1:E2)		
3	South	3	January				**Answer**		
4	North	5	February				10		
5	South	7	February						

```
=DPRODUCT(A1:C5, "Sales", E1:E2)
```

Result: 10
Explanation: The function multiplies the sales values for the "North" region (2 * 5 = 10).

Explore Further with GPT:
Ask GPT how to combine DPRODUCT with other database functions like DSUM and DAVERAGE for advanced data analysis.

Tips for Using DPRODUCT

- **Criteria format:** Ensure the criteria range includes a header matching the database and values for filtering.
- **Error handling:** If no records meet the criteria, the function returns #VALUE!.

DROP Function

Lookup & Reference Functions

Introduction

The DROP function removes a specified number of rows or columns from the beginning or end of an array. It is commonly used in data analysis to filter or reshape data dynamically.

Simple explanation: Removes rows or columns from an array.

Common use cases: Used in filtering datasets, skipping headers, or creating dynamic ranges in data analysis.

When to use this function: Use when you need to exclude a specific number of rows or columns from a dataset for further analysis.

Syntax

```
=DROP(array, rows, [columns])
```

- **array**: The array or range to modify.
- **rows**: The number of rows to remove (positive to remove from the top, negative to remove from the bottom).
- **[columns]** *(optional)*: The number of columns to remove (positive to remove from the left, negative to remove from the right)

Worked Example

Challenge: Remove the first row from the array

Formula:

```
=DROP(A1:C3, 1)
```

Result:

A B C

4 5 6

7 8 9

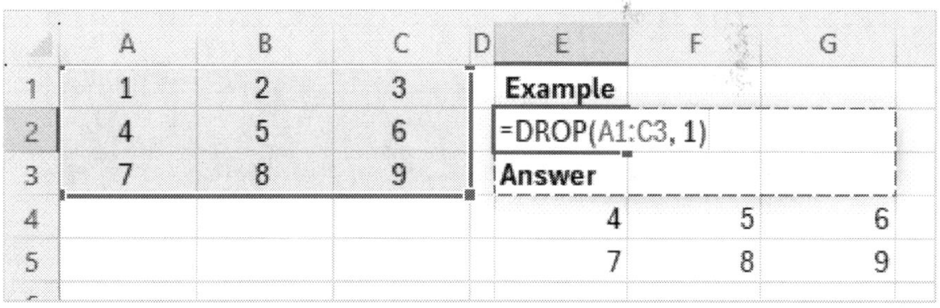

	A	B	C	D	E	F	G
1	1	2	3		Example		
2	4	5	6		=DROP(A1:C3, 1)		
3	7	8	9		Answer		
4					4	5	6
5					7	8	9

Explanation: The first row is removed, leaving the rest of the array intact.

Explore Further with GPT:
Ask GPT how to use DROP with other array functions like TAKE or FILTER for more complex data transformations.

Tips for Using DROP

- **Combining rows and columns:** Use both rows and columns arguments to simultaneously remove rows and columns:

  ```
  =DROP(A1:C3, 1, 1)
  ```

- **Alternative slicing:** Pair with TAKE to extract specific portions of an array while ignoring others

DSTDEV Function

Database Functions

Introduction

The DSTDEV function estimates the standard deviation of a population based on values from a specified field (column) in a database that meet given criteria. It is used in statistical analysis to measure the spread of data points around the mean.

Simple explanation: Returns the estimated population standard deviation of values in a column that meet specified criteria.

Common use cases: Used in statistical modeling, data analysis, and assessing variability in structured datasets.

When to use this function: Use when analyzing the variability of a population subset based on filtering conditions.

Syntax

```
=DSTDEV(database, field, criteria)
```

- **database**: The range of cells containing the database, including headers.
- **field**: The column to calculate the standard deviation for, specified as a column header (in quotes) or column number.
- **criteria**: The range of cells defining the filter criteria.

Worked Example

Challenge: Calculate the standard deviation of sales for the "North" region from a dataset.

Formula:

```
=DSTDEV(A1:C5, "Sales", E1:E2)
```

Result: 141.42

Explanation: The function calculates the standard deviation of sales values (100 and 300) for the "North" region.

	A	B	C	D	E	F	G	H	I
1	Region	Sales	Month		Region		Example		
2	North	100	January		North		=DSTDEV(A1:C5, "Sales", E1:E2)		
3	South	200	January				Answer		
4	North	300	February				141.42		
5	South	400	February						
6									

Tips for Using DSTDEV

- **Criteria format:** Ensure the criteria range includes a header matching the database and values for filtering.
- **Population vs. sample:** Use DSTDEV for sample standard deviation; for population standard deviation, use DSTDEVP.

DSTDEVP Function

Database Functions

Introduction

The DSTDEVP function calculates the standard deviation of an entire population based on values from a specified field (column) in a database that meet given criteria. It is used in statistical analysis to measure the spread of a complete dataset.

Simple explanation: Returns the population standard deviation of values in a column that meet specified criteria.

Common use cases: Used in statistical modeling, data analysis, and assessing variability in structured datasets for an entire population.

When to use this function: Use when analyzing the variability of a complete dataset based on filtering conditions.

Syntax

```
=DSTDEVP(database, field, criteria)
```

- **database**: The range of cells containing the database, including headers.
- **field**: The column to calculate the standard deviation for, specified as a column header (in quotes) or column number.
- **criteria**: The range of cells defining the filter criteria.

Worked Example

Challenge: Calculate the population standard deviation of sales for the "North" region from a dataset.

Result: 100
Explanation: The function calculates the population standard deviation of sales values (100 and 300) for the "North" region.

	A	B	C	D	E	F	G	H	I
1	**Region**	**Sales**	**Month**		**Region**		**Example**		
2	North	100	January		North		=DSTDEVP(A1:C5, "Sales", E1:E2)		
3	South	200	January				**Answer**		
4	North	300	February				100.00		
5	South	400	February						
6									

Explore Further with GPT: Ask GPT how to use DSTDEVP for larger datasets or to compare it with DSTDEV for sample standard deviation calculations.

Tips for Using DSTDEVP

- **Criteria format:** Ensure the criteria range includes a header matching the database and values for filtering.
- **Population vs. sample:** Use DSTDEVP for population standard deviation; for sample standard deviation, use DSTDEV.

DSUM Function

Database Functions

Introduction

The DSUM function calculates the sum of values in a specified field (column) of a database that meet given criteria. It is commonly used for filtering and aggregating data in structured datasets.

Simple explanation: Returns the sum of values in a column that meet specified criteria.

Common use cases: Used in data analysis, financial modeling, and reporting to compute conditional totals.

When to use this function: Use when working with structured datasets to calculate the sum of filtered numeric values.

Syntax

```
=DSUM(database, field, criteria)
```

- **database**: The range of cells containing the database, including headers.
- **field**: The column to sum values from, specified as a column header (in quotes) or column number.
- **criteria**: The range of cells defining the filter criteria.

Worked Example

Challenge: Calculate the total sales for the "North" region from a dataset.

Formula:

```
=DSUM(A1:C5, "Sales", E1:E2)
```

Result: 400

Explanation: The function adds the sales values (100 and 300) for the "North" region based on the criteria range.

	A	B	C	D	E	F	G	H	I
1	**Region**	**Sales**	**Month**		**Region**		**Example**		
2	North	100	January		North		=DSUM(A1:C5, "Sales", E1:E2)		
3	South	200	January				**Answer**		
4	North	300	February				400.00		
5	South	400	February						
6									

Explore Further with GPT:
Ask GPT how to use DSUM for more advanced filtering scenarios or to compare it with modern Excel functions like SUMIFS.

Tips for Using DSUM

- **Criteria format:** Ensure the criteria range includes a header matching the database and values for filtering.
- **Dynamic analysis:** Combine with dynamic ranges or named ranges for more flexible criteria.
- **Modern alternatives:** Use SUMIFS for simpler syntax and multiple criteria handling:

  ```
  =SUMIFS(B2:B5, A2:A5, "North")
  ```

- **Combine with other database functions:** Use alongside DCOUNT and DAVERAGE for comprehensive data analysis.

DURATION Function

Financial Functions

Introduction

The DURATION function calculates the Macauley duration for an assumed par value of 100 currency units. It measures the weighted average time to receive cash flows from a bond and is commonly used in bond pricing and interest rate sensitivity analysis.

Simple explanation: Returns the duration of a bond based on cash flow timings and interest rate sensitivity.

Common use cases: Used in bond valuation, portfolio management, and interest rate risk analysis.

When to use this function: Use when analyzing the sensitivity of a bond's price to changes in interest rates.

Syntax

```
=DURATION(settlement, maturity, coupon, yld, frequency, [basis])
```

- **settlement**: The bond's settlement date (the date the buyer purchases the bond).
- **maturity**: The bond's maturity date (when it is redeemed).
- **coupon**: The bond's annual coupon rate as a decimal (e.g., 0.05 for 5%).
- **yld**: The bond's annual yield as a decimal (e.g., 0.06 for 6%).
- **frequency**: The number of coupon payments per year:
  - 1 for annual payments; 2 for semi-annual payments; 4 for quarterly payments;
- **[basis]** *(optional)*: The day count basis:
  - 0: US (NASD) 30/360 (default); 1: Actual/actual; 2: Actual/360; 3: Actual/365; 4: European 30/360.

Worked Example

Challenge: Calculate the duration of a bond with the following details:

- Settlement date: 01-Jan-2023
- Maturity date: 01-Jan-2028
- Annual coupon rate: 5%
- Annual yield: 6%
- Payment frequency: 2 (semi-annual)
- Basis: 0 (US 30/360 day count).

	A	B	C	D	E	F
1	**Example**					
2	=DURATION(DATE(2023,1,1), DATE(2028,1,1), 0.05, 0.06, 2, 0)					
3	**Answer**					
4	4.47					

Formula:

```
=DURATION(DATE(2023,1,1), DATE(2028,1,1), 0.05, 0.06, 2, 0)
```

Result: 4.47

Explanation: The bond has a Macauley duration of 4.47 years, indicating the weighted average time to receive cash flows.

DVAR Function

Database Functions

Introduction

The DVAR function estimates the variance of a population based on values in a specified field (column) of a database that meet given criteria. Variance measures the spread of data points around the mean, making this function useful for statistical analysis of filtered datasets.

Simple explanation: Returns the estimated population variance of values in a column that meet specified criteria.

Common use cases: Used in data analysis, statistical modeling, and performance evaluation to assess variability.

When to use this function: Use when working with structured datasets to calculate variance for a filtered subset.

Syntax

```
=DVAR(database, field, criteria)
```

- **database**: The range of cells containing the database, including headers.
- **field**: The column to calculate the variance for, specified as a column header (in quotes) or column number.
- **criteria**: The range of cells defining the filter criteria.

Worked Example

Challenge: Calculate the variance of sales for the "North" region from a dataset.

Formula:

```
=DVAR(A1:C5, "Sales", E1:E2)
```

Result: 20,000

Explanation:

- For the "North" region, the sales values are 100 and 300.
- The mean is (100 + 300) / 2 = 200.
- Deviations are 100 - 200 = -100 and 300 - 200 = 100.
- Variance is ((-100)^2 + (100)^2) / (2 - 1) = 20,000.

	A	B	C	D	E	F	G	H	I
1	**Region**	**Sales**	**Month**		**Region**		**Example**		
2	North	100	January		North		=DVAR(A1:C5, "Sales", E1:E2)		
3	South	200	January				**Answer**		
4	North	300	February				20000.00		
5	South	400	February						
6									

Tips for Using DVAR

- **Criteria format:** Ensure the criteria range includes a header matching the database and values for filtering.
- **Population vs. sample:** Use DVAR for sample variance; for population variance, use DVARP.

DVARP Function

Database Functions

Introduction

The DVARP function calculates the variance of an entire population based on values in a specified field (column) of a database that meet given criteria. It measures how data points are spread around the mean, making it useful in statistical analysis of filtered datasets.

Simple explanation: Returns the population variance of values in a column that meet specified criteria.

Common use cases: Used in data analysis, quality control, and performance evaluation to assess variability across a complete population.

When to use this function: Use when analyzing the variance of a complete dataset based on specific filtering conditions.

Syntax

```
=DVARP(database, field, criteria)
```

- **database**: The range of cells containing the database, including headers.
- **field**: The column to calculate the variance for, specified as a column header (in quotes) or column number.
- **criteria**: The range of cells defining the filter criteria

Worked Example

Challenge: Calculate the population variance of sales for the "North" region from a dataset.

Formula:

```
=DVARP(A1:C5,
"Sales", E1:E2)
```

	A	B	C	D	E	F	G	H	I
1	Region	Sales	Month		Region		Example		
2	North	100	January		North		=DVARP(A1:C5, "Sales", E1:E2)		
3	South	200	January				Answer		
4	North	300	February				10,000		
5	South	400	February						

Result: 10,000
Explanation:

- For the "North" region, the sales values are 100 and 300.
- The mean is (100 + 300) / 2 = 200.
- Deviations are 100 - 200 = -100 and 300 - 200 = 100.
- Variance is ((-100)^2 + (100)^2) / 2 = 10,000.

Explore Further with GPT:
Ask GPT how to use DVARP alongside DVAR for comparative statistical analysis or how to implement it in large datasets.

EDATE Function

Date & Time Functions

Introduction

The EDATE function calculates a date that is a specified number of months before or after a given date. It is commonly used in scheduling, financial modeling, and project management to determine future or past dates based on a time offset.

Simple explanation: Returns a date that is a specified number of months before or after a given date.

Common use cases: Used in loan schedules, subscription management, and planning timelines.

When to use this function: Use when calculating exact dates offset by a certain number of months.

Syntax

```
=EDATE(start_date, months)
```

- **start_date**: The initial date as a valid Excel date.
- **months**: The number of months to offset:
  - Positive values move the date forward.
  - Negative values move the date backward

Worked Example

Challenge: Calculate the date three months after 01-Jan-2023.

Formula:

```
=EDATE(DATE(2023, 1, 1), 3)
```

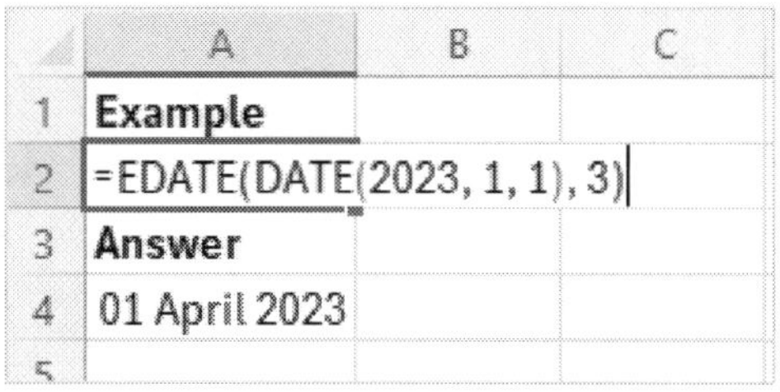

Result: 01-Apr-2023
Explanation: The function adds three months to the start date, resulting in 01-Apr-2023.

Explore Further with GPT:
Ask GPT how to combine EDATE with EOMONTH to calculate the last day of the offset month or integrate it into financial models.

Tips for Using EDATE

- **Date format:** Ensure start_date is a valid Excel date to avoid #VALUE! errors.
- **Dynamic dates:** Combine with TODAY() to calculate future or past dates dynamically:

  ```
  =EDATE(TODAY(), 6)
  ```

- **Partner with EOMONTH:** Use EOMONTH for end-of-month adjustments:

  ```
  =EOMONTH(EDATE(DATE(2023, 1, 1), 3), 0)
  ```

EFFECT Function

Financial Functions

Introduction

The EFFECT function calculates the effective annual interest rate given the nominal annual interest rate and the number of compounding periods per year. It is used in financial analysis to compare interest rates with different compounding frequencies.

Simple explanation: Returns the effective annual interest rate based on the nominal rate and compounding periods.

Common use cases: Used in loan analysis, investment evaluation, and financial modeling to determine comparable interest rates.

When to use this function: Use when converting nominal rates to effective rates for accurate comparisons.

Syntax

```
=EFFECT(nominal_rate, npery)
```

- **nominal_rate**: The nominal annual interest rate as a decimal (e.g., 0.05 for 5%).
- **npery**: The number of compounding periods per year (e.g., 12 for monthly compounding).

Worked Example

Challenge: Calculate the effective annual interest rate for a nominal rate of 5% with monthly compounding.

Formula:

```
=EFFECT(0.05, 12)
```

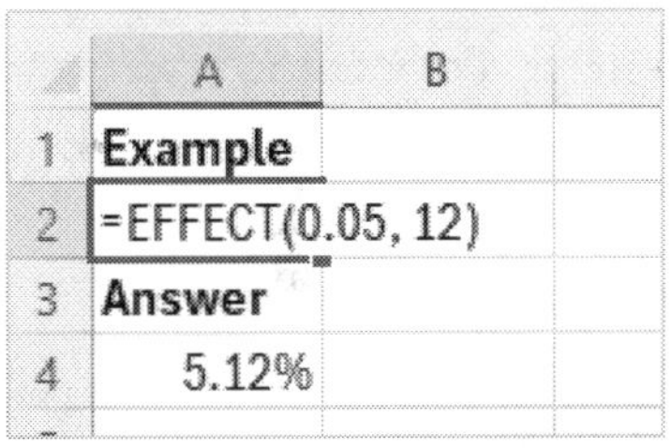

Result: 0.05116 (or 5.12%)
Explanation: The effective annual interest rate is slightly higher than the nominal rate due to monthly compounding.

Explore Further with GPT:
Ask GPT how to use EFFECT alongside NOMINAL to convert between effective and nominal rates or integrate it into loan analysis models.

Tips for Using EFFECT

- **Compounding periods:** Ensure the npery argument accurately reflects the compounding frequency (e.g., 1 for annual, 12 for monthly).

  ```
  =EFFECT(0.06, 12) - EFFECT(0.06, 4)
  ```

- **Partner with NOMINAL:** Convert back to nominal rates using the NOMINAL function:

  ```
  =NOMINAL(EFFECT(0.05, 12), 12)
  ```

ENCODEURL Function

Web Functions

Introduction

The ENCODEURL function encodes a text string into a format suitable for use in a URL. It replaces special characters with their percent-encoded equivalents, ensuring the text is safe for web requests.

Simple explanation: Converts a text string into a URL-safe format by encoding special characters.

Common use cases: Used in creating URLs for web APIs, linking to dynamic queries, and generating encoded strings for web applications.

When to use this function: Use when creating or modifying URLs programmatically to include special characters.

Syntax

```
=ENCODEURL(text)
```

- **text**: The text string to encode.

Worked Example

Challenge: Encode the text "Hello World!" into a URL-safe format.

Formula:

```
=ENCODEURL("Hello World!")
```

Result: Hello%20World%21

Explanation: The function replaces the space with %20 and the exclamation mark with %21, which are the percent-encoded equivalents.

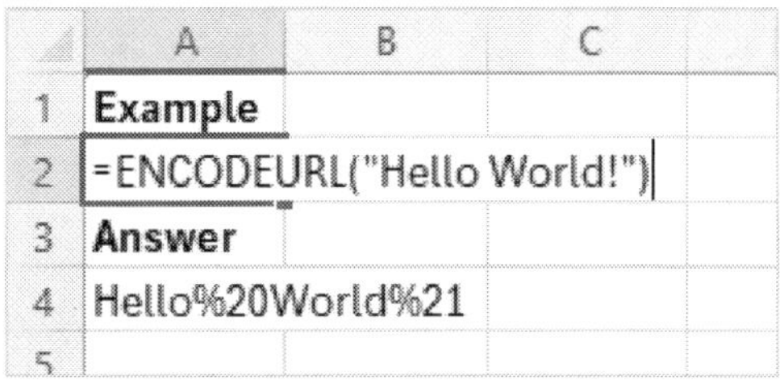

	A	B	C
1	**Example**		
2	=ENCODEURL("Hello World!")		
3	**Answer**		
4	Hello%20World%21		
5			

Explore Further with GPT:
Ask GPT how to combine ENCODEURL with functions like WEBSERVICE for dynamic API calls or to decode encoded URLs.

Tips for Using ENCODEURL

- **Web APIs:** Combine with functions like CONCAT to build complete URLs dynamically:

  ```
  =ENCODEURL("https://api.example.com/search?query=" & A1)
  ```

- **Decoding URLs:** Excel does not have a native DECODEURL function; use external tools or code for decoding if needed.

- **Error handling:** If the input text contains invalid characters, the function may return unexpected results or errors.

EOMONTH Function

Date & Time Functions

Introduction

The EOMONTH function returns the last day of the month that is a specified number of months before or after a given date. It is commonly used in financial modeling, project planning, and scheduling.

Simple explanation: Returns the last day of a month, offset by a specified number of months.

Common use cases: Used in loan schedules, fiscal period calculations, and determining month-end dates.

When to use this function: Use when calculating the end of a specific month relative to a start date.

Syntax

```
=EOMONTH(start_date, months)
```

- **start_date**: The initial date as a valid Excel date.
- **months**: The number of months to offset:
    - Positive values move forward in time.
    - Negative values move backward in time.

Worked Example

Challenge: Calculate the last day of the month three months after 15-Jan-2023.

Formula:

```
=EOMONTH(DATE(2023, 1, 15), 3)
```

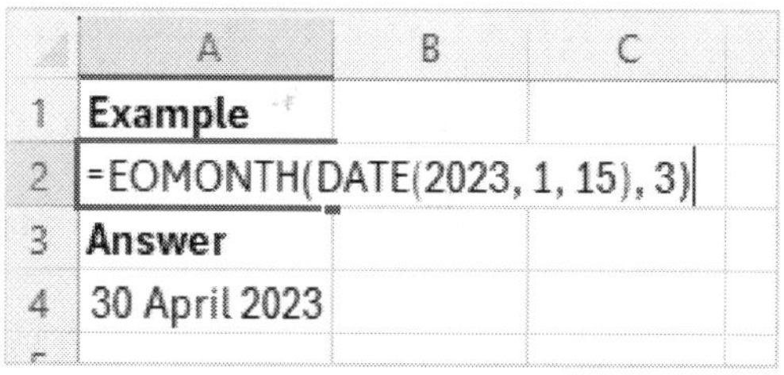

Result: 30-Apr-2023
Explanation: The function calculates the last day of April, which is three months after the start date.

Explore Further with GPT:
Ask GPT how to use EOMONTH with EDATE for more complex date calculations or to integrate it into fiscal year analyses.

Tips for Using EOMONTH

- **Dynamic dates:** Combine with TODAY() to calculate the current or future month-end:

  ```
  =EOMONTH(TODAY(), 0)
  ```

- **Partner with EDATE:** Use EOMONTH to calculate month-end dates and EDATE for exact offsets within months:

  ```
  =EOMONTH(EDATE(DATE(2023,1,1), 3), 0)
  ```

- **Error handling:** Ensure start_date is a valid Excel date to avoid #VALUE! errors.

ERF Function

Engineering Functions

Introduction

The ERF function returns the error function, which is a statistical function widely used in probability, statistics, and partial differential equations to model Gaussian distributions. It calculates the integral of the error function between a lower limit and an upper limit.

Simple explanation: Computes the error function for a range of values, useful in probability and statistics.

Common use cases: Used in statistical modeling, data analysis, and engineering to analyze error rates or Gaussian distributions.

When to use this function: Use when working with error or probability calculations based on Gaussian functions.

Syntax

```
=ERF(lower_limit, [upper_limit])
```

- **lower_limit**: The lower bound for the range of integration.
- **[upper_limit]** *(optional)*: The upper bound for the range of integration. If omitted, the function calculates from 0 to lower_limit.

Worked Example

Challenge: Calculate the error function for the range 0 to 1.5.

Formula:

```
=ERF(0, 1.5)
```

Result: 0.966105
Explanation: The function calculates the integral of the error function from 0 to 1.5.

	A	B
1	**Example**	
2	=ERF(0, 1.5)	
3	**Answer**	
4	0.966105	

Explore Further with GPT:
Ask GPT how to use ERF alongside ERFC for complementary error function calculations or its applications in probability distributions.

Tips for Using ERF

- **Single argument:** If only lower_limit is provided, Excel assumes the integral starts from 0.
- **Complementary function:** Use ERFC to calculate the complementary error function:

  ```
  =ERFC(1.5)
  ```

- **Error handling:** Ensure the inputs are valid numeric values to avoid #VALUE! errors.
- **Applications:** Combine with statistical functions like NORM.DIST or NORM.INV to analyze probabilities in Gaussian distributions.

ERF.PRECISE Function

Engineering Functions

Introduction

The ERF.PRECISE function returns the error function integrated between 0 and a specified lower limit. It is a statistical function often used in probability, data analysis, and engineering to evaluate Gaussian distributions.

Simple explanation: Computes the error function from 0 to a specified value with high precision.

Common use cases: Used in probability theory, statistical modeling, and error analysis related to Gaussian distributions.

When to use this function: Use when you need a precise calculation of the error function for Gaussian or probabilistic models.

Syntax

```
=ERF.PRECISE(x)
```

- **x**: The value up to which the error function is calculated (the upper limit). The function assumes the lower limit is 0.

Worked Example

Challenge: Calculate the error function from 0 to 1.5.

Formula:

```
=ERF.PRECISE(1.5)
```

Result: 0.966105
Explanation: The function calculates the integral of the error function from 0 to 1.5

	A	B	C
1	**Example**		
2	=ERF.PRECISE(1.5)		
3	**Answer**		
4	0.966105		

Explore Further with GPT:
Ask GPT how to use ERF.PRECISE alongside ERF or how it compares in accuracy for Gaussian and probability-based models.

Tips for Using ERF.PRECISE

- **Precision advantage:** This function is more accurate and reliable for numerical calculations compared to the legacy ERF function.
- **Handling negatives:** The function handles both positive and negative values of x, providing directionally accurate results.
- **Applications:** Combine with other statistical functions for advanced data analysis or error modeling:

  ```
  =ERFC.PRECISE(1.5) + ERF.PRECISE(1.5)
  ```

  This sums the error function and its complement for a total probability calculation.

ERFC Function

Engineering Functions

Introduction

The ERFC function calculates the complementary error function, which is 1 - ERF(x). It represents the tail probability of the Gaussian distribution and is widely used in probability, statistics, and engineering.

Simple explanation: Computes the complementary error function for a specified value.

Common use cases: Used in probability theory, error analysis, and evaluating tail probabilities of Gaussian distributions.

When to use this function: Use when analyzing the probability in the tail of a Gaussian distribution or calculating 1 - ERF(x).

Syntax

```
=ERFC(x)
```

- **x**: The value at which to calculate the complementary error function. It integrates the Gaussian distribution from x to infinity

Worked Example

Challenge: Calculate the complementary error function for 1.5.

Formula:

```
=ERFC(1.5)
```

	A	B
1	**Example**	
2	=ERFC(1.5)	
3	**Answer**	
4	0.033895	

Result: 0.033895
Explanation: The function computes the tail probability from 1.5 to infinity in the Gaussian distribution.

Explore Further with GPT:
Ask GPT how to combine ERFC with ERF for comprehensive probability analysis or how to interpret its results in Gaussian models.

Tips for Using ERFC

- **Complementary function:** Use ERFC with ERF to validate probability results:

  ```
  =ERF(1.5) + ERFC(1.5)  'Result: 1
  ```

- **Handling negatives:** For negative values of x, the function integrates from x to infinity and produces larger results.

- **Error handling:** Ensure x is a valid numeric value to avoid #VALUE! errors

ERFC.PRECISE Function

Engineering Functions

Introduction

The ERFC.PRECISE function calculates the complementary error function with high precision. It integrates the Gaussian distribution from a given value to infinity and is commonly used in probability, statistics, and error analysis.

Simple explanation: Computes the complementary error function from a specified value to infinity with improved accuracy.

Common use cases: Used in statistical analysis, probability calculations, and Gaussian modeling.

When to use this function: Use when high precision is required for tail probabilities or complementary Gaussian error functions.

Syntax

```
=ERFC.PRECISE(x)
```

- **x**: The value at which to calculate the complementary error function. The function integrates from x to infinity

Worked Example

Challenge: Calculate the complementary error function for 1.5.

Formula:

```
=ERFC.PRECISE(1.5)
```

Result: 0.033895
Explanation: The function computes the tail probability from 1.5 to infinity with high precision.

	A	B
1	**Example**	
2	=ERFC.PRECISE(1.5)	
3	**Answer**	
4	0.033895	

Explore Further with GPT:
Ask GPT how to use ERFC.PRECISE for advanced Gaussian calculations or to compare its use cases with ERF.PRECISE.

Tips for Using ERFC.PRECISE

- **Enhanced precision:** Use this function for more accurate calculations than the legacy ERFC function.
- **Handling negatives:** For negative values of x, the function integrates from x to infinity, producing larger results.
- **Validate with ERF.PRECISE:** Combine with ERF.PRECISE for complementary probability checks:

  ```
  =ERF.PRECISE(1.5) + ERFC.PRECISE(1.5)
  ```

  Result: 1

ERROR.TYPE Function

Information Functions

Introduction

The ERROR.TYPE function returns a numeric code corresponding to a specific error value in Excel. It helps in error handling by identifying the type of error and providing custom responses or actions.

Simple explanation: Identifies the type of error in a formula or cell by returning a numeric code.

Common use cases: Used in troubleshooting, error tracking, and creating custom error messages or actions in formulas.

When to use this function: Use when analyzing or managing errors in complex formulas or datasets.

Syntax

```
=ERROR.TYPE(error_value)
```

- **error_value**: The error to identify. It can be a direct error value (e.g., #DIV/0!) or a reference to a cell containing an error.

Error Codes and Their Meanings

Error Value	Returned Code	Description
#NULL!	1	Null intersection error
#DIV/0!	2	Division by zero
#VALUE!	3	Invalid data type
#REF!	4	Invalid cell reference
#NAME?	5	Undefined name or function
#NUM!	6	Invalid numeric calculation
#N/A	7	Value not available
Any other error	#N/A	Not an error or unrecognized

Worked Example

Challenge: Identify the error type in cell A1 containing #DIV/0!.

Formula:

```
=ERROR.TYPE(A1)
```

Result: 2
Explanation: The function identifies the error in cell A1 as a division by zero error, corresponding to code 2.

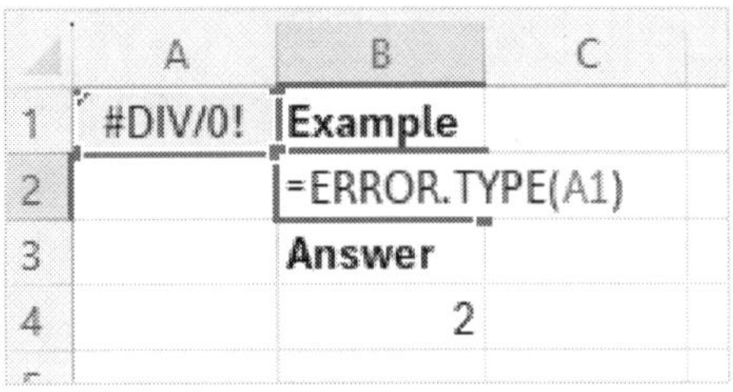

Explore Further with GPT:
Ask GPT how to combine ERROR.TYPE with IFERROR or ISERROR to build robust error-handling workflows.

EVEN Function

Math & Trigonometry Functions

Introduction

The EVEN function rounds a number up to the nearest even integer. It always rounds away from zero, regardless of whether the input is positive or negative. This function is useful in mathematical calculations and scenarios where even integers are required.

Simple explanation: Rounds a number up to the nearest even integer.

Common use cases: Used in calculations requiring even numbers, such as packaging, inventory grouping, or grid alignment.

When to use this function: Use when rounding numbers to the nearest even integer is necessary.

Syntax

```
=EVEN(number)
```

- **number**: The numeric value to round.

Worked Example

Challenge: Round the number 3.2 to the nearest even integer.

Formula:

```
=EVEN(3.2)
```

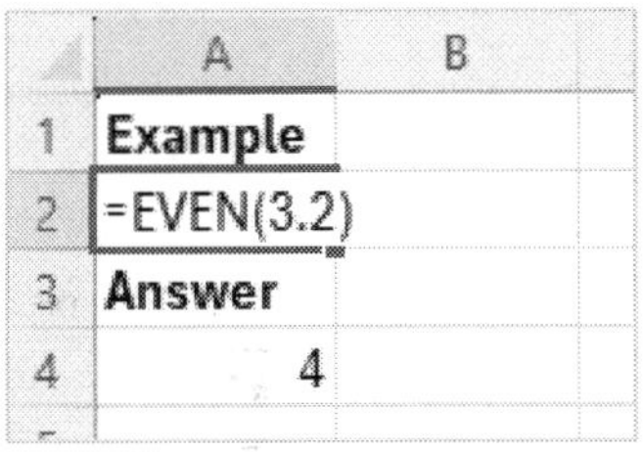

Result: 4
Explanation: The function rounds 3.2 up to the nearest even integer, which is 4.

Explore Further with GPT:
Ask GPT how to combine EVEN with other rounding functions like ODD or ROUND for custom rounding scenarios.

Tips for Using EVEN

- **Always rounds up (away from zero):** The function rounds positive numbers up and negative numbers down to the next even integer.
- **Applications with ODD:** Pair with the ODD function for scenarios requiring alternation between even and odd values:

  ```
  =ODD(3.2)  'Result: 5
  ```

- **Error handling:** Ensure the input number is numeric to avoid #VALUE! errors.

EXACT Function

Text Functions

Introduction

The EXACT function compares two text strings and returns TRUE if they are exactly the same, including case sensitivity, or FALSE otherwise. It is commonly used in data validation, case-sensitive comparisons, and duplicate detection.

Simple explanation: Compares two text strings and checks if they are exactly the same (case-sensitive).

Common use cases: Used in data cleaning, case-sensitive matching, and validating text inputs.

When to use this function: Use when precise, case-sensitive comparisons between two text strings are needed.

Syntax

```
=EXACT(text1, text2)
```

- **text1**: The first text string to compare.
- **text2**: The second text string to compare

Worked Example

Challenge: Compare the strings "Hello" and "hello".

Formula:

```
=EXACT("Hello", "hello")
```

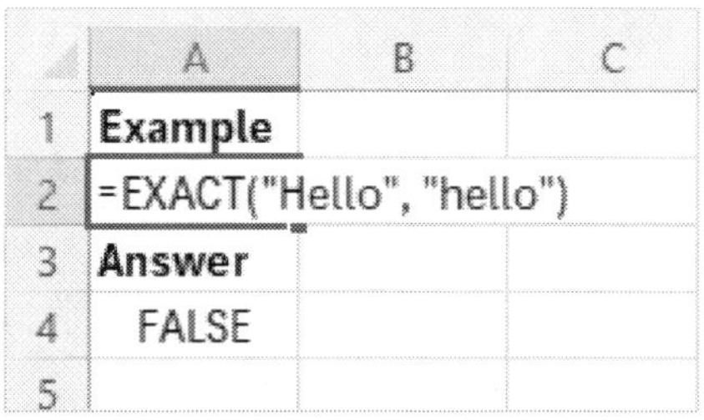

Result: FALSE
Explanation: The function returns FALSE because the text strings differ in case (uppercase H vs. lowercase h).

Explore Further with GPT:
Ask GPT how to use EXACT in combination with functions like IF or SEARCH for advanced text validation or comparison workflows.

Tips for Using EXACT

- **Case sensitivity:** Unlike = or IF, the EXACT function is case-sensitive, making it ideal for precise matching scenarios.
- **Error handling:** Ensure both text1 and text2 are valid text values to avoid unexpected results.
- **Combine with conditional logic:** Use alongside IF to trigger specific actions based on text matching:

  ```
  =IF(EXACT(A1, B1), "Match", "No Match")
  ```

- **Array comparisons:** Combine with array formulas or FILTER for bulk text comparisons in datasets.

EXP Function

Math & Trigonometry Functions

Introduction

The EXP function returns the result of raising the mathematical constant **e** (approximately 2.718281) to the power of a given number. It is commonly used in exponential growth calculations, scientific modeling, and natural logarithm-related computations.

Simple explanation: Calculates e^x, where **e** is the base of natural logarithms, and ***x*** is the input number.

Common use cases: Used in exponential growth/decay models, compound interest calculations, and scientific formulas.

When to use this function: Use when exponential growth or e^x calculations are required in your dataset.

Syntax

```
=EXP(number)
```

- **number**: The exponent to which ***e*** is raised.

Worked Example

Challenge: Calculate e^2.

Formula:

```
=EXP(2)
```

	A	B
1	**Example**	
2	=EXP(2)	
3	**Answer**	
4	7.389056	

Result: 7.389056
Explanation: The function calculates e^2, which is approximately 7.389.

Explore Further with GPT:
Ask GPT how to use EXP alongside LN (natural logarithm) for reverse calculations or in exponential regression models.

Tips for Using EXP

- **Combine with logarithms:** Use with LN for operations involving natural logarithms:

  ```
  =LN(EXP(2))  'Result: 2
  ```

- **Growth modeling:** Pair with ^ and other arithmetic functions to create exponential growth/decay models:

  ```
  =100 * EXP(0.05 * A1)  'Exponential growth
  ```

- **Scientific applications:** Ideal for physics, biology, and economics calculations involving natural exponential relationships.

EXPAND Function

Lookup & Reference Functions

Introduction

The EXPAND function resizes an array to a specified number of rows and columns, filling additional spaces with a provided value if necessary. It is useful for reshaping data and creating dynamic arrays for analysis or visualization.

Simple explanation: Adjusts the size of an array by adding or reducing rows and columns.

Common use cases: Used in creating dynamic data ranges, filling tables, and ensuring consistent array dimensions for analysis.

When to use this function: Use when resizing an array for specific dimensions or filling missing data.

Syntax

```
=EXPAND(array, rows, columns, [default])
```

- **array**: The array to resize.
- **rows**: The desired number of rows in the output array.
- **columns**: The desired number of columns in the output array.
- **[default]** *(optional)*: The value to fill in additional spaces. Defaults to 0 if omitted.

Worked Example

Challenge: Expand the array {1, 2; 3, 4} to 4 rows and 3 columns, filling with 0.

Formula:

```
=EXPAND({1, 2; 3, 4}, 4, 3, 0)
```

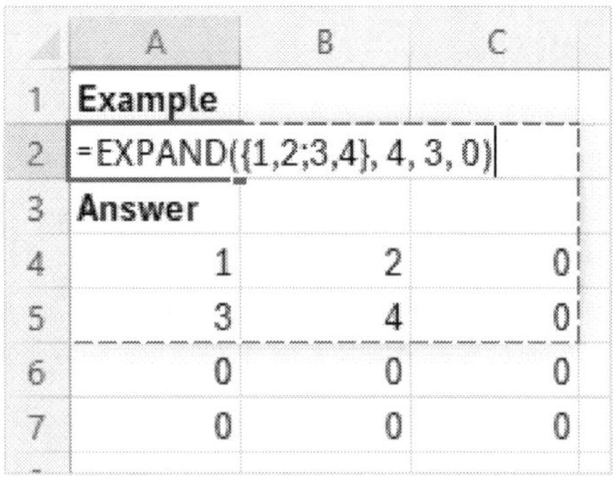

Result:

1	**2**	**0**
3	**4**	**0**
0	**0**	**0**
0	**0**	**0**

Explanation: The array is resized to 4 rows and 3 columns, with extra cells filled with 0.

Explore Further with GPT:
Ask GPT how to use EXPAND in combination with SEQUENCE or FILTER to create dynamic data tables or reshape arrays for analysis.

Tips for Using EXPAND

- **Default values:** Use the default argument to control how extra spaces are filled, particularly for non-numeric arrays:

```
=EXPAND({1, 2}, 3, 3, "N/A")
```

EXPON.DIST Function

Statistical Functions

Introduction

The EXPON.DIST function returns the exponential distribution, a probability distribution commonly used to model the time between events in a Poisson process. It can compute either the probability density function (PDF) or the cumulative distribution function (CDF).

Simple explanation: Calculates probabilities using the exponential distribution.

Common use cases: Used in reliability analysis, queuing theory, and modeling time between events.

When to use this function: Use when analyzing or modeling data involving exponentially distributed time intervals.

Syntax

```
=EXPON.DIST(x, lambda, cumulative)
```

- **x**: The value of the random variable.
- **lambda**: The rate parameter of the distribution (must be > 0).
- **cumulative**: A logical value:
    - TRUE for the CDF (cumulative probability up to x).
    - FALSE for the PDF (probability density at x).

Worked Example

Challenge: Calculate the probability density (PDF) for x=2 with a rate parameter λ=0.5.

Formula:

```
=EXPON.DIST(2, 0.5, FALSE)
```

Result: 0.18394

Explanation: The function computes the PDF of the exponential distribution at x=2.

	A	B	C
1	**Example**		
2	=EXPON.DIST(2, 0.5, FALSE)		
3	**Answer**		
4	0.18394		
5			

Explore Further with GPT:
Ask GPT how to interpret EXPON.DIST results in reliability analysis or how it relates to the Poisson distribution.

Tips for Using EXPON.DIST

- **Rate parameter:** Ensure λ\lambdaλ is positive to avoid #NUM! errors.
- **Applications in reliability:** Pair with functions like NORM.DIST or POISSON.DIST to model more complex distributions.
- **Visualizing distributions:** Use EXPON.DIST in a range of values to plot the exponential distribution:

  ```
  =EXPON.DIST(A1, 0.5, FALSE)
  ```

- **CDF vs. PDF:** Use TRUE for cumulative probabilities when analyzing total probabilities up to a point, and FALSE for specific point probabilities.

EXPONDIST Function

Compatibility Functions

Introduction

The EXPONDIST function calculates the exponential distribution for a given value of xxx and a specified rate parameter λ. It can compute the probability density function (PDF) or the cumulative distribution function (CDF). This function has been replaced by EXPON.DIST in modern versions of Excel.

Simple explanation: Calculates the exponential distribution using older Excel syntax.

Common use cases: Used in earlier Excel versions for modeling time intervals in a Poisson process.

When to use this function: Use when working with older Excel versions requiring backward compatibility.

Syntax

```
=EXPONDIST(x, lambda, cumulative)
```

- **x**: The value of the random variable.
- **lambda**: The rate parameter of the distribution (must be > 0).
- **cumulative**: A logical value:
  - TRUE for the CDF (cumulative probability up to ***x***).
  - FALSE for the PDF (probability density at ***x***).

Worked Example

Challenge: Calculate the cumulative probability for x=2 with λ=0.5.

Formula:

```
=EXPONDIST(2, 0.5, TRUE)
```

Result: 0.632121
Explanation: The function computes the cumulative probability for x=2 with the exponential distribution.

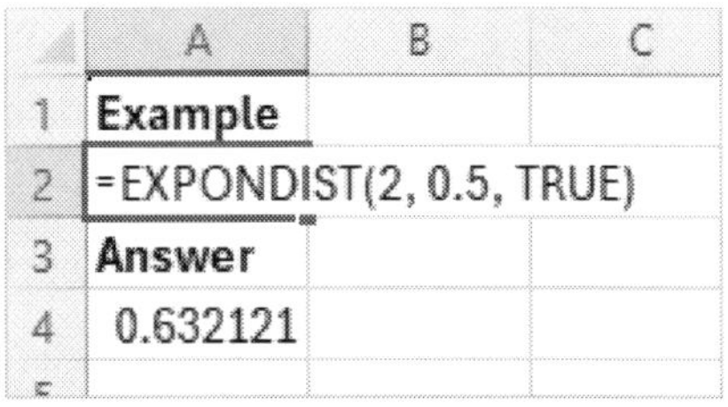

Explore Further with GPT:
Ask GPT how to update older Excel files using EXPONDIST to the newer EXPON.DIST function or to compare their performance and accuracy.

Tips for Using EXPONDIST

- **Use EXPON.DIST if available:** For modern Excel users, EXPON.DIST offers the same functionality with updated naming.
- **Rate parameter:** Ensure λ is greater than zero to avoid #NUM! errors.
- **Backward compatibility:** This function is maintained for older Excel files but is not recommended for new projects.
- **Plotting distributions:** Use in conjunction with Excel charts to visualize probabilities across a range of ***x*** values

FACT Function

Math & Trigonometry Functions

Introduction

The FACT function calculates the factorial of a given non-negative number. The factorial of a number n is the product of all positive integers less than or equal to n. This function is widely used in statistics, combinatorics, and mathematical analysis.

Simple explanation: Returns the factorial of a number (n!).

Common use cases: Used in probability, statistics, and permutations or combinations calculations.

When to use this function: Use when factorials are needed in statistical or combinatorial computations.

Syntax

```
=FACT(number)
```

- **number**: The non-negative integer for which to calculate the factorial.

Worked Example

Challenge: Calculate the factorial of 5.

Formula:

```
=FACT(5)
```

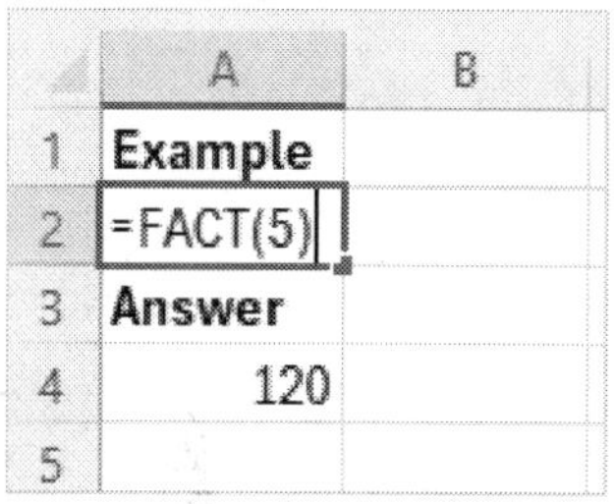

Result: 120
Explanation: The factorial of 5 is 5×4×3×2×1=120.

Explore Further with GPT

Ask GPT how to use FACT alongside logarithmic functions for large factorial approximations, such as Stirling's approximation, or in advanced probability models.

Tips for Using FACT

- **Non-negative inputs only:** The function returns a #NUM! error if the input is negative.
- **Use with combinations:** Combine with COMBIN or PERMUT for calculating permutations and combinations:

  ```
  =COMBIN(5, 3)   'Result: 10
  ```

- **Large numbers:** For very large numbers, factorials grow quickly, and the result may exceed Excel's numeric limit.

FACTDOUBLE Function

Math & Trigonometry Functions

Introduction

The FACTDOUBLE function calculates the double factorial of a given non-negative integer. The double factorial of a number n is the product of all integers of the same parity (odd or even) less than or equal to n.

Simple explanation: Returns the double factorial of a number, multiplying every second integer.

Common use cases: Used in advanced mathematics, combinatorics, and probability, especially for simplifying complex factorial-related expressions.

When to use this function: Use when working with double factorials in mathematical or statistical models.

Syntax

```
=FACTDOUBLE(number)
```

- **number**: The non-negative integer for which to calculate the double factorial.

Worked Example

Challenge: Calculate the double factorial of 6.

Formula:

```
=FACTDOUBLE(6)
```

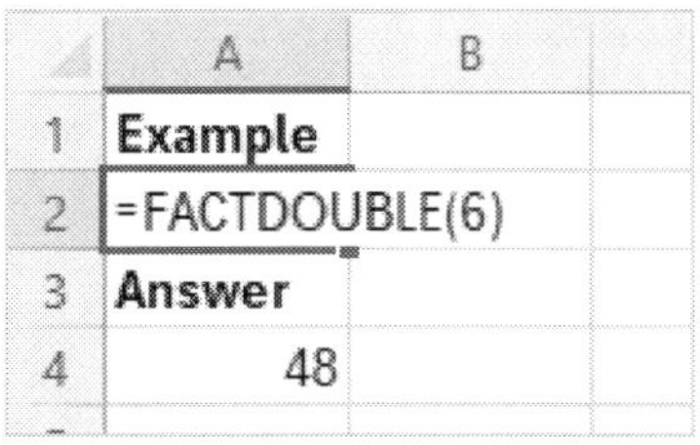

Result: 48
Explanation: The double factorial of 6 is 6×4×2=486.

Explore Further with GPT

Ask GPT how to use FACTDOUBLE in combinatorial problems or how it compares to regular factorials in simplifying formulas for odd and even sequences.

Tips for Using FACTDOUBLE

- **Non-negative inputs only:** The function returns a #NUM! error if the input is negative.
- **Combine with other functions:** Use with FACT or COMBIN for advanced mathematical operations.
- **Special case:** For n=0 or n=−1, the double factorial is defined as 1.

FALSE Function

Logical Functions

Introduction

The FALSE function returns the logical value FALSE. It is primarily used in logical comparisons and conditional expressions to represent a negative or untrue condition. While it is rarely used alone, it is useful in building formulas and logical operations.

Simple explanation: Returns the logical value FALSE.

Common use cases: Used in logical formulas, comparisons, and testing conditions.

When to use this function: Use when you need to explicitly include FALSE in logical operations or comparisons.

Syntax

```
=FALSE()
```

- This function takes no arguments and always returns the logical value FALSE.

Worked Example

Challenge: Use the FALSE function in a logical formula to test if a value equals 10.

Formula:

```
=IF(A1=10, TRUE, FALSE())
```

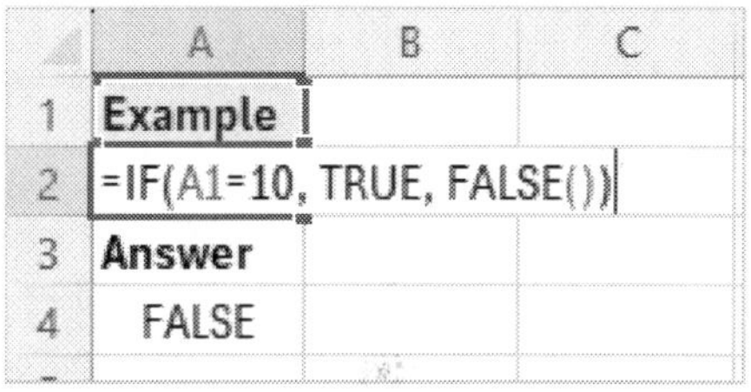

Result: FALSE (if A1 is not equal to 10).
Explanation: The formula returns FALSE when the condition A1=10 is not met.

Explore Further with GPT

Ask GPT how to combine FALSE with logical functions like IF, AND, or OR for more complex logical operations.

Tips for Using FALSE

- **Shortcut:** Instead of using FALSE(), you can directly type FALSE in most logical operations (e.g., =IF(A1>10, TRUE, FALSE)).
- **Logical functions:** Combine with AND, OR, or NOT for conditional expressions:

  ```
  =AND(A1>10, FALSE())
  ```

- **Use with TRUE:** Pair with the TRUE function to toggle between logical states or create conditional outcomes.

F.DIST Function

Statistical Functions

Introduction

The F.DIST function calculates the F-distribution, a probability distribution commonly used in hypothesis testing, particularly for comparing variances between two datasets. It can return either the cumulative distribution function (CDF) or the probability density function (PDF).

Simple explanation: Returns the F-distribution for comparing variances between two datasets.

Common use cases: Used in ANOVA (Analysis of Variance) and other statistical tests for comparing variability.

When to use this function: Use when performing statistical tests involving the F-distribution.

Syntax

```
=F.DIST(x, deg_freedom1, deg_freedom2, cumulative)
```

- **x**: The value at which to evaluate the distribution.
- **deg_freedom1**: Degrees of freedom for the numerator.
- **deg_freedom2**: Degrees of freedom for the denominator.
- **cumulative**: A logical value:
  - TRUE for the CDF (cumulative probability).
  - FALSE for the PDF (probability density).

Worked Example

Challenge: Calculate the cumulative F-distribution for x=2.5x = 2.5x=2.5, with 555 numerator degrees of freedom and 101010 denominator degrees of freedom.

Formula:

```
=F.DIST(2.5, 5, 10, TRUE)
```

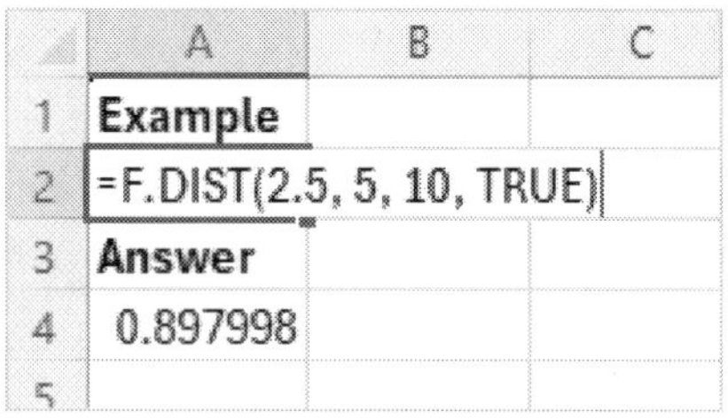

Result: 0.897998
Explanation: The function calculates the cumulative probability of obtaining an F-statistic less than or equal to 2.5.

Explore Further with GPT

Ask GPT how to use F.DIST alongside F.INV or F.TEST for complete hypothesis testing workflows, or how to interpret results in statistical models.

Tips for Using F.DIST

- **Valid degrees of freedom:** Ensure deg_freedom1 and deg_freedom2 are positive integers to avoid #NUM! errors.
- **Combine with other statistical functions:** Use F.DIST alongside F.TEST for hypothesis testing or F.INV to find critical values.

FDIST Function

Compatibility Functions

Introduction

The FDIST function is a legacy function used to return the F-distribution. It has been replaced by the modern F.DIST function but is still available in Excel for backward compatibility. It calculates the probability of obtaining an F-statistic for given numerator and denominator degrees of freedom.

Simple explanation: Returns the cumulative F-distribution probability for comparing variances between two datasets.

Common use cases: Used in statistical hypothesis testing, particularly in older Excel models, to evaluate variability.

When to use this function: Use when working with older Excel versions requiring backward compatibility.

Syntax

```
=FDIST(x, deg_freedom1, deg_freedom2)
```

- **x**: The value at which to evaluate the distribution.
- **deg_freedom1**: Degrees of freedom for the numerator.
- **deg_freedom2**: Degrees of freedom for the denominator.

Worked Example

Challenge: Calculate the cumulative F-distribution for x=2.5, with 5 numerator degrees of freedom and 10 denominator degrees of freedom.

Formula:

```
=FDIST(2.5, 5, 10)
```

Result: 0.102002
Explanation: The function calculates the cumulative probability of obtaining an F-statistic less than or equal to 2.5.

	A	B
1	**Example**	
2	=FDIST(2.5, 5, 10)	
3	**Answer**	
4	0.102002	

Explore Further with GPT

Ask GPT how to update formulas using FDIST to the newer F.DIST function, or how to integrate it into hypothesis testing workflows.

Tips for Using FDIST

- **Backward compatibility:** Use FDIST only when working with older Excel files. For modern applications, use F.DIST.
- **Modern alternatives:** Switch to F.DIST for enhanced functionality and to include probability density (PDF) calculations:

  ```
  =F.DIST(2.5, 5, 10, TRUE)  'Cumulative
  ```

- **Valid inputs:** Ensure degrees of freedom and xxx are positive values to avoid errors.

F.DIST.RT Function

Statistical Functions

Introduction

The F.DIST.RT function returns the right-tailed F-distribution, commonly used in hypothesis testing to determine the significance of observed variance differences between two datasets. The function calculates the probability that an F-statistic is greater than a given value.

Simple explanation: Returns the right-tailed F-distribution probability for comparing variances.

Common use cases: Used in ANOVA (Analysis of Variance) and other statistical tests to evaluate differences in variability.

When to use this function: Use when analyzing the probability of observing an F-statistic greater than a given value in hypothesis testing.

Syntax

```
=F.DIST.RT(x, deg_freedom1, deg_freedom2)
```

- **x**: The F-statistic value.
- **deg_freedom1**: Degrees of freedom for the numerator.
- **deg_freedom2**: Degrees of freedom for the denominator.

Worked Example

Challenge: Calculate the right-tailed F-distribution probability for x=2.5, with 5 numerator degrees of freedom and 10 denominator degrees of freedom.

Formula:

```
=F.DIST.RT(2.5, 5, 10)
```

Result: 0.102002
Explanation: The function calculates the probability of obtaining an F-statistic greater than 2.5.

	A	B
1	**Example**	
2	=F.DIST.RT(2.5, 5, 10)	
3	**Answer**	
4	0.102002	
5		

Explore Further with GPT

Ask GPT how to combine F.DIST.RT with F.INV.RT for critical value calculations or how to interpret its results in ANOVA and other statistical tests.

Tips for Using F.DIST.RT

- **Right-tailed focus:** This function always calculates the probability in the right tail, making it suitable for one-tailed F-tests.
- **Use with modern statistical tools:** Combine with F.INV.RT to determine critical thresholds for hypothesis testing:

  ```
  =F.INV.RT(0.05, 5, 10)
  ```

- **Legacy considerations:** For backward compatibility, the older FDIST function also calculates right-tailed probabilities but lacks the clarity of the newer naming conventions.

FILTER Function

Lookup & Reference Functions

Introduction

The FILTER function returns an array of values that meet a specified condition. It is a dynamic array function, meaning its results spill into adjacent cells automatically. The function is widely used for extracting data, creating subsets, and building dynamic dashboards.

Simple explanation: Filters a range of data based on a condition.

Common use cases: Used in dynamic reporting, data analysis, and creating interactive dashboards.

When to use this function: Use when you need to extract specific rows or columns from a dataset that meet certain criteria.

Syntax

```
=FILTER(array, include, [if_empty])
```

- **array**: The range or array to filter.
- **include**: A condition that determines which values to include (evaluates to TRUE or FALSE).
- **[if_empty]** *(optional)*: The value to return if no entries match the condition. If omitted, the function returns #CALC!.

Worked Example

Challenge: Extract all rows where the sales are greater than 200.

Formula:

```
=FILTER(A1:B4, B1:B4>200, "No matching data")
```

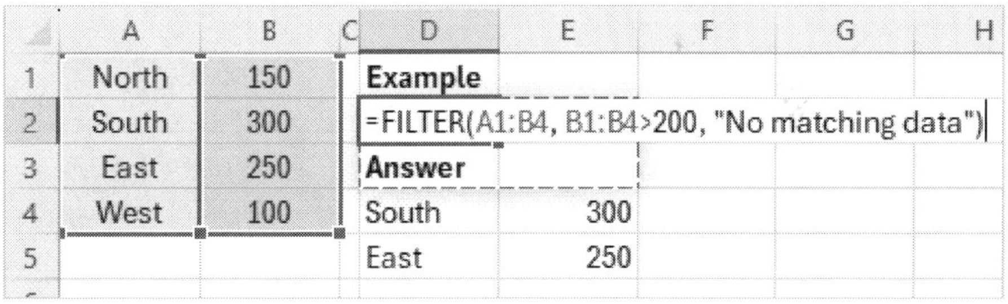

Result:

South	300
East	250

Explanation: The function filters the rows where the sales value is greater than 200.

Explore Further with GPT

Ask GPT how to combine FILTER with nested functions for complex data extraction, or how to handle large datasets dynamically in Excel.

Tips for Using FILTER

- **Dynamic arrays:** Ensure there is enough space for the results to spill into adjacent cells; otherwise, Excel returns a #SPILL! error.

FILTERXML Function

Web Functions

Introduction

The FILTERXML function parses an XML string and returns specific data using XPath queries. It is commonly used for extracting structured data from web services, APIs, or XML documents directly within Excel.

Simple explanation: Extracts data from XML strings based on a specified XPath query.

Common use cases: Used in data analysis, web scraping, and processing XML-based API responses.

When to use this function: Use when extracting specific elements or attributes from an XML string for analysis or visualization.

Syntax

```
=FILTERXML(xml, xpath)
```

- **xml**: A valid XML string to parse.
- **xpath**: The XPath query to extract data from the XML string.

Worked Example

Challenge: Extract the names of employees from the following XML string:

<employees>
<employee>
<name>John</name>
<age>30</age>
</employee>
<employee>
<name>Jane</name>
<age>25</age>
</employee>
</employees>

	A
1	**Example**
2	=FILTERXML("<employees><employee><name>John</name><age>30</age></employee><employee><name>Jane</name><age>25</age></employee></employees>", "//name")
3	**Answer**
4	John
5	Jane

Formula:

```
=FILTERXML("<employees><employee><name>John</name><age>30</age></employee><employee><name>Jane</name><age>25</age></employee></employees>", "//name")
```

Result:
John (spills into adjacent cells if dynamic arrays are enabled)
Jane

Explanation: The XPath query //name retrieves all <name> elements within the XML structure.

FIND Function

Text Functions

Introduction

The FIND function returns the position of a specified substring within a text string. It is case-sensitive and does not support wildcard characters, making it ideal for exact text searches.

Simple explanation: Finds the position of a substring in a text string (case-sensitive).

Common use cases: Used in data cleaning, text analysis, and extracting specific substrings.

When to use this function: Use when you need to locate the position of a specific substring in a larger text string.

Syntax

```
=FIND(find_text, within_text, [start_num])
```

- **find_text**: The substring you want to find.
- **within_text**: The text string to search within.
- **[start_num]** *(optional)*: The position in the text string to start the search. Defaults to 1.

Worked Example

Challenge: Find the position of "cat" in the text "concatenation".

Formula:

```
=FIND("cat", "concatenation")
```

Result: 4
Explanation: The substring "cat" starts at the 4th character in "concatenation".

	A	B	C
1	**Example**		
2	=FIND("cat", "concatenation")		
3	**Answer**		
4	4		

Explore Further with GPT

Ask GPT how to use FIND alongside MID or LEFT for extracting specific parts of text or how to handle case-insensitive searches with alternatives like SEARCH.

Tips for Using FIND

- **Case-sensitive:** The FIND function distinguishes between uppercase and lowercase letters. Use SEARCH for case-insensitive searches.
- **Error handling:** If the substring is not found, FIND returns a #VALUE! error. Wrap with IFERROR for custom handling:

  ```
  =IFERROR(FIND("dog", "cat"), "Not Found")
  ```

- **Use with text functions:** Combine FIND with MID, LEFT, or RIGHT to extract substrings:

  ```
  =MID(A1, FIND("-", A1) + 1, 5)
  ```

FINDB Function

Text Functions

Introduction

The FINDB function returns the position of a specified substring within a text string, similar to the FIND function. However, FINDB is designed for double-byte character set (DBCS) languages, such as Chinese, Japanese, or Korean. It treats each double-byte character as two bytes when DBCS is set as the default language.

Simple explanation: Finds the position of a substring in a text string, treating double-byte characters appropriately for DBCS languages.

Common use cases: Used in text analysis for DBCS languages where characters can occupy more than one byte.

When to use this function: Use when working with DBCS languages to locate the position of a substring in text.

Syntax

```
=FINDB(find_text, within_text, [start_num])
```

- **find_text**: The substring you want to find.
- **within_text**: The text string to search within.
- **[start_num]** *(optional)*: The position in the text string to start the search. Defaults to 1.

Worked Example

Challenge: Find the position of "字" in the text "文字列" (a string in Japanese).

Formula:

```
=FINDB("字", "文字列")
```

Result: 2
Explanation: In a DBCS language setup, "字" starts at the 2nd byte in "文字列".

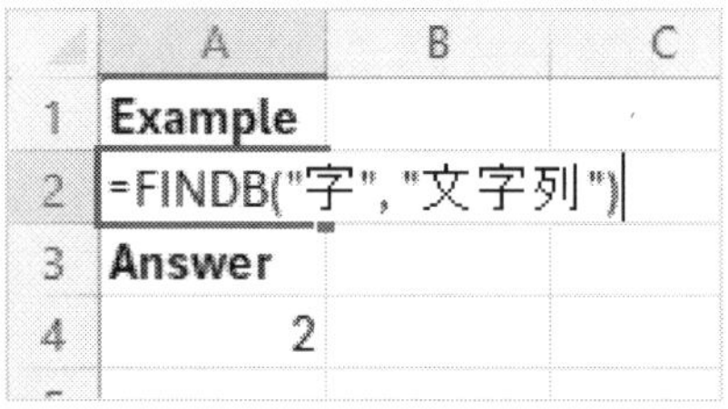

Explore Further with GPT

Ask GPT how to use FINDB in combination with text extraction functions like MIDB or how to handle mixed single-byte and double-byte character sets effectively.

Tips for Using FINDB

- **DBCS support:** This function is most useful in DBCS language environments. In non-DBCS languages, FINDB behaves the same as FIND.
- **Error handling:** If the substring is not found, FINDB returns a #VALUE! error. Wrap with IFERROR for graceful error handling:

  ```
  =IFERROR(FINDB("字", "文字列"), "Not Found")
  ```

F.INV Function

Statistical Functions

Introduction

The F.INV function calculates the inverse of the F-distribution. It determines the F-statistic value for a given cumulative probability and degrees of freedom. This function is commonly used in hypothesis testing and analysis of variance (ANOVA).

Simple explanation: Returns the F-statistic value corresponding to a given cumulative probability.

Common use cases: Used in statistical hypothesis testing, critical value calculations, and variance analysis.

When to use this function: Use when you need to find the F-statistic value for a specific cumulative probability in an F-distribution.

Syntax

```
=F.INV(probability, deg_freedom1, deg_freedom2)
```

- **probability**: The cumulative probability for which to compute the F-statistic.
- **deg_freedom1**: Degrees of freedom for the numerator.
- **deg_freedom2**: Degrees of freedom for the denominator.

Worked Example

Challenge: Find the F-statistic value corresponding to a cumulative probability of 0.95, with 5 numerator degrees of freedom and 10 denominator degrees of freedom.

Formula:

```
=F.INV(0.95, 5, 10)
```

Result: 3.325835

Explanation: The function calculates the F-statistic value such that the cumulative probability up to this value is 0.95.

	A	B
1	**Example**	
2	=F.INV(0.95, 5, 10)	
3	**Answer**	
4	3.325835	

Explore Further with GPT

Ask GPT how to use F.INV for critical region analysis in hypothesis testing or how it complements F.DIST in statistical workflows.

Tips for Using F.INV

- **Valid probability range:** Ensure the probability value is between 0 and 1 to avoid #NUM! errors.
- **Degrees of freedom:** Input positive integers for both numerator and denominator degrees of freedom to avoid errors.
- **Combine with F.DIST.RT:** Use F.DIST.RT to calculate the right-tail probability for the F-statistic obtained with F.INV:

  ```
  =F.DIST.RT(F.INV(0.95, 5, 10), 5, 10)
  ```

- **Hypothesis testing:** Use to determine the critical F-value for rejection regions in ANOVA or other variance tests.

F.INV.RT Function

Statistical Functions

Introduction

The F.INV.RT function calculates the inverse of the right-tailed F-distribution. It returns the F-statistic value for a given probability in the right tail and specified degrees of freedom. This function is commonly used in hypothesis testing, especially for determining critical values in ANOVA and other variance analyses.

- **Simple explanation:** Returns the F-statistic value corresponding to a given right-tail probability.
- **Common use cases:** Used in hypothesis testing to determine critical F-values for rejection regions.
- **When to use this function:** Use when analyzing right-tailed probabilities in the F-distribution, such as in one-tailed tests.

Syntax

```
=F.INV.RT(probability, deg_freedom1, deg_freedom2)
```

- **probability**: The right-tail probability for which to compute the F-statistic.
- **deg_freedom1**: Degrees of freedom for the numerator.
- **deg_freedom2**: Degrees of freedom for the denominator.

Worked Example

Challenge: Find the F-statistic value corresponding to a right-tail probability of 0.05, with 5 numerator degrees of freedom and 10 denominator degrees of freedom.

Formula:

```
=F.INV.RT(0.05, 5, 10)
```

Result: 3.325835
Explanation: The function calculates the F-statistic value such that the area to the right under the curve is 0.05.

	A	B	C
1	**Example**		
2	=F.INV.RT(0.05, 5, 10)		
3	**Answer**		
4	3.325835		

Explore Further with GPT

Ask GPT how to use F.INV.RT alongside F.DIST.RT to confirm critical F-values or integrate it into a complete hypothesis testing workflow.

Tips for Using F.INV.RT

- **Valid probability range:** Ensure the probability value is between 0 and 1 to avoid #NUM! errors.
- **Right-tailed focus:** This function is specifically for right-tail probabilities. Use F.INV for cumulative probabilities.
- **Combine with F.DIST.RT:** Validate your critical F-value by plugging it into F.DIST.RT:

  ```
  =F.DIST.RT(F.INV.RT(0.05, 5, 10), 5, 10)  'Result: 0.05
  ```

- **Applications in ANOVA:** Use to determine rejection thresholds for variance analysis and other F-tests.

FINV Function

Compatibility Functions

Introduction

The FINV function is a legacy function used to calculate the inverse of the F-distribution. It determines the F-statistic value for a given right-tail probability and specified degrees of freedom. This function has been replaced by F.INV.RT in modern versions of Excel but is maintained for backward compatibility.

Simple explanation: Returns the F-statistic value corresponding to a right-tail probability.

Common use cases: Used in older Excel models for hypothesis testing and determining critical values in variance analysis.

When to use this function: Use when working with older Excel versions that do not support F.INV.RT.

Syntax

```
=FINV(probability, deg_freedom1, deg_freedom2)
```

- **probability**: The right-tail probability for which to compute the F-statistic.
- **deg_freedom1**: Degrees of freedom for the numerator.
- **deg_freedom2**: Degrees of freedom for the denominator.

Worked Example

Challenge: Find the F-statistic value corresponding to a right-tail probability of 0.05, with 5 numerator degrees of freedom and 10 denominator degrees of freedom.

Formula:

```
=FINV(0.05, 5, 10)
```

Result: 3.325835
Explanation: The function calculates the F-statistic value such that the area to the right under the curve is 0.05.

	A	B
1	**Example**	
2	=FINV(0.05, 5, 10)	
3	**Answer**	
4	3.325835	

Explore Further with GPT

Ask GPT how to update formulas using FINV to the newer F.INV.RT function or how to integrate it into modern statistical workflows.

Tips for Using FINV

- **Backward compatibility:** Use FINV only when working with older Excel files. For modern projects, use F.INV.RT.
- **Combine with FDIST:** Validate the result by calculating the right-tail probability:

  ```
  =FDIST(FINV(0.05, 5, 10), 5, 10)  'Result: 0.05
  ```

- **Modern alternatives:** Switch to F.INV.RT for better readability and compatibility with modern Excel:

  ```
  =F.INV.RT(0.05, 5, 10)
  ```

FISHER Function

Statistical Functions

Introduction

The FISHER function returns the Fisher transformation of a given value. This transformation is used in statistics to convert a Pearson correlation coefficient into a form that is approximately normally distributed, enabling hypothesis testing and confidence intervals for correlations.

Simple explanation: Transforms a correlation coefficient into a value suitable for statistical testing.

Common use cases: Used in hypothesis testing, statistical modeling, and transforming correlation coefficients.

When to use this function: Use when analyzing or testing correlations in datasets.

Syntax

```
=FISHER(x)
```

- **x**: The numeric value to transform, typically a correlation coefficient between -1 and 1.

Worked Example

Challenge: Perform a Fisher transformation on the correlation coefficient 0.8.

Formula:

```
=FISHER(0.8)
```

Result: 1.098612
Explanation: The function transforms the correlation coefficient of 0.8 into its Fisher-transformed value.

	A	B
1	**Example**	
2	=FISHER(0.8)	
3	**Answer**	
4	1.098612	

Explore Further with GPT

Ask GPT how to use FISHER alongside FISHERINV for reverse transformations or in building confidence intervals for correlation coefficients.

Tips for Using FISHER

- **Input range:** Ensure xxx is between -1 and 1 (inclusive). Values outside this range result in a #NUM! error.
- **Reverse transformation:** Use FISHERINV to revert the Fisher-transformed value back to a correlation coefficient:

  ```
  =FISHERINV(1.098612289)  'Result: 0.8
  ```

- **Statistical applications:** Use FISHER to analyze correlations in conjunction with CORREL:

  ```
  =FISHER(CORREL(A1:A10, B1:B10))
  ```

- **Confidence intervals:** Pair with standard error calculations to derive confidence intervals for correlation coefficients.

FISHERINV Function

Statistical Functions

Introduction

The FISHERINV function returns the inverse Fisher transformation of a value. It converts a Fisher-transformed value back into a correlation coefficient, making it useful for interpreting results from statistical analyses involving the Fisher transformation.

Simple explanation: Converts a Fisher-transformed value back to a correlation coefficient.

Common use cases: Used in statistical modeling and analysis to interpret transformed correlation coefficients.

When to use this function: Use when converting Fisher-transformed values back to their original correlation coefficient form.

Syntax

```
=FISHERINV(y)
```

- **y**: The numeric value to invert, typically the output of a FISHER function.

Worked Example

Challenge: Convert the Fisher-transformed value 1.098612289 back to a correlation coefficient.

Formula:

```
=FISHERINV(1.098612289)
```

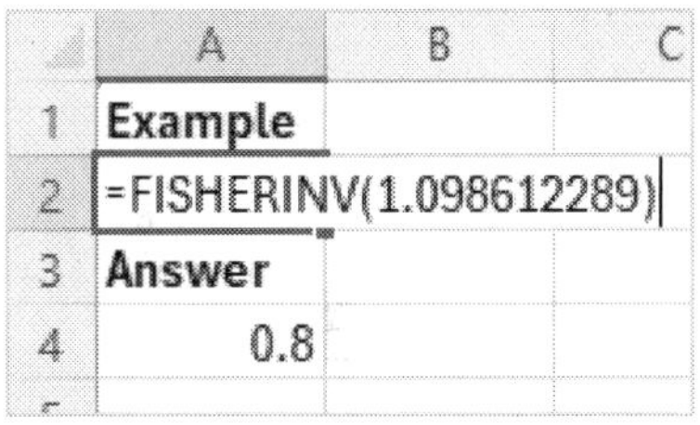

Result: 0.8
Explanation: The function reverses the Fisher transformation, converting the value back to a correlation coefficient of 0.8.

Explore Further with GPT

Ask GPT how to combine FISHERINV with FISHER for bidirectional transformations or how to use it in constructing confidence intervals for correlations.

Tips for Using FISHERINV

- **Input considerations:** The input should be a Fisher-transformed value; it may not produce meaningful results for arbitrary values.
- **Combine with FISHER:** Use FISHERINV to verify transformations are reversible:

  ```
  =FISHERINV(FISHER(0.8))  'Result: 0.8
  ```

- **Statistical applications:** Pair with confidence interval calculations and the CORREL function for analyzing correlation data:

  ```
  =FISHERINV(FISHER(CORREL(A1:A10, B1:B10)))
  ```

- **Error handling:** Ensure inputs are numeric to avoid #VALUE! errors.

FIXED Function

Text Functions

Introduction

The FIXED function rounds a number to a specified number of decimal places and returns the result as text. It can optionally include or exclude commas for thousands separators, making it useful for formatting numbers for display or reporting.

Simple explanation: Rounds a number and formats it as text with optional thousands separators.

Common use cases: Used in financial reports, dashboards, and formatted text-based number displays.

When to use this function: Use when you need to display numbers with specific decimal formatting or as text.

Syntax

```
=FIXED(number, [decimals], [no_commas])
```

- **number**: The number to format.
- **[decimals]** *(optional)*: The number of decimal places to include. Defaults to 2.
- **[no_commas]** *(optional)*: A logical value indicating whether to omit commas:
  - FALSE (or omitted): Includes commas.
  - TRUE: Omits commas.

Worked Example

Challenge: Format the number 1234.5678 with 2 decimal places and include commas.

Formula:

```
=FIXED(1234.5678, 2)
```

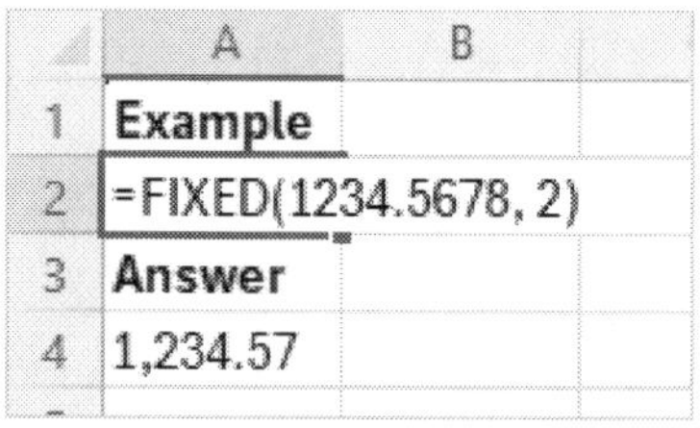

Result: "1,234.57"
Explanation: The function rounds the number to 2 decimal places and includes a comma as a thousands separator

Explore Further with GPT

Ask GPT how to combine FIXED with other text functions like TEXT for customized formatting or how to use it in creating formatted reports.

Tips for Using FIXED

- **Text output:** The result is always a text string, not a number. Use VALUE to convert it back to a numeric format if needed:

  ```
  =VALUE(FIXED(1234.5678, 2))
  ```

- **Alternative function:** Use TEXT for more flexible formatting options:

  ```
  =TEXT(1234.5678, "#,##0.00")
  ```

FLOOR Function

Compatibility Functions

Introduction

The FLOOR function rounds a number down to the nearest multiple of a specified significance. It is particularly useful in financial calculations, inventory management, and any scenario requiring rounding to specified increments.

Simple explanation: Rounds a number down to the nearest specified multiple.

Common use cases: Used in financial modeling, pricing calculations, and rounding values to standardized increments.

When to use this function: Use when you need to round down numbers to a multiple of your choice.

Syntax

```
=FLOOR(number, significance)
```

- **number**: The number to round.
- **significance**: The multiple to which the number should be rounded down

Worked Example

Challenge: Round the number 27.8 down to the nearest multiple of 5.

Formula:

```
=FLOOR(27.8, 5)
```

Result: 25

Explanation: The function rounds 27.8 down to the nearest multiple of 5, which is 25.

	A	B
1	**Example**	
2	=FLOOR(27.8, 5)	
3	**Answer**	
4	25	

Explore Further with GPT

Ask GPT how to use FLOOR with other rounding functions like CEILING or ROUND for precise number manipulation.

Tips for Using FLOOR

- **Positive and negative numbers:** The function always rounds down, regardless of whether the number is positive or negative.
- **Significance sign matters:** The significance argument must have the same sign as the number, or the function will return a #NUM! error.
- **Alternative functions:** Use FLOOR.MATH for additional flexibility in rounding behavior with positive or negative numbers:

  ```
  =FLOOR.MATH(-27.8, 5)
  ```

- **Practical applications:** Use FLOOR to standardize values like currency denominations or time intervals

FLOOR.MATH Function

Math & Trigonometry Functions

Introduction

The FLOOR.MATH function rounds a number down to the nearest multiple of a specified significance. It provides greater flexibility compared to the FLOOR function by allowing control over how negative numbers are rounded.

Simple explanation: Rounds a number down to the nearest multiple, with more control over negative number behavior.

Common use cases: Used in financial calculations, inventory management, and time rounding, especially when working with both positive and negative numbers.

When to use this function: Use when rounding numbers to specific increments with greater control over rounding direction for negative values.

Syntax

```
=FLOOR.MATH(number, [significance], [mode])
```

- **number**: The number to round.
- **[significance]** *(optional)*: The multiple to which the number should be rounded. Defaults to 1.
- **[mode]** *(optional)*: A logical value determining how negative numbers are rounded:
    - 0 or omitted: Rounds negative numbers down (away from zero).
    - 1: Rounds negative numbers up (toward zero).

Worked Example

Challenge: Round 27.8 down to the nearest multiple of 5.

Formula:

```
=FLOOR.MATH(27.8, 5)
```

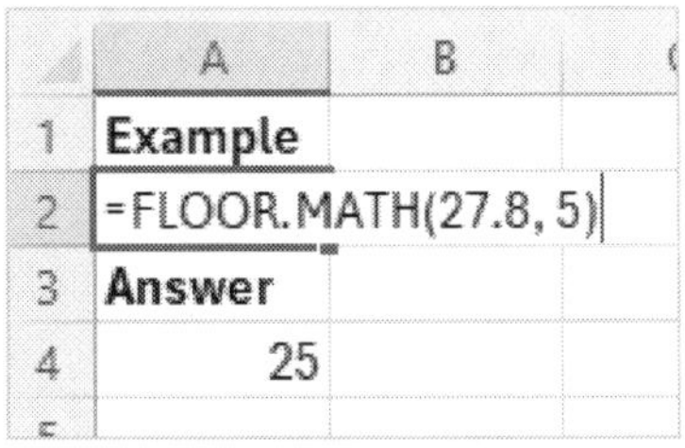

Result: 25
Explanation: The function rounds 27.8 down to the nearest multiple of 5, which is 25.

Tips for Using FLOOR.MATH

- **Default behavior:** If no significance or mode is specified, the function defaults to rounding to the nearest integer down.
- **Control over negatives:** The mode argument offers flexibility for handling negative numbers, making it more versatile than FLOOR.
- **Significance and sign:** The significance argument must match the sign of the number, or the function will return a #NUM! error.

FLOOR.PRECISE Function

Math & Trigonometry Functions

Introduction

The FLOOR.PRECISE function rounds a number down to the nearest multiple of a specified significance. Unlike the FLOOR function, it always rounds numbers toward zero, providing consistent behavior for both positive and negative values.

Simple explanation: Rounds a number down to the nearest multiple, always toward zero.

Common use cases: Used in financial calculations, inventory management, and rounding tasks requiring consistent treatment of positive and negative numbers.

When to use this function: Use when rounding numbers with consistent "toward zero" behavior for both positive and negative values is necessary.

Syntax

```
=FLOOR.PRECISE(number, [significance])
```

- **number**: The number to round.
- **[significance]** *(optional)*: The multiple to which the number should be rounded. Defaults to 1

Worked Example

Challenge: Round 27.8 down to the nearest multiple of 5.

Formula:

```
=FLOOR.PRECISE(27.8, 5)
```

	A	B	C
1	**Example**		
2	=FLOOR.PRECISE(27.8, 5)		
3	**Answer**		
4	25		
5			

Result: 25
Explanation: The function rounds 27.8 down to the nearest multiple of 5, which is 25.

Explore Further with GPT

Ask GPT how to use FLOOR.PRECISE alongside CEILING.PRECISE for consistent rounding in datasets or how it compares to FLOOR and FLOOR.MATH.

Tips for Using FLOOR.PRECISE

- **Sign-consistent rounding:** Unlike FLOOR, the rounding behavior is always toward zero, regardless of the number's sign.
- **Default significance:** If no significance is provided, the function defaults to rounding down to the nearest integer.
- **Use cases in finance:** Ideal for consistent rounding of amounts, such as taxes or discounts, that require uniform behavior for both gains and losses:

  ```
  =FLOOR.PRECISE(123.45, 0.1)   'Rounds to the nearest 0.1
  ```

- **Significance sign ignored:** Unlike FLOOR, the sign of the significance argument is ignored, allowing more flexible usage.

FORECAST Function

Statistical Functions

Introduction

The FORECAST function predicts a future value based on a linear trend derived from existing data points. It uses the least-squares method to calculate the relationship between the dependent variable (known values) and the independent variable (known x-values).

Simple explanation: Predicts a value using a linear trend from existing data.

Common use cases: Used in sales forecasting, trend analysis, and predictive modeling.

When to use this function: Use when you need to estimate future outcomes based on historical data trends.

Syntax

```
=FORECAST(x, known_y's, known_x's)
```

- **x**: The data point for which you want to predict a value.
- **known_y's**: The range of dependent data (y-values).
- **known_x's**: The range of independent data (x-values).

Worked Example

Challenge: Predict the sales for a new product after 7 months based on historical data.

Formula:

```
=FORECAST(7, B2:B6, A2:A6)
```

Result: 500
Explanation: The function predicts sales of 500 units after 7 months based on the linear trend.

	A	B	C	D	E	F
1	Months (x)	Sales (y)		Example		
2	1	200		=FORECAST(7, B2:B6, A2:A6)		
3	2	250		Answer		
4	3	300		500		
5	4	350				
6	5	400				
7						

Explore Further with GPT

Ask GPT how to use FORECAST in combination with more advanced functions like FORECAST.LINEAR or for non-linear trend predictions using exponential or polynomial models.

Tips for Using FORECAST

- **Linear trends only:** This function assumes a linear relationship between x and y. For non-linear trends, consider other methods or functions like FORECAST.ETS.
- **Match data types:** Ensure the known_y's and known_x's are numeric and correspond to each other in size.
- **Error handling:** If known_x's and known_y's are of different lengths, the function returns a #N/A error.
- **Alternative functions:** Use FORECAST.LINEAR in modern Excel for the same functionality with updated naming conventions.

FORECAST.ETS Function

Statistical Functions

Introduction

The FORECAST.ETS function predicts a future value using an exponential smoothing algorithm. It accounts for seasonality in time series data, making it ideal for forecasting trends with periodic patterns, such as sales, inventory levels, or website traffic.

Simple explanation: Predicts future values based on exponential smoothing and seasonality.

Common use cases: Used in sales forecasting, financial modeling, and analyzing seasonal data trends.

When to use this function: Use when forecasting time series data with recurring patterns or seasonality.

Syntax

```
=FORECAST.ETS(target_date, values, timeline, [seasonality], [data_completion], [aggregation])
```

- **target_date**: The point in time for which you want to forecast a value.
- **values**: The historical data points (dependent variable).
- **timeline**: The corresponding timeline (independent variable).
- **[seasonality]** *(optional)*: A numeric value indicating the seasonal pattern:
    - 0: No seasonality (detect automatically).
    - 1: No seasonality (ignore it).
    - Positive integer: Specifies the number of data points in a seasonal cycle.
- **[data_completion]** *(optional)*: Logical value determining how to handle missing data:
    - TRUE (default): Interpolates missing points.
    - FALSE: Treats missing points as zeros.
- **[aggregation]** *(optional)*: Specifies how to aggregate data with duplicate timestamps (e.g., AVERAGE, SUM, MAX).

Worked Example

Challenge: Forecast sales for Month 13 based on monthly sales data with seasonality.

Formula:

```
=FORECAST.ETS(13, B2:B13, A2:A13)
```

Result: Predicted sales for Month 13 (e.g., 300 depending on the seasonal trend).

	A	B	C	D	E	F
1	Month	Sales		Example		
2	1	200		=FORECAST.ETS(13, B2:B13, A2:A13)		
3	2	250		Answer		
4	3	300		238.15		
5	4	400				
6	5	150				
7	6	200				
8	7	250				
9	8	300				
10	9	400				
11	10	150				
12	11	200				
13	12	250				

FORECAST.ETS.CONFINT Function

Statistical Functions

Introduction

The FORECAST.ETS.CONFINT function calculates the confidence interval for a forecasted value returned by the FORECAST.ETS function.

Simple explanation: Returns the range of confidence around a forecast, indicating prediction reliability.

Common use cases: Used in financial modeling, projections, and risk analysis to assess forecast accuracy.

When to use this function: Use when forecasting with FORECAST.ETS to include confidence intervals for more informed decision-making.

Syntax

```
=FORECAST.ETS.CONFINT(target_date, values, timeline, [confidence_level], [seasonality], [data_completion], [aggregation])
```

- **target_date**: The point in time for which to calculate the confidence interval.
- **values**: The historical data points (dependent variable).
- **timeline**: The corresponding timeline (independent variable).
- **[confidence_level]** *(optional)*: A numeric value (between 0 and 1) indicating the confidence level for the interval. Defaults to 95% (0.95).
- **[seasonality]** *(optional)*: Specifies the seasonal pattern:
  - See above;
- **[data_completion]** *(optional)***:** Logical value for handling missing data (TRUE for interpolation, FALSE for zeros).
- **[aggregation]** *(optional)***:** Specifies how to aggregate duplicate timestamps (e.g., AVERAGE, SUM).

Worked Example

Challenge: Calculate the 95% confidence interval for Month 13 sales based on seasonal sales data.

Formula:

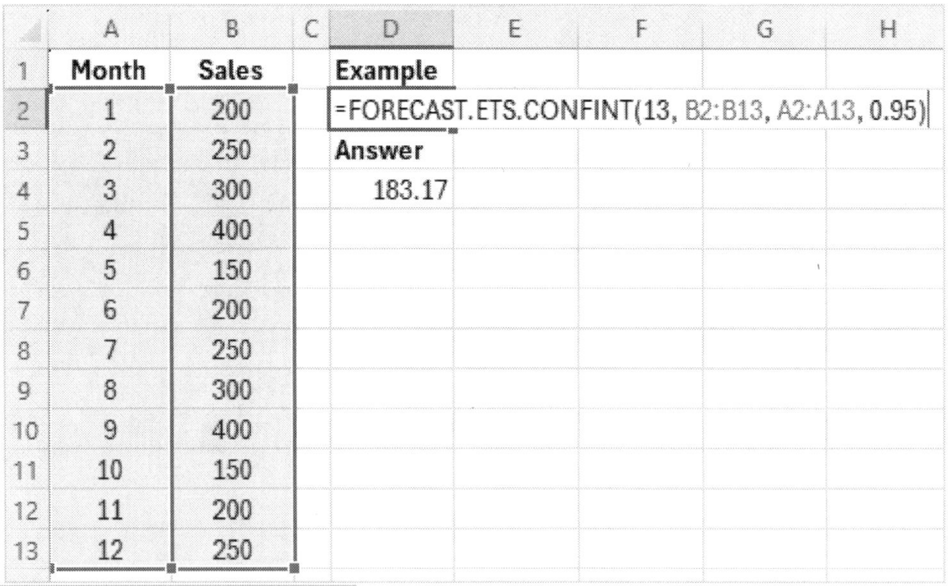

	A	B	C	D	E	F	G	H
1	Month	Sales		Example				
2	1	200		=FORECAST.ETS.CONFINT(13, B2:B13, A2:A13, 0.95)				
3	2	250		Answer				
4	3	300		183.17				
5	4	400						
6	5	150						
7	6	200						
8	7	250						
9	8	300						
10	9	400						
11	10	150						
12	11	200						
13	12	250						

```
=FORECAST.ETS.CONFINT(13, B2:B13, A2:A13, 0.95)
```

Result: Returns a confidence interval range, such as 50.

Explanation: This indicates the forecasted value for Month 13 is ±50 within the 95% confidence level.

FORECAST.ETS.SEASONALITY Function

Statistical Functions

Introduction

The FORECAST.ETS.SEASONALITY function detects the length of the seasonal pattern in time series data. It helps identify recurring trends or cycles, which can then be used to improve forecasting accuracy with the FORECAST.ETS function.

Simple explanation: Returns the number of data points in a recurring seasonal pattern.

Common use cases: Used in sales forecasting, trend analysis, and understanding seasonality in time series data.

When to use this function: Use when you need to determine the seasonality of your dataset for more accurate forecasting.

Syntax

```
=FORECAST.ETS.SEASONALITY(values, timeline, [data_completion], [aggregation])
```

- **values**: The historical data points (dependent variable).
- **timeline**: The corresponding timeline (independent variable).
- **[data_completion]** *(optional)*: Logical value determining how to handle missing data:
  - TRUE (default): Interpolates missing points.
  - FALSE: Treats missing points as zeros.
- **[aggregation]** *(optional)***:** Specifies how to aggregate data with duplicate timestamps (e.g., AVERAGE, SUM).

Worked Example

Challenge: Detect the seasonality in monthly sales data.

Formula:

	A	B	C	D	E	F	G	H
1	**Date**	**Sales**		**Example**				
2	Jan-09	2,644,539		=FORECAST.ETS.SEASONALITY(B2:B57, A2:A57, TRUE)				
3	Feb-09	2,359,800		**Answer**				
4	Mar-09	2,925,918		12				
54	May-13	3,933,016						
55	Jun-13	4,146,797						
56	Jul-13	4,176,486						
57	Aug-13	4,347,059						
58								

```
=FORECAST.ETS.SEASONALITY(B2:B13, A2:A13)
```

Result: 12 (The function detects a seasonal cycle of 12 data points, indicating the data follows a yearly seasonal pattern.)

Explore Further with GPT

Ask GPT how to integrate the detected seasonality into FORECAST.ETS models or how to handle irregular seasonality in datasets.

FORECAST.ETS.STAT Function

Statistical Functions

Introduction

The FORECAST.ETS.STAT function calculates various statistical metrics to evaluate the quality and accuracy of a forecast generated by the FORECAST.ETS function. These metrics help in understanding the reliability and performance of the forecast.

Simple explanation: Returns a statistical metric related to the accuracy of an ETS forecast.

Common use cases: Used in data analysis, model evaluation, and forecasting accuracy assessments.

When to use this function: Use when you need to evaluate the reliability and accuracy of forecasts generated by FORECAST.ETS.

Syntax

```
=FORECAST.ETS.STAT(values, timeline, statistic_type, [seasonality], [data_completion], [aggregation])
```

- **values**: The historical data points (dependent variable).
- **timeline**: The corresponding timeline (independent variable).
- **statistic_type**: A numeric value specifying the desired statistical metric:
  - 1: Alpha;2: Beta; 3: Gamma; 4: MASE (Mean Absolute Scaled Error); 5: RMSE (Root Mean Square Error); 6: SMAPE (Symmetric Mean Absolute Percentage Error).
- **[seasonality]** *(optional)*: Specifies the seasonal pattern:
  - 0: Automatic detection; 1: No seasonality; Positive integer: Specifies the number of data points in a seasonal cycle.
- **[data_completion]** *(optional)*: Logical value determining how to handle missing data (TRUE for interpolation, FALSE for zeros).
- **[aggregation]** *(optional)*: Specifies how to aggregate duplicate timestamps (e.g., AVERAGE, SUM)

Worked Example

Challenge: Calculate the RMSE (Root Mean Square Error) for a forecasted sales model.

Formula:

```
=FORECAST.ETS.STAT(B2:B9, A2:A9, 5)
```

Result: 0.26

Explanation: The function calculates the RMSE for the forecasted model, providing a measure of forecast accuracy.

	A	B	C	D	E	F	G
1	Month	Sales		Example			
2	1	200		=FORECAST.ETS.STAT(B2:B9, A2:A9, 5)			
3	2	250		Answer			
4	3	300		0.26			
5	4	400					
6	5	150					
7	6	200					
8	7	250					
9	8	300					
10							

FORECAST.LINEAR Function

Statistical Functions

Introduction

The FORECAST.LINEAR function predicts a future value based on a linear trend derived from existing data points. It is functionally identical to the older FORECAST function, providing a more descriptive name for modern Excel users.

Simple explanation: Predicts a value using a linear trend from existing data.

Common use cases: Used in sales forecasting, trend analysis, and predictive modeling where linear relationships exist.

When to use this function: Use when you need to estimate future outcomes based on historical data trends in a linear context.

Syntax

```
=FORECAST.LINEAR(x, known_y's, known_x's)
```

- **x**: The data point for which you want to predict a value.
- **known_y's**: The range of dependent data (y-values).
- **known_x's**: The range of independent data (x-values).

Worked Example

Challenge: Predict the sales for a new product after 7 months based on historical data.

Formula:

```
=FORECAST.LINEAR(7, B2:B6,
A2:A6)
```

Result: 530

Explanation: The function predicts sales of 530 units after 7 months based on the linear trend.

	A	B	C	D	E	F
1	Month	Sales		Example		
2	1	200		=FORECAST.LINEAR(7, B2:B6, A2:A6)		
3	2	250		Answer		
4	3	300		530		
5	4	400				
6	5	400				
7						

Explore Further with GPT

Ask GPT how to enhance linear forecasts by combining FORECAST.LINEAR with statistical tools like regression analysis or to compare its output with exponential or seasonal forecasts.

Tips for Using FORECAST.LINEAR

- **Linear trends only:** This function assumes a linear relationship between x and y. For non-linear trends, consider other forecasting methods such as FORECAST.ETS.
- **Ensure data alignment:** The known_y's and known_x's ranges must be the same size and correspond directly to avoid #N/A errors.
- **Backward compatibility:** Use FORECAST.LINEAR instead of the older FORECAST function for clarity in modern Excel workbooks.

FORMULATEXT Function

Lookup & Reference Functions

Introduction

The FORMULATEXT function returns a text string that displays the formula in a specified cell. It is useful for auditing, documenting, or explaining formulas in a workbook.

Simple explanation: Displays the formula used in a specific cell as text.

Common use cases: Used in formula auditing, creating documentation, or sharing formula logic with others.

When to use this function: Use when you want to show the actual formula in a cell instead of its calculated result.

Syntax

```
=FORMULATEXT(reference)
```

- **reference**: The cell or range containing the formula you want to display.

Worked Example

Challenge: Display the formula used in cell A2.

1. Suppose cell A2 contains the following formula:

```
=SUM(B1:B10)
```

Formula:

```
=FORMULATEXT(A2)
```

Result: =SUM(B1:B10)
Explanation: The function displays the exact formula from cell A2 as a text string.

	A	B	C
1	**Example**		
2	=SUM(B1:B10)		
3	**Answer**		
4	=SUM(B1:B10)		
5			

Explore Further with GPT

Ask GPT how to use FORMULATEXT for automated formula documentation or combine it with conditional logic to audit spreadsheets.

Tips for Using FORMULATEXT

- **Reference limitations:** The function only works with formulas. It returns #N/A if the referenced cell contains static values or is empty.
- **Use with dynamic ranges:** Combine with functions like INDIRECT to display formulas from dynamically referenced cells:

```
=FORMULATEXT(INDIRECT("A1"))
```

- **Spreadsheet documentation:** Use FORMULATEXT in summary sheets to create a self-documenting workbook by showing key formulas alongside their results.
- **Error handling:** Wrap the function in IFERROR to handle non-formula cells gracefully:

```
=IFERROR(FORMULATEXT(A1), "No formula")
```

FREQUENCY Function

Statistical Functions

Introduction

The FREQUENCY function calculates how often values occur within a range of numbers and returns an array of frequencies. It is typically used to create frequency distributions or histograms.

Simple explanation: Counts how many values fall into specific intervals (bins).

Common use cases: Used in data analysis, summarizing large datasets, and creating histograms.

When to use this function: Use when analyzing data distributions or grouping data into intervals.

Syntax

```
=FREQUENCY(data_array, bins_array)
```

- **data_array**: The range of numbers to analyze.
- **bins_array**: The intervals (bins) into which you want to group the data

Worked Example

Challenge: Count how many test scores fall into specific intervals.

Bins: 50, 70, 90

Formula:

```
=FREQUENCY(A2:A9, B2:B4)
```

Result (array):

Bins	Frequency
≤50	1
51-70	3
71-90	4
>90	0

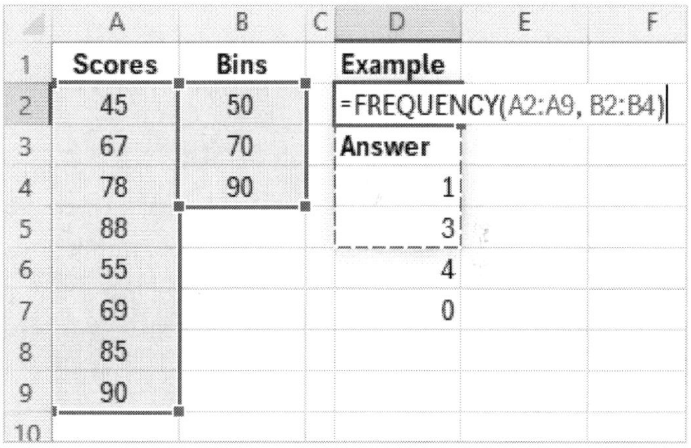

Explanation: The function counts how many scores fall into each bin and spills the result into adjacent cells.

Explore Further with GPT

Ask GPT how to visualize frequency distributions as histograms or how to adjust bin sizes dynamically based on data range.

Tips for Using FREQUENCY

- **Array function:** This function returns an array of values. Select a range of cells for the output and press CTRL+SHIFT+ENTER (or simply enter in modern Excel with dynamic arrays).
- **Additional bin:** The result always includes an extra bin for values greater than the largest bin in bins_array.

F.TEST Function

Statistical Functions

Introduction

The F.TEST function returns the result of an F-test, which determines whether there is a significant difference between the variances of two datasets. It is commonly used in hypothesis testing to compare the variability of two populations.

Simple explanation: Calculates the probability that two datasets have the same variance.

Common use cases: Used in ANOVA (Analysis of Variance), statistical modeling, and hypothesis testing.

When to use this function: Use when comparing the variances of two datasets to test for statistical significance.

Syntax

```
=F.TEST(array1, array2)
```

- **array1**: The first dataset (numeric values).
- **array2**: The second dataset (numeric values).

Worked Example

Challenge: Compare the variances of two datasets.

Formula:

```
=F.TEST(A2:A6, B2:B6)
```

Result: 0.433763

Explanation: The function returns the probability that the variances of the two groups are not significantly different. In this case, a p-value of 0.433763 suggests no strong evidence to reject the null hypothesis (equal variances).

	A	B	C	D	E
1	Group A	Group B		Example	
2	10	8		=F.TEST(A2:A6, B2:B6)	
3	12	9		Answer	
4	14	11		0.433763	
5	16	12			
6	18	13			
7					

Explore Further with GPT

Ask GPT how to interpret p-values in F-tests or how to combine F.TEST with other statistical methods like T.TEST or ANOVA.

Tips for Using F.TEST

- **Interpret p-values:** A p-value below 0.05 typically indicates a significant difference in variances. A larger p-value suggests the variances are not significantly different.
- **Assumptions:** The test assumes the data in each array are normally distributed.
- **Error handling:** Ensure both arrays contain numeric values and have at least two data points each. Otherwise, the function will return a #DIV/0! error.
- **Use with F-statistics:** Use the p-value with F-statistic results for a complete hypothesis testing workflow.

FTEST Function

Compatibility Function

Introduction

The FTEST function is a legacy function used to perform an F-test, returning the p-value that indicates whether the variances of two datasets are significantly different. It has been replaced by the modern F.TEST function but is still available for backward compatibility.

Simple explanation: Calculates the p-value for comparing the variances of two datasets.

Common use cases: Used in hypothesis testing, statistical analysis, and older Excel workbooks.

When to use this function: Use when working with older Excel versions that do not support the F.TEST function.

Syntax

```
=FTEST(array1, array2)
```

- **array1**: The first dataset (numeric values).
- **array2**: The second dataset (numeric values)

Worked Example

Challenge: Compare the variances of two datasets.

Formula:

```
=FTEST(A2:A6, B2:B6)
```

Result: 0.433763

Explanation: The function calculates the p-value, which represents the probability that the variances of the two datasets are not significantly different. A p-value of 0.4338 suggests no strong evidence to reject the null hypothesis (equal variances).

	A	B	C	D	E
1	Group A	Group B		Example	
2	10	8		=FTEST(A2:A6, B2:B6)	
3	12	9		Answer	
4	14	11		0.433763	
5	16	12			
6	18	13			

Explore Further with GPT

Ask GPT how to transition from using FTEST to F.TEST or how to interpret p-values in the context of hypothesis testing.

Tips for Using FTEST

- **Backward compatibility:** Use FTEST only when working with older Excel workbooks. For modern Excel versions, use F.TEST.
- **Interpret p-values:** A smaller p-value (e.g., < 0.05) indicates significantly different variances, while a larger p-value suggests similarity.
- **Modern alternative:** Replace FTEST with F.TEST in new projects for enhanced clarity and functionality:

  ```
  =F.TEST(A2:A6, B2:B6)
  ```

FV Function

Financial Functions

Introduction

The FV function calculates the future value of an investment based on periodic, constant payments and a constant interest rate. It is widely used in financial analysis for savings, investments, and loan forecasting.

Simple explanation: Calculates the future value of an investment or loan.

Common use cases: Used in financial planning, retirement savings calculations, and investment forecasting.

When to use this function: Use when determining how much an investment will grow over time with regular contributions and a fixed interest rate.

Syntax

```
=FV(rate, nper, pmt, [pv], [type])
```

- **rate**: The interest rate per period.
- **nper**: The total number of payment periods.
- **pmt**: The payment made each period (must remain constant).
- **[pv]** *(optional)*: The present value (initial amount). Defaults to 0.
- **[type]** *(optional)*: Specifies when payments are due:
  - 0 or omitted: At the end of the period.
  - 1: At the beginning of the period.

Worked Example

Challenge: Calculate the future value of saving $200 per month for 5 years with a 5% annual interest rate, compounded monthly.

Data:

- **Rate**: 5% / 12 (monthly interest rate).
- **Nper**: 5 * 12 (5 years, 12 months per year).
- **Pmt**: -200 (negative because it's an outgoing payment).
- **Pv**: 0 (no initial investment).
- **Type**: 0 (payments at the end of the period).

	A	B	C
1	**Example**		
2	=FV(5%/12, 5*12, -200, 0, 0)		
3	**Answer**		
4	13,601.22		

Formula:

```
=FV(5%/12, 5*12, -200, 0, 0)
```

Result: 13,601.22
Explanation: Saving $200 per month at 5% annual interest results in $13,601.22 after 5 years.

FVSCHEDULE Function

Financial Functions

Introduction

The FVSCHEDULE function calculates the future value of an investment based on an initial principal and a schedule of varying interest rates. This function is useful when dealing with investments that have different rates over time, rather than a fixed rate.

Simple explanation: Calculates the future value of an investment with a series of changing interest rates.

Common use cases: Used in investment analysis, forecasting returns, and evaluating variable-rate savings or loans.

When to use this function: Use when an investment's interest rate changes over time, requiring a more dynamic calculation.

Syntax

```
=FVSCHEDULE(principal, schedule)
```

- **principal**: The initial investment amount.
- **schedule**: An array or range of interest rates applied over time.

Worked Example

Challenge: Calculate the future value of a $1,000 investment with varying annual interest rates over three years: 5%, 3%, and 4%.

Formula:

```
=FVSCHEDULE(1000, B2:B4)
```

	A	B	C	D	E	F
1	Year	Rate		Example		
2	1	5%		=FVSCHEDULE(1000, B2:B4)		
3	2	3%		Answer		
4	3	4%		1,124.76		

Result: 1,124.76

Explanation: The function calculates the compounded future value of $1,000 over three years with the rates 5%, 3%, and 4% applied sequentially:

- Year 1: 1000×(1+0.05)= 1050
- Year 2: 1050×(1+0.03)=1081.50
- Year 3: 1081.50×(1+0.04)=1124.76

Explore Further with GPT

Ask GPT how to combine `FVSCHEDULE` with scenario analysis or how to create custom schedules dynamically with Excel formulas.

Tips for Using FVSCHEDULE

- **Interest rates as decimals:** Ensure that the rates in the schedule are entered as decimals (e.g., 5% as 0.05).
- **Negative principal:** If the principal is an outflow (e.g., a loan), enter it as a negative value to reflect cash flow direction.

GAMMA Function

Statistical Functions

Introduction

The GAMMA function calculates the Gamma function for a specified value. The Gamma function is an extension of the factorial function to non-integer and complex numbers, widely used in statistics, probability, and advanced mathematics.

Simple explanation: Returns the Gamma function value for a given input.

Common use cases: Used in probability distributions (e.g., Gamma and Beta distributions), statistical modeling, and advanced mathematical computations.

When to use this function: Use when you need to calculate the Gamma function for a given number.

Syntax

```
=GAMMA(x)
```

- **x**: The number for which to calculate the Gamma function. Must be positive or a non-zero negative number.

Worked Example

Challenge: Calculate the Gamma function value for 5.

Formula:

```
=GAMMA(5)
```

	A
1	**Example**
2	=GAMMA(5)
3	**Answer**
4	24

Result: 24

Explanation: The Gamma function for a positive integer n is equivalent to (n−1)!(n-1)!(n−1)!. Therefore, Γ(5)=4!=24.

Explore Further with GPT

Ask GPT how the Gamma function relates to probability distributions like the Gamma or Beta distributions, or how to apply it in advanced statistical scenarios.

Tips for Using GAMMA

- **Non-integer inputs:** The Gamma function works for non-integer values, unlike the factorial function, which only applies to integers.
- **Positive domain:** The function is undefined for zero or negative integers and will return a #NUM! error.
- **Statistical applications:** Combine with other statistical functions like GAMMALN (natural logarithm of the Gamma function) for advanced modeling:

  ```
  =GAMMALN(2.5)   'Result: 0.28468287
  ```

- **Error handling:** Ensure inputs are valid (e.g., positive or non-zero negative numbers) to avoid errors.

GAMMA.DIST Function

Statistical Functions

Introduction

The GAMMA.DIST function returns the Gamma distribution, which is commonly used in probability and statistics for modeling wait times, reliability, and other distributions involving positive continuous variables. It can calculate either the probability density function (PDF) or the cumulative distribution function (CDF).

Simple explanation: Returns the Gamma distribution for a given value, either as a probability density (PDF) or cumulative probability (CDF).

Common use cases: Used in reliability analysis, queuing models, and probability studies involving wait times or variability.

When to use this function: Use when analyzing data modeled by the Gamma distribution or calculating probabilities for such data.

Syntax

```
=GAMMA.DIST(x, alpha, beta, cumulative)
```

- **x**: The value at which to evaluate the function. Must be ≥0.
- **alpha**: The shape parameter (also known as k).
- **beta**: The scale parameter (also known as θ\thetaθ). Must be >0> 0>0.
- **cumulative**: A logical value:
  - TRUE: Returns the cumulative distribution function (CDF).
  - FALSE: Returns the probability density function (PDF).

Worked Example

Challenge: Calculate the cumulative Gamma distribution for x=10, with α=2 and β=3.

Formula:

```
=GAMMA.DIST(10, 2, 3, TRUE)
```

	A	B	C
1	**Example**		
2	=GAMMA.DIST(10, 2, 3, TRUE)		
3	**Answer**		
4	0.845413		

Result: 0.845412695
Explanation: The function calculates the cumulative probability for the Gamma distribution up to x=10 with the given parameters.

Explore Further with GPT

Ask GPT how to fit a Gamma distribution to real-world data or how the parameters α\alphaα and β\betaβ influence the shape and scale of the distribution.

Tips for Using GAMMA.DIST

- **Positive constraints:** Ensure x≥0, α>0, and β>0, or the function will return a #NUM! error.
- **Cumulative vs. PDF:** Use TRUE for cumulative probabilities (e.g., the likelihood of X≤x) and FALSE for probability densities at a specific point.

GAMMADIST Function

Compatibility Function

Introduction

The GAMMADIST function is a legacy function used to calculate the Gamma distribution, either as a probability density function (PDF) or a cumulative distribution function (CDF). It has been replaced by the modern GAMMA.DIST function but is retained for backward compatibility.

Simple explanation: Returns the Gamma distribution for a given value, similar to GAMMA.DIST.

Common use cases: Used in older workbooks for reliability analysis, modeling variability, and calculating probabilities based on the Gamma distribution.

When to use this function: Use when working with older Excel versions that do not support GAMMA.DIST.

Syntax

```
=GAMMADIST(x, alpha, beta, cumulative)
```

- **x**: The value at which to evaluate the function. Must be ≥0\geq 0≥0.
- **alpha**: The shape parameter (also known as kkk).
- **beta**: The scale parameter (also known as θ\thetaθ). Must be >0> 0>0.
- **cumulative**: A logical value:
  - TRUE: Returns the cumulative distribution function (CDF).
  - FALSE: Returns the probability density function (PDF).

Worked Example

Challenge: Calculate the cumulative Gamma distribution for x=10, with α=2 and β=3.

Formula:

```
=GAMMADIST(10, 2, 3, TRUE)
```

Result: 0.845413

Explanation: The function calculates the cumulative probability for the Gamma distribution up to x=10 with the given parameters.

	A	B	C
1	**Example**		
2	=GAMMADIST(10, 2, 3, TRUE)		
3	**Answer**		
4	0.845413		

Explore Further with GPT

Ask GPT how to transition formulas from GAMMADIST to GAMMA.DIST or how the Gamma distribution applies to real-world scenarios like modeling wait times or reliability.

Tips for Using GAMMADIST

- **Backward compatibility:** Use GAMMADIST only in older Excel versions. For modern workbooks, replace it with GAMMA.DIST for clarity and compatibility.
- **Positive constraints:** Ensure x≥0, α>>0, and β>0, or the function will return a #NUM! error.

GAMMA.INV Function

Statistical Functions

Introduction

The GAMMA.INV function calculates the inverse of the cumulative Gamma distribution. It returns the value x for which the cumulative Gamma distribution equals a given probability. This function is used in probability and statistics to determine critical values or thresholds in Gamma-distributed data.

Simple explanation: Finds the value x for a given cumulative probability in the Gamma distribution.

Common use cases: Used in hypothesis testing, reliability analysis, and statistical modeling to determine thresholds or critical points.

When to use this function: Use when solving for the input value x in Gamma-distributed data corresponding to a known cumulative probability.

Syntax

```
=GAMMA.INV(probability, alpha, beta)
```

- **probability**: The cumulative probability (must be between 0 and 1).
- **alpha**: The shape parameter (also known as k).
- **beta**: The scale parameter (also known as θ). Must be >0.

Worked Example

Challenge: Find the value xxx such that the cumulative Gamma distribution equals 0.95 with α=2 and β=3.

Formula:

```
=GAMMA.INV(0.95, 2, 3)
```

	A	B	C
1	**Example**		
2	=GAMMA.INV(0.95, 2, 3)		
3	**Answer**		
4	14.23159		
5			

Result: 14.23159
Explanation: The function determines that the cumulative probability reaches 0.95 at x=14.23159 for the given parameters.

Explore Further with GPT

Ask GPT how to use GAMMA.INV in hypothesis testing workflows or how to apply it in reliability engineering scenarios.

Tips for Using GAMMA.INV

- **Input constraints:** Ensure the probability is between 0 and 1, and both α\alphaα and β\betaβ are positive. Invalid inputs will result in a #NUM! error.
- **Pair with GAMMA.DIST:** Use GAMMA.INV to find xxx values and confirm their cumulative probabilities with GAMMA.DIST:

  ```
  =GAMMA.DIST(GAMMA.INV(0.95, 2, 3), 2, 3, TRUE)  'Result: 0.95
  ```

- **Statistical applications:** Commonly used in reliability engineering to calculate failure thresholds or critical values in Gamma-distributed data.

GAMMAINV Function

Compatibility Functions

Introduction

The GAMMAINV function is a legacy function used to calculate the inverse of the cumulative Gamma distribution. It returns the value xxx for which the cumulative Gamma distribution equals a given probability. This function has been replaced by GAMMA.INV in modern Excel versions but remains available for backward compatibility.

Simple explanation: Finds the value xxx corresponding to a cumulative probability in the Gamma distribution.

Common use cases: Used in older Excel workbooks for hypothesis testing, reliability analysis, and determining critical values.

When to use this function: Use when working with older Excel versions that do not support GAMMA.INV.

Syntax

```
=GAMMAINV(probability, alpha, beta)
```

- **probability**: The cumulative probability (must be between 0 and 1).
- **alpha**: The shape parameter (also known as k).
- **beta**: The scale parameter (also known as θ). Must be >0.

Worked Example

Challenge: Find the value xxx such that the cumulative Gamma distribution equals 0.95 with α=2 and β=3.

Formula:

```
=GAMMAINV(0.95, 2, 3)
```

Result: 14.23159
Explanation: The function determines that the cumulative probability reaches 0.95 at x=14.23159 for the given parameters.

	A	B	C
1	**Example**		
2	=GAMMAINV(0.95, 2, 3)		
3	**Answer**		
4	14.23159		

Explore Further with GPT

Ask GPT how to transition formulas from GAMMAINV to GAMMA.INV or how to apply inverse Gamma calculations in practical scenarios like reliability engineering.

Tips for Using GAMMAINV

- **Backward compatibility:** Use GAMMAINV only for older Excel workbooks. For new projects, switch to GAMMA.INV for improved clarity and compatibility:

  ```
  =GAMMA.INV(0.95, 2, 3)
  ```

- **Input constraints:** Ensure the probability is between 0 and 1, and both α\alphaα and β\betaβ are positive. Invalid inputs result in a #NUM! error.

GAMMALN Function

Statistical Functions

Introduction

The GAMMALN function returns the natural logarithm of the Gamma function for a specified positive number. It is often used in probability and statistics to simplify calculations involving large factorials or Gamma distributions.

Simple explanation: Computes the natural logarithm of the Gamma function for a given value.

Common use cases: Used in statistical modeling, probability distribution calculations, and simplifying large computations involving Gamma functions.

When to use this function: Use when working with Gamma distributions or calculating large factorials that require logarithmic values.

Syntax

```
=GAMMALN(x)
```

- **x**: The number for which to calculate the natural logarithm of the Gamma function. Must be positive.

Worked Example

Challenge: Find the natural logarithm of the Gamma function for x=5.

Formula:

```
=GAMMALN(5)
```

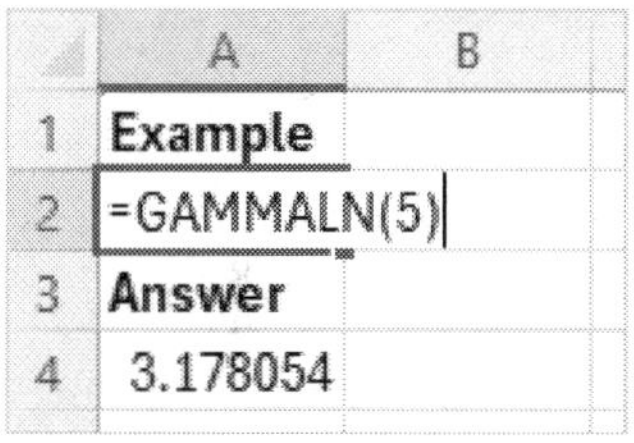

Result: 3.178054
Explanation: The function computes the natural logarithm of Γ(5). Since Γ(5)=4!= 24, the natural logarithm of 24 is ln(24)=3.178054.

Explore Further with GPT

Ask GPT how to use GAMMALN in conjunction with other statistical functions like GAMMA.DIST or how to apply it in statistical modeling and large data computations.

Tips for Using GAMMALN

- **Positive inputs only:** The input x must be positive; otherwise, the function returns a #NUM! error.
- **Simplifies calculations:** Use GAMMALN for calculations involving large Gamma values to avoid computational overflow or underflow.
- **Statistical applications:** Combine with EXP to calculate the Gamma function directly:

  ```
  =EXP(GAMMALN(5))  'Result: 24
  ```

- **Error handling:** Use IFERROR to manage invalid inputs gracefully:

  ```
  =IFERROR(GAMMALN(A1), "Invalid input")
  ```

GAMMALN.PRECISE Function

Statistical Functions

Introduction

The GAMMALN.PRECISE function calculates the natural logarithm of the Gamma function for a specified positive number. It is an updated version of GAMMALN, providing better clarity and compatibility with modern Excel naming conventions.

Simple explanation: Computes the natural logarithm of the Gamma function for a given value.

Common use cases: Used in statistical modeling, probability distributions, and large computations involving Gamma functions.

When to use this function: Use when working with Gamma distributions or factorial calculations requiring logarithmic values.

Syntax

```
=GAMMALN.PRECISE(x)
```

- **x**: The number for which to calculate the natural logarithm of the Gamma function. Must be positive.

Worked Example

Challenge: Find the natural logarithm of the Gamma function for x=5.

Formula:

```
=GAMMALN.PRECISE(5)
```

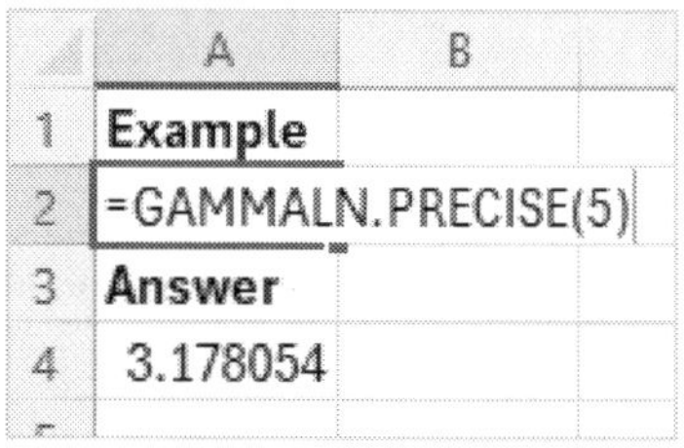

Result: 3.178054
Explanation: The function computes the natural logarithm of Γ(5). Since Γ(5)=4!=24, the natural logarithm of 24 is ln(24)=3.178054.

Explore Further with GPT

Ask GPT how to use GAMMALN.PRECISE in conjunction with other statistical functions like GAMMA.DIST or how to apply it in advanced mathematical models.

Tips for Using GAMMALN.PRECISE

- **Positive inputs only:** The input x must be positive; otherwise, the function returns a #NUM! error.
- **Avoid overflow:** Use GAMMALN.PRECISE in calculations involving large Gamma values to prevent computational errors.
- **Combine with EXP:** Use EXP to calculate the Gamma function directly from the natural logarithm:

  ```
  =EXP(GAMMALN.PRECISE(5))  'Result: 24
  ```

- **Error handling:** Use IFERROR to manage invalid inputs gracefully:

  ```
  =IFERROR(GAMMALN.PRECISE(A1), "Invalid input")
  ```

GAUSS Function

Statistical Functions

Introduction

The GAUSS function calculates the probability that a random variable from a standard normal distribution lies between the mean (0) and a specified number of standard deviations. It is based on the cumulative distribution function (CDF) of the standard normal distribution.

Simple explanation: Returns the probability that a value from a standard normal distribution is between 0 and a given value.

Common use cases: Used in probability analysis, statistics, and areas involving normal distributions.

When to use this function: Use when you need to calculate probabilities for standard normal distributions within a specific range.

Syntax

```
=GAUSS(z)
```

- **z**: The number of standard deviations from the mean (0) for which you want to calculate the probability.

Worked Example

Challenge: Find the probability that a value from a standard normal distribution lies between 0 and 1 standard deviation.

Formula:

```
=GAUSS(1)
```

	A
1	**Example**
2	=GAUSS(1)
3	**Answer**
4	0.341345

Result: 0.341345
Explanation: The function calculates the probability that a standard normal random variable lies between 0 and 1, which is approximately 34.13%.

Explore Further with GPT

Ask GPT how to combine GAUSS with other statistical functions like NORM.DIST or how to use it for z-score calculations in hypothesis testing.

Tips for Using GAUSS

- **Standard normal distribution only:** The GAUSS function assumes a mean of 0 and a standard deviation of 1. For other distributions, use NORM.DIST.
- **Relationship to NORM.S.DIST:** The GAUSS function is equivalent to:

  ```
  =NORM.S.DIST(z, TRUE) - 0.5
  ```

- **Negative values:** The function works symmetrically for negative z-scores, returning negative probabilities.
- **Applications in statistics:** Combine with z-scores to calculate probabilities for real-world data:

  ```
  =GAUSS((x - mean) / std_dev)
  ```

GCD Function

Math & Trigonometry Functions

Introduction

The GCD function calculates the greatest common divisor (GCD) of two or more integers. The GCD is the largest integer that divides all the given numbers without leaving a remainder.

Simple explanation: Finds the largest number that divides all given integers exactly.

Common use cases: Used in mathematics, number theory, and applications requiring simplification of fractions or ratios.

When to use this function: Use when you need to find the greatest common divisor for two or more integers.

Syntax

```
=GCD(number1, [number2], ...)
```

- **number1, number2, ...**: Integers for which you want to calculate the greatest common divisor. At least one number is required.

Worked Example

Challenge: Find the greatest common divisor of 36 and 60.

Formula:

```
=GCD(36, 60)
```

Result: 12
Explanation: The largest number that divides both 36 and 60 without a remainder is 12.

	A	B
1	**Example**	
2	=GCD(36, 60)	
3	**Answer**	
4	12	

Explore Further with GPT

Ask GPT how to use GCD in advanced mathematical operations or how it applies to real-world scenarios like simplifying ratios or solving Diophantine equations.

Tips for Using GCD

- **Positive integers only:** The function works only with positive integers. Negative numbers are treated as their absolute values.
- **Zero as an argument:** If any number is 0, the result is the GCD of the remaining numbers. If all numbers are 0, the function returns 0.
- **Applications with LCM:** Combine GCD with LCM (least common multiple) to solve ratio problems:

  ```
  =LCM(number1, number2) / GCD(number1, number2)
  ```

- **Error handling:** Ensure all inputs are integers to avoid errors.

GEOMEAN Function

Statistical Functions

Introduction

The GEOMEAN function calculates the geometric mean of a set of positive numbers. The geometric mean is the nth root of the product of nnn numbers and is used to find average growth rates, particularly in financial and statistical contexts.

Simple explanation: Returns the average growth rate of a set of positive numbers.

Common use cases: Used in finance for calculating compound interest, investment returns, and population growth rates.

When to use this function: Use when working with datasets involving ratios, percentages, or growth rates.

Syntax

```
=GEOMEAN(number1, [number2], ...)
```

- **number1, number2, ...**: Positive numbers for which you want to calculate the geometric mean. Can be numbers, ranges, or arrays.

Worked Example

Challenge: Calculate the geometric mean of 2, 8, and 16.

Formula:

```
=GEOMEAN(2, 8, 16)
```

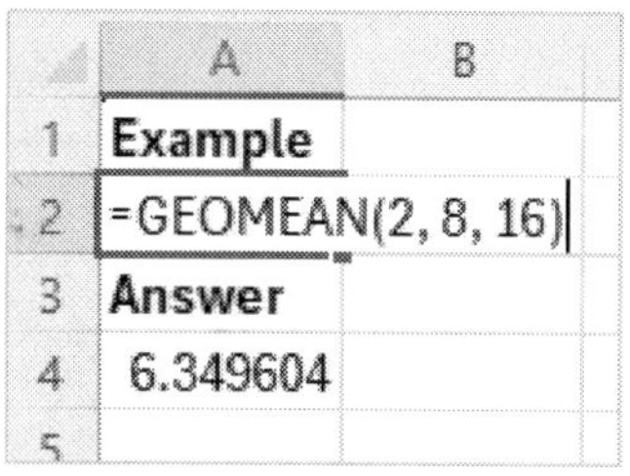

Result: 6.349604

Example with a Range

Challenge: Calculate the geometric mean of values in the range A1:A5 where the data is: 4, 5, 6, 7, and 8.

Formula:

```
=GEOMEAN(A1:A5)
```

Result: 5.6347896
Explanation: The function calculates the geometric mean of all values in the range.

Explore Further with GPT

Ask GPT how to apply GEOMEAN in analyzing investment returns or how it compares to AVERAGE in specific datasets.

Tips for Using GEOMEAN

- **Positive numbers only:** All numbers in the input must be positive. Negative or zero values will result in a #NUM! error.
- **Comparison with arithmetic mean:** Use GEOMEAN when dealing with rates or percentages instead of AVERAGE, which is more appropriate for additive data.

GESTEP Function

Engineering Functions

Introduction

The GESTEP function tests whether a number is greater than or equal to a specified step value. It returns 1 if the number is greater than or equal to the step value and 0 otherwise. It is commonly used in logical tests and comparisons in data analysis.

Simple explanation: Checks if a number is greater than or equal to a threshold and returns 1 if true or 0 if false.

Common use cases: Used in logical comparisons, data filtering, and conditional calculations.

When to use this function: Use when you need a binary output based on whether a number meets or exceeds a threshold.

Syntax

```
=GESTEP(number, [step])
```

- **number**: The value to test.
- **[step]** *(optional)*: The threshold value. Defaults to 0 if omitted.

Worked Example

Challenge: Test if the number 10 is greater than or equal to the step value 5.

Formula:

```
=GESTEP(10, 5)
```

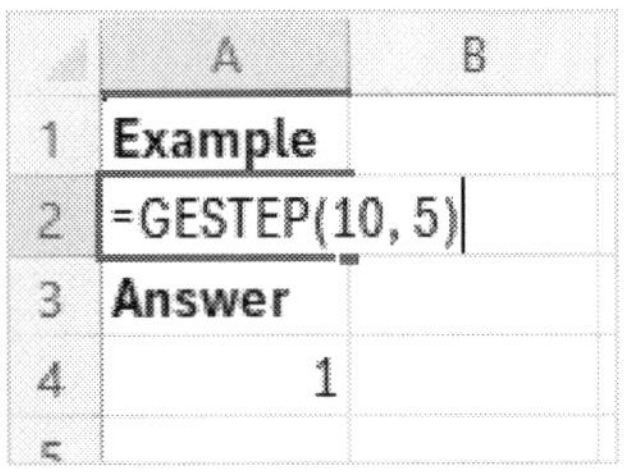

Result: 1
Explanation: Since 10 is greater than or equal to 5, the function returns 1.

Explore Further with GPT

Ask GPT how to use GESTEP in conditional analysis, such as filtering datasets or creating binary classifiers in Excel.

Tips for Using GESTEP

- **Combine with arrays:** Use GESTEP with arrays to test multiple values simultaneously in modern Excel:

  ```
  =GESTEP({1, -1, 5, 10}, 5)
  ```

  Output: {0, 0, 1, 1}

- **Applications in data analysis:** Combine GESTEP with SUM or COUNT to calculate the number of values exceeding a threshold:

  ```
  =SUM(GESTEP(A1:A10, 5))
  ```

- **Error handling:** Ensure all inputs are numeric to avoid #VALUE! errors

GETPIVOTDATA Function

Lookup & Reference Functions

Introduction

The GETPIVOTDATA function retrieves specific data from a PivotTable based on field and item names. It allows for precise referencing of data in PivotTables, even if the layout changes, making it highly useful for dynamic reporting and analysis.

Simple explanation: Extracts data from a PivotTable using specified fields and items.

Common use cases: Used in dynamic dashboards, custom reports, and automated data extraction from PivotTables.

When to use this function: Use when you need to reference specific data points in a PivotTable reliably, regardless of layout changes.

Syntax

```
=GETPIVOTDATA(data_field, pivot_table, [field1, item1, field2, item2], ...)
```

- **data_field**: The name of the value field you want to retrieve (as a string).
- **pivot_table**: A cell reference within the PivotTable you want to extract data from.
- **field1, item1, ...** *(optional)*: Pairs of field names and item names that specify the data to extract.

Worked Example

Challenge: Retrieve the total sales for the "North" region from a PivotTable.

PivotTable Layout:

Region Sales

North 500

South 300

Formula:

`=GETPIVOTDATA("Sales", E1, "Region", "North")`

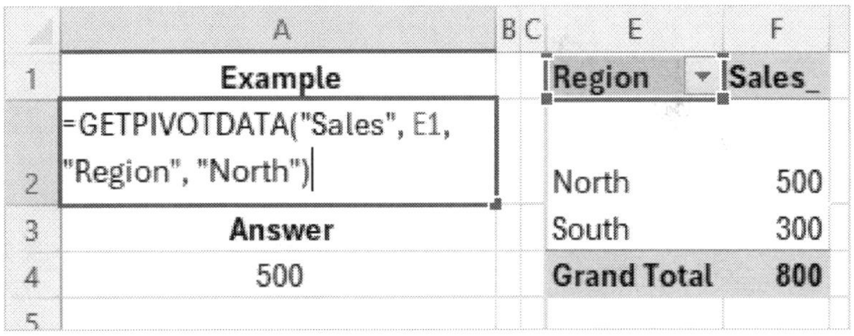

Result: 500
Explanation: The function retrieves the total sales for the "North" region by specifying the data_field ("Sales") and the Region field with the "North" item.

Explore Further with GPT

Ask GPT how to use GETPIVOTDATA for creating dynamic reports or how to automate complex data extraction workflows from PivotTables.

Tips for Using GETPIVOTDATA

- **Dynamic referencing:** The function adapts to layout changes in the PivotTable, ensuring references remain accurate.

GROWTH Function

Statistical Functions

Introduction

The GROWTH function calculates predicted exponential growth based on existing data. It uses the least-squares method to determine the best exponential curve for the given data points, making it useful for forecasting and trend analysis.

Simple explanation: Predicts future values based on an exponential growth trend.

Common use cases: Used in financial forecasting, population studies, and analyzing exponential trends.

When to use this function: Use when you need to model or predict exponential growth trends in your data.

Syntax

```
=GROWTH(known_y's, [known_x's], [new_x's], [const])
```

- **known_y's**: The dependent data points (y-values).
- **[known_x's]** *(optional)*: The independent data points (x-values). Defaults to sequential values if omitted.
- **[new_x's]** *(optional)*: The x-values for which to calculate predicted y-values. Defaults to the same as known_x's if omitted.
- **[const]** *(optional)*: Logical value:
    - TRUE (default): Fits the exponential curve $y=b \cdot m^x$.
    - FALSE: Fits the curve $y=m^x$ (forces b=1).

Worked Example

Challenge: Predict sales for Month 4 based on exponential growth from historical data.

Formula:

```
=GROWTH(B2:B4, A2:A4, {4})
```

Result: 1600

Explanation: The function predicts that sales for Month 4 will be 1600 based on the exponential growth trend in the given data.

	A	B	C	D	E	F
1	Month	Sales		Example		
2	1	200		=GROWTH(B2:B4, A2:A4, {4})		
3	2	400		Answer		
4	3	800		1600		
5						

Explore Further with GPT

Ask GPT how to use GROWTH for multi-variable datasets or to compare it with TREND for linear growth analysis.

Tips for Using GROWTH

- **Logarithmic relationship:** The function assumes an exponential relationship between x and y. For linear trends, use TREND.
- **New x-values:** The new_x's argument allows you to extend predictions into the future:

  ```
  =GROWTH(B2:B10, A2:A10, {11,12,13})
  ```

HARMEAN Function

Statistical Functions

Introduction

The HARMEAN function calculates the harmonic mean of a set of positive numbers. The harmonic mean is a type of average that is particularly useful when dealing with rates or ratios, such as speed or cost per unit.

Simple explanation: Returns the harmonic mean, which is the reciprocal of the arithmetic mean of reciprocals.

Common use cases: Used in calculating average rates, such as travel speeds or financial metrics involving ratios.

When to use this function: Use when averaging rates or proportions to ensure accuracy in weighted calculations.

Syntax

```
=HARMEAN(number1, [number2], ...)
```

- **number1, number2, ...**: Positive numbers for which to calculate the harmonic mean. Can be individual numbers, ranges, or arrays.

Worked Example

Challenge: Calculate the harmonic mean of 4, 5, and 6.

Formula:

```
=HARMEAN(4, 5, 6)
```

Result: 4.864865

	A	B
1	**Example**	
2	=HARMEAN(4, 5, 6)	
3	**Answer**	
4	4.864865	

Explore Further with GPT

Ask GPT how to use HARMEAN in financial calculations or compare it with other means like AVERAGE and GEOMEAN in different scenarios.

Tips for Using HARMEAN

- **Positive numbers only:** The function only works with positive numbers. Negative or zero values will result in a #NUM! error.
- **Comparison with arithmetic and geometric means:**
  - Harmonic mean ≤ Geometric mean ≤ Arithmetic mean (for the same dataset).
- **Ideal for rates and ratios:** Use the harmonic mean when working with datasets involving rates, such as speeds, densities, or financial returns.

HEX2BIN Function

Engineering Functions

Introduction

The HEX2BIN function converts a hexadecimal number to a binary number. This is commonly used in computing and engineering applications where hexadecimal and binary numeral systems are prevalent.

Simple explanation: Converts a hexadecimal number into its binary equivalent.

Common use cases: Used in computing, digital systems design, and converting between numeral systems.

When to use this function: Use when you need to translate hexadecimal values into binary for analysis or processing.

Syntax

```
=HEX2BIN(number, [places])
```

- **number**: The hexadecimal number to convert. This can be a string or numeric value.
- **[places]** *(optional)*: The number of characters to pad the result with. If omitted, the function returns the shortest possible binary representation.

Worked Example

Challenge: Convert the hexadecimal number A to binary.

Formula:

```
=HEX2BIN("A")
```

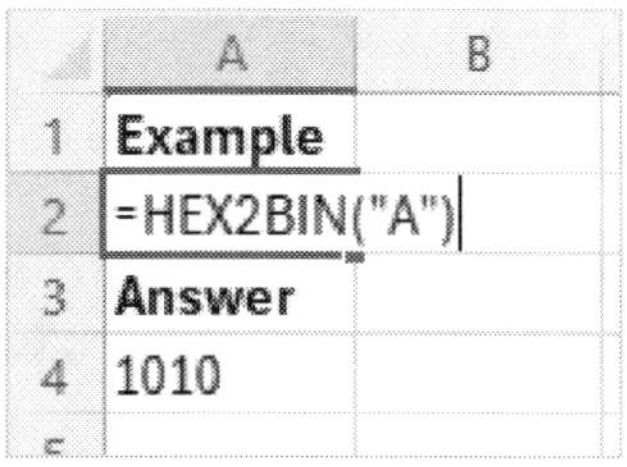

Result: 1010
Explanation: The hexadecimal number A is equivalent to the binary number 1010.

Explore Further with GPT

Ask GPT how to use HEX2BIN in combination with other conversion functions like BIN2DEC or how to automate numeral system conversions in Excel.

Tips for Using HEX2BIN

- **Maximum binary length:** The function supports up to 10 characters in the binary output, corresponding to a hexadecimal input of up to 40 bits.

- **Padding with places:** If the binary result exceeds the specified `places`, the function returns a `#NUM!` error. Ensure the `places` value is large enough for the output:

```
=HEX2BIN("A", 2) 'Result: #NUM! (binary '1010' exceeds 2 places)
```

- **Error handling:** Use `IFERROR` to manage invalid inputs gracefully:

```
=IFERROR(HEX2BIN(A1), "Invalid input")
```

HEX2DEC Function

Engineering Functions

Introduction

The HEX2DEC function converts a hexadecimal number to its decimal equivalent. This function is widely used in computing, engineering, and mathematical contexts to work with different numeral systems.

Simple explanation: Converts a hexadecimal number into its decimal equivalent.

Common use cases: Used in data processing, digital systems design, and numerical conversions.

When to use this function: Use when translating hexadecimal values into decimal for analysis or computations.

Syntax

```
=HEX2DEC(number)
```

- **number**: The hexadecimal number to convert. This can be a string or numeric value.

Worked Example

Challenge: Convert the hexadecimal number A to decimal.

Formula:

```
=HEX2DEC("A")
```

Result: 10
Explanation: The hexadecimal number A is equivalent to the decimal number 10.

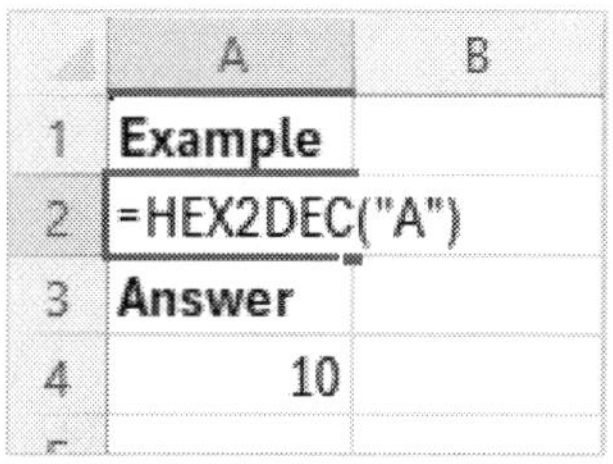

Explore Further with GPT

Ask GPT how to combine HEX2DEC with other numeral system conversions or how to automate multi-step conversions in Excel.

Tips for Using HEX2DEC

- **Maximum input length:** The function supports hexadecimal inputs up to 10 characters, corresponding to 40 bits.
- **Signed numbers:** The function interprets hexadecimal numbers as signed 32-bit integers:

  ```
  =HEX2DEC("7FFFFFFF")  'Result: 2147483647
  ```

  ```
  =HEX2DEC("FFFFFFFF")  'Result: -1
  ```

- **Avoid errors with invalid inputs:** Ensure the number argument contains valid hexadecimal characters (0–9, A–F).

HEX2OCT Function

Engineering Functions

Introduction

The HEX2OCT function converts a hexadecimal number to its octal equivalent. This is particularly useful in computing and engineering applications where hexadecimal and octal numeral systems are commonly used.

Simple explanation: Converts a hexadecimal number into its octal equivalent.

Common use cases: Used in computing, digital systems design, and numeral system conversions.

When to use this function: Use when translating hexadecimal values into octal for analysis or processing.

Syntax

```
=HEX2OCT(number, [places])
```

- **number**: The hexadecimal number to convert. This can be a string or numeric value.
- **[places]** *(optional)*: The number of characters to pad the result with. If omitted, the function returns the shortest possible octal representation.

Worked Example

Challenge: Convert the hexadecimal number A to octal.

Formula:

```
=HEX2OCT("A")
```

Result: 12
Explanation: The hexadecimal number A is equivalent to the octal number 12.

	A	B
1	**Example**	
2	=HEX2OCT("A")	
3	**Answer**	
4	12	

Explore Further with GPT

Ask GPT how to use HEX2OCT in combination with other conversion functions like OCT2BIN or how to apply numeral system conversions in Excel for advanced workflows.

Tips for Using HEX2OCT

- **Maximum output length:** The function supports octal outputs up to 10 characters, corresponding to a hexadecimal input of up to 40 bits.
- **Padding with places:** If the octal result exceeds the specified `places`, the function returns a `#NUM!` error. Ensure the `places` value is large enough for the output:

```
=HEX2OCT("A", 2)  'Result: #NUM! (octal '12' exceeds 2 places)
```

- **Error handling:** Use `IFERROR` to manage invalid inputs gracefully:

```
=IFERROR(HEX2OCT(A1), "Invalid input")
```

HLOOKUP Function

Lookup & Reference Functions

Introduction

The HLOOKUP function searches for a value in the first row of a table and returns a value in the same column from a specified row. It is often used for horizontal lookups where data is organized in rows rather than columns.

Simple explanation: Searches for a value in the first row and returns a value from a specified row in the same column.

Common use cases: Used in data retrieval, report generation, and dynamic referencing in horizontally structured datasets.

When to use this function: Use when working with horizontal tables where you need to find a value based on a key in the first row.

Syntax

```
=HLOOKUP(lookup_value, table_array, row_index_num, [range_lookup])
```

- **lookup_value**: The value to search for in the first row of the table.
- **table_array**: The table or range of data to search.
- **row_index_num**: The row number (relative to the table_array) from which to return a value.
- **[range_lookup]** *(optional)*:
    - TRUE (default): Approximate match.
    - FALSE: Exact match.

Worked Example

Challenge: Look up the sales for "Product B" from the table

Formula:

```
=HLOOKUP("Product B", A1:D2, 2, FALSE)
```

Result: 200

Explanation: The function searches for "Product B" in the first row and returns the corresponding value from the second row.

	A	B	C	D
1	**Product**	**Product A**	**Product B**	**Product C**
2	Sales	100	200	300
3				
4	**Example**			
5	=HLOOKUP("Product B", A1:D2, 2, FALSE)			
6	**Answer**			
7	200			

Explore Further with GPT

Ask GPT how to optimize HLOOKUP for dynamic references or how to switch to XLOOKUP for enhanced functionality in modern Excel.

Tips for Using HLOOKUP

- **Exact vs. approximate matches:** Use FALSE for exact matches to avoid unexpected results when the lookup value is not in the first row.

HOUR Function

Date & Time Functions

Introduction

The HOUR function extracts the hour component from a given time value. It returns an integer ranging from 0 (12:00 AM) to 23 (11:00 PM), making it useful for time-based calculations and data analysis.

Simple explanation: Retrieves the hour from a time value.

Common use cases: Used in time tracking, scheduling, and calculating time differences.

When to use this function: Use when you need to extract or analyze the hour component of a time value.

Syntax

```
=HOUR(serial_number)
```

- **serial_number**: A time value, a cell containing a time, or a formula that returns a time.

Worked Example

Challenge: Extract the hour from the time 14:45.

Formula:

```
=HOUR(TIME(14, 45, 0))
```

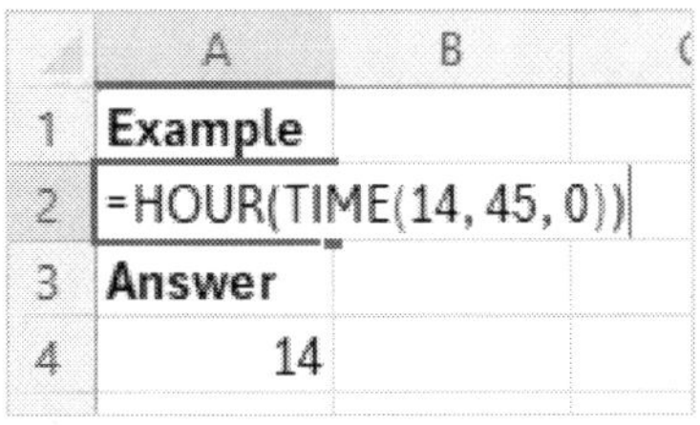

Result: 14
Explanation: The function extracts the hour component (14) from the given time.

Explore Further with GPT

Ask GPT how to use HOUR in time-based calculations like work shift analysis or scheduling automation.

Tips for Using HOUR

- **Time formatting:** Ensure the input cell contains a valid time or a serial number representing a time.
- **Combining with other functions:** Use HOUR alongside MINUTE and SECOND for detailed time analysis:

  ```
  =HOUR(A1) & ":" & MINUTE(A1) & ":" & SECOND(A1)
  ```

- **Error handling:** Wrap the function in IFERROR to handle invalid inputs:

  ```
  =IFERROR(HOUR(A1), "Invalid time")
  ```

HSTACK Function

Lookup & Reference Functions

Introduction

The HSTACK function horizontally stacks multiple arrays, creating a single array by placing each input array side-by-side. The rows in each array remain intact, resulting in a combined array where the arrays are joined horizontally.

- **Simple explanation:** Combines arrays horizontally, preserving their row structures.
- **Common use cases:** Used in data manipulation, combining datasets, and creating horizontally structured arrays.
- **When to use this function:** Use when you need to merge multiple arrays or values into a wider array.

Syntax

```
=HSTACK(array1, [array2], ...)
```

- **array1, array2, ...**: Arrays, ranges, or values to be combined horizontally.

Worked Example

Challenge: Horizontally combine values in ranges A2:A4 and B2:B4.

Formula:

```
=HSTACK(A2:A4, B2:B4)
```

Result:

1	4
2	5
3	6

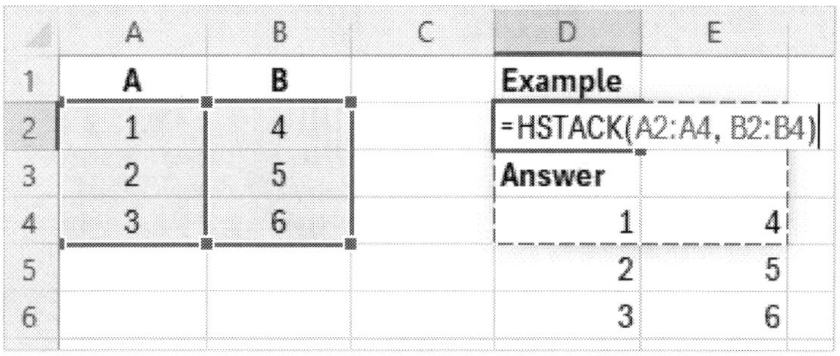

Explanation: The function places values from A2:A4 and B2:B4 side-by-side into a single array.

Explore Further with GPT

Ask GPT how to combine HSTACK with other array manipulation functions like VSTACK or how to use it in data transformation workflows.

Tips for Using HSTACK

- **Dynamic arrays:** The function automatically spills results into adjacent cells. Ensure there is enough space to display the result; otherwise, you'll see a #SPILL! error.
- **Combine with other functions:** Use `HSTACK` with `TRANSPOSE` or `VSTACK` for advanced array manipulations:

```
=VSTACK(HSTACK(A2:A4, B2:B4))
```

HYPERLINK Function

Lookup & Reference Functions

Introduction

The HYPERLINK function creates a clickable link to a specified URL, file path, or cell reference. It enables easy navigation within workbooks or to external resources, enhancing interactivity in your spreadsheets.

Simple explanation: Creates a clickable link to a web page, file, or cell reference.

Common use cases: Used for linking to external websites, opening files, or navigating within workbooks.

When to use this function: Use when you need to add clickable links to simplify navigation.

Syntax

```
=HYPERLINK(link_location, [friendly_name])
```

- **link_location**: The URL, file path, or cell reference to link to.
- **[friendly_name]** *(optional)*: The text or value displayed in the cell. If omitted, the link_location is displayed as the link.

Worked Example

Challenge: Create a hyperlink to the OpenAI website with a user-friendly display name.

Formula:

```
=HYPERLINK("https://www.google.com", "Visit Google")
```

Result:
The cell displays "Visit Google" as a clickable link. Clicking it navigates to the Google website.

Example with File Path

Challenge: Create a hyperlink to a file located at C:\Documents\Report.xlsx.

Formula:

```
=HYPERLINK("C:\Documents\Report.xlsx", "Open Report")
```

Result:
The cell displays "Open Report" as a clickable link. Clicking it opens the specified file.

Explore Further with GPT

Ask GPT how to dynamically generate hyperlinks based on cell data or automate navigation within complex workbooks.

Tips for Using HYPERLINK

- **Dynamic links:** Combine HYPERLINK with other functions like CONCAT or TEXT to create dynamic links:

  ```
  =HYPERLINK("https://example.com/page?id=" & A1, "Open Page")
  ```

HYPGEOM.DIST Function

Statistical Functions

Introduction

The HYPGEOM.DIST function calculates the hypergeometric distribution, which gives the probability of a certain number of successes in a fixed-size sample drawn from a population without replacement. This is commonly used in quality control, card games, and statistical studies involving finite populations.

Simple explanation: Computes the probability of successes in a sample drawn from a finite population.

Common use cases: Used in quality control testing, card probability calculations, and population studies.

When to use this function: Use when analyzing probabilities in scenarios with finite populations and sampling without replacement.

Syntax

```
=HYPGEOM.DIST(sample_s, number_sample, population_s, number_pop, cumulative)
```

- **sample_s**: The number of successes in the sample.
- **number_sample**: The size of the sample.
- **population_s**: The total number of successes in the population.
- **number_pop**: The total size of the population.
- **cumulative**: Logical value:
    - TRUE: Returns the cumulative distribution function (CDF).
    - FALSE: Returns the probability mass function (PMF).

Worked Example

Challenge: Calculate the probability of drawing exactly 2 defective items in a sample of 5 items from a batch of 20 items, where 4 items in the batch are defective.

Formula:

```
=HYPGEOM.DIST(2, 5, 4, 20, FALSE)
```

	A	B	C	D
1	**Example**			
2	=HYPGEOM.DIST(2, 5, 4, 20, FALSE)			
3	**Answer**			
4	0.216718			
5				

Result: 0.216718
Explanation: The function calculates the probability mass function (PMF), which determines the exact probability of selecting 2 defective items in the sample.

Explore Further with GPT

Ask GPT how to use HYPGEOM.DIST for card game probabilities or how to apply it in quality control scenarios.

Tips for Using HYPGEOM.DIST

- **Finite population assumption:** This function is appropriate for sampling without replacement from a finite population. For sampling with replacement, consider using BINOM.DIST.
- **Applications in card games:** Calculate probabilities for specific hands, such as drawing a certain number of hearts in a hand of cards..

HYPGEOMDIST Function

Compatibility Functions

Introduction

The HYPGEOMDIST function is a legacy function that calculates the hypergeometric distribution, which gives the probability of a specific number of successes in a sample drawn from a population without replacement. It has been replaced by the modern HYPGEOM.DIST function in newer versions of Excel but is still available for backward compatibility.

Simple explanation: Computes the probability of successes in a sample drawn from a finite population.

Common use cases: Used in quality control testing, card probability calculations, and population studies.

When to use this function: Use when working with older Excel versions that do not support HYPGEOM.DIST.

Syntax

```
=HYPGEOMDIST(sample_s, number_sample, population_s, number_pop)
```

- **sample_s**: The number of successes in the sample.
- **number_sample**: The size of the sample.
- **population_s**: The total number of successes in the population.
- **number_pop**: The total size of the population.

Worked Example

Challenge: Calculate the probability of drawing exactly 2 defective items in a sample of 5 items from a batch of 20 items, where 4 items in the batch are defective.

Formula:

```
=HYPGEOMDIST(2, 5, 4, 20)
```

Result: 0.216718
Explanation: The function calculates the probability of selecting exactly 2 defective items in the sample.

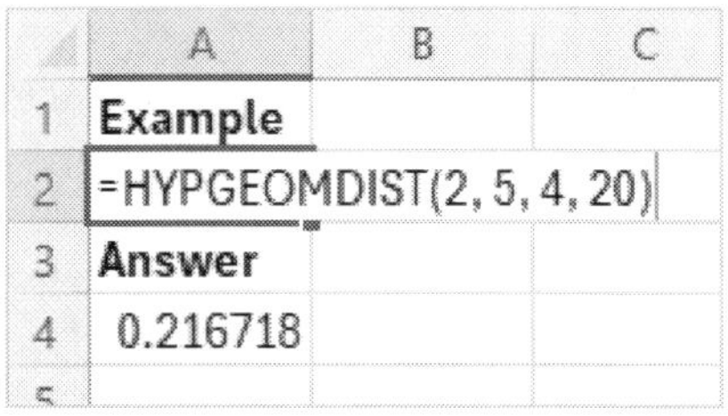

	A	B	C
1	**Example**		
2	=HYPGEOMDIST(2, 5, 4, 20)		
3	**Answer**		
4	0.216718		

Explore Further with GPT

Ask GPT how to transition formulas from HYPGEOMDIST to HYPGEOM.DIST or how to use hypergeometric probabilities in real-world scenarios like card games or quality control.

Tips for Using HYPGEOMDIST

- **Backward compatibility:** Use HYPGEOMDIST only for older Excel workbooks. For new projects, replace it with HYPGEOM.DIST for enhanced functionality:

  ```
  =HYPGEOM.DIST(sample_s, number_sample, population_s, number_pop, FALSE)
  ```

- **Finite population assumption:** This function assumes sampling without replacement. For sampling with replacement, use BINOM.DIST.
- **Error handling:** Ensure all inputs are valid (non-negative integers) to avoid #NUM! or #VALUE! errors.

IF Function

Logical Functions

Introduction

The IF function performs a logical test and returns one value if the condition is TRUE and another value if it is FALSE. It is one of the most versatile functions in Excel, commonly used in conditional calculations and decision-making.

Simple explanation: Checks a condition and returns one value if true and another if false.

Common use cases: Used in decision-making, conditional formatting, and dynamic reporting.

When to use this function: Use when you need different outcomes based on a logical test.

Syntax

```
=IF(logical_test, value_if_true, value_if_false)
```

- **logical_test**: The condition to evaluate (e.g., A1 > 10).
- **value_if_true**: The value to return if the condition is TRUE.
- **value_if_false**: The value to return if the condition is FALSE.

Worked Example

Challenge: Determine if a student passed or failed based on their score.

Formula (for B2):

=IF(B2 >= 50, "Pass", "Fail")

	A	B	C	D	E	F
1	**Student**	**Score**		**Example**		
2	Alice	75		=IF(B2 >= 50, "Pass", "Fail")		
3	Bob	45		**Answer**		
4				Pass		
5						

Result:

- For Alice (Score: 75): Pass
- For Bob (Score: 45): Fail

Explanation: The function evaluates whether the score is greater than or equal to 50 and returns "Pass" or "Fail" accordingly.

Explore Further with GPT

Ask GPT how to use IF with other logical functions like AND or OR or how to simplify complex decision-making scenarios with alternatives like IFS.

Tips for Using IF

- **Combine with other logical functions:** Use AND, OR, and NOT for more complex conditions:

  ```
  =IF(AND(A1 > 10, B1 < 20), "True", "False")
  ```

IFERROR Function

Logical Functions

Introduction

The IFERROR function checks for errors in a formula and returns a specified value if an error occurs. If no error is found, it returns the result of the formula. This is a highly useful function for error handling in Excel, making workbooks more user-friendly and less prone to displaying disruptive error messages.

Simple explanation: Returns a custom value when a formula results in an error; otherwise, returns the formula's result.

Common use cases: Used to handle errors like #DIV/0!, #VALUE!, and #N/A in calculations and reports.

When to use this function: Use when you want to suppress errors or provide alternate values for invalid calculations.

Syntax

```
=IFERROR(value, value_if_error)
```

- **value**: The formula or expression to evaluate.
- **value_if_error**: The value to return if an error is detected

Worked Example

Challenge: Prevent a division-by-zero error when calculating a ratio.

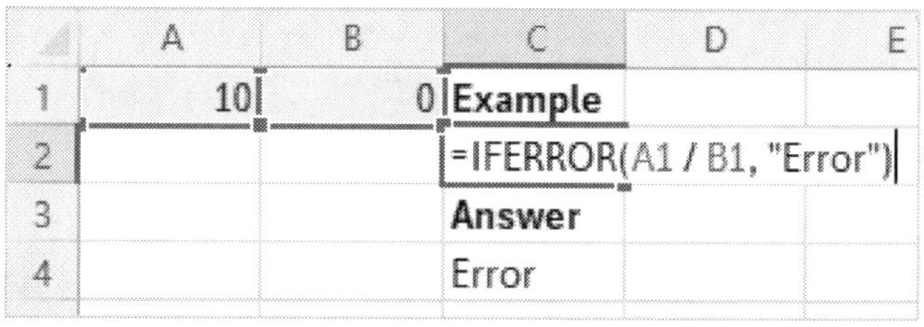

Formula:

```
=IFERROR(A1 / B1, "Error")
```

Result:

- If A1 = 10 and B1 = 2, the result is 5.
- If A1 = 10 and B1 = 0, the result is "Error".

Explanation: The function evaluates the division. If an error occurs (e.g., dividing by zero), it returns the specified value "Error".

Explore Further with GPT

Ask GPT how to use IFERROR in combination with lookup functions like VLOOKUP or dynamic calculations to improve data workflows.

Tips for Using IFERROR

- **Suppressing errors:** Use IFERROR to prevent disruptive error messages in reports or dashboards:

  ```
  =IFERROR(VLOOKUP(A1, B1:D10, 2, FALSE), "Not Found")
  ```

- **Provide meaningful feedback:** Instead of blank outputs, return clear messages or alternate calculations:

  ```
  =IFERROR(A1 / B1, "Invalid Input: Check B1")
  ```

IFNA Function

Logical Functions

Introduction

The IFNA function checks for #N/A errors in a formula and returns a specified value if such an error occurs. If no #N/A error is found, it returns the result of the formula. This function is particularly useful when working with lookup functions like VLOOKUP or XLOOKUP, where #N/A is a common error.

Simple explanation: Returns a custom value when a formula results in a #N/A error; otherwise, returns the formula's result.

Common use cases: Used to handle missing data or mismatches in lookup operations.

When to use this function: Use when suppressing or replacing #N/A errors is necessary, especially in lookup scenarios.

Syntax

```
=IFNA(value, value_if_na)
```

- **value**: The formula or expression to evaluate.
- **value_if_na**: The value to return if a #N/A error is detected.

Worked Example

Challenge: Handle missing values in a VLOOKUP.

Formula:

	A	B	C	D	E	F
1	J	**Sales Area**	**Rep**	**Target**		**Example**
2		A	Jack	100000		=IFNA(VLOOKUP(A1,
3		B	Jill	20000		B1:D10, 2, FALSE), "Not
4		C	John	50000		Found")
5		D	Sue	45000		
6		E	Adam	35000		
7		F	Abdul	120000		**Answer**
8		G	Nik	25000		Not Found
9		H	Fara	35000		
10		I	Raul	66000		
11						

```
=IFNA(VLOOKUP(A1, B1:D10, 2, FALSE), "Not Found")
```

Result:

- If VLOOKUP finds a match, it returns the corresponding value.
- If VLOOKUP results in #N/A, the formula returns "Not Found".

Tips for Using IFNA

- **Targeting specific errors:** Unlike IFERROR, which handles all errors, IFNA specifically targets #N/A errors, making it ideal for lookup functions like VLOOKUP, HLOOKUP, or XLOOKUP.
- **Provide meaningful output:** Instead of generic messages, return contextually helpful information for users:

  ```
  =IFNA(XLOOKUP(A1, B1:B10, C1:C10), "Data Not Found")
  ```

IFS Function

Logical Functions

Introduction

The IFS function evaluates multiple conditions in the order they are provided and returns the corresponding result for the first condition that evaluates to TRUE. It simplifies writing multiple nested IF statements, making your formulas cleaner and easier to read.

Simple explanation: Evaluates multiple conditions and returns the result for the first TRUE condition.

Common use cases: Used for decision-making scenarios with multiple conditions.

When to use this function: Use when you need to evaluate multiple conditions sequentially.

Syntax

```
=IFS(logical_test1, value_if_true1, [logical_test2, value_if_true2], ...)
```

- **logical_test1, logical_test2, ...**: Conditions to evaluate, in order.
- **value_if_true1, value_if_true2, ...**: Results to return for the corresponding conditions if TRUE

Worked Example

Challenge: Categorize scores as "High," "Medium," or "Low."

Formula:

```
=IFS(A2 > 80, "High", A2 > 50, "Medium", TRUE, "Low")
```

	A	B	C	D	E	F	G
1	Score		Example				
2	85		=IFS(A2 > 80, "High", A2 > 50, "Medium", TRUE, "Low")				
3	65		Answer				
4	45		High				

Result:

- For a score of 85: High
- For a score of 65: Medium
- For a score of 45: Low

Explanation: The function evaluates each condition in sequence. The first TRUE condition determines the result.

Explore Further with GPT

Ask GPT how to combine IFS with other logical functions like AND or OR or how to transition from nested IF formulas to IFS.

Tips for Using IFS

- **Order matters:** The function evaluates conditions in the order provided and stops at the first TRUE condition. Place the most specific conditions first:

  ```
  =IFS(A1 > 100, "Very High", A1 > 80, "High", TRUE, "Default")
  ```

- **Default value:** Use TRUE as the final logical test to act as a catch-all for unmatched conditions.

IMABS Function

Engineering Functions

Introduction

The IMABS function calculates the absolute value (modulus) of a complex number. The absolute value of a complex number is the distance from the origin in the complex plane, defined as ***sqrt{a² + b²}*** for a complex number ***a+bi***.

Simple explanation: Returns the absolute value (modulus) of a complex number.

Common use cases: Used in engineering, physics, and mathematical applications involving complex numbers.

When to use this function: Use when analyzing or performing calculations with complex numbers.

Syntax

```
=IMABS(inumber)
```

- **inumber**: The complex number for which to calculate the absolute value. This can be a string like "***a+bi***" or "***a-bi***" or a result of a function returning a complex number (e.g., COMPLEX).

Worked Example

Challenge: Calculate the absolute value of the complex number 3+4i3 + 4i3+4i.

Formula:

```
=IMABS("3+4i")
```

Result: 5

	A	B
1	**Example**	
2	=IMABS("3+4i")	
3	**Answer**	
4	5	

Explore Further with GPT

Ask GPT how to use IMABS in conjunction with other complex number functions like IMAGINARY, IMREAL, and COMPLEX for advanced calculations.

Tips for Using IMABS

- **Input as a string or formula:** The inumber can be a manually entered string like "***4+3i***" or the result of a calculation using COMPLEX.
- **Applications in engineering:** Use IMABS to compute magnitudes of impedances or other complex quantities in electrical engineering:

  ```
  =IMABS(COMPLEX(3, 4))  'Result: 5
  ```

- **Error handling:** Ensure the input is a valid complex number format; otherwise, the function returns a #NUM! error.

IMAGE Function

Lookup & Reference Functions

Introduction

The IMAGE function inserts an image into a cell from a given source, such as a URL. It dynamically displays the image as part of the worksheet, enabling visual representations alongside data for enhanced interactivity and presentation.

Simple explanation: Displays an image from a URL directly in a cell.

Common use cases: Used for creating dashboards, visual reports, and adding context to data through images.

When to use this function: Use when you need to integrate images into your spreadsheet for a more engaging presentation.

Syntax

```
=IMAGE(source, [alt_text], [sizing], [height], [width])
```

- **source**: The URL or path to the image.
- **[alt_text]** *(optional)*: Text to display if the image cannot be rendered.
- **[sizing]** *(optional)*:
  - 0: Fit the image to the cell.
  - 1: Maintain the original size of the image.
  - 2: Fit the image while maintaining its aspect ratio.
  - 3: Custom size based on height and width arguments.
- **[height]** *(optional)*: The height of the image (only used with sizing = 3).
- **[width]** *(optional)*: The width of the image (only used with sizing = 3).

Worked Example

Challenge: Insert an image a sphere into a cell.

Formula:

```
=IMAGE("https://support.content.office.net/en-us/media/2d9e717a-0077-438f-8e5e-f85a1305d4ad.jpg", "Sphere",0)
```

Result:
The cell displays the sphere image, resized to fit the cell.

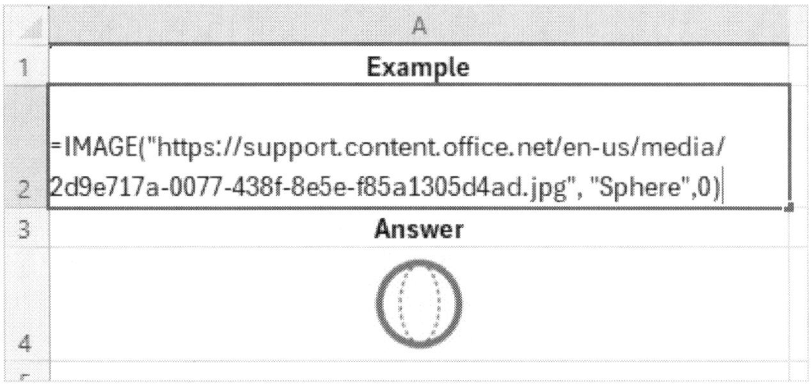

Explore Further with GPT

Ask GPT how to integrate the IMAGE function into dynamic dashboards or automate image updates based on cell values.

IMAGINARY Function

Engineering Functions

Introduction

The IMAGINARY function returns the imaginary coefficient of a complex number. A complex number has the form ***a+bi***, where a is the real part and b is the imaginary coefficient. This function extracts b.

Simple explanation: Returns the imaginary part of a complex number.

Common use cases: Used in engineering, physics, and mathematical computations involving complex numbers.

When to use this function: Use when analyzing or performing operations on the imaginary components of complex numbers.

Syntax

```
=IMAGINARY(inumber)
```

- **inumber**: The complex number from which to extract the imaginary coefficient. This can be a string like "***a+bi***" or "***a-bi***" or the result of a formula returning a complex number (e.g., COMPLEX).

Worked Example

Challenge: Extract the imaginary part from the complex number ***3+4i***.

Formula:

```
=IMAGINARY("3+4i")
```

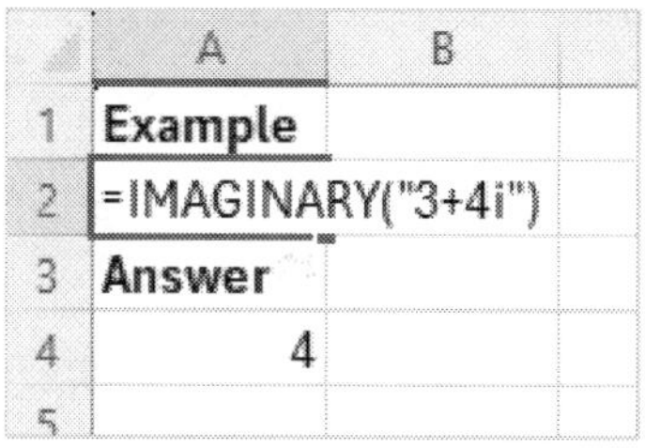

Result: 4
Explanation: The function returns the imaginary coefficient ***b=4*** from ***3+4i***.

Explore Further with GPT

Ask GPT how to use IMAGINARY in conjunction with other complex number functions like IMREAL, IMABS, and COMPLEX for advanced mathematical modeling.

Tips for Using IMAGINARY

- **Input as string or formula:** The inumber can be a manually entered string like "***4-3i***" or the result of a function such as COMPLEX.
- **Applications in engineering:** Use IMAGINARY to analyze components of impedances or phasors in electrical engineering:

  ```
  =IMAGINARY(COMPLEX(3, -4))  'Result: -4
  ```

IMARGUMENT Function

Engineering Functions

Introduction

The IMARGUMENT function returns the argument (angle) of a complex number in radians. The argument is the angle in the complex plane between the positive real axis and the line representing the complex number. It's particularly useful in polar coordinate analysis of complex numbers.

Simple explanation: Returns the angle (in radians) of a complex number relative to the positive real axis.

Common use cases: Used in engineering, physics, and mathematical computations involving polar forms of complex numbers.

When to use this function: Use when analyzing the phase or direction of a complex number in the complex plane.

Syntax

```
=IMARGUMENT(inumber)
```

- **inumber**: The complex number for which to calculate the argument. This can be a string like "***a+bi***" or "***a-bi***" or the result of a formula returning a complex number (e.g., COMPLEX).

Worked Example

Challenge: Calculate the argument of the complex number ***1+ \sqrt{3i}***.

Formula:

```
=IMARGUMENT("1+1.732i")
```

Result: 1.047185

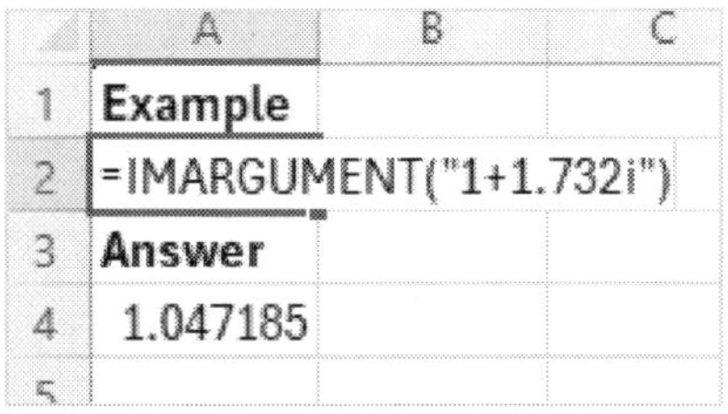

Explore Further with GPT

Ask GPT how to combine IMARGUMENT with other functions like IMABS and IMCONJUGATE to analyze polar forms of complex numbers.

Tips for Using IMARGUMENT

- **Units in radians:** The result is always in radians. To convert to degrees, multiply by 180/π:

  ```
  =IMARGUMENT("1+1.732i") * 180 / PI()
  ```

- **Valid inputs:** Ensure the input is in a valid complex number format; otherwise, the function returns a #NUM! error.

- **Zero handling:** If the input is 0, the function returns 0 radians.

IMCONJUGATE Function

Engineering Functions

Introduction

The IMCONJUGATE function returns the complex conjugate of a given complex number. The complex conjugate of a+bia + bia+bi is a−bia - bia−bi. It is used in various mathematical and engineering applications, particularly in simplifying expressions involving complex numbers.

Simple explanation: Returns the complex conjugate of a complex number by reversing the sign of its imaginary part.

Common use cases: Used in engineering, physics, and signal processing for simplifying complex number operations.

When to use this function: Use when analyzing or manipulating the conjugate of a complex number in mathematical computations.

Syntax

```
=IMCONJUGATE(inumber)
```

- **inumber**: The complex number for which to calculate the conjugate. This can be a string like "***a+bi***" or "***a-bi***" or the result of a formula returning a complex number (e.g., COMPLEX).

Worked Example

Challenge: Calculate the conjugate of the complex number ***3+4i***.

Formula:

```
=IMCONJUGATE("3+4i")
```

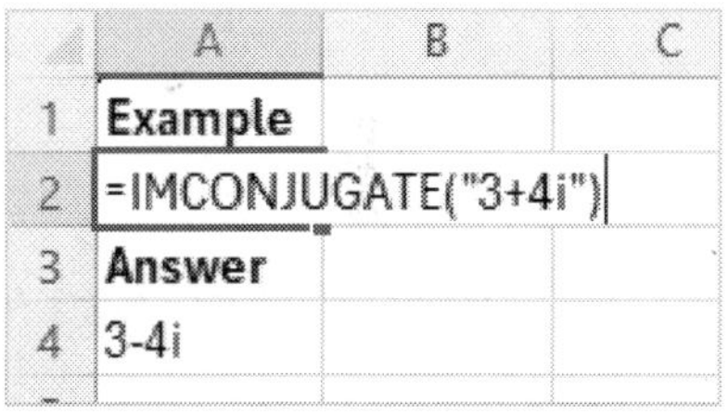

	A	B	C
1	**Example**		
2	=IMCONJUGATE("3+4i")		
3	**Answer**		
4	3-4i		

Result: 3-4i
Explanation: The complex conjugate of ***3+4i*** is ***3−4i***, as the sign of the imaginary part is reversed.

Explore Further with GPT

Ask GPT how to combine IMCONJUGATE with other functions like IMPRODUCT or IMABS to simplify and analyze expressions involving complex numbers.

Tips for Using IMCONJUGATE

- **Input formats:** The inumber can be a manually entered string like "4-3i" or the result of a function such as COMPLEX.
- **Applications in simplifications:** Use IMCONJUGATE to simplify calculations involving the product or division of complex numbers:

```
=IMPRODUCT("3+4i", IMCONJUGATE("3+4i"))  'Result: 25
```

This works because the product of a complex number and its conjugate equals the square of its magnitude.

IMCOS Function

Engineering Functions

Introduction

The IMCOS function returns the cosine of a given complex number. For a complex number ***z=a+bi***, the cosine is computed using the formula:

$$\cos(z)=\cos(a)\cosh(b)-i\sin(a)\sinh(b)$$

It is widely used in engineering and mathematical applications involving complex numbers.

Simple explanation: Calculates the cosine of a complex number.

Common use cases: Used in signal processing, electrical engineering, and mathematical analysis involving trigonometric functions of complex numbers.

When to use this function: Use when analyzing trigonometric properties of complex numbers.

Syntax

```
=IMCOS(inumber)
```

- **inumber**: The complex number for which to calculate the cosine. This can be a string like "a+bi" or "a-bi" or the result of a formula returning a complex number (e.g., COMPLEX)

Worked Example

Challenge: Calculate the cosine of the complex number ***1+i***.

Formula:

```
=IMCOS("1+1i")
```

Result: 0.833730025131149-0.988897705762865i

	A	B	C	D
1	**Example**			
2	=IMCOS("1+1i")			
3	**Answer**			
4	0.833730025131149-0.988897705762865i			

Explore Further with GPT

Ask GPT how to combine IMCOS with other trigonometric complex functions like IMSIN and IMEXP for solving equations or modeling waveforms.

Tips for Using IMCOS

- **Input as string or formula:** The inumber can be entered as a string like "***1-2i***" or as the result of a function such as COMPLEX.
- **Applications in engineering:** Use IMCOS in signal processing to analyze oscillations or waves represented by complex numbers.

IMCOSH Function

Engineering Functions

Introduction

The IMCOSH function returns the hyperbolic cosine of a given complex number. For a complex number ***z=a+bi***, the hyperbolic cosine is calculated as:

$$cosh(z)=cosh(a)cos(b)+isinh(a)sinb)$$

This function is widely used in engineering and mathematical fields involving hyperbolic trigonometric calculations with complex numbers.

Simple explanation: Calculates the hyperbolic cosine of a complex number.

Common use cases: Used in physics, signal processing, and engineering to analyze waveforms and hyperbolic properties of complex numbers.

When to use this function: Use when performing hyperbolic trigonometric operations on complex numbers.

Syntax

```
=IMCOSH(inumber)
```

- **inumber**: The complex number for which to calculate the hyperbolic cosine. This can be a string like "***a+bi***" or "***a-bi***" or the result of a formula returning a complex number (e.g., COMPLEX)

Worked Example

Challenge: Calculate the hyperbolic cosine of the complex number ***1+i***.

Formula:

```
=IMCOSH("1+1i")
```

Result: 0.833730025131149+0.988897705762865i

	A	B	C	D
1	**Example**			
2	=IMCOSH("1+1i")			
3	**Answer**			
4	0.833730025131149+0.988897705762865i			
5				

Explore Further with GPT

Ask GPT how to combine IMCOSH with other hyperbolic functions like IMSINH and IMEXP for advanced mathematical modeling or signal processing.

Tips for Using IMCOSH

- **Input as string or formula:** The inumber can be entered as a string like "***1+2i***" or as the result of a function such as COMPLEX.
- **Applications in physics and engineering:** Use IMCOSH in calculations involving wave equations or heat transfer in complex systems.

IMCOT Function

Engineering Functions

Introduction

The IMCOT function returns the cotangent of a given complex number. For a complex number ***z=a+bi***, the cotangent is calculated as the reciprocal of the tangent:

cot(z)=cos(z)/sin(z)

This function is useful in engineering, physics, and mathematical applications involving trigonometric calculations of complex numbers.

Simple explanation: Calculates the cotangent of a complex number.

Common use cases: Used in electrical engineering, signal processing, and advanced mathematics to analyze complex trigonometric properties.

When to use this function: Use when working with the reciprocal of the tangent function for complex numbers.

Syntax

```
=IMCOT(inumber)
```

- **inumber**: The complex number for which to calculate the cotangent. This can be a string like "a+bi" or "a-bi" or the result of a formula returning a complex number (e.g., COMPLEX).

Worked Example

Challenge: Calculate the cotangent of the complex number 1+i1 + i1+i.

Formula:

```
=IMCOT("1+1i")
```

Result: 0.217621561854403-0.868014142895925i

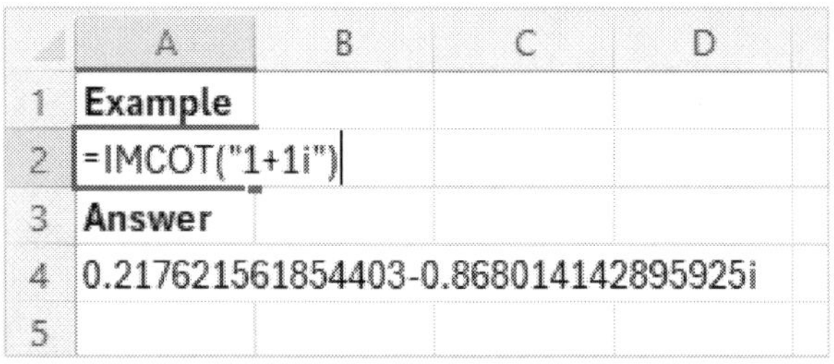

	A	B	C	D
1	**Example**			
2	=IMCOT("1+1i")			
3	**Answer**			
4	0.217621561854403-0.868014142895925i			
5				

Explore Further with GPT

Ask GPT how to combine IMCOT with other trigonometric functions like IMSIN and IMCOS for solving complex equations or analyzing waveforms.

Tips for Using IMCOT

- **Input as string or formula:** The inumber can be a manually entered string like "***2-3i***" or the result of a formula such as COMPLEX.
- **Applications in engineering:** Use IMCOT to calculate impedance, phase angles, or oscillatory behavior in electrical circuits.

IMCSC Function

Engineering Functions

Introduction

The IMCSC function returns the cosecant of a given complex number. For a complex number ***z=a+bi***, the cosecant is calculated as the reciprocal of the sine:

csc(z)=1/sin(z)

This function is commonly used in engineering, physics, and mathematical computations involving trigonometric relationships with complex numbers.

Simple explanation: Calculates the cosecant (reciprocal of sine) of a complex number.

Common use cases: Used in signal processing, wave analysis, and solving trigonometric equations involving complex numbers.

When to use this function: Use when working with the reciprocal of the sine function for complex numbers.

Syntax

```
=IMCSC(inumber)
```

- **inumber**: The complex number for which to calculate the cosecant. This can be a string like "***a+bi***" or "***a-bi***" or the result of a formula returning a complex number (e.g., COMPLEX).

Worked Example

Challenge: Calculate the cosecant of the complex number ***1+i***.

Formula:

```
=IMCSC("1+1i")
```

Result: 0.621518017170428-0.303931001628427i

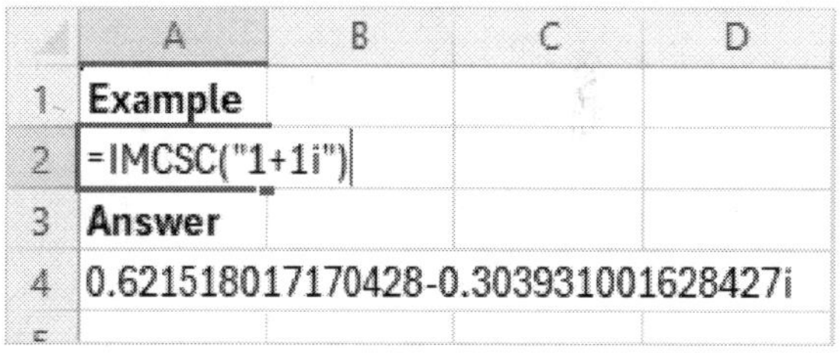

Explore Further with GPT

Ask GPT how to combine IMCSC with other trigonometric functions like IMSIN and IMCOT to solve equations or model waveforms.

Tips for Using IMCSC

- **Input as string or formula:** The inumber can be entered as a string like "***1-2i***" or the result of a function such as COMPLEX.
- **Applications in engineering:** Use IMCSC in calculations for wave analysis, electrical impedance, or oscillatory behavior in complex systems.

IMCSCH Function

Engineering Functions

Introduction

The IMCSCH function returns the hyperbolic cosecant of a given complex number. For a complex number ***z=a+bi***, the hyperbolic cosecant is calculated as the reciprocal of the hyperbolic sine:

csch(z)=1/sinh(z)

This function is commonly used in engineering, physics, and mathematical computations involving hyperbolic trigonometric relationships with complex numbers.

Simple explanation: Calculates the hyperbolic cosecant (reciprocal of hyperbolic sine) of a complex number.

Common use cases: Used in signal processing, advanced physics, and mathematical modeling involving hyperbolic functions.

When to use this function: Use when analyzing the hyperbolic reciprocal properties of complex numbers.

Syntax

```
=IMCSCH(inumber)
```

- **inumber**: The complex number for which to calculate the hyperbolic cosecant. This can be a string like "***a+bi***" or "***a-bi***" or the result of a formula returning a complex number (e.g., COMPLEX).

Worked Example

Challenge: Calculate the hyperbolic cosecant of the complex number ***1+i***.

Formula:

```
=IMCSCH("1+1i")
```

Result: 0.303931001628426-0.621518017170429i

	A	B	C	D
1	**Example**			
2	=IMCSCH("1+1i")			
3	**Answer**			
4	0.303931001628426-0.621518017170429i			
5				

Explore Further with GPT

Ask GPT how to use IMCSCH with other hyperbolic trigonometric functions like IMSINH and IMCOSH for advanced mathematical and engineering applications.

Tips for Using IMCSCH

- **Input as string or formula:** The inumber can be entered as a string like "***1-2i***" or the result of a function such as COMPLEX.
- **Applications in engineering:** Use IMCSCH in calculations for wave propagation, signal analysis, or hyperbolic modeling of complex systems.

IMDIV Function

Engineering Functions

Introduction

The IMDIV function returns the quotient of two complex numbers. For two complex numbers $z_1=a+bi$ and $z_2=c+di$, the division is calculated as:

$z_1/z_2=(a+bi)(c-di)/c^2+d^2$

This function is essential in mathematical, engineering, and signal processing calculations involving complex numbers.

Simple explanation: Divides one complex number by another.

Common use cases: Used in electrical engineering, control systems, and advanced mathematical computations.

When to use this function: Use when dividing complex numbers in mathematical or engineering applications.

Syntax

```
=IMDIV(inumber1, inumber2)
```

- **inumber1**: The numerator (complex number to be divided).
- **inumber2**: The denominator (complex number dividing the numerator).

Worked Example

Challenge: Divide ***3+4i*** by ***1−2i***

Formula:

```
=IMDIV("3+4i", "1-2i")
```

Result: -1.4+2.2i

	A	B
1	**Example**	
2	=IMDIV("3+4i", "1-2i")	
3	**Answer**	
4	-1+2i	
5		

Explore Further with GPT

Ask GPT how to combine IMDIV with other functions like IMCONJUGATE and IMABS for advanced analysis and simplifications involving complex numbers.

Tips for Using IMDIV

- **Input as string or formula:** Both inumber1 and inumber2 can be manually entered as strings like "3+4i" or generated using the COMPLEX function.
- **Applications in engineering:** Use IMDIV in signal analysis, impedance calculations, or control systems involving complex transfer functions.

IMEXP Function

Engineering Functions

Introduction

The IMEXP function returns the exponential of a given complex number. For a complex number ***z=a+bi***, the exponential is calculated as:

$e^z = e^a \cdot (\cos(b) + i\sin(b))$

This function is commonly used in engineering, physics, and mathematics, particularly in solving equations and modeling exponential growth or decay in the complex domain.

Simple explanation: Calculates the exponential of a complex number.

Common use cases: Used in signal processing, quantum mechanics, and differential equations involving complex numbers.

When to use this function: Use when solving problems involving the exponential growth or oscillatory behavior of complex numbers.

Syntax

```
=IMEXP(inumber)
```

- **inumber**: The complex number for which to calculate the exponential. This can be a string like "***a+bi***" or "***a-bi***" or the result of a formula returning a complex number (e.g., COMPLEX).

Worked Example

Challenge: Calculate the exponential of the complex number ***1+i***.

Formula:

```
=IMEXP("1+1i")
```

Result: 1.46869393991589+2.28735528717884i

	A	B	C	D
1	**Example**			
2	=IMEXP("1+1i")			
3	**Answer**			
4	1.46869393991589+2.28735528717884i			

Explore Further with GPT

Ask GPT how to use IMEXP with other functions like IMLOG or IMPOWER to solve advanced equations or analyze growth and oscillation models

Tips for Using IMEXP

- **Input as string or formula:** The inumber can be entered as a string like "***1-2i***" or the result of a function such as COMPLEX.
- **Applications in physics and engineering:** Use IMEXP for wave analysis, Fourier transforms, or solving differential equations in the complex domain.

IMLN Function

Engineering Functions

Introduction

The IMLN function returns the natural logarithm of a given complex number. For a complex number $z=a+bi$, the natural logarithm is calculated as:

$$\ln(z)=\ln(|z|)+i\theta$$

Where $|z|=\sqrt{a^2+b^2}$ is the magnitude of the complex number, and $\theta=\tan^{-1}(b/a)$ is the argument (angle) of the complex number.

Simple explanation: Calculates the natural logarithm of a complex number.

Common use cases: Used in engineering, physics, and mathematics for solving equations involving logarithms and complex numbers.

When to use this function: Use when performing logarithmic operations on complex numbers in advanced mathematical or engineering problems.

Syntax

```
=IMLN(inumber)
```

- **inumber**: The complex number for which to calculate the natural logarithm. This can be a string like "***a+bi***" or "***a-bi***" or the result of a formula returning a complex number (e.g., COMPLEX).

Worked Example

Challenge: Calculate the natural logarithm of the complex number ***1+i***.

Formula:

```
=IMLN("1+1i")
```

Result: 0.346573590279973+0.785398163397448i

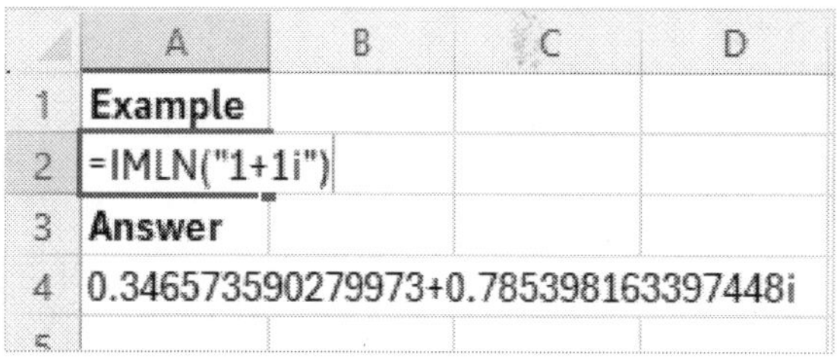

Explore Further with GPT

Ask GPT how to use IMLN with other functions like IMEXP and IMPOWER for solving logarithmic and exponential equations involving complex numbers.

Tips for Using IMLN

- **Input as string or formula:** The inumber can be entered as a string like "***1-2i***" or the result of a function such as COMPLEX.
- **Applications in engineering:** Use IMLN in signal processing, electrical engineering, or solving logarithmic equations involving complex impedance.

IMLOG10 Function

Engineering Functions

Introduction

The IMLOG10 function returns the base-10 logarithm of a given complex number. For a complex number ***z=a+bi***, the base-10 logarithm is calculated as:

$$log_{10}(z)=ln(|z|)/ln(10)+i(\theta/ln(10))$$

Where $|z|= sqrt\{a^2 + b^2\}$ is the magnitude, and $\theta=tan^{-1}(b/a)$ is the argument of the complex number.

Simple explanation: Calculates the base-10 logarithm of a complex number.

Common use cases: Used in mathematical, engineering, and scientific computations involving logarithmic scaling of complex numbers.

When to use this function: Use when solving equations or analyzing logarithmic relationships in the complex domain.

Syntax

```
=IMLOG10(inumber)
```

- **inumber**: The complex number for which to calculate the base-10 logarithm. This can be a string like "***a+bi***" or "***a-bi***" or the result of a formula returning a complex number (e.g., COMPLEX)

Worked Example

Challenge: Calculate the base-10 logarithm of the complex number ***1+i***.

Formula:

```
=IMLOG10("1+1i")
```

Result: 0.150514997831991+0.34109408846046i

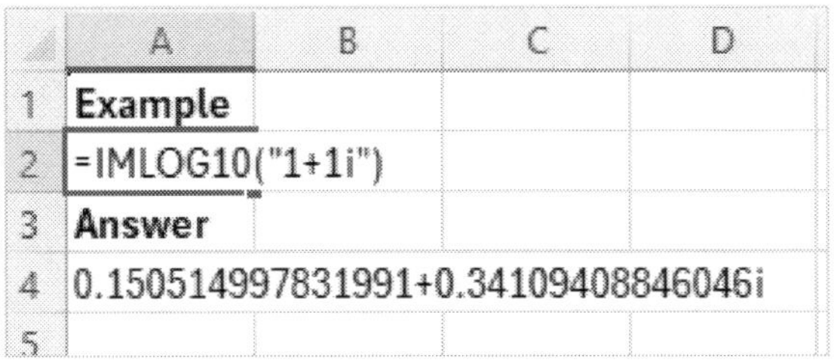

	A	B	C	D
1	Example			
2	=IMLOG10("1+1i")			
3	Answer			
4	0.150514997831991+0.34109408846046i			
5				

Explore Further with GPT

Ask GPT how to combine IMLOG10 with functions like IMEXP and IMPOWER for solving advanced equations involving logarithmic relationships in the complex domain.

Tips for Using IMLOG10

- **Input as string or formula:** The inumber can be entered as a string like "***2-3i***" or the result of a function such as COMPLEX.
- **Applications in engineering:** Use IMLOG10 in signal processing, frequency analysis, or scaling problems involving complex numbers.

IMLOG2 Function

Engineering Functions

Introduction

The IMLOG2 function returns the base-2 logarithm of a given complex number. For a complex number ***z=a+bi***, the base-2 logarithm is calculated as:

$\log_2(z)=\ln(|z|)/\ln(2)+i(\theta/\ln(2))$

Where $|z|=\mathrm{sqrt}\{a^2+b^2\}$ is the magnitude, and $\theta=\tan^{-1}(b/a)$ is the argument of the complex number.

Simple explanation: Calculates the base-2 logarithm of a complex number.

Common use cases: Used in mathematical, engineering, and scientific computations involving logarithmic scaling with base 2.

When to use this function: Use when solving equations or analyzing binary logarithmic relationships in the complex domain.Syntax

Syntax

```
=IMLOG2(inumber)
```

- **inumber**: The complex number for which to calculate the base-2 logarithm. This can be a string like "***a+bi***" or "***a-bi***" or the result of a formula returning a complex number (e.g., COMPLEX).

Worked Example

Challenge: Calculate the base-2 logarithm of the complex number ***1+i***.

Formula:

```
=IMLOG2("1+1i")
```

	A	B
1	**Example**	
2	=IMLOG2("1+1i")	
3	**Answer**	
4	0.5+1.1330900354568i	

Result: 0.5+1.1330900354568i

Explore Further with GPT

Ask GPT how to combine IMLOG2 with functions like IMEXP and IMPOWER for solving equations involving binary logarithmic relationships in the complex domain.

Tips for Using IMLOG2

- **Input as string or formula:** The inumber can be entered as a string like "***2-3i***" or the result of a function such as COMPLEX.
- **Applications in engineering:** Use IMLOG2 in signal processing, binary scaling problems, or binary systems analysis involving complex numbers.

IMPOWER Function

Engineering Functions

Introduction

The IMPOWER function returns a complex number raised to a given power. For a complex number ***z=a+bi*** raised to a power ***n***, the result is calculated as:

$z^n=|z|^n \cdot (\cos(n\theta)+i\sin(n\theta))$

Where $|z|$ is the magnitude and θ is the argument (angle) of the complex number.

Simple explanation: Calculates the result of raising a complex number to a power.

Common use cases: Used in engineering, physics, and mathematical applications involving powers of complex numbers.

When to use this function: Use when solving equations or analyzing powers of complex numbers.

Syntax

```
=IMPOWER(inumber, number)
```

- **inumber**: The base complex number to raise to a power. This can be a string like "***a+bi***" or "***a-bi***" or the result of a formula returning a complex number (e.g., COMPLEX).
- **number**: The exponent to which the base complex number is raised

Worked Example

Challenge: Calculate $(1+i)^3$

Formula:

```
=IMPOWER("1+1i", 3)
```

Result: -2+2i

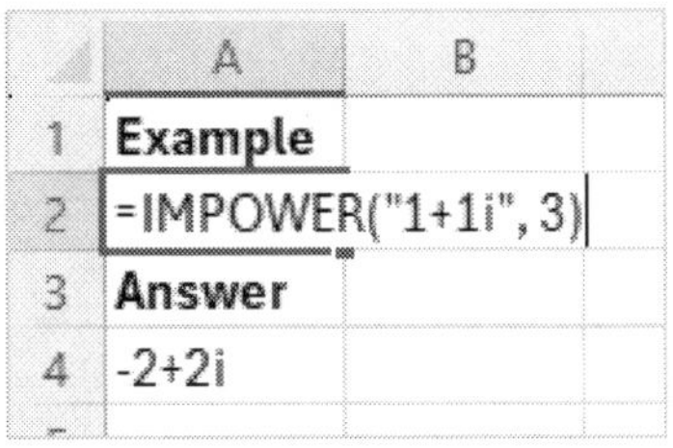

Explore Further with GPT

Ask GPT how to use IMPOWER with functions like IMABS and IMARGUMENT for deeper analysis of powers in polar form.

Tips for Using IMPOWER

- **Input as string or formula:** The inumber can be a string like "***1-2i***" or the result of a function like COMPLEX.
- **Applications in engineering:** Use IMPOWER to analyze oscillations, resonance, or complex systems with power relationships.

IMPRODUCT Function

Engineering Functions

Introduction

The IMPRODUCT function calculates the product of two or more complex numbers. For two complex numbers $z_1=a+bi$ and $z_2=c+di$, the product is calculated as:

$z_1 \cdot z_2=(ac-bd)+(ad+bc)i$

This function is commonly used in engineering, physics, and mathematical applications involving complex number multiplication.

Simple explanation: Multiplies two or more complex numbers.

Common use cases: Used in signal processing, electrical engineering, and solving equations involving products of complex numbers.

When to use this function: Use when multiplying complex numbers in mathematical or engineering computations.

Syntax

```
=IMPRODUCT(inumber1, [inumber2], ...)
```

- **inumber1, inumber2, ...**: The complex numbers to multiply. These can be strings like "***a+bi***", "***a-bi***", or results of formulas returning complex numbers (e.g., COMPLEX).

Worked Example

Challenge: Multiply ***2+3i*** by ***1−4i***

Formula:

```
=IMPRODUCT("2+3i", "1-4i")
```

Result: 14-5i

	A	B	C
1	**Example**		
2	=IMPRODUCT("2+3i", "1-4i")		
3	**Answer**		
4	14-5i		

Explore Further with GPT

Ask GPT how to use IMPRODUCT with other functions like IMDIV and IMCONJUGATE for solving advanced problems involving complex numbers.

Tips for Using IMPRODUCT

- **Input as string or formula:** The inputs can be entered as strings like "***2-3i***" or as the result of formulas like COMPLEX.
- **Applications in engineering:** Use IMPRODUCT in impedance calculations, phasor analysis, or power calculations involving complex systems.

IMREAL Function

Engineering Functions

Introduction

The IMREAL function returns the real part of a complex number. For a complex number ***z=a+bi***, the real part is ***a***. This function is useful for extracting and analyzing the real component in mathematical, engineering, and scientific computations involving complex numbers.

Simple explanation: Extracts the real part of a complex number.

Common use cases: Used in engineering, signal processing, and mathematical analysis to separate real and imaginary components.

When to use this function: Use when you need to isolate and work with the real component of a complex number.

Syntax

```
=IMREAL(inumber)
```

- **inumber**: The complex number from which to extract the real part. This can be a string like "***a+bi***" or "***a-bi***" or the result of a formula returning a complex number (e.g., COMPLEX).

Worked Example

Challenge: Extract the real part of the complex number ***3+4i***.

Formula:

```
=IMREAL("3+4i")
```

Result: 3

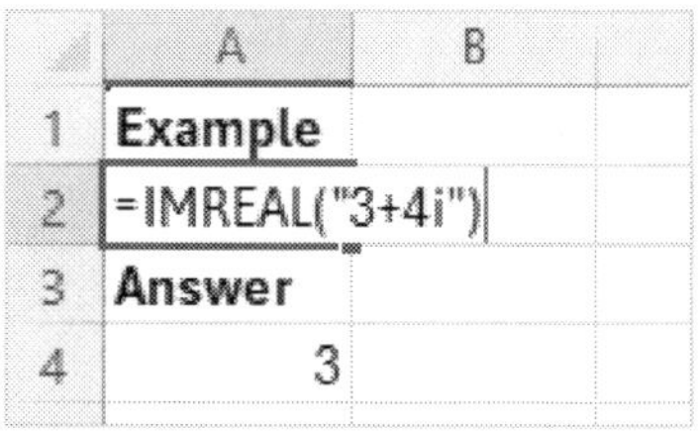

Explore Further with GPT

Ask GPT how to use IMREAL alongside IMAGINARY and IMABS to fully analyze and manipulate complex numbers.

Tips for Using IMREAL

- **Input as string or formula:** The inumber can be a string like "***4-3i***" or the result of a function like COMPLEX.
- **Applications in engineering:** Use IMREAL in impedance calculations, phasor analysis, or signal decomposition to separate real and imaginary parts.

IMSEC Function

Engineering Functions

Introduction

The IMSEC function returns the secant of a given complex number. For a complex number ***z=a+bi***, the secant is calculated as the reciprocal of the cosine:

sec(z)=1/cos(z)

This function is useful in engineering, physics, and mathematical applications that involve trigonometric relationships with complex numbers.

Simple explanation: Calculates the secant (reciprocal of cosine) of a complex number.

Common use cases: Used in signal processing, wave analysis, and solving trigonometric equations involving complex numbers.

When to use this function: Use when analyzing the reciprocal of the cosine function for complex numbers.

Syntax

```
=IMSEC(inumber)
```

- **inumber**: The complex number for which to calculate the secant. This can be a string like "***a+bi***" or "***a-bi***" or the result of a formula returning a complex number (e.g., COMPLEX).

Worked Example

Challenge: Calculate the secant of the complex number ***1+i***.

Formula:

```
=IMSEC("1+1i")
```

Result: 0.498337030555187+0.591083841721045i

	A	B	C	D
1	**Example**			
2	=IMSEC("1+1i")			
3	**Answer**			
4	0.498337030555187+0.591083841721045i			
5				

Explore Further with GPT

Ask GPT how to use IMSEC with other trigonometric functions like IMCOS and IMCOT to solve equations or model waveforms involving complex numbers.

Tips for Using IMSEC

- **Input as string or formula:** The inumber can be entered as a string like "***1-2i***" or the result of a function such as COMPLEX.

- **Applications in engineering:** Use IMSEC in calculations for signal analysis, wave propagation, or oscillatory behavior in complex systems.

IMSECH Function

Engineering Functions

Introduction

The IMSECH function returns the hyperbolic secant of a given complex number. For a complex number ***z=a+bi***, the hyperbolic secant is calculated as the reciprocal of the hyperbolic cosine:

sech(z)=1/cosh(z)

This function is commonly used in engineering, physics, and mathematical computations involving hyperbolic trigonometric relationships with complex numbers.

Simple explanation: Calculates the hyperbolic secant (reciprocal of hyperbolic cosine) of a complex number.

Common use cases: Used in signal processing, advanced physics, and mathematical modeling involving hyperbolic functions.

When to use this function: Use when analyzing the hyperbolic reciprocal properties of complex numbers.

Syntax

```
=IMSECH(inumber)
```

- **inumber**: The complex number for which to calculate the hyperbolic secant. This can be a string like "***a+bi***" or "***a-bi***" or the result of a formula returning a complex number (e.g., COMPLEX).

Worked Example

Challenge: Calculate the hyperbolic secant of the complex number ***1+i***.

Formula:

```
=IMSECH("1+1i")
```

Result: 0.498337030555187-0.591083841721045i

	A	B	C	D
1	**Example**			
2	=IMSECH("1+1i")			
3	**Answer**			
4	0.498337030555187-0.591083841721045i			

Explore Further with GPT

Ask GPT how to combine IMSECH with other hyperbolic functions like IMCOSH and IMSINH for advanced mathematical modeling or signal processing.

Tips for Using IMSECH

- **Input as string or formula:** The inumber can be entered as a string like "***1-2i***" or the result of a function such as COMPLEX.
- **Applications in engineering:** Use IMSECH in calculations for wave propagation, signal analysis, or hyperbolic modeling of complex systems.

IMSIN Function

Engineering Functions

Introduction

The IMSIN function returns the sine of a given complex number. For a complex number ***z=a+bi***, the sine is calculated as:

sin(z)=sin(a)cosh(b)+icos(a)sinh(b)

This function is commonly used in engineering, physics, and mathematical computations involving trigonometric properties of complex numbers.

- **Simple explanation:** Calculates the sine of a complex number.
- **Common use cases:** Used in signal processing, wave analysis, and solving trigonometric equations involving complex numbers.
- **When to use this function:** Use when analyzing the sine function for complex numbers.

Syntax

```
=IMSIN(inumber)
```

- **inumber**: The complex number for which to calculate the sine. This can be a string like "***a+bi***" or "***a-bi***" or the result of a formula returning a complex number (e.g., COMPLEX).

Worked Example

Challenge: Calculate the sine of the complex number ***1+i***.

Formula:

```
=IMSIN("1+1i")
```

Result: 1.29845758141598+0.634963914784736i

Explore Further with GPT

Ask GPT how to combine IMSIN with functions like IMCOS and IMCOT to solve equations or analyze waveforms involving complex numbers.

Tips for Using IMSIN

- **Input as string or formula:** The inumber can be entered as a string like "***1-2i***" or the result of a function such as COMPLEX.
- **Applications in engineering:** Use IMSIN in calculations for wave propagation, signal analysis, or oscillatory behavior in complex systems.

IMSINH Function

Engineering Functions

Introduction

The IMSINH function returns the hyperbolic sine of a given complex number. For a complex number ***z=a+bi***, the hyperbolic sine is calculated as:

sinh(z)=sinh(a)cos(b)+icosh(a)sin(b)

This function is useful in engineering, physics, and mathematical applications involving hyperbolic functions of complex numbers.

Simple explanation: Calculates the hyperbolic sine of a complex number.

Common use cases: Used in signal processing, heat transfer, and advanced mathematical modeling involving hyperbolic functions.

When to use this function: Use when analyzing the hyperbolic properties of complex numbers.

Syntax

```
=IMSINH(inumber)
```

- **inumber**: The complex number for which to calculate the hyperbolic sine. This can be a string like "***a+bi***" or "***a-bi***" or the result of a formula returning a complex number (e.g., COMPLEX).

Worked Example

Challenge: Calculate the hyperbolic sine of the complex number ***1+i***.

Formula:

```
=IMSINH("1+1i")
```

Result: 0.634963914784736+1.29845758141598i

	A	B	C	D
1	**Example**			
2	=IMSINH("1+1i")			
3	**Answer**			
4	0.634963914784736+1.29845758141598i			

Explore Further with GPT

Ask GPT how to use IMSINH with functions like IMCOSH and IMSECH to solve equations or model systems involving hyperbolic trigonometric relationships.

Tips for Using IMSINH

- **Input as string or formula:** The inumber can be entered as a string like "***1-2i***" or the result of a function such as COMPLEX.
- **Applications in engineering:** Use IMSINH in heat transfer, wave propagation, or signal analysis problems involving complex systems.

IMSQRT Function

Engineering Functions

Introduction

The IMSQRT function returns the square root of a given complex number. For a complex number ***z=a+bi***, the square root is calculated as:

z=sqrt{(|z| + a)/2} + i.sign(b) . sqrt{(|z| - })/2 }

Where ***/z/=sqrt{a2 + b2}*** is the magnitude of the complex number.

Simple explanation: Calculates the square root of a complex number.

Common use cases: Used in engineering, physics, and mathematical computations involving roots of complex numbers.

When to use this function: Use when analyzing or solving problems involving square roots of complex numbers.

Syntax

```
=IMSQRT(inumber)
```

- **inumber**: The complex number for which to calculate the square root. This can be a string like "***a+bi***" or "***a-bi***" or the result of a formula returning a complex number (e.g., COMPLEX)

Worked Example

Challenge: Calculate the square root of the complex number ***3+4i***.

Formula:

```
=IMSQRT("3+4i")
```

Result: 2+1i

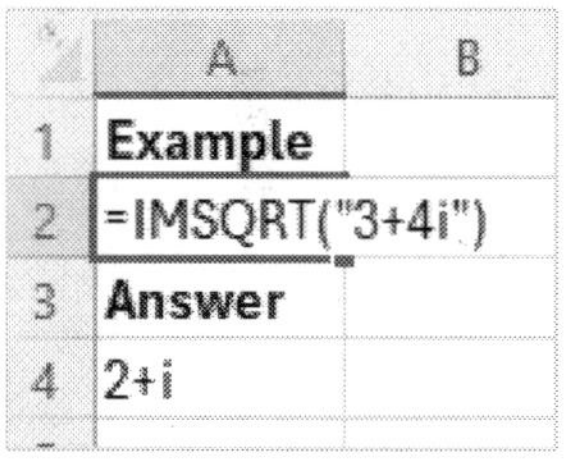

Explore Further with GPT

Ask GPT how to combine IMSQRT with functions like IMPOWER or IMPRODUCT to solve equations involving roots of complex numbers.

Tips for Using IMSQRT

- **Input as string or formula:** The inumber can be a string like "***4-3i***" or the result of a function like COMPLEX.
- **Applications in engineering:** Use IMSQRT in impedance calculations, phasor analysis, or signal decomposition involving square roots of complex numbers.

IMSUB Function

Engineering Functions

Introduction

The IMSUB function returns the difference between two complex numbers. For two complex numbers $z^1=a+bi$ and $z^2=c+di$, the subtraction is calculated as:

$z_1-z_2=(a-c)+(b-d)i$

This function is commonly used in engineering, physics, and mathematical applications where subtracting complex numbers is necessary.

Simple explanation: Subtracts one complex number from another.

Common use cases: Used in signal processing, electrical engineering, and solving equations involving differences of complex numbers.

When to use this function: Use when subtracting complex numbers in mathematical or engineering computations.

Syntax

```
=IMSUB(inumber1, inumber2)
```

- **inumber1**: The complex number to subtract from (minuend).
- **inumber2**: The complex number to subtract (subtrahend). These can be strings like "***a+bi***", "***a-bi***", or results of formulas returning complex numbers (e.g., COMPLEX).

Worked Example

Challenge: Subtract ***1−4i*** from ***2+3i***.

Formula:

```
=IMSUB("2+3i", "1-4i")
```

Result: 1+7i

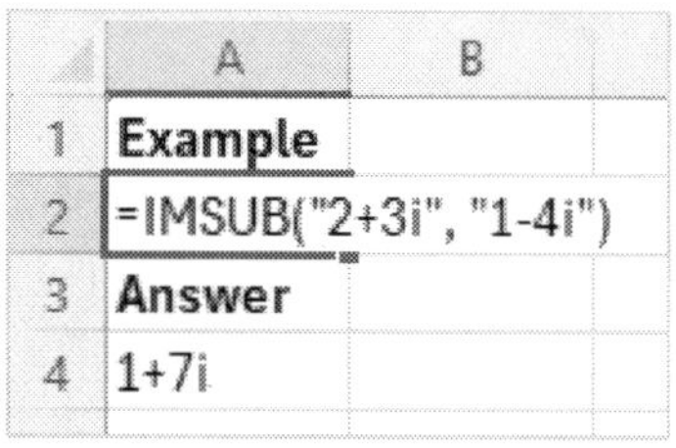

Explore Further with GPT

Ask GPT how to combine IMSUB with other functions like IMADD or IMCONJUGATE for solving equations involving operations on complex numbers.

Tips for Using IMSUB

- **Input as string or formula:** The inputs can be entered as strings like "***3+4i***" or as the result of formulas like COMPLEX.
- **Applications in engineering:** Use IMSUB in calculations for signal differences, impedance changes, or phasor subtraction.

IMSUM Function

Engineering Functions

Introduction

The IMSUM function returns the sum of two or more complex numbers. For two complex numbers $z_1=a+bi$ and $z_2=c+di$, the addition is calculated as:

$z_1+z_2=(a+c)+(b+d)i$

This function is commonly used in engineering, physics, and mathematical applications where adding complex numbers is necessary.

Simple explanation: Adds two or more complex numbers.

Common use cases: Used in signal processing, electrical engineering, and solving equations involving sums of complex numbers.

When to use this function: Use when adding complex numbers in mathematical or engineering computations.

Syntax

```
=IMSUM(inumber1, [inumber2], ...)
```

- **inumber1, inumber2, ...**: The complex numbers to sum. These can be strings like "***a+bi***", "***a-bi***", or results of formulas returning complex numbers (e.g., COMPLEX).

Worked Example

Challenge: Add ***2+3i*** and ***1−4i***.

Formula:

```
=IMSUM("2+3i", "1-4i")
```

Result: 3-1i

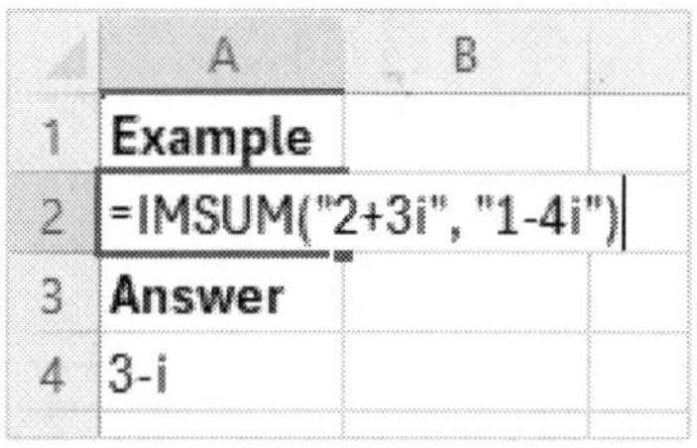

Explore Further with GPT

Ask GPT how to use IMSUM with functions like IMSUB or IMPRODUCT for solving equations involving complex numbers.

Tips for Using IMSUM

- **Input as string or formula:** The inputs can be entered as strings like "***3+4i***" or as the result of formulas like COMPLEX.
- **Applications in engineering:** Use IMSUM in signal combination, impedance addition, or phasor summation.

IMTAN Function

Engineering Functions

Introduction

The IMTAN function returns the tangent of a given complex number. For a complex number ***z=a+bi***, the tangent is calculated as:

tan(z)=sin(z)/cos(z)

This function is commonly used in engineering, physics, and mathematical applications that involve trigonometric relationships with complex numbers.

Simple explanation: Calculates the tangent of a complex number.

Common use cases: Used in signal processing, wave analysis, and solving trigonometric equations involving complex numbers.

When to use this function: Use when analyzing the tangent function for complex numbers.

Syntax

```
=IMTAN(inumber)
```

- **inumber**: The complex number for which to calculate the tangent. This can be a string like "***a+bi***" or "***a-bi***" or the result of a formula returning a complex number (e.g., COMPLEX).

Worked Example

Challenge: Calculate the tangent of the complex number ***1+i***.

Formula:

```
=IMTAN("1+1i")
```

Result: 0.271752585319512+1.08392332733869i

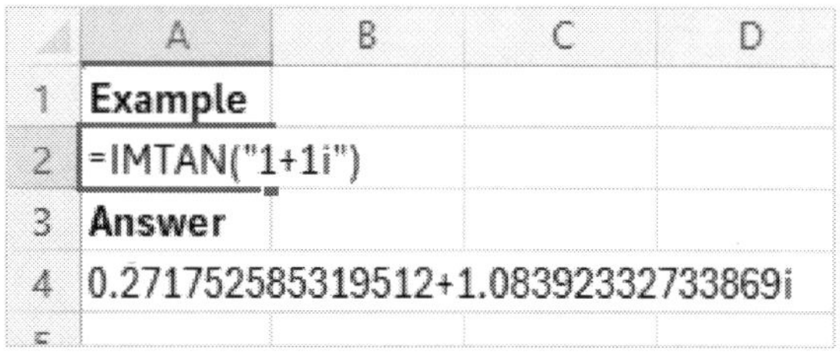

Explore Further with GPT

Ask GPT how to use IMTAN with functions like IMCOT, IMCOS, and IMSIN to solve equations or model waveforms involving complex numbers.

Tips for Using IMTAN

- **Input as string or formula:** The inumber can be entered as a string like "***1-2i***" or the result of a function such as COMPLEX.
- **Applications in engineering:** Use IMTAN in calculations for wave propagation, signal analysis, or oscillatory behavior in complex systems.

INDEX Function

Lookup & Reference Functions

Introduction

The INDEX function returns the value of a cell or an array element based on specified row and column numbers. It is a powerful tool for retrieving data from tables or arrays.

Simple explanation: Retrieves the value of a specific cell or element in a table or array.

Common use cases: Used in data analysis, table lookups, and dynamic report generation.

When to use this function: Use when you need to extract data from a specific location in a table or array.

Syntax

```
=INDEX(array, row_num, [column_num], [area_num])
```

- **array**: The range or array from which to retrieve the value.
- **row_num**: The row number in the array.
- **[column_num]** *(optional)*: The column number in the array.
- **[area_num]** *(optional)*: The specific range or area to use if the array spans multiple ranges.

Worked Example

Challenge: Retrieve the sales value for the 3rd row and 2nd column in a table

Formula:

```
=INDEX(A1:C4, 3, 2)
```

Result: 150

Explanation: The function retrieves the value from the 3rd row and 2nd column, which is 150.

	A	B	C	D	E	F
1	**Product**	**Sales**	**Units**		**Example**	
2	Apple	200	50		=INDEX(A1:C4, 3, 2)	
3	Banana	150	30		**Answer**	
4	Cherry	300	40		150	
5						

Explore Further with GPT

Ask GPT how to combine INDEX with other functions like MATCH and IF for advanced lookups or conditional data retrieval.

Tips for Using INDEX

- **Combining with MATCH:** Use INDEX with MATCH for dynamic lookups:

  ```
  =INDEX(A1:C4, MATCH("Banana", A1:A4, 0), MATCH("Sales", A1:C1, 0))
  ```

  This retrieves the sales value for "Banana."

INDIRECT Function

Lookup & Reference Functions

Introduction

The INDIRECT function returns the reference specified by a text string. This allows you to dynamically refer to cells, ranges, or named ranges, enabling flexible and dynamic spreadsheet models.

Simple explanation: Converts a text string into a valid cell or range reference.

Common use cases: Used in dynamic referencing, dependent dropdowns, and data validation.

When to use this function: Use when you need to create flexible references that adjust dynamically based on input or formulas.

Syntax

```
=INDIRECT(ref_text, [a1])
```

- **ref_text**: A text string that specifies the reference. This can be a cell address, range, or named range.
- **[a1]** *(optional)*: A logical value indicating the reference style. Default is TRUE (A1 style). Set to FALSE for R1C1 style.

Worked Example

Challenge: Retrieve the value from cell B2 using a dynamic reference

Formula:

`=INDIRECT("B2")`

Result: 200
Explanation: The text string "B2" is converted into a reference, and the value in B2 is retrieved.

	A	B	C	D	E	F
1	**Name**	**Sales**	**Units**		**Example**	
2	**Apple**	200	50		=INDIRECT("B2")	
3	**Banana**	150	30		**Answer**	
4					200	
5						

Explore Further with GPT

Ask GPT how to use INDIRECT with functions like ADDRESS, ROW, and COLUMN for dynamic referencing or creating flexible models.

Tips for Using INDIRECT

- **Referencing named ranges:** Use INDIRECT to reference named ranges dynamically:

  `=INDIRECT("SalesData")`

- **Create dynamic ranges:** Combine with ROW and COLUMN to create dynamic ranges:

  `=SUM(INDIRECT("A1:A" & ROW()))`

  This sums all rows in column A up to the current row.

INFO Function

Information Functions

Introduction

The INFO function returns information about the current operating environment in which Excel is running, such as the operating system, directory paths, or recalculation mode.

Simple explanation: Retrieves information about the system environment or Excel settings.

Common use cases: Used in debugging, system analysis, or creating dynamic models that adapt to the operating environment.

When to use this function: Use when you need to obtain system-related details or environment-specific information.

Syntax

```
=INFO(type_text)
```

type_text: A text value specifying the type of information to return. The following are valid options:

- "directory": Current directory or folder path.
- "numfile": Number of active worksheets in all open workbooks.
- "origin": Reference of the top-left cell visible in the Excel window (e.g., $A$1).
- "osversion": Current operating system version.
- "recalc": Recalculation mode (Automatic or Manual).
- "release": Excel version number.
- "system": Current operating system name.

Worked Example

Challenge: Retrieve the current operating system name.

Formula:

```
=INFO("system")
```

	A	B
1	**Example**	
2	=INFO("system")	
3	**Answer**	
4	pcdos	

Result: "pcdos" (for Windows systems).
Explanation: The function returns "pcdos" to indicate the Windows operating system.

Explore Further with GPT

Ask GPT how to use INFO in conjunction with functions like CELL or ENVIRON (VBA) for advanced system diagnostics or dynamic workbook adjustments.

Tips for Using INFO

- **System insights:** Use INFO to understand the operating environment dynamically for better debugging or conditional workflows:

  ```
  =IF(INFO("system")="pcdos", "Windows Environment", "Other OS")
  ```

INT Function

Math & Trigonometry Functions

Introduction

The INT function rounds a number down to the nearest integer. It always rounds numbers towards negative infinity, meaning positive numbers are rounded down to the nearest whole number, and negative numbers are rounded further away from zero.

Simple explanation: Rounds a number down to the nearest integer.

Common use cases: Used in financial modeling, data analysis, and situations where truncation of decimal values is required.

When to use this function: Use when you need to round numbers down to their nearest whole value.

Syntax

```
=INT(number)
```

- **number**: The real number you want to round down.

Worked Example

Challenge: Round the number 4.7 down to the nearest integer.

Formula:

```
=INT(4.7)
```

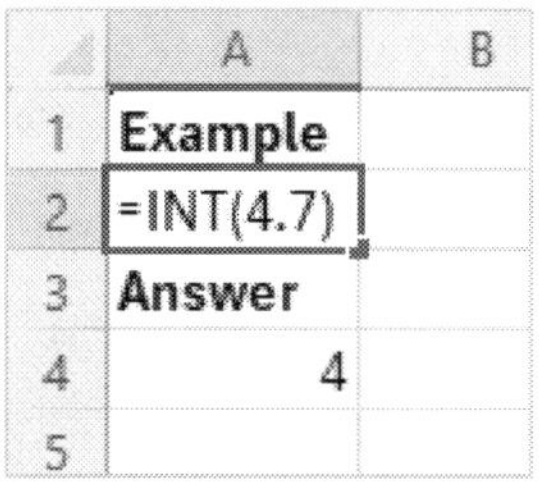

Result: 4
Explanation: The function rounds 4.7 down to the nearest whole number, which is 4.

Explore Further with GPT

Ask GPT how to use INT with functions like MOD or ROUND to create advanced rounding logic or conditionally process numeric data.

Tips for Using INT

- **Combining with MOD for integer division:** Use INT with MOD to perform integer division:

  ```
  =INT(A1/B1) & " remainder " & MOD(A1, B1)
  ```

- **Handling decimal truncation:** If you need to truncate numbers without rounding, use TRUNC instead of INT.

- **Negative number behavior:** Remember that INT rounds down towards negative infinity, which can differ from rounding functions like ROUND.

INTERCEPT Function

Statistical Functions

Introduction

The INTERCEPT function calculates the point at which a line will intersect the y-axis, based on a set of known x and y values. It assumes a linear relationship between the variables, fitting the line using the least-squares method.

Simple explanation: Finds the y-intercept of a line based on known data points.

Common use cases: Used in statistical modeling, data analysis, and regression analysis to understand trends and relationships.

When to use this function: Use when analyzing linear relationships between two variables and determining where the line crosses the y-axis.

Syntax

```
=INTERCEPT(known_y's, known_x's)
```

- **known_y's**: The dependent data values (y-values).
- **known_x's**: The independent data values (x-values).

Worked Example

Challenge: Calculate the y-intercept of a line based on the following data:

Formula:

```
=INTERCEPT(B2:B5, A2:A5)
```

(Assuming A2:A5 contains X values and B2:B5 contains Y values.)

Result: 1

Explanation: The line that fits the data points ***(1,3),(2,5),(3,7),(4,9)*** has a slope of 2 and a y-intercept of 1, described by the equation ***y=2x+1*** .

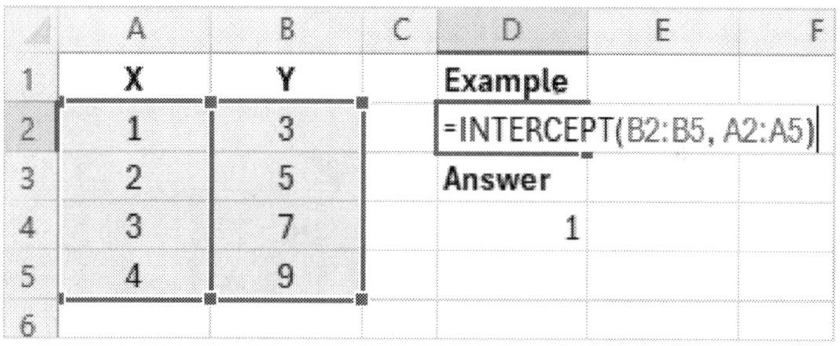

	A	B	C	D	E	F
1	X	Y		Example		
2	1	3		=INTERCEPT(B2:B5, A2:A5)		
3	2	5		Answer		
4	3	7		1		
5	4	9				
6						

Explore Further with GPT

Ask GPT how to combine INTERCEPT with SLOPE, TREND, or FORECAST functions to create complete regression models or make predictions.

Tips for Using INTERCEPT

- **Combining with SLOPE:** Use INTERCEPT with SLOPE to describe a full line equation:

  ```
  =SLOPE(B2:B5, A2:A5) & "x + " & INTERCEPT(B2:B5, A2:A5)
  ```

- **Error handling:** Ensure the ranges for known_y's and known_x's are of the same size; otherwise, the function returns a #N/A error.

- **Data validation:** Ensure data points represent a linear relationship for meaningful results.

INTRATE Function

Financial Functions

Introduction

The INTRATE function calculates the effective interest rate for a fully invested security, given its price, redemption value, and the duration between settlement and maturity.

Simple explanation: Computes the effective interest rate for a security investment.

Common use cases: Used in financial modeling, bond analysis, and investment calculations.

When to use this function: Use when analyzing the interest rate of a fully invested security based on its price and return.

Syntax

```
=INTRATE(settlement, maturity, investment, redemption, [basis])
```

- **settlement**: The date the security is purchased (settlement date).
- **maturity**: The date the security matures (maturity date).
- **investment**: The amount invested in the security.
- **redemption**: The amount received at maturity (redemption value).
- **[basis]** *(optional)*: The day-count basis for the calculation:
    - 0 or omitted: US (NASD) 30/360; 1: Actual/actual; 2: Actual/360; 3: Actual/365; 4: European 30/360.

Worked Example

Challenge: Calculate the interest rate for a bond with the following details:

- Settlement date: January 1, 2023.
- Maturity date: December 31, 2023.
- Investment amount: $1,000.
- Redemption value: $1,050.
- Basis: Actual/actual.

Formula:

```
=INTRATE(DATE(2023,1,1),
DATE(2023,12,31), 1000, 1050, 1)
```

	A	B	C	D	E	F
1	**Example**					
2	=INTRATE(DATE(2023,1,1), DATE(2023,12,31), 1000, 1050, 1)					
3	**Answer**					
4	5%					

Result: 0.05 or 5%

Explanation: The function calculates an effective interest rate of 5%5\%5% for the investment based on the provided inputs.

IPMT Function

Financial Functions

Introduction

The IPMT function calculates the interest portion of a payment for a specific period of a loan or investment. This is particularly useful for creating loan amortization schedules, analyzing investment returns, or understanding interest versus principal payments.

Simple explanation: Determines how much of a payment goes towards interest for a specific period.

Common use cases: Used in financial planning, loan management, and amortization schedules.

When to use this function: Use when calculating the interest portion of periodic payments for loans or investments.

Syntax

```
=IPMT(rate, per, nper, pv, [fv], [type])
```

- **rate**: The interest rate per period.
- **per**: The specific payment period to calculate interest for (must be between 1 and nper).
- **nper**: Total number of payment periods.
- **pv**: Present value of the loan or investment (total principal amount).
- **[fv]** *(optional)*: Future value, or the desired balance after the last payment (default is 0).
- **[type]** *(optional)*: When payments are due:
    - 0 or omitted: Payments are made at the end of the period.
    - 1: Payments are made at the beginning of the period.

Worked Example

Challenge: Calculate the interest portion of the 2nd payment on a $15,000 loan, repaid over 5 years with monthly payments, at an annual interest rate of 4.5%.

Details:

- Loan amount (pv): $15,000.
- Annual interest rate: 4.5%.
- Loan term: 5 years (60 months).
- Payments made at the end of each period.

	A	B	C
1	**Example**		
2	=IPMT(4.5%/12, 2, 60, 15000)		
3	**Answer**		
4	-£55.41		

Formula:

```
=IPMT(4.5%/12, 2, 60, 15000)
```

Result: -55.41

Explanation: The interest portion of the 2nd monthly payment is $55.41. The negative value indicates that this is an outgoing payment.

IRR Function

Financial Functions

Introduction

The IRR function calculates the internal rate of return (IRR) for a series of periodic cash flows. The IRR is the discount rate at which the net present value (NPV) of the cash flows equals zero. This is a critical metric for evaluating the profitability of investments or projects.

Simple explanation: Finds the annualized rate of return for a series of cash flows.

Common use cases: Used in investment analysis, capital budgeting, and financial modeling.

When to use this function: Use when you need to evaluate the rate of return on an investment based on cash inflows and outflows.

Syntax

```
=IRR(values, [guess])
```

- **values**: An array or range of cells containing the cash flows, including the initial investment (must be negative).
- **[guess]** *(optional)*: An estimate of the expected IRR. If omitted, Excel assumes 10% as the initial guess.

Worked Example

Challenge: Calculate the internal rate of return for a project with given cash flows:

Formula:

```
=IRR(B2:B6)
```

Result: 8%

Explanation: The IRR for this project is 8%, meaning the project is expected to yield an annualized return of 8%.

	A	B	C	D
1	Year	Cash Flow		Example
2	0	- 10,000.00		=IRR(B2:B6)
3	1	3,000.00		Answer
4	2	3,000.00		8%
5	3	3,000.00		
6	4	3,000.00		
7				

Explore Further with GPT

Ask GPT how to combine IRR with functions like NPV or XIRR to analyze projects with irregular cash flows or varying discount rates.

Tips for Using IRR

- **Negative and positive cash flows:** Ensure the cash flow series includes at least one negative value (outflow) and one positive value (inflow); otherwise, IRR cannot calculate a valid return.
- **Dynamic ranges:** Use IRR with named ranges or dynamic arrays for flexible financial models.
- **Multiple IRRs:** If there are multiple sign changes in the cash flows, IRR may return multiple rates or fail to converge. In such cases, use NPV to test different rates.

ISBLANK Function

Information Functions

Introduction

The ISBLANK function checks whether a specified cell is empty. It returns TRUE if the cell is empty and FALSE otherwise. This is useful for validating data, identifying gaps, or creating dynamic formulas that respond to empty cells.

Simple explanation: Checks if a cell is empty.

Common use cases: Used in data validation, error checking, and conditional logic.

When to use this function: Use when you need to determine if a cell contains data or is empty.

Syntax

```
=ISBLANK(value)
```

- **value**: The reference to the cell you want to check.

Worked Example

Challenge: Determine if cell A1 is empty.

Data in A1: *(Empty)*

Formula:

```
=ISBLANK(A1)
```

Result: TRUE
Explanation: The ISBLANK function returns TRUE because A1 is empty.

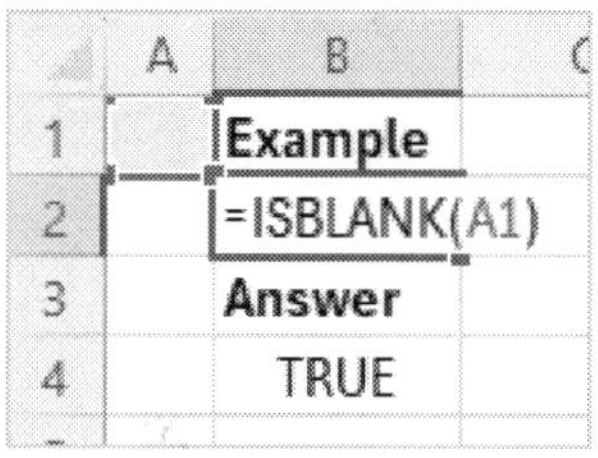

Explore Further with GPT

Ask GPT how to use ISBLANK with other functions like IF, COUNTA, or ISERROR to build advanced validation or data-cleaning workflows.

Tips for Using ISBLANK

- **Combine with IF:** Use ISBLANK to create conditional logic for handling empty cells:

  ```
  =IF(ISBLANK(A1), "Cell is empty", "Cell contains data")
  ```

- **Handling cells with formulas:** If a cell contains a formula that evaluates to "" (blank text), ISBLANK returns FALSE. Use this formula to check for blank-like outputs instead:

  ```
  =A1=""
  ```

ISERR Function

Information Functions

Introduction

The ISERR function checks whether a value results in an error, excluding the #N/A error. If the value is an error other than #N/A, the function returns TRUE; otherwise, it returns FALSE. This is useful for handling errors in formulas or creating conditional logic that excludes #N/A.

Simple explanation: Checks for errors (excluding #N/A).

Common use cases: Used in error handling, debugging, and building robust formulas.

When to use this function: Use when you need to identify and handle errors in data or calculations, excluding #N/A.

Syntax

```
=ISERR(value)
```

- **value**: The value or expression to check for an error.

Worked Example

Challenge: Check if dividing by zero results in an error.

Formula:

```
=ISERR(1/0)
```

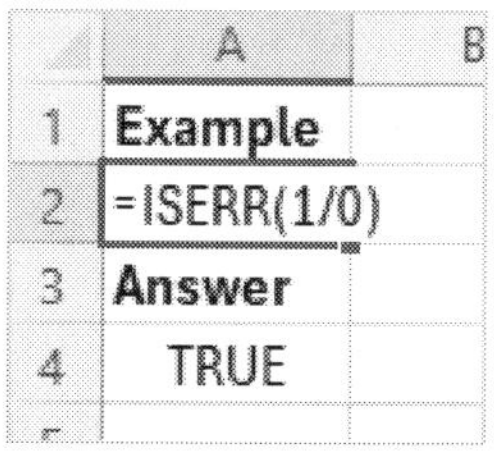

Result: TRUE
Explanation: Dividing by zero generates a #DIV/0! error, which ISERR identifies as an error

Explore Further with GPT

Ask GPT how to use ISERR with other functions like IFERROR, ISERROR, or IF to build advanced error-handling formulas.

Tips for Using ISERR

- **Combine with IF:** Create conditional formulas to handle errors dynamically:

  ```
  =IF(ISERR(A1), "Error detected", A1)
  ```

- **Difference from ISERROR:** Use ISERR to exclude #N/A from error detection, or ISERROR to include all errors:

  ```
  =ISERROR(A1)    ' Detects all errors
  ```

  ```
  =ISERR(A1)      ' Excludes #N/A
  ```

- **For error-specific handling:** Use error-specific functions like IFERROR or IFNA to target specific error types.

ISERROR Function

Information Functions

Introduction

The ISERROR function checks whether a value results in any error. It returns TRUE if the value results in an error (including #N/A), and FALSE otherwise. This function is useful for identifying and handling errors in formulas or datasets.

Simple explanation: Checks for any error in a value or formula.

Common use cases: Used in error handling, debugging, and building formulas that adapt dynamically to errors.

When to use this function: Use when you need to identify all error types in data or calculations.

Syntax

```
=ISERROR(value)
```

- **value**: The value, expression, or cell reference to check for an error.

Worked Example

Challenge: Check if dividing by zero results in an error.

Formula:

```
=ISERROR(1/0)
```

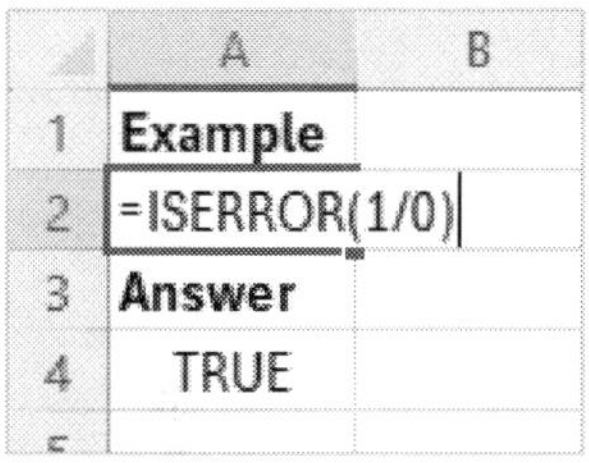

Result: TRUE
Explanation: Dividing by zero generates a #DIV/0! error, which ISERROR identifies as an error

Explore Further with GPT

Ask GPT how to combine ISERROR with functions like IFERROR, ISNA, or IF to create robust formulas that handle all potential errors.

Tips for Using ISERROR

- **Combine with IF:** Use ISERROR to create conditional formulas for error handling:

  ```
  =IF(ISERROR(A1), "Error detected", A1)
  ```

- **Handling errors in calculations:** For simpler error management, use IFERROR, which combines error checking and fallback value assignment:

  ```
  =IFERROR(A1/B1, "Invalid calculation")
  ```

ISEVEN Function

Information Functions

Introduction

The ISEVEN function checks whether a number is even. It returns TRUE if the number is even and FALSE if it is odd. This function is helpful in data validation, conditional formatting, and logical calculations.

Simple explanation: Determines if a number is even.

Common use cases: Used in data validation, logical operations, and numerical analysis.

When to use this function: Use when you need to identify even numbers in a dataset or create conditions based on even numbers.

Syntax

```
=ISEVEN(number)
```

- **number**: The numeric value or reference to check for evenness

Worked Example

Challenge: Check if the number 10 is even.

Formula:

```
=ISEVEN(10)
```

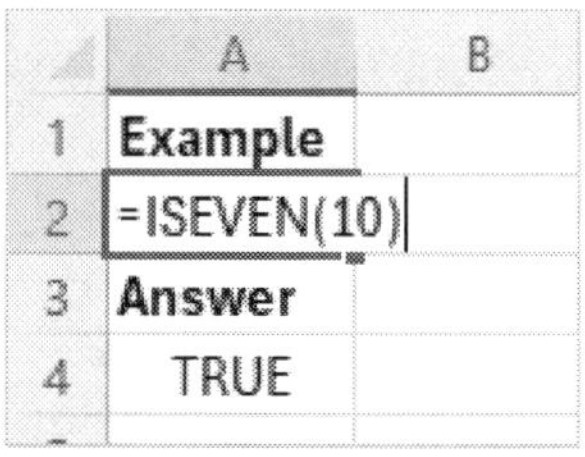

Result: TRUE
Explanation: The number 10 is even, so the function returns TRUE.

Explore Further with GPT

Ask GPT how to combine ISEVEN with functions like IF, MOD, or FILTER to analyze datasets or create conditional formatting rules.

Tips for Using ISEVEN

- **Combine with IF:** Use ISEVEN to create conditional logic:

  ```
  =IF(ISEVEN(A1), "Even", "Odd")
  ```

- **Use with arrays:** Identify even numbers in a range using dynamic arrays:

  ```
  =FILTER(A1:A10, ISEVEN(A1:A10))
  ```

ISFORMULA Function

Information Functions

Introduction

The ISFORMULA function checks whether a specified cell contains a formula. It returns TRUE if the cell contains a formula and FALSE otherwise. This function is useful for auditing spreadsheets, validating data, or debugging.

Simple explanation: Checks if a cell contains a formula.

Common use cases: Used in data validation, error checking, and auditing spreadsheets.

When to use this function: Use when you need to identify cells with formulas for further analysis or conditional logic.

Syntax

```
=ISFORMULA(reference)
```

- **reference**: The cell reference to check for a formula.

Worked Example

Challenge: Check if cell A1 contains a formula.

Data in A1**:** =SUM(B1:B10)

Formula:

```
=ISFORMULA(A1)
```

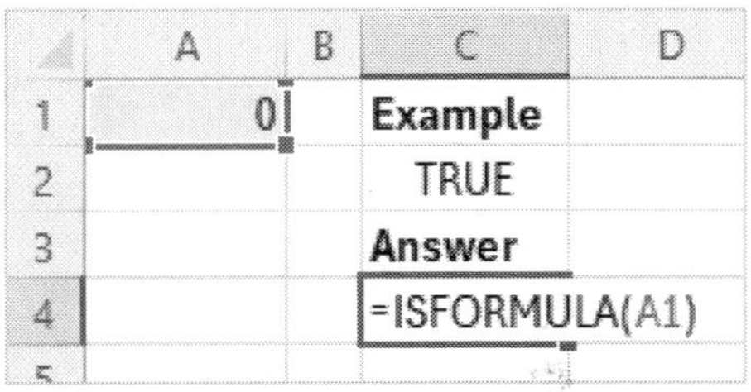

Result: TRUE
Explanation: The cell A1 contains a formula (=SUM(B1:B10)), so the function returns TRUE.

Explore Further with GPT

Ask GPT how to use ISFORMULA with functions like IF, COUNTIF, or FILTER to analyze spreadsheets or highlight formula cells dynamically.

Tips for Using ISFORMULA

- **Combine with IF:** Use ISFORMULA to build conditional logic:

  ```
  =IF(ISFORMULA(A1), "Contains formula", "Static value")
  ```

- **Error handling:** Ensure the reference is valid; otherwise, the function returns a #VALUE! error

ISLOGICAL Function

Information Functions

Introduction

The ISLOGICAL function checks whether a value is a logical value, such as TRUE or FALSE. It returns TRUE if the value is logical and FALSE otherwise. This function is useful for validating logical expressions or identifying logical values in datasets.

Simple explanation: Checks if a value is a logical TRUE or FALSE.

Common use cases: Used in data validation, debugging, and building conditional logic.

When to use this function: Use when analyzing or validating logical values in formulas or datasets.

Syntax

```
=ISLOGICAL(value)
```

- **value**: The value or cell reference to check for a logical value.

Worked Example

Challenge: Check if a formula result is logical.

Data in A1: =A2>A3 *(Evaluates to TRUE)*

Formula:

```
=ISLOGICAL(A1)
```

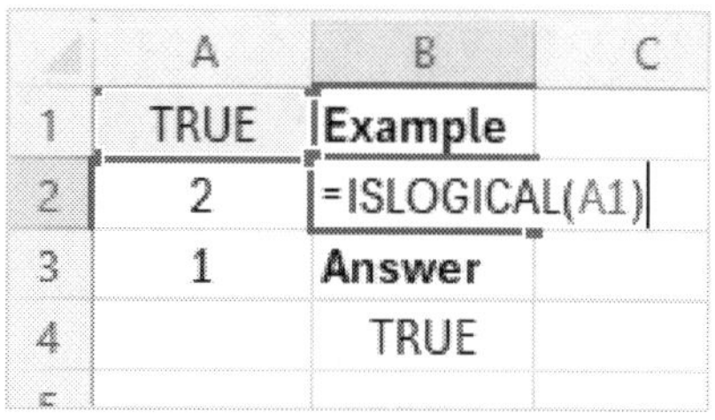

Result: TRUE
Explanation: The formula in A1 evaluates to a logical TRUE, so ISLOGICAL returns TRUE.

Explore Further with GPT

Ask GPT how to use ISLOGICAL with functions like IF, AND, or OR to build advanced logical expressions or dynamic models.

Tips for Using ISLOGICAL

- **Error handling:** Ensure the reference is valid; otherwise, the function may return a #VALUE! error.
- **Dynamic formulas:** Pair ISLOGICAL with logical functions like AND, OR, or NOT to validate inputs or simplify conditions.
- **Combine with `IF`:** Use `ISLOGICAL` to create conditional logic based on logical values:

```
=IF(ISLOGICAL(A1), "Logical value", "Not logical")
```

ISNA Function

Information Functions

Introduction

The ISNA function checks whether a value or expression results in the #N/A error. It returns TRUE if the value is #N/A and FALSE otherwise. This is useful for handling missing data or avoiding errors in formulas that depend on external lookups.

Simple explanation: Checks if a value is the #N/A error.

Common use cases: Used in data validation, error handling, and managing missing data in lookups.

When to use this function: Use when identifying or handling missing values returned as #N/A.

Syntax

```
=ISNA(value)
```

- **value**: The value, expression, or cell reference to check for the #N/A error.

Worked Example

Challenge: Check if a VLOOKUP formula returns #N/A.

Formula in C1:

```
=VLOOKUP(103, A1:B3, 2, FALSE)
```

(This results in #N/A because ID 103 does not exist.)

ISNA Formula:

```
=ISNA(C1)
```

	A	B	C	D	E
1	**ID**	**Name**	#N/A		**Example**
2	101	Alice			=ISNA(C1)
3	102	Bob			**Answer**
4					TRUE
5					

Result: TRUE
Explanation: The VLOOKUP formula in C1 returns #N/A, so ISNA identifies the error and returns TRUE.

Explore Further with GPT

Ask GPT how to use ISNA with functions like IF, IFERROR, or MATCH to handle missing data or improve lookup formulas.

Tips for Using ISNA

- **Combine with IF:** Use ISNA to create custom error handling:

  ```
  =IF(ISNA(C1), "Not found", C1)
  ```

- **Difference from ISERROR:** While ISERROR checks for all errors, ISNA focuses specifically on #N/A.

ISNONTEXT Function

Information Functions

Introduction

The ISNONTEXT function checks whether a value is not text. It returns TRUE if the value is not text and FALSE if it is text. This includes numbers, blank cells, logical values (TRUE or FALSE), and errors, which are considered non-text.

Simple explanation: Checks if a value is not text.

Common use cases: Used in data validation, filtering, and cleaning datasets to identify non-text values.

When to use this function: Use when distinguishing between text and non-text values in datasets or formulas.

Syntax

```
=ISNONTEXT(value)
```

- **value**: The value or cell reference to check for non-text content.

Worked Example

Challenge: Check if a numeric value is non-text.

Data in A1: 123

Formula:

```
=ISNONTEXT(A1)
```

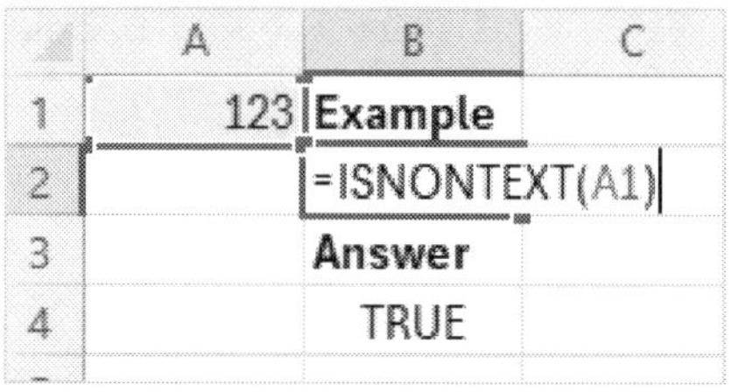

Result: TRUE
Explanation: The value in A1 is a number, which is not text, so ISNONTEXT returns TRUE.

Explore Further with GPT

Ask GPT how to use ISNONTEXT with functions like IF, ISTEXT, or COUNTA to clean data or create validation rules.

Tips for Using ISNONTEXT

- **Combine with IF:** Use ISNONTEXT to create conditional logic:

  ```
  =IF(ISNONTEXT(A1), "Not text", "Text")
  ```

- **Highlight non-text values:** Use conditional formatting to highlight cells that are not text:

  1. Select the range (e.g., A1:A10).
  2. Go to **Conditional Formatting** → **New Rule**.
  3. Use the formula:

  ```
  =ISNONTEXT(A1)
  ```

ISNUMBER Function

Information Functions

Introduction

The ISNUMBER function checks whether a value is a number. It returns TRUE if the value is numeric and FALSE otherwise. This function is useful for data validation, filtering, and logical operations involving numerical data.

Simple explanation: Checks if a value is a number.

Common use cases: Used in data validation, filtering, and cleaning datasets to identify numerical values.

When to use this function: Use when distinguishing between numeric and non-numeric values in datasets or formulas.

Syntax

```
=ISNUMBER(value)
```

- **value**: The value or cell reference to check for numeric content.

Worked Example

Challenge: Check if a numeric value is a number.

Data in A1: 123

Formula:

```
=ISNUMBER(A1)
```

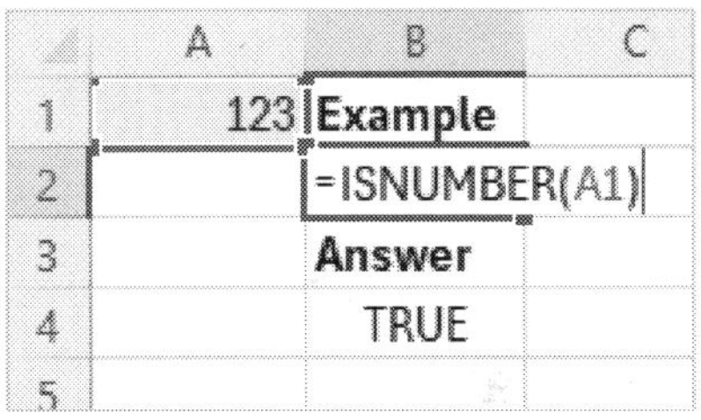

Result: TRUE
Explanation: The value in A1 is a number, so ISNUMBER returns TRUE.

Explore Further with GPT

Ask GPT how to combine ISNUMBER with functions like IF, COUNTIF, or FILTER to create dynamic data analysis models or validation rules.

Tips for Using ISNUMBER

- **Combine with IF:** Use ISNUMBER to create conditional logic:

  ```
  =IF(ISNUMBER(A1), "Valid number", "Not a number")
  ```

- **Detect numbers in arrays:** Combine ISNUMBER with array functions for advanced filtering:

  ```
  =FILTER(A1:A10, ISNUMBER(A1:A10))
  ```

- **Error handling:** Ensure valid references to avoid errors.

ISODD Function

Information Functions

Introduction

The ISODD function checks whether a number is odd. It returns TRUE if the number is odd and FALSE if it is even. This function is helpful in data validation, conditional formatting, and logical calculations.

Simple explanation: Checks if a number is odd.

Common use cases: Used in data validation, logical operations, and numerical analysis.

When to use this function: Use when you need to identify odd numbers in a dataset or create conditions based on odd numbers.

Syntax

```
=ISODD(number)
```

- **number**: The numeric value or reference to check for oddness.

Worked Example

Challenge: Check if the number 7 is odd.

Formula:

```
=ISODD(7)
```

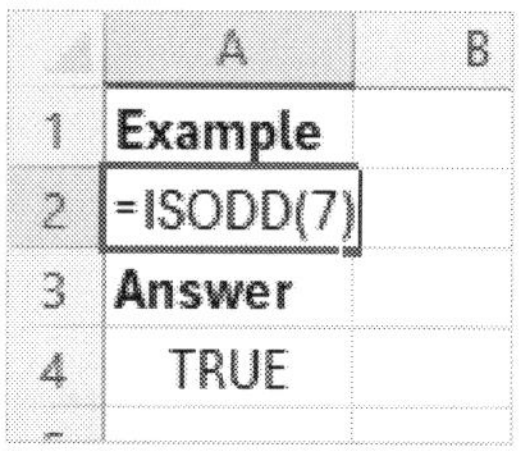

Result: TRUE
Explanation: The number 7 is odd, so the function returns TRUE.

Explore Further with GPT

Ask GPT how to combine ISODD with functions like IF, MOD, or FILTER to analyze datasets or create conditional formatting rules.

Tips for Using ISODD

- **Combine with IF:** Use ISODD to create conditional logic:

  ```
  =IF(ISODD(A1), "Odd", "Even")
  ```

- **Decimal numbers:** If the input is a decimal, ISODD truncates it to an integer before evaluation. For example:

  ```
  =ISODD(7.9)    ' Returns TRUE (7 is odd)
  ```

ISOMITTED Function

Information Functions

Introduction

The ISOMITTED function checks whether a value has been explicitly omitted from a function's arguments. It returns TRUE if the argument is omitted and FALSE otherwise. This function is particularly useful in custom Excel functions created using **LAMBDA** to handle optional parameters.

Simple explanation: Checks if an argument is missing in a function call.

Common use cases: Used in custom formulas or functions to handle optional arguments dynamically.

When to use this function: Use when creating or troubleshooting LAMBDA functions that include optional parameters.

Syntax

```
=ISOMITTED(parameter)
```

- **parameter**: The argument or parameter to check for omission.

Worked Example

Challenge: Detect if an optional parameter in a LAMBDA function is omitted.

1. **Define a LAMBDA function:**

```
=LAMBDA(x, y, IF(ISOMITTED(y), "y is missing", "y is provided"))
```

2. **Invoke the LAMBDA function:**

```
=MyLambda(10,)
```

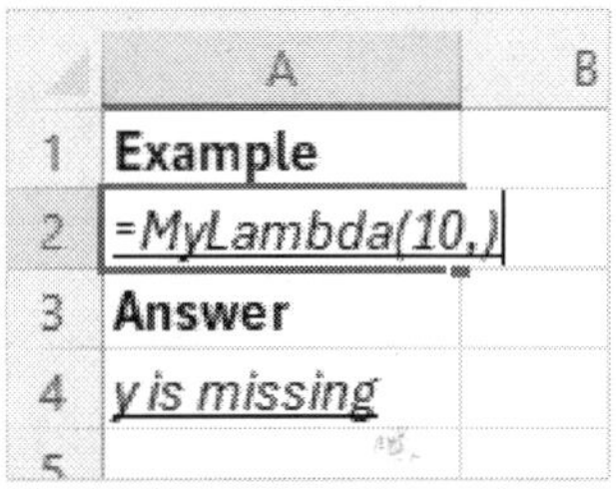

Result: "y is missing"
Explanation: The function MyLambda is called with only one argument (x), so ISOMITTED detects that y is omitted.

Explore Further with GPT

Ask GPT how to use ISOMITTED to handle complex optional logic in LAMBDA functions or how to design custom reusable formulas with optional parameters.

Tips for Using ISOMITTED

- **Combine with IF:** Use ISOMITTED to provide default values for omitted parameters:

  ```
  =LAMBDA(x, y, IF(ISOMITTED(y), x*2, x*y))
  ```

  This doubles x if y is omitted; otherwise, it multiplies x by y.

- **Error-proof LAMBDA functions:** Use ISOMITTED to prevent errors caused by missing parameters in custom functions.

ISREF Function

Information Functions

Introduction

The ISREF function checks whether a value is a valid reference. It returns TRUE if the value is a reference and FALSE otherwise. This function is useful for validating cell references in formulas or identifying invalid references.

Simple explanation: Checks if a value is a valid cell or range reference.

Common use cases: Used in data validation, error checking, and debugging formulas that rely on dynamic references.

When to use this function: Use when you need to confirm that a value or input is a valid reference.

Syntax

```
=ISREF(value)
```

- **value**: The value or expression to check for a reference.

Worked Example

Challenge: Check if a cell reference is valid.

Data in A1: =B1

Formula:

```
=ISREF(A1)
```

Result: TRUE
Explanation: The value A1 is a valid cell reference, so ISREF returns TRUE.

	A	B
1	Example	**Example**
2		=ISREF(A1)
3		**Answer**
4		TRUE

Explore Further with GPT

Ask GPT how to use ISREF with functions like INDIRECT, IF, or ERROR.TYPE to build robust formulas and dynamic models.

Tips for Using ISREF

- **Combine with IF:** Use ISREF to conditionally handle references:

  ```
  =IF(ISREF(A1), "Valid reference", "Not a reference")
  ```

- **Dynamic reference checks:** Combine ISREF with INDIRECT to validate references generated from text:

  ```
  =IF(ISREF(INDIRECT(A1)), "Valid reference", "Invalid reference")
  ```

ISTEXT Function

Information Functions

Introduction

The ISTEXT function checks whether a value is text. It returns TRUE if the value is text and FALSE otherwise. This function is useful for data validation, cleaning datasets, and building logical conditions.

Simple explanation: Checks if a value is text.

Common use cases: Used in data validation, error checking, and identifying text entries in datasets.

When to use this function: Use when you need to distinguish between text and non-text values in formulas or data analysis.

Syntax

```
=ISTEXT(value)
```

- **value**: The value or cell reference to check for text.

Worked Example

Challenge: Check if a cell contains text.

Data in A1: "Hello World"

Formula:

```
=ISTEXT(A1)
```

Result: TRUE
Explanation: The value in A1 is text, so ISTEXT returns TRUE.

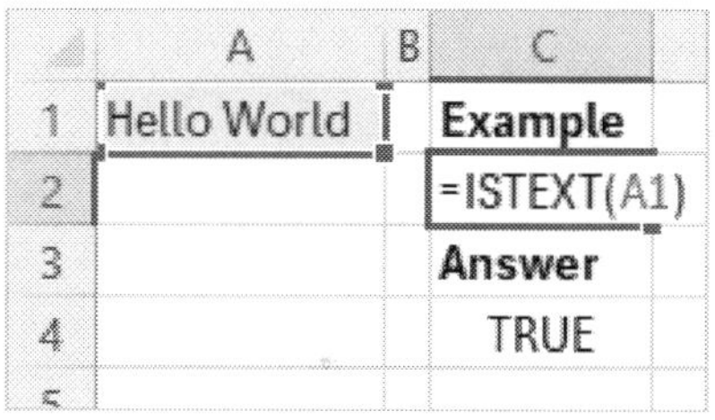

Explore Further with GPT

Ask GPT how to combine ISTEXT with functions like IF, ISNUMBER, or COUNTIF to build dynamic formulas or analyze datasets.

Tips for Using ISTEXT

- **Combine with IF:** Use ISTEXT to create conditional logic:

  ```
  =IF(ISTEXT(A1), "Text value", "Not text")
  ```

- **Detect text in arrays:** Combine ISTEXT with array functions for filtering:

  ```
  =FILTER(A1:A10, ISTEXT(A1:A10))
  ```

ISO.CEILING Function

Math & Trigonometry Functions

Introduction

The ISO.CEILING function rounds a number up to the nearest multiple of a specified significance, regardless of the number's sign. Unlike the CEILING.MATH function, ISO.CEILING always rounds numbers away from zero, ensuring consistency for both positive and negative numbers.

Simple explanation: Rounds a number up to the nearest specified multiple, consistently away from zero.

Common use cases: Used in financial modeling, inventory management, and calculations requiring standardized rounding.

When to use this function: Use when you need consistent rounding for positive and negative numbers.

Syntax

```
=ISO.CEILING(number, [significance])
```

- **number**: The value to be rounded.
- **[significance]** *(optional)*: The multiple to which the number is rounded. The default is 1.

Worked Example

Challenge: Round 5.3 up to the nearest whole number.

Formula:

```
=ISO.CEILING(5.3)
```

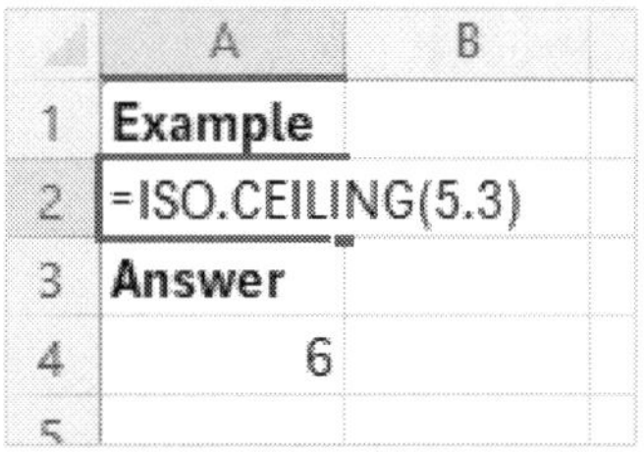

Result: 6
Explanation: The function rounds 5.3 up to the nearest multiple of 1.

Explore Further with GPT

Ask GPT how to combine ISO.CEILING with other functions like FLOOR, ROUND, or MROUND to create custom rounding logic.

Tips for Using ISO.CEILING

- **Default significance:** If the significance argument is omitted, the function defaults to rounding to the nearest integer.
- **Consistency for negatives:** Unlike CEILING.MATH, which depends on the mode argument, ISO.CEILING always rounds away from zero, making it consistent.
- **Combining with financial models:** Use ISO.CEILING for rounding financial values, such as currency or batch sizes, to the nearest specified increment.

ISOWEEKNUM Function

Date & Time Functions

Introduction

The ISOWEEKNUM function returns the ISO week number for a given date. According to the ISO 8601 standard, weeks begin on Monday, and the first week of the year is the one containing January 4. This is useful for aligning with international date and time standards in project management, reporting, or planning.

Simple explanation: Determines the ISO week number for a date.

Common use cases: Used in project timelines, reporting dashboards, and international calendars.

When to use this function: Use when working with week numbers following the ISO 8601 standard.

Syntax

```
=ISOWEEKNUM(date)
```

- **date**: The date for which you want to find the ISO week number. This must be a valid Excel date.

Worked Example

Challenge: Find the ISO week number for January 1, 2023.

Formula:

```
=ISOWEEKNUM(DATE(2023,1,1))
```

Result: 52
Explanation: According to the ISO standard, January 1, 2023, falls in the 52nd week of 2022 because the first ISO week of 2023 starts on January 2, 2023.

	A	B	C
1	**Example**		
2	=ISOWEEKNUM(DATE(2023,1,1))		
3	**Answer**		
4	52		

Explore Further with GPT

Ask GPT how to combine ISOWEEKNUM with functions like WEEKNUM, DATE, or TEXT to create custom time-based calculations or reporting frameworks.

Tips for Using ISOWEEKNUM

- **Difference from WEEKNUM:** While WEEKNUM calculates week numbers based on configurable starting days, ISOWEEKNUM strictly follows the ISO 8601 standard, where weeks start on Monday.
- **Data validation:** Ensure the input is a valid Excel date; otherwise, the function returns a #VALUE! error.
- **Project tracking:** Combine ISOWEEKNUM with date functions to dynamically calculate weekly progress in project plans.

ISPMT Function

Financial Functions

Introduction

The ISPMT function calculates the interest paid during a specific period of an investment or loan with constant periodic payments and a constant interest rate. Unlike IPMT, which calculates interest for a single payment, ISPMT calculates simple interest over the specified period.

Simple explanation: Calculates the interest for a specific period of a loan or investment.

Common use cases: Used in financial modeling, loan schedules, and investment analysis.

When to use this function: Use when analyzing the interest portion of an investment or loan in a specific period.

Syntax

```
=ISPMT(rate, per, nper, pv)
```

- **rate**: The interest rate per period.
- **per**: The period for which the interest is calculated (must be between 1 and nper).
- **nper**: The total number of payment periods.
- **pv**: The present value of the loan or investment (principal amount).

Worked Example

Challenge: Calculate the interest for the 2nd month of a $10,000 loan repaid over 12 months with an annual interest rate of 6%.

Details:

- Loan amount (pv): $10,000.
- Annual interest rate (rate): 6% (convert to monthly rate).
- Loan term (nper): 12 months.
- Period to calculate (per): 2.

	A	B	C
1	**Example**		
2	=ISPMT(6%/12, 2, 12, 10000)		
3	**Answer**		
4	-41.67		

Formula:

```
=ISPMT(6%/12, 2, 12, 10000)
```

Result: -41.67
Explanation: The function calculates that $41.67 is the interest for the 2nd month of the loan. The negative sign indicates an outgoing payment.

Explore Further with GPT

Ask GPT how to combine ISPMT with functions like IPMT, PMT, or FV to create complete financial models or amortization schedules.

KURT Function

Statistical Functions

Introduction

The KURT function calculates the kurtosis of a dataset, which measures the sharpness (peakedness) or flatness of its distribution. A positive kurtosis indicates a sharper peak (leptokurtic), while a negative kurtosis suggests a flatter distribution (platykurtic).

Simple explanation: Measures how peaked or flat a data distribution is.

Common use cases: Used in statistical analysis, financial modeling, and risk assessment.

When to use this function: Use when analyzing the shape of data distributions to understand variability and identify outliers.

Syntax

```
=KURT(number1, [number2], ...)
```

- **number1, number2, ...:** 1 to 255 numerical values or ranges to calculate kurtosis.

Worked Example

Challenge: Calculate the kurtosis for a dataset

Formula:

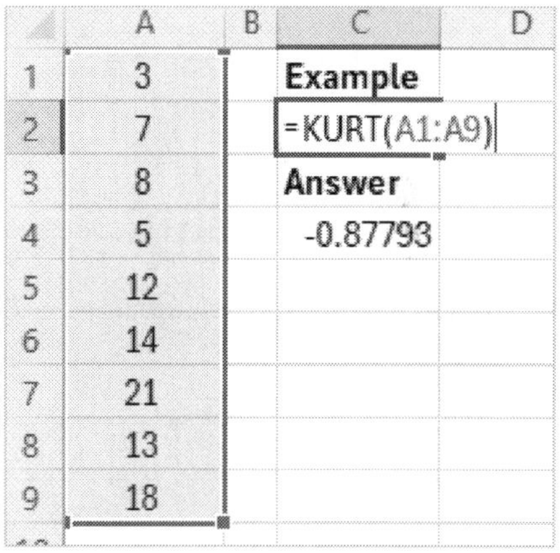


```
=KURT(A1:A9)
```

Result: -0.877934165
Explanation: The negative kurtosis value indicates the dataset has a flatter distribution (platykurtic) compared to a normal distribution.

Explore Further with GPT

Ask GPT how to combine KURT with other statistical functions like SKEW, STDEV, or AVERAGE to perform advanced data analysis.

Tips for Using KURT

- **Minimum data size:** The dataset must include at least 4 values; otherwise, the function returns a #DIV/0! error.

- **Outliers impact:** Outliers significantly affect kurtosis, as the function measures the weight of the distribution tails.

LAMBDA Function

Logical Functions

Introduction

The LAMBDA function allows you to create custom reusable functions directly in Excel without requiring VBA or macros. These functions can take input parameters, perform calculations, and return results, just like built-in Excel functions.

Simple explanation: Creates custom functions using Excel formulas.

Common use cases: Used for simplifying repetitive calculations, building modular formulas, and sharing reusable logic across workbooks.

When to use this function: Use when you need custom functionality that isn't available in Excel's built-in functions.

Syntax

```
=LAMBDA([parameter1, parameter2, …], calculation)
```

- **parameter1, parameter2, ...** *(optional)*: Names for input parameters used in the calculation.
- **calculation**: The formula or logic to be performed using the parameters

Worked Example

Challenge: Create a custom function to calculate the square of a number.

Formula:

=LAMBDA(x, x^2)

Usage:

=LAMBDA(x, x^2)(5)

Result: 25

Explanation: The function calculates the square of 5 by squaring the parameter x.

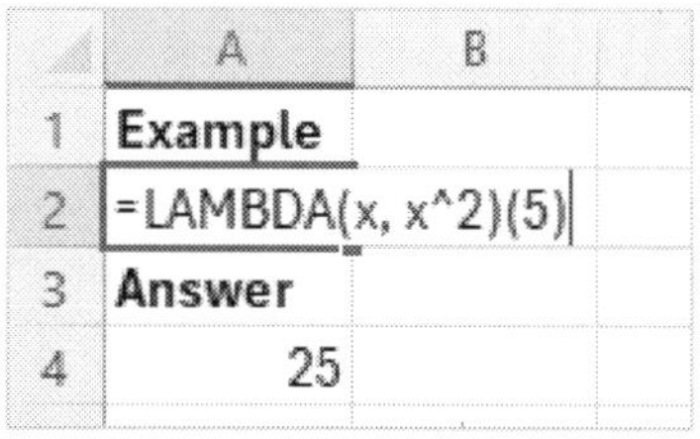

Explore Further with GPT

Ask GPT how to create advanced LAMBDA functions involving IF, FILTER, or LET for dynamic calculations and conditional logic.

Tips for Using LAMBDA

- **Error handling:** Use IFERROR within the LAMBDA function to manage invalid inputs:

  ```
  =LAMBDA(x, IFERROR(x^2, "Invalid input"))
  ```

- **Nesting:** Combine LAMBDA with other functions like MAP, REDUCE, or SCAN to perform advanced calculations across arrays.
- **Named functions:** Save reusable LAMBDA formulas with meaningful names to make them accessible throughout the workbook.

LARGE Function

Statistical Functions

Introduction

The LARGE function returns the k-th largest value in a dataset. This is useful for identifying top-performing values, ranking data, or extracting specific statistical metrics.

Simple explanation: Finds the k-th largest value in a dataset.

Common use cases: Used in data analysis, ranking, and identifying top values in a list.

When to use this function: Use when you need to extract specific high-ranking values from a dataset.

Syntax

```
=LARGE(array, k)
```

- **array**: The range or array of numeric values to evaluate.
- **k**: The rank (1 for the largest, 2 for the second largest, etc.) of the value to return.

Worked Example

Challenge: Find the 2nd largest value in a dataset.

Formula:

```
=LARGE(A1:A5, 2)
```

Result: 20
Explanation: The second largest value in the dataset is 20.

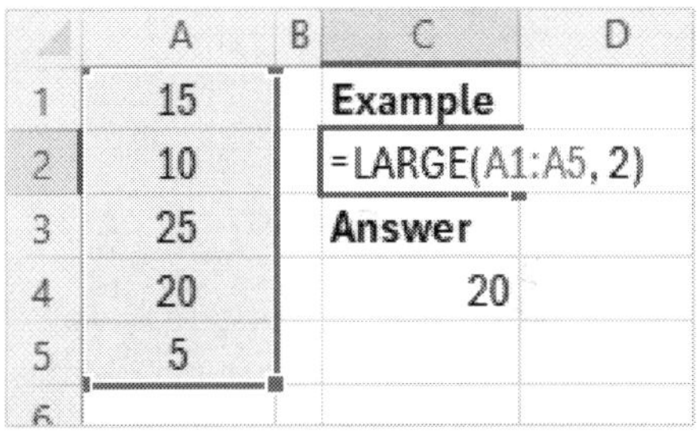

	A	B	C	D
1	15		**Example**	
2	10		=LARGE(A1:A5, 2)	
3	25		**Answer**	
4	20		20	
5	5			
6				

Explore Further with GPT

Ask GPT how to combine LARGE with functions like IF, FILTER, or INDEX to perform advanced ranking and data extraction.

Tips for Using LARGE

- **Error handling:** If k is less than 1 or greater than the number of values in the array, the function returns a #NUM! error. Use IFERROR to handle this:

  ```
  =IFERROR(LARGE(A1:A5, B1), "Invalid rank")
  ```

- **Sorting alternative:** Use LARGE instead of sorting to quickly extract top values without altering the dataset.

LCM Function

Math & Trigonometry Functions

Introduction

The LCM function calculates the least common multiple (LCM) of two or more integers. The LCM is the smallest positive integer that is evenly divisible by all the given numbers. This is useful in mathematical modeling, scheduling, and solving problems involving repeated patterns.

Simple explanation: Finds the smallest number divisible by all given integers.

Common use cases: Used in scheduling tasks, synchronizing cycles, and solving mathematical problems.

When to use this function: Use when you need to find a common multiple of integers.

Syntax

```
=LCM(number1, [number2], ...)
```

- **number1, number2, ...**: 1 to 255 integers for which you want to calculate the least common multiple.

Worked Example

Challenge: Find the least common multiple of 4 and 6.

Formula:

```
=LCM(4, 6)
```

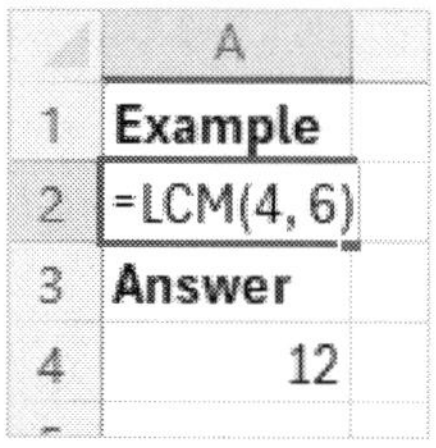

Result: 12
Explanation: The smallest number that is evenly divisible by both 4 and 6 is 12.

Explore Further with GPT

Ask GPT how to combine LCM with functions like GCD, MOD, or IF to solve advanced mathematical or scheduling problems.

Tips for Using LCM

- **Non-integer inputs:** The LCM function ignores decimal values; ensure the inputs are integers.
- **Large numbers:** The function may return a #NUM! error if the result exceeds Excel's numeric limit.
- **Combine with GCD:** Use the greatest common divisor (GCD) in conjunction with LCM to analyze relationships between numbers:

  ```
  =GCD(4, 6)
  ```

  ```
  =LCM(4, 6)
  ```

LEFT Function

Text Functions

Introduction

The LEFT function extracts a specified number of characters from the beginning (left side) of a text string. It is useful for text manipulation, data cleaning, and extracting key components from larger strings.

Simple explanation: Extracts characters from the start of a text string.

Common use cases: Used for cleaning data, parsing codes, or extracting prefixes.

When to use this function: Use when you need to isolate the beginning part of a string.

Syntax

```
=LEFT(text, [num_chars])
```

- **text**: The text string from which characters will be extracted.
- **[num_chars]** *(optional)*: The number of characters to extract. Defaults to 1 if omitted.

Worked Example

Challenge: Extract the first 4 characters from the text "Excel Tips".

Data in A1: "Excel Tips"

Formula:

```
=LEFT(A1, 4)
```

Result: "Exce"
Explanation: The function extracts the first 4 characters from the string in A1.

	A	B	C
1	Excel Tips		**Example**
2			=LEFT(A1, 4)
3			**Answer**
4			Exce

Explore Further with GPT

Ask GPT how to use LEFT with functions like MID, RIGHT, or FIND to handle complex text extraction scenarios.

Tips for Using LEFT

- **Ensure text input:** Numbers are treated as text. To avoid unexpected results, explicitly convert numeric values to text using TEXT:

  ```
  =LEFT(TEXT(A1, "0"), 3)
  ```

- **Working with multibyte characters:** For text in double-byte character sets (e.g., Japanese or Chinese), use the LEFTB function to extract a specific number of bytes instead of characters:

  ```
  =LEFTB(A1, 4)
  ```

  (Useful for text in languages where characters may require more than one byte.)

LEN Function

Text Functions

Introduction

The LEN function calculates the number of characters in a text string, including spaces, numbers, and special characters. It is widely used for text manipulation, data validation, and cleaning.

Simple explanation: Counts the number of characters in a text string.

Common use cases: Used to validate input length, find text lengths, and clean data.

When to use this function: Use when analyzing or verifying the length of text data.

Syntax

```
=LEN(text)
```

- **text**: The text string whose length you want to calculate.

Worked Example

Challenge: Count the number of characters in the text "Excel Tips".

Data in A1: "Excel Tips"

Formula:

```
=LEN(A1)
```

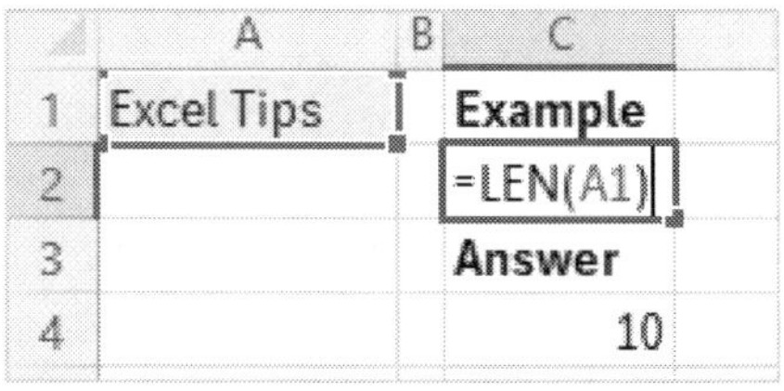

Result: 10
Explanation: The function counts all characters in "Excel Tips", including the space, and returns 10.

Explore Further with GPT

Ask GPT how to combine LEN with functions like TRIM, MID, or IF to clean and analyze text data dynamically.

Tips for Using LEN

- **Count characters after trimming:** Combine LEN with TRIM to calculate the length of text without leading or trailing spaces:

  ```
  =LEN(TRIM(A1))
  ```

- **Working with multibyte characters:** For text in double-byte character sets (e.g., Japanese or Chinese), use the LENB function to count the number of bytes rather than characters:

  ```
  =LENB(A1)
  ```

LET Function

Logical Functions

Introduction

The LET function allows you to define variables and assign them values within a formula, simplifying complex calculations and improving performance. By reusing values within the same formula, you avoid redundant calculations and make formulas easier to read and maintain.

Simple explanation: Assigns values to variables and uses them within a formula.

Common use cases: Used for simplifying long formulas, improving readability, and reducing repetitive calculations.

When to use this function: Use when building complex formulas that reuse intermediate values.

Syntax

```
=LET(name1, value1, [name2, value2, …], calculation)
```

- **name1, value1, ...**: Variable names and their corresponding values.
- **calculation**: The formula or logic that uses the defined variables.

Worked Example

Challenge: Calculate the area of a rectangle, reusing the length and width values.

Formula:

```
=LET(length, 10, width, 5, length * width)
```

Result: 50
Explanation: The formula assigns 10 to length and 5 to width, then calculates length * width.

	A	B	C	D
1	**Example**			
2	=LET(length, 10, width, 5, length * width)			
3	**Answer**			
4	50			
5				

Explore Further with GPT

Ask GPT how to use LET in combination with LAMBDA, FILTER, or SEQUENCE for creating dynamic, efficient, and reusable formulas.

Tips for Using LET

- **Improve readability:** Use descriptive variable names to make complex formulas easier to understand:

  ```
  =LET(total, SUM(A1:A10), avg, total/10, avg)
  ```

- **Combine with dynamic arrays:** Use LET with functions like FILTER or SORT to process dynamic datasets more efficiently.
- **Nested LET functions:** You can define multiple levels of variables by nesting LET functions, but ensure the formula remains readable.

LINEST Function

Statistical Functions

Introduction

The LINEST function calculates the statistics for a linear regression line that best fits a dataset. It returns the slope, intercept, and additional regression statistics, such as the R-squared value, to measure the relationship between dependent and independent variables.

Simple explanation: Performs linear regression analysis and returns the line equation and additional statistics.

Common use cases: Used in trend analysis, predictive modeling, and statistical forecasting.

When to use this function: Use when analyzing linear relationships between variables or predicting outcomes based on trends.

Syntax

```
=LINEST(known_y's, [known_x's], [const], [stats])
```

- **known_y's**: The dependent variable (y-values).
- **[known_x's]** *(optional)*: The independent variable (x-values). Defaults to {1, 2, 3, ...} if omitted.
- **[const]** *(optional)*: Logical value indicating whether to force the intercept to 0. Defaults to TRUE (include the intercept).
- **[stats]** *(optional)*: Logical value indicating whether to return additional regression statistics. Defaults to FALSE.

Worked Example

Challenge: Find the slope and intercept for the equation ***y=mx+b***, given a dataset:

Formula:

```
=LINEST(B2:B6, A2:A6)
```

Result: {2.2, -1}
Explanation: The slope is 2, and the intercept is 0. This indicates the equation of the line is ***y=2.2x-1***

	A	B	C	D	E
1	X	Y		Example	
2	1	2		=LINEST(B2:B6, A2:A6)	
3	2	3		Answer	
4	3	5		2.2	-1
5	4	7			
6	5	11			
7					

Explore Further with GPT

Ask GPT how to combine LINEST with visualization tools like charts or functions like FORECAST.LINEAR to create dynamic models.

Tips for Using LINEST

- **Array output:** LINEST returns an array of values. Use CTRL+SHIFT+ENTER (for legacy Excel) or spill behavior (for Excel 365/2021) to view results.
- **R-squared value:** When stats is set to TRUE, the R-squared value indicates the goodness of fit. A value close to 1 signifies a strong linear relationship.
- **Forcing intercept to zero:** Set const to FALSE if the intercept should be zero

LN Function

Math & Trigonometry Functions

Introduction

The LN function calculates the natural logarithm of a given number. The natural logarithm is based on the constant eee (approximately equal to 2.718), which is the base of the natural exponential function.

Simple explanation: Calculates the natural logarithm of a number.

Common use cases: Used in financial modeling, growth analysis, and solving mathematical problems involving exponential relationships.

When to use this function: Use when working with exponential growth, decay, or other problems involving **e**.

Syntax

```
=LN(number)
```

- **number**: A positive numeric value for which you want the natural logarithm.

Worked Example

Challenge: Find the natural logarithm of 20.

Formula:

```
=LN(20)
```

	A
1	**Example**
2	=LN(20)
3	**Answer**
4	2.995732

Result: 2.995732
Explanation: The natural logarithm of 20 is approximately 2.996.

Explore Further with GPT

Ask GPT how to combine LN with other mathematical functions like EXP, LOG, or POWER to model growth, decay, or scaling problems.

Tips for Using LN

- **Convert to other bases:** To calculate logarithms in other bases, use the LOG function. For example, to calculate base-10 logarithms:

  ```
  =LOG(A1, 10)
  ```

- **Relationship with EXP:** The EXP function is the inverse of LN. For example:

  ```
  =EXP(LN(10))  ' Returns 10
  ```

- **Real-world applications:** Use LN to model natural growth (e.g., population growth) or decay (e.g., radioactive decay).

LOG Function

Math & Trigonometry Functions

Introduction

The LOG function calculates the logarithm of a number for a specified base. By default, if the base is omitted, it assumes base 10. This function is useful for scaling data, solving exponential equations, and performing mathematical analysis.

Simple explanation: Calculates the logarithm of a number for a specified base.

Common use cases: Used in scientific calculations, data scaling, and financial modeling.

When to use this function: Use when you need to calculate logarithms in any base.

Syntax

```
=LOG(number, [base])
```

- **number**: A positive numeric value for which to calculate the logarithm.
- **[base]** *(optional)*: The base for the logarithm. Defaults to 10 if omitted.

Worked Example

Challenge: Find the logarithm of 1000 in base 10.

Formula:

```
=LOG(1000, 10)
```

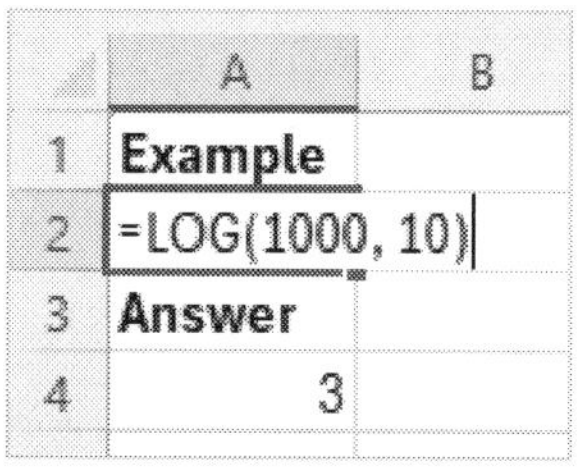

	A	B
1	**Example**	
2	=LOG(1000, 10)	
3	**Answer**	
4	3	

Result: 3
Explanation: 10^3=1000, so the logarithm of 1000 in base 10 is 3.

Explore Further with GPT

Ask GPT how to combine LOG with functions like EXP, LN, or POWER to model exponential growth, scaling, or data normalization.

Tips for Using LOG

- **Default base:** When the base argument is omitted, LOG assumes base 10. To calculate the natural logarithm, use base ***e*** (approximately 2.718):

  ```
  =LOG(A1, EXP(1))
  ```

- **Convert between bases:** To calculate logarithms in a different base, use:

  ```
  =LOG(number, base)
  ```

  For example, LOG(16, 2) calculates the base-2 logarithm of 16, which is 4.

LOG10 Function

Math & Trigonometry Functions

Introduction

The LOG10 function calculates the base-10 logarithm of a given number. It is often used in scientific and financial calculations, especially when working with powers of 10 or scaling data for analysis.

Simple explanation: Calculates the base-10 logarithm of a number.

Common use cases: Used in scientific notation, scaling data, and solving exponential equations.

When to use this function: Use when working specifically with base-10 logarithms.

Syntax

```
=LOG10(number)
```

- **number**: A positive numeric value for which to calculate the base-10 logarithm.

Worked Example

Challenge: Find the base-10 logarithm of 0.01.

Formula:

```
=LOG10(0.01)
```

	A	B
1	**Example**	
2	=LOG10(0.01)	
3	**Answer**	
4	-2	

Result: -2

Explanation: 10^{-2}=0.01, so the base-10 logarithm of 0.01 is −2.

Tips for Using LOG10

- **Handling small values:** LOG10 returns negative values for inputs between 000 and 111, as these represent fractions.
- **Error handling:** The LOG10 function returns a #NUM! error if the input is less than or equal to 000. Use IFERROR for safer formulas:

  ```
  =IFERROR(LOG10(A1), "Invalid input")
  ```

- **Relationship with POWER**: The LOG10 function is the inverse of POWER for base 10:

  ```
  =POWER(10, LOG10(1000))  ' Returns 1000
  ```

LOGEST Function

Statistical Functions

Introduction

The LOGEST function calculates an exponential curve that best fits a dataset and returns an array of values describing the curve. It is useful for exponential growth or decay analysis, where data relationships follow the form $y=b \cdot m^x$.

Simple explanation: Performs exponential regression to fit data to the equation $y=b \cdot m^x$.

Common use cases: Used in growth analysis, population modeling, and financial forecasting.

When to use this function: Use when analyzing exponential relationships in datasets.

Syntax

```
=LOGEST(known_y's, [known_x's], [const], [stats])
```

- **known_y's**: The dependent variable (y-values).
- **[known_x's]** *(optional)*: The independent variable (x-values). Defaults to {1, 2, 3, ...} if omitted.
- **[const]** *(optional)*: Logical value indicating whether to force the constant ***b*** to equal 1. Defaults to TRUE (include the constant).
- **[stats]** *(optional)*: Logical value indicating whether to return additional regression statistics. Defaults to FALSE.

Worked Example

Challenge: Find the exponential equation for a dataset.

Formula:

```
=LOGEST(B2:B6, A2:A6)
```

Result (array): {2.72, 1}
Explanation: The exponential equation y=2.71 . e^{x}, with b=2.71 and m=1.

	A	B	C	D	E
1	X	Y		Example	
2	1	2.7		=LOGEST(B2:B6, A2:A6)	
3	2	7.4		Answer	
4	3	20.1		2.72	1.00
5	4	54.6			
6	5	148			

Explore Further with GPT

Ask GPT how to combine LOGEST with visualization tools like charts or functions like GROWTH to create predictive models and visualize trends.

Tips for Using LOGEST

- **Array output:** LOGEST returns an array of values. Use CTRL+SHIFT+ENTER (for legacy Excel) or spill behavior (for Excel 365/2021) to display results.
- **Interpretation:** The first value in the result is the base ***b*** and subsequent values are the exponents ***m***.
- **R-squared value:** When stats is set to TRUE, the R-squared value indicates the fit of the model. A value close to 1 indicates a strong fit.

LOGINV Function

Compatibility Functions

Introduction

The LOGINV function calculates the inverse of the lognormal cumulative distribution for a specified mean and standard deviation of the natural logarithm. It returns the value xxx such that the cumulative lognormal distribution is equal to a given probability.

Simple explanation: Finds the value ***x*** for a given probability in a lognormal distribution.

Common use cases: Used in financial modeling, risk analysis, and statistical modeling to determine thresholds or specific points in lognormal distributions.

When to use this function: Use when analyzing data that follows a lognormal distribution and you need to calculate specific values.

Syntax

```
=LOGINV(probability, mean, standard_dev)
```

- **probability**: A probability associated with the lognormal distribution (must be between 0 and 1).
- **mean**: The mean of the natural logarithm of the distribution.
- **standard_dev**: The standard deviation of the natural logarithm of the distribution.

Worked Example

Challenge: Find the value ***x*** for a lognormal distribution where:

- Probability: 0.95
- Mean: 1.5
- Standard Deviation: 0.5

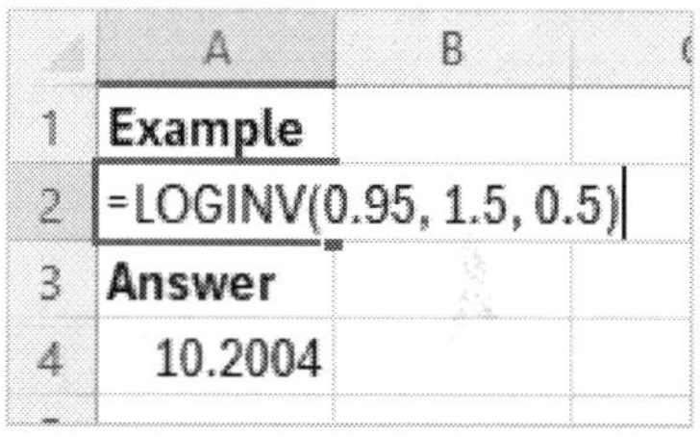

Formula:

```
=LOGINV(0.95, 1.5, 0.5)
```

Result: 10.2004
Explanation: For a cumulative probability of 0.95, the value ***x*** in the lognormal distribution with the specified mean and standard deviation is approximately 10.2004.

Tips for Using LOGINV

- **Input constraints:** Ensure the probability is between 000 and 111. Any value outside this range will result in a #NUM! error.
- **Modeling lognormal data:** Use LOGINV to calculate specific points in scenarios like financial risk analysis (e.g., stock prices) or environmental studies.
- **Excel compatibility:** The LOGINV function is available in Excel 2007 and earlier. For later versions (Excel 2010+), use LOGNORM.INV.

LOGNORM.DIST Function

Statistical Functions

Introduction

The LOGNORM.DIST function returns the lognormal distribution for a specified mean and standard deviation of the natural logarithm. This function is often used in statistical analysis, financial modeling, and risk assessment for data that follows a lognormal distribution.

Simple explanation: Calculates the probability or cumulative probability for a lognormal distribution.

Common use cases: Used in financial risk modeling, environmental studies, and reliability analysis.

When to use this function: Use when analyzing datasets with lognormally distributed values.

Syntax

```
=LOGNORM.DIST(x, mean, standard_dev, cumulative)
```

- **x**: The value at which to evaluate the lognormal distribution (must be > 0).
- **mean**: The mean of the natural logarithm of the distribution.
- **standard_dev**: The standard deviation of the natural logarithm of the distribution.
- **cumulative**: A logical value specifying whether to return the cumulative distribution function (TRUE) or the probability density function (FALSE).

Worked Example

Challenge: Find the cumulative probability for x=5, mean 1.5, and standard deviation 0.5.

Formula:

```
=LOGNORM.DIST(5, 1.5, 0.5, TRUE)
```

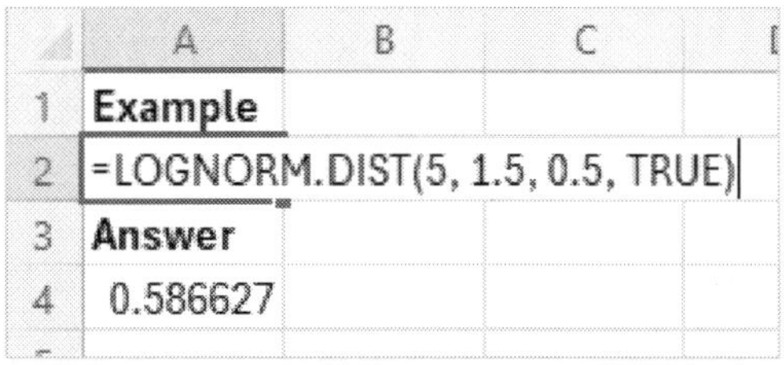

Result: 0.586627
Explanation: The cumulative probability of x=5 under the given lognormal distribution is approximately 0.586627.

Explore Further with GPT

Ask GPT how to use LOGNORM.DIST with LOGINV, NORM.DIST, or EXP to model lognormal distributions, calculate thresholds, or solve real-world problems.

Tips for Using LOGNORM.DIST

- **Input constraints:** Ensure x>0; otherwise, the function returns a #NUM! error.
- **Cumulative vs. probability density:** Use TRUE for cumulative probabilities and FALSE for the probability density at a specific xxx:

  ```
  =LOGNORM.DIST(x, mean, standard_dev, TRUE)   ' Cumulative
  ```

  ```
  =LOGNORM.DIST(x, mean, standard_dev, FALSE)  ' Probability density
  ```

- **Modeling distributions:** Combine with LOGINV to calculate specific thresholds or percentiles in a lognormal distribution:

  ```
  =LOGINV(0.95, mean, standard_dev)  ' 95th percentile
  ```

LOGNORMDIST Function

Compatibility Functions

Introduction

The LOGNORMDIST function calculates the cumulative lognormal distribution for a specified mean and standard deviation of the natural logarithm. It is commonly used in financial and statistical analysis to model values that follow a lognormal distribution.

Simple explanation: Calculates the cumulative probability for a lognormal distribution.

Common use cases: Used in modeling financial returns, risk analysis, and data following a lognormal distribution.

When to use this function: Use when analyzing the cumulative behavior of datasets with lognormal characteristics.

Syntax

```
=LOGNORMDIST(x, mean, standard_dev)
```

- **x**: The value at which to evaluate the cumulative distribution (must be > 0).
- **mean**: The mean of the natural logarithm of the distribution.
- **standard_dev**: The standard deviation of the natural logarithm of the distribution

Worked Example

Challenge: Find the cumulative probability for x=5, mean 1.5, and standard deviation 0.5.

Formula:

```
=LOGNORMDIST(5, 1.5, 0.5)
```

	A	B	C
1	**Example**		
2	=LOGNORMDIST(5, 1.5, 0.5)		
3	**Answer**		
4	0.586627		
5			

Result: 0.586627
Explanation: The cumulative probability of x=5 under the given lognormal distribution is approximately 0.586627.

Explore Further with GPT

Ask GPT how to use LOGNORMDIST alongside other statistical functions like LOGINV or LOGNORM.DIST to model and interpret lognormal distributions effectively.

Tips for Using LOGNORMDIST

- **Legacy function:** The LOGNORMDIST function has been replaced by LOGNORM.DIST in Excel 2010 and later versions. For backward compatibility, LOGNORMDIST is still supported in older Excel versions.
- **Input constraints:** Ensure x>0; otherwise, the function returns a #NUM! error.
- **Cumulative distribution only:** Unlike LOGNORM.DIST, which offers both cumulative and probability density options, LOGNORMDIST only calculates the cumulative probability.

LOGNORM.INV Function

Statistical Functions

Introduction

The LOGNORM.INV function calculates the inverse of the lognormal cumulative distribution for a specified mean and standard deviation of the natural logarithm. It returns the value xxx such that the cumulative lognormal distribution equals a given probability.

Simple explanation: Finds the value xxx for a given probability in a lognormal distribution.

Common use cases: Used in financial modeling, risk analysis, and statistical analysis to calculate thresholds or specific points in lognormal distributions.

When to use this function: Use when you need to determine the value corresponding to a specific cumulative probability in a lognormal distribution.

Syntax

```
=LOGNORM.INV(probability, mean, standard_dev)
```

- **probability**: The cumulative probability associated with the lognormal distribution (must be between 0 and 1).
- **mean**: The mean of the natural logarithm of the distribution.
- **standard_dev**: The standard deviation of the natural logarithm of the distribution

Worked Example

Challenge: Find the value x for a lognormal distribution with:

- Probability: 0.95
- Mean: 1.5
- Standard Deviation: 0.50

	A	B	C
1	**Example**		
2	=LOGNORM.INV(0.95, 1.5, 0.5)		
3	**Answer**		
4	10.2004		

Formula:

```
=LOGNORM.INV(0.95, 1.5, 0.5)
```

Result: 10.2004

Explanation: For a cumulative probability of 0.95, the value in the lognormal distribution is approximately 10.2004.

Tips for Using LOGNORM.INV

- **Input constraints:** Ensure the probability is between 0 and 1; values outside this range result in a #NUM! error.
- **Modeling thresholds:** Use LOGNORM.INV to calculate specific percentiles in a distribution, such as:

```
=LOGNORM.INV(0.95, mean, standard_dev)  ' 95th percentile
```

LOOKUP Function

Lookup & Reference Functions

Introduction

The LOOKUP function searches for a value in a single row or column and returns a corresponding value from another row or column. It is useful for retrieving data from a dataset when you know part of the data.

Simple explanation: Searches for a value in one range and returns a corresponding value from another range.

Common use cases: Used in data retrieval, creating reports, and matching values across tables.

When to use this function: Use when you need to find a corresponding value in a dataset with sorted data.

Syntax

```
=LOOKUP(lookup_value, lookup_vector, [result_vector])
```

- **lookup_value**: The value to search for in the lookup range.
- **lookup_vector**: A single row or column containing sorted data where the search is performed.
- **[result_vector]** *(optional)*: A single row or column containing the values to return. If omitted, the function returns a value from the lookup_vector.

Worked Example

Challenge: Find the grade for a score of 85 based on a dataset:

Formula:

```
=LOOKUP(85, A2:A6, B1:B5)
```

	A	B	C	D	E	F
1	**Score**	**Grade**		**Example**		
2	50	F		=LOOKUP(85, A2:A6, B2:B6)		
3	60	D		**Answer**		
4	70	C		B		
5	80	B				
6	90	A				
7						

Result: B
Explanation: The function searches for 85 in the Score column. Since 85 is between 80 and 90, it returns the corresponding value B from the Grade column

Explore Further with GPT

Ask GPT how to use LOOKUP with functions like MATCH, INDEX, or IF to handle more complex data retrieval tasks.

Tips for Using LOOKUP

- **Sorted data requirement:** The lookup_vector must be sorted in ascending order. If the data is unsorted, use VLOOKUP, HLOOKUP, or XLOOKUP instead.
- **Approximate match:** If the exact lookup_value is not found, LOOKUP returns the largest value less than or equal to the lookup_value.
- **Alternative functions:** Use `XLOOKUP` for more flexibility, such as exact matches and reverse lookups:

  ```
  =XLOOKUP(lookup_value, lookup_vector, result_vector)
  ```

LOWER Function

Text Functions

Introduction

The LOWER function converts all uppercase letters in a text string to lowercase. It leaves numbers, special characters, and already lowercase letters unchanged. This function is commonly used in text standardization and formatting.

Simple explanation: Converts text to all lowercase letters.

Common use cases: Used for standardizing text in datasets, ensuring consistency in email addresses, and formatting text fields.

When to use this function: Use when you need to transform text to a consistent lowercase format.

Syntax

```
=LOWER(text)
```

- **text**: The text string to convert to lowercase. This can be a reference to a cell, a hardcoded string, or a formula result.

Worked Example

Challenge: Convert "Excel Functions" in cell A1 to lowercase.

Formula:

=LOWER(A1)

Result: "excel functions"
Explanation: The function converts all uppercase letters (E and F) to lowercase, leaving the rest unchanged.

	A	B	C
1	Excel Functions		**Example**
2			=LOWER(A1)
3			**Answer**
4			excel functions
5			

Explore Further with GPT

Ask GPT how to combine LOWER with other functions like UPPER, PROPER, or TRIM for cleaning and standardizing text data.

Tips for Using LOWER

- **Text standardization:** Combine LOWER with TRIM and CLEAN to remove extra spaces and non-printable characters:

  `=LOWER(TRIM(CLEAN(A1)))`

- **Email validation:** Use LOWER to ensure consistent email formatting in data validation rules.

MAKEARRAY Function

Logical Functions

Introduction

The MAKEARRAY function generates an array by applying a custom formula to each cell in a specified row and column range. It enables the creation of dynamic arrays using custom logic for each cell's value.

Simple explanation: Creates an array by applying a formula to each cell in a defined range.

Common use cases: Used for generating custom tables, dynamic data simulations, or performing cell-by-cell calculations across an array.

When to use this function: Use when you need to dynamically generate arrays with custom formulas.

Syntax

```
=MAKEARRAY(rows, columns, lambda(row, column))
```

- **rows**: The number of rows in the array.
- **columns**: The number of columns in the array.
- **lambda(row, column)**: A custom formula, defined using the LAMBDA function, to calculate the value for each cell

Worked Example

Challenge: Create a 3x3 array where each cell contains the sum of its row and column indices.

Formula:

```
=MAKEARRAY(3, 3, LAMBDA(row,
column, row + column))
```

Result:

	1	2	3
1	2	3	4
2	3	4	5
3	4	5	6

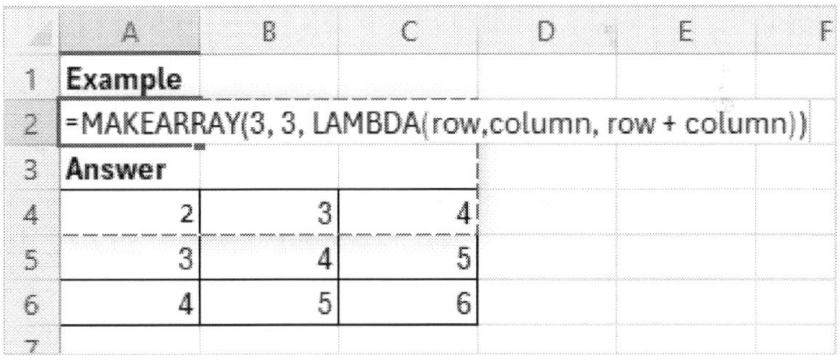

	A	B	C	D	E	F
1	**Example**					
2	=MAKEARRAY(3, 3, LAMBDA(row,column, row + column))					
3	**Answer**					
4	2	3	4			
5	3	4	5			
6	4	5	6			
7						

Explanation: Each cell is the sum of its row and column indices (e.g., cell (2, 3) contains 2 + 3 = 5).

Explore Further with GPT

Ask GPT how to combine MAKEARRAY with functions like SEQUENCE, RAND, or INDEX to generate dynamic tables, random data, or advanced simulations.

Tips for Using MAKEARRAY

- **Complex logic:** Use LAMBDA to apply conditional or more advanced logic to each cell:

  ```
  =MAKEARRAY(4, 4, LAMBDA(row, column, IF(MOD(row + column, 2) = 0, "Even", "Odd")))
  ```

MAP Function

Logical Functions

Introduction

The MAP function applies a custom formula to each element of one or more arrays and returns a new array containing the results. It is useful for applying transformations or calculations to array elements dynamically.

Simple explanation: Applies a custom formula to each element of one or more arrays.

Common use cases: Used for array transformations, element-wise calculations, or creating new datasets based on existing arrays.

When to use this function: Use when you need to perform element-wise operations across one or more arrays.

Syntax

```
=MAP(array1, [array2, …], lambda(element1, [element2, …]))
```

- **array1, array2, ...**: One or more arrays to transform.
- **lambda(element1, element2, ...)**: A custom formula, defined using the LAMBDA function, to apply to each element.

Worked Example

Challenge: Multiply each element of an array by 2.

Formula:

```
=MAP(A1:A5, LAMBDA(x, x * 2))
```

Result:

1	2
2	4
3	6
4	8
5	10

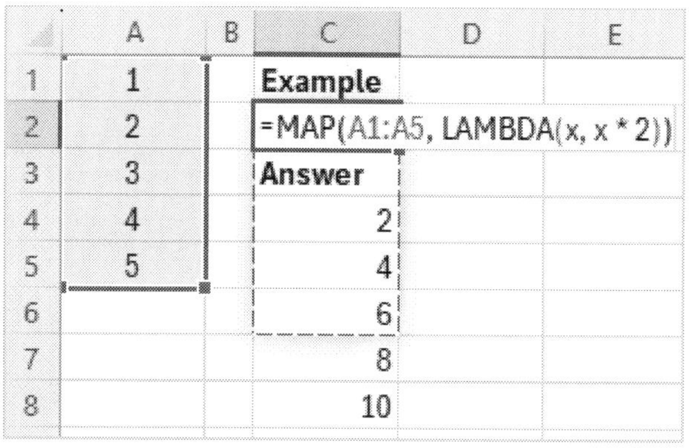

Explanation: Each element in A1:A5 is multiplied by 2 using the LAMBDA function.

Explore Further with GPT

Ask GPT how to combine MAP with functions like FILTER, REDUCE, or SCAN to perform advanced array operations and dynamic calculations.

Tips for Using MAP

- **Dynamic arrays:** The result of MAP spills into adjacent cells if enough space is available.
- **Multiple arrays:** You can use MAP with multiple arrays as long as they have the same dimensions.

MATCH Function

Lookup & Reference Functions

Introduction

The MATCH function searches for a specified value in a range and returns its relative position. It is commonly used for locating values within lists or arrays and is often combined with other functions like INDEX.

Simple explanation: Finds the position of a value in a range.

Common use cases: Used for locating values in datasets, creating dynamic ranges, and working with data lookups.

When to use this function: Use when you need the position of a value rather than the value itself.

Syntax

```
=MATCH(lookup_value, lookup_array, [match_type])
```

- **lookup_value**: The value you want to find.
- **lookup_array**: The range of cells or array to search.
- **[match_type]** *(optional)*: Determines how the function matches the value:
    - 1 (default): Finds the largest value less than or equal to lookup_value (requires sorted data in ascending order).
    - 0: Finds the exact match.
    - -1: Finds the smallest value greater than or equal to lookup_value (requires sorted data in descending order).

Worked Example

Challenge: Find the position of the value 20 in the dataset.

Formula:

```
=MATCH(20, A1:A5, 0)
```

Result: 3
Explanation: The value 20 is located in the third position of the range A1:A5.

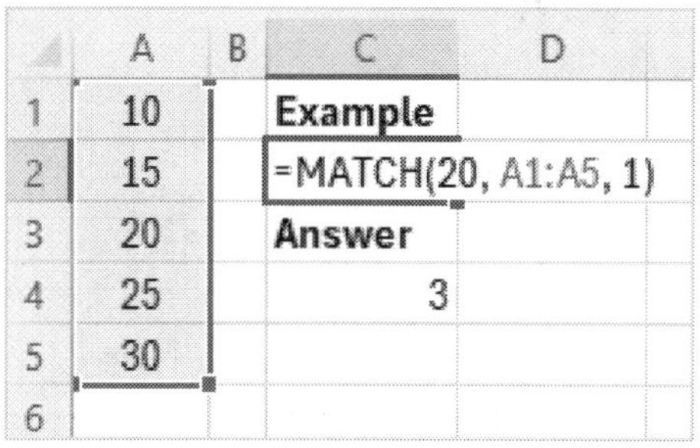

	A	B	C	D
1	10		**Example**	
2	15		=MATCH(20, A1:A5, 1)	
3	20		**Answer**	
4	25		3	
5	30			
6				

Explore Further with GPT

Ask GPT how to combine MATCH with INDEX, VLOOKUP, or XLOOKUP for advanced lookup and data retrieval tasks.

Tips for Using MATCH

- **Exact vs. approximate:** Use 0 for exact matches and 1 or -1 for approximate matches. Ensure the data is sorted appropriately for approximate matches.
- **Combine with `INDEX`:** Use `MATCH` to find the position of a value and feed it into `INDEX` for value retrieval:

```
=INDEX(B1:B5, MATCH(lookup_value, A1:A5, 0))
```

MAX Function

Statistical Functions

Introduction

The MAX function returns the largest numeric value in a specified range or list of numbers. It is commonly used in data analysis to identify maximum values in datasets.

Simple explanation: Finds the largest value in a range or list.

Common use cases: Used to identify peak values, track maximum metrics, or validate data.

When to use this function: Use when you need the highest value from a dataset.

Syntax

```
=MAX(number1, [number2], ...)
```

- **number1, number2, ...**: 1 to 255 numeric values, cell references, or ranges to evaluate.

Worked Example

Challenge: Find the largest number in a dataset.

Formula:

`=MAX(A1:A5)`

Result: 30
Explanation: The largest value in the range A1:A5 is 30.

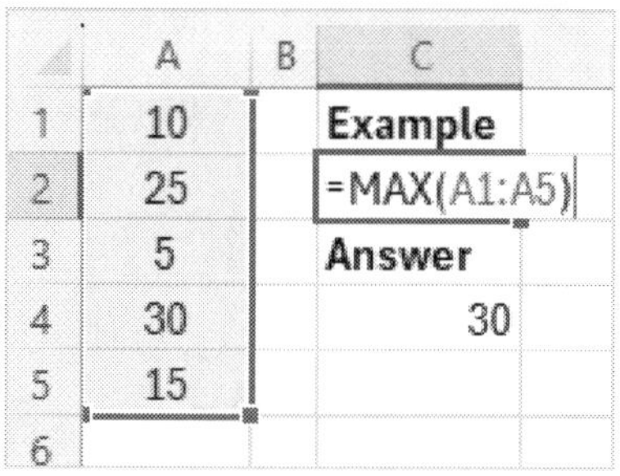

Explore Further with GPT

Ask GPT how to use MAX in combination with other functions like IF, ARRAYFORMULA, or FILTER to perform advanced calculations or data analysis.

Tips for Using MAX

- **Ignoring non-numeric values:** The MAX function automatically ignores text, blank cells, and logical values (TRUE, FALSE).
- **Combine with conditional logic:** Use `MAX` with `IF` to find the maximum value that meets specific criteria:

  `=MAX(IF(A1:A5>10, A1:A5))`

  (Use `CTRL+SHIFT+ENTER` for array formulas in legacy Excel versions.)

MAXA Function

Statistical Functions

Introduction

The MAXA function returns the largest numeric value in a specified range or list of values, similar to MAX. However, unlike MAX, it evaluates text and logical values. Text is treated as 0, and logical values are treated as 1 for TRUE and 0 for FALSE.

Simple explanation: Finds the largest value in a range, treating logical values and text differently than MAX.

Common use cases: Used when datasets include logical values or text that need to be factored into the calculation.

When to use this function: Use when your data includes logical values or text and their evaluation is important.

Syntax

```
=MAXA(value1, [value2], ...)
```

- **value1, value2, ...**: 1 to 255 numeric values, cell references, or ranges to evaluate.

Worked Example

Challenge: Find the largest value in a dataset that includes logical values.

Formula:

```
=MAXA(A1:A5)
```

Result: 20

Explanation: The largest numeric value is 20. The logical value TRUE is treated as 1, and the text "Text" is treated as 0.

	A	B	C
1	10		**Example**
2	15		=MAXA(A1:A5)
3	TRUE		**Answer**
4	"Text"		20
5	20		

Explore Further with GPT

Ask GPT how to combine MAXA with functions like IF, FILTER, or ARRAYFORMULA to create more complex and dynamic analyses.

Tips for Using MAXA

- **Logical values:** TRUE is treated as 1, and FALSE is treated as 0. This differs from MAX, which ignores logical values.
- **Text as zero:** Text values, including empty strings (""), are treated as 0.
- **Combine with conditional logic:** Use MAXA with IF to include specific conditions:

  ```
  =MAXA(IF(A1:A5>10, A1:A5))
  ```

  (Use CTRL+SHIFT+ENTER for array formulas in legacy Excel versions.)

MAXIFS Function

Statistical Functions

Introduction

The MAXIFS function returns the largest numeric value from a range that meets one or more specified criteria. It allows for conditional maximum calculations, making it ideal for filtering data based on specific conditions.

Simple explanation: Finds the largest value in a range that meets specified conditions.

Common use cases: Used for data analysis, filtering results, and conditional calculations.

When to use this function: Use when you need to find the maximum value based on criteria.

Syntax

```
=MAXIFS(max_range, criteria_range1, criteria1, [criteria_range2, criteria2], ...)
```

- **max_range**: The range of values to find the maximum value from.
- **criteria_range1**: The range to evaluate against the first criterion.
- **criteria1**: The condition to apply to criteria_range1.
- **[criteria_range2, criteria2]** *(optional)*: Additional ranges and criteria to apply.

Worked Example

Challenge: Find the maximum sales value for Region "North" in the dataset

Formula:

```
=MAXIFS(B2:B6, A2:A6, "North")
```

	A	B	C	D	E	F
1	**Region**	**Sales**		**Example**		
2	North	200		=MAXIFS(B2:B6, A2:A6, "North")		
3	South	150		**Answer**		
4	North	300		300		
5	East	250				
6	North	180				

Result: 300

Explanation: The function searches the Sales range (B2:B6) and returns the maximum value where Region (A2:A6) is North.

Explore Further with GPT

Ask GPT how to combine MAXIFS with functions like MINIFS, FILTER, or SORT for dynamic filtering and ranking analyses.

Tips for Using MAXIFS

- **Criteria flexibility:** Criteria can include wildcards (* for multiple characters, ? for a single character) and operators (e.g., ">=100").
- **Blank cells:** Blank cells in the max_range or criteria_range are ignored.
- **Combine with dynamic criteria:** Use cell references for criteria to make the formula adaptable:

  ```
  =MAXIFS(B2:B6, A2:A6, D1)
  ```

  (Where D1 contains the desired criterion, such as North.)

MDETERM Function

Math & Trigonometry Functions

Introduction

The MDETERM function calculates the determinant of a square matrix. Determinants are useful in linear algebra for solving systems of linear equations, performing transformations, and analyzing matrix properties.

Simple explanation: Calculates the determinant of a square matrix.

Common use cases: Used in linear algebra, solving equations, and mathematical modeling.

When to use this function: Use when working with square matrices in mathematical or scientific computations.

Syntax

```
=MDETERM(array)
```

- **array**: A square matrix (same number of rows and columns) of numeric values.

Worked Example

Challenge: Calculate the determinant of a 2x2 matrix.

Matrix in A1:B2:

A	B
3 (a)	8 (b)
4 (c)	6 (d)

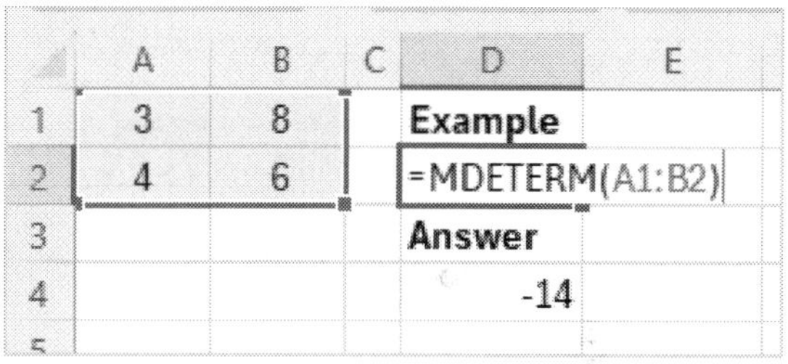

Formula:

```
=MDETERM(A1:B2)
```

Result: -14

Explanation: The determinant of a 2x2 matrix is calculated as (a·d)−(b·c). For this matrix:

(3·6)−(8·4)=18−32=−14

Explore Further with GPT

Ask GPT how to combine MDETERM with functions like MINVERSE and MMULT to perform advanced matrix operations, such as solving systems of equations.

Tips for Using MDETERM

- **Square matrices only:** The MDETERM function works only with square matrices. If the matrix is not square, the function returns a #VALUE! error.
- **Numeric values:** Ensure all cells in the matrix contain numeric values. Non-numeric values or blank cells result in a #VALUE! error.
- **Matrix size limit:** The maximum size of the matrix is constrained by Excel's memory and array size limits (e.g., 32x32 matrix in older versions).

MDURATION Function

Financial Functions

Introduction

The MDURATION function calculates the modified Macaulay duration of a security with periodic interest payments. This financial metric measures the sensitivity of a bond's price to changes in interest rates, adjusted for the bond's yield.

Simple explanation: Calculates the adjusted duration of a bond based on interest rates and yield.

Common use cases: Used in bond analysis, risk management, and portfolio optimization.

When to use this function: Use when assessing interest rate risk or comparing bond durations.

Syntax

```
=MDURATION(settlement, maturity, coupon, yld, frequency, [basis])
```

- **settlement**: The bond's settlement date (the date the bond is purchased).
- **maturity**: The bond's maturity date (the date the bond expires).
- **coupon**: The bond's annual coupon rate (as a decimal).
- **yld**: The bond's annual yield (as a decimal).
- **frequency**: The number of coupon payments per year (1 for annual, 2 for semi-annual, 4 for quarterly).
- **[basis]** *(optional)*: The day count basis to use (defaults to 0 for 30/360 US).
    - 0: 30/360 (US); 1: Actual/actual; 2: Actual/360; 3: Actual/365;4: 30/360 (European)

Worked Example

Challenge: Calculate the modified duration of a bond.

Inputs:

- Settlement date: 01-Jan-2023
- Maturity date: 01-Jan-2028
- Coupon rate: 5% (0.05)
- Yield: 6% (0.06)
- Frequency: 2 (semi-annual)
- Basis: 0 (30/360 US)

	A	B	C	D	E	F
1	**Example**					
2	=MDURATION(DATE(2023,1,1), DATE(2028,1,1), 0.05, 0.06, 2, 0)					
3	**Answer**					
4	4.34					

Formula:

```
=MDURATION(DATE(2023,1,1), DATE(2028,1,1), 0.05, 0.06, 2, 0)
```

Result: 4.34

Explanation: The bond's modified duration is approximately 4.34 years, meaning its price would change by about 4.34% for a 1% change in yield.

MEDIAN Function

Statistical Functions

Introduction

The MEDIAN function returns the median (middle value) of a set of numbers. If the dataset contains an odd number of values, the function returns the middle value; if even, it returns the average of the two middle values. This is useful for understanding the central tendency of a dataset, especially when it contains outliers.

Simple explanation: Finds the middle value in a dataset.

Common use cases: Used in statistical analysis, data cleaning, and measuring central tendency.

When to use this function: Use when you need a central value that isn't skewed by outliers.

Syntax

```
=MEDIAN(number1, [number2], ...)
```

- **number1, number2, ...**: 1 to 255 numeric values, cell references, or ranges to evaluate.

Worked Example

Challenge: Find the median of a dataset

Formula:

```
=MEDIAN(A1:A7)
```

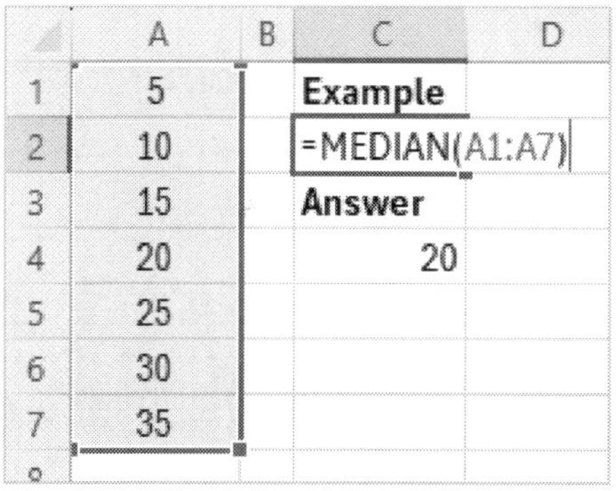

Result: 20
Explanation: The dataset has an odd number of values, so the median is the middle value when sorted.

Explore Further with GPT

Ask GPT how to use MEDIAN in combination with AVERAGE, MODE, or STDEV to perform more comprehensive statistical analyses.

Tips for Using MEDIAN

- **Ignores non-numeric values:** The MEDIAN function automatically excludes text, logical values, and blank cells from calculations.
- **Error handling:** If the dataset contains no numeric values, MEDIAN returns a #NUM! error. Use IFERROR to handle this:

  ```
  =IFERROR(MEDIAN(A1:A7), "No numeric values")
  ```

- **Comparison with AVERAGE:** Use MEDIAN instead of AVERAGE when the dataset has significant outliers, as MEDIAN is less affected.

MID Function

Text Functions

Introduction

The MID function extracts a specified number of characters from a text string, starting at a given position. It is useful for parsing and manipulating text, such as extracting specific substrings or splitting text into components.

Simple explanation: Extracts a substring from a text string, starting at a specified position.

Common use cases: Used for parsing data, extracting codes or identifiers, and working with structured text.

When to use this function: Use when you need to isolate a specific part of a text string.

Syntax

```
=MID(text, start_num, num_chars)
```

- **text**: The text string to extract from.
- **start_num**: The position of the first character to extract (1-based index).
- **num_chars**: The number of characters to extract.

Worked Example

Challenge: Extract the word "Tips" from the text "Excel Tips".

Formula:

```
=MID(A1, 7, 4)
```

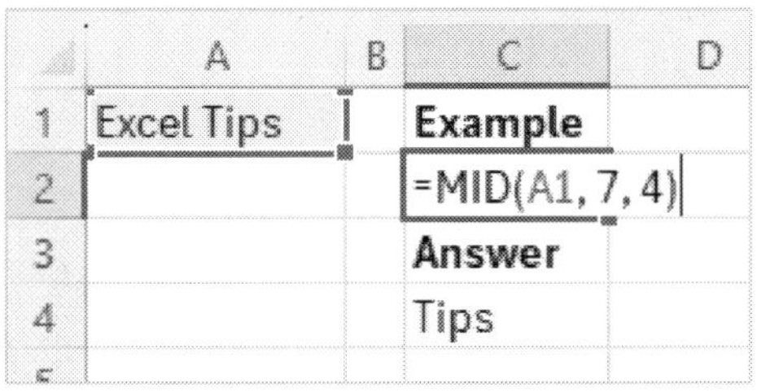

Result: "Tips"
Explanation: The function starts at position 7 and extracts 4 characters, resulting in "Tips".

Explore Further with GPT

Ask GPT how to combine MID with functions like SEARCH, FIND, or LEN to dynamically extract substrings based on specific patterns or conditions.

Tips for Using MID

- **Start position:** If start_num is less than 1, the function returns a #VALUE! error. Ensure the start position is valid.
- **Length exceeds text:** If num_chars exceeds the remaining length of the text string, the function returns all characters from the start position to the end of the string.
- **Working with double-byte characters:** For text in languages that use double-byte character sets (e.g., Japanese or Chinese), use the `MIDB` function. This function operates similarly to `MID` but counts each byte instead of each character:

  ```
  =MIDB(A1, 3, 4) (Extracts 4 bytes starting at position 3.)
  ```

MIN Function

Statistical Functions

Introduction

The MIN function returns the smallest numeric value in a specified range or list of numbers. It is commonly used in data analysis to identify the minimum values in datasets.

Simple explanation: Finds the smallest value in a range or list.

Common use cases: Used to identify minimum metrics, validate data, or find lower thresholds.

When to use this function: Use when you need the lowest value from a dataset.

Syntax

```
=MIN(number1, [number2], ...)
```

- **number1, number2, ...**: 1 to 255 numeric values, cell references, or ranges to evaluate.

Worked Example

Challenge: Find the smallest number in a dataset

Formula:

```
=MIN(A1:A7)
```

Result: 5
Explanation: The smallest value in the range A1:A7 is 5.

	A	B	C	D
1	5		**Example**	
2	10		=MIN(A1:A7)	
3	15		**Answer**	
4	20		5	
5	25			
6	30			
7	35			
8				

Explore Further with GPT

Ask GPT how to use MIN in combination with conditional functions like IF or dynamic functions like FILTER for more complex data analysis.

Tips for Using MIN

- **Ignores non-numeric values:** The MIN function automatically excludes text, blank cells, and logical values (TRUE, FALSE) from calculations.
- **Dynamic ranges:** Combine with `OFFSET` or `INDEX` to create dynamic ranges:

  ```
  =MIN(OFFSET(A1, 0, 0, 5, 1))
  ```

MINIFS Function

Statistical Functions

Introduction

The MINIFS function returns the smallest numeric value in a range that meets one or more specified criteria. It allows for conditional minimum calculations, making it ideal for filtering data based on specific conditions.

Simple explanation: Finds the smallest value in a range that meets specified conditions.

Common use cases: Used for data analysis, filtering results, and conditional calculations.

When to use this function: Use when you need to find the minimum value based on criteria.

Syntax

```
=MINIFS(min_range, criteria_range1, criteria1, [criteria_range2, criteria2], ...)
```

- **min_range**: The range of values to find the minimum value from.
- **criteria_range1**: The range to evaluate against the first criterion.
- **criteria1**: The condition to apply to criteria_range1.
- **[criteria_range2, criteria2]** *(optional)*: Additional ranges and criteria to apply.

Worked Example

Challenge: Find the minimum sales value for Region North

Formula:

```
=MINIFS(B2:B6, A2:A6, "North")
```

Result: 180

Explanation: The function searches the Sales range (B2:B6) and returns the smallest value where Region (A2:A6) is North.

	A	B	C	D	E	F
1	Region	Sales		Example		
2	North	200		=MINIFS(B2:B6, A2:A6, "North")		
3	South	150		Answer		
4	North	300		180		
5	East	250				
6	North	180				
7						

Explore Further with GPT

Ask GPT how to combine MINIFS with functions like MAXIFS, FILTER, or SORT for dynamic filtering and ranking analyses.

Tips for Using MINIFS

- **Criteria flexibility:** Criteria can include wildcards (* for multiple characters, ? for a single character) and operators (e.g., ">=100").
- **Blank cells:** Blank cells in the min_range or criteria_range are ignored.
- **Combine with dynamic criteria:** Use cell references for criteria to make the formula adaptable:

  ```
  =MINIFS(B2:B6, A2:A6, D1)
  ```

  (Where D1 contains the desired criterion, such as North.)

MINA Function

Statistical Functions

Introduction

The MINA function returns the smallest value in a specified range or list of values. Unlike MIN, it evaluates text and logical values in addition to numbers. Text is treated as 0, and logical values are treated as 1 for TRUE and 0 for FALSE.

Simple explanation: Finds the smallest value in a range, treating logical values and text differently than MIN.

Common use cases: Used when datasets include logical values or text that need to be factored into the calculation.

When to use this function: Use when your data includes logical values or text and their evaluation is important.

Syntax

```
=MINA(value1, [value2], ...)
```

- **value1, value2, ...**: 1 to 255 numeric values, cell references, or ranges to evaluate.

Worked Example

Challenge: Find the smallest value in a dataset that includes logical values.

Formula:

```
=MINA(A1:A5)
```

Result: 0
Explanation: The smallest value is 0, as the text "Text" is treated as 0 and TRUE is treated as 1.

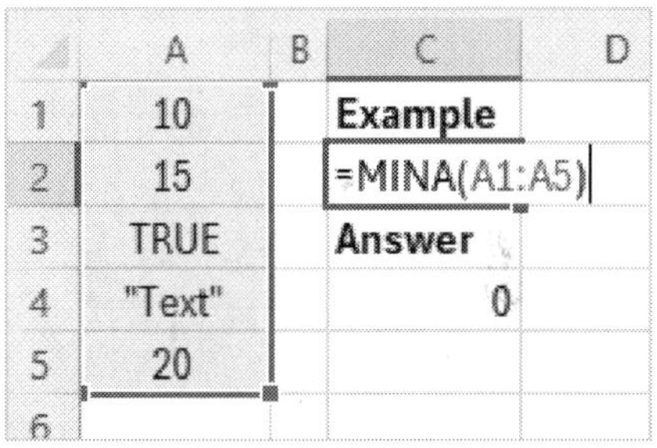

	A	B	C	D
1	10		**Example**	
2	15		=MINA(A1:A5)	
3	TRUE		**Answer**	
4	"Text"		0	
5	20			
6				

Explore Further with GPT

Ask GPT how to combine MINA with functions like IF, FILTER, or SORT for advanced conditional filtering and ranking.

Tips for Using MINA

- **Logical values:** TRUE is treated as 1, and FALSE is treated as 0. This differs from MIN, which ignores logical values.
- **Text as zero:** Text values, including empty strings (""), are treated as 0.
- **Combine with conditional logic:** Use MINA with IF to include specific conditions:

  ```
  =MINA(IF(A1:A5 > 10, A1:A5))
  ```

  (Use CTRL+SHIFT+ENTER for array formulas in legacy Excel versions.)

MINUTE Function

Date & Time Functions

Introduction

The MINUTE function extracts the minute component from a time value. It returns an integer between 0 and 59, representing the minute part of the specified time.

Simple explanation: Extracts the minute from a time value.

Common use cases: Used for time analysis, scheduling, or extracting specific time components for calculations.

When to use this function: Use when you need to isolate the minute value from a time.

Syntax

```
=MINUTE(serial_number)
```

- **serial_number**: A time value from which to extract the minute. This can be a cell reference, a result of a formula, or a time entered as text in a recognized format.

Worked Example

Challenge: Extract the minute from the time 12:45 PM.

Formula:

`=MINUTE(A1)`

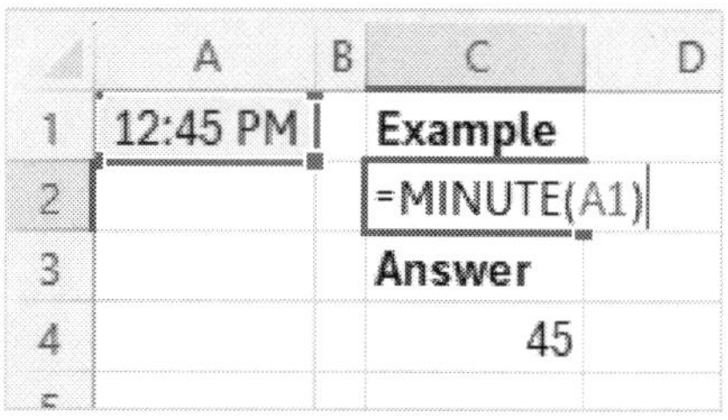

Result: 45
Explanation: The MINUTE function extracts the minute portion (45) from the time.

Explore Further with GPT

Ask GPT how to use MINUTE with other time functions like HOUR, SECOND, or TIMEVALUE for advanced time analysis and manipulation.

Tips for Using MINUTE

- **Time formats:** Ensure the input time is in a valid Excel-recognized format. If the value is not a valid time, the function will return a #VALUE! error.
- **Combine with TIMEVALUE:** Use TIMEVALUE to convert a time string into a serial number if needed:

  `=MINUTE(TIMEVALUE("14:30"))`

- **Dynamic updates:** Combine with NOW or TODAY for real-time time analysis

MINVERSE Function

Math & Trigonometry Functions

Introduction

The MINVERSE function calculates the inverse of a square matrix. The inverse of a matrix is used in linear algebra for solving systems of linear equations, performing transformations, and other mathematical computations.

Simple explanation: Finds the inverse of a square matrix.

Common use cases: Used in solving linear equations, mathematical modeling, and performing matrix algebra.

When to use this function: Use when you need the inverse of a square matrix for further calculations.

Syntax

```
=MINVERSE(array)
```

- **array**: A square matrix (same number of rows and columns) of numeric values.

Worked Example

Challenge: Calculate the inverse of a 2x2 matrix.

Matrix in A1:B2:

A	B
2 (a)	3 (b)
1 (c)	4 (d)

Formula:

```
=MINVERSE(A1:B2)
```

Result (array):

	A	B
1	0.8	-0.6
2	-0.2	0.4

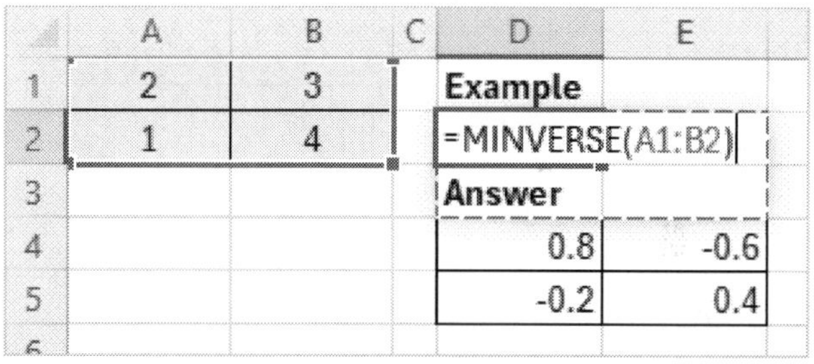

Explanation: The inverse of a 2x2 matrix is calculated as:

$$\frac{1}{ad - bc} \cdot \begin{bmatrix} d & -b \\ -c & a \end{bmatrix}$$

Explore Further with GPT

Ask GPT how to combine MINVERSE with functions like MMULT and MDETERM to solve linear equations or validate matrix properties.

MIRR Function

Financial Functions

Introduction

The MIRR function calculates the Modified Internal Rate of Return (MIRR) for an investment based on periodic cash flows and the financing and reinvestment rates. Unlike the standard IRR, the MIRR accounts for the cost of investment and the return on reinvested cash flows, providing a more realistic profitability measure.

Simple explanation: Calculates the profitability of an investment, considering financing and reinvestment rates.

Common use cases: Used in financial modeling, project evaluation, and investment analysis.

When to use this function: Use when you need a more accurate rate of return that accounts for financing and reinvestment assumptions.

Syntax

```
=MIRR(values, finance_rate, reinvest_rate)
```

- **values**: An array or range of cells representing the series of cash flows. Cash outflows (investments) should be negative, and inflows should be positive.
- **finance_rate**: The interest rate paid on the initial investment (cost of financing).
- **reinvest_rate**: The interest rate earned on reinvested cash flows.

Worked Example

Challenge: Calculate the MIRR for a project with given cash flows:

1. **Finance Rate:** 10% (0.1)
2. **Reinvestment Rate:** 12% (0.12)

Formula:

```
=MIRR(A2:A6, 0.1, 0.12)
```

Result: 0.126 (12.6%)

Explanation: The MIRR function calculates the return on the project, factoring in the cost of financing and the rate of reinvestment for the cash flows.

	A	B	C	D
1	Cash Flow		Example	
2	-1000		=MIRR(A2:A6, 0.1, 0.12)	
3	200		Answer	
4	300		12.6%	
5	400			
6	500			
7				

Explore Further with GPT

Ask GPT how to compare MIRR with IRR and NPV for evaluating investment profitability and project viability.

Tips for Using MIRR

- **Include all cash flows:** Ensure the values array includes the initial investment (typically a negative value) and all subsequent cash flows.
- **Finance and reinvestment rates:** Use realistic values for the finance_rate and reinvest_rate to reflect the cost of capital and expected return on reinvested funds.

MMULT Function

Math & Trigonometry Functions

Introduction

The MMULT function performs matrix multiplication, returning the product of two arrays. Matrix multiplication is commonly used in linear algebra for solving systems of equations, performing transformations, and analyzing data relationships.

Simple explanation: Multiplies two matrices and returns the resulting matrix.

Common use cases: Used in statistical modeling, data transformations, and solving linear systems.

When to use this function: Use when you need the product of two matrices in calculations or modeling.

Syntax

```
=MMULT(array1, array2)
```

- **array1**: The first matrix in the multiplication.
- **array2**: The second matrix in the multiplication.

Note: The number of columns in array1 must equal the number of rows in array2.

Worked Example

Challenge: Multiply the given matrices:

Formula:

```
=MMULT(A1:B2, C1:D2)
```

Result (Spill Array):

	C	D
1	19	22
2	43	50

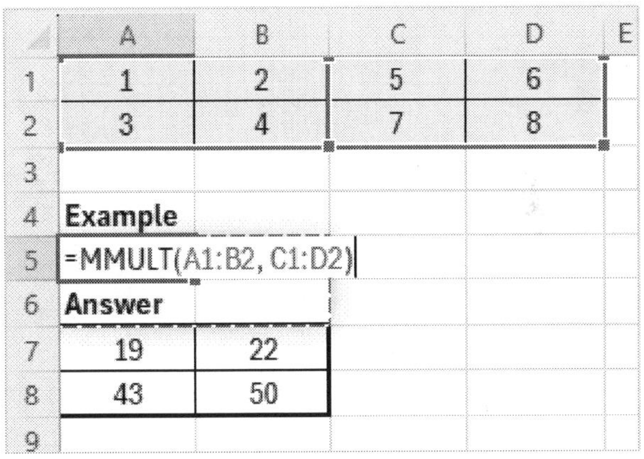

	A	B	C	D	E
1	1	2	5	6	
2	3	4	7	8	
3					
4	Example				
5	=MMULT(A1:B2, C1:D2)				
6	Answer				
7	19	22			
8	43	50			
9					

Explanation: The product of two matrices is calculated as:

$$\text{Result}_{i,j} = \sum(\text{Row } i \text{ of A} \times \text{Column } j \text{ of B})$$

For the first cell, (1·5)+(2·7)=19

Tips for Using MMULT

- **Matrix dimensions:** Ensure the number of columns in array1 matches the number of rows in array2. If not, the function will return a #VALUE! error.

MOD Function

Math & Trigonometry Functions

Introduction

The MOD function returns the remainder after dividing one number by another. It is useful for repetitive calculations, identifying cycles, or working with even/odd numbers.

Simple explanation: Finds the remainder when one number is divided by another.

Common use cases: Used in modular arithmetic, scheduling tasks, and identifying patterns.

When to use this function: Use when you need to calculate the remainder from a division operation.

Syntax

```
=MOD(number, divisor)
```

- **number**: The dividend (the number to be divided).
- **divisor**: The divisor (the number by which to divide).

Worked Example

Challenge: Find the remainder when dividing 17 by 5.

Formula:

```
=MOD(17, 5)
```

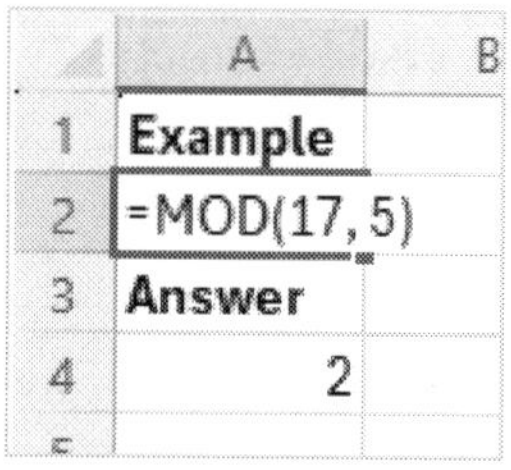

Result: 2
Explanation: 17÷5=3, remainder 2.

Explore Further with GPT

Ask GPT how to combine MOD with IF, ROW, or COLUMN for tasks like alternating row formatting or custom data grouping.

Tips for Using MOD

- **Even or odd checks:** Use MOD to check if a number is even or odd:

  ```
  =IF(MOD(A1, 2) = 0, "Even", "Odd")
  ```

- **Repeat patterns:** Use MOD for creating cyclic patterns, such as alternating row formatting:

  ```
  =MOD(ROW(), 2) = 0
  ```

- **Handling negative numbers:** The result of MOD always has the same sign as the divisor.

MODE Function

Compatibility Functions

Introduction

The MODE function returns the most frequently occurring number in a dataset. It helps identify patterns or central tendencies in numerical data. If multiple values occur with the same frequency, it returns the first one found.

Simple explanation: Finds the most common number in a range or list.

Common use cases: Used in statistical analysis, data validation, and identifying trends.

When to use this function: Use when you need the most frequently occurring number in a dataset.

Syntax

```
=MODE(number1, [number2], ...)
```

- **number1, number2, ...**: 1 to 255 numeric values, cell references, or ranges to evaluate.

Note: The MODE function has been replaced by MODE.SNGL in modern Excel versions but is still supported for compatibility.

Worked Example

Challenge: Find the most frequently occurring number in a dataset.

Formula:

```
=MODE(A1:A7)
```

Result: 10
Explanation: The number 10 occurs most frequently in the dataset (3 times).

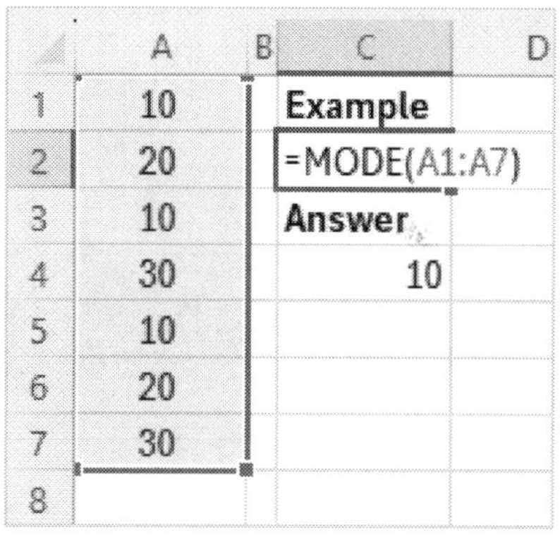

Explore Further with GPT

Ask GPT how to use MODE alongside MODE.SNGL, MODE.MULT, or FREQUENCY for deeper insights into data trends.

Tips for Using MODE

- **Error handling:** Use IFERROR to handle cases where no mode exists:

  ```
  =IFERROR(MODE(A1:A10), "No mode")
  ```

- **Combine with other functions:** Use MODE with FREQUENCY for detailed statistical analysis:

```
=INDEX(A1:A10, MATCH(MAX(FREQUENCY(A1:A10, A1:A10)), FREQUENCY(A1:A10, A1:A10), 0))
```

(This returns the most frequent value in the range.)

- **Non-numeric data:** The MODE function ignores text, logical values, and blank cells.
- **Excel compatibility:** The MODE function is available in all Excel versions but is replaced by MODE.SNGL in newer versions.

MODE.MULT Function

Statistical Functions

Introduction

The MODE.MULT function returns a vertical array of the most frequently occurring numbers in a dataset. Unlike MODE.SNGL, which returns only one mode, MODE.MULT identifies all modes in the dataset when there are multiple values with the same frequency.

Simple explanation: Finds all the most common numbers in a range or list.

Common use cases: Used in statistical analysis to identify all modes in a dataset with multiple peaks.

When to use this function: Use when you need all the modes, not just the first one.

Syntax

```
=MODE.MULT(number1, [number2], ...)
```

- **number1, number2, ...**: 1 to 255 numeric values, cell references, or ranges to evaluate.

Note: The formula must be entered as an array formula in versions of Excel before 365/2021.

Worked Example

Challenge: Find all modes in a dataset with multiple peaks.

Formula:

Result (Spill Array):

20
30

Explanation: The numbers 20 and 30 each occur with the highest frequency (2 times) and are returned as separate rows in the spill array.

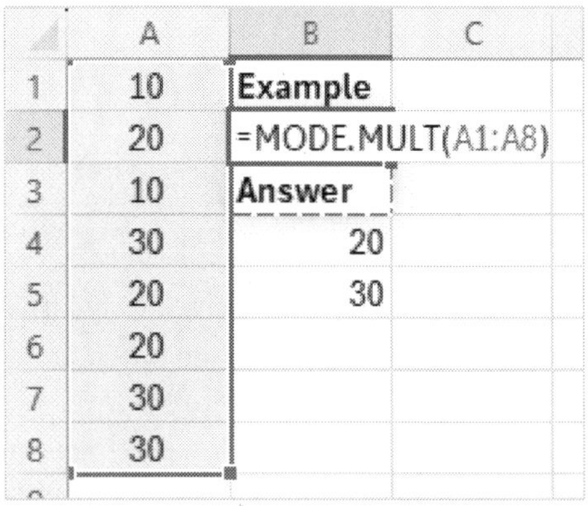

Explore Further with GPT

Ask GPT how to combine MODE.MULT with functions like FREQUENCY or SORT to create custom frequency analyses or data visualizations.

Tips for Using MODE.MULT

- **Spill arrays:** In Excel 365/2021, the result spills into adjacent cells automatically. For older Excel versions, enter the formula as an array formula using CTRL+SHIFT+ENTER.
- **Error handling:** If no value occurs more than once, MODE.MULT returns a #N/A error. Use IFERROR to handle this:

  ```
  =IFERROR(MODE.MULT(A1:A8), "No mode")
  ```

MODE.SNGL Function

Statistical Functions

Introduction

The MODE.SNGL function returns the most frequently occurring number in a dataset. If multiple values have the same frequency, it returns the first mode it encounters. It is the modern replacement for the older MODE function.

Simple explanation: Finds the most common number in a range or list.

Common use cases: Used in statistical analysis, trend identification, and data cleaning.

When to use this function: Use when you need the most frequent number in a dataset.

Syntax

```
=MODE.SNGL(number1, [number2], ...)
```

- **number1, number2, ...**: 1 to 255 numeric values, cell references, or ranges to evaluate.

Worked Example

Challenge: Find the most frequently occurring number in a dataset.

Formula:

```
=MODE.SNGL(A1:A8)
```

Result: 15
Explanation: The number 15 occurs most frequently in the dataset (3 times).

	A	B	C	D
1	15		**Example**	
2	20		=MODE.SNGL(A1:A8)	
3	15		**Answer**	
4	30		15	
5	15			
6	20			
7	30			
8	40			
9				

Explore Further with GPT

Ask GPT how to use MODE.SNGL with functions like COUNTIF, FREQUENCY, or SORT for advanced statistical and trend analysis.

Tips for Using MODE.SNGL

- **Error handling:** Use IFERROR to handle cases where no mode exists:

  ```
  =IFERROR(MODE.SNGL(A1:A10), "No mode")
  ```

- **Combine with other functions:** Use MODE.SNGL with COUNTIF to calculate the frequency of the returned mode:

  ```
  =COUNTIF(A1:A10, MODE.SNGL(A1:A10))
  ```

  (This returns the count of the mode in the dataset.)

MONTH Function

Date & Time Functions

Introduction

The MONTH function extracts the month as a number (1–12) from a date. It is useful for analyzing, sorting, or categorizing data based on months.

Simple explanation: Returns the month of a given date as a number.

Common use cases: Used in time-based analyses, reporting, and organizing data by months.

When to use this function: Use when you need to extract or work with the month part of a date.

Syntax

```
=MONTH(serial_number)
```

- **serial_number**: A valid Excel date from which to extract the month. This can be a cell reference, a formula result, or a date entered as text in a recognized format.

Worked Example

Challenge: Extract the month from a specific date.

Formula:

```
=MONTH(A1)
```

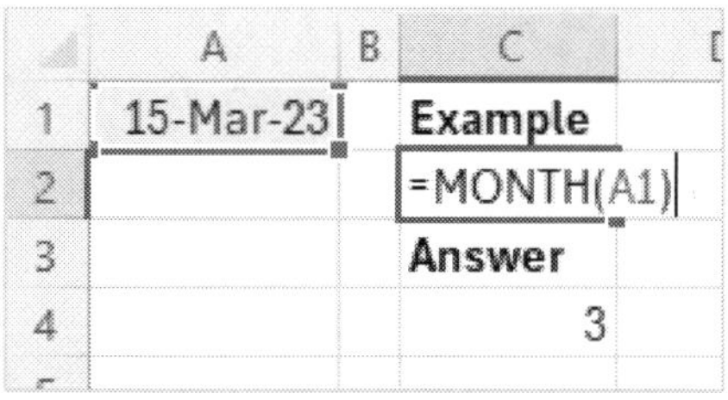

Result: 3
Explanation: The date 15-Mar-2023 corresponds to the third month of the year, so the function returns 3.

Explore Further with GPT

Ask GPT how to combine MONTH with functions like YEAR, DAY, or TEXT for comprehensive date manipulations and formatting.

Tips for Using MONTH

- **Valid dates only:** Ensure the input is a valid Excel date. If not, the function returns a #VALUE! error.
- **Combine with DATEVALUE:** Convert text to a date first if needed:

  ```
  =MONTH(DATEVALUE("April 15, 2023"))
  ```

- **Custom formatting:** Use TEXT to display the month's name instead of its number:

  ```
  =TEXT(A1, "mmmm")
  ```

  (This displays "March" for a March date.)

MROUND Function

Math & Trigonometry

Introduction

The MROUND function rounds a number to the nearest multiple of a specified value. It is particularly useful for financial calculations, time rounding, or aligning values to specific intervals.

Simple explanation: Rounds a number to the nearest specified multiple.

Common use cases: Used in financial modeling, time calculations, and ensuring consistent value increments.

When to use this function: Use when you need to round numbers to a specific multiple.

Syntax

```
=MROUND(number, multiple)
```

- **number**: The value to round.
- **multiple**: The multiple to which you want to round the number.

Worked Example

Challenge: Round the number 27 to the nearest multiple of 5.

Formula:

```
=MROUND(27, 5)
```

Result: 25
Explanation: The closest multiple of 5 to 27 is 25.

	A	B
1	**Example**	
2	=MROUND(27, 5)	
3	**Answer**	
4	25	
5		

Explore Further with GPT

Ask GPT how to combine MROUND with functions like ROUND, CEILING, or FLOOR for more precise rounding in complex scenarios.

Tips for Using MROUND

- **Same sign for inputs:** Both number and multiple must have the same sign (positive or negative). Otherwise, the function returns a #NUM! error.
- **Zero behavior:** If the number is 0, the function always returns 0.
- **Alternative functions:** Use ROUND, CEILING, or FLOOR for different rounding behaviors:

```
=CEILING(27, 5)  // Rounds up to the nearest multiple
=FLOOR(27, 5)    // Rounds down to the nearest multiple
```

MULTINOMIAL Function

Math & Trigonometry

Introduction

The MULTINOMIAL function calculates the ratio of the factorial of the sum of a set of numbers to the product of the factorials of the numbers. It is used in probability and statistics, especially in multinomial distributions.

Simple explanation: Computes the multinomial coefficient for a set of numbers.

Common use cases: Used in statistics for multinomial probabilities and combinatorial calculations.

When to use this function: Use when working with multinomial probabilities or calculating large combinatorial values.

Syntax

```
=MULTINOMIAL(number1, [number2], ...)
```

- **number1, number2, ...**: 1 to 255 non-negative numbers or references to evaluate.

Worked Example

Challenge: Calculate the multinomial coefficient for 2, 3, and 4.

Formula:

`=MULTINOMIAL(2, 3, 4)`

	A	B	C
1	**Example**		
2	=MULTINOMIAL(2, 3, 4)		
3	**Answer**		
4	1260		

Result: 1260
Explanation: The formula calculates as:

$$\frac{(2+3+4)!}{2!\cdot 3!\cdot 4!} = \frac{9!}{2!\cdot 3!\cdot 4!}$$

Explore Further with GPT

Ask GPT how to combine MULTINOMIAL with functions like FACT, COMBIN, or PERMUT for more advanced combinatorial and statistical analyses.

Tips for Using MULTINOMIAL

- **Non-negative inputs:** All input numbers must be non-negative. Negative numbers will result in a #NUM! error.
- **Handling decimals:** Decimal inputs are truncated to integers before calculation.
- **Excel compatibility:** The `MULTINOMIAL` function is available in all modern Excel versions.

MUNIT Function

Math & Trigonometry

Introduction

The MUNIT function generates a unit matrix (also known as an identity matrix) of a specified size. In a unit matrix, all diagonal elements are 1, and all other elements are 0. This function is commonly used in linear algebra.

Simple explanation: Creates an identity matrix of the specified size.

Common use cases: Used in matrix operations such as solving linear equations, transformations, or verifying matrix properties.

When to use this function: Use when you need a unit (identity) matrix for calculations or as a base for other matrix operations.

Syntax

```
=MUNIT(dimension)
```

- **dimension**: The size of the identity matrix (number of rows and columns). Must be a positive integer.

Worked Example

Challenge: Create a 3x3 identity matrix.

Formula:

=MUNIT(3)

Result (Spill Array):

	A	B	C
1	1	0	0
2	0	1	0
3	0	0	1

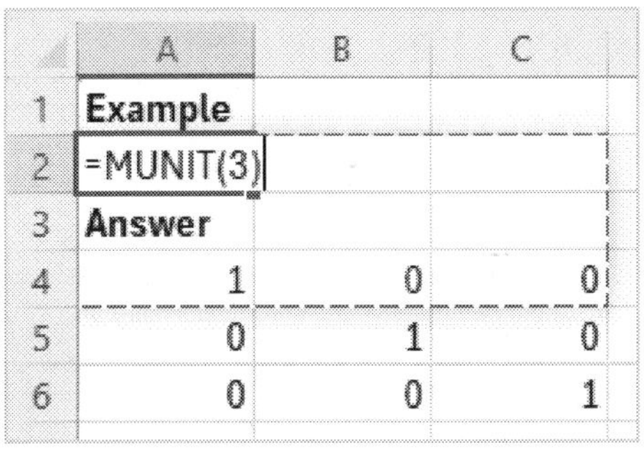

Explanation: The MUNIT function generates a 3x3 identity matrix where the diagonal elements are 1 and all other elements are 0.

Explore Further with GPT

Ask GPT how to combine MUNIT with MMULT, MINVERSE, or TRANSPOSE for solving linear equations or performing matrix operations.

Tips for Using MUNIT

- **Square matrices only:** The MUNIT function always creates a square matrix of the specified size.
- **Dynamic arrays:** In Excel 365/2021, the result spills into adjacent cells automatically. For older versions, ensure enough cells are selected before entering the formula as an array formula (CTRL+SHIFT+ENTER).

N Function

Information Functions

Introduction

The N function converts a value to a numeric representation. If the value is a number, it remains unchanged. For non-numeric values, such as text, logical values, or errors, the function returns specific predefined results.

Simple explanation: Converts a value to its numeric equivalent or returns 0 for non-numeric inputs like text.

Common use cases: Used for ensuring numeric inputs in calculations or checking numeric status.

When to use this function: Use when you need to handle mixed data types and extract numeric values for processing.

Syntax

```
=N(value)
```

- **value**: The value to convert to a number. This can be a number, text, logical value, or reference.

Behavior of N Function:

Input Type	**Result**
Number	Retuns the number itself
Date	Returns the serial number of the date
Logical Value	TRUE returns 1, FALSE returns 0
Text	Returns 0
Error Value	Returns the error

Worked Example

Challenge: Convert a variety of data types to numeric values

Formula:

`=N(A1)`

Result in B1:B5:

42
0
1
0
44927

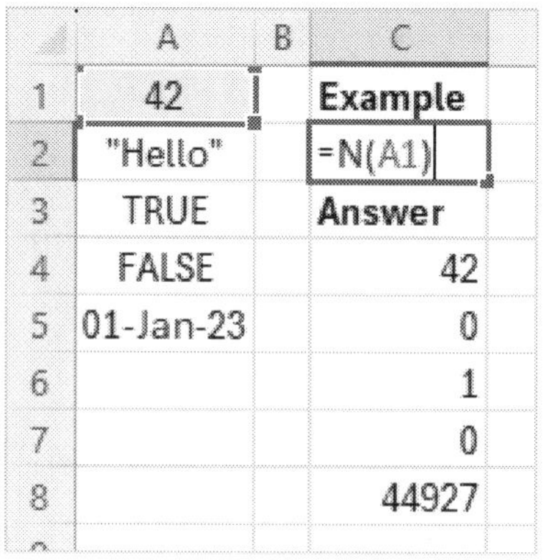

	A	B	C
1	42		**Example**
2	"Hello"		=N(A1)
3	TRUE		**Answer**
4	FALSE		42
5	01-Jan-23		0
6			1
7			0
8			44927

Explore Further with GPT

Ask GPT how to combine N with functions like IF, TEXT, or VALUE for advanced data cleaning and numerical conversions.

NA Function

Information Functions

Introduction

The NA function returns the error value #N/A, which stands for "Not Available." This function is useful when you need to signal missing data in a dataset. It can also be used to generate #N/A errors intentionally for testing or compatibility purposes.

Simple explanation: Generates the #N/A error, indicating that data is missing or unavailable.

Common use cases: Used in testing, data validation, and as a placeholder for missing data.

When to use this function: Use when you need to indicate unavailable data or trigger an #N/A error.

Syntax

```
=NA()
```

- The function takes no arguments.

Worked Example

Challenge: Insert an #N/A error to indicate missing data.

Formula:

```
=NA()
```

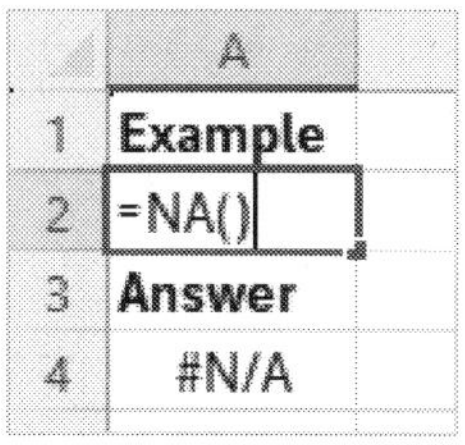

Result: #N/A

Explanation: The NA function returns the #N/A error to signal that data is unavailable.

Explore Further with GPT

Ask GPT how to combine NA with functions like IFERROR, LOOKUP, or ISNA for advanced error handling and data cleanup.

- **Testing scenarios:** Use NA to simulate missing data for debugging or testing formulas:

  ```
  =IF(B1=NA(), "Error in data", B1)
  ```

- **Highlight missing data:** Combine with conditional formatting to visually highlight #N/A values in your spreadsheet.
- **Error propagation:** If a formula refers to a cell with #N/A, the error propagates. Use this to flag dependencies on missing data.

NEGBINOM.DIST Function

Statistical Functions

Introduction

The NEGBINOM.DIST function calculates the negative binomial distribution. This distribution represents the probability of a certain number of failures before achieving a set number of successes in a series of independent and identically distributed Bernoulli trials.

Simple explanation: Computes the probability of observing a specified number of failures before reaching a target number of successes.

Common use cases: Used in probability, statistics, and predictive modeling to analyze outcomes in scenarios like quality control or repeated experiments.

When to use this function: Use when modeling the probability of failures before successes in trials.

Syntax

```
=NEGBINOM.DIST(number_f, number_s, probability_s, cumulative)
```

- **number_f**: The number of failures.
- **number_s**: The number of successes required.
- **probability_s**: The probability of success in each trial (0 ≤ probability_s ≤ 1).
- **cumulative**: A logical value. If TRUE, the function returns the cumulative probability; if FALSE, it returns the probability mass function.

Worked Example

Challenge: Calculate the probability of observing exactly 5 failures before achieving 3 successes in a scenario where the probability of success in each trial is 0.6.

Inputs:

- number_f: 5
- number_s: 3
- probability_s: 0.6
- cumulative: FALSE

	A	B	C	D
1	**Example**			
2	=NEGBINOM.DIST(5, 3, 0.6, FALSE)			
3	**Answer**			
4	0.046449			
5				

Formula:

```
=NEGBINOM.DIST(5, 3, 0.6, FALSE)
```

Result: 0.046449
Explanation: The function calculates the probability mass function for 5 failures before 3 successes.

Explore Further with GPT

Ask GPT how to use NEGBINOM.DIST in combination with BINOM.DIST, POISSON.DIST, or NORM.DIST for comparing different probabilistic models.

NEGBINOMDIST Function

Compatibility Functions

Introduction

The NEGBINOMDIST function calculates the probability of observing a specified number of failures before a target number of successes in a series of independent Bernoulli trials. It is the legacy version of the modern NEGBINOM.DIST function and is retained for compatibility.

Simple explanation: Computes the probability of a given number of failures before reaching a target number of successes.

Common use cases: Used in probability and statistics for modeling repeated experiments, quality control, or trials with a fixed success probability.

When to use this function: Use when working in older Excel versions or maintaining compatibility with legacy formulas.

Syntax

```
=NEGBINOMDIST(number_f, number_s, probability_s)
```

- **number_f**: The number of failures.
- **number_s**: The number of successes required.
- **probability_s**: The probability of success in each trial (0 ≤ probability_s ≤ 1).

Worked Example

Challenge: Calculate the probability of observing exactly 5 failures before achieving 3 successes in a scenario where the probability of success in each trial is 0.6.

Inputs:

- number_f: 5
- number_s: 3
- probability_s: 0.6

	A	B	C
1	**Example**		
2	=NEGBINOMDIST(5, 3, 0.6)		
3	**Answer**		
4	0.046449		

Formula:

```
=NEGBINOMDIST(5, 3, 0.6)
```

Result: 0.046449
Explanation: The function calculates the probability mass function for 5 failures before 3 successes

Comparison with NEGBINOM.DIST

The NEGBINOMDIST function is equivalent to using NEGBINOM.DIST with the cumulative parameter set to FALSE. For cumulative probabilities, switch to NEGBINOM.DIST for enhanced functionality.

Explore Further with GPT

Ask GPT how to combine NEGBINOMDIST with BINOMDIST or POISSON for evaluating different probabilistic models.

NETWORKDAYS Function

Date & Time Functions

Introduction

The NETWORKDAYS function calculates the number of whole working days (excluding weekends and optionally specified holidays) between two dates. It is commonly used in project management, payroll, and scheduling tasks to determine work durations.

Simple explanation: Counts the number of working days between two dates, excluding weekends and optional holidays.

Common use cases: Used for tracking work durations, calculating deadlines, and determining billable days.

When to use this function: Use when you need to calculate working days between two dates

Syntax

```
=NETWORKDAYS(start_date, end_date, [holidays])
```

- **start_date**: The start date of the period.
- **end_date**: The end date of the period.
- **[holidays]** *(optional)*: A range of dates to exclude as non-working days (e.g., public holidays).

Worked Example

Challenge: Calculate the number of working days between 01-Jan-2023 and 15-Jan-2023, excluding a holiday on 06-Jan-2023.

Inputs:

- Start date: 01-Jan-2023; End date: 15-Jan-2023
- Holiday: 06-Jan-2023

Formula:

```
=NETWORKDAYS(DATE(2023,1,1), DATE(2023,1,15),
DATE(2023,1,6))
```

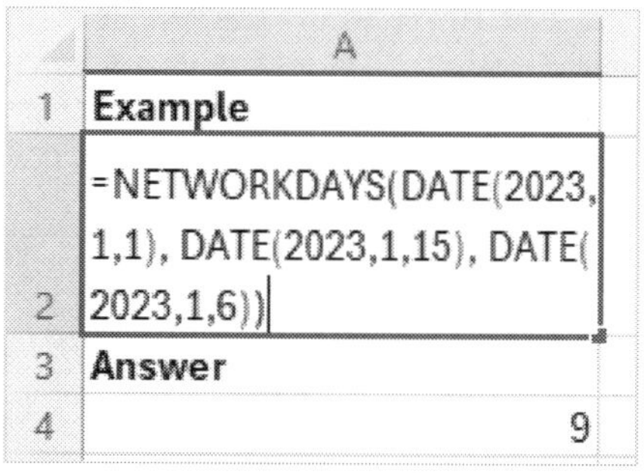

Result: 9

Explanation: The function counts weekdays between 01-Jan-2023 and 15-Jan-2023 and excludes weekends and the specified holiday.

Explore Further with GPT

Ask GPT how to combine NETWORKDAYS with WORKDAY, TODAY, or custom date ranges for advanced scheduling and deadline tracking.

Tips for Using NETWORKDAYS

- **Default weekends:** The function assumes Saturdays and Sundays as weekends. For custom weekend definitions, use NETWORKDAYS.INTL.
- **Holidays as a range:** Provide a range of dates for multiple holidays. Example:

  `=NETWORKDAYS(A1, B1, C1:C5) (Where C1:C5 contains holiday dates.)`

NETWORKDAYS.INTL Function

Date & Time Functions

Introduction

The NETWORKDAYS.INTL function calculates the number of whole working days (excluding weekends and optionally specified holidays) between two dates. It offers flexibility by allowing custom definitions for weekends, making it useful for organizations with non-standard workweeks.

Simple explanation: Counts the number of working days between two dates, with customizable weekends and optional holidays.

Common use cases: Used for tracking work durations in custom work schedules or across different countries with unique weekend definitions.

When to use this function: Use when calculating working days for non-standard workweeks or specific holiday schedules.

Syntax

```
=NETWORKDAYS.INTL(start_date, end_date, [weekend], [holidays])
```

- **start_date**: The start date of the period.
- **end_date**: The end date of the period.
- **[weekend]** *(optional)*: A code or string that specifies which days are weekends (defaults to 1, Saturday and Sunday).
- **[holidays]** *(optional)*: A range of dates to exclude as non-working days (e.g., public holidays).

Weekend Codes

1: Saturday, Sunday; 2: Sunday, Monday; 3: Monday, Tuesday; 4: Tuesday, Wednesday; 5: Wednesday, Thursday; 6: Thursday, Friday; 7: Friday, Saturday; 11: Sunday only; 12: Monday only; 13: Tuesday only; 14: Wednesday only; 15: Thursday only; 16: Friday only; 17: Saturday only

Worked Example

Challenge: Calculate the number of working days between 01-Jan-2023 and 15-Jan-2023, excluding holidays and with Friday and Saturday as weekends.

Formula:

```
=NETWORKDAYS.INTL(DATE(2023,1,1), DATE(2023,1,15), 7,
DATE(2023,1,6))
```

Result: 10

Explanation: The function calculates weekdays between 01-Jan-2023 and 15-Jan-2023, excluding Fridays, Saturdays, and the specified holiday.

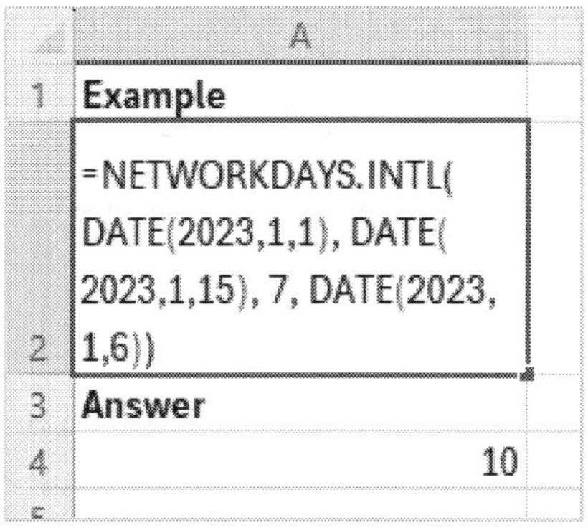

NOMINAL Function

Financial Functions

Introduction

The NOMINAL function calculates the nominal annual interest rate based on the effective annual interest rate and the number of compounding periods per year. It is useful for financial calculations to compare nominal and effective interest rates.

Simple explanation: Converts an effective annual interest rate into a nominal annual interest rate.

Common use cases: Used in financial modeling, loan comparisons, and understanding interest rates in compounding scenarios.

When to use this function: Use when you need the nominal rate from an effective rate for financial comparisons.

Syntax

```
=NOMINAL(effect_rate, npery)
```

- **effect_rate**: The effective annual interest rate (as a decimal).
- **npery**: The number of compounding periods per year. Must be a positive integer.

Worked Example

Challenge: Calculate the nominal annual interest rate for an effective rate of 5% with monthly compounding.

Formula:

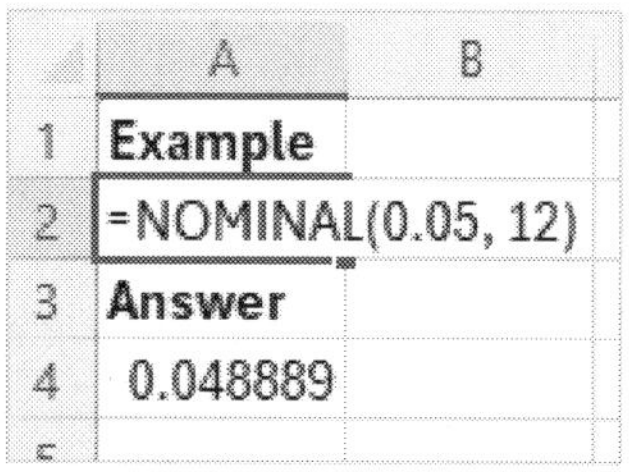

Result: 0.04889 (4.889%)
Explanation: The nominal annual interest rate is slightly less than the effective rate because of monthly compounding.

Explore Further with GPT

Ask GPT how to compare NOMINAL with EFFECT to analyze differences in interest rates across different compounding frequencies.

Tips for Using NOMINAL

- **Effective rate as decimal:** Ensure the effect_rate is entered as a decimal (e.g., 5% should be entered as 0.05).
- **Compounding periods:** The npery value must be a positive integer. Non-integer or zero values result in a #NUM! error.

NORM.DIST Function

Statistical Functions

Introduction

The NORM.DIST function calculates the normal (Gaussian) distribution for a specified mean and standard deviation. It can return the probability density function (PDF) or the cumulative distribution function (CDF), depending on the input. This function is used widely in statistics and probability analysis.

Simple explanation: Calculates the probability or cumulative value for a normal distribution.

Common use cases: Used in hypothesis testing, statistical modeling, and analyzing data distributions.

When to use this function: Use when analyzing or working with normally distributed data.

Syntax

```
=NORM.DIST(x, mean, standard_dev, cumulative)
```

- **x**: The value for which you want the distribution.
- **mean**: The mean of the distribution.
- **standard_dev**: The standard deviation of the distribution. Must be greater than 0.
- **cumulative**: A logical value. If TRUE, returns the cumulative distribution function (CDF); if FALSE, returns the probability density function (PDF).

Worked Example

Challenge: Calculate the cumulative probability for a normal distribution with mean 50, standard deviation 10, and a value of 60.

Formula:

```
=NORM.DIST(60, 50, 10, TRUE)
```

	A	B	C
1	**Example**		
2	=NORM.DIST(60, 50, 10, TRUE)		
3	**Answer**		
4	0.8413		

Result: 0.8413
Explanation: The cumulative probability that a random variable is less than or equal to 60 in this distribution is approximately 84.13%.

Explore Further with GPT

Ask GPT how to combine NORM.DIST with NORM.S.DIST and NORM.INV for statistical analyses, such as calculating z-scores or confidence intervals.

Tips for Using NORM.DIST

- **Cumulative or PDF:** Use TRUE for cumulative probabilities (CDF) and FALSE for point probabilities (PDF).
- **Standard deviation constraints:** The standard_dev parameter must be greater than 0. Otherwise, the function returns a #NUM! error.
- **Mean and symmetry:** For symmetric data, the mean is the center of the distribution

NORMDIST Function

Compatibility Functions

Introduction

The NORMDIST function calculates the normal (Gaussian) distribution for a given mean and standard deviation. This function is the legacy version of the modern NORM.DIST and is included for compatibility with older Excel versions.

Simple explanation: Computes the probability or cumulative value for a normal distribution.

Common use cases: Used in older Excel spreadsheets for statistical analysis, hypothesis testing, and probability computations.

When to use this function: Use when maintaining compatibility with older Excel files or systems.

Syntax

```
=NORMDIST(x, mean, standard_dev, cumulative)
```

- **x**: The value for which you want the distribution.
- **mean**: The mean of the distribution.
- **standard_dev**: The standard deviation of the distribution. Must be greater than 0.
- **cumulative**: A logical value. If TRUE, returns the cumulative distribution function (CDF); if FALSE, returns the probability density function (PDF).

Worked Example

Challenge: Calculate the cumulative probability for a normal distribution with mean 50, standard deviation 10, and a value of 60.

Formula:

```
=NORMDIST(60, 50, 10, TRUE)
```

Result: 0.8413
Explanation: The cumulative probability that a random variable is less than or equal to 60 is approximately 84.13%.

	A	B	C
1	**Example**		
2	=NORMDIST(60, 50, 10, TRUE)		
3	**Answer**		
4	0.8413		

Explore Further with GPT

Ask GPT how to transition from NORMDIST to NORM.DIST or how to use related functions like NORM.INV and NORM.S.DIST for advanced statistical modeling.

Tips for Using NORMDIST

- **Legacy usage:** Use NORMDIST only for compatibility with older Excel versions. In Excel 2010 and later, NORM.DIST is preferred.
- **Error handling:** Use IFERROR to manage invalid inputs:

  ```
  =IFERROR(NORMDIST(A1, B1, C1, TRUE), "Invalid input")
  ```

NORMINV Function

Statistical Functions

Introduction

The NORMINV function returns the inverse of the normal cumulative distribution for a given probability, mean, and standard deviation. It essentially finds the value (x) for which the cumulative probability equals the specified probability. This function is the legacy version of the modern NORM.INV.

Simple explanation: Calculates the value at a given cumulative probability for a normal distribution.

Common use cases: Used in statistical analysis for setting thresholds, hypothesis testing, and simulating data.

When to use this function: Use when working with cumulative probabilities to find corresponding values in a normal distribution.

Syntax

```
=NORMINV(probability, mean, standard_dev)
```

- **probability**: The cumulative probability for which you want the value. Must be between 0 and 1.
- **mean**: The mean of the normal distribution.
- **standard_dev**: The standard deviation of the distribution. Must be greater than 0

Worked Example

Challenge: Find the value corresponding to the 95th percentile of a normal distribution with mean 50 and standard deviation 10.

Formula:

```
=NORMINV(0.95, 50, 10)
```

	A	B
1	**Example**	
2	=NORMINV(0.95, 50, 10)	
3	**Answer**	
4	66.449	

Result: 66.449
Explanation: The value 66.449 corresponds to the 95th percentile of the distribution

Explore Further with GPT

Ask GPT how to combine NORMINV with functions like RAND or RANDBETWEEN for generating random numbers from a normal distribution.

Tips for Using NORMINV

- **Probability range:** Ensure the probability is between 0 and 1. Values outside this range return a #NUM! error.
- **Error handling:** Use IFERROR to manage invalid inputs:

  ```
  =IFERROR(NORMINV(A1, B1, C1), "Invalid input")
  ```

NORM.INV Function

Compatibility Functions

Introduction

The NORM.INV function calculates the inverse of the normal cumulative distribution for a specified probability, mean, and standard deviation. It is commonly used to find the value (x) corresponding to a given cumulative probability in a normal distribution.

Simple explanation: Finds the value for a given cumulative probability in a normal distribution.

Common use cases: Used in statistical analysis, hypothesis testing, and setting thresholds for normal distributions.

When to use this function: Use when you need to find the value associated with a specific percentile or cumulative probability.

Syntax

```
=NORM.INV(probability, mean, standard_dev)
```

- **probability**: The cumulative probability for which you want the corresponding value. Must be between 0 and 1.
- **mean**: The mean of the normal distribution.
- **standard_dev**: The standard deviation of the distribution. Must be greater than 0

Worked Example

Challenge: Find the value corresponding to the 90th percentile in a normal distribution with mean 50 and standard deviation 10.

Formula:

```
=NORM.INV(0.90, 50, 10)
```

Result: 62.8155
Explanation: The value 62.8155 corresponds to the 90th percentile of the given normal distribution.

	A	B
1	**Example**	
2	=NORM.INV(0.9, 50, 10)	
3	**Answer**	
4	62.8155	

Explore Further with GPT

Ask GPT how to use NORM.INV with functions like RAND or RANDBETWEEN to generate random values from a normal distribution.

Tips for Using NORM.INV

- **Probability range:** Ensure probability is between 0 and 1. Values outside this range return a #NUM! error.
- **Simulating normal random variables:** Combine with `RAND` to create random values from a normal distribution:

  ```
  =NORM.INV(RAND(), mean, standard_dev)
  ```

NORM.S.DIST Function

Statistical Functions

Introduction

The NORM.S.DIST function calculates the standard normal distribution (a normal distribution with a mean of 0 and a standard deviation of 1) for a given value. It can return the probability density function (PDF) or the cumulative distribution function (CDF).

Simple explanation: Computes the standard normal distribution probability or cumulative value for a given z-score.

Common use cases: Used in z-score calculations, statistical hypothesis testing, and probability analysis.

When to use this function: Use when working with z-scores or standard normal distributions.

Syntax

```
=NORM.S.DIST(z, cumulative)
```

- **z**: The z-score (number of standard deviations from the mean).
- **cumulative**: A logical value. If TRUE, returns the cumulative distribution function (CDF); if FALSE, returns the probability density function (PDF).

Worked Example

Challenge: Calculate the cumulative probability for a z-score of 1.5.

Formula:

```
=NORM.S.DIST(1.5, TRUE)
```

Result: 0.9332
Explanation: The cumulative probability that a value is less than or equal to a z-score of 1.5 is approximately 93.32%.

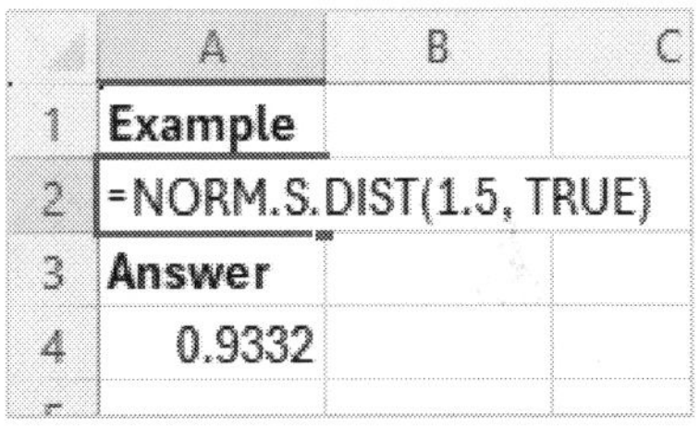

	A	B	C
1	**Example**		
2	=NORM.S.DIST(1.5, TRUE)		
3	**Answer**		
4	0.9332		

Explore Further with GPT

Ask GPT how to combine NORM.S.DIST with functions like NORM.DIST, NORM.INV, or STANDARDIZE for advanced statistical and probability calculations.

Tips for Using NORM.S.DIST

- **Cumulative or PDF:** Use TRUE for cumulative probabilities (CDF) and FALSE for point probabilities (PDF).
- **Relationship to NORM.DIST:** For distributions with a non-zero mean or non-unit standard deviation, use NORM.DIST instead.

  ```
  =NORM.DIST(x, mean, standard_dev, TRUE)
  ```

NORMSDIST Function

Compatibility Functions

Introduction

The NORMSDIST function calculates the cumulative standard normal distribution (a normal distribution with a mean of 0 and a standard deviation of 1) for a given z-score. This function is the legacy version of the modern NORM.S.DIST and is retained for backward compatibility.

Simple explanation: Returns the cumulative probability for a z-score in the standard normal distribution.

Common use cases: Used in older Excel spreadsheets for statistical analysis, z-score calculations, and hypothesis testing.

When to use this function: Use when maintaining compatibility with older Excel files or systems

Syntax

```
=NORMSDIST(z)
```

- **z**: The z-score (number of standard deviations from the mean).

Worked Example

Challenge: Calculate the cumulative probability for a z-score of 1.5.

Formula:

```
=NORMSDIST(1.5)
```

	A	B
1	**Example**	
2	=NORMSDIST(1.5)	
3	**Answer**	
4	0.9332	

Result: 0.9332
Explanation: The cumulative probability that a value is less than or equal to a z-score of 1.5 is approximately 93.32%.

Explore Further with GPT

Ask GPT how to transition from NORMSDIST to NORM.S.DIST or how to use related functions like STANDARDIZE and NORM.INV for z-score analysis.

Tips for Using NORMSDIST

- **Cumulative probabilities only:** The function always returns the cumulative probability (CDF). To compute the probability density function (PDF), use:

  ```
  =NORM.S.DIST(z, FALSE)
  ```

- **Z-score applications:** Combine with STANDARDIZE to calculate cumulative probabilities for values from non-standard distributions:

  ```
  =NORMSDIST(STANDARDIZE(x, mean, standard_dev))
  ```

NORM.S.INV Function

Statistical Functions

Introduction

The NORM.S.INV function calculates the inverse of the standard normal cumulative distribution. It returns the z-score for a given cumulative probability in the standard normal distribution (mean = 0, standard deviation = 1).

Simple explanation: Finds the z-score for a given cumulative probability in the standard normal distribution.

Common use cases: Used in hypothesis testing, statistical modeling, and determining thresholds for probabilities in standard normal distributions.

When to use this function: Use when you need the z-score corresponding to a specific cumulative probability.

Syntax

```
=NORM.S.INV(probability)
```

- **probability**: The cumulative probability for which you want the z-score. Must be between 0 and 1.

Worked Example

Challenge: Find the z-score corresponding to the 95th percentile in a standard normal distribution.

Formula:

```
=NORM.S.INV(0.95)
```

Result: 1.6449
Explanation: A cumulative probability of 0.95 corresponds to a z-score of approximately 1.6449 in the standard normal distribution.

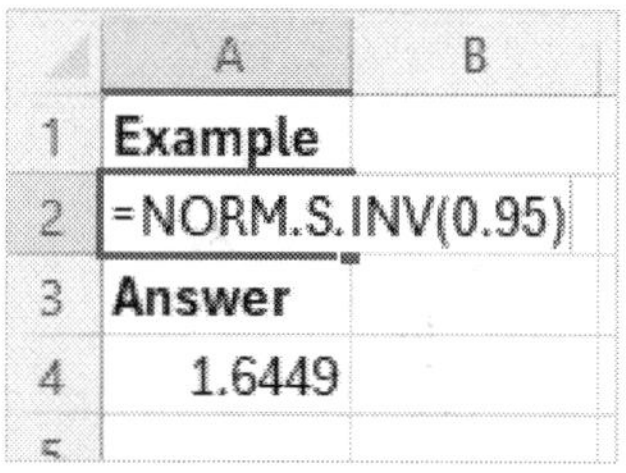

Explore Further with GPT

Ask GPT how to combine NORM.S.INV with RAND to generate random z-scores for simulations and statistical experiments.

Tips for Using NORM.S.INV

- **Probability range:** Ensure the probability is between 0 and 1. Values outside this range return a #NUM! error.
- **Simulating z-scores:** Combine with RAND to generate random z-scores:

  ```
  =NORM.S.INV(RAND())
  ```

  (This formula generates random z-scores from the standard normal distribution.)

NORMSINV Function

Compatibility Functions

Introduction

The NORMSINV function calculates the inverse of the standard normal cumulative distribution. It returns the z-score corresponding to a given cumulative probability in the standard normal distribution (mean = 0, standard deviation = 1). This is the legacy version of the modern NORM.S.INV function.

Simple explanation: Finds the z-score for a given cumulative probability in a standard normal distribution.

Common use cases: Used in older Excel spreadsheets for statistical modeling, hypothesis testing, and z-score analysis.

When to use this function: Use when maintaining compatibility with older Excel files or systems.

Syntax

```
=NORMSINV(probability)
```

- **probability**: The cumulative probability for which you want the z-score. Must be between 0 and 1.

Worked Example

Challenge: Find the z-score corresponding to the 90th percentile in a standard normal distribution.

Formula:

```
=NORMSINV(0.90)
```

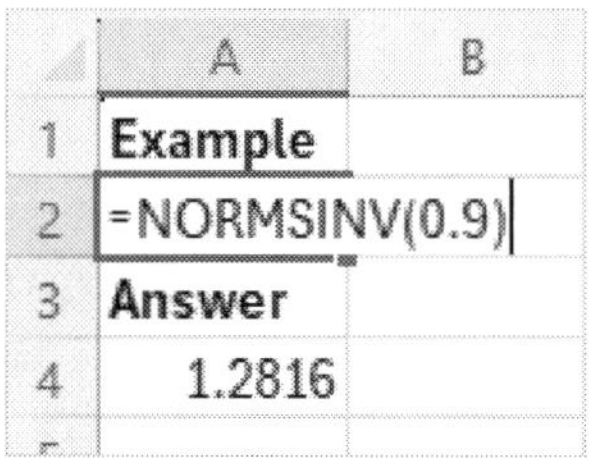

Result: 1.2816
Explanation: A cumulative probability of 0.90 corresponds to a z-score of approximately 1.2816 in the standard normal distribution.

Explore Further with GPT

Ask GPT how to use NORMSINV alongside functions like RAND or STANDARDIZE for generating random z-scores and performing statistical analyses.

Tips for Using NORMSINV

- **Probability range:** Ensure the probability is between 0 and 1. Values outside this range result in a #NUM! error.
- **Simulating z-scores:** Combine with RAND to generate random z-scores:

  ```
  =NORMSINV(RAND())
  ```

  (This formula generates random z-scores from the standard normal distribution.)

NOT Function

Logical Functions

Introduction

The NOT function reverses the logical value of its argument. It converts TRUE to FALSE and FALSE to TRUE. This function is commonly used in logical tests and decision-making processes.

Simple explanation: Returns the opposite of a given logical value.

Common use cases: Used in decision-making, conditional formatting, and building complex logical expressions.

When to use this function: Use when you need to invert a logical value or condition.

Syntax

```
=NOT(logical)
```

- **logical**: A value or expression that evaluates to TRUE or FALSE.

Worked Example

Challenge: Determine if a number is *not greater than 10*.

Formula:

=NOT(A1 > 10)

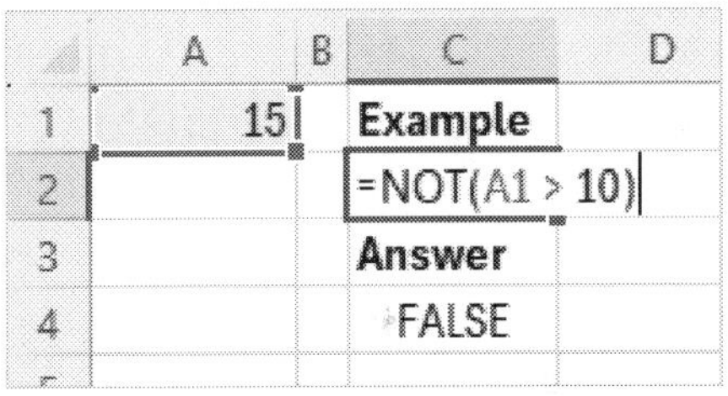

Result: FALSE
Explanation: The expression A1 > 10 evaluates to TRUE because 15 > 10. The NOT function inverts this to FALSE.

Explore Further with GPT

Ask GPT how to combine NOT with functions like AND, OR, and IF to build more advanced logical conditions.

Tips for Using NOT

- **Combine with other functions:** The NOT function is often used with AND, OR, or IF to build complex logical expressions. Example:

  ```
  =IF(NOT(OR(A1 > 10, B1 < 5)), "Valid", "Invalid")
  ```

  (This checks if neither A1 > 10 nor B1 < 5 is true.)

- **Invert conditions:** Use NOT to simplify logic inversion in formulas:

  ```
  =NOT(A1 = "Complete")
  ```

  (This checks if A1 is not "Complete.")

NOW Function

Date & Time Functions

Introduction

The NOW function returns the current date and time based on the system's clock. It is useful for time-stamping entries, calculating durations, or creating dynamic reports that update automatically.

Simple explanation: Returns the current date and time.

Common use cases: Used for time-stamping data, tracking time-sensitive events, or creating dynamic reports.

When to use this function: Use when you need the current date and time to automatically update.

Syntax

```
=NOW()
```

- No arguments are required for this function.

Worked Example

Challenge: Display the current date and time.

Formula:

`=NOW()`

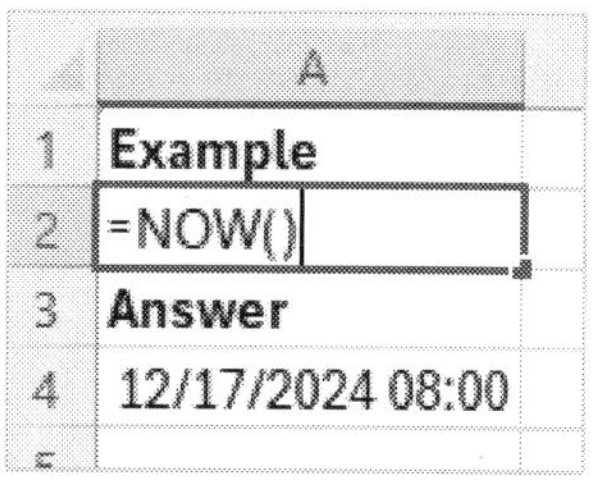

Result: 12/17/2024 08:00 (depending on your system's current date and time)
Explanation: The function returns the current date and time based on the system's clock.

Explore Further with GPT

Ask GPT how to combine NOW with other functions like DATEDIF or TODAY to calculate durations, deadlines, or automate time-sensitive reporting.

Tips for Using NOW

- **Dynamic updates:** The NOW function recalculates automatically whenever the worksheet is recalculated.
- **Date-only format:** To display only the date without the time, use TEXT or format the cell as a date.

  `=TEXT(NOW(), "mm/dd/yyyy")`

- **Time-only format:** To display only the time, use:

  `=TEXT(NOW(), "hh:mm:ss")`

- **Excel compatibility:** The NOW function is available in all Excel versions.

NPER Function

Financial Functions

Introduction

The NPER function calculates the number of payment periods required to pay off a loan or reach an investment goal, based on constant periodic payments and a constant interest rate.

Simple explanation: Determines how many periods it takes to pay off a loan or investment.

Common use cases: Used for loan amortization, retirement planning, and investment forecasting.

When to use this function: Use when you need to determine the duration needed to achieve a financial target.

Syntax

```
=NPER(rate, pmt, pv, [fv], [type])
```

- **rate**: The interest rate per period.
- **pmt**: The payment made each period (negative for outgoing payments).
- **pv**: The present value (loan principal or current investment).
- **[fv]** *(optional)*: The future value you want to achieve (default is 0).
- **[type]** *(optional)*: Specifies when payments are due:
    - 0 (default): Payments are due at the end of the period.
    - 1: Payments are due at the beginning of the period.

Worked Example

Challenge: Calculate the number of periods required to repay a loan of $10,000 at a 5% annual interest rate, with monthly payments of $200.

Formula:

```
=NPER(0.004167, -200, 10000)
```

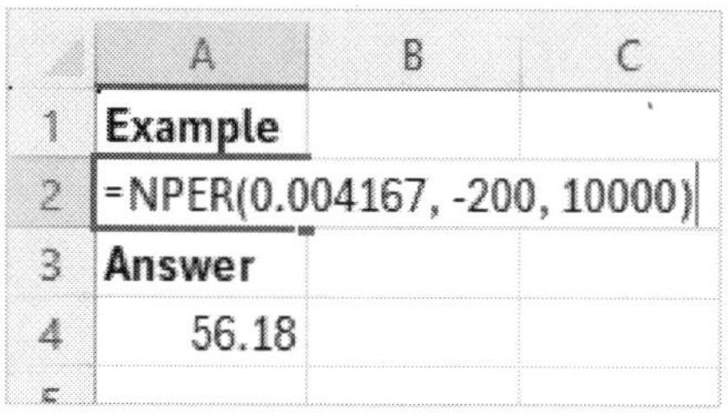

Result: 56.18
Explanation: It will take approximately 56 months to repay the loan.

Tips for Using NPER

- **Signs for cash flow:** Payments (pmt) and present value (pv) should have opposite signs. For example:
    - Use a negative sign for payments (outflows).
    - Use a positive sign for present value (inflows).
- **Adjust interest rates:** Ensure the interest rate matches the payment frequency. For example:
    - Monthly payments → Divide the annual interest rate by 12.
    - Quarterly payments → Divide the annual interest rate by 4.

NPV Function

Financial Functions

Introduction

The NPV function calculates the Net Present Value (NPV) of an investment based on a series of periodic cash flows and a constant discount rate. NPV measures the value of future cash flows in today's terms, helping determine whether an investment is profitable.

Simple explanation: Computes the present value of future cash flows based on a given discount rate.

Common use cases: Used in investment analysis, project evaluations, and financial modeling to assess profitability.

When to use this function: Use when evaluating cash flows to determine the net present value of an investment.

Syntax

```
=NPV(rate, value1, [value2], ...)
```

- **rate**: The discount rate per period (e.g., monthly, quarterly, annually).
- **value1, value2, ...**: The series of cash flows (e.g., payments or returns), where:
  - Positive values represent inflows (e.g., revenues).
  - Negative values represent outflows (e.g., costs).

Worked Example

Challenge: Calculate the Net Present Value of an investment with an annual discount rate of 10% and the following cash flows:

- Initial investment (outflow): -1000; Year 1: 300; Year 2: 420; Year 3: 680

Formula:

```
=NPV(10%, 300, 420, 680) + (-1000)
```

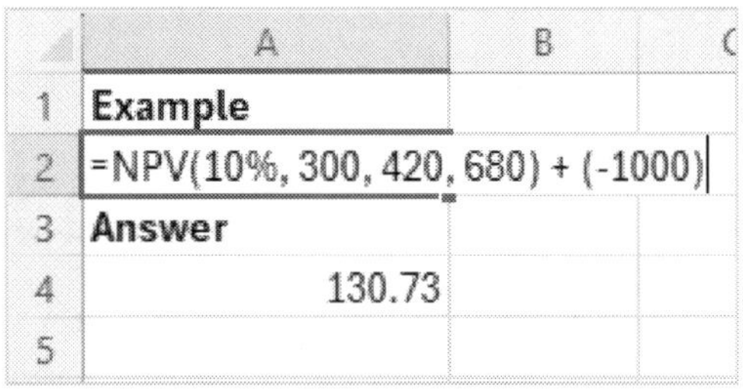

	A	B	C
1	**Example**		
2	=NPV(10%, 300, 420, 680) + (-1000)		
3	**Answer**		
4	130.73		
5			

Result: 130.73
Explanation:

- The NPV function calculates the present value of the future cash inflows (300, 420, and 680) at a discount rate of 10%.
- Subtracting the initial investment (1000) gives the final NPV. A positive NPV indicates that the investment is profitable.

Tips for Using NPV

- **Include initial investment:** The initial investment (cash outflow) must be added separately to the result of the NPV function:

  ```
  =NPV(rate, value1, value2, ...) + initial_investment
  ```

NUMBERVALUE Function

Text Functions

Introduction

The NUMBERVALUE function converts text that appears as a number into a numeric value, using specified decimal and group separators. It is useful for handling numbers stored as text in various formats or regional settings.

Simple explanation: Converts a number stored as text into a numeric value.

Common use cases: Used in data cleaning, importing data with inconsistent number formats, and converting numbers from text in different locales.

When to use this function: Use when you need to transform text numbers into usable numeric values for calculations.

Syntax

```
=NUMBERVALUE(text, [decimal_separator], [group_separator])
```

- **text**: The text to convert to a number.
- **[decimal_separator]** *(optional)*: The character used as the decimal separator (e.g., . or ,).
- **[group_separator]** *(optional)*: The character used as the grouping separator (e.g., , or .).

Worked Example

Challenge: Convert text "1.234,56" (using a comma as the decimal separator) into a number.

Formula:

```
=NUMBERVALUE("1.234,56", ",", ".")
```

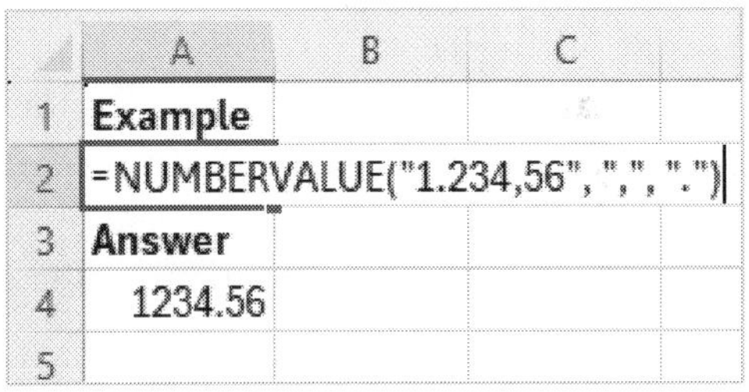

	A	B	C
1	**Example**		
2	=NUMBERVALUE("1.234,56", ",", ".")		
3	**Answer**		
4	1234.56		
5			

Result: 1234.56
Explanation: The function interprets "1.234,56" as 1234.56 by using "," as the decimal separator and "." as the grouping separator.

Explore Further with GPT

Ask GPT how to use NUMBERVALUE in combination with functions like TEXT, VALUE, or TEXTSPLIT for advanced data parsing and formatting tasks.

Tips for Using NUMBERVALUE

- **Locale-specific separators:** Use the appropriate decimal_separator and group_separator for data from different locales. For example:
  - For French numbers: NUMBERVALUE("1 234,56", ",", " ")
  - For German numbers: NUMBERVALUE("1.234,56", ",", ".")
- **Handles extra spaces:** The function automatically trims leading and trailing spaces in the text.

OCT2BIN Function

Engineering Functions

Introduction

The OCT2BIN function converts an octal (base-8) number to its binary (base-2) equivalent. This function is useful for engineers, computer scientists, and anyone working with numerical systems and conversions.

Simple explanation: Converts an octal number to a binary number.

Common use cases: Used in computer science, engineering, and digital systems where conversions between numerical systems are required.

When to use this function: Use when you need to transform octal values into binary format.

Syntax

```
=OCT2BIN(number, [places])
```

- **number**: The octal number to convert. Must be a valid octal number (digits 0–7).
- **[places]** *(optional)*: The number of characters to pad the binary result with leading zeros. If omitted, Excel uses the minimum required digits.

Worked Example

Challenge: Convert the octal number 7 to binary.

Formula:

```
=OCT2BIN(7)
```

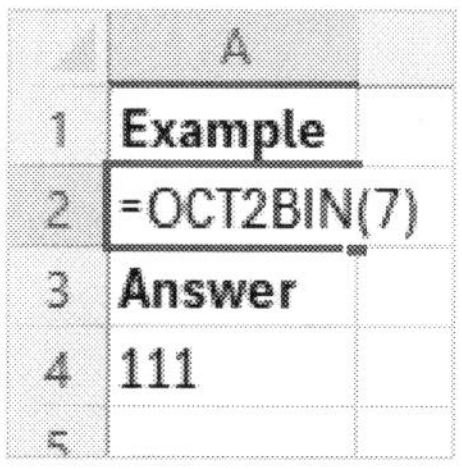

Result: 111
Explanation: The octal number 7 is equivalent to the binary number 111.

Explore Further with GPT

Ask GPT how to combine OCT2BIN with functions like BIN2DEC, OCT2HEX, or DEC2BIN for full numerical system conversions.

Tips for Using OCT2BIN

- **Valid octal inputs:** Ensure the number contains only digits 0–7. Invalid numbers return a #NUM! error.
- **Padding behavior:** If the binary result exceeds the specified number of places, Excel ignores the places value and returns the full binary result.
- **Leading zeros:** Use the places parameter to add leading zeros for uniform binary representations.

OCT2DEC Function

Engineering Functions

Introduction

The OCT2DEC function converts an octal (base-8) number to its decimal (base-10) equivalent. This function is commonly used in computer science, engineering, and mathematics for numerical system conversions.

Simple explanation: Converts an octal number to a decimal number.

Common use cases: Used in programming, digital systems, and scientific calculations requiring base-8 to base-10 conversions.

When to use this function: Use when you need to interpret octal numbers in decimal format.

Syntax

```
=OCT2DEC(number)
```

- **number**: The octal number to convert. Must be a valid octal number (digits 0–7).

Worked Example

Challenge: Convert the octal number 10 to decimal.

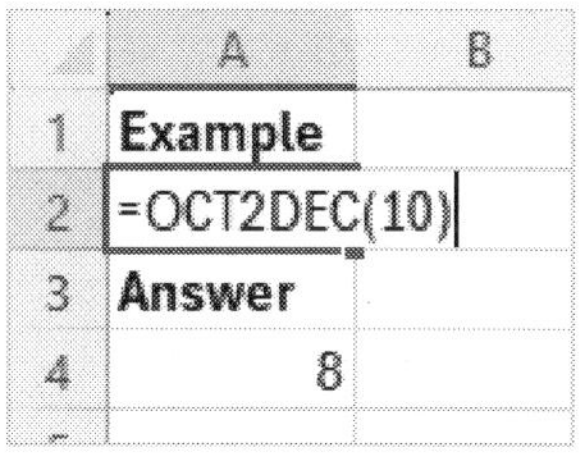

Formula:

```
=OCT2DEC(10)
```

Result: 8
Explanation: The octal number 10 corresponds to the decimal number 8.

Explore Further with GPT

Ask GPT how to combine OCT2DEC with functions like DEC2BIN, OCT2HEX, or DEC2OCT for a complete numerical system conversion toolkit.

Tips for Using OCT2DEC

- **Valid octal inputs:** Ensure the number consists only of digits 0–7. Invalid inputs return a #NUM! error.
- **Two's complement for negatives:** For octal numbers interpreted as negatives, Excel uses two's complement representation.

OCT2HEX Function

Engineering Functions

Introduction

The OCT2HEX function converts an octal (base-8) number to its hexadecimal (base-16) equivalent. This function is useful in digital systems and computer science for working with numerical system conversions.

Simple explanation: Converts an octal number into a hexadecimal number.

Common use cases: Used in programming, engineering, and digital system design where conversions between octal and hexadecimal are required.

When to use this function: Use when interpreting or converting octal values into hexadecimal format.

Syntax

```
=OCT2HEX(number, [places])
```

- **number**: The octal number to convert. Must be a valid octal number (digits 0–7).
- **[places]** *(optional)*: The number of characters to pad the hexadecimal result with leading zeros. If omitted, Excel uses the minimum required digits.

Worked Example

Challenge: Convert the octal number 10 to hexadecimal.

Formula:

```
=OCT2HEX(10)
```

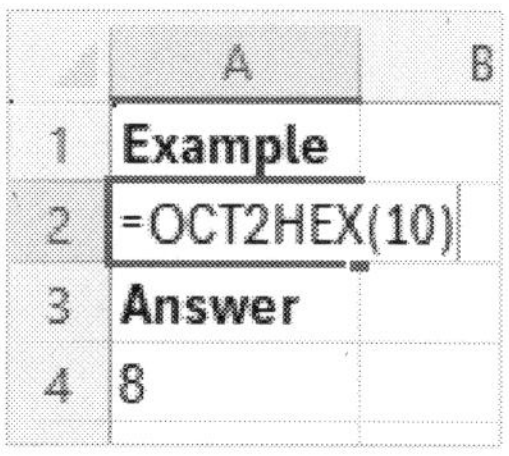

Result: 8

Explanation: The octal number 10 corresponds to the decimal number 8, which is equivalent to 8 in hexadecimal.

Explore Further with GPT

Ask GPT how to combine OCT2HEX with functions like HEX2DEC, OCT2DEC, or DEC2HEX for full numerical system conversions.

Tips for Using OCT2HEX

- **Valid octal inputs:** Ensure the number contains only digits 0–7. Invalid inputs return a #NUM! error.
- **Padding behavior:** If the hexadecimal result exceeds the specified number of places, Excel ignores the places value and returns the full hexadecimal result.
- **Leading zeros:** Use the places parameter to add leading zeros for uniform hexadecimal representations.

ODD Function

Math & Trigonometry Functions

Introduction

The ODD function rounds a number up to the nearest odd integer. If the number is already odd, it remains unchanged. This function works with both positive and negative numbers.

Simple explanation: Rounds a number up to the next odd integer.

Common use cases: Used in statistical calculations, rounding operations, and scenarios requiring odd-numbered values.

When to use this function: Use when you need odd integers for calculations or constraints.

Syntax

```
=ODD(number)
```

- **number**: The number to be rounded to the nearest odd integer.

Worked Example

Challenge: Round the number 6.3 up to the nearest odd integer.

Formula:

```
=ODD(6.3)
```

Result: 7
Explanation: The function rounds 6.3 up to the next odd integer, which is 7.

	A
1	**Example**
2	=ODD(6.3)
3	**Answer**
4	7

Explore Further with GPT

Ask GPT how to combine ODD with functions like EVEN, ROUND, or INT for more advanced rounding operations.

Tips for Using ODD

- **Positive and negative numbers:** The function always rounds away from zero to the next odd integer.
- **Zero input:** If the input is 0, the result is 1.
- **Use with other rounding functions:** Combine with functions like ROUND or CEILING for customized rounding logic:

  ```
  =ODD(ROUND(A1, 0))
  ```

ODDFPRICE Function

Financial Functions

Introduction

The ODDFPRICE function calculates the price per $100 face value of a security with an odd (irregular) first period. This function is used in financial modeling for bonds and other securities with irregular initial coupon payment schedules.

Simple explanation: Calculates the price of a bond with an irregular first coupon period.

Common use cases: Used in bond pricing, investment analysis, and financial forecasting for bonds with non-standard first payment periods.

When to use this function: Use when evaluating the price of a bond with an odd first coupon period.

Syntax

```
=ODDFPRICE(settlement, maturity, issue, first_coupon, rate, yld, redemption, frequency, [basis])
```

- **settlement**: The settlement date of the security (when the buyer acquires the security).
- **maturity**: The maturity date of the security (when it expires).
- **issue**: The issue date of the security.
- **first_coupon**: The date of the first coupon payment.
- **rate**: The annual coupon rate.
- **yld**: The annual yield of the security.
- **redemption**: The redemption value per $100 face value (usually 100).
- **frequency**: The number of coupon payments per year:
    - 1 = Annual; 2 = Semi-annual; 4 = Quarterly.
- **[basis]** *(optional)*: The day count basis to use (default is 0):
    - 0 = US (NASD) 30/360; 1 = Actual/actual; 2 = Actual/360; 3 = Actual/365; 4 = European 30/360.

Worked Example

Challenge: Calculate the price of a bond with a rate of % and a yield of 4%

Formula:

```
=ODDFPRICE(DATE(2024,1,1), DATE(2028,1,1),
DATE(2023,7,1), DATE(2024,7,1), 0.05, 0.04, 100, 2, 0)
```

Result: 103.61
Explanation: The bond's price is calculated based on the odd first coupon period, yield, and other parameters.

	A
1	**Example**
2	=ODDFPRICE(DATE(2024,1,1), DATE(2028,1,1), DATE(2023,7,1), DATE(2024,7,1), 0.05, 0.04, 100, 2, 0)
3	**Answer**
4	103.61

ODDFYIELD Function

Financial Functions

Introduction

The ODDFYIELD function calculates the yield of a security with an odd (irregular) first period. This function is commonly used in financial modeling for bonds or securities with non-standard initial payment schedules.

Simple explanation: Calculates the yield of a bond with an irregular first coupon period.

Common use cases: Used in bond valuation, investment analysis, and financial forecasting for securities with non-standard first payment schedules.

When to use this function: Use when determining the yield for a bond with an odd first period.

Syntax

```
=ODDFYIELD(settlement, maturity, issue, first_coupon, rate, pr, redemption, frequency, [basis])
```

- **settlement**: The settlement date of the security (when the buyer acquires the security).
- **maturity**: The maturity date of the security (when it expires).
- **issue**: The issue date of the security.
- **first_coupon**: The date of the first coupon payment.
- **rate**: The annual coupon rate.
- **pr**: The price of the security per $100 face value.
- **redemption**: The redemption value per $100 face value (usually 100).
- **frequency**: The number of coupon payments per year:
  - 1 = Annual; 2 = Semi-annual; 4 = Quarterly.
- **[basis]** *(optional)*: The day count basis to use (default is 0):
  - 0 = US (NASD) 30/360; 1 = Actual/actual; 2 = Actual/360; 3 = Actual/365; 4 = European 30/360.

Worked Example

Challenge: Calculate the yield of a bond

Formula:

```
=ODDFYIELD(DATE(2024,1,1), DATE(2028,1,1), DATE(2023,7,1), DATE(2024,7,1), 0.05, 104.25, 100, 2, 0)
```

Result: 3.83%
Explanation: The function calculates the annual yield for the bond, accounting for the odd first coupon period and the given inputs.

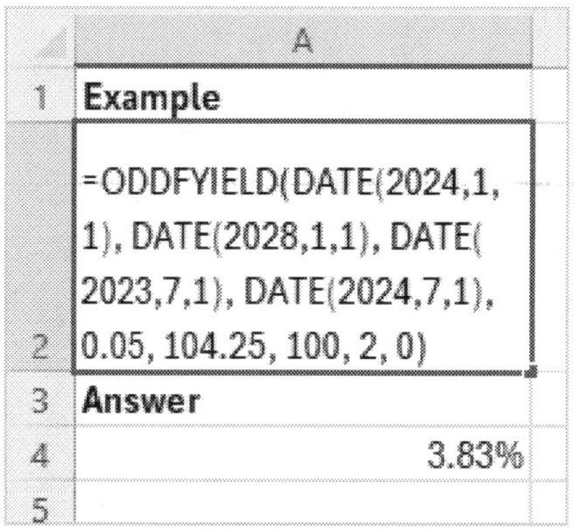

ODDLPRICE Function

Financial Functions

Introduction

The ODDLPRICE function calculates the price per $100 face value of a security with an odd (irregular) last period. This function is commonly used for bonds or securities with non-standard final payment schedules.

Simple explanation: Calculates the price of a bond with an irregular last coupon period.

Common use cases: Used in bond pricing, investment analysis, and financial modeling for securities with non-standard last payment schedules.

When to use this function: Use when evaluating the price of a bond with an odd last period.

Syntax

```
=ODDLPRICE(settlement, maturity, last_interest, rate, yld, redemption, frequency, [basis])
```

- **settlement**: The settlement date of the security (when the buyer acquires the security).
- **maturity**: The maturity date of the security (when it expires).
- **last_interest**: The date of the last interest payment before maturity.
- **rate**: The annual coupon rate.
- **yld**: The annual yield of the security.
- **redemption**: The redemption value per $100 face value (usually 100).
- **frequency**: The number of coupon payments per year:
  - 1 = Annual; 2 = Semi-annual; 4 = Quarterly.
- **[basis]** *(optional)*: The day count basis to use (default is 0):
  - 0 = US (NASD) 30/360; 1 = Actual/actual; 2 = Actual/360; 3 = Actual/365; 4 = European 30/360.

Worked Example

Challenge: Calculate the price of a bond:

Formula:

```
=ODDLPRICE(DATE(2017,4,14), DATE(2017,6,30),
DATE(2017,1,31), 0.05, 0.035, 100, 2, 0)
```

Result: 100.31
Explanation: The function calculates the bond's price based on the odd last period, annual yield, coupon rate, and other parameters.

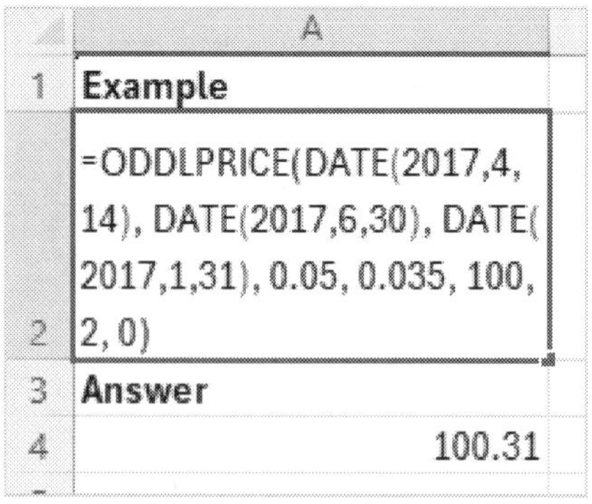

Explore Further with GPT

Ask GPT how to combine ODDLPRICE with ODDLYIELD, PRICE, or YIELD for more comprehensive bond analysis and valuation.

ODDLYIELD Function

Financial Functions

Introduction

The ODDLYIELD function calculates the yield of a security with an odd (irregular) last period. This function is often used for bonds or securities with non-standard final payment schedules, helping investors understand the annualized return.

Simple explanation: Calculates the annualized yield for a bond with an irregular last coupon period.

Common use cases: Used in bond analysis, investment evaluation, and financial modeling for securities with non-standard payment schedules.

When to use this function: Use when determining the yield of a bond with an odd final period.

Syntax

```
=ODDLYIELD(settlement, maturity, last_interest, rate, pr, redemption, frequency, [basis])
```

- **settlement**: The date the buyer acquires the bond.
- **maturity**: The date the bond expires.
- **last_interest**: The last coupon payment date before maturity.
- **rate**: The annual coupon rate of the bond.
- **pr**: The market price of the bond per $100 face value.
- **redemption**: The redemption value of the bond per $100 face value (usually 100).
- **frequency**: The number of coupon payments per year:
    - 1 = Annual; 2 = Semi-annual; 4 = Quarterly.
- **[basis]** *(optional)*: The day count basis to use (default is 0):
    - 0 = US (NASD) 30/360; 1 = Actual/actual; 2 = Actual/360; 3 = Actual/365; 4 = European 30/360.

Worked Example

Challenge: Calculate the yield of a bond

Formula:

```
=ODDLYIELD(DATE(2017,4,14), DATE(2017,6,30),
DATE(2017,1,31), 0.05, 100, 100, 2, 0)
```

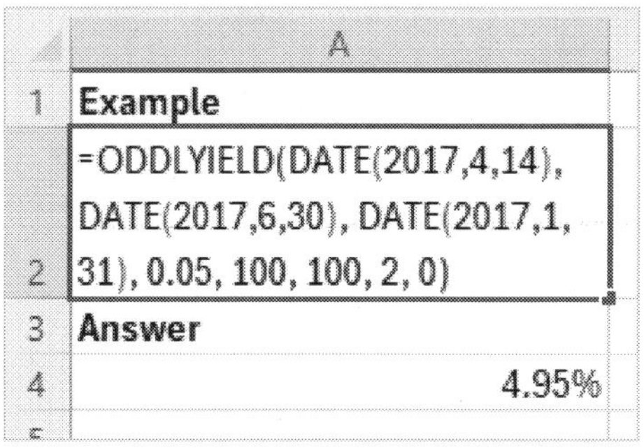

Result: 4.95%
Explanation: The annualized yield of the bond is calculated based on the odd last period, market price, redemption value, and other inputs.

Tips for Using ODDLYIELD

- **Date Order:** Ensure the settlement date occurs after the last interest date but before the maturity date: Last Interest < Settlement < Maturity.

OFFSET Function

Lookup & Reference Functions

Introduction

The OFFSET function returns a reference to a range that is a specified number of rows and columns away from a given starting point. You can also specify the height and width of the range in rows and columns.

Simple explanation: Dynamically references a range by shifting rows and columns from a starting point.

Common use cases: Used for creating dynamic ranges, dynamic charts, and complex formulas.

When to use this function: Use when you need to reference a range that changes based on other criteria or values.

Syntax

```
=OFFSET(reference, rows, cols, [height], [width])
```

- **reference**: The starting cell or range.
- **rows**: The number of rows to move up (negative) or down (positive) from the reference.
- **cols**: The number of columns to move left (negative) or right (positive) from the reference.
- **[height]** *(optional)*: The number of rows in the returned range (default is 1).
- **[width]** *(optional)*: The number of columns in the returned range (default is 1).

Worked Example

Challenge: Return the value from a cell 2 rows below and 3 columns to the right of cell A1.

Formula:

```
=OFFSET(A1, 2, 3)
```

Result: Pear
Explanation: Starting at A1, the formula moves 2 rows down and 3 columns to the right, landing at cell D3.

	A	B	C	D	E	F	G	H
1	Apple	Banana	Cherry	Date	Elder		**Example**	
2	Fig	Grape	Honey	Kiwi	Lemon		=OFFSET(A1, 2, 3)	
3	Mango	Nectar	Olive	Pear	Quince		**Answer**	
4							Pear	
5								

Explore Further with GPT

Ask GPT how to combine OFFSET with functions like COUNTA, SUM, or AVERAGE to create dynamic named ranges and enhance formulas.

Tips for Using OFFSET

- **Dynamic Named Ranges:** Combine with COUNTA to create dynamic ranges:

  ```
  =OFFSET(A1, 0, 0, COUNTA(A:A), 1)
  ```

  (This creates a range from A1 down to the last non-blank cell in column A.)

- **Performance Considerations:** The OFFSET function is volatile, meaning it recalculates whenever the workbook changes. This can slow down large workbooks.

OR Function

Logical Functions

Introduction

The OR function returns TRUE if any of the conditions in its arguments evaluate to TRUE; otherwise, it returns FALSE. It is commonly used in logical tests to combine multiple criteria.

Simple explanation: Checks if at least one condition is true.

Common use cases: Used in decision-making, conditional formatting, and combining multiple logical criteria.

When to use this function: Use when you need to test multiple conditions and return TRUE if any of them are met.

Syntax

```
=OR(logical1, [logical2], ...)
```

- **logical1, logical2, ...**: Conditions or logical expressions to evaluate. These can reference cells, values, or expressions.

Worked Example

Challenge: Determine if either A1 > 10 or B1 < 5.

Formula:

```
=OR(A1 > 10, B1 < 5)
```

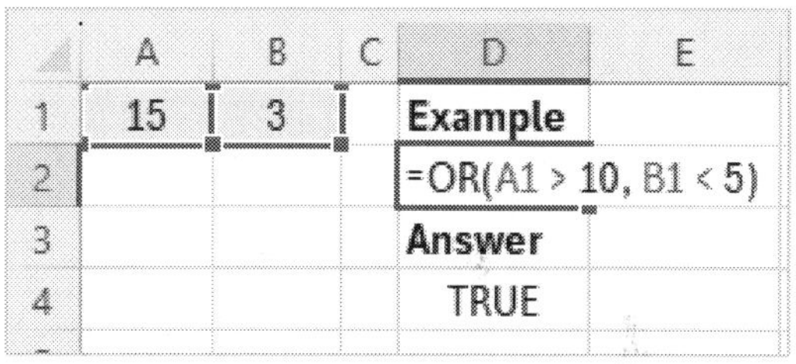

Result: TRUE
Explanation: The first condition A1 > 10 evaluates to TRUE because 15 > 10. Therefore, the OR function returns TRUE.

Tips for Using OR

- **Combine with IF:** Use OR inside an IF function to create conditional results:

  ```
  =IF(OR(A1 > 10, B1 < 5), "Pass", "Fail")
  ```

  (This returns "Pass" if either condition is met.)

- **Array Formulas:** Use OR with arrays by entering the formula as an array formula (Ctrl + Shift + Enter in older Excel versions):

  ```
  =OR(A1:A10 > 10)
  ```

PDURATION Function

Financial Functions

Introduction

The PDURATION function calculates the number of periods required for an investment to grow to a specified future value at a constant interest rate. It is a helpful tool for financial planning and investment analysis.

Simple explanation: Determines how long it takes for an investment to grow to a target amount.

Common use cases: Used in financial forecasting, compound interest calculations, and investment growth modeling.

When to use this function: Use when you need to calculate the time required to achieve a financial goal based on a given interest rate.

Syntax

```
=PDURATION(rate, pv, fv)
```

- **rate**: The constant interest rate per period.
- **pv**: The present value (initial amount of the investment).
- **fv**: The future value (target amount).

Worked Example

Challenge: Calculate how many years it will take for an investment of $10,000 to grow to $20,000 at an annual interest rate of 5%.

Formula:

```
=PDURATION(0.05, 10000, 20000)
```

Result: 14.21
Explanation: At an annual interest rate of 5%, it will take approximately 14.21 years for $10,000 to grow to $20,000.

	A	B	C
1	**Example**		
2	=PDURATION(0.05, 10000, 20000)		
3	**Answer**		
4	14.21		
5			

Explore Further with GPT

Ask GPT how to combine PDURATION with functions like RATE, FV, or NPER for comprehensive financial analysis.

Tips for Using PDURATION

- **Interest rate consistency:** Ensure the rate corresponds to the compounding period:
  - For annual interest rates, enter the annual rate.
  - For monthly rates, divide the annual rate by 12.
- **Positive values:** Both pv and fv must be positive. If either is negative, Excel returns a #NUM! error.

PEARSON Function

Statistical Functions

Introduction

The PEARSON function calculates the Pearson correlation coefficient between two data sets. This coefficient measures the strength and direction of a linear relationship between two variables.

Simple explanation: Measures how strongly two sets of data are linearly related.

Common use cases: Used in statistics, data analysis, and predictive modeling to assess relationships between variables.

When to use this function: Use when you need to quantify the linear correlation between two data sets.

Syntax

```
=PEARSON(array1, array2)
```

- **array1**: The first set of data points.
- **array2**: The second set of data points.

Worked Example

Challenge: Calculate the Pearson correlation coefficient for two data sets.

Formula:

```
=PEARSON(A2:A6, B2:B6)
```

	A	B	C	D	E	F
1	X (Array1)	Y (Array2)		Example		
2	1	2		=PEARSON(A2:A6, B2:B6)		
3	2	3		Answer		
4	3	4		1		
5	4	5				
6	5	6				
7						

Result: 1

Explanation: The correlation coefficient of 1 indicates a perfect positive linear relationship between X and Y.

Explore Further with GPT

Ask GPT how to interpret Pearson correlation values and combine PEARSON with functions like SLOPE or FORECAST for deeper statistical insights.

Tips for Using PEARSON

- **Correlation value range:** The result will always be between -1 and 1:
  - 1: Perfect positive linear relationship.
  - -1: Perfect negative linear relationship.
  - 0: No linear relationship.
- **Array lengths must match:** array1 and array2 must have the same number of data points. Mismatched arrays return a #N/A error.

PERCENTILE.EXC Function

Statistical Functions

Introduction

The PERCENTILE.EXC function returns the k-th percentile of a data set, where k is between 0 and 1, excluding the smallest and largest values in the data set. It is useful for statistical analysis and identifying thresholds within data.

Simple explanation: Calculates the percentile value of a data set, excluding the extremes.

Common use cases: Used in statistical analysis, outlier detection, and performance benchmarking.

When to use this function: Use when you need to calculate a percentile while excluding the smallest and largest values in the data set.

Syntax

```
=PERCENTILE.EXC(array, k)
```

- **array**: The data set (a range of values).
- **k**: The desired percentile (a number between 0 and 1, exclusive).

Worked Example

Challenge: Find the 80th percentile of the data set {10, 20, 30, 40, 50}.

Formula:

```
=PERCENTILE.EXC(A1:A5, 0.8)
```

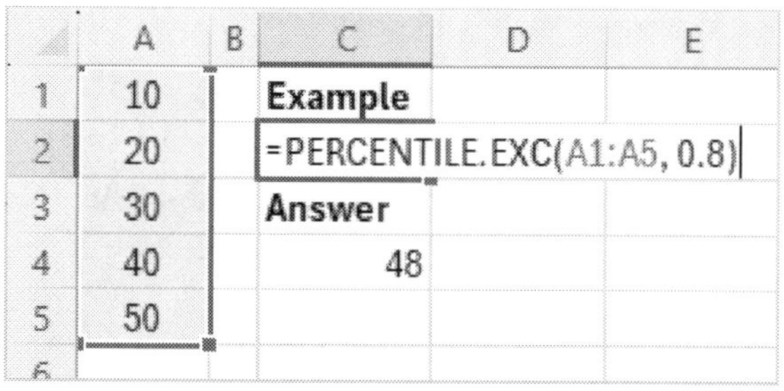

Result: 48
Explanation: The 80th percentile value of the data set is 48, calculated while excluding the smallest and largest values.

Explore Further with GPT

Ask GPT how to use PERCENTILE.EXC in combination with PERCENTILE.INC, QUARTILE.EXC, or MEDIAN for deeper statistical insights.

Tips for Using PERCENTILE.EXC

- **Valid range for k:** The k value must be strictly between 0 and 1. Values of 0 or 1 will return a #NUM! error.
- **Array requirements:** Ensure the array contains at least two data points; otherwise, the function returns a #NUM! error.
- **Difference from PERCENTILE.INC:** Use PERCENTILE.INC to include the smallest and largest values in the data set.

PERCENTILE.INC Function

Statistical Functions

Introduction

The PERCENTILE.INC function returns the k-th percentile of a data set, where k is between 0 and 1, including the smallest and largest values in the data set. It is a useful tool for analyzing data distribution and determining thresholds.

Simple explanation: Calculates the percentile value of a data set, including the extremes.

Common use cases: Used in statistical analysis, performance evaluation, and data segmentation.

When to use this function: Use when you need to calculate a percentile while including the smallest and largest values in the data set.

Syntax

```
=PERCENTILE.INC(array, k)
```

- **array**: The data set (a range of values).
- **k**: The desired percentile (a number between 0 and 1, inclusive)

Worked Example

Challenge: Find the 80th percentile of the data set {10, 20, 30, 40, 50}.

Formula:

```
=PERCENTILE.INC(A1:A5, 0.8)
```

Result: 42

Explanation: The 80th percentile value of the data set is 42, calculated while including the smallest and largest values.

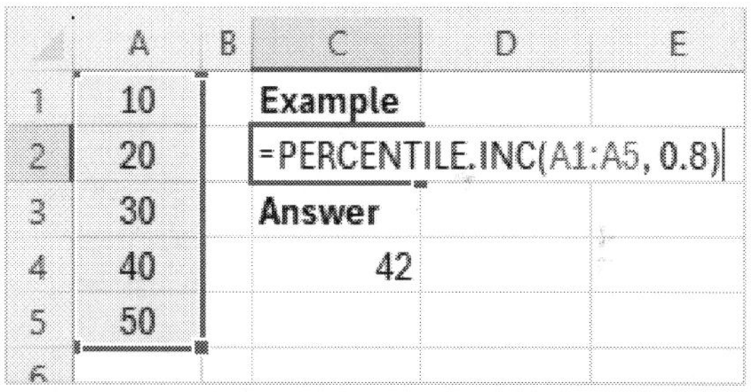

	A	B	C	D	E
1	10		Example		
2	20		=PERCENTILE.INC(A1:A5, 0.8)		
3	30		Answer		
4	40		42		
5	50				

Explore Further with GPT

Ask GPT how to use PERCENTILE.INC in combination with QUARTILE.INC, AVERAGE, or MEDIAN to gain deeper insights into data distribution.

Tips for Using PERCENTILE.INC

- **Valid range for k:** The k value must be between 0 and 1, inclusive. Values outside this range return a #NUM! error.
- **Include boundary values:** This function includes the smallest (0th percentile) and largest (100th percentile) values in the data set.
- **Difference from PERCENTILE.EXC:** Use PERCENTILE.EXC to exclude the smallest and largest values.

PERCENTILE Function

Compatibility Functions

Introduction

The PERCENTILE function is a legacy function used to calculate the k-th percentile of a data set. While it has been replaced by PERCENTILE.INC and PERCENTILE.EXC, it remains available in Excel for backward compatibility.

Simple explanation: Calculates the percentile value of a data set, including the smallest and largest values.

Common use cases: Used in legacy spreadsheets for statistical analysis and performance evaluation.

When to use this function: Use for compatibility with older Excel versions or when updating legacy files.

Syntax

```
=PERCENTILE(array, k)
```

- **array**: The data set (a range of values).
- **k**: The desired percentile (a number between 0 and 1, inclusive).

Worked Example

Challenge: Find the 80th percentile of the data set {10, 20, 30, 40, 50}.

Formula:

```
=PERCENTILE(A1:A5, 0.8)
```

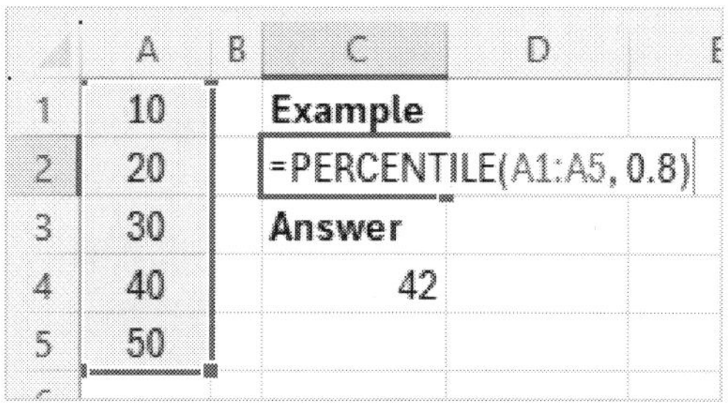

Result: 42
Explanation: The 80th percentile value of the data set is 42, calculated while including the smallest and largest values.

Explore Further with GPT

Ask GPT how to migrate legacy PERCENTILE formulas to PERCENTILE.INC or PERCENTILE.EXC for modern Excel usage.

Tips for Using PERCENTILE

- **Use for backward compatibility:** Consider replacing PERCENTILE with PERCENTILE.INC or PERCENTILE.EXC in newer workbooks.
- **k must be valid:** Ensure k is between 0 and 1. Values outside this range will return a #NUM! error.
- **Legacy feature:** Available for backward compatibility; use PERCENTILE.INC for identical functionality in modern workbooks.

PERCENTRANK.EXC Function

Statistical Functions

Introduction

The PERCENTRANK.EXC function returns the rank of a value in a data set as a percentage (between 0 and 1), excluding the smallest and largest values. It is useful for statistical analysis and identifying a value's relative standing in a data set.

Simple explanation: Calculates the percentage rank of a value in a data set, excluding extremes.

Common use cases: Used in data analysis to understand the relative position of a value in a range.

When to use this function: Use when you need a value's percentile rank without considering the smallest and largest data points.

Syntax

```
=PERCENTRANK.EXC(array, x, [significance])
```

- **array**: The data set (a range of numeric values).
- **x**: The value for which to determine the percentage rank.
- **[significance]** *(optional)*: The number of significant digits to include in the result (default is 3).

Worked Example

Challenge: Calculate the percentage rank of 35 in the data set {10, 20, 30, 40, 50}.

Formula:

```
=PERCENTRANK.EXC(A1:A5, 35)
```

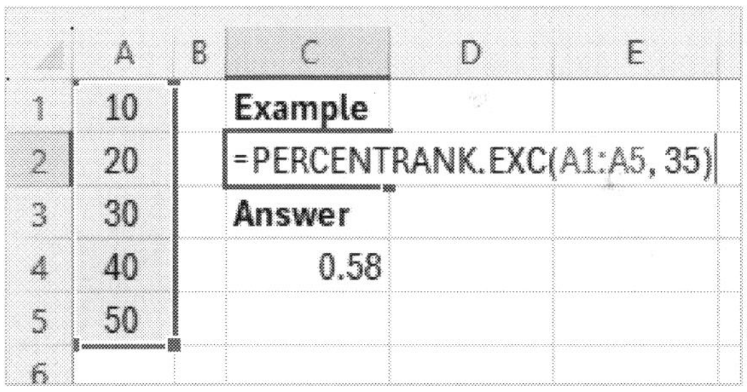

	A	B	C	D	E
1	10		**Example**		
2	20		=PERCENTRANK.EXC(A1:A5, 35)		
3	30		**Answer**		
4	40		0.58		
5	50				
6					

Result: 0.58
Explanation: The value 35 ranks at the 58th percentile of the data set, excluding the smallest and largest values.

Explore Further with GPT

Ask GPT how to combine PERCENTRANK.EXC with functions like QUARTILE.EXC, PERCENTILE.EXC, or RANK.EQ for deeper data insights.

Tips for Using PERCENTRANK.EXC

- **Excludes extremes:** Unlike PERCENTRANK.INC, this function does not consider the smallest and largest values when calculating ranks.
- **Valid input values:** The x value must fall within the data range. If x is smaller than the smallest value or larger than the largest value, the function returns #N/A.
- **Significance parameter:** Use the significance argument to control the number of decimal places in the result.

PERCENTRANK.INC Function

Statistical Functions

Introduction

The PERCENTRANK.INC function returns the rank of a value in a data set as a percentage (between 0 and 1), including the smallest and largest values. It is a helpful tool for understanding a value's relative standing in a data range.

Simple explanation: Calculates the percentage rank of a value in a data set, including extremes.

Common use cases: Used in statistical analysis, performance evaluation, and data comparison.

When to use this function: Use when you need a value's percentile rank, including the smallest and largest data points.

Syntax

```
=PERCENTRANK.INC(array, x, [significance])
```

- **array**: The data set (a range of numeric values).
- **x**: The value for which to determine the percentage rank.
- **[significance]** *(optional)*: The number of significant digits to include in the result (default is 3).

Worked Example

Challenge: Calculate the percentage rank of 35 in the data set {10, 20, 30, 40, 50}.

Formula:

```
=PERCENTRANK.INC(A1:A5, 35)
```

Result: 0.63
Explanation: The value 35 ranks at the 63rd percentile of the data set, including the smallest (10) and largest (50) values.

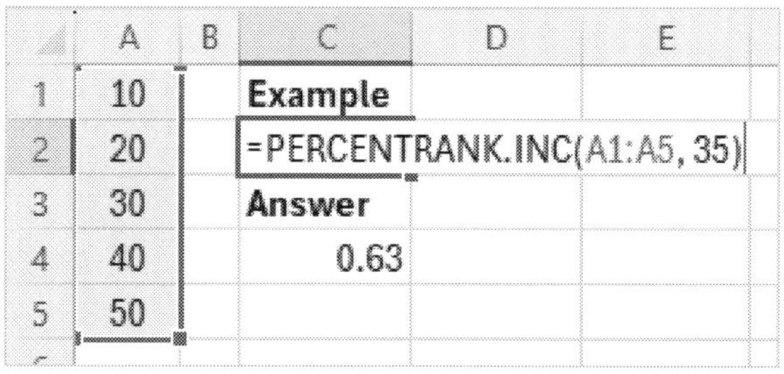

Explore Further with GPT

Ask GPT how to use PERCENTRANK.INC in combination with PERCENTILE.INC, RANK.EQ, or QUARTILE.INC for deeper insights into data distribution.

Tips for Using PERCENTRANK.INC

- **Includes extremes:** Unlike PERCENTRANK.EXC, this function considers the smallest and largest values when calculating ranks.
- **Valid input values:** The x value must fall within the data range. If x is smaller than the smallest value or larger than the largest value, the function returns #N/A.
- **Significance parameter:** Use the significance argument to control the number of decimal places in the result.

PERCENTRANK Function

Compatibility Functions

Introduction

The PERCENTRANK function is a legacy function used to calculate the rank of a value in a data set as a percentage. While it has been replaced by PERCENTRANK.INC and PERCENTRANK.EXC, it remains available for backward compatibility.

Simple explanation: Calculates the percentage rank of a value in a data set, including the smallest and largest values.

Common use cases: Used in legacy spreadsheets for data ranking and statistical analysis.

When to use this function: Use for compatibility with older Excel versions or when updating legacy files.

Syntax

```
=PERCENTRANK(array, x, [significance])
```

- **array**: The data set (a range of numeric values).
- **x**: The value for which to determine the percentage rank.
- **[significance]** *(optional)*: The number of significant digits to include in the result (default is 3)

Worked Example

Challenge: Calculate the percentage rank of 35 in the data set {10, 20, 30, 40, 50}.

Formula:

```
=PERCENTRANK(A1:A5, 35)
```

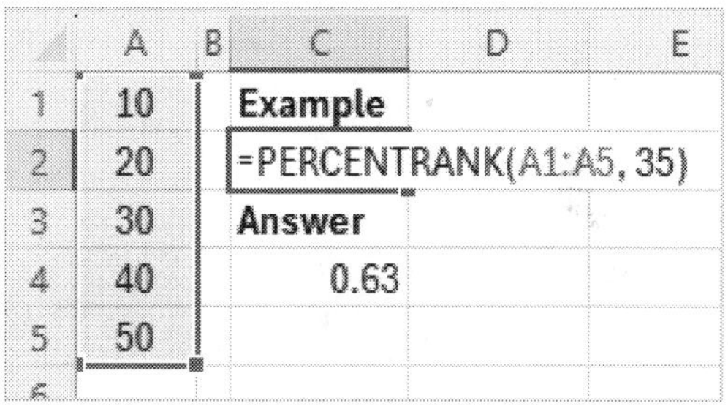

Result: 0.63
Explanation: The value 35 ranks at the 63rd percentile of the data set, including the smallest and largest values.

Explore Further with GPT

Ask GPT how to migrate legacy PERCENTRANK formulas to PERCENTRANK.INC or PERCENTRANK.EXC for modern Excel usage.

Tips for Using PERCENTRANK

- **Use for backward compatibility:** Consider replacing PERCENTRANK with PERCENTRANK.INC or PERCENTRANK.EXC in newer workbooks.
- **Valid input values:** The x value must fall within the data range. If x is smaller than the smallest value or larger than the largest value, the function returns #N/A.
- **Significance parameter:** Use the significance argument to control the number of decimal places in the result.

PERMUT Function

Statistical Functions

Introduction

The PERMUT function calculates the number of permutations for a given number of items, where order matters. Permutations are arrangements of items in a specific order, useful in probability, statistics, and combinatorics.

Simple explanation: Counts the ways to arrange a subset of items where order matters.

Common use cases: Used in probability, scheduling, and ranking scenarios.

When to use this function: Use when determining the number of possible ordered arrangements of a subset of items.

Syntax

```
=PERMUT(number, number_chosen)
```

- **number**: The total number of items.
- **number_chosen**: The number of items to arrange.

Worked Example

Challenge: Calculate the number of ways to arrange 3 items chosen from a set of 5 items.

Formula:

```
=PERMUT(5, 3)
```

	A	B
1	**Example**	
2	=PERMUT(5, 3)	
3	**Answer**	
4	60	

Result: 60
Explanation: There are 60 ways to arrange 3 items from a set of 5 where order matters.

Explore Further with GPT

Ask GPT how to combine PERMUT with COMBIN or FACT to solve advanced combinatorics problems or compare permutations and combinations.

Tips for Using PERMUT

- **Order matters:** Use PERMUT when the arrangement sequence is important.
- **Error handling:** If number_chosen is greater than number or either value is non-numeric, the function returns #NUM! or #VALUE!.
- **Related functions:**
  - Use COMBIN when order doesn't matter.
  - Use FACT to calculate factorials for entire sets.

PERMUTATIONA Function

Statistical Functions

Introduction

The PERMUTATIONA function calculates the number of permutations for a given number of items, where repetition of items is allowed. This function is useful in scenarios where duplicates are permitted in ordered arrangements.

Simple explanation: Counts the number of ordered arrangements of items where repetition is allowed.

Common use cases: Used in probability, combinations with repetition, and problem-solving scenarios involving duplicate items.

When to use this function: Use when calculating the number of arrangements with repetition allowed.

Syntax

```
=PERMUTATIONA(number, number_chosen)
```

- **number**: The total number of items available.
- **number_chosen**: The number of items to arrange.

Worked Example

Challenge: Calculate the number of ways to arrange 3 items chosen from a set of 5 items, allowing repetition.

Formula:

```
=PERMUTATIONA(5, 3)
```

Result: 125

Explanation: Each of the 3 positions can be filled by any of the 5 items, and repetition is allowed, resulting in $5^3=125$ arrangements.

	A	B
1	**Example**	
2	=PERMUTATIONA(5, 3)	
3	**Answer**	
4	125	

Explore Further with GPT

Ask GPT how to combine PERMUTATIONA with PERMUT or COMBIN to solve advanced combinatorics problems involving permutations with or without repetition.

Tips for Using PERMUTATIONA

- **Repetition matters:** Use PERMUTATIONA when duplicate selections are allowed in ordered arrangements.
- **Error handling:** If number or number_chosen is non-numeric or negative, the function returns a #NUM! or #VALUE! error.
- **Related functions:**
  - Use PERMUT for permutations without repetition.
  - Use COMBIN or COMBINA for combinations (where order doesn't matter).

PHI Function

Statistical Functions

Introduction

The PHI function returns the value of the standard normal probability density function (PDF) for a given number. It is based on the standard normal distribution curve, where the mean is 0 and the standard deviation is 1.

Simple explanation: Calculates the height of the standard normal distribution curve at a given point.

Common use cases: Used in statistics, probability, and financial modeling to evaluate normal distributions.

When to use this function: Use when working with standard normal probability density functions.

Syntax

```
=PHI(x)
```

- **x**: The numeric value for which to calculate the probability density function.

Worked Example

Challenge: Calculate the standard normal PDF value for 1.5.

Formula:

```
=PHI(1.5)
```

Result: 0.12952
Explanation: The value of the standard normal PDF at x = 1.5 is approximately 0.12952.

	A	B
1	**Example**	
2	=PHI(1.5)	
3	**Answer**	
4	0.12952	

Explore Further with GPT

Ask GPT how to combine PHI with functions like NORM.DIST, NORM.S.DIST, or EXP for advanced statistical and probabilistic calculations.

Tips for Using PHI

- **Normal distribution:** The PHI function only applies to the standard normal distribution (mean = 0, standard deviation = 1).
- **Error handling:** If x is non-numeric, the function returns a #VALUE! error.
- **Graphing the PDF:** Use PHI in conjunction with a range of x values to plot the standard normal distribution curve.

PI Function

Math & Trigonometry Functions

Introduction

The PI function returns the mathematical constant π (pi), which is approximately equal to 3.14159265358979. Pi represents the ratio of a circle's circumference to its diameter and is widely used in geometry, trigonometry, and engineering calculations.

Simple explanation: Provides the value of the constant π.

Common use cases: Used in geometry, trigonometry, and scientific calculations involving circles, arcs, and oscillations.

When to use this function: Use when you need the constant π in calculations.

Syntax

```
=PI()
```

- The function takes no arguments.

Worked Example

Challenge: Calculate the circumference of a circle with a diameter of 10.

Formula:

```
=PI() * 10
```

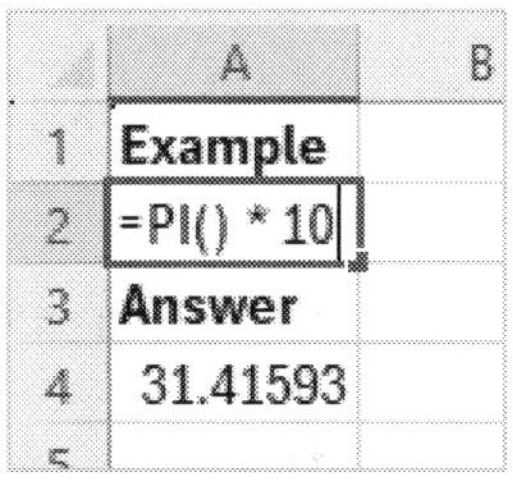

Result: 31.41593
Explanation: The formula calculates the circumference of a circle using $C=\pi\times\text{diameter}$, where π is returned by the PI function.

Explore Further with GPT

Ask GPT how to use PI in trigonometric formulas, arc length calculations, or solving oscillation equations.

Tips for Using PI

- **Precision:** The PI function provides π to 15 decimal places for accurate calculations.
- **Common formulas using π:** Use PI for formulas involving:
  - Circumference: $C=\pi\times d$ or $C=2\pi r$
  - Area of a circle: $A=\pi r^2$
  - Volume of a sphere: $V=(4/3)\pi r^3$
- **No arguments:** The PI function does not require any input arguments.
- **Excel compatibility:** The PI function is available in all modern Excel versions

PMT Function

Financial Functions

Introduction

The PMT function calculates the payment required to fully amortize a loan or investment based on constant payments and a constant interest rate. It is widely used in financial modeling for loans, mortgages, and savings plans.

Simple explanation: Computes the regular payment amount for a loan or investment.

Common use cases: Used in loan repayment schedules, mortgage calculations, and savings planning.
When to use this function: Use when determining the regular payment amount needed to repay a loan or achieve an investment target.

Syntax

```
=PMT(rate, nper, pv, [fv], [type])
```

- **rate**: The interest rate per period.
- **nper**: The total number of payment periods.
- **pv**: The present value (the loan amount or investment).
- **[fv]** *(optional)*: The future value, or the desired balance after the last payment (default is 0).
- **[type]** *(optional)*: Specifies when payments are due:
  - 0 = End of the period (default).
  - 1 = Beginning of the period.

Worked Example

Challenge: Calculate the monthly payment for a loan of $10,000 with an annual interest rate of 6% over 5 years.

Formula:

```
=PMT(0.005, 60, 10000)
```

Result: -193.33
Explanation: The monthly payment required to repay the loan is $193.33. A negative amount indicates a repayment.

	A	B	C
1	**Example**		
2	=PMT(0.005, 60, 10000)		
3	**Answer**		
4	- 193.33		
5			

Explore Further with GPT

Ask GPT how to combine `PMT` with `IPMT`, `PPMT`, or `FV` to build complete loan or savings schedules.

Tips for Using PMT

- **Cash flow convention:** Payments (outflows) are negative, and loan amounts or deposits (inflows) are positive.
- **Consistent periods:** Ensure the rate and nper use the same time period (e.g., monthly, quarterly).

POISSON.DIST Function

Statistical Functions

Introduction

The POISSON.DIST function calculates probabilities for events that occur at a fixed rate within a specified interval. It is used in statistics to model the number of events in a given time or space.

Simple explanation: Computes the probability of a certain number of events occurring within a fixed interval.

Common use cases: Used in queuing theory, call center analytics, traffic flow analysis, and inventory management.

When to use this function: Use when modeling the probability of discrete events happening independently at a constant rate.

Syntax

```
=POISSON.DIST(x, mean, cumulative)
```

- **x**: The number of events.
- **mean**: The expected number of events within the interval.
- **cumulative**: A logical value:
  - TRUE: Returns the cumulative probability (probability of up to x events).
  - FALSE: Returns the probability mass function (probability of exactly x events).

Worked Example

Challenge: Calculate the probability of observing exactly 3 calls in an hour if the average number of calls is 5 per hour.

Formula:

```
=POISSON.DIST(3, 5, FALSE)
```

Result: 0.14037
Explanation: The probability of receiving exactly 3 calls in an hour is approximately 14.04%.

	A	B	C
1	**Example**		
2	=POISSON.DIST(3, 5, FALSE)		
3	**Answer**		
4	0.14037		

Explore Further with GPT

Ask GPT how to combine POISSON.DIST with other functions like AVERAGE, STDEV, or NORM.DIST for advanced statistical modeling and comparison.

Tips for Using POISSON.DIST

- **Discrete events only:** Use POISSON.DIST for discrete events that occur at a constant rate and independently of each other.
- **Mean consistency:** Ensure the mean value reflects the expected number of events in the same interval as the observed x value.
- **Cumulative option:** Use TRUE for cumulative probabilities and FALSE for exact probabilities.

POISSON Function

Compatibility Functions

Introduction

The POISSON function calculates probabilities for events that occur at a fixed rate within a specified interval. It is a legacy function replaced by POISSON.DIST in modern Excel versions but remains available for backward compatibility.

Simple explanation: Computes the probability of a certain number of events occurring within a fixed interval.

Common use cases: Used in legacy spreadsheets for queuing theory, inventory management, and statistical analysis of discrete events.

When to use this function: Use for compatibility with older Excel versions or when working with legacy files.

Syntax

```
=POISSON(x, mean, cumulative)
```

- **x**: The number of events.
- **mean**: The expected number of events within the interval.
- **cumulative**: A logical value:
  - TRUE: Returns the cumulative probability (probability of up to x events).
  - FALSE: Returns the probability mass function (probability of exactly x events).

Worked Example

Challenge: Calculate the probability of observing exactly 3 calls in an hour if the average number of calls is 5 per hour.

Formula:

```
=POISSON(3, 5, FALSE)
```

Result: 0.14037
Explanation: The probability of receiving exactly 3 calls in an hour is approximately 14.04%

	A	B
1	**Example**	
2	=POISSON(3, 5, FALSE)	
3	**Answer**	
4	0.14037	

Explore Further with GPT

Ask GPT how to migrate legacy POISSON formulas to POISSON.DIST for modern statistical analysis and compatibility.

Tips for Using POISSON

- **Use for backward compatibility:** Consider replacing POISSON with POISSON.DIST in newer workbooks.
- **Discrete events only:** Suitable for modeling independent events that occur at a constant rate.
- **Error handling:** If x is negative, or mean is less than or equal to zero, the function returns a #NUM! error.

POWER Function

Math & Trigonometry Functions

Introduction

The POWER function returns the result of a number raised to a specified power (exponent). It simplifies calculations involving exponential growth, mathematical modeling, and engineering problems.

Simple explanation: Computes a number raised to a specified exponent.

Common use cases: Used in scientific calculations, exponential growth modeling, and algebraic expressions.

When to use this function: Use when performing calculations that involve powers or exponents.

Syntax

```
=POWER(number, power)
```

- **number**: The base number to raise to a power.
- **power**: The exponent to which the base number is raised.

Worked Example

Challenge: Calculate 2^3 (2 raised to the power of 3).

Formula:

```
=POWER(2, 3)
```

Result: 8
Explanation: $2^3=2\times2\times2=8$

	A	B
1	**Example**	
2	=POWER(2, 3)	
3	**Answer**	
4	8	
5		

Explore Further with GPT

Ask GPT how to use POWER in combination with functions like EXP, LOG, or SQRT for advanced mathematical modeling.

Tips for Using POWER

- **Equivalent operator:** You can use the caret (^) operator for the same result:

  ```
  =2^3
  ```

- **Negative exponents:** Use negative powers to calculate reciprocals:

  ```
  =POWER(2, -3)    // Result: 0.125
  ```

- **Fractional powers:** Use fractional exponents for roots (e.g., 0.333 for cube roots).

PPMT Function

Financial Functions

Introduction

The PPMT function calculates the principal portion of a payment for a specific period of a loan or investment based on constant payments and a constant interest rate. It is commonly used in loan amortization schedules to break down payments into principal and interest components.

Simple explanation: Determines the principal amount paid in a specific period.

Common use cases: Used in loan repayment schedules, mortgage calculations, and investment planning.

When to use this function: Use when you need to calculate how much of a payment goes toward reducing the loan balance.

Syntax

```
=PPMT(rate, per, nper, pv, [fv], [type])
```

- **rate**: The interest rate per period.
- **per**: The specific period for which to calculate the principal payment (must be between 1 and nper).
- **nper**: The total number of payment periods.
- **pv**: The present value (the loan amount or investment).
- **[fv]** *(optional)*: The future value, or the desired balance after the last payment (default is 0).
- **[type]** *(optional)*: Specifies when payments are due:
  - 0 = End of the period (default).
  - 1 = Beginning of the period.

Worked Example

Challenge: Calculate the principal portion of the first monthly payment for a $10,000 loan with an annual interest rate of 6% over 5 years.

Formula:

```
=PPMT(0.005, 1, 60, -10000)
```

Result: -143.33
Explanation: The first payment includes $143.33 applied to the principal balance. The negative sign indicates a cash outflow.

	A	B	C
1	**Example**		
2	=PPMT(0.005, 1, 60, 10000)		
3	**Answer**		
4	- 143.33		
5			

Tips for Using PPMT

- **Consistency in inputs:** Ensure rate and nper match the payment frequency (e.g., monthly, quarterly).
- **Cash flow convention:** Payments (outflows) are negative, and loan amounts or deposits (inflows) are positive.

PRICE Function

Financial Functions

Introduction

The PRICE function calculates the price per $100 face value of a bond that pays periodic interest. It is used in financial modeling to determine the fair value of bonds based on interest rates, maturity, and coupon payments.

Simple explanation: Computes the price of a bond based on its yield, coupon rate, and maturity.

Common use cases: Used in bond pricing, investment analysis, and financial portfolio management.

When to use this function: Use when determining the fair value of a bond given its yield and terms.

Syntax

```
=PRICE(settlement, maturity, rate, yld, redemption, frequency, [basis])
```

- **settlement**: The date the bond is purchased (settlement date).
- **maturity**: The date the bond matures.
- **rate**: The bond's annual coupon rate.
- **yld**: The bond's annual yield.
- **redemption**: The redemption value of the bond per $100 face value.
- **frequency**: The number of coupon payments per year:
    - 1 = Annual; 2 = Semi-annual; 4 = Quarterly
- **[basis]** *(optional)*: The day count basis to use:
    - 0 = US 30/360; 1 = Actual/actual; 2 = Actual/360; 3 = Actual/365; 4 = European 30/360

Challenge: Calculate the price of a bond with a settlement date of January 1, 2023, maturity date of January 1, 2028, an annual coupon rate of 5%, an annual yield of 6%, and a redemption value of $100. The bond pays interest semi-annually.

Formula:

```
=PRICE(DATE(2023,1,1), DATE(2028,1,1), 0.05, 0.06, 100, 2, 0)
```

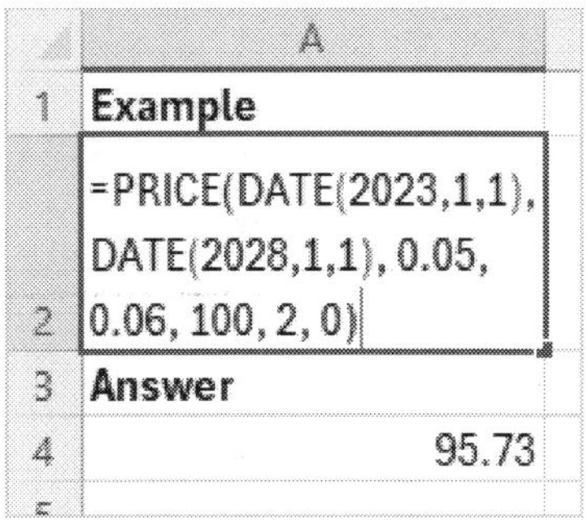

Result: 95.73
Explanation: The bond is priced at 95.73 per $100 face value, reflecting the higher yield compared to the coupon rate.

Tips for Using PRICE

- **Settlement and maturity dates:** The settlement date must be earlier than the maturity date.
- **Frequency alignment:** Ensure the coupon frequency matches the bond's payment schedule (1, 2, or 4).

PRICEDISC Function

Financial Functions

Introduction

The PRICEDISC function calculates the price per $100 face value of a discounted security. A discounted security is sold at a lower price than its face value and does not pay periodic interest.

Simple explanation: Computes the price of a discounted security based on its discount rate and maturity.

Common use cases: Used in bond pricing, short-term investment evaluation, and financial modeling for discounted securities.

When to use this function: Use when calculating the price of a zero-coupon bond or a discounted Treasury bill.

Syntax

```
=PRICEDISC(settlement, maturity, discount, redemption, [basis])
```

- **settlement**: The date the security is purchased (settlement date).
- **maturity**: The date the security matures.
- **discount**: The annual discount rate of the security.
- **redemption**: The redemption value of the security per $100 face value.
- **[basis]** *(optional)*: The day count basis to use:
    - 0 = US 30/360; 1 = Actual/actual; 2 = Actual/360; 3 = Actual/365; 4 = European 30/360

Worked Example

Challenge: Calculate the price of a discounted Treasury bill with a settlement date of January 1, 2023, maturity date of April 1, 2023, a discount rate of 3%, and a redemption value of $100.

Formula:

```
=PRICEDISC(DATE(2023,1,1), DATE(2023,4,1), 0.03, 100, 0)
```

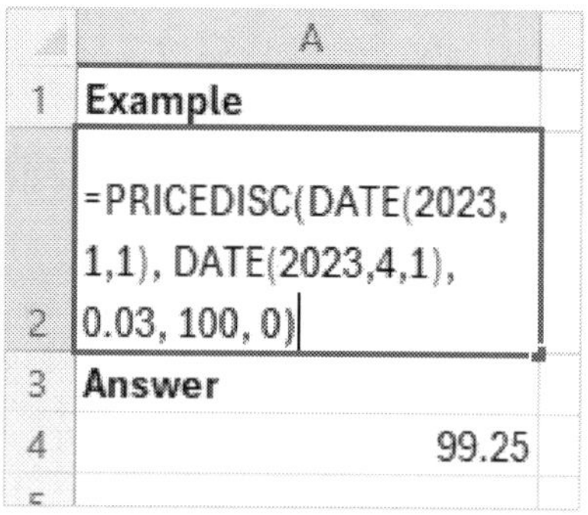

Result: 99.25

Explanation: The discounted security is priced at 99.25 per $100 face value, reflecting the time to maturity and discount rate.

Tips for Using PRICEDISC

- **Settlement and maturity dates:** Ensure the settlement date is earlier than the maturity date.
- **Day count basis:** Select the appropriate basis for your calculation (e.g., Actual/actual or US 30/360).
- **Discount rate precision:** Provide the discount rate as a decimal (e.g., 3% as 0.03).

PRICEMAT Function

Financial Functions

Introduction

The PRICEMAT function calculates the price per $100 face value of a security that pays interest at maturity. It is used for valuing bonds and other fixed-income securities that pay interest only at the end of their term.

Simple explanation: Computes the price of a bond or security that pays interest at maturity.

Common use cases: Used in bond pricing, investment evaluation, and financial modeling for securities with interest payable at maturity.

When to use this function: Use when calculating the price of a bond or security with interest accrued until maturity.

Syntax

```
=PRICEMAT(settlement, maturity, issue, rate, yld, [basis])
```

- **settlement**: The date the security is purchased (settlement date).
- **maturity**: The date the security matures.
- **issue**: The issue date of the security.
- **rate**: The annual coupon rate of the security.
- **yld**: The annual yield of the security.
- **[basis]** *(optional)*: The day count basis to use:
  - 0 = US 30/360; 1 = Actual/actual; 2 = Actual/360; 3 = Actual/365; 4 = European 30/360

Worked Example

Challenge: Calculate the price of a bond with the following details: Issue date: January 1, 2023; Settlement date: March 1, 2023; Maturity date: January 1, 2025; Annual coupon rate: 4%; Annual yield: 5%

Formula:

```
=PRICEMAT(DATE(2023,3,1), DATE(2025,1,1), DATE(2023,1,1),
0.04, 0.05, 0)
```

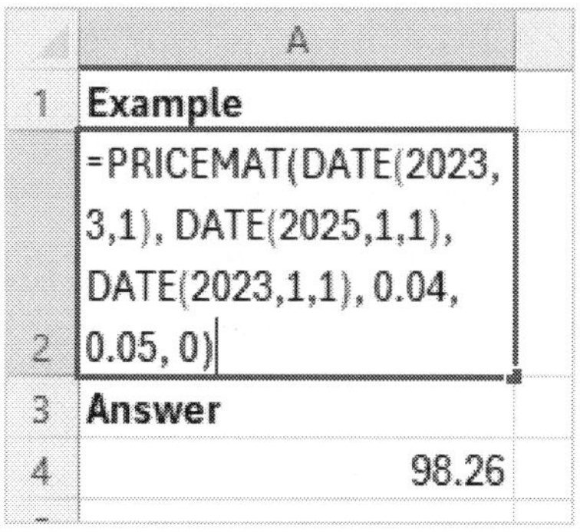

Result: 98.26
Explanation: The bond is priced at 98.26 per $100 face value, reflecting the annual yield and time to maturity.

Tips for Using PRICEMAT

- **Date consistency:** Ensure the settlement date is between the issue date and maturity date.
- **Day count basis:** Select the correct basis for your calculation, as it affects interest accrual.
- **Annualized inputs:** Provide the rate and yld as annualized values (e.g., 4% as 0.04).

PROB Function

Statistical Functions

Introduction

The PROB function calculates the probability that a value from a data set falls within a specified range, based on a given probability distribution. It is often used in statistical analysis and probability modeling.

Simple explanation: Computes the probability of values occurring within a specific range.

Common use cases: Used in risk assessment, statistical analysis, and decision-making under uncertainty.

When to use this function: Use when working with data sets and their corresponding probability distributions.

Syntax

```
=PROB(x_range, prob_range, [lower_limit], [upper_limit])
```

- **x_range**: The range of numeric values in the data set.
- **prob_range**: The range of probabilities associated with the values in x_range.
- **[lower_limit]** *(optional)*: The lower boundary of the range.
- **[upper_limit]** *(optional)*: The upper boundary of the range. If omitted, the function calculates the probability of values equal to lower_limit.

Worked Example

Challenge: Calculate the probability of values between 30 and 40 in the data set

Formula:

```
=PROB(A2:A6, B2:B6, 30, 40)
```

Result: 0.6

Explanation: The probability of values between 30 and 40 is 0.3 + 0.3 = 0.6.

	A	B	C	D
1	X (x_range)	P (prob_range)		Example
2	10	0.1		
3	20	0.2		=PROB(A2:A6, B2:B6, 30, 40)
4	30	0.3		
5	40	0.3		Answer
6	50	0.1		0.6

Explore Further with GPT

Ask GPT how to use PROB in combination with statistical functions like AVERAGE, STDEV, or NORM.DIST for advanced probability modeling.

Tips for Using PROB

- **Probabilities must sum to 1:** The prob_range values should sum to 1. If they don't, the function may produce incorrect results.
- **Matching ranges:** Ensure x_range and prob_range are the same size; otherwise, the function returns a #N/A error.
- **Handling missing upper limits:** If upper_limit is omitted, the function calculates the probability for values equal to lower_limit.

PRODUCT Function

Math & Trigonometry Functions

Introduction

The PRODUCT function multiplies all the numbers provided as arguments and returns the result. It is a convenient way to calculate the product of multiple numbers or ranges without using the * operator repeatedly.

Simple explanation: Multiplies numbers or ranges of numbers together.

Common use cases: Used in mathematical calculations, geometric mean determination, and financial modeling involving compounding.

When to use this function: Use when multiplying multiple values or ranges efficiently.

Syntax

```
=PRODUCT(number1, [number2], ...)
```

- **number1**: The first number or range to include in the multiplication.
- **[number2], ...** *(optional)*: Additional numbers or ranges to multiply

Challenge: Multiply the values in the range {2, 3, 4}.

Formula:

```
=PRODUCT(A1:A3)
```

Result: 24
Explanation: The PRODUCT function multiplies 2 × 3 × 4 to return 24.

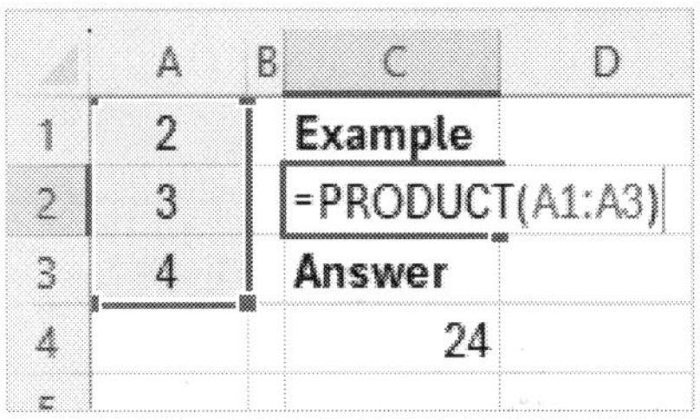

	A	B	C	D
1	2		Example	
2	3		=PRODUCT(A1:A3)	
3	4		Answer	
4			24	

Explore Further with GPT

Ask GPT how to combine PRODUCT with functions like POWER, SQRT, or AVERAGE for more advanced mathematical operations.

Tips for Using PRODUCT

- **Works with ranges:** The function can handle ranges and individual numbers simultaneously:

  ```
  =PRODUCT(A1:A3, 10)
  ```

  Multiplies all values in A1:A3 by 10.

- **Zeros in the range:** Any 0 in the input results in a product of 0.

PROPER Function

Text Functions

Introduction

The PROPER function converts the first letter of each word in a text string to uppercase and all other letters to lowercase. It is often used for formatting text, such as names or titles, to ensure consistent capitalization.

Simple explanation: Capitalizes the first letter of each word in a text string while converting other letters to lowercase.

Common use cases: Used for formatting names, titles, and other text entries in a consistent style.

When to use this function: Use when you need to standardize text capitalization.

Syntax

```
=PROPER(text)
```

- **text**: The text string or cell reference containing the text to format.

Worked Example

Challenge: Format the text "john DOE" to proper case.

Formula:

`=PROPER(A1)`

Result: John Doe
Explanation: The PROPER function capitalizes the first letter of each word and converts the remaining letters to lowercase.

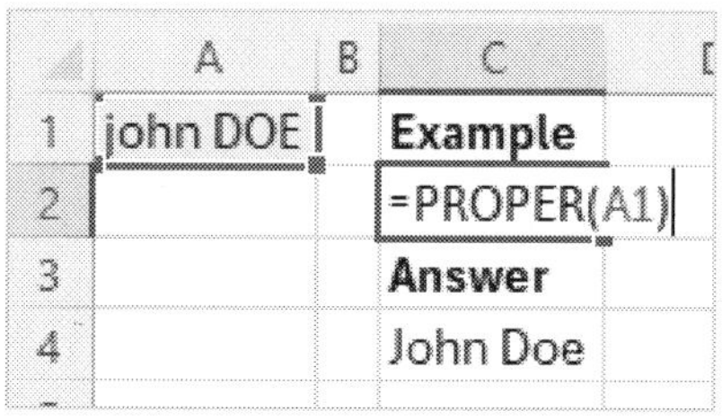

Explore Further with GPT

Ask GPT how to combine PROPER with UPPER, LOWER, or TEXTJOIN for advanced text processing and formatting tasks.

Tips for Using PROPER

- **Handles punctuation:** Words separated by spaces, hyphens, or other punctuation are individually capitalized. For example:

  `=PROPER("john-doe") Result: John-Doe`

- **Ignores non-text characters:** The function does not alter numbers, symbols, or punctuation marks.
- **Error handling:** If text is blank or contains invalid references, the function returns an empty result or a #VALUE! error.
- **Works with formulas:** Use PROPER in combination with other functions like CONCAT or TRIM for enhanced text formatting.

PV Function

Financial Functions

Introduction

The PV function calculates the present value of an investment or loan based on constant payments and a constant interest rate. It helps determine the current worth of future payments or cash flows.

Simple explanation: Computes the current value of future cash flows.

Common use cases: Used in financial modeling, loan amortization schedules, and investment planning.

When to use this function: Use when evaluating loans, mortgages, or investments with regular payments or returns.

Syntax

```
=PV(rate, nper, pmt, [fv], [type])
```

- **rate**: The interest rate per period.
- **nper**: The total number of payment periods.
- **pmt**: The payment made each period (outflow).
- **[fv]** *(optional)*: The future value, or the desired balance after the last payment (default is 0).
- **[type]** *(optional)*: Specifies when payments are due:
  - 0 = End of the period (default).
  - 1 = Beginning of the period.

Worked Example

Challenge: Calculate the present value of a loan with monthly payments of $500, an annual interest rate of 6%, and a term of 5 years.

Formula:

```
=PV(0.005, 60, -500)
```

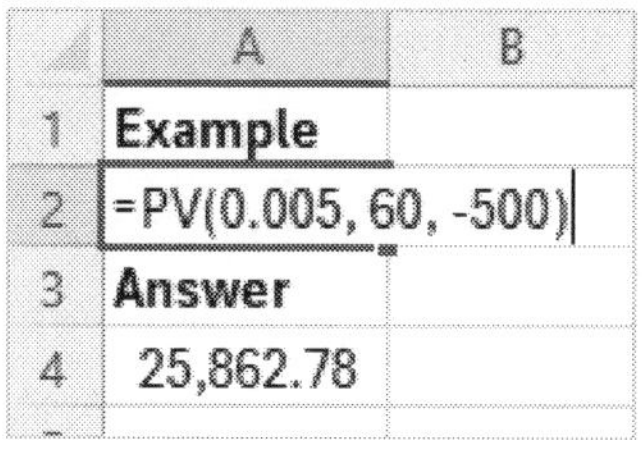

	A	B
1	**Example**	
2	=PV(0.005, 60, -500)	
3	**Answer**	
4	25,862.78	

Result: 25,862.78
Explanation: The present value of the loan is $25,862.78, which represents the amount borrowed (a positive inflow).

Tips for Using PV

- **Cash flow convention:** Payments (outflows) are negative, and investments or loans (inflows) are positive.
- **Consistent periods:** Ensure the rate and nper match the payment frequency (e.g., monthly, quarterly).
- **Related functions:**
  - Use FV to calculate the future value of cash flows.
  - Use PMT to calculate the periodic payment required.

QUARTILE Function

Compatibility Functions

Introduction

The QUARTILE function calculates the quartiles of a data set, dividing it into four equal parts. Quartiles are useful for understanding data distribution and identifying outliers. It has been replaced by QUARTILE.INC and QUARTILE.EXC in modern Excel versions but remains available for backward compatibility.

Simple explanation: Returns a specific quartile of a data set.

Common use cases: Used in statistical analysis to describe data spread and identify boundaries for outliers.

When to use this function: Use for compatibility with older Excel files or when calculating quartiles using inclusive methods.

Syntax

```
=QUARTILE(array, quart)
```

- **array**: The data set (a range of values).
- **quart**: The quartile to return:
    - 0 = Minimum value (0th percentile).
    - 1 = First quartile (25th percentile).
    - 2 = Median (50th percentile).
    - 3 = Third quartile (75th percentile).
    - 4 = Maximum value (100th percentile).

Worked Example

Challenge: Calculate the first quartile for the data set {10, 20, 30, 40, 50}

Formula:

```
=QUARTILE(A1:A5, 1)
```

Result: 20

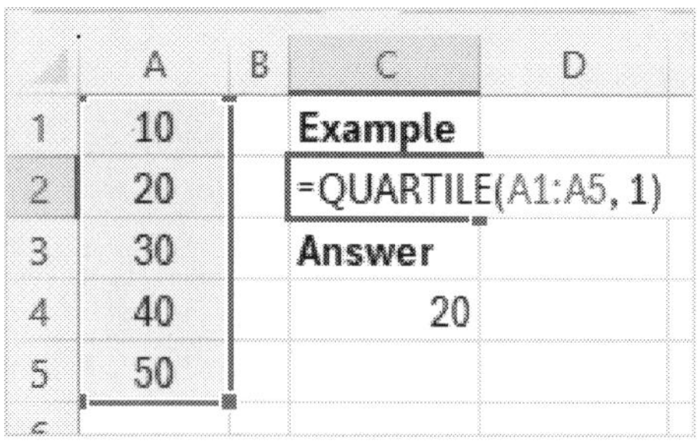

Explanation: The QUARTILE function divides the data set into four equal parts, with 20 at the 25th percentile.

Explore Further with GPT

Ask GPT how to use QUARTILE alongside PERCENTILE, AVERAGE, or STDEV for deeper data analysis.

Tips for Using QUARTILE

- **Consider using modern functions:** Replace QUARTILE with QUARTILE.INC or QUARTILE.EXC for more precise control in modern Excel.

QUARTILE.EXC Function

Statistical Functions

Introduction

The QUARTILE.EXC function returns the quartiles of a data set, excluding the smallest and largest values. Quartiles divide data into four equal parts and are useful for analyzing the distribution of a data set and identifying outliers.

Simple explanation: Calculates quartiles, excluding the extremes of the data set.

Common use cases: Used in statistical analysis, data distribution analysis, and outlier detection.

When to use this function: Use when quartiles should be calculated with the exclusion of minimum and maximum values.

Syntax

```
=QUARTILE.EXC(array, quart)
```

- **array**: The data set (a range of numeric values).
- **quart**: The quartile to return:
  - 1 = First quartile (25th percentile).
  - 2 = Median (50th percentile).
  - 3 = Third quartile (75th percentile).

Worked Example

Challenge: Calculate the third quartile for the data set {10, 20, 30, 40, 50}.

Formula:

```
=QUARTILE.EXC(A1:A5, 3)
```

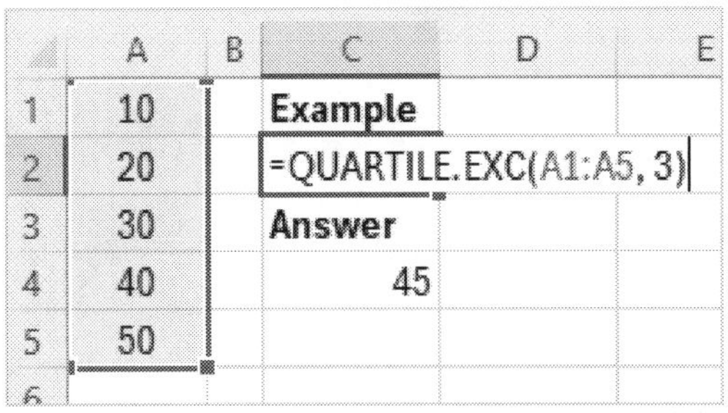

	A	B	C	D	E
1	10		Example		
2	20		=QUARTILE.EXC(A1:A5, 3)		
3	30		Answer		
4	40		45		
5	50				
6					

Result: Q3: 45
Explanation: The QUARTILE.EXC function excludes the smallest and largest values when calculating quartiles.

Explore Further with GPT

Ask GPT how to use QUARTILE.EXC with other statistical functions like PERCENTILE.EXC, AVERAGE, or STDEV for advanced data analysis.

Tips for Using QUARTILE.EXC

- **Excludes extreme values:** Unlike QUARTILE.INC, this function excludes the smallest and largest data points when calculating quartiles.
- **Error handling:** If the data set is too small to exclude minimum and maximum values, the function returns a #NUM! error.

QUARTILE.INC Function

Statistical Functions

Introduction

The QUARTILE.INC function returns the quartiles of a data set, including the smallest and largest values. Quartiles divide data into four equal parts and are used for analyzing the distribution of data and identifying outliers.

Simple explanation: Calculates quartiles, including the minimum and maximum values of the data set.

Common use cases: Used in statistical analysis, descriptive statistics, and outlier detection.

When to use this function: Use when quartiles should be calculated with the inclusion of all values in the data set.

Syntax

```
=QUARTILE.INC(array, quart)
```

- **array**: The data set (a range of numeric values).
- **quart**: The quartile to return:
    - 0 = Minimum value (0th percentile).
    - 1 = First quartile (25th percentile).
    - 2 = Median (50th percentile).
    - 3 = Third quartile (75th percentile).
    - 4 = Maximum value (100th percentile).

Worked Example

Challenge: Calculate the first quartile for the data set {10, 20, 30, 40, 50}.

Formula:

```
=QUARTILE.INC(A1:A5, 1)
```

Result: Q1: 20

Explanation: The QUARTILE.INC function calculates quartiles including the minimum and maximum values of the data set.

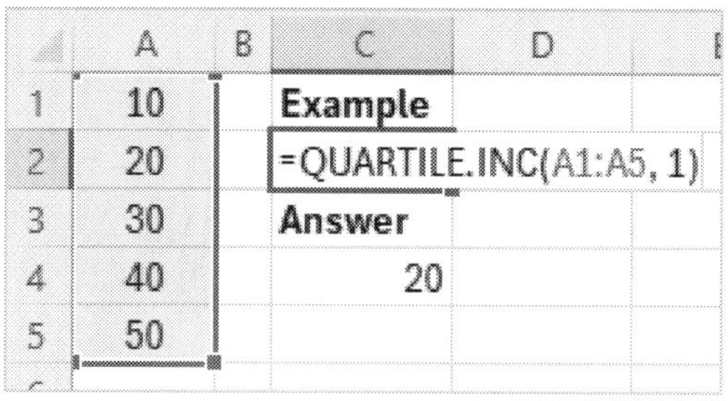

Explore Further with GPT

Ask GPT how to combine QUARTILE.INC with other functions like PERCENTILE.INC, AVERAGE, or STDEV for advanced statistical analysis.

Tips for Using QUARTILE.INC

- **Includes all values:** Unlike QUARTILE.EXC, this function considers the smallest and largest values when calculating quartiles.
- **Works for all quartiles:** Use the appropriate quart argument to retrieve minimum, Q1, median, Q3, or maximum values.

QUOTIENT Function

Math & Trigonometry Functions

Introduction

The QUOTIENT function returns the integer portion of a division, discarding any remainder. It is useful when you only need whole numbers from a division operation.

Simple explanation: Divides two numbers and returns only the whole number result, ignoring any remainder.

Common use cases: Used in financial modeling, inventory management, and scenarios requiring whole number calculations.

When to use this function: Use when you need the integer part of a division without rounding or decimal places.

Syntax

```
=QUOTIENT(numerator, denominator)
```

- **numerator**: The number to be divided.
- **denominator**: The number by which to divide the numerator.

Worked Example

Challenge: Divide 11 by 3 and return only the integer part of the result.

Formula:

```
=QUOTIENT(11, 3)
```

	A	B
1	**Example**	
2	=QUOTIENT(11, 3)	
3	**Answer**	
4	3	

Result: 3
Explanation: The integer portion of 11÷3 is 3, with a remainder of 2 (ignored by QUOTIENT).

Explore Further with GPT

Ask GPT how to combine QUOTIENT with other functions like MOD, ROUND, or INT for complete division calculations, including remainders.

Tips for Using QUOTIENT

- **Ignores remainders:** Use MOD alongside QUOTIENT to calculate the remainder:

  `=MOD(11, 3) Result: 2.`

- **Handles zero:** If the denominator is 0, the function returns a #DIV/0! error.

- **Decimal truncation:** The function truncates any decimals in the result without rounding.

RADIANS Function

Math & Trigonometry Functions

Introduction

The RADIANS function converts angles measured in degrees to radians. Radians are often used in trigonometry and mathematical calculations involving angles.

Simple explanation: Converts an angle from degrees to radians.

Common use cases: Used in trigonometric functions (e.g., SIN, COS, TAN) that require angle inputs in radians.

When to use this function: Use when working with trigonometric calculations or converting angles from degrees to radians.

Syntax

```
=RADIANS(angle)
```

- **angle**: The angle in degrees to convert to radians.

Worked Example

Challenge: Convert 180 degrees to radians.

Formula:

```
=RADIANS(180)
```

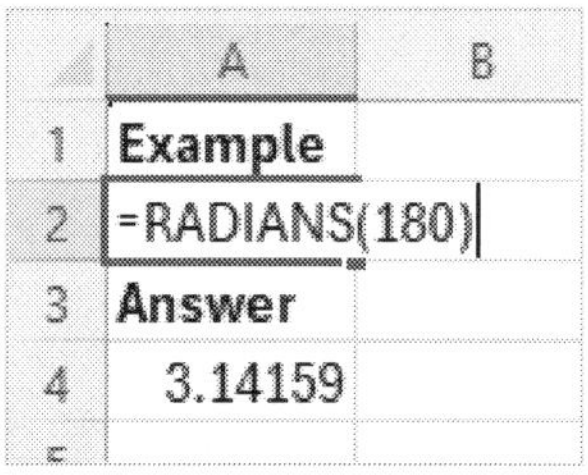

Result: 3.14159
Explanation: The RADIANS function converts 180 degrees to π radians, which is approximately 3.14159.

Explore Further with GPT

Ask GPT how to combine RADIANS with other functions like DEGREES, SIN, or PI to perform advanced trigonometric calculations.

Tips for Using RADIANS

- **Conversion formula:** The function uses the formula Radians=Degrees×π180\text{Radians} = \text{Degrees} \times \frac{\pi}{180}Radians=Degrees×180π.
- **Use with trigonometric functions:** Most trigonometric functions (SIN, COS, etc.) in Excel require input in radians, making RADIANS essential for angle conversions.
- **Reversing the conversion:** Use the DEGREES function to convert radians back to degrees:

  `=DEGREES(PI()) Result: 180.`

RAND Function

Math & Trigonometry Functions

Introduction

The RAND function generates a random decimal number between 0 (inclusive) and 1 (exclusive). It is useful for simulations, statistical sampling, and generating random test data.

Simple explanation: Creates a random number between 0 and 1.

Common use cases: Used in simulations, randomized experiments, and creating dummy data for analysis.

When to use this function: Use when you need random decimal values within a defined range.

Syntax

```
=RAND()
```

- The function does not take any arguments.

Worked Example

Challenge: Generate a random decimal number between 0 and 1.

Formula:

```
=RAND()
```

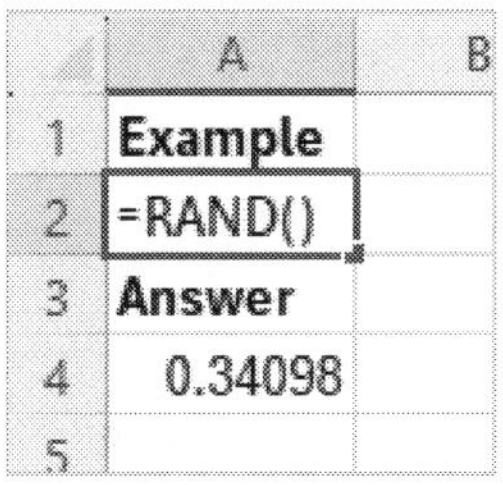

Result: A random number such as 0.34098
Explanation: Each time the worksheet recalculates, the RAND function generates a new random number between 0 and 1.

Explore Further with GPT

Ask GPT how to combine RAND with functions like RANDBETWEEN, ROUND, or IF for advanced randomization and simulations.

Tips for Using RAND

- **Recalculation behavior:** The RAND function generates a new number whenever the worksheet recalculates (e.g., when you edit a cell or press F9).
- **Freezing the value:** Copy and paste the value as static if you want to prevent it from changing:
  - Select the cell → Right-click → Copy → Right-click → Paste Values.
- **Range scaling:** Use multiplication and addition to scale the random number to any desired range.
- **Error handling:** The function does not produce errors but may require additional logic for specific use cases.

RANDARRAY Function

Math & Trigonometry Functions

Introduction

The RANDARRAY function generates an array of random numbers. You can specify the size of the array and define whether the random numbers should be integers or decimals within a specified range. It is an advanced alternative to RAND.

Simple explanation: Creates an array of random numbers with customizable dimensions and ranges.

Common use cases: Used in simulations, statistical modeling, and generating random datasets.

When to use this function: Use when you need multiple random values in a specific array structure or range.

Syntax

```
=RANDARRAY([rows], [columns], [min], [max], [integer])
```

- **rows** *(optional)*: The number of rows in the array.
- **columns** *(optional)*: The number of columns in the array.
- **min** *(optional)*: The minimum value of the random numbers (default is 0).
- **max** *(optional)*: The maximum value of the random numbers (default is 1).
- **integer** *(optional)*: A logical value (TRUE or FALSE) specifying whether to return integers (TRUE) or decimals (FALSE, default).

Worked Example

Challenge: Generate a 3x3 array of random decimal numbers between 0 and 1.

Formula:

```
=RANDARRAY(3, 3)
```

Result:

0.065147	0.916372	0.023874
0.56074	0.641363	0.977729
0.828031	0.653922	0.204542

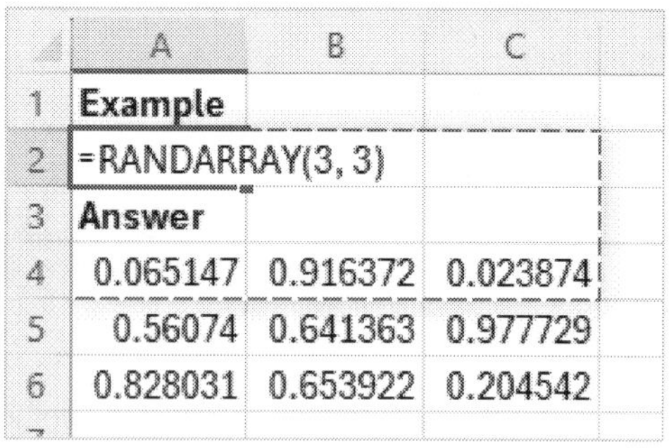

Explanation: The RANDARRAY function generates a 3x3 grid of random decimal numbers between 0 and 1.

Explore Further with GPT

Ask GPT how to combine RANDARRAY with functions like INDEX, SORT, or FILTER to generate advanced randomized datasets or subsets.

Tips for Using RANDARRAY

- **Dynamic array behavior:** RANDARRAY spills its output dynamically into adjacent cells. Ensure there's enough space for the array; otherwise, the function returns a #SPILL! error.

RANDBETWEEN Function

Math & Trigonometry Functions

Introduction

The RANDBETWEEN function generates a random integer between two specified numbers, inclusive. It is ideal for scenarios requiring whole number randomization within a range.

Simple explanation: Generates a random integer between two specified values.

Common use cases: Used in simulations, random sampling, and creating test data.

When to use this function: Use when you need random whole numbers within a specific range.

Syntax

```
=RANDBETWEEN(bottom, top)
```

- **bottom**: The smallest integer in the range.
- **top**: The largest integer in the range.

Worked Example

Challenge: Generate a random integer between 10 and 50.

Formula:

```
=RANDBETWEEN(10, 50)
```

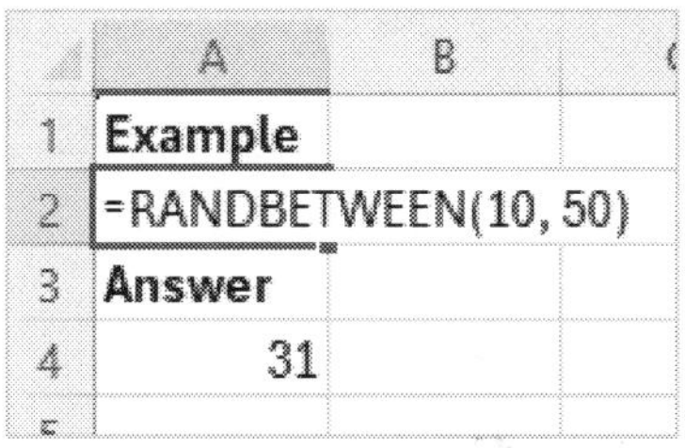

Result: A random integer, such as 31.
Explanation: The RANDBETWEEN function generates a random integer between 10 and 50, inclusive.

Explore Further with GPT

Ask GPT how to combine RANDBETWEEN with other functions like INDEX, SEQUENCE, or CHOOSE for generating randomized lists or selections.

Tips for Using RANDBETWEEN

- **Dynamic recalculation:** The function recalculates every time the worksheet recalculates. To freeze the value, use Copy → Paste Values.
- **Handles inclusive ranges:** Both the bottom and top values are included in the result
- **Related functions:** Use RANDARRAY for generating multiple random values, and RAND for random decimals.

RANK.AVG Function

Statistical Functions

Introduction

The RANK.AVG function returns the rank of a number within a list of numbers, with average rankings assigned to duplicate values. It is useful for ranking data with ties while maintaining fair ranking.

Simple explanation: Ranks a number within a list, assigning tied values the average of their ranks.

Common use cases: Used in statistical analysis, ranking competition results, and grading systems.

When to use this function: Use when ranking values in a list and ties need to be handled with averaged ranks.

Syntax

```
=RANK.AVG(number, ref, [order])
```

- **number**: The number to rank.
- **ref**: The range of numbers to rank within.
- **[order]** *(optional)*:
    - 0 or omitted: Ranks in descending order (largest value = rank 1).
    - 1: Ranks in ascending order (smallest value = rank 1).

Worked Example

Challenge: Rank the value 86 in the data set, using descending order

Formula:

```
=RANK.AVG(86, A1:A5)
```

Result: 3.5
Explanation: The value 86 occurs twice in the data set. RANK.AVG assigns both instances the average of ranks 3 and 4, resulting in 3.5.

	A	B	C	D
1	100		**Example**	
2	90		=RANK.AVG(86, A1:A5)	
3	86		**Answer**	
4	86		3.5	
5	70			

Explore Further with GPT

Ask GPT how to combine RANK.AVG with functions like IF, COUNTIF, or SORT for advanced ranking systems and analysis.

Tips for Using RANK.AVG

- **Handles ties:** Unlike RANK.EQ, RANK.AVG assigns tied values the average of their ranks.
- **Sorting order:** Use the order argument to rank in ascending (1) or descending (0) order.
- **Dynamic ranges:** Use absolute references ($A$1:$A$5) for ranges to ensure consistency when copying the formula.
- **Error handling:** If number is not in the range ref, the function returns a #N/A error.

RANK.EQ Function

Statistical Functions

Introduction

The RANK.EQ function returns the rank of a number in a list of numbers, resolving ties by assigning the same rank to all tied values. It is commonly used for ranking data in a straightforward manner without averaging tied ranks.

Simple explanation: Ranks a number within a list, with tied values receiving the same rank.

Common use cases: Used in ranking competition results, grading systems, and data analysis.

When to use this function: Use when ranking values in a list without averaging ties.

Syntax

```
=RANK.EQ(number, ref, [order])
```

- **number**: The number to rank.
- **ref**: The range of numbers to rank within.
- **[order]** *(optional)*:
  - 0 or omitted: Ranks in descending order (largest value = rank 1).
  - 1: Ranks in ascending order (smallest value = rank 1).

Worked Example

Challenge: Rank the value 86 in the data set, using descending order.

Formula:

```
=RANK.EQ(86, A1:A5)
```

Result: 3
Explanation: Both instances of 86 are ranked as 3, and the next value (70) is ranked 5.

	A	B	C	D
1	100		**Example**	
2	90		=RANK.EQ(86, A1:A5)	
3	86		**Answer**	
4	86		3	
5	70			
6				

Explore Further with GPT

Ask GPT how to combine RANK.EQ with functions like IF, COUNTIF, or SORT for creating advanced ranking systems.

Tips for Using RANK.EQ

- **Handles ties equally:** Tied values receive the same rank, and subsequent ranks are skipped.
- **Sorting order:** Use the order argument to rank in ascending (1) or descending (0) order.
- **Dynamic ranges:** Use absolute references ($A$1:$A$5) to ensure consistency when copying the formula.

RANK Function

Compatibility Functions

Introduction

The RANK function returns the rank of a number in a list of numbers. It resolves ties by assigning the same rank to tied values, skipping subsequent ranks. This function has been replaced by RANK.EQ and RANK.AVG in modern Excel versions but remains available for backward compatibility.

Simple explanation: Ranks a number in a list, with tied values receiving the same rank.

Common use cases: Used in ranking competition results, grading systems, and older Excel spreadsheets.

When to use this function: Use when working with legacy spreadsheets requiring rank calculations.

Syntax

```
=RANK(number, ref, [order])
```

- **number**: The number to rank.
- **ref**: The range of numbers to rank within.
- **[order]** *(optional)*:
    - 0 or omitted: Ranks in descending order (largest value = rank 1).
    - 1: Ranks in ascending order (smallest value = rank 1).

Worked Example

Challenge: Rank the value 86 in the data set, using descending order

Formula:

```
=RANK(86, A1:A5)
```

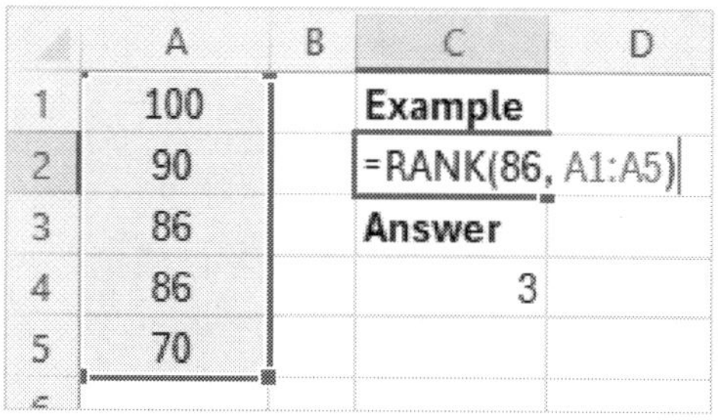

Result: 3
Explanation: Both instances of 86 are ranked as 3, skipping rank 4.

Explore Further with GPT

Ask GPT how to transition from RANK to RANK.EQ or RANK.AVG for more modern and flexible ranking calculations.

Tips for Using RANK

- **Compatibility note:** Use RANK.EQ or RANK.AVG for modern spreadsheets to handle ties more flexibly.
- **Handles ties:** Tied values receive the same rank, and subsequent ranks are skipped.
- **Sorting order:** Use the order argument to rank in ascending (1) or descending (0) order

RATE Function

Financial Functions

Introduction

The RATE function calculates the interest rate per period of an investment, loan, or annuity based on constant payments and a fixed payment schedule. It is widely used in financial analysis to determine the rate of return or cost of borrowing.

Simple explanation: Computes the interest rate per period for a loan or investment.

Common use cases: Used in loan calculations, investment planning, and financial modeling.

When to use this function: Use when determining the periodic interest rate based on payments, loan terms, and future value.

Syntax

```
=RATE(nper, pmt, pv, [fv], [type], [guess])
```

- **nper**: Total number of payment periods.
- **pmt**: The payment made each period (outflow).
- **pv**: The present value (loan amount or investment).
- **[fv]** *(optional)*: The future value (default is 0).
- **[type]** *(optional)*:
    - 0 = Payments due at the end of the period (default).
    - 1 = Payments due at the beginning of the period.
- **[guess]** *(optional)*: Your initial estimate of the interest rate (default is 10% or 0.1).

Worked Example

Challenge: Calculate the monthly interest rate for a loan of $10,000 with a term of 5 years, a monthly payment of $200, and a future value of $0.

Formula:

```
=RATE(60, -200, 10000)
```

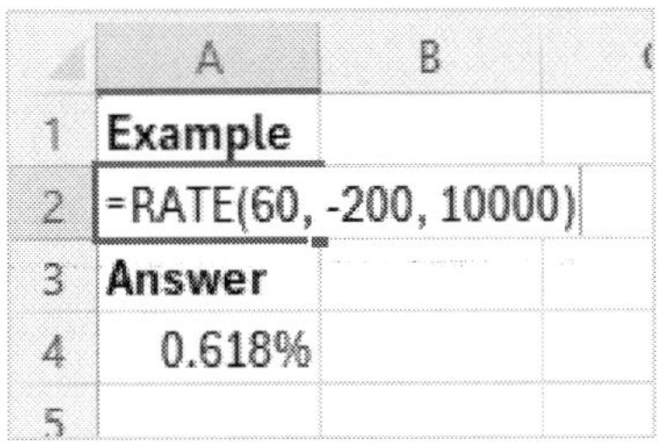

Result: 0.00618
Explanation: The monthly interest rate is approximately 0.618%. To convert to an annual rate, multiply by 12 (approximately 7.42% per year).

Explore Further with GPT

Ask GPT how to combine RATE with NPV, PMT, or FV to perform comprehensive financial modeling and investment analysis.

Tips for Using RATE

- **Guess parameter:** Use the guess argument if the function fails to converge on a solution.
- **Rate per period:** The result is the rate per period. For an annual rate, multiply by the number of periods per year.

RECEIVED Function

Financial Functions

Introduction

The RECEIVED function calculates the amount received at maturity for a fully invested security. It is used to determine the maturity value of securities such as Treasury bills or zero-coupon bonds.

Simple explanation: Computes the maturity value of an investment or security.

Common use cases: Used in bond pricing, Treasury bill analysis, and investment calculations.

When to use this function: Use when determining the total amount received at maturity for a discounted or interest-bearing security.

Syntax

```
=RECEIVED(settlement, maturity, investment, discount, [basis])
```

- **settlement**: The date the investment is purchased (settlement date).
- **maturity**: The date the investment matures.
- **investment**: The initial amount invested.
- **discount**: The annual discount rate of the security.
- **[basis]** *(optional)*: The day count basis to use:
    - 0 = US 30/360 (default); 1 = Actual/actual; 2 = Actual/360; 3 = Actual/365; 4 = European 30/360.

Worked Example

Challenge: Calculate the amount received at maturity for a Treasury bill with the following details:

- Purchase date: January 1, 2023; Maturity date: July 1, 2023; Initial investment: $10,000; Annual discount rate: 5%.

Formula:

```
=RECEIVED(DATE(2023,1,1), DATE(2023,7,1), 10000, 0.05, 0)
```

Result: 10,256.41
Explanation: The total amount received at maturity is $10,256.41, including the discount accrued over the period.

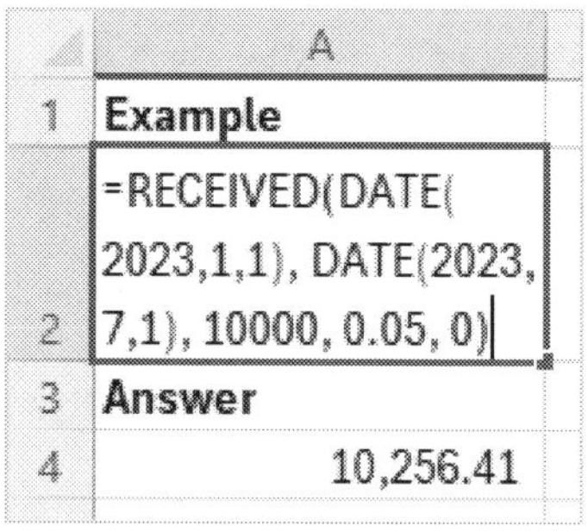

Explore Further with GPT

Ask GPT how to combine RECEIVED with functions like YIELD, DISC, or PRICE for comprehensive financial modeling and investment analysis.

Tips for Using RECEIVED

- **Settlement and maturity dates:** Ensure the settlement date is earlier than the maturity date.
- **Investment consistency:** The investment represents the amount fully invested at the purchase date.
- **Day count basis:** Select the appropriate basis for your security type (e.g., US 30/360 or Actual/actual).

REDUCE Function

Logical Functions

Introduction

The REDUCE function reduces an array to a single accumulated value by applying a custom lambda function to each element in the array. It is a powerful tool for advanced calculations and data transformations.

Simple explanation: Aggregates an array into a single value using a custom-defined operation.

Common use cases: Used in custom aggregations, cumulative calculations, and advanced array processing.

When to use this function: Use when performing iterative calculations over an array or accumulating values based on a custom formula.

Syntax

```
=REDUCE([initial_value], array, lambda(accumulator, value))
```

- **initial_value** *(optional)*: The starting value for the accumulator.
- **array**: The array to be reduced.
- **lambda**: A custom function that defines how the reduction operates:
  - accumulator: The running total or accumulated value.
  - value: The current element in the array being processed.

Worked Example

Challenge: Calculate the sum of the numbers {1, 2, 3, 4, 5} using REDUCE.

Formula:

```
=REDUCE(0, {1,2,3,4,5}, LAMBDA(a, v, a+v))
```

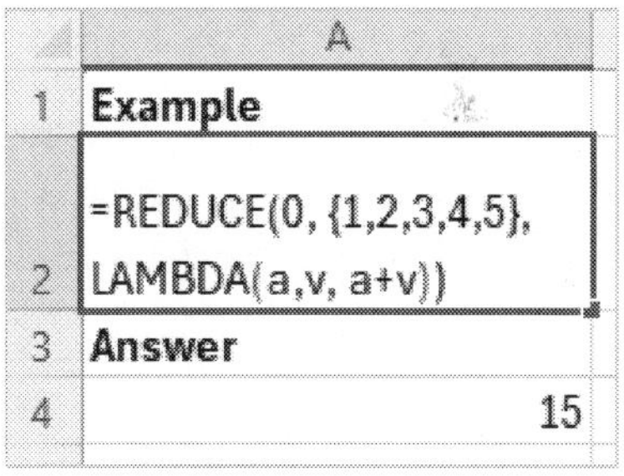

Result: 15
Explanation: The function iterates through the array {1, 2, 3, 4, 5}, adding each value to the accumulator. Starting with 0, the accumulated value becomes 15.

Explore Further with GPT

Ask GPT how to combine REDUCE with other array functions like SCAN, MAP, or FILTER for advanced data processing.

Tips for Using REDUCE

- **Initial value matters:** The initial_value sets the starting point for the accumulation. For addition, use 0; for multiplication, use 1.
- **Custom logic:** Leverage the LAMBDA function to define any operation, including conditional logic and advanced calculations.
- **Dynamic arrays:** Works seamlessly with dynamic arrays, spilling results into adjacent cells when used with other functions.

REGISTER.ID Function

Add-in & Automation Functions

Introduction

The REGISTER.ID function returns the registration ID of a dynamic link library (DLL) or code resource that has been previously registered. This function is primarily used in advanced Excel applications for interacting with external libraries or resources.

Simple explanation: Retrieves the registration ID of a previously registered external DLL or code resource.

Common use cases: Used in advanced custom solutions, macros, or Excel add-ins requiring integration with external code.

When to use this function: Use when working with Excel's ability to integrate external DLLs or code resources.

Syntax

```
=REGISTER.ID(library_text, proc_name, [type_text])
```

- **library_text**: The name of the DLL (e.g., "user32.dll") or code resource.
- **proc_name**: The name of the procedure or function within the DLL or resource.
- **[type_text]** *(optional)*: A text string specifying the argument and return types for the procedure.

Worked Example

Challenge: Retrieve the registration ID of a procedure in a DLL named "myLibrary.dll" for a function named "myFunction".

Formula:

```
=REGISTER.ID("myLibrary.dll", "myFunction")
```

	A
1	**Example**
2	=REGISTER.ID("myLibrary.dll", "myFunction")
3	**Answer**
4	1000234
5	

Result: A numeric ID or #VALUE! if the registration fails.
Explanation: The function returns the registration ID of myFunction from myLibrary.dll, which can be used in further calls or for debugging.

Explore Further with GPT

Ask GPT how to use REGISTER.ID in combination with VBA and CALL to create robust Excel-integrated solutions leveraging external libraries.

Tips for Using REGISTER.ID

- **Pre-registration required:** The DLL or code resource must be registered before using this function.
- **For advanced users:** This function is intended for advanced Excel users and developers.
- **Security considerations:** Ensure the external DLL or resource is from a trusted source to avoid potential security risks.

REPLACE Function

Text Functions

Introduction

The REPLACE and REPLACEB functions replace part of a text string with new text, starting at a specified position and for a specified number of characters. While REPLACE operates on characters, REPLACEB operates on bytes and is designed for double-byte character set (DBCS) languages like Japanese or Chinese.

Simple explanation: Substitutes part of a text string with new text.

Common use cases: Used for modifying text, such as updating formatting, replacing substrings, or correcting data.

When to use these functions: Use REPLACE for single-byte languages (e.g., English) and REPLACEB for DBCS languages.

Syntax

```
=REPLACE(old_text, start_num, num_chars, new_text)
```

- **old_text**: The original text string.
- **start_num**: The position of the character to begin replacing.
- **num_chars**: The number of characters to replace.
- **new_text**: The new text to insert

Worked Example for REPLACE

Challenge: Replace the first 5 characters of "ExcelFunctions" with "Data".

Formula:

```
=REPLACE("ExcelFunctions", 1, 5, "Data")
```

Result: DataFunctions
Explanation: The first 5 characters of "ExcelFunctions" are replaced with "Data".

	A	B	C	D
1	**Example**			
2	=REPLACE("ExcelFunctions", 1, 5, "Data")			
3	**Answer**			
4	DataFunctions			
5				

Explore Further with GPT

Ask GPT how to combine REPLACE or REPLACEB with TEXT, SEARCH, or LEN for advanced text manipulation.

Tips for Using REPLACE and REPLACEB

- **Case sensitivity:** The functions are case-sensitive when replacing text.
- **DBCS behavior:** REPLACEB counts each double-byte character as 2 if the DBCS language is enabled (e.g., Japanese, Chinese). Otherwise, it behaves like REPLACE.
- **Dynamic inputs:** Combine with SEARCH to locate positions dynamically:

  ```
  =REPLACE(A1, SEARCH("old", A1), 3, "new")
  ```

- **Excel compatibility:** Both functions are available in all modern Excel versions, but REPLACEB is relevant only in DBCS-enabled environments.

REPT Function

Text Functions

Introduction

The REPT function repeats a text string a specified number of times. It is useful for creating visual representations, padding text, or generating repeated patterns in cells.

Simple explanation: Repeats a given text string a specified number of times.

Common use cases: Used for creating repeated patterns, simple visualizations, or padding text with characters.

When to use this function: Use when you need to repeat text or symbols programmatically.

Syntax

```
=REPT(text, number_times)
```

- **text**: The text string to repeat.
- **number_times**: The number of times to repeat the text.

Worked Example

Challenge: Repeat the word "Excel" three times.

Formula:

```
=REPT("Excel", 3)
```

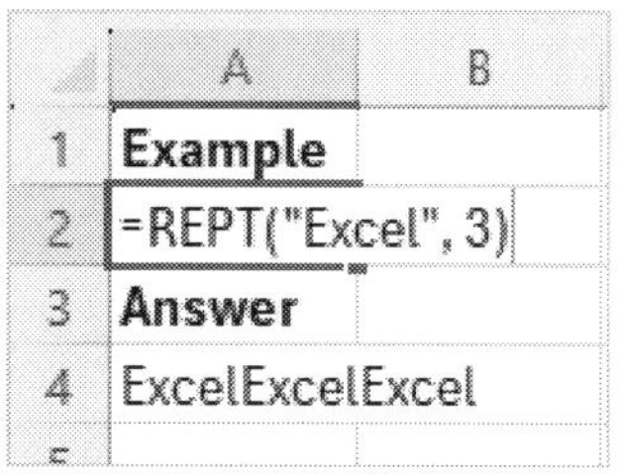

	A	B
1	**Example**	
2	=REPT("Excel", 3)	
3	**Answer**	
4	ExcelExcelExcel	

Result: ExcelExcelExcel
Explanation: The REPT function concatenates "Excel" three times into a single string.

Explore Further with GPT

Ask GPT how to use REPT with functions like LEN, CONCAT, or TEXT to create custom visualizations or formatted outputs.

Tips for Using REPT

- **Dynamic repetition:** Combine with other functions to dynamically control repetitions:

  ```
  =REPT("*", A1)
  ```

  Repeats * as many times as the value in A1.

- **Character limit:** The result cannot exceed 32,767 characters.
- **Error handling:** If number_times is less than 0, the function returns an empty string ("").

RIGHT Function

Text Functions

Introduction

The RIGHT and RIGHTB functions extract a specified number of characters from the end of a text string. While RIGHT works with characters, RIGHTB works with bytes, making it suitable for double-byte character set (DBCS) languages like Japanese or Chinese.

Simple explanation: Extracts text from the end of a string.

Common use cases: Used for substring extraction, formatting, and working with fixed-width data.

When to use these functions: Use RIGHT for single-byte languages (e.g., English) and RIGHTB for DBCS languages.

Syntax

```
=RIGHT(text, [num_chars])
```

- **text**: The original text string.
- **num_chars** *(optional)*: The number of characters to extract (default is 1).

Worked Example for RIGHT

Challenge: Extract the last 4 characters of "ExcelFunctions".

Formula:

```
=RIGHT("ExcelFunctions", 4)
```

	A	B	C
1	**Example**		
2	=RIGHT("ExcelFunctions", 4)		
3	**Answer**		
4	ions		
5			

Result: ions
Explanation: The RIGHT function extracts the last 4 characters from the string.

Explore Further with GPT

Ask GPT how to combine RIGHT or RIGHTB with functions like SEARCH, LEN, or MID for advanced text parsing and manipulation.

Tips for Using RIGHT and RIGHTB

- **Default behavior:** If num_chars or num_bytes is omitted, the function defaults to extracting 1 character or byte.
- **DBCS behavior:** RIGHTB treats each double-byte character as 2 bytes when a DBCS language is enabled. Otherwise, it behaves like RIGHT.
- **Error handling:** If num_chars or num_bytes is negative, the function returns a #VALUE! error.
- **Excel compatibility:** Both functions are available in all modern Excel versions, with RIGHTB being relevant only in DBCS-enabled environments.

ROMAN Function

Math & Trigonometry Functions

Introduction

The ROMAN function converts an Arabic numeral (standard number) to a Roman numeral as text. It supports different levels of Roman numeral formatting to suit specific needs.

Simple explanation: Converts a number into Roman numeral format.

Common use cases: Used in historical documents, formatting, and numbering sections or chapters in reports.

When to use this function: Use when a Roman numeral representation is required for styling or presentation.

Syntax

```
=ROMAN(number, [form])
```

- **number**: The Arabic numeral to convert. Must be a positive integer between 1 and 3999.
- **[form]** *(optional)*: A value that specifies the type of Roman numeral formatting:
    - 0 or omitted: Classic form (e.g., IV for 4).
    - 1-4: Simplified forms with increasing levels of abbreviation.
    - TRUE: Same as 0.
    - FALSE: Same as 4 (simplest form).

Worked Example

Challenge: Convert the number 2023 into a Roman numeral.

Formula:

```
=ROMAN(2023)
```

Result: MMXXIII
Explanation: The ROMAN function converts 2023 into its classical Roman numeral form.

	A	B
1	**Example**	
2	=ROMAN(2023)	
3	**Answer**	
4	MMXXIII	

Explore Further with GPT

Ask GPT how to combine ROMAN with other functions like VALUE, TEXT, or CONCAT for enhanced formatting and customization.

Tips for Using ROMAN

- **Range limitation:** The number must be between 1 and 3999; otherwise, the function returns a #VALUE! error.
- **Format variations:** Use the form argument to choose the level of abbreviation:
    - 0: Classic format (e.g., CDXCIX for 499).
    - 1-4: Abbreviated formats (e.g., LDVLIV for 499 in form 4)

ROUND Function

Math & Trigonometry Functions

Introduction

The ROUND function rounds a number to a specified number of digits. It is a versatile tool for ensuring numerical consistency and managing precision in calculations.

Simple explanation: Rounds a number to a specific number of decimal places.

Common use cases: Used in financial modeling, reporting, and controlling precision in calculations.

When to use this function: Use when you need a rounded number to avoid excessive decimal places or for presentation purposes.

Syntax

```
=ROUND(number, num_digits)
```

- **number**: The number to be rounded.
- **num_digits**: The number of digits to round to:
  - Positive values: Number of decimal places (e.g., 2 rounds to two decimal places).
  - 0: Rounds to the nearest integer.
  - Negative values: Rounds to the left of the decimal point (e.g., -1 rounds to the nearest ten).

Worked Example

Challenge: Round the value 123.456 to two decimal places.

Formula:

```
=ROUND(123.456, 2)
```

Result: 123.46
Explanation: The ROUND function rounds the value to two decimal places, increasing the last digit based on standard rounding rules.

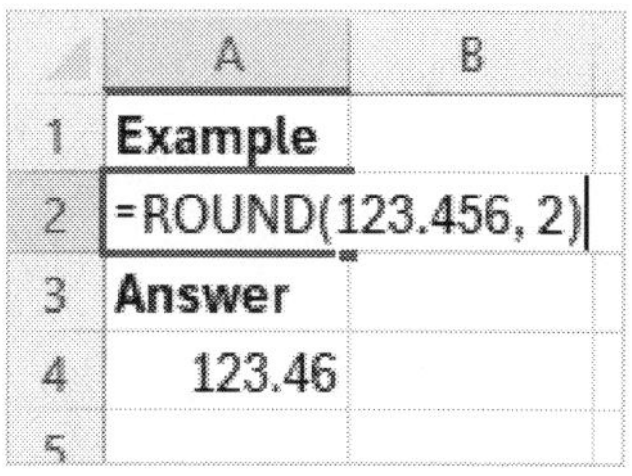

Explore Further with GPT

Ask GPT how to combine ROUND with functions like AVERAGE, SUM, or TEXT to control output formatting in complex calculations.

Tips for Using ROUND

- **Standard rounding rules:** Numbers are rounded up if the digit immediately after the rounding position is 5 or greater.
- **Handling precision:** Combine with ROUND to standardize outputs for consistent calculations:

  ```
  =ROUND(SUM(A1:A10), 2)
  ```

ROUNDDOWN Function

Math & Trigonometry Functions

Introduction

The ROUNDDOWN function rounds a number down toward zero to a specified number of digits. It always truncates digits beyond the specified position, regardless of their value.

- **Simple explanation:** Rounds a number down by removing digits beyond the specified position.
- **Common use cases:** Used in financial calculations, reporting, and scenarios where conservative rounding is required.
- **When to use this function:** Use when you need to truncate a number rather than apply standard rounding rules.

Syntax

```
=ROUNDDOWN(number, num_digits)
```

- **number**: The number to be rounded down.
- **num_digits**: The number of digits to retain:
  - Positive values: Number of decimal places.
  - 0: Rounds down to the nearest integer.
  - Negative values: Rounds down to the left of the decimal point (e.g., nearest tens, hundreds).

Worked Example

Challenge: Round 456.789 down to two decimal places.

Formula:

```
=ROUNDDOWN(456.789, 2)
```

	A	B	C
1	**Example**		
2	=ROUNDDOWN(456.789, 2)		
3	**Answer**		
4	456.78		

Result: 456.78
Explanation: The ROUNDDOWN function truncates the number to two decimal places, ignoring the digit 9.

Explore Further with GPT

Ask GPT how to combine ROUNDDOWN with other functions like IF, MOD, or INT to build custom logic for calculations and reporting.

Tips for Using ROUNDDOWN

- **Always truncates:** The function always truncates digits, regardless of their value.
- **Handling negative digits:** Use negative num_digits to truncate numbers at higher place values (e.g., tens, hundreds).
- **Dynamic rounding:** Combine with other functions to perform conditional rounding:

  ```
  =ROUNDDOWN(A1/B1, 2)
  ```

  Rounds down the result of a division to two decimal places.

ROUNDUP Function

Math & Trigonometry Functions

Introduction

The ROUNDUP function rounds a number up, away from zero, to a specified number of digits. Unlike ROUND, it always increases the magnitude of the number, regardless of the digits being removed.

- **Simple explanation:** Rounds a number up, regardless of the digit being rounded.
- **Common use cases:** Used in financial modeling, reporting, and calculations where upward rounding is required.
- **When to use this function:** Use when you need to round numbers up consistently, ensuring that no values are rounded down.

Syntax

```
=ROUNDUP(number, num_digits)
```

- **number**: The number to be rounded up.
- **num_digits**: The number of digits to retain:
  - Positive values: Number of decimal places to retain.
  - 0: Rounds up to the nearest integer.
  - Negative values: Rounds up to the left of the decimal point (e.g., nearest tens, hundreds).

Worked Example

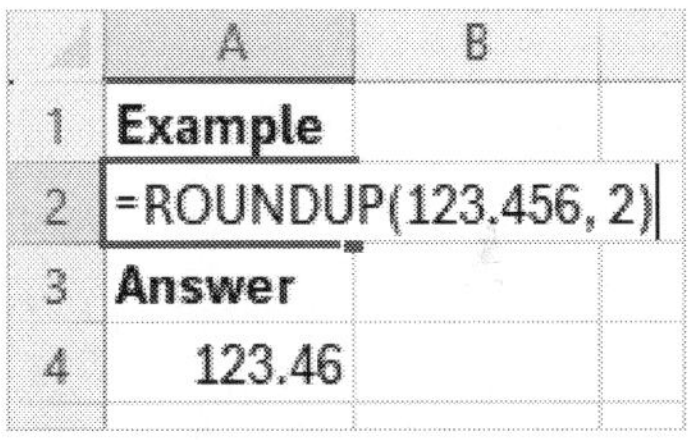

Challenge: Round 123.456 up to two decimal places.

Formula:

```
=ROUNDUP(123.456, 2)
```

Result: 123.46
Explanation: The ROUNDUP function increases the last retained digit by 1, rounding the number up to two decimal places.

Explore Further with GPT

Ask GPT how to combine ROUNDUP with other functions like FLOOR, CEILING, or MOD to create custom rounding solutions.

Tips for Using ROUNDUP

- **Always rounds up:** The function always rounds up, increasing the magnitude of the number, regardless of the next digit's value.
- **Handling negative digits:** Use negative num_digits to round up to higher place values (e.g., tens, hundreds).

ROW Function

Lookup & Reference Functions

Introduction

The ROW function returns the row number of a reference. If no reference is provided, it returns the row number of the cell where the function is used. It is useful for indexing, referencing, and creating dynamic ranges in Excel.

- **Simple explanation:** Returns the row number of a cell or range.
- **Common use cases:** Used in creating dynamic row references, numbering rows, and in combination with other functions for advanced formulas.
- **When to use this function:** Use when you need the row number of a specific cell or when working with dynamic row-based formulas.

Syntax

```
=ROW([reference])
```

- **reference** *(optional)*: The cell or range for which to return the row number. If omitted, it returns the row number of the cell where the formula is entered.

Worked Example

Challenge: Find the row number of cell B5.

Formula:

```
=ROW(B5)
```

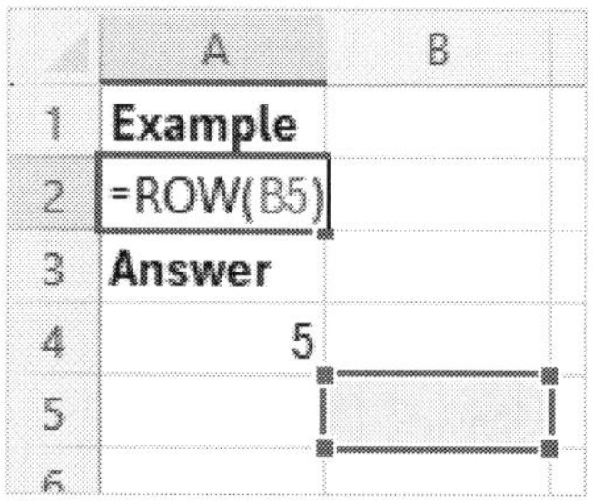

Result: 5
Explanation: The function returns 5, as cell B5 is in row 5.

Explore Further with GPT

Ask GPT how to use ROW in combination with INDEX, OFFSET, or MATCH to create advanced lookup or dynamic range formulas.

Tips for Using ROW

- **Dynamic numbering:** Use ROW to create sequential numbers in a column:

  ```
  =ROW() - 1
  ```

  If starting in row 2, this will return 1, 2, 3, etc.

- **Error handling:** If reference is invalid or refers to a deleted cell, the function returns a #REF! error.

ROWS Function

Lookup & Reference Functions

Introduction

The ROWS function returns the number of rows in a given range. It is commonly used for dynamic range calculations, iterative processes, and determining the size of arrays.

- **Simple explanation:** Counts the number of rows in a specified range.
- **Common use cases:** Used in data analysis, dynamic range creation, and table manipulations.
- **When to use this function:** Use when you need to determine the number of rows in a range or array.

Syntax

```
=ROWS(array)
```

- **array**: The range or array for which to count the rows.

Worked Example

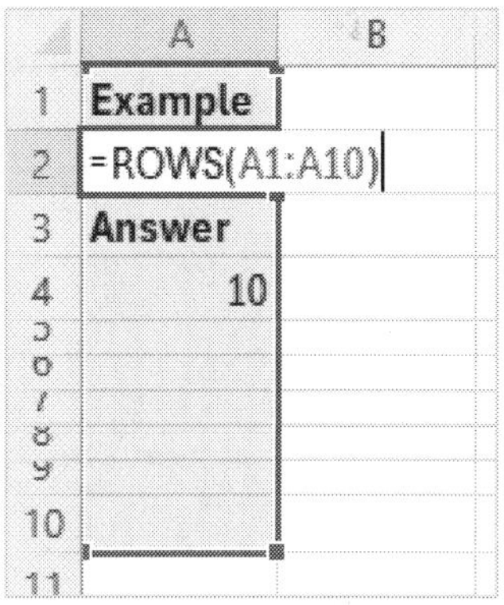

Challenge: Find the number of rows in the range A1:A10.

Formula:

```
=ROWS(A1:A10)
```

Result: 10
Explanation: The ROWS function counts the number of rows in the specified range, returning 10.

Explore Further with GPT

Ask GPT how to combine ROWS with functions like INDEX, OFFSET, or SEQUENCE for dynamic range creation and advanced array handling.

Tips for Using ROWS

- **Dynamic ranges:** Use ROWS in combination with INDEX or OFFSET to create dynamic ranges:

  ```
  =SUM(A1:INDEX(A:A, ROWS(A1:A10)))
  ```

  This sums the first 10 rows dynamically.

- **Counting rows in tables:** Use ROWS with structured references in Excel tables:

  ```
  =ROWS(Table1[Column1])
  ```

  Counts the number of rows in a specified table column

- **Error handling:** Ensure the array argument is valid; otherwise, the function returns a #VALUE! or #REF! error.

RRI Function

Financial Functions

Introduction

The RRI function calculates the equivalent interest rate for an investment or loan based on the number of periods, the present value, and the future value. It is useful for determining the compound annual growth rate (CAGR) of an investment.

- **Simple explanation:** Computes the annualized growth rate required for an investment to grow from its present value to a future value over a specified number of periods.
- **Common use cases:** Used in investment analysis, financial planning, and compound interest calculations.
- **When to use this function:** Use when determining the consistent rate of return required to achieve a specific future value.

Syntax

```
=RRI(nper, pv, fv)
```

- **nper**: The total number of periods.
- **pv**: The present value (initial amount).
- **fv**: The future value (final amount).

Worked Example

Challenge: Calculate the annual growth rate required to grow an investment of $5,000 to $10,000 in 5 years.

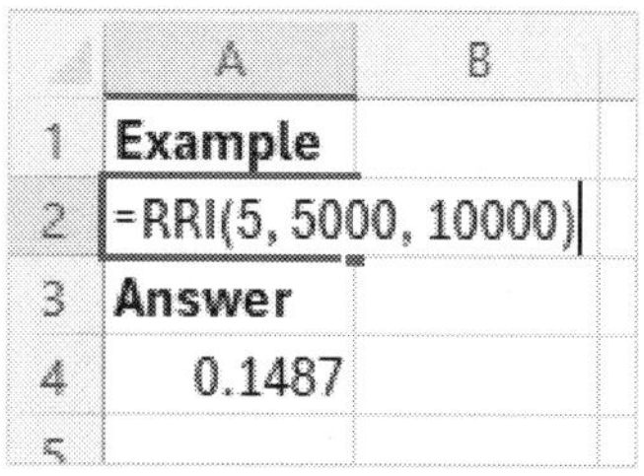

Inputs:

- nper: 5 (years); pv: 5000; fv: 10000

Formula:

```
=RRI(5, 5000, 10000)
```

Result: 0.1487 (or 14.87%)
Explanation: The function returns 0.1487, meaning the investment needs to grow at an annualized rate of 14.87% to double in 5 years.

Explore Further with GPT

Ask GPT how to combine RRI with functions like FV, NPV, or IRR to create more advanced financial models.

Tips for Using RRI

- **Consistent periods:** Ensure nper represents the correct number of compounding periods (e.g., use years for annual rates, quarters for quarterly rates).
- **Positive future value:** Both pv and fv must be positive, or Excel will return a #NUM! error.
- **Error handling:** Use IFERROR to handle invalid inputs:

  ```
  =IFERROR(RRI(A1, A2, A3), "Invalid input")
  ```

RSQ Function

Statistical Functions

Introduction

The RSQ function returns the square of the Pearson correlation coefficient (R^2) between two data sets. It measures how well the data in the two sets fit a linear regression model. The closer the result is to 1, the stronger the linear relationship.

- **Simple explanation:** Computes the coefficient of determination (R^2), indicating how well a linear regression model fits the data.
- **Common use cases:** Used in regression analysis, trend evaluation, and statistical modeling.
- **When to use this function:** Use when you need to measure the goodness of fit of a linear relationship between two variables.

Syntax

```
=RSQ(known_y's, known_x's)
```

- **known_y's**: The dependent data set (y-values).
- **known_x's**: The independent data set (x-values).

Worked Example

Challenge: Calculate the R^2 value for a data set:

Formula:

```
=RSQ(B2:B6, A2:A6)
```

Result: 1

Explanation: The RSQ function returns 1, indicating a perfect linear relationship between X and Y.

	A	B	C	D	E
1	**X (known_x's)**	**Y (known_y's)**		**Example**	
2	1	2		=RSQ(B2:B6, A2:A6)	
3	2	3		**Answer**	
4	3	4		1	
5	4	5			
6	5	6			

Explore Further with GPT

Ask GPT how to use RSQ with other functions like LINEST, SLOPE, or INTERCEPT for deeper regression analysis and trendline creation.

Tips for Using RSQ

- **Equal-sized arrays:** Ensure that known_y's and known_x's contain the same number of data points. If not, Excel returns a #N/A error.
- **Use with regression functions:** Combine RSQ with LINEST or FORECAST for complete regression analysis.
- **Handling non-linear relationships:** If the relationship is non-linear, consider using polynomial or exponential regression models.
- **Excel compatibility:** The RSQ function is available in all modern Excel versions.

RTD Function

Lookup & Reference Functions

Introduction

The RTD function retrieves real-time data from a program that supports COM (Component Object Model) automation. It is commonly used to display live data in Excel from external sources, such as financial markets, inventory systems, or IoT sensors.

- **Simple explanation:** Connects to an external COM server to display real-time data in Excel.
- **Common use cases:** Used for live financial data feeds, stock prices, sensor data, and dynamic reporting from third-party applications.
- **When to use this function:** Use when you need to display continuously updating real-time data from an external source.

Syntax

```
=RTD(progID, server, topic1, [topic2], ...)
```

- **progID**: The programmatic identifier (ProgID) of the COM automation add-in (e.g., "Bloomberg.Excel.RTD").
- **server** *(optional)*: The name of the server where the add-in is running. If running locally, leave this blank.
- **topic1, [topic2], ...**: One or more topics that specify the data to retrieve. The number of topics and their meaning depend on the COM server being used.

Worked Example

Challenge: Retrieve the live stock price for Microsoft (MSFT) from a hypothetical real-time data server.

Formula:

```
=RTD("MarketData.Server", , "StockPrice", "MSFT")
```

Result: A continuously updating stock price for Microsoft.
Explanation: The RTD function connects to the external COM server "MarketData.Server" and retrieves the live stock price for "MSFT".

Explore Further with GPT

Ask GPT how to set up a COM server or integrate real-time data sources with Excel using the RTD function.

Tips for Using RTD

- **Local vs. remote servers:** Leave the server argument blank for local servers. Specify a server name for remote connections.
- **COM server requirement:** The RTD function requires a registered COM server that supports real-time data.
- **Security considerations:** Ensure the COM server comes from a trusted source to avoid security risks.

SCAN Function

Logical Functions

Introduction

The SCAN function processes each element of an array and returns an array of intermediate values by applying a custom lambda function. It performs cumulative calculations, making it useful for creating running totals or custom cumulative results.

- **Simple explanation:** Applies a custom operation to each element of an array and returns a running list of results.
- **Common use cases:** Used for creating running totals, cumulative calculations, and iterative transformations.
- **When to use this function:** Use when you need intermediate results from applying a custom function cumulatively across an array.

Syntax

```
=SCAN([initial_value], array, lambda(accumulator, value))
```

- **initial_value** *(optional)*: The starting value for the accumulator.
- **array**: The array to process.
- **lambda**: A custom function that defines the operation to apply:
    - accumulator: The running total or accumulated value.
    - value: The current element in the array being processed.

Worked Example

Challenge: Create a running total for the array {1, 2, 3, 4, 5}.

Formula:

```
=SCAN(0, {1, 2, 3, 4, 5}, LAMBDA(a, v, a + v))
```

	A	B	C	D	E
1	**Example**				
2	=SCAN(0, {1,2,3,4,5}, LAMBDA(a,v, a + v))				
3	**Answer**				
4	1	3	6	10	15
5					

Result: {1, 3, 6, 10, 15}

Explanation: The SCAN function adds each element to the accumulator, returning an array of running totals.

Explore Further with GPT

Ask GPT how to combine SCAN with other functions like REDUCE, SEQUENCE, or FILTER for advanced iterative calculations and array transformations.

Tips for Using SCAN

- **Initial value:** The initial_value sets the starting point for the accumulator. For running totals, use 0; for products, use 1.
- **Custom logic:** Leverage the LAMBDA function to apply any custom operation, including arithmetic, logical, or string operations.

SEARCH Function

Text Functions

Introduction

The SEARCH and SEARCHB functions return the position of a substring within a larger text string. Unlike FIND, SEARCH is case-insensitive. The SEARCHB function is similar but counts bytes instead of characters, making it suitable for double-byte character set (DBCS) languages like Japanese or Chinese.

- **Simple explanation:** Finds the position of one text string within another, ignoring case.
- **Common use cases:** Used for text parsing, locating specific substrings, and building dynamic formulas.
- **When to use these functions:** Use SEARCH for case-insensitive searches in single-byte languages and SEARCHB when working with DBCS languages.

Syntax

```
=SEARCH(find_text, within_text, [start_num])
```

- **find_text**: The substring to search for.
- **within_text**: The text string to search within.
- **[start_num]** *(optional)*: The position in within_text to start the search (default is 1)

Worked Example

Challenge: Find the position of the substring "Excel" in the text "Learn Excel Functions".

Formula:

```
=SEARCH("Excel", "Learn Excel Functions")
```

	A	B	C	D
1	**Example**			
2	=SEARCH("Excel", "Learn Excel Functions")			
3	**Answer**			
4	7			

Result: 7
Explanation: The substring "Excel" starts at the 7th character in the text "Learn Excel Functions".

Explore Further with GPT

Ask GPT how to use SEARCH with functions like MID, LEFT, or LEN for advanced text parsing and extraction.

Tips for Using SEARCH

- **Case-insensitivity:** SEARCH is case-insensitive, unlike FIND, which is case-sensitive.
- **start_num parameter:** Use the start_num argument to find subsequent occurrences of a substring.
- **DBCS behavior:** SEARCHB counts each double-byte character as 2 bytes if a DBCS language is enabled (e.g., Japanese, Chinese). Otherwise, it behaves like SEARCH.
- **Excel compatibility:** Both SEARCH and SEARCHB are available in all modern Excel versions. SEARCHB is relevant only when a DBCS language is enabled.

SEC Function

Math & Trigonometry Functions

Introduction

The SEC function returns the secant of an angle specified in radians. The secant of an angle is defined as ***sec(x)=1/cos(x)***. It is commonly used in trigonometry and mathematical modeling.

- **Simple explanation:** Calculates the secant of an angle given in radians.
- **Common use cases:** Used in trigonometry, geometry, physics, and engineering for calculations involving secant functions.
- **When to use this function:** Use when solving problems that require the secant of an angle in radians.

Syntax

```
=SEC(number)
```

- **number**: The angle in radians for which to calculate the secant.

Worked Example

Challenge: Calculate the secant of π4\frac{\pi}{4}4π radians.

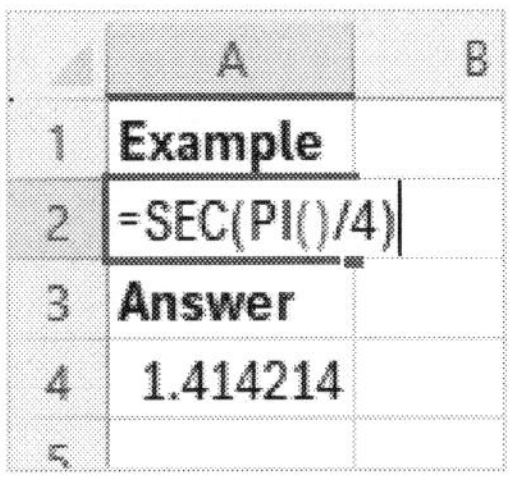

Formula:

```
=SEC(PI()/4)
```

Result: 1.414214
Explanation: The secant of π/4 radians is 1/cos(π/4) = sqrt{2} [approx 1.414214].

Explore Further with GPT

Ask GPT how to combine SEC with other trigonometric functions like COS, TAN, or COT for advanced mathematical modeling.

Tips for Using SEC

- **Radians input:** Ensure the input is in radians. Use the RADIANS function to convert degrees to radians if necessary.
- **Inverse function:** To find the inverse secant (arcsecant), use ACOS(1/x) since Excel does not have a built-in inverse secant function.
- **Error handling:** The SEC function returns a #NUM! error if the input is an odd multiple of π/2 (90°, 270°, etc.), where the cosine is zero and secant is undefined.
- **Excel compatibility:** The SEC function is available in Excel 2013 and later versions

SECH Function

Math & Trigonometry Functions

Introduction

The SECH function returns the hyperbolic secant of a number. The hyperbolic secant is defined as ***sech(x)=2/(e^x+e^-x)***, where ***e*** is Euler's number. It is commonly used in advanced mathematics, engineering, and physics.

- **Simple explanation:** Calculates the hyperbolic secant of a number.
- **Common use cases:** Used in mathematical modeling, physics, and hyperbolic geometry for solving problems involving hyperbolic functions.
- **When to use this function:** Use when working with hyperbolic functions in equations or models.

Syntax

```
=SECH(number)
```

- **number**: The real number for which to calculate the hyperbolic secant.

Worked Example

	A
1	**Example**
2	=SECH(1)
3	**Answer**
4	0.648054
5	

Challenge: Calculate the hyperbolic secant of 1.

Formula:

```
=SECH(1)
```

Result: 0.648054
Explanation: The SECH function computes $2/(e^{1}+e^{-1}) \approx 0.648054$

Explore Further with GPT

Ask GPT how to use SECH with other hyperbolic functions like SINH, COSH, or TANH to solve complex mathematical problems.

Tips for Using SECH

- **Works with real numbers:** The function accepts both positive and negative real numbers.
- **Hyperbolic relationships:** The hyperbolic secant is related to the hyperbolic cosine by sech(x)=1/cosh(x) .

SECOND Function

Date & Time Functions

Introduction

The SECOND function returns the second component of a given time value as a number between 0 and 59. It is useful for extracting the seconds from a time value or performing calculations involving time.

- **Simple explanation:** Extracts the number of seconds from a time value.
- **Common use cases:** Used in time-based calculations, data logging, and timestamp analysis.
- **When to use this function:** Use when you need to retrieve or manipulate the seconds part of a time value.

Syntax

```
=SECOND(serial_number)
```

- **serial_number**: A valid Excel time value or a cell reference containing the time. Excel stores time values as fractions of a day.

Worked Example

Challenge: Extract the seconds from the time 12:34:56.

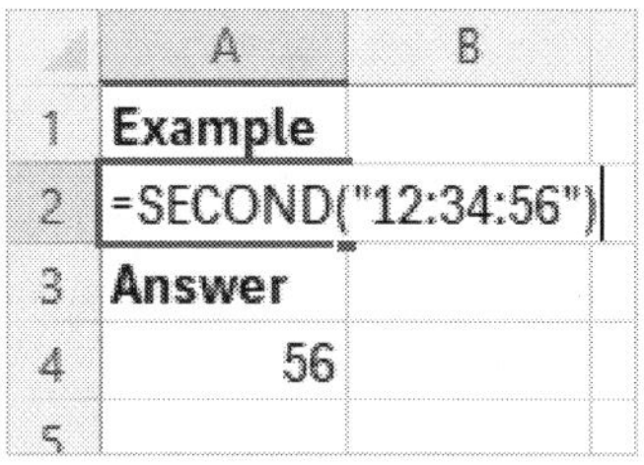

Formula:

```
=SECOND("12:34:56")
```

Result: 56
Explanation: The SECOND function extracts the seconds component (56) from the given time.

Explore Further with GPT

Ask GPT how to combine SECOND with functions like HOUR, MINUTE, or TIME to create custom time-based calculations.

Tips for Using SECOND

- **Handles fractional times:** The function works with fractional time values, where 1 represents a full day.
- **Dynamic updates:** Use with NOW or TIME for dynamically changing time values.
- **Error handling:** If serial_number is not a valid time or number, the function returns a #VALUE! error. Use IFERROR to manage this:

  ```
  =IFERROR(SECOND(A1), "Invalid time")
  ```

- **Excel compatibility:** The SECOND function is available in all modern Excel versions

SEQUENCE Function

Math & Trigonometry Functions

Introduction

The SEQUENCE function generates an array of sequential numbers, either in a single row or column, or in a matrix with multiple rows and columns. It is useful for creating numbered lists, grids, or dynamic ranges.

- **Simple explanation:** Creates an array of sequential numbers in rows, columns, or both.
- **Common use cases:** Used in generating dynamic lists, matrices, indexing, and iteration in calculations.
- **When to use this function:** Use when you need to create a sequence of numbers for calculations or as an index.

Syntax

```
=SEQUENCE(rows, [columns], [start], [step])
```

- **rows** *(optional)*: The number of rows to return.
- **columns** *(optional)*: The number of columns to return (default is 1).
- **start** *(optional)*: The starting number (default is 1).
- **step** *(optional)*: The increment between numbers (default is 1).

Worked Example

Challenge: Create a 3x4 matrix of sequential numbers starting from 5 with a step of 2.

Formula:

```
=SEQUENCE(3, 4, 5, 2)
```

Result:

A	B	C	D
5	7	9	11
13	15	17	19
21	23	25	27

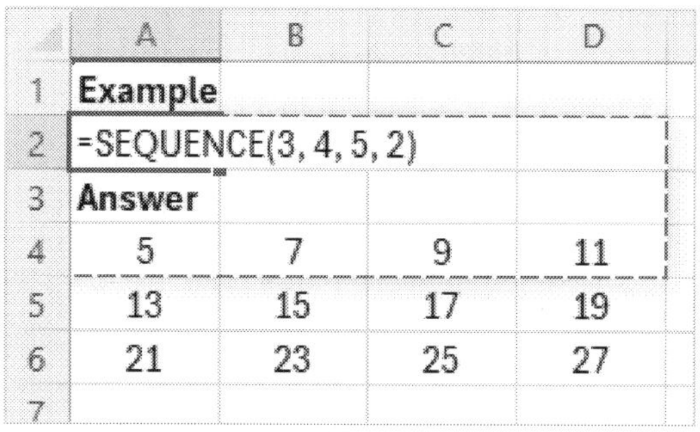

	A	B	C	D
1	**Example**			
2	=SEQUENCE(3, 4, 5, 2)			
3	**Answer**			
4	5	7	9	11
5	13	15	17	19
6	21	23	25	27
7				

Explore Further with GPT

Ask GPT how to combine SEQUENCE with functions like INDEX, SORT, or FILTER to create dynamic ranges and custom lists.

Tips for Using SEQUENCE

- **Dynamic arrays:** The function spills its output dynamically into adjacent cells. Ensure there's enough space for the array, or Excel will return a #SPILL! error.

SERIESSUM Function

Math & Trigonometry Functions

Introduction

The SERIESSUM function returns the sum of a power series based on the provided coefficients, exponents, and a given input value. It is useful in mathematical modeling and scientific calculations involving polynomial expansions.

- **Simple explanation:** Calculates the sum of a power series using an input value and given coefficients.
- **Common use cases:** Used in polynomial approximations, numerical analysis, and scientific computations.
- **When to use this function:** Use when summing a power series with varying coefficients and exponents.

Syntax

```
=SERIESSUM(x, n, m, coefficients)
```

- **x**: The input value for the power series.
- **n**: The initial exponent applied to x.
- **m**: The increment added to the exponent for each term in the series.
- **coefficients**: An array or range of coefficients corresponding to each term in the series

Worked Example

Challenge: Calculate the sum of the power series $\boldsymbol{1+2x+3x^2+4x^3}$ when $\boldsymbol{x=2}$.

Inputs:

- x: 2; n: 0 (initial exponent); m: 1 (increment for each term); coefficients: {1, 2, 3, 4}

Formula:

```
=SERIESSUM(2, 0, 1, {1, 2, 3, 4})
```

	A	B	C
1	**Example**		
2	=SERIESSUM(2, 0, 1, {1,2,3,4})		
3	**Answer**		
4	49		

Result: 49

Explanation: The function evaluates the power series as $1x2^0+2x2^1+3x2^2+4x2^3$ = 1+4+12+32=49.

Explore Further with GPT

Ask GPT how to combine SERIESSUM with functions like FACT, PI, or EXP for more advanced series calculations.

Tips for Using SERIESSUM

- **Array handling:** Ensure the coefficients argument is entered as an array or range.

SHEET Function

Information Functions

Introduction

The SHEET function returns the sheet number of a specified sheet or reference. If no argument is provided, it returns the sheet number of the sheet containing the formula. It is useful for managing large workbooks with multiple sheets or dynamic references.

- **Simple explanation:** Returns the number of a sheet in the workbook.
- **Common use cases:** Used for dynamic references, troubleshooting, and creating formulas that adapt to changes in sheet order.
- **When to use this function:** Use when you need to identify or work with sheet numbers dynamically.

Syntax

```
=SHEET([value])
```

- **value** *(optional)*: A reference or sheet name for which to return the sheet number. If omitted, the function returns the sheet number of the current sheet.

Worked Example

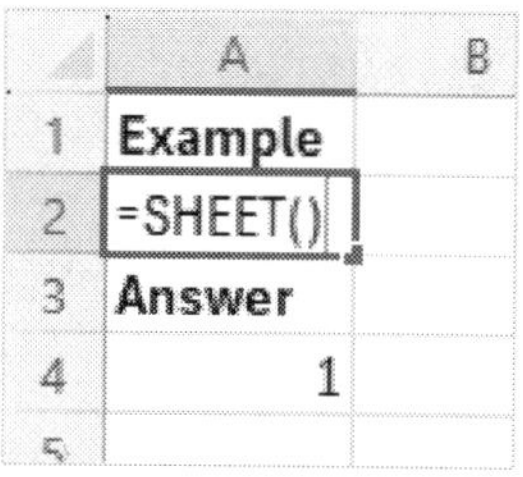

Challenge: Find the sheet number of the current sheet.

Formula:

```
=SHEET()
```

Result: 1, 2, or any other number depending on the position of the current sheet in the workbook.
Explanation: The function returns the number of the sheet where the formula is entered

Explore Further with GPT

Ask GPT how to combine SHEET with functions like CELL, SHEETS, or INDIRECT to build dynamic and adaptable references across large workbooks.

Tips for Using SHEET

- **Reference requirement:** If the specified reference or sheet name does not exist, the function returns a #REF! error.
- **Dynamic sheet management:** Use SHEET in combination with INDIRECT to create dynamic references based on sheet numbers.
- **Error handling:** Use IFERROR to manage errors when referencing non-existent sheets:

  ```
  =IFERROR(SHEET(INDIRECT("'MissingSheet'!A1")), "Sheet not found")
  ```

- **Excel compatibility:** The SHEET function is available in Excel 2013 and later versions

SHEETS Function

Information Functions

Introduction

The SHEETS function returns the number of sheets in a reference or the entire workbook if no reference is provided. It is useful for managing large workbooks and dynamic calculations that depend on the number of sheets.

- **Simple explanation:** Counts the total number of sheets in a workbook or a specified reference.
- **Common use cases:** Used for workbook management, dynamic referencing, and generating reports based on the number of sheets.
- **When to use this function:** Use when you need to count the number of sheets in a workbook or within a specific group of sheets.

Syntax

```
=SHEETS([reference])
```

- **reference** *(optional)*: A reference to a sheet or range of sheets. If omitted, the function returns the total number of sheets in the workbook.

Worked Example

Challenge: Count the total number of sheets in a workbook.

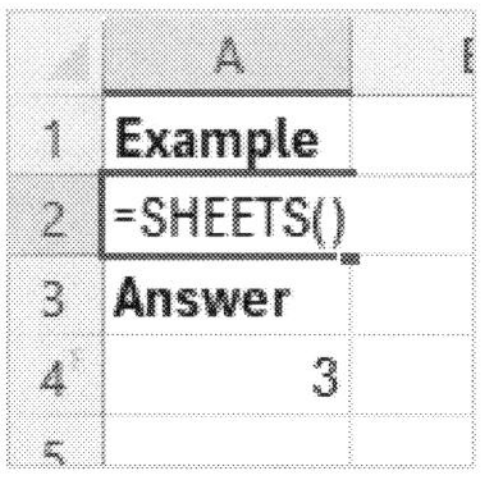

Formula:

```
=SHEETS()
```

Result: 3 (or the actual number of sheets in your workbook).
Explanation: The function returns the total number of sheets in the workbook.

Explore Further with GPT

Ask GPT how to combine SHEETS with functions like INDEX, INDIRECT, or CELL for advanced workbook management and navigation.

Tips for Using SHEETS

- **No reference counts all sheets:** If no reference is provided, the function counts all sheets in the workbook.
- **3D references:** Use 3D references to count specific groups of sheets. For example:

  ```
  =SHEETS(Sheet1:Sheet5!A1)
  ```

  Counts the sheets from Sheet1 to Sheet5.
- **Dynamic referencing:** Combine SHEETS with INDIRECT to create dynamic formulas based on the total number of sheets:

  ```
  =INDIRECT("Sheet" & SHEETS() & "!A1")
  ```

SIGN Function

Math & Trigonometry Functions

Introduction

The SIGN function returns the sign of a number, indicating whether the number is positive, negative, or zero. It outputs 1 for positive numbers, -1 for negative numbers, and 0 if the input is zero.

- **Simple explanation:** Identifies whether a number is positive, negative, or zero.
- **Common use cases:** Used in mathematical models, data analysis, and custom logic for handling positive and negative values.
- **When to use this function:** Use when you need to classify numbers by their sign.

Syntax

```
=SIGN(number)
```

- **number**: The number for which to determine the sign.

Worked Example

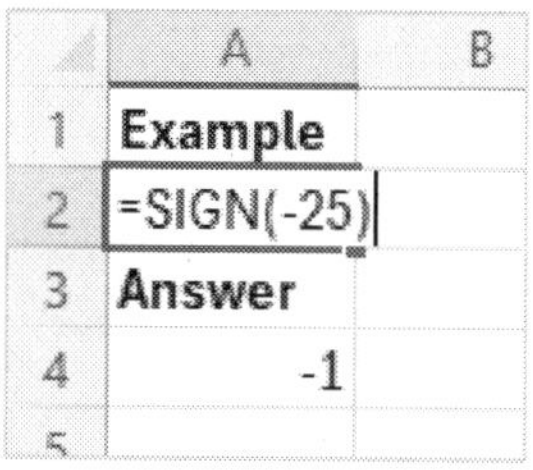

Challenge: Determine the sign of -25.

Formula:

```
=SIGN(-25)
```

Result: -1
Explanation: The function returns -1 because the input number is negative.

Explore Further with GPT

Ask GPT how to use SIGN with functions like IF, ABS, or ROUND to create custom formulas for handling different types of numbers.

Tips for Using SIGN

- **Zero handling:** The function returns 0 if the input is exactly zero.
- **Combining with IF:** Create custom logic based on the sign of a number:

  ```
  =IF(SIGN(A1)=1, "Positive", IF(SIGN(A1)=-1, "Negative", "Zero"))
  ```

  Classifies numbers as positive, negative, or zero.
- **Excel compatibility:** The SIGN function is available in all modern Excel versions

SIN Function

Math & Trigonometry Functions

Introduction

The SIN function returns the sine of an angle specified in radians. It is commonly used in trigonometry to solve problems involving right triangles and periodic phenomena like waves and oscillations.

- **Simple explanation:** Computes the sine of an angle given in radians.
- **Common use cases:** Used in trigonometry, physics, engineering, and wave modeling.
- **When to use this function:** Use when solving problems requiring the sine of an angle.

Syntax

```
=SIN(number)
```

- **number**: The angle in radians for which to calculate the sine.

Worked Example

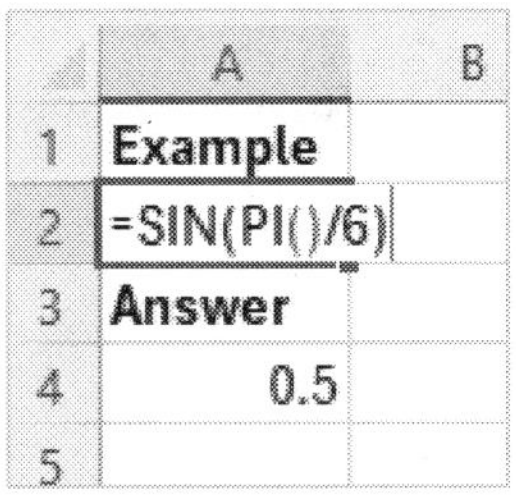

Challenge: Calculate the sine of π/6 radians.

Formula:

```
=SIN(PI()/6)
```

Result: 0.5
Explanation: The sine of π/6 radians is 0.5.

Explore Further with GPT

Ask GPT how to use SIN with functions like COS, TAN, or PI for advanced trigonometric and wave calculations.

Tips for Using SIN

- **Radians input:** Ensure the input is in radians. Use the RADIANS function to convert degrees to radians when necessary.
- **Periodic properties:** The sine function is periodic with a period of 2π, meaning sin(x+2π)=sin(x).
- **Combining with other functions:** Use SIN in conjunction with COS and TAN for solving complex trigonometric problems:

  ```
  =SIN(A1) + COS(A1)
  ```

  Computes the sum of the sine and cosine of the value in cell A1.

SINH Function

Math & Trigonometry Functions

Introduction

The SINH function returns the hyperbolic sine of a number. The hyperbolic sine is defined as ***sinh(x)=(e^{x}−e^{-x})/2***, where ***e*** is Euler's number. It is commonly used in advanced mathematics, physics, and engineering.

- **Simple explanation:** Computes the hyperbolic sine of a number.
- **Common use cases:** Used in hyperbolic geometry, physics simulations, and mathematical modeling.
- **When to use this function:** Use when solving problems involving hyperbolic trigonometric functions.

Syntax

```
=SINH(number)
```

- **number**: The real number for which to calculate the hyperbolic sine.

Worked Example

Challenge: Calculate the hyperbolic sine of 1.

Formula:

```
=SINH(1)
```

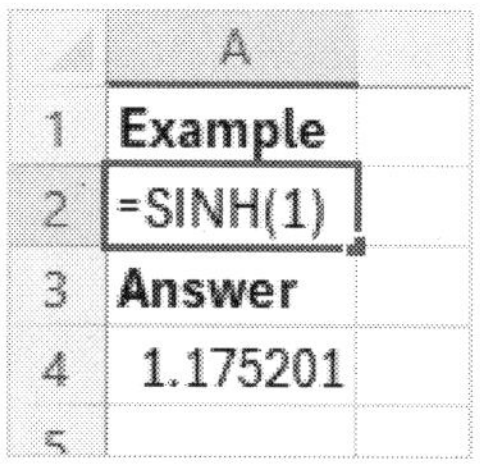

	A
1	**Example**
2	=SINH(1)
3	**Answer**
4	1.175201
5	

Result: 1.175201
Explanation: The function calculates $(e^{1}-e^{-1})/2 \approx 1.175201$

Explore Further with GPT

Ask GPT how to combine SINH with other hyperbolic functions like COSH, TANH, or EXP for advanced mathematical solutions

Tips for Using SINH

- **Handles real numbers:** The function accepts both positive and negative real numbers.
- **Hyperbolic identities:** The hyperbolic sine is related to the hyperbolic cosine by the identity $\cosh^2(x)-\sinh^2(x)=1$
- **Dynamic input:** Combine SINH with other functions for dynamic calculations:

  ```
  =SINH(A1)
  ```

  Computes the hyperbolic sine of the value in cell A1.

SKEW Function

Statistical Functions

Introduction

The SKEW function returns the skewness of a distribution, which measures the asymmetry of data around the mean. A positive skew indicates a distribution with a longer tail on the right side, while a negative skew indicates a longer tail on the left side.

- **Simple explanation:** Computes the asymmetry of a data set's distribution around its mean.
- **Common use cases:** Used in statistical analysis, risk assessment, and financial modeling to understand the shape of data distributions.
- **When to use this function:** Use when analyzing whether a data set is symmetric or skewed

Syntax

`=SKEW(number1, [number2], ...)`

- **number1, [number2], ...**: Numeric values or ranges representing the data set. You can provide up to 254 arguments.

Worked Example

Challenge: Calculate the skewness of the data set {3, 6, 8, 10, 15}.

Formula:

`=SKEW(A1:A5)`

Result: 0.54776
Explanation: The SKEW function computes the skewness of the data set, returning a positive value, indicating a distribution with a longer tail on the right side.

	A	B	C
1	3	**Example**	
2	6	=SKEW(A1:A5)	
3	8	**Answer**	
4	10	0.54776	
5	15		
6			

Explore Further with GPT

Ask GPT how to use SKEW alongside KURT, STDEV, or AVERAGE to perform advanced statistical analysis.

Tips for Using SKEW

- **Interpretation:**
  - Positive result → Right-skewed distribution (longer right tail).
  - Negative result → Left-skewed distribution (longer left tail).
  - Result near 0 → Symmetrical distribution.
- **Sufficient data points:** Ensure your data set contains at least three values; otherwise, the function returns a #DIV/0! error.
- **Error handling:** Use IFERROR to manage errors:

  `=IFERROR(SKEW(A1:A10), "Insufficient data")`

SKEW.P Function

Statistical Functions

Introduction

The SKEW.P function returns the population skewness of a distribution, which measures the asymmetry of the entire population around its mean. Unlike SKEW, which calculates sample skewness, SKEW.P assumes the data represents the entire population.

- **Simple explanation:** Computes the asymmetry of a population distribution around its mean.
- **Common use cases:** Used in statistical analysis, population data modeling, and risk assessment to understand the distribution's shape.
- **When to use this function:** Use when you have data representing the entire population and want to measure its skewness.

Syntax

```
=SKEW.P(number1, [number2], ...)
```

- **number1, [number2], ...:** Numeric values or ranges representing the population data set. You can provide up to 254 arguments.

Worked Example

Challenge: Calculate the population skewness of the data set {3, 6, 8, 10, 15}.

Formula:

```
=SKEW.P(A1:A5)
```

Result: 0.36745
Explanation: The SKEW.P function computes the population skewness, returning a positive value, indicating a distribution with a longer right tail.

Explore Further with GPT

Ask GPT how to use SKEW.P with other statistical functions like STDEV.P, KURT, or AVERAGE for population-level statistical analysis.

Tips for Using SKEW.P

- **Interpretation:**
  - Positive result → Right-skewed population (longer right tail).
  - Negative result → Left-skewed population (longer left tail).
  - Result near 0 → Symmetrical population distribution.
- **Sufficient data points:** Ensure your data set contains at least three values; otherwise, the function returns a #DIV/0! error.
- **Error handling:** Use IFERROR to handle invalid data or insufficient data points:

  ```
  =IFERROR(SKEW.P(A1:A10), "Insufficient data")
  ```

SLN Function

Financial Functions

Introduction

The SLN function calculates the straight-line depreciation of an asset for one period. Straight-line depreciation spreads the cost of an asset evenly over its useful life, making it one of the simplest methods for calculating depreciation.

- **Simple explanation:** Computes the depreciation of an asset using the straight-line method, where depreciation is the same for each period.
- **Common use cases:** Used in financial modeling, accounting, and asset management to track the reduction in value of fixed assets over time.
- **When to use this function:** Use when calculating fixed, equal depreciation amounts for an asset over its useful life.

Syntax

```
=SLN(cost, salvage, life)
```

- **cost**: The initial cost of the asset.
- **salvage**: The value of the asset at the end of its useful life (salvage value).
- **life**: The useful life of the asset, in periods (e.g., years).

Worked Example

Challenge: Calculate the annual straight-line depreciation of an asset with an initial cost of $50,000, a salvage value of $5,000, and a useful life of 10 years.

	A	B
1	**Example**	
2	=SLN(50000, 5000, 10)	
3	**Answer**	
4	4,500.00	
5		

Inputs:

- cost: 50000; salvage: 5000; life: 10

Formula:

```
=SLN(50000, 5000, 10)
```

Result: 4500
Explanation: The function calculates the annual depreciation as (50000−5000)/10 = 4500.

Explore Further with GPT

Ask GPT how to use SLN alongside DB, DDB, or SYD to model different depreciation methods and compare their effects on asset value.

Tips for Using SLN

- **Consistent depreciation:** The straight-line method results in equal depreciation amounts for each period.
- **Units of life:** Ensure that the life argument matches the desired depreciation period (e.g., years, months).

SLOPE Function

Statistical Functions

Introduction

The SLOPE function returns the slope of the linear regression line through a set of data points. The slope represents the rate of change between the dependent and independent variables and is useful in statistical analysis and predictive modeling.

- **Simple explanation:** Computes the slope of the best-fit line through a set of data points.
- **Common use cases:** Used in trend analysis, regression modeling, and forecasting to determine how one variable changes in relation to another.
- **When to use this function:** Use when analyzing the relationship between two variables or when performing linear regression.

Syntax

```
=SLOPE(known_y's, known_x's)
```

- **known_y's**: The dependent data set (y-values).
- **known_x's**: The independent data set (x-values).

Worked Example

Challenge: Calculate the slope of the line for a set of data points:

Formula:

`=SLOPE(B2:B6, A2:A6)`

Result: 2.2

Explanation: The slope indicates that for each unit increase in X, Y increases by 2.2.

	A	B	C	D	E
1	X (known_x's)	Y (known_y's)		Example	
2	1	2		=SLOPE(B2:B6, A2:A6)	
3	2	3		Answer	
4	3	5		2.2	
5	4	7			
6	5	11			
7					

Explore Further with GPT

Ask GPT how to use SLOPE with functions like INTERCEPT, LINEST, or FORECAST to build predictive models and perform advanced regression analysis.

Tips for Using SLOPE

- **Equal-sized arrays:** Ensure known_y's and known_x's have the same number of data points; otherwise, the function returns a #N/A error.
- **Interpreting slope:**
  - Positive slope → As X increases, Y increases.
  - Negative slope → As X increases, Y decreases.
  - Zero slope → No relationship between X and Y.
- **Dynamic references:** Use absolute references ($A$1:$A$10) to fix ranges when copying the formula across cells.

SMALL Function

Statistical Functions

Introduction

The SMALL function returns the k-th smallest value in a data set. It is useful for extracting specific ranked values, such as the minimum, second smallest, or any k-th smallest value in a range.

- **Simple explanation:** Finds the k-th smallest value in a list of numbers.
- **Common use cases:** Used in ranking, filtering data, and statistical analysis.
- **When to use this function:** Use when you need to find the smallest values or specific ranks in a dataset.

Syntax

```
=SMALL(array, k)
```

- **array**: The range or array containing numeric values.
- **k**: The position (rank) of the value to return, where 1 returns the smallest value, 2 returns the second smallest, and so on.

Worked Example

Challenge: Find the second smallest value in the data set {10, 25, 15, 5, 30}.

Formula:

`=SMALL(A1:A5, 2)`

Result: 10
Explanation: The second smallest value in the data set is 10

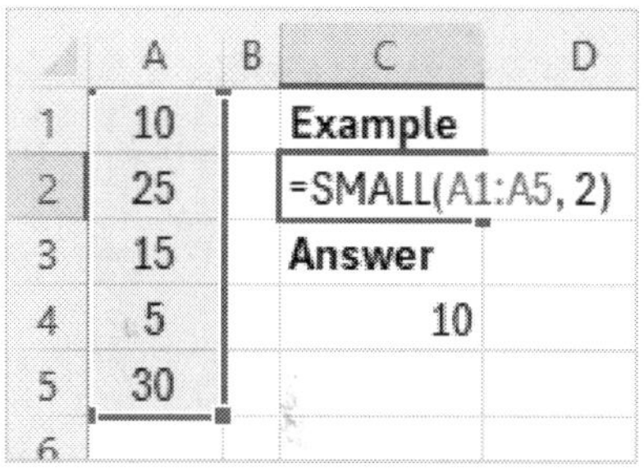

Explore Further with GPT

Ask GPT how to combine SMALL with functions like IF, INDEX, or SORT for advanced data extraction and analysis.

Tips for Using SMALL

- **Dynamic ranking:** Combine SMALL with ROW to return the smallest values dynamically:

  `=SMALL(A1:A10, ROW(A1))`

  This returns the smallest value for the first row, the second smallest for the second row, and so on.

- **Error handling:** If k is less than 1 or greater than the number of elements in array, the function returns a #NUM! error. Use IFERROR to manage errors:

  `=IFERROR(SMALL(A1:A10, B1), "Invalid input")`

- **Non-numeric values:** The function ignores non-numeric values in the array

SORT Function

Lookup & Reference Functions

Introduction

The SORT function sorts the contents of a range or array based on one or more columns. You can sort data in ascending or descending order and return the results as a dynamic array.

- **Simple explanation:** Arranges a range or array in ascending or descending order.
- **Common use cases:** Used for sorting data dynamically without altering the original range, creating sorted lists, or organizing data for analysis.
- **When to use this function:** Use when you need to sort data without manually rearranging it.

Syntax

```
=SORT(array, [sort_index], [sort_order], [by_col])
```

- **array**: The range or array to sort.
- **[sort_index]** *(optional)*: The column or row number to sort by. Default is 1 (first column or row).
- **[sort_order]** *(optional)*: The order to sort by:
    - 1 = Ascending (default).
    - -1 = Descending.
- **[by_col]** *(optional)*: A logical value specifying the direction to sort:
    - FALSE or omitted = Sort by rows (default).
    - TRUE = Sort by columns.

Worked Example

Challenge: Sort the range {10, 25, 15, 5, 30} in ascending order.

Formula:

```
=SORT(A1:A5)
```

Result: (5, 10, 15, 25, 30)

Explanation: The function sorts the range in ascending order by default.

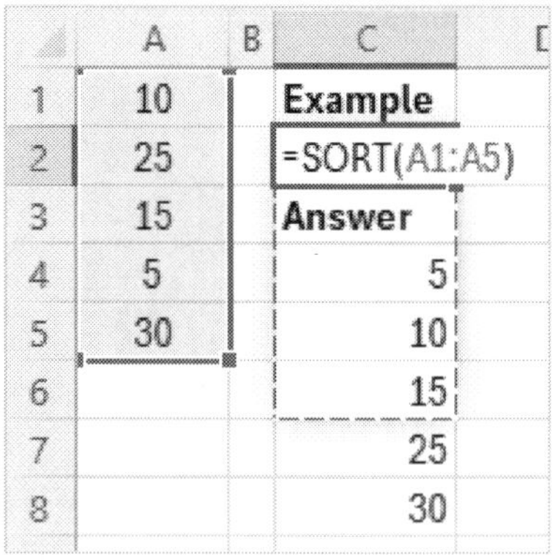

Explore Further with GPT

Ask GPT how to use SORT with functions like FILTER, UNIQUE, or SEQUENCE to build advanced dynamic tables and dashboards.

Tips for Using SORT

- **Dynamic sorting:** Since SORT returns a dynamic array, any changes to the source data automatically update the sorted result.
- **Multi-level sorting:** Combine SORT with SORTBY for multi-level sorting.

SORTBY Function

Lookup & Reference Functions

Introduction

The SORTBY function sorts the contents of a range or array based on one or more columns or arrays, in ascending or descending order. It offers more flexibility than SORT, as it allows sorting by multiple criteria.

- **Simple explanation:** Sorts a range or array based on one or more specified criteria.
- **Common use cases:** Used for dynamic multi-level sorting, creating sorted lists, and organizing complex data.
- **When to use this function:** Use when sorting data by multiple columns or when the sorting order depends on custom criteria.

Syntax

```
=SORTBY(array, by_array1, [sort_order1], [by_array2], [sort_order2], ...)
```

- **array**: The range or array to sort.
- **by_array1**: The first array or column to sort by.
- **[sort_order1]** *(optional)*: The sort order for by_array1:
    - 1 = Ascending (default); -1 = Descending.
- **[by_array2], [sort_order2]**, ... *(optional)*: Additional arrays and their corresponding sort orders for multi-level sorting.

Worked Example

Challenge: Sort a list of students by their scores in descending order.

Formula:

```
=SORTBY(A2:B5, B2:B5, -1)
```

Explanation: The function sorts the list in descending order based on the scores in column B.

	A	B	C	D	E	F
1	**Name**	**Score**		**Example**		
2	John	80		=SORTBY(A2:B5, B2:B5, -1)		
3	Alice	95		**Answer**		
4	Bob	70		Alice	95	
5	Mark	85		Mark	85	
6				John	80	
7				Bob	70	
8						

Explore Further with GPT

Ask GPT how to combine SORTBY with functions like FILTER, UNIQUE, or INDEX for creating complex data tables and reports.

Tips for Using SORTBY

- **Multi-level sorting:** Unlike SORT, SORTBY allows sorting by multiple arrays or columns, each with its own order.
- **Dynamic updates:** The sorted output updates automatically when the source data changes, as SORTBY returns a dynamic array.

SQRT Function

Math & Trigonometry Functions

Introduction

The SQRT function returns the positive square root of a number. The square root of a number is a value that, when multiplied by itself, gives the original number.

- **Simple explanation:** Computes the positive square root of a given number.
- **Common use cases:** Used in mathematical modeling, geometry, and scientific calculations.
- **When to use this function:** Use when you need to find the positive square root of a number.

Syntax

```
=SQRT(number)
```

- **number**: The number for which to calculate the square root. It must be greater than or equal to zero.

Worked Example

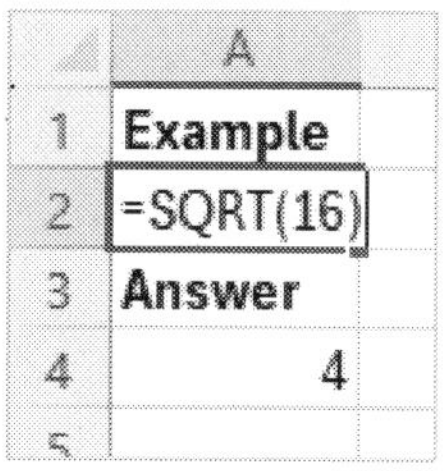

Challenge: Find the square root of 16.

Formula:

```
=SQRT(16)
```

Result: 4
Explanation: The function computes the square root of 16, which is 4, because 4×4=16.

Explore Further with GPT

Ask GPT how to combine SQRT with functions like POWER, ABS, or ROUND for more advanced mathematical operations.

Tips for Using SQRT

- **Positive results only:** The function returns only the positive square root.
- **Avoiding errors:** Use ABS to ensure non-negative inputs:

  ```
  =SQRT(ABS(A1))
  ```

  This ensures that the input is non-negative, preventing #NUM! errors.

SQRTPI Function

Math & Trigonometry Functions

Introduction

The SQRTPI function returns the square root of the product of a given number and π (pi $\approx$ 3.14159). It simplifies calculations involving circles and geometry where the product of a number and π is common.

- **Simple explanation:** Computes the square root of number$\times\pi$.
- **Common use cases:** Used in geometry, trigonometry, and physics for calculations involving circular or spherical shapes.
- **When to use this function:** Use when calculating the square root of a number multiplied by π.

Syntax

```
=SQRTPI(number)
```

- **number**: The number to multiply by π before taking the square root. It must be greater than or equal to zero.

Worked Example

Challenge: Find the square root of 5$\times\pi$.

Formula:

```
=SQRTPI(5)
```

Result: 3.963327
Explanation: The function computes sqrt{5 x π} = sqrt{15.70795} $\approx$ 3.963327.

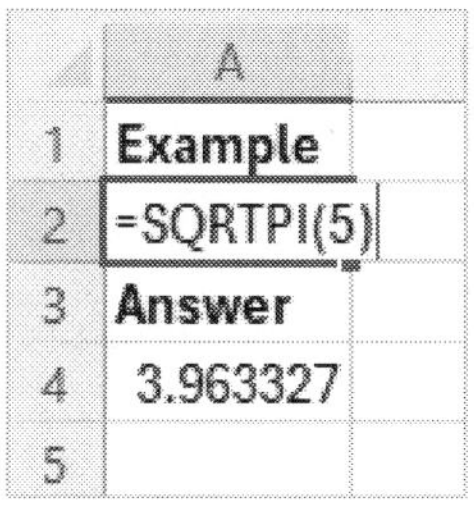

	A
1	**Example**
2	=SQRTPI(5)
3	**Answer**
4	3.963327
5	

Explore Further with GPT

Ask GPT how to combine SQRTPI with functions like PI, POWER, or SIN for advanced geometric and trigonometric calculations.

Tips for Using SQRTPI

- **Positive results only:** The function returns only the positive square root.
- **Avoid errors:** Ensure the number argument is non-negative to avoid #NUM! errors. Use IF or IFERROR to handle negative inputs:

  ```
  =IF(number>=0, SQRTPI(number), "Invalid input")
  ```

- **Related functions:**
  - Use PI to manually calculate sqrt{number$\times\pi$}:

    ```
    =SQRT(A1 * PI())
    ```

  - Use SQRT for general square root calculations.

STANDARDIZE Function

Statistical Functions

Introduction

The STANDARDIZE function returns a normalized value (z-score) based on a given mean and standard deviation. The z-score represents how many standard deviations a value is from the mean, which is useful in comparing data points from different distributions.

- **Simple explanation:** Computes the z-score of a value by normalizing it using the mean and standard deviation of the data set.
- **Common use cases:** Used in statistical analysis, hypothesis testing, and data normalization.
- **When to use this function:** Use when standardizing data to compare values across different scales.

Syntax

```
=STANDARDIZE(x, mean, standard_dev)
```

- **x**: The value to standardize.
- **mean**: The arithmetic mean of the distribution.
- **standard_dev**: The standard deviation of the distribution.

Worked Example

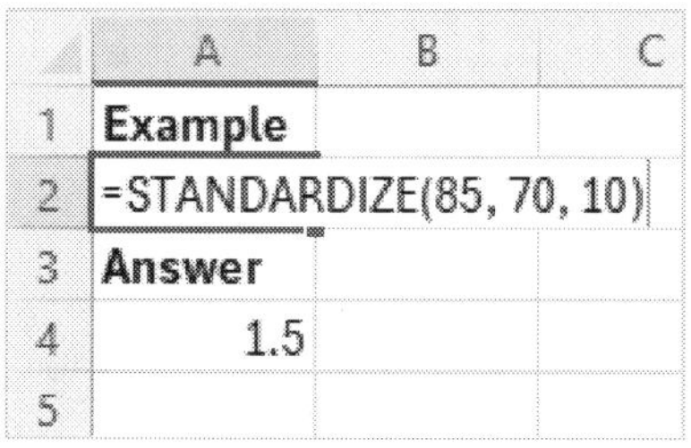

Challenge: Standardize the value 85 given a mean of 70 and a standard deviation of 10.

Inputs:

- x: 85; mean: 70; standard_dev: 10

Formula:

```
=STANDARDIZE(85, 70, 10)
```

Result: 1.5
Explanation: The z-score of 85 is 1.5, meaning the value is 1.5 standard deviations above the mean.

Explore Further with GPT

Ask GPT how to use STANDARDIZE with functions like AVERAGE, STDEV, or NORM.DIST to perform advanced statistical analysis or create standard normal distributions.

Tips for Using STANDARDIZE

- **Z-score interpretation:**
    - A positive z-score indicates the value is above the mean.
    - A negative z-score indicates the value is below the mean.
    - A z-score of 0 means the value is exactly at the mean.

STOCKHISTORY Function

Financial Functions

Introduction

The STOCKHISTORY function retrieves historical financial data, such as stock prices, for a specified time period. It provides data on open, high, low, close prices, and trading volume, making it useful for financial analysis and tracking stock performance over time.

- **Simple explanation:** Retrieves historical stock price data for a given ticker symbol and date range.
- **Common use cases:** Used in financial analysis, portfolio tracking, and investment research.
- **When to use this function:** Use when you need historical financial data for stocks, ETFs, or other securities.

Syntax

```
=STOCKHISTORY(stock, start_date, [end_date], [interval], [headers], [properties])
```

- **stock**: The ticker symbol or financial instrument (in quotes or as a reference).
- **start_date**: The start date for retrieving data.
- **[end_date]** *(optional)*: The end date for retrieving data. If omitted, only data for the start date is returned.
- **[interval]** *(optional)*: The time interval for the data:
    - 0 = Daily (default); 1 = Weekly; 2 = Monthly.
- **[headers]** *(optional)*: A logical value indicating whether to include headers (0 = No, 1 = Yes, default).
- **[properties]** *(optional)*: One or more properties to return:
    - 0 = Date (mandatory); 1 = Close (default); 2 = Open; 3 = High; 4 = Low; 5 = Volume.

Worked Example

Challenge: Retrieve daily historical data for Microsoft (MSFT) from January 1, 2023, to January 10, 2023.

Formula:

```
=STOCKHISTORY("MSFT", DATE(2023,1,1), DATE(2023,1,10))
```

Result: A a range of cells covering Jan 1st 2023 to Jan 10th 2023.

	A	B
1	**Example**	
2	=STOCKHISTORY("MSFT", DATE(2023,1,	
3	1), DATE(2023,1,10))	
4	Date	Close
5	03/01/2023	$ 239.58
6	04/01/2023	$ 229.10
7	05/01/2023	$ 222.31
8	06/01/2023	$ 224.93
9	09/01/2023	$ 227.12
10	10/01/2023	$ 228.85
11		

Explore Further with GPT

Ask GPT how to use STOCKHISTORY with other functions like AVERAGE, MAX, or LINEST.

Tips for Using STOCKHISTORY

- **Date handling:** Ensure start_date and end_date are valid Excel dates. Use the DATE function for consistency.

STDEV Function

Compatibility Functions

Introduction

The STDEV function returns the standard deviation of a data set, which measures how much the values deviate from the mean. This function is designed for sample data and helps in understanding the variability or spread of data.

- **Simple explanation:** Computes the standard deviation of a sample data set.
- **Common use cases:** Used in statistical analysis, quality control, and risk management to measure variability.
- **When to use this function:** Use when calculating the standard deviation for a sample rather than an entire population.

Syntax

```
=STDEV(number1, [number2], ...)
```

- **number1, [number2], ...**: Numeric values or ranges representing the sample data set. You can provide up to 254 arguments.

Worked Example

Challenge: Calculate the standard deviation for the data set {5, 10, 15, 20, 25}.

Formula:

```
=STDEV(A1:A5)
```

Result: 7.905694
Explanation: The function computes the sample standard deviation of the values, which measures how much the values deviate from the mean.

	A	B	C	D
1	5		**Example**	
2	10		=STDEV(A1:A5)	
3	15		**Answer**	
4	20		7.905694	
5	25			
6				

Explore Further with GPT

Ask GPT how to use STDEV with functions like AVERAGE, VAR, or STDEVP for advanced statistical analysis.

Tips for Using STDEV

- **Sample vs. population:** Use STDEV when working with a sample. For population data, use STDEVP or STDEV.P.
- **Modern equivalent:** In newer versions of Excel, STDEV is replaced by STDEV.S for sample standard deviation.
- **Handling non-numeric values:** The function ignores non-numeric values in the range.
- **Excel compatibility:** The STDEV function is available in all Excel versions but is replaced by STDEV.S in Excel 2010 and later versions.

STDEV.P Function

Statistical Functions

Introduction

The STDEV.P function calculates the standard deviation of a population, which measures how much the values in a data set deviate from the mean. Unlike STDEV.S, which is used for sample data, STDEV.P assumes the data represents the entire population.

- **Simple explanation:** Computes the standard deviation for an entire population.
- **Common use cases:** Used in statistical analysis, population-level data modeling, and quality control.
- **When to use this function:** Use when calculating the standard deviation for a complete data set rather than a sample.

Syntax

```
=STDEV.P(number1, [number2], ...)
```

- **number1, [number2], ...:** Numeric values or ranges representing the population data set. You can provide up to 254 arguments.

Worked Example

Challenge: Calculate the population standard deviation for the data set {5, 10, 15, 20, 25}.

Formula:

```
=STDEV.P(A1:A5)
```

Result: 7.071068
Explanation: The function computes the population standard deviation, which measures how much the values deviate from the mean for the entire data set.

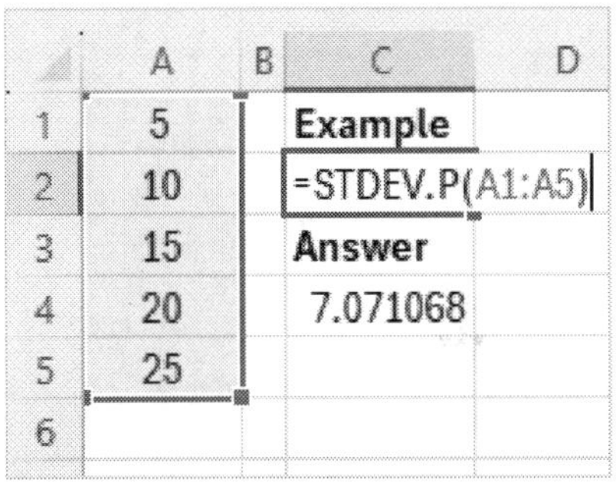

	A	B	C	D
1	5		**Example**	
2	10		=STDEV.P(A1:A5)	
3	15		**Answer**	
4	20		7.071068	
5	25			
6				

Explore Further with GPT

Ask GPT how to use STDEV.P with functions like AVERAGE, VAR.P, or MEDIAN for advanced statistical analysis.

Tips for Using STDEV.P

- **Population vs. sample:** Use STDEV.P when you have the entire population. For sample data, use STDEV.S.
- **Non-numeric values:** The function ignores non-numeric values in the range.
- **Dynamic ranges:** Combine STDEV.P with FILTER or IF to compute standard deviation for specific subsets of data:

  ```
  =STDEV.P(FILTER(A1:A10, A1:A10>10))
  ```

  This computes the population standard deviation for values greater than 10.

STDEV.S Function

Statistical Functions

Introduction

The STDEV.S function calculates the standard deviation of a sample data set, measuring how much the values deviate from the mean. It uses Bessel's correction, dividing by ***n−1*** instead of ***n***, making it appropriate for sample data analysis.

- **Simple explanation:** Computes the standard deviation for a sample data set.
- **Common use cases:** Used in statistical analysis, hypothesis testing, and data modeling when working with a sample rather than the entire population.
- **When to use this function:** Use when calculating the standard deviation for a sample of data, not the entire population.

Syntax

```
=STDEV.S(number1, [number2], ...)
```

- **number1, [number2], ...:** Numeric values or ranges representing the sample data set. You can provide up to 254 arguments.

Worked Example

Challenge: Calculate the sample standard deviation for the data set {5, 10, 15, 20, 25}

Formula:

```
=STDEV.S(A1:A5)
```

Result: 7.905694
Explanation: The function computes the sample standard deviation, which measures how much the values deviate from the mean for a sample.

	A	B	C	D
1	5		**Example**	
2	10		=STDEV.S(A1:A5)	
3	15		**Answer**	
4	20		7.905694	
5	25			
6				

Explore Further with GPT

Ask GPT how to use STDEV.S with functions like AVERAGE, VAR.S, or STDEV.P to perform advanced statistical analysis.

Tips for Using STDEV.S

- **Sample vs. population:** Use STDEV.S when working with a sample. For population data, use STDEV.P.
- **Non-numeric values:** The function ignores non-numeric values in the range.
- **Dynamic ranges:** Combine STDEV.S with FILTER or IF to compute the standard deviation for specific subsets of data:

  ```
  =STDEV.S(FILTER(A1:A10, A1:A10>10))
  ```

  This computes the sample standard deviation for values greater than 10.

STDEVA Function

Statistical Functions

Introduction

The STDEVA function calculates the standard deviation of a sample data set, considering both numeric and text values. Unlike STDEV.S, which only evaluates numeric values, STDEVA treats text and logical values differently:

- Logical values TRUE and FALSE are treated as 1 and 0, respectively.
- Text values are treated as 0.
- **Simple explanation:** Computes the standard deviation of a sample, including logical and text values as part of the data set.
- **Common use cases:** Used in statistical analysis when working with data sets that include both numbers and non-numeric data like logical values.
- **When to use this function:** Use when calculating the sample standard deviation for data sets containing both numbers and text or logical values.

Syntax

```
=STDEVA(number1, [number2], ...)
```

- **number1, [number2], ...:** Numeric values, logical values, or text representing the sample data set. You can provide up to 254 arguments.

Worked Example

Challenge: Calculate the sample standard deviation for the data set {5, 10, TRUE, "Text", FALSE}

Formula:

`=STDEVA(A1:A5)`

Result: 4.32435
Explanation:

- 5 and 10 are treated as numbers.
- TRUE is treated as 1.
- "Text" and FALSE are treated as 0.
  The function calculates the sample standard deviation for the values {5, 10, 1, 0, 0}.

	A	B	C	D
1	5		**Example**	
2	10		=STDEVA(A1:A5)	
3	TRUE		**Answer**	
4	Text		4.32435	
5	FALSE			
6				

Explore Further with GPT

Ask GPT how to use `STDEVA` with functions like `AVERAGEA`, `STDEV.S`, or `VARA` for statistical analysis

Tips for Using STDEVA

- **Handling logical values:** TRUE is counted as 1, and FALSE is counted as 0.
- **Handling text values:** All text values, including empty strings (""), are treated as 0

STDEVP Function

Compatibility Functions

Introduction

The STDEVP function calculates the standard deviation for an entire population. It measures how much the values in a population deviate from the mean. Unlike STDEV, which is used for sample data, STDEVP assumes the data set represents the entire population. In modern versions of Excel, STDEVP has been replaced by STDEV.P, but it remains available for compatibility with older Excel versions.

- **Simple explanation:** Computes the standard deviation for a complete population.
- **Common use cases:** Used in population-level statistical analysis, quality control, and financial modeling.
- **When to use this function:** Use when calculating the standard deviation for a complete data set, not a sample.

Syntax

```
=STDEVP(number1, [number2], ...)
```

- **number1, [number2], ...:** Numeric values or ranges representing the population data set. You can provide up to 254 arguments.

Worked Example

Challenge: Calculate the population standard deviation for the data set {5, 10, 15, 20, 25}.

Formula:

```
=STDEVP(A1:A5)
```

Result: 7.071068

Explanation: The function computes the population standard deviation, indicating how much the values in the population deviate from the mean

	A	B	C	D
1	5		**Example**	
2	10		=STDEVP(A1:A5)	
3	15		**Answer**	
4	20		7.071068	
5	25			
6				

Explore Further with GPT

Ask GPT how to use STDEVP with functions like AVERAGE, VARP, or MEDIAN for advanced statistical analysis.

Tips for Using STDEVP

- **Population vs. sample:** Use STDEVP when you have the entire population. For sample data, use STDEV or STDEV.S.
- **Non-numeric values:** The function ignores non-numeric values in the range.
- **Dynamic ranges:** Combine STDEVP with FILTER or IF to compute standard deviation for specific subsets of data:

  ```
  =STDEVP(FILTER(A1:A10, A1:A10>10))
  ```

  This computes the population standard deviation for values greater than 10

STDEVPA Function

Statistical Functions

Introduction

The STDEVPA function calculates the population standard deviation, including both numeric and non-numeric values in the data set. Unlike STDEV.P, which only evaluates numeric values, STDEVPA treats logical and text values differently:

- Logical values TRUE and FALSE are treated as 1 and 0, respectively.
- Text values are treated as 0.
- **Simple explanation:** Computes the population standard deviation, including logical and text values as part of the data set.
- **Common use cases:** Used in statistical analysis when working with complete data sets containing both numbers and non-numeric data like logical values.
- **When to use this function:** Use when calculating the population standard deviation for a complete data set that includes both numbers and non-numeric values.

Syntax

```
=STDEVPA(number1, [number2], ...)
```

- **number1, [number2], ...**: Numeric values, logical values, or text representing the population data set. You can provide up to 254 arguments.

Worked Example

Challenge: Calculate the population standard deviation for the data set {5, 10, TRUE, "Text", FALSE}

Formula:

`=STDEVPA(A1:A5)`

Result: 3.867816

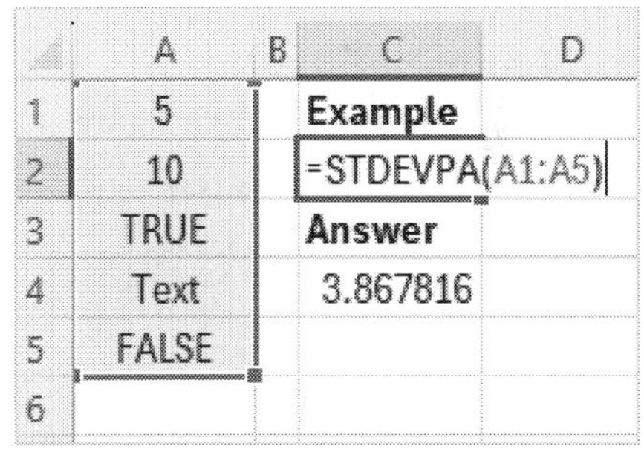

	A	B	C	D
1	5		**Example**	
2	10		=STDEVPA(A1:A5)	
3	TRUE		**Answer**	
4	Text		3.867816	
5	FALSE			
6				

Explanation: 5 and 10 are treated as numbers, TRUE is treated as 1, "Text" and FALSE are treated as 0. The function calculates the population standard deviation for the values {5, 10, 1, 0, 0}

Explore Further with GPT

Ask GPT how to use STDEVPA with functions like VAR.PA, AVERAGEA, or COUNTIF for advanced population-level statistical analysis

Tips for Using STDEVPA

- **Handling logical values:** TRUE is counted as 1, and FALSE is counted as 0.
- **Handling text values:** All text values, including empty strings (""), are treated as 0.

STEYX Function

Statistical Functions

Introduction

The STEYX function returns the standard error of the predicted y-value for each x in a linear regression. The standard error is a measure of the accuracy of predictions made by a regression line. A smaller value indicates a more accurate prediction.

- **Simple explanation:** Computes the standard error of the predicted y-values based on a linear regression.
- **Common use cases:** Used in statistical analysis, predictive modeling, and hypothesis testing to evaluate the precision of a regression model.
- **When to use this function:** Use when assessing the reliability of predictions made by a linear regression model.

Syntax

```
=STEYX(known_y's, known_x's)
```

- **known_y's**: The dependent data set (y-values).
- **known_x's**: The independent data set (x-values).

Worked Example

Challenge: Calculate the standard error for a data set.

Formula:

```
=STEYX(B2:B6, A2:A6)
```

Result: 0.894427

Explanation: The function computes the standard error of the predicted y-values for each x-value in the given data set.

	A	B	C	D	E
1	X (known_x's)	Y (known_y's)		Example	
2	1	2		=STEYX(B2:B6, A2:A6)	
3	2	4		Answer	
4	3	5		0.894427	
5	4	4			
6	5	5			
7					

Explore Further with GPT

Ask GPT how to combine STEYX with functions like LINEST, SLOPE, or INTERCEPT to create more comprehensive regression models.

Tips for Using STEYX

- **Equal-sized arrays:** Ensure that known_y's and known_x's have the same number of data points; otherwise, the function returns a #N/A error.
- **Interpreting the result:**
  - A smaller standard error indicates that the regression line is a better fit for the data.
  - A larger standard error suggests greater variability and less reliable predictions.

SUBSTITUTE Function

Text Functions

Introduction

The SUBSTITUTE function replaces occurrences of a specific text string within another text string. Unlike REPLACE, which works based on position, SUBSTITUTE works by identifying exact text matches and replacing them.

- **Simple explanation:** Replaces specific occurrences of a text string within another text string.
- **Common use cases:** Used for text cleanup, data transformation, and replacing specific substrings.
- **When to use this function:** Use when you need to replace specific text within a string based on its content rather than position.

Syntax

```
=SUBSTITUTE(text, old_text, new_text, [instance_num])
```

- **text**: The original text string.
- **old_text**: The text to be replaced.
- **new_text**: The text to replace old_text with.
- **[instance_num]** *(optional)*: Specifies which occurrence of old_text to replace. If omitted, all occurrences are replaced.

Worked Example

Challenge: Replace all instances of "apple" with "orange" in the text "I like apple pie and apple juice."

Formula:

```
=SUBSTITUTE("I like apple pie and apple juice",
"apple", "orange")
```

Result: I like orange pie and orange juice
Explanation: The function replaces every occurrence of "apple" with "orange."

	A	B
1	**Example**	
2	=SUBSTITUTE("I like apple pie and apple juice", "apple", "orange")	
3	**Answer**	
4	I like orange pie and orange juice	
5		

Explore Further with GPT

Ask GPT how to use SUBSTITUTE with functions like TRIM, LEN, or TEXT for text manipulation and data cleansing.

Tips for Using SUBSTITUTE

- **Case sensitivity:** The function is case-sensitive. To perform a case-insensitive replacement, combine with LOWER or UPPER.
- **Dynamic replacement:** Use cell references for dynamic text replacement:

  ```
  =SUBSTITUTE(A1, B1, C1)
  ```

  This replaces occurrences of the text in B1 with the text in C1 in the string from A1

SUBTOTAL Function

Math & Trigonometry Functions

Introduction

The SUBTOTAL function returns a subtotal in a list or database. It provides various aggregation operations, such as sum, average, count, and more. Unlike regular functions, SUBTOTAL can exclude manually hidden rows or filtered-out rows, making it ideal for working with filtered data.

- **Simple explanation:** Computes a specified aggregation (e.g., sum, average, count) on a list while optionally ignoring hidden or filtered rows.
- **Common use cases:** Used in summarizing data in filtered lists, creating dynamic reports, and calculating totals in structured data.
- **When to use this function:** Use when you need a subtotal or aggregate value that adapts to filtering or hiding rows.

Syntax

```
=SUBTOTAL(function_num, ref1, [ref2], ...)
```

- **function_num**: A number specifying the type of subtotal to calculate.
- **ref1, [ref2], ...**: One or more ranges to aggregate.

Function Numbers for SUBTOTAL:

- ***[function_num {includes hidden rows}.function_num {ignores hidden rows}, Associated Function]***
- [1, 101, AVERAGE] ; [2, 102, COUNT] ; [3, 103, COUNTA] ; [4, 104,MAX] ; [5, 105, MIN] ; [6, 106, PRODUCT] ; [7, 107, STDEV] ; [8, 108, STDEVP] ; [9, 109, SUM] ; [10, 110, VAR] ; [11, 111, VARP]

Worked Example

Challenge: Calculate the sum of the range {10, 20, 30, 40, 50} while ignoring manually hidden rows.

Formula:

```
=SUBTOTAL(109, A1:A5)
```

Result: 150
Explanation: The function calculates the sum of the range while ignoring any hidden rows, using 109 as the function number for SUM with hidden rows excluded.

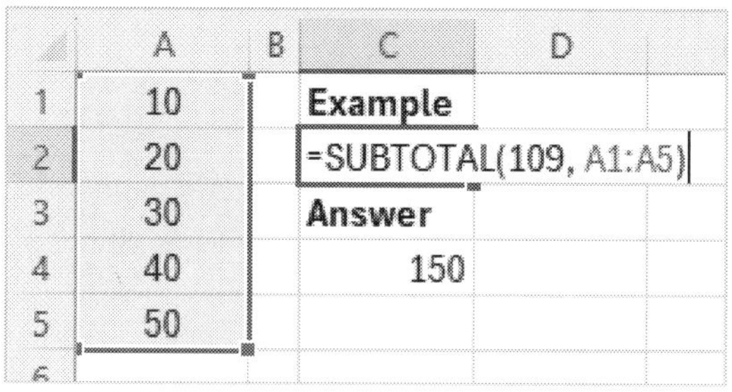

Tips for Using SUBTOTAL

- **Dynamic recalculation:** The result updates automatically when rows are hidden or filtered.
- **Combining with other functions:** Use SUBTOTAL with functions like FILTER or INDEX to create more dynamic reports:

  ```
  =SUBTOTAL(109, FILTER(A1:A10, B1:B10="Category"))
  ```

  This calculates the sum of values in A1:A10 for rows where B1:B10 equals "Category".

SUM Function

Math & Trigonometry Functions

Introduction

The SUM function adds all the numbers provided as arguments. It is one of the most commonly used functions in Excel for performing basic arithmetic operations on a range or list of values.

- **Simple explanation:** Computes the total sum of a range or list of numbers.
- **Common use cases:** Used in financial analysis, data aggregation, and reporting to calculate totals.
- **When to use this function:** Use when you need to sum a range of values or specific numbers.

Syntax

```
=SUM(number1, [number2], ...)
```

- **number1, [number2], ...**: Numeric values, cell references, or ranges to sum. You can provide up to 254 arguments.

Worked Example

Challenge: Calculate the sum of the numbers {10, 20, 30, 40, 50}

Formula:

```
=SUM(A1:A5)
```

Result: 150
Explanation: The function adds all the values in the range A1:A5 to return a total of 150.

	A	B	C
1	10		**Example**
2	20		=SUM(A1:A5)
3	30		**Answer**
4	40		150
5	50		
6			

Explore Further with GPT

Ask GPT how to combine SUM with functions like IF, SUBTOTAL, or FILTER for advanced dynamic calculations.

Tips for Using SUM

- **Ignoring non-numeric values:** The function ignores non-numeric values (e.g., text) in the specified range.
- **Dynamic ranges:** Combine with FILTER to sum only specific values:

  ```
  =SUM(FILTER(A1:A10, B1:B10="Category"))
  ```

  This sums values in A1:A10 where B1:B10 equals "Category".
- **Alternative functions:** Use SUMIF or SUMIFS for conditional summing.
- **Excel compatibility:** The SUM function is available in all modern Excel versions

SUMIF Function

Math & Trigonometry Functions

Introduction

The SUMIF function adds the values in a range that meet a specified condition. It allows conditional summing based on a single criterion, making it ideal for data analysis and reporting.

- **Simple explanation:** Adds values that meet a specific condition.
- **Common use cases:** Used in financial analysis, data filtering, and conditional summing based on criteria such as numbers, text, or dates.
- **When to use this function:** Use when you need to sum a range based on a single condition.

Syntax

```
=SUMIF(range, criteria, [sum_range])
```

- **range**: The range of cells to evaluate against the condition (criteria).
- **criteria**: The condition to apply (e.g., ">=10", "Apple", B1).
- **[sum_range]** *(optional)*: The range of cells to sum. If omitted, range is used for both evaluating the condition and summing.

Worked Example

Challenge: Sum the sales amounts where the corresponding product is "Apple."

Formula:

```
=SUMIF(A2:A5, "Apple", B2:B5)
```

Result: 300
Explanation: The function sums the values in B2:B5 where the corresponding cells in A2:A5 are "Apple."

	A	B	C	D	E	F
1	**Product**	**Sales**		**Example**		
2	Apple	100		=SUMIF(A2:A5, "Apple", B2:B5)		
3	Banana	150		**Answer**		
4	Apple	200		300		
5	Orange	120				
6						

Explore Further with GPT

Ask GPT how to combine SUMIF with functions like AVERAGEIF, COUNTIF, or FILTER for advanced conditional calculations.

Tips for Using SUMIF

- **Logical operators:** You can use logical operators such as >, <, =, <>, combined with numbers or cell references:

  ```
  =SUMIF(B1:B10, ">=50")
  ```

- **Wildcard support:** Use * to match any number of characters and ? to match a single character:

  ```
  =SUMIF(A1:A10, "App*")
  ```

SUMIFS Function

Math & Trigonometry Functions

Introduction

The SUMIFS function adds the values in a range that meet multiple criteria. It allows for conditional summing based on several conditions, making it more versatile than SUMIF.

- **Simple explanation:** Adds values that meet multiple conditions.
- **Common use cases:** Used in financial modeling, multi-criteria data analysis, and dynamic reporting where multiple conditions need to be applied.
- **When to use this function:** Use when you need to sum a range based on multiple criteria.

Syntax

```
=SUMIFS(sum_range, criteria_range1, criteria1, [criteria_range2], [criteria2], ...)
```

- **sum_range**: The range of cells to sum.
- **criteria_range1**: The range to evaluate against the first condition.
- **criteria1**: The condition to apply to criteria_range1.
- **[criteria_range2], [criteria2], ...** *(optional)*: Additional ranges and their corresponding conditions

Worked Example

Challenge: Sum the sales amounts where the product is "Apple" and the region is "North."

Formula:

```
=SUMIFS(C2:C5, A2:A5, "Apple", B2:B5, "North")
```

Result: 220

Explanation: The function sums the values in C2:C5 where the corresponding cells in A2:A5 are "Apple" and in B2:B5 are "North".

	A	B	C	D	E
1	**Product**	**Region**	**Sales**		**Example**
2	Apple	North	100		=SUMIFS(C2:C5,
3	Banana	North	150		A2:A5, "Apple",
4	Apple	South	200		B2:B5, "North")
5	Apple	North	120		**Answer**
6					220
7					

Explore Further with GPT

Ask GPT how to combine SUMIFS with functions like AVERAGEIFS, COUNTIFS, or FILTER for advanced data analysis.

Tips for Using SUMIFS

- **Text criteria:** Use quotes when specifying text criteria:

  ```
  =SUMIFS(A1:A10, B1:B10, "Apple")
  ```

- **Logical operators:** Use logical operators (>, <, =, <>) for numeric criteria:

  ```
  =SUMIFS(A1:A10, B1:B10, ">=50")
  ```

  This sums values where the corresponding cells are greater than or equal to 50.

SUMPRODUCT Function

Math & Trigonometry Functions

Introduction

The SUMPRODUCT function multiplies corresponding elements in one or more arrays and returns the sum of those products. It is commonly used for weighted averages, conditional summing, and complex data analysis without the need for helper columns.

- **Simple explanation:** Multiplies elements in arrays and returns the sum of the resulting products.
- **Common use cases:** Used for calculating weighted averages, conditional sums, and combining multiple criteria in financial and statistical analysis.
- **When to use this function:** Use when you need to multiply and sum arrays or ranges in a single step.

Syntax

```
=SUMPRODUCT(array1, [array2], ...)
```

- **array1, [array2], ...**: Arrays or ranges to multiply and sum. All arrays must have the same dimensions.

Worked Example

Challenge: Calculate the total revenue from products sold, where the quantities and unit prices are provided.

Formula:

```
=SUMPRODUCT(A2:A4, B2:B4)
```

Result: 230
Explanation: The function multiplies each pair of corresponding elements (5*10, 8*15, 3*20) and sums the products (50 + 120 + 60 = 230).

Explore Further with GPT

Ask GPT how to use SUMPRODUCT with functions like IF, ABS, or INDEX to create advanced dynamic reports.

Tips for Using SUMPRODUCT

- **Handling conditions:** Use logical expressions inside SUMPRODUCT to apply conditions dynamically:

  ```
  =SUMPRODUCT((B1:B10="Category")*A1:A10)
  ```

  This sums values in A1:A10 where the corresponding cells in B1:B10 are equal to "Category".
- **Boolean logic:** When using conditions, Excel treats TRUE as 1 and FALSE as 0.
- **Array dimensions:** Ensure all arrays have the same dimensions; otherwise, the function returns a #VALUE! error.

SUMSQ Function

Math & Trigonometry Functions

Introduction

The SUMSQ function returns the sum of the squares of the provided arguments. It squares each number and sums the results, making it useful for statistical analysis, such as calculating variance and standard deviation.

- **Simple explanation:** Computes the sum of the squares of numbers.
- **Common use cases:** Used in statistical calculations, regression analysis, and error minimization problems.
- **When to use this function:** Use when you need to sum the squares of numbers or ranges.

Syntax

```
=SUMSQ(number1, [number2], ...)
```

- **number1, [number2], ...:** Numeric values or ranges to be squared and summed. You can provide up to 254 arguments.

Worked Example

Challenge: Calculate the sum of the squares of the numbers {3, 4, 5}

Formula:

```
=SUMSQ(A1:A3)
```

Result: 50

Explanation: The function computes $3^2+4^2+5^2 = 9+16+25=50$.

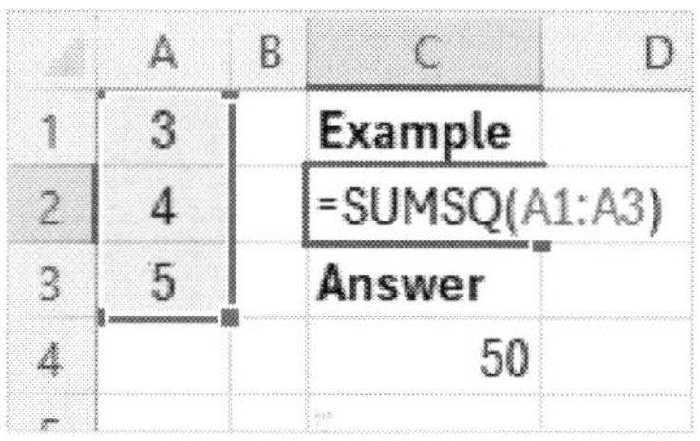

Explore Further with GPT

Ask GPT how to combine SUMSQ with functions like AVERAGE, STDEV, or SQRT for advanced statistical calculations.

Tips for Using SUMSQ

- **Handling ranges and arrays:** The function can handle a combination of individual numbers, ranges, and arrays:

  ```
  =SUMSQ(A1:A10, B1:B10, 5)
  ```

  This sums the squares of all values in A1:A10 and B1:B10, plus 5^2.

- **Non-numeric values:** The function ignores non-numeric values in ranges.

SUMX2MY2 Function

Math & Trigonometry Functions

Introduction

The SUMX2MY2 function returns the sum of the difference of squares of corresponding values in two arrays. It squares each value in the arrays, subtracts the second array's squared value from the first array's squared value for each pair, and sums the results.

- **Simple explanation:** Computes the sum of the differences of squares of corresponding elements in two arrays.
- **Common use cases:** Used in statistical analysis and mathematical modeling, especially when working with quadratic relationships.
- **When to use this function:** Use when you need to calculate the sum of the differences of squared values in two data sets.

Syntax

```
=SUMX2MY2(array_x, array_y)
```

- **array_x**: The first array or range of numeric values.
- **array_y**: The second array or range of numeric values. Both arrays must have the same dimensions.

Worked Example

Challenge: Calculate the sum of the difference of squares for the arrays {3, 4, 5} and {1, 2, 3}

Formula:

```
=SUMX2MY2(A1:A3, B1:B3)
```

Result: 36

Explanation: The function computes:

$(3^2-1^2)+(4^2-2^2)+(5^2-3^2) = (9-1)+(16-4)+(25-9)=8+12+16 = 36$

	A	B	C	D	E	F
1	3	1		Example		
2	4	2		=SUMX2MY2(A1:A3, B1:B3)		
3	5	3		Answer		
4				36		

Explore Further with GPT

Ask GPT how to use SUMX2MY2 with functions like SUMX2PY2, SUMXMY2, or SUMPRODUCT for advanced mathematical and statistical analysis.

Tips for Using SUMX2MY2

- **Equal-sized arrays:** Ensure that array_x and array_y have the same number of elements; otherwise, the function returns a #VALUE! error.
- **Non-numeric values:** The function ignores non-numeric values in the arrays.
- **Dynamic arrays:** Combine SUMX2MY2 with FILTER or INDEX to calculate results for specific subsets of data:

  ```
  =SUMX2MY2(FILTER(A1:A10, B1:B10>0), FILTER(C1:C10, B1:B10>0))
  ```

  This computes the sum of the difference of squares for positive values in B1:B10.

SUMX2PY2 Function

Math & Trigonometry Functions

Introduction

The SUMX2PY2 function returns the sum of the sum of squares of corresponding values in two arrays. It squares each value in both arrays, adds the squares for each pair of corresponding elements, and then sums the results.

- **Simple explanation:** Computes the sum of the sums of squares of corresponding elements in two arrays.
- **Common use cases:** Used in statistical analysis, vector calculations, and mathematical modeling involving quadratic relationships.
- **When to use this function:** Use when you need to calculate the sum of the sums of squares for corresponding values in two data sets.

Syntax

```
=SUMX2PY2(array_x, array_y)
```

- **array_x:** The first array or range of numeric values.
- **array_y:** The second array or range of numeric values. Both arrays must have the same dimensions.

Worked Example

Challenge: Calculate the sum of the sums of squares for the arrays {3, 4, 5} and {1, 2, 3}

Formula:

```
=SUMX2PY2(A1:A3, B1:B3)
```

Result: 64
Explanation: The function computes:

$(3^2+1^2)+(4^2+2^2)+(5^2+3^2) = (9+1)+(16+4)+(25+9) = 10+20+40=64$

Explore Further with GPT

Ask GPT how to use SUMX2PY2 with functions like SUMX2MY2, SUMPRODUCT, or SUMSQ to solve advanced mathematical problems and perform vector operations.

Tips for Using SUMX2PY2

- **Equal-sized arrays:** Ensure that array_x and array_y have the same number of elements; otherwise, the function returns a #VALUE! error.
- **Dynamic arrays:** Use FILTER or INDEX with SUMX2PY2 to compute sums for specific subsets of data:

  ```
  =SUMX2PY2(FILTER(A1:A10, B1:B10>0), FILTER(C1:C10, B1:B10>0))
  ```

  This computes the sum of the sums of squares only for rows where B1:B10 contains positive values.

SUMXMY2 Function

Math & Trigonometry Functions

Introduction

The SUMXMY2 function returns the sum of the squares of the differences between corresponding values in two arrays. It subtracts the second array's values from the first array's values for each pair, squares the differences, and sums the results.

- **Simple explanation:** Computes the sum of the squares of differences between corresponding elements in two arrays.
- **Common use cases:** Used in statistical analysis, regression models, and error measurement, such as calculating the sum of squared errors (SSE).
- **When to use this function:** Use when you need to measure the squared differences between two data sets.

Syntax

```
=SUMXMY2(array_x, array_y)
```

- **array_x**: The first array or range of numeric values.
- **array_y**: The second array or range of numeric values. Both arrays must have the same dimensions.

Worked Example

Challenge: Calculate the sum of the squares of differences for the arrays {3, 4, 5} and {1, 2, 3}

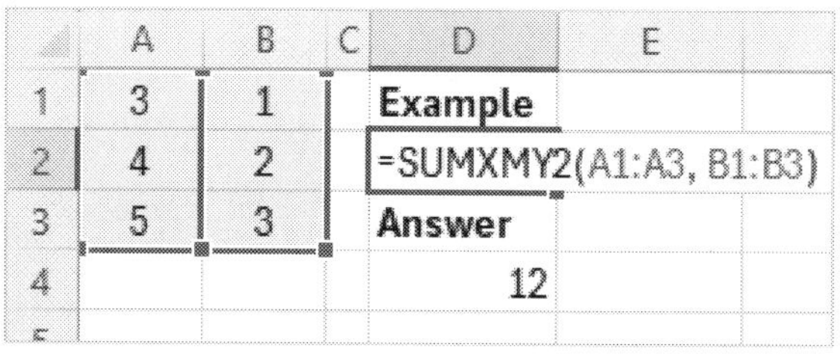

Formula:

```
=SUMXMY2(A1:A3, B1:B3)
```

Result: 12
Explanation: The function computes:

$(3-1)^2+(4-2)^2+(5-3)^2 = 2^2+2^2+2^2=4+4+4=12$

Explore Further with GPT

Ask GPT how to combine SUMXMY2 with functions like LINEST, SLOPE, or RSQ for advanced regression and error analysis.

Tips for Using SUMXMY2

- **Equal-sized arrays:** Ensure that array_x and array_y have the same number of elements; otherwise, the function returns a #VALUE! error.
- **Non-numeric values:** The function ignores non-numeric values in the arrays.
- **Dynamic arrays:** Combine SUMXMY2 with FILTER to calculate the sum of squared differences for specific subsets of data:

  ```
  =SUMXMY2(FILTER(A1:A10, B1:B10>0), FILTER(C1:C10, B1:B10>0))
  ```

  This computes the sum of squared differences only for positive values in B1:B10.

SWITCH Function

Logical Functions

Introduction

The SWITCH function evaluates an expression against a list of values and returns the corresponding result for the first matching value. If no match is found, it returns an optional default value. It simplifies nested IF statements by allowing multiple conditions to be handled more cleanly.

- **Simple explanation:** Returns a value based on matching an expression with a list of possible values.
- **Common use cases:** Used for creating decision trees, mapping inputs to specific outputs, and simplifying complex nested IF statements.
- **When to use this function:** Use when you need to evaluate an expression against multiple possible values and return corresponding results.

Syntax

```
=SWITCH(expression, value1, result1, [value2, result2], ..., [default])
```

- **expression**: The value or expression to evaluate.
- **value1, result1, [value2, result2], ...**: Pairs of values and corresponding results.
- **[default]** *(optional)*: The value to return if no match is found.

Worked Example

Challenge: Map a numeric grade to a letter grade using a given scale.

Formula:

```
=SWITCH(TRUE, A1>=90, "A", A1>=80,
"B", A1>=70, "C", A1>=60, "D",
"F")
```

	A	B	C	D	E
1	85	Grade	Letter		Example
2		90	A		=SWITCH(TRUE, A1>=90, "A",
3		80	B		A1>=80, "B", A1>=70, "C", A1>=
4		70	C		60, "D", "F")
5		60	D		Answer
6		Below 60	F		B
7					

Result: If A1 = 85, the result is B.

Explanation: The function checks the conditions in order, and since A1 = 85 satisfies A1>=80, it returns B.

Explore Further with GPT

Ask GPT how to use SWITCH with other functions like CHOOSE, IF, or VLOOKUP to create dynamic decision-making models.

Tips for Using SWITCH

- **Order matters:** The function checks the values in order, returning the result for the first match it finds.
- **Default value:** Always include a default value to handle cases where no match is found:

```
=SWITCH(A1, 1, "Yes", 0, "No", "Unknown")
```

SYD Function

Financial Functions

Introduction

The SYD function calculates the sum-of-years' digits depreciation of an asset for a specified period. This method accelerates depreciation, meaning more depreciation is recognized in earlier periods of the asset's useful life.

- **Simple explanation:** Computes depreciation using the sum-of-years' digits method, which depreciates an asset faster in the early years.
- **Common use cases:** Used in accounting and financial modeling to calculate accelerated depreciation for assets.
- **When to use this function:** Use when you need to apply the sum-of-years' digits method to calculate depreciation.

Syntax

```
=SYD(cost, salvage, life, per)
```

- **cost**: The initial cost of the asset.
- **salvage**: The value of the asset at the end of its useful life (salvage value).
- **life**: The total useful life of the asset (in periods).
- **per**: The period for which to calculate depreciation (must be between 1 and life).

Worked Example

Challenge: Calculate the depreciation for an asset with an initial cost of $10,000, a salvage value of $2,000, a useful life of 5 years, and for the second year.

Inputs:

- cost: 10000; salvage: 2000; life: 5; per: 2

Formula:

```
=SYD(10000, 2000, 5, 2)
```

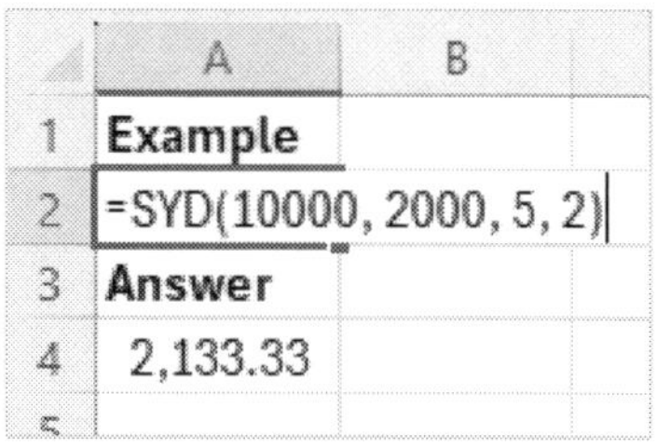

Result: 2133.33

Explanation: The function calculates the depreciation for the second year using the sum-of-years' digits method. The total depreciation for the 5-year life is spread more heavily over the earlier years

Explore Further with GPT

Ask GPT how to compare the SYD method with other depreciation methods, such as SLN (straight-line) and DB (declining balance), for financial modeling.

Tips for Using SYD

- **Accelerated depreciation:** The sum-of-years' digits method results in higher depreciation in the earlier periods and lower depreciation in the later periods.

T Function

Text Functions

Introduction

The T function returns the text of a given value. If the value is text, it returns the text itself. If the value is anything other than text (e.g., a number, date, or logical value), it returns an empty string (""). This function is useful when ensuring that only text values are returned in formulas.

- **Simple explanation:** Returns the text of a value or an empty string if the value is not text.
- **Common use cases:** Used in data cleaning, conditional formatting, and formulas that require only text values.
- **When to use this function:** Use when you want to extract or ensure text values in a formula or cell reference.

Syntax

```
=T(value)
```

- **value**: The value or cell reference to check. It can be text, a number, a logical value, or an error.

Worked Example

Challenge: Return the text from various data types.

Result: Text values are returned; non-text values are not.

Explanation: The T function returns the text from A2, while it returns an empty string for numeric, logical, or error values in other cells.

	A	B	C	D
1	**Input**	**Output**		**Example**
2	Hello	Hello		=T(A2)
3	123			**Answer**
4	TRUE			Hello
5	#DIV/0!	#DIV/0!		
6				

Explore Further with GPT

Ask GPT how to use T in combination with functions like IF, ISTEXT, or CONCAT for advanced text manipulation.

Tips for Using T

- **Handling non-text values:** The function returns an empty string for numbers, logical values, and errors.
- **Use with text-specific functions:** Combine with TEXT, CONCAT, or TRIM to clean or format text-based data.
- **Error handling:** Since T handles errors by returning an empty string, it can help in cleaning up error-prone data without additional error-handling functions.
- **Excel compatibility:** The T function is available in all modern Excel versions.

TAN Function

Math & Trigonometry Functions

Introduction

The TAN function returns the tangent of an angle specified in radians. The tangent of an angle is defined as the ratio of the sine to the cosine of that angle. It is commonly used in trigonometry and geometry.

- **Simple explanation:** Computes the tangent of a given angle in radians.
- **Common use cases:** Used in trigonometry, geometry, engineering, and wave analysis to solve problems involving right triangles or periodic functions.
- **When to use this function:** Use when solving problems that require the tangent of an angle in radians.

Syntax

```
=TAN(number)
```

- **number**: The angle in radians for which to calculate the tangent.

Worked Example

Challenge: Calculate the tangent of π/4 radians.

Formula:

```
=TAN(PI()/4)
```

Result: 1

Explanation: The tangent of π/4 radians is 1 because tan(π/4) = sin(π/4) / cos(π/4) = 1 .

	A
1	**Example**
2	=TAN(PI()/4)
3	**Answer**
4	1
5	

Explore Further with GPT

Ask GPT how to combine TAN with functions like SIN, COS, or ATAN to solve advanced trigonometric problems.

Tips for Using TAN

- **Radians input:** Ensure the input is in radians. Use the RADIANS function to convert degrees to radians if necessary:

  ```
  =TAN(RADIANS(30))
  ```

  This calculates the tangent of 30 degrees.
- **Periodicity:** The tangent function is periodic with a period of π, meaning tan(x+nπ)=tan(x) for any integer n.
- **Undefined values:** The function returns a #DIV/0! error if the angle is an odd multiple of π/2 (90°, 270°, etc.), where the cosine of the angle is zero.

TANH Function

Introduction

The TANH function returns the hyperbolic tangent of a number. The hyperbolic tangent is defined as tanh(x) = sinh(x)/cosh(x) = ($e^x - e^{-x}/e^x + e^{-x}$). It is commonly used in mathematical modeling, neural networks, and signal processing.

- **Simple explanation:** Computes the hyperbolic tangent of a number.
- **Common use cases:** Used in advanced mathematics, physics, and engineering, especially in solving differential equations and in neural network activation functions.
- **When to use this function:** Use when working with hyperbolic functions or in models requiring hyperbolic transformations.

Syntax

```
=TANH(number)
```

- **number**: The real number for which to calculate the hyperbolic tangent.

Worked Example

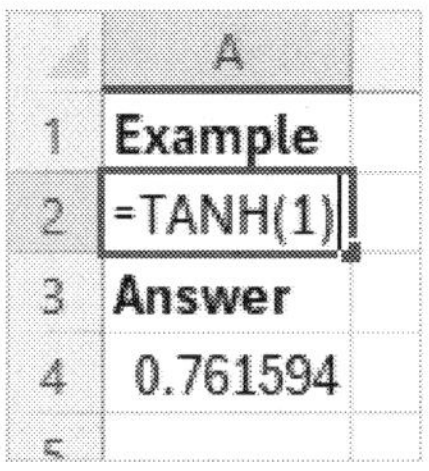

	A
1	Example
2	=TANH(1)
3	Answer
4	0.761594

Challenge: Calculate the hyperbolic tangent of 1.

Formula:

```
=TANH(1)
```

Result: 0.761594

Explanation: The function computes the hyperbolic tangent of 1 using the formula $(e^1 - e^{-1})/(e^1 + e^{-1}) \approx 0.761594$.

Explore Further with GPT

Ask GPT how to combine TANH with other hyperbolic functions like SINH, COSH, or EXP for advanced mathematical solutions.

Tips for Using TANH

- **Range of results:** The result of TANH is always between -1 and 1.
- **Symmetry:** The hyperbolic tangent is an odd function, meaning tanh(−x) = −tanh(x)

TAKE Function

Lookup & Reference Functions

Introduction

The TAKE function returns a specified number of rows or columns from the start or end of an array. It is useful for extracting subsets of data without manually selecting ranges.

- **Simple explanation:** Extracts a specific number of rows or columns from an array.
- **Common use cases:** Used in dynamic table creation, extracting subsets of data, and simplifying range manipulation in large datasets.
- **When to use this function:** Use when you need to dynamically extract a fixed number of rows or columns from a data set.

Syntax

```
=TAKE(array, [rows], [columns])
```

- **array**: The array or range from which to extract data.
- **[rows]** *(optional)*: The number of rows to return. A positive number extracts rows from the top, while a negative number extracts rows from the bottom.
- **[columns]** *(optional)*: The number of columns to return. A positive number extracts columns from the left, while a negative number extracts columns from the right.

Worked Example

Challenge: Extract the first 3 rows from a data set.

Formula:

`=TAKE(A1:B5, 3)`

Result: 1 10, 2 20, 3 30

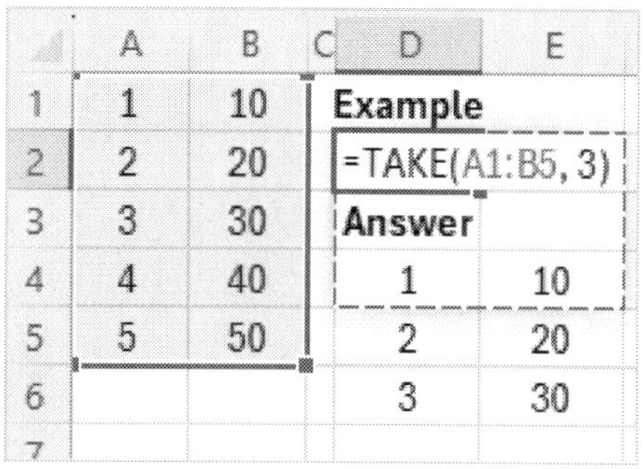

Explanation: The function extracts the first 3 rows from the range A1:B5.

Explore Further with GPT

Ask GPT how to combine TAKE with functions like DROP, FILTER, or SORT to build advanced dynamic data manipulation tools.

Tips for Using TAKE

- **Omitting rows or columns:** You can omit either the rows or columns argument to extract only in one dimension.
- **Negative values:** Use negative values to extract from the end of the array instead of the start.
- **Dynamic extraction:** Combine TAKE with SEQUENCE or INDEX to extract dynamically changing subsets:

  `=TAKE(SORT(A1:B10, 2, -1), 5)`

  This extracts the top 5 rows after sorting by the second column in descending order.

TBILLEQ Function

Financial Functions

Introduction

The TBILLEQ function returns the bond-equivalent yield for a Treasury bill. It converts the discount rate of a Treasury bill into an annualized bond-equivalent yield, allowing comparisons with other interest-bearing investments.

- **Simple explanation:** Converts the discount rate of a Treasury bill into an annualized yield for comparison with bonds.
- **Common use cases:** Used in financial analysis, investment evaluation, and comparing short-term Treasury bills with longer-term bonds.
- **When to use this function:** Use when you need to evaluate the equivalent yield of a Treasury bill relative to other fixed-income securities.

Syntax

```
=TBILLEQ(settlement, maturity, discount)
```

- **settlement**: The settlement date of the Treasury bill (the date when the bill is purchased).
- **maturity**: The maturity date of the Treasury bill (the date when the bill matures).
- **discount**: The discount rate of the Treasury bill (expressed as a decimal or percentage).

Worked Example

Challenge: Calculate the bond-equivalent yield for a Treasury bill with a settlement date of January 1, 2024, a maturity date of April 1, 2024, and a discount rate of 5%.

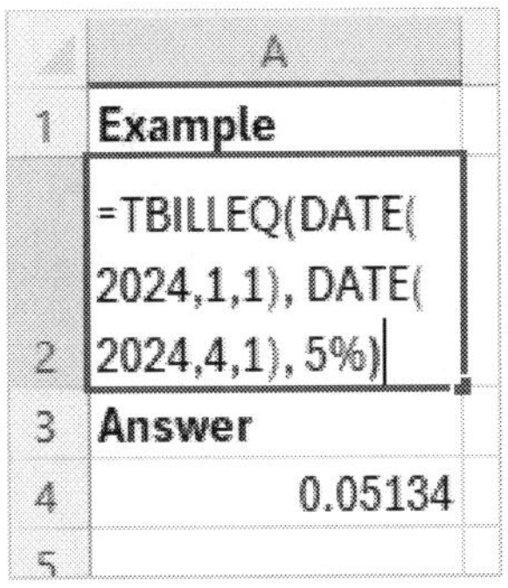

Inputs:

- settlement: 01-Jan-2024; maturity: 01-Apr-2024; discount: 5%

Formula:

```
=TBILLEQ(DATE(2024,1,1), DATE(2024,4,1), 5%)
```

Result: 0.05134 (or 5.134%)
Explanation: The function computes the bond-equivalent yield for the given Treasury bill.

Explore Further with GPT

Ask GPT how to compare TBILLEQ with other yield functions like TBILLPRICE, TBILLYIELD, or YIELD for advanced fixed-income analysis.

Tips for Using TBILLEQ

- **Date handling:** Ensure valid Excel dates. Use the DATE function to input dates explicitly:

  ```
  =TBILLEQ(DATE(2024,1,1), DATE(2024,4,1), 5%)
  ```

- **Discount rate:** Enter the discount as a decimal (e.g., 0.05) or a percentage (e.g., 5%).

TBILLPRICE Function

Financial Functions

Introduction

The TBILLPRICE function returns the price per $100 face value of a Treasury bill based on its settlement date, maturity date, and discount rate. This function is useful for determining how much an investor would pay for a Treasury bill at a given discount rate.

- **Simple explanation:** Computes the price per $100 face value of a Treasury bill based on its discount rate and time to maturity.
- **Common use cases:** Used in bond pricing, fixed-income investment analysis, and Treasury bill valuation.
- **When to use this function:** Use when calculating the purchase price of a Treasury bill given its discount rate and maturity.

Syntax

```
=TBILLPRICE(settlement, maturity, discount)
```

- **settlement**: The settlement date of the Treasury bill (the date when the bill is purchased).
- **maturity**: The maturity date of the Treasury bill (the date when the bill matures).
- **discount**: The discount rate of the Treasury bill (expressed as a decimal or percentage).

Worked Example

Challenge: Calculate the price of a Treasury bill with a settlement date of January 1, 2024, a maturity date of April 1, 2024, and a discount rate of 5%.

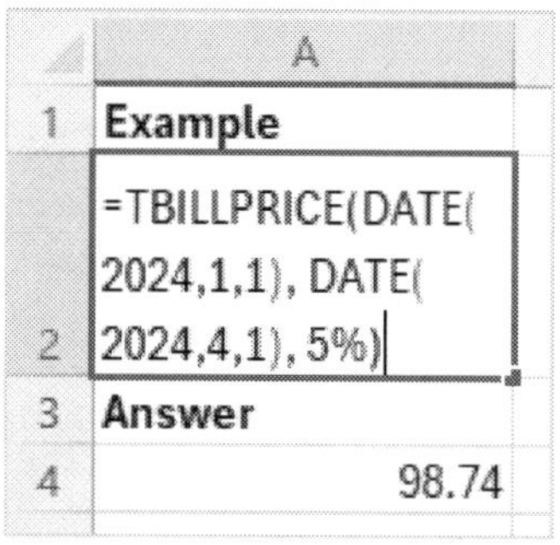

Inputs:

- settlement: 01-Jan-2024; maturity: 01-Apr-2024; discount: 5%

Formula:

```
=TBILLPRICE(DATE(2024,1,1), DATE(2024,4,1), 5%)
```

Result: 98.74
Explanation: The function returns 98.74, meaning the price per $100 face value is $98.74. This reflects the discount rate applied over the time to maturity

Explore Further with GPT

Ask GPT how to use TBILLPRICE alongside other functions like TBILLYIELD, TBILLEQ, or YIELD for comprehensive fixed-income analysis.

Tips for Using TBILLPRICE

- **Date handling:** Ensure that settlement and maturity are valid Excel dates. Use the DATE function to input dates explicitly:

  ```
  =TBILLPRICE(DATE(2024,1,1), DATE(2024,4,1), 5%)
  ```

TBILLYIELD Function

Financial Functions

Introduction

The TBILLYIELD function returns the yield of a Treasury bill based on its settlement date, maturity date, and price. It calculates the annualized yield for a Treasury bill, helping investors evaluate the return on short-term government securities.

- **Simple explanation:** Computes the annual yield of a Treasury bill based on its price and time to maturity.
- **Common use cases:** Used in bond yield analysis, investment evaluation, and comparing Treasury bills with other fixed-income securities.
- **When to use this function:** Use when calculating the annual yield of a Treasury bill to compare it with other investments.

Syntax

```
=TBILLYIELD(settlement, maturity, price)
```

- **settlement**: The settlement date of the Treasury bill (the date when the bill is purchased).
- **maturity**: The maturity date of the Treasury bill (the date when the bill matures).
- **price**: The price per $100 face value of the Treasury bill.

Worked Example

Challenge: Calculate the yield of a Treasury bill with a settlement date of January 1, 2024, a maturity date of April 1, 2024, and a price of $98.75 per $100 face value.

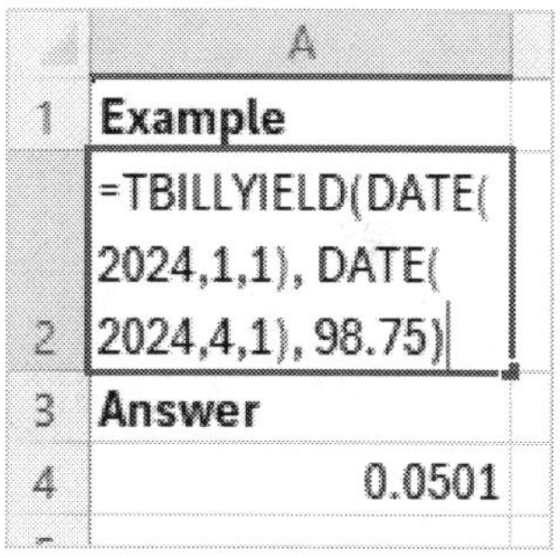

Inputs:

- settlement: 01-Jan-2024; maturity: 01-Apr-2024; price: 98.75

Formula:

```
=TBILLYIELD(DATE(2024,1,1), DATE(2024,4,1), 98.75)
```

Result: 0.0501 (or 5.01%)
Explanation: The function computes the annual yield, indicating a return of 5.063% based on the given price and time to maturity.

Explore Further with GPT

Ask GPT how to compare TBILLYIELD with functions like TBILLEQ, TBILLPRICE, or YIELD to evaluate different types of fixed-income securities.

Tips for Using TBILLYIELD

- **Price input:** Enter the price per $100 face value of the Treasury bill.

T.DIST Function

Statistical Functions

Introduction

The T.DIST function returns the left-tailed probability of the Student's t-distribution. This distribution is commonly used in hypothesis testing when working with small sample sizes or when the population standard deviation is unknown.

- **Simple explanation:** Computes the cumulative probability of a value in the Student's t-distribution.
- **Common use cases:** Used in hypothesis testing, confidence interval estimation, and t-tests.
- **When to use this function:** Use when calculating probabilities or p-values for a given t-statistic in a Student's t-distribution.

Syntax

```
=T.DIST(x, degrees_freedom, cumulative)
```

- **x**: The t-value for which to calculate the distribution.
- **degrees_freedom**: The degrees of freedom, typically equal to the sample size minus one.
- **cumulative**: A logical value specifying the type of distribution:
  - TRUE: Returns the cumulative distribution function (CDF).
  - FALSE: Returns the probability density function (PDF).

Worked Example

	A	B
1	**Example**	
2	=T.DIST(2.5, 10, TRUE)	
3	**Answer**	
4	0.984277	
5		

Challenge: Calculate the cumulative probability of a t-value of 2.5 with 10 degrees of freedom.

Inputs:

- x: 2.5; degrees_freedom: 10; cumulative: TRUE

Formula:

```
=T.DIST(2.5, 10, TRUE)
```

Result: 0.984277
Explanation: The function returns 0.984277, meaning the cumulative probability up to a t-value of 2.5 with 10 degrees of freedom is approximately 98.42%.

Explore Further with GPT

Ask GPT how to combine T.DIST with functions like T.INV, T.DIST.2T, or T.TEST for advanced statistical hypothesis testing.

Tips for Using T.DIST

- **Cumulative vs. probability density:**
  - Use TRUE for cumulative probability (left-tailed p-value).
  - Use FALSE for the probability density at a specific point.

T.DIST.2T Function

Statistical Functions

Introduction

The T.DIST.2T function returns the two-tailed probability of the Student's t-distribution. This function is commonly used in hypothesis testing, where the probability of observing a value as extreme as or more extreme than the given t-value (in both tails of the distribution) is required.

- **Simple explanation:** Computes the two-tailed probability for a given t-value in a Student's t-distribution.
- **Common use cases:** Used in two-tailed hypothesis tests, such as t-tests for differences in means.
- **When to use this function:** Use when calculating the p-value for a two-tailed t-test or when evaluating probabilities in both tails of the distribution.

Syntax

```
=T.DIST.2T(x, degrees_freedom)
```

- **x**: The absolute t-value for which to calculate the two-tailed probability.
- **degrees_freedom**: The degrees of freedom, typically equal to the sample size minus one.

Worked Example

Challenge: Calculate the two-tailed probability for a t-value of 2.5 with 10 degrees of freedom.

Inputs:

- x: 2.5; degrees_freedom: 10

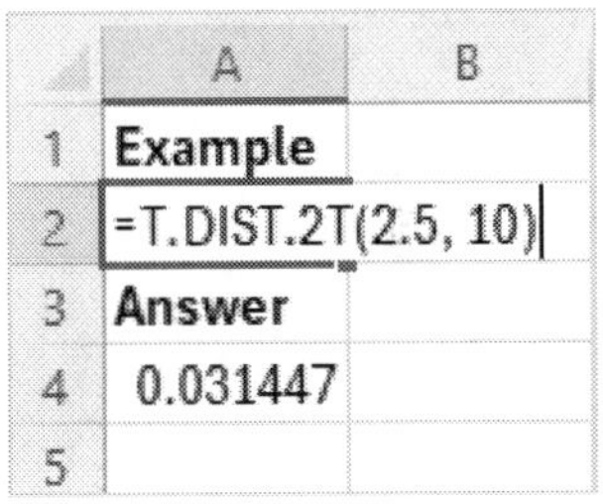

Formula:

```
=T.DIST.2T(2.5, 10)
```

Result: 0.031447
Explanation: The function returns 0.031477, meaning the probability of observing a t-value as extreme as ±2.5 in a Student's t-distribution with 10 degrees of freedom is approximately 3.14%.

Explore Further with GPT

Ask GPT how to use T.DIST.2T with functions like T.DIST, T.INV.2T, or T.TEST for advanced hypothesis testing and p-value calculations.

Tips for Using T.DIST.2T

- **Absolute t-value:** Ensure the x value is positive. The function automatically accounts for both tails of the distribution.
- **Degrees of freedom:** The degrees_freedom argument must be greater than 0. If it is less than or equal to 0, the function returns a #NUM! error.
- **Error handling:** Use IFERROR to handle invalid inputs gracefully:

```
=IFERROR(T.DIST.2T(A1, B1), "Invalid input")
```

T.DIST.RT Function

Statistical Functions

Introduction

The T.DIST.RT function returns the right-tailed probability of the Student's t-distribution. It is commonly used in one-tailed hypothesis tests where the probability of observing a t-value as extreme as or more extreme than the given value in the right tail is needed.

- **Simple explanation:** Computes the right-tailed probability for a given t-value in a Student's t-distribution.
- **Common use cases:** Used in one-tailed t-tests, hypothesis testing, and p-value calculations for right-tailed tests.
- **When to use this function:** Use when performing a right-tailed t-test or calculating a one-sided p-value.

Syntax

```
=T.DIST.RT(x, degrees_freedom)
```

- **x**: The t-value for which to calculate the right-tailed probability.
- **degrees_freedom**: The degrees of freedom, typically equal to the sample size minus one.

Worked Example

Challenge: Calculate the right-tailed probability for a t-value of 2.5 with 10 degrees of freedom.

Inputs:

- x: 2.5; degrees_freedom: 10

Formula:

```
=T.DIST.RT(2.5, 10)
```

	A	B
1	**Example**	
2	=T.DIST.RT(2.5, 10)	
3	**Answer**	
4	0.015723	
5		

Result: 0.015723
Explanation: The function returns 0.015723, meaning the probability of observing a t-value greater than 2.5 in a Student's t-distribution with 10 degrees of freedom is approximately 1.57%.

Explore Further with GPT

Ask GPT how to use T.DIST.RT with functions like T.DIST, T.INV.RT, or T.TEST for advanced one-tailed hypothesis testing.

Tips for Using T.DIST.RT

- **Right-tailed p-value:** The function only returns the probability in the right tail of the distribution.
- **Degrees of freedom:** Ensure the degrees_freedom argument is greater than 0. If it is less than or equal to 0, the function returns a #NUM! error.

TDIST Function

Compatibility Functions

Introduction

The TDIST function returns the probability associated with the Student's t-distribution. It supports one-tailed and two-tailed tests. This function is used in hypothesis testing, especially when working with small sample sizes or unknown population standard deviations.

Note: In newer versions of Excel, TDIST has been replaced by T.DIST, T.DIST.RT, and T.DIST.2T, but it remains available for compatibility with older Excel versions.

- **Simple explanation:** Computes the probability for a given t-value in a Student's t-distribution, supporting one-tailed or two-tailed tests.
- **Common use cases:** Used in t-tests, hypothesis testing, and p-value calculations.
- **When to use this function:** Use when performing statistical analysis involving the Student's t-distribution in older Excel versions.

Syntax

```
=TDIST(x, degrees_freedom, tails)
```

- **x**: The t-value for which to calculate the probability.
- **degrees_freedom**: The degrees of freedom, typically equal to the sample size minus one.
- **tails**: The number of tails for the test:
    - 1 = One-tailed test.
    - 2 = Two-tailed test.

Worked Example

Challenge: Calculate the two-tailed probability for a t-value of 2.5 with 10 degrees of freedom.

Inputs:

- x: 2.5; degrees_freedom: 10; tails: 2

	A	B
1	**Example**	
2	=TDIST(2.5, 10, 2)	
3	**Answer**	
4	0.031447	
5		

Formula:

```
=TDIST(2.5, 10, 2)
```

Result: 0.031447

Explanation: The function returns 0.031447, meaning the probability of observing a t-value as extreme as ±2.5 in a two-tailed test with 10 degrees of freedom is approximately 3.14%.

Tips for Using TDIST

- **Tails argument:** Always specify 1 for one-tailed tests and 2 for two-tailed tests. Omitting this argument will result in an error.

TEXT Function

Text Functions

Introduction

The TEXT function formats a number and converts it to text according to a specified format. It is useful for controlling the display of numbers, dates, times, and other values, ensuring consistency in reports and dashboards.

- **Simple explanation:** Converts a number to text in a specific format.
- **Common use cases:** Used for formatting dates, times, percentages, currency, and custom text output.
- **When to use this function:** Use when you need to display numbers in a specific format or when combining numbers with text in a formula.

Syntax

```
=TEXT(value, format_text)
```

- **value**: The number, date, or time to be formatted.
- **format_text**: A text string specifying the desired format.

Common Format Codes

Type	Format Code Example	Result Example
Number	"0.00"	123.45 → 123.45
Percentage	"0.00%"	0.1234 → 12.34%
Currency	"$#,##0.00"	1234.5 → $1,234.50
Date	"dd/mm/yyyy"	01-Jan-2024 → 01/01/2024
Time	"hh:mm AM/PM"	14:30 → 2:30 PM
Text with Number	"Total: #,##0"	1000 → Total: 1,000

Worked Example

Challenge: Format the number 1234.567 as currency with two decimal places.

Formula:

```
=TEXT(1234.567, "$#,##0.00")
```

Result: $1,234.57

Explanation: The function formats the number as currency, including commas for thousands and rounding to two decimal places.

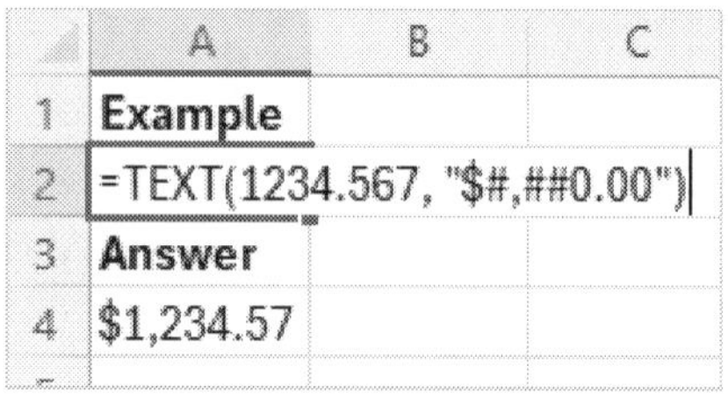

Explore Further with GPT

Ask GPT how to use TEXT with functions like CONCAT, IF, or NOW to create dynamic, well-formatted reports.

TEXTAFTER Function

Text Functions

Introduction

The TEXTAFTER function returns the portion of a text string that appears after a specified delimiter. It is useful for extracting parts of a string based on specific characters or substrings.

- **Simple explanation:** Extracts text from a string after a given delimiter.
- **Common use cases:** Used for splitting data, extracting values from delimited strings, and working with structured text data such as CSV or logs.
- **When to use this function:** Use when you need to retrieve the portion of a string following a specific character or word.

Syntax

```
=TEXTAFTER(text, delimiter, [instance_num], [match_mode], [match_end], [if_not_found])
```

- **text**: The text string to search.
- **delimiter**: The character(s) or substring after which the function extracts text.
- **[instance_num]** *(optional)*: Specifies which occurrence of the delimiter to use (default is 1). Positive numbers count from the start, and negative numbers count from the end.
- **[match_mode]** *(optional)*: Specifies case sensitivity:
    - 0 = Case-sensitive (default).
    - 1 = Case-insensitive.
- **[match_end]** *(optional)*: Determines whether to match the delimiter at the end of the text:
    - 0 = Don't match at the end (default).
    - 1 = Match at the end.
- **[if_not_found]** *(optional)*: The value to return if the delimiter is not found. If omitted, an error is returned.

Worked Example

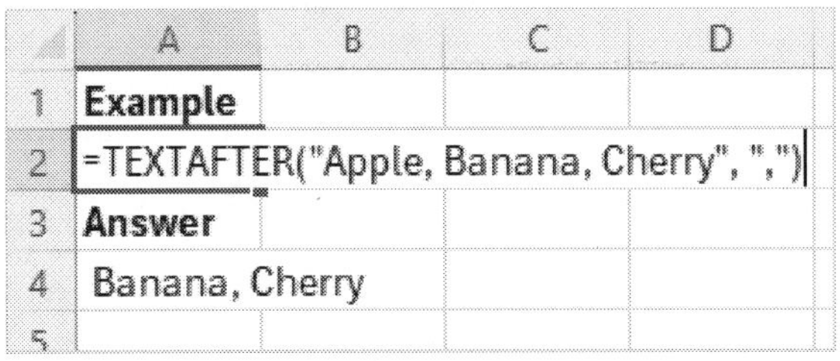

Challenge: Extract the text after the first comma in the string "Apple, Banana, Cherry".

Formula:

```
=TEXTAFTER("Apple, Banana, Cherry", ",")
```

Result: " Banana, Cherry"
Explanation: The function returns the text after the first comma, including the space before "Banana".

TEXTBEFORE Function

Text Functions

Introduction

The TEXTBEFORE function returns the portion of a text string that appears before a specified delimiter. It is useful for extracting parts of a string based on specific characters or substrings.

- **Simple explanation:** Extracts text from a string before a given delimiter.
- **Common use cases:** Used for splitting data, extracting values from structured text, and parsing delimited strings such as file paths, CSV data, or logs.
- **When to use this function:** Use when you need to retrieve the portion of a string preceding a specific character or word.

Syntax

```
=TEXTBEFORE(text, delimiter, [instance_num], [match_mode], [match_end], [if_not_found])
```

- **text**: The text string to search.
- **delimiter**: The character(s) or substring before which the function extracts text.
- **[instance_num]** *(optional)*: Specifies which occurrence of the delimiter to use (default is 1). Positive numbers count from the start, and negative numbers count from the end.
- **[match_mode]** *(optional)*: Specifies case sensitivity:
  - = Case-sensitive (default).
  - = Case-insensitive.
- **[match_end]** *(optional)*: Determines whether to match the delimiter at the end of the text:
  - = Don't match at the end (default).
  - = Match at the end.
- **[if_not_found]** *(optional)*: The value to return if the delimiter is not found. If omitted, an error is returned.

Worked Example

Challenge: Extract the text before the first comma in the string "Apple, Banana, Cherry".

Formula:

```
=TEXTBEFORE("Apple, Banana, Cherry", ",")
```

Result: "Apple"
Explanation: The function returns the text before the first comma, which is "Apple".

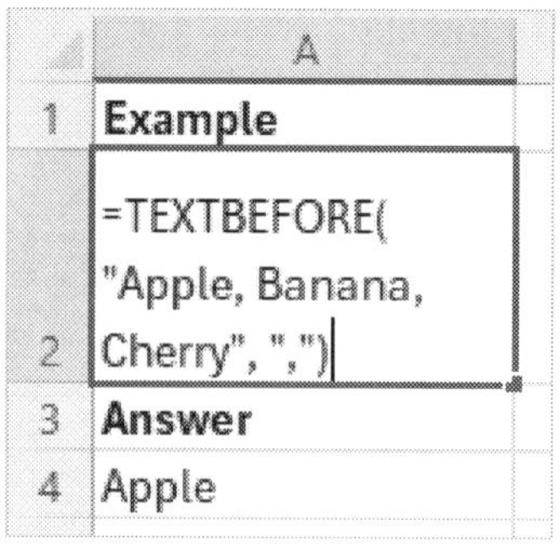

	A
1	**Example**
2	=TEXTBEFORE("Apple, Banana, Cherry", ",")
3	**Answer**
4	Apple

Explore Further with GPT

Ask GPT how to combine TEXTBEFORE with TEXTAFTER, SPLIT, or LEN for advanced text parsing and dynamic extraction.

TEXTJOIN Function

Text Functions

Introduction

The TEXTJOIN function concatenates (joins) multiple text strings into one, using a specified delimiter. Unlike CONCAT or CONCATENATE, TEXTJOIN allows you to include or exclude empty cells and provides more flexibility when working with arrays.

- **Simple explanation:** Joins multiple text strings into one, separated by a specified delimiter.
- **Common use cases:** Used for combining text values, creating delimited lists, and generating formatted reports.
- **When to use this function:** Use when you need to join multiple text values with a delimiter and optionally exclude empty values.

Syntax

```
=TEXTJOIN(delimiter, ignore_empty, text1, [text2], ...)
```

- **delimiter**: The text to use as a separator between joined values (e.g., a comma, space, or hyphen).
- **ignore_empty**: A logical value (TRUE or FALSE) indicating whether to ignore empty cells or values.
    - TRUE: Ignores empty values.
    - FALSE: Includes empty values.
- **text1, [text2],** ...: One or more text strings or ranges to join.

Worked Example

Challenge: Join the words "Apple", "Banana", and "Cherry" with a comma separator.

Formula:

```
=TEXTJOIN(", ", TRUE, "Apple", "Banana", "Cherry")
```

Result: "Apple, Banana, Cherry"
Explanation: The function joins the text strings with a comma and a space as the delimiter.

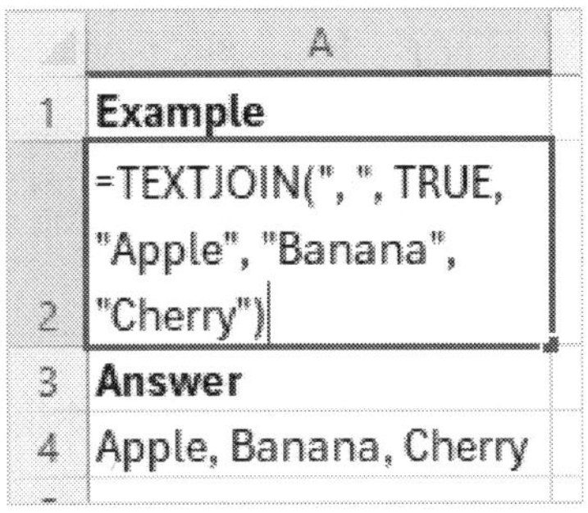

	A
1	**Example**
2	=TEXTJOIN(", ", TRUE, "Apple", "Banana", "Cherry")
3	**Answer**
4	Apple, Banana, Cherry

Explore Further with GPT

Ask GPT how to use TEXTJOIN with functions like FILTER, SORT, or UNIQUE to create dynamic lists and formatted reports.

Tips for Using TEXTJOIN

- **Ignoring empty values:** Set ignore_empty to TRUE to exclude empty cells or values from the result.
- **Joining ranges:** You can join entire ranges or arrays:

  ```
  =TEXTJOIN(", ", TRUE, A1:A10) --This joins all non-empty values in the range A1:A10.
  ```

TEXTSPLIT Function

Text Functions

Introduction

The TEXTSPLIT function splits a text string into multiple cells based on specified delimiters. It can split by rows, columns, or both, making it useful for parsing structured data such as CSV files or logs.

- **Simple explanation:** Splits a text string into multiple cells using a specified delimiter.
- **Common use cases:** Used for parsing delimited strings, extracting data from structured text, and transforming single-cell data into multiple columns or rows.
- **When to use this function:** Use when you need to split a text string into parts based on a specific character or set of characters.

Syntax

```
=TEXTSPLIT(text, col_delimiter, [row_delimiter], [ignore_empty], [match_mode])
```

- **text**: The text string to split.
- **col_delimiter**: The delimiter used to split text into columns.
- **[row_delimiter]** *(optional)*: The delimiter used to split text into rows.
- **[ignore_empty]** *(optional)*: A logical value (TRUE or FALSE) indicating whether to ignore empty cells:
  - TRUE: Ignores empty cells (default).
  - FALSE: Includes empty cells.
- **[match_mode]** *(optional)*: Specifies case sensitivity for delimiters:
  - 0 = Case-sensitive (default).
  - 1 = Case-insensitive.

Worked Example

Challenge: Split the string "Apple, Banana, Cherry" into separate cells using a comma as the delimiter.

Formula:

```
=TEXTSPLIT("Apple, Banana, Cherry", ", ")
```

Result: Apple Banana Cherry

Explanation: The function splits the text at each comma followed by a space, placing each resulting word in a separate column.

	A	B	C	D
1	**Example**			
2	=TEXTSPLIT("Apple, Banana, Cherry", ", ")			
3	**Answer**			
4	Apple	Banana	Cherry	
5				

Explore Further with GPT

Ask GPT how to combine TEXTSPLIT with functions like TEXTAFTER, TEXTBEFORE, or TEXTJOIN for advanced string manipulation and data parsing.

TIME Function

Date & Time Functions

Introduction

The TIME function returns a time value based on specified hour, minute, and second components. It converts these components into a decimal number that represents time in Excel, allowing easy manipulation of time values in formulas.

- **Simple explanation:** Creates a time value from hour, minute, and second inputs.
- **Common use cases:** Used for constructing time values, performing time arithmetic, and formatting custom time outputs.
- **When to use this function:** Use when you need to create a valid time value from separate hour, minute, and second inputs.

Syntax

```
=TIME(hour, minute, second)
```

- **hour**: A number from 0 to 23 representing the hour.
- **minute**: A number from 0 to 59 representing the minute.
- **second**: A number from 0 to 59 representing the second.

Worked Example

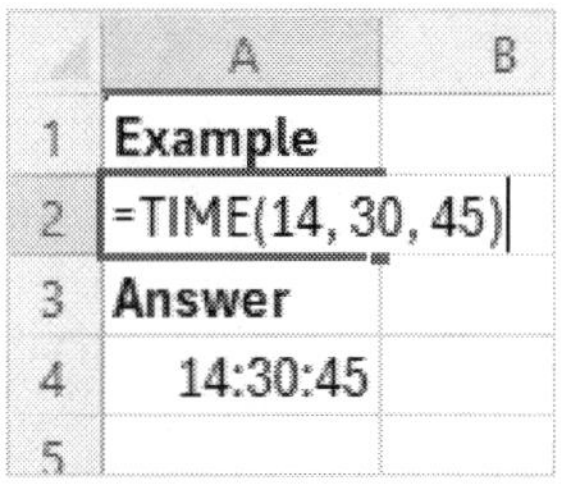

	A	B
1	Example	
2	=TIME(14, 30, 45)	
3	Answer	
4	14:30:45	
5		

Challenge: Create a time value for 14:30:45 (2:30:45 PM).

Formula:

```
=TIME(14, 30, 45)
```

Result: 14:30:45

Explanation: The function combines 14 hours, 30 minutes, and 45 seconds to create the time value 14:30:45.

Explore Further with GPT

Ask GPT how to combine TIME with functions like NOW, HOUR, MINUTE, or SECOND to create dynamic time calculations and perform time-based operations.

Tips for Using TIME

- **Handling overflow:** The function automatically adjusts for overflow values in hour, minute, or second:

  ```
  =TIME(25, 120, 90)
  ```

  This results in 02:02:30 the next day (25 hours becomes 1 hour the next day, 120 minutes becomes 2 hours, and 90 seconds becomes 1 minute and 30 seconds).

- **Time arithmetic:** Combine TIME with NOW or TODAY to perform dynamic calculations involving dates and times:

  ```
  =TODAY() + TIME(14, 30, 0) --This adds 14:30 (2:30 PM) to the current date.
  ```

TIMEVALUE Function

Date & Time Functions

Introduction

The TIMEVALUE function converts a time represented as a text string into an Excel time value. This allows you to perform arithmetic operations or apply formatting to time strings that would otherwise be treated as text.

- **Simple explanation:** Converts a time in text format into a numeric time value that Excel recognizes.
- **Common use cases:** Used when importing or processing time data stored as text, converting it into a usable time format for calculations.
- **When to use this function:** Use when you need to convert a time string into a valid Excel time for arithmetic operations or formatting.

Syntax

```
=TIMEVALUE(time_text)
```

- **time_text**: A text string representing a time, such as "14:30:00" or "2:30 PM".

Worked Example

Challenge: Convert the time string "14:30:00" into a numeric time value.

Formula:

`=TIMEVALUE("14:30:00")`

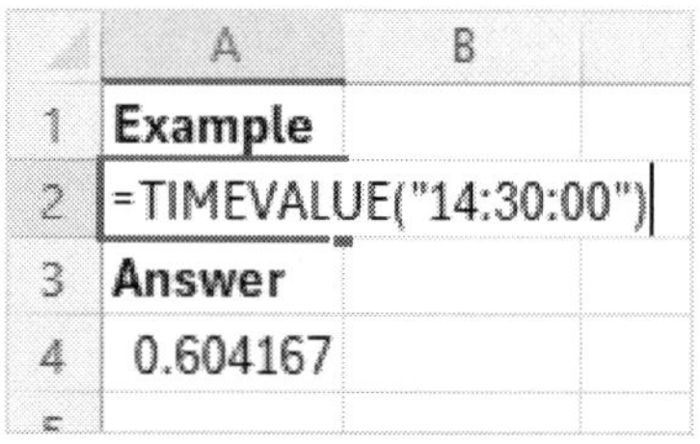

	A	B
1	Example	
2	=TIMEVALUE("14:30:00")	
3	Answer	
4	0.604167	

Result: 0.604167
Explanation: Excel represents time as a fraction of a 24-hour day. The result 0.604167 corresponds to 14:30:00 or 2:30 PM, which is 60.42% of the day.

Explore Further with GPT

Ask GPT how to combine TIMEVALUE with functions like TEXT, HOUR, or MINUTE to create dynamic time-based calculations.

Tips for Using TIMEVALUE

- **Date handling:** The TIMEVALUE function ignores any date portion in the input string and only processes the time.
- **Text format:** Ensure time_text is in a recognizable time format (e.g., "hh:mm:ss" or "h:mm AM/PM").
- **Combining with date values:** To create a full datetime value, add the result of TIMEVALUE to a date:

  `=DATE(2024, 1, 1) + TIMEVALUE("14:30:00")`

  This results in 01-Jan-2024 14:30.

T.INV Function

Statistical Functions

Introduction

The T.INV function returns the inverse of the Student's t-distribution for a given probability and degrees of freedom. It is used in hypothesis testing, confidence interval estimation, and other statistical applications where critical t-values are required.

- **Simple explanation:** Computes the t-value corresponding to a given probability and degrees of freedom for a one-tailed t-test.
- **Common use cases:** Used in hypothesis testing to find critical t-values for confidence intervals and t-tests.
- **When to use this function:** Use when you need the critical t-value for a one-tailed test or when calculating confidence intervals for small sample sizes.

Syntax

```
=T.INV(probability, degrees_freedom)
```

- **probability**: The probability associated with the one-tailed Student's t-distribution (between 0 and 1).
- **degrees_freedom**: The degrees of freedom, typically equal to the sample size minus one.

Worked Example

Challenge: Find the t-value for a one-tailed probability of 0.05 with 10 degrees of freedom.

Inputs:

- probability: 0.05
- degrees_freedom: 10

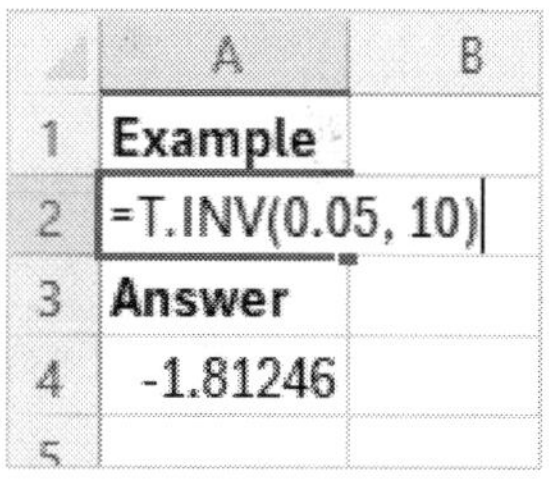

	A	B
1	Example	
2	=T.INV(0.05, 10)	
3	Answer	
4	-1.81246	
5		

Formula:

```
=T.INV(0.05, 10)
```

Result: -1.81246
Explanation: The function returns -1.81246, which is the critical t-value for a one-tailed test at a 5% significance level with 10 degrees of freedom.

Explore Further with GPT

Ask GPT how to combine T.INV with functions like T.DIST, T.INV.2T, or CONFIDENCE.T to perform advanced hypothesis testing and interval estimation.

Tips for Using T.INV

- **One-tailed vs. two-tailed tests:**
  - For a one-tailed test, use the desired probability directly.
  - For a two-tailed test, use $1-\alpha/2$ as the probability (where α is the significance level).

T.INV.2T Function

Statistical Functions

Introduction

The T.INV.2T function returns the two-tailed inverse of the Student's t-distribution. It is used to find the critical t-value for a two-tailed t-test, commonly required in hypothesis testing and confidence interval calculations.

- **Simple explanation:** Computes the t-value for a given two-tailed probability and degrees of freedom.
- **Common use cases:** Used in two-tailed hypothesis tests and confidence interval estimation when critical t-values are needed.
- **When to use this function:** Use when calculating the critical t-value for a two-tailed t-test or constructing a confidence interval.

Syntax

```
=T.INV.2T(probability, degrees_freedom)
```

- **probability**: The total probability in both tails of the distribution (between 0 and 1).
- **degrees_freedom**: The degrees of freedom, typically equal to the sample size minus one.

Worked Example

Challenge: Find the two-tailed t-value for a 95% confidence interval with 10 degrees of freedom.

Inputs:

- probability: 0.05 (5% in both tails, corresponding to a 95% confidence level); degrees_freedom: 10

Formula:

```
=T.INV.2T(0.05, 10)
```

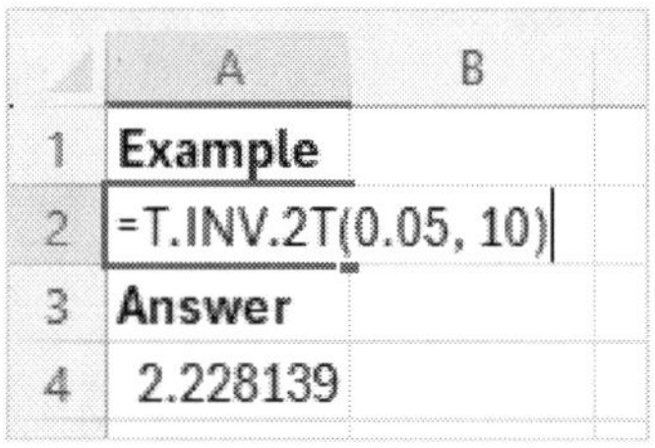

Result: 2.228139
Explanation: The function returns 2.228139, which is the critical t-value for a 95% confidence interval with 10 degrees of freedom.

Explore Further with GPT

Ask GPT how to combine T.INV.2T with functions like T.DIST.2T, CONFIDENCE.T, or AVERAGE to perform advanced hypothesis testing and confidence interval calculations.

Tips for Using T.INV.2T

- **Two-tailed probability:** The probability argument represents the total area in both tails. For example:
  - For a 95% confidence interval, use 0.05.
  - For a 99% confidence interval, use 0.01.
- **Degrees of freedom:** Ensure degrees_freedom is greater than 0. If it is less than or equal to 0, the function returns a #NUM! error.

TINV Function

Compatibility Functions

Introduction

The TINV function returns the two-tailed inverse of the Student's t-distribution. It is used to find the critical t-value for a specified probability and degrees of freedom in two-tailed hypothesis testing.

Note: In newer versions of Excel, TINV has been replaced by T.INV.2T, but it remains available for compatibility with older Excel versions.

- **Simple explanation:** Computes the t-value for a given two-tailed probability and degrees of freedom.
- **Common use cases:** Used in hypothesis testing, confidence interval estimation, and statistical analysis.
- **When to use this function:** Use when performing a two-tailed t-test or constructing a confidence interval in older versions of Excel.

Syntax

```
=TINV(probability, degrees_freedom)
```

- **probability**: The total probability in both tails of the distribution (between 0 and 1).
- **degrees_freedom**: The degrees of freedom, typically equal to the sample size minus one.

Worked Example

Challenge: Find the two-tailed t-value for a 95% confidence interval with 10 degrees of freedom.

Inputs:

- probability: 0.05 (5% in both tails, corresponding to a 95% confidence level); degrees_freedom: 10

Formula:

```
=TINV(0.05, 10)
```

Result: 2.228139
Explanation: The function returns 2.228139, which is the critical t-value for a 95% confidence interval with 10 degrees of freedom.

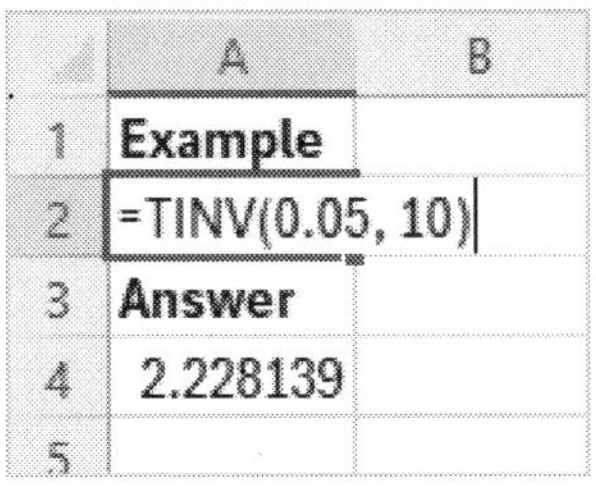

Explore Further with GPT

Ask GPT how to replace TINV with T.INV.2T in newer versions of Excel for improved statistical analysis.

Tips for Using TINV

- **Two-tailed probability:** The probability argument represents the total area in both tails. For example:
  - For a 95% confidence interval, use 0.05.
  - For a 99% confidence interval, use 0.01.
- **Degrees of freedom:** Ensure degrees_freedom is greater than 0. If it is less than or equal to 0, the function returns a #NUM! error.

TOCOL Function

Lookup & Reference Functions

Introduction

The TOCOL function transforms an array or range into a single column by stacking its elements vertically. It is useful for reshaping data, consolidating multi-dimensional arrays, and preparing data for analysis.

- **Simple explanation:** Converts a range or array into a single column by stacking the values vertically.
- **Common use cases:** Used for flattening tables, extracting data from arrays, and transforming matrix data into a column.
- **When to use this function:** Use when you need to convert multi-dimensional data into a single column.

Syntax

```
=TOCOL(array, [ignore], [scan_by_column])
```

- **array**: The range or array to be transformed into a column.
- **[ignore]** *(optional)*: Specifies which types of values to ignore:
  - 0: Do not ignore any values (default).
  - 1: Ignore blanks.
  - 2: Ignore errors.
- **[scan_by_column]** *(optional)*: Specifies the direction of scanning:
  - FALSE or omitted: Scan by row first (row-major order).
  - TRUE: Scan by column first (column-major order).

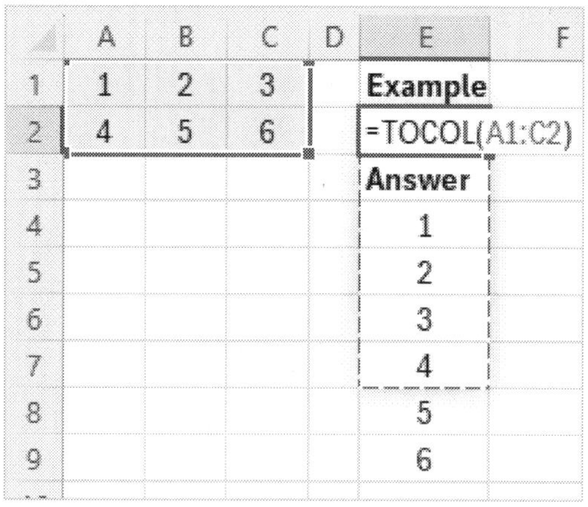

	A	B	C	D	E	F
1	1	2	3		**Example**	
2	4	5	6		=TOCOL(A1:C2)	
3					**Answer**	
4					1	
5					2	
6					3	
7					4	
8					5	
9					6	

Worked Example

Challenge: Convert a 2x3 table into a single column.

Formula:

```
=TOCOL(A1:C2)
```

Result: A 1 column, 6 row range containing the numbers 1-6

Explore Further with GPT

Ask GPT how to combine TOCOL with functions like UNIQUE, SORT, or FILTER to perform advanced data transformations.

Tips for Using TOCOL

- **Handling blanks and errors:** Use the ignore argument to exclude blanks or errors:

  ```
  =TOCOL(A1:C10, 2)
  ```

  This ignores any errors in the range A1:C10.

TOROW Function

Lookup & Reference Functions

Introduction

The TOROW function transforms an array or range into a single row by stacking its elements horizontally. It is useful for reshaping data, flattening arrays, and preparing data for analysis or presentation.

- **Simple explanation:** Converts a range or array into a single row by stacking values horizontally.
- **Common use cases:** Used for flattening tables, reshaping matrices, and extracting data into a horizontal format.
- **When to use this function:** Use when you need to convert multi-dimensional data into a single row.

Syntax

```
=TOROW(array, [ignore], [scan_by_column])
```

- **array**: The range or array to be transformed into a row.
- **[ignore]** *(optional)*: Specifies which types of values to ignore:
  - 0: Do not ignore any values (default).
  - 1: Ignore blanks.
  - 2: Ignore errors.
- **[scan_by_column]** *(optional)*: Specifies the direction of scanning:
  - FALSE or omitted: Scan by row first (row-major order).
  - TRUE: Scan by column first (column-major order).

Worked Example

Challenge: Convert a 2x3 table into a row.

Formula:

```
=TOROW(A1:C2)
```

Result: The function stacks the elements row-wise into a single row.

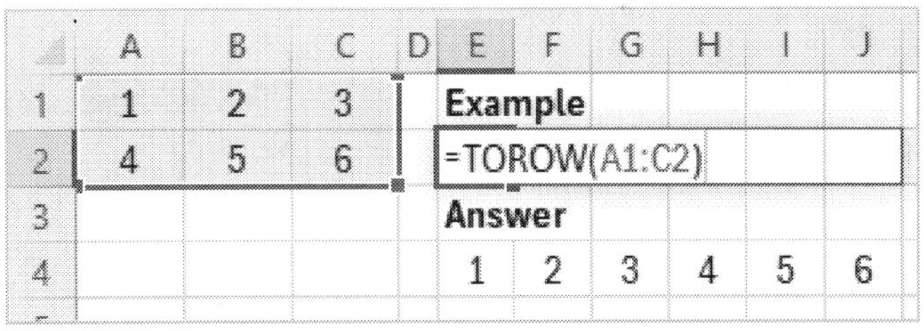

Explore Further with GPT

Ask GPT how to combine TOROW with functions like UNIQUE, SORT, or TEXTJOIN for advanced data manipulation and list generation.

Tips for Using TOROW

- **Direction control:** Use the scan_by_column argument to control whether the function stacks values row-wise or column-wise.

TODAY Function

Date & Time Functions

Introduction

The TODAY function returns the current date as a serial number without the time component. It dynamically updates whenever the worksheet is recalculated, making it useful for creating dynamic date-based reports and tracking time-sensitive data.

- **Simple explanation:** Returns the current date without the time.
- **Common use cases:** Used in dynamic date calculations, generating reports, and creating date-based conditions (e.g., due dates or age calculations).
- **When to use this function:** Use when you need the current date to update automatically in your calculations.

Syntax

```
=TODAY()
```

- The function takes no arguments.

Worked Example

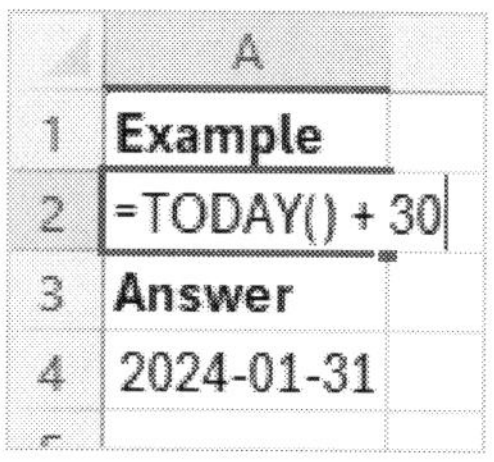

Challenge: Calculate a due date that is 30 days from today.

Formula:

`=TODAY() + 30`

Result: 2024-01-31 (if today is 2024-01-01).
Explanation: The function adds 30 days to the current date, returning the date 30 days from today.

Explore Further with GPT

Ask GPT how to combine TODAY with functions like DATEDIF, TEXT, or EDATE to build custom date-based calculations and reports.

Tips for Using TODAY

- **Date formatting:** Use custom date formats to display the result as needed (e.g., "dd-mmm-yyyy" or "yyyy/mm/dd").
- **Combining with other functions:** Use TODAY with functions like YEAR, MONTH, or DAY to extract specific parts of the current date:

  `=YEAR(TODAY())`

  This returns the current year.
- **Dynamic updates:** The result of TODAY updates automatically whenever the worksheet is recalculated (e.g., when you open the workbook or press F9).

TRANSPOSE Function

Lookup & Reference Functions

Introduction

The TRANSPOSE function converts a vertical range of cells into a horizontal range (or vice versa) by flipping rows into columns and columns into rows. It is useful when you need to reorganize data without manually copying and pasting.

- **Simple explanation:** Converts rows to columns or columns to rows in a range or array.
- **Common use cases:** Used for data reorganization, converting lists to tables, and preparing data for analysis.
- **When to use this function:** Use when you need to switch the orientation of data from vertical to horizontal or vice versa.

Syntax

```
=TRANSPOSE(array)
```

- **array**: The range or array to transpose.

Worked Example

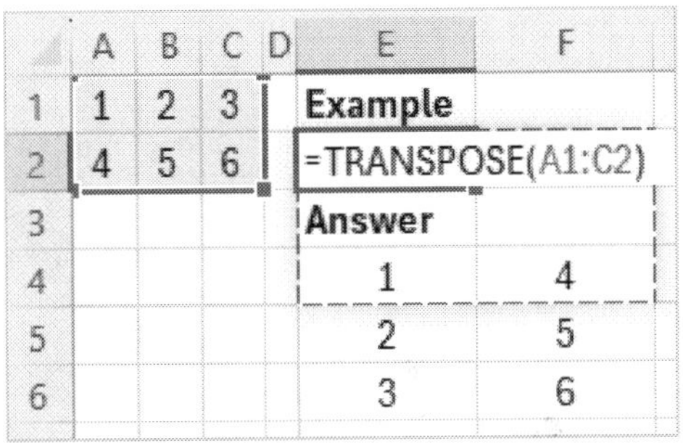

Challenge: Transpose a 2x3 range into a 3x2 range.

Formula:
Select a 3x2 empty range (e.g., D1:E3), then enter:

```
=TRANSPOSE(A1:C2)
```

Press Ctrl + Shift + Enter (for Excel versions prior to Excel 365) to enter the formula as an array formula.

Result: The function converts the rows in A1:C2 into columns in D1:E3.

Explore Further with GPT

Ask GPT how to use TRANSPOSE with functions like INDEX, SEQUENCE, or FILTER to build dynamic tables and reshaped data views.

Tips for Using TRANSPOSE

- **Error handling:** If the target range is smaller than the transposed range, Excel returns a #SPILL! error.
- **Combining with other functions:** Use TRANSPOSE with UNIQUE or SORT to create dynamic transposed lists:

  ```
  =TRANSPOSE(UNIQUE(A1:A10))
  ```

  This creates a transposed list of unique values from A1:A10.
- **Excel compatibility:** The TRANSPOSE function is available in all modern Excel versions. In Excel versions prior to Excel 365, it requires entering as an array formula using Ctrl + Shift + Enter.

TREND Function

Statistical Functions

Introduction

The TREND function returns values along a linear trend by fitting a straight line to the given data using the least squares method. It can be used to predict future values based on existing data or to interpolate missing values in a dataset.

- **Simple explanation:** Predicts values along a linear trend based on known data points.
- **Common use cases:** Used in forecasting, regression analysis, and predicting trends in sales, financial data, or other numerical datasets.
- **When to use this function:** Use when you need to model data with a linear trend or make predictions based on historical data.

Syntax

```
=TREND(known_y's, [known_x's], [new_x's], [const])
```

- **known_y's**: The dependent data set (y-values).
- **[known_x's]** *(optional)*: The independent data set (x-values). If omitted, Excel assumes known_x's = {1, 2, 3, ...}.
- **[new_x's]** *(optional)*: The x-values for which to return predicted y-values. If omitted, Excel uses the same x-values as known_x's.
- **[const]** *(optional)*: A logical value specifying whether to force the y-intercept to 0:
    - TRUE (default): Calculates the intercept normally.
    - FALSE: Forces the intercept to 0.

Worked Example

Challenge: Predict y-values for a given linear trend based on known data.

Formula: Predict y-values for X = 5, 6 based on the existing trend.

```
=TREND(B2:B5, A2:A5, {5, 6})
```

	A	B	C	D	E	F
1	**X (known_x's)**	**Y (known_y's)**		**Example**		
2	1	5		=TREND(B2:B5, A2:A5, {5,6})		
3	2	7		**Answer**		
4	3	9		13	15	
5	4	11				
6						

Result: {13, 15}

Explanation: The function calculates the linear trend based on the known data and predicts that when X = 5, Y = 13, and when X = 6, Y = 15.

Tips for Using TREND

- **Multiple linear regression:** The TREND function can handle multiple sets of known_x's for multivariate regression:

```
=TREND(B1:B10, C1:D10) -- This predicts y-values based on two independent
variables in C1:D10.
```

TRIM Function

Text Functions

Introduction

The TRIM function removes all extra spaces from a text string, leaving only single spaces between words. It is useful for cleaning up text data that may contain leading, trailing, or multiple spaces.

- **Simple explanation:** Removes extra spaces from a text string, keeping only single spaces between words.
- **Common use cases:** Used for data cleaning, text formatting, and ensuring consistent spacing in text fields.
- **When to use this function:** Use when you need to clean up text data with unnecessary spaces.

Syntax

```
=TRIM(text)
```

- **text**: The text string from which to remove extra spaces.

Worked Example

Challenge: Remove extra spaces from the string " Excel is fun ".

Formula:

```
=TRIM("   Excel   is   fun   ")
```

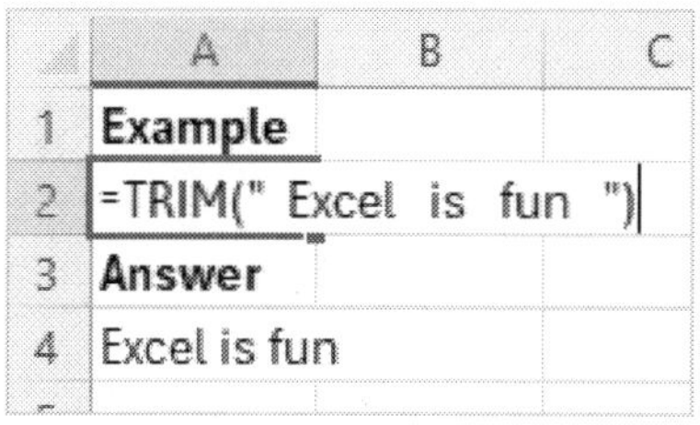

Result: "Excel is fun"
Explanation: The function removes all leading and trailing spaces and reduces multiple spaces between words to a single space.

Explore Further with GPT

Ask GPT how to combine TRIM with functions like CLEAN, TEXT, or SUBSTITUTE to perform advanced text manipulation

Tips for Using TRIM

- **Combining with other functions:** Use TRIM with CLEAN to remove both extra spaces and non-printable characters:

  ```
  =TRIM(CLEAN(A1))
  ```

  This cleans up both spaces and unwanted characters in A1.

- **Preserves single spaces:** The function retains single spaces between words, ensuring proper readability.

TRIMMEAN Function

Statistical Functions

Introduction

The TRIMMEAN function returns the mean (average) of a data set, excluding a specified percentage of data points from the top and bottom tails. It is useful for reducing the influence of outliers on the calculated average.

- **Simple explanation:** Computes the mean of a data set after excluding a specified percentage of extreme values from both ends.
- **Common use cases:** Used in statistical analysis, especially when dealing with data sets that may contain outliers.
- **When to use this function:** Use when you want a more robust average that minimizes the effect of extreme values.

Syntax

```
=TRIMMEAN(array, percent)
```

- **array**: The range or array of numeric values.
- **percent**: The fraction (between 0 and 1) of data points to exclude from the calculation. This percentage is split equally between the top and bottom of the data set.

Worked Example

Challenge: Calculate the trimmed mean of the data set {5, 10, 15, 20, 25, 30, 35, 40} excluding 20% of the extreme values.

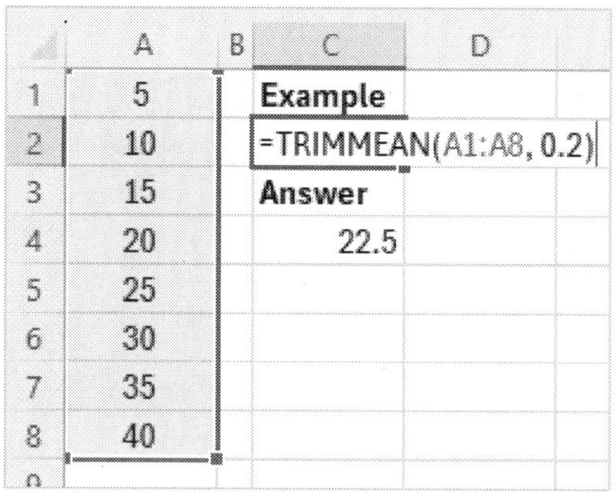

Formula:

```
=TRIMMEAN(A1:A8, 0.2)
```

Result: 22.5

Explanation: The function excludes 20% of the total data points (16% from each tail, i.e., 1 value from the top and 1 from the bottom), leaving {10, 15, 20, 25, 30, 35}. The mean of these remaining values is 22.5.

Explore Further with GPT

Ask GPT how to use TRIMMEAN with functions like AVERAGE, MEDIAN, or STDEV to compare different measures of central tendency.

Tips for Using TRIMMEAN

- **Percent value:** Ensure that percent is between 0 and 1. If it is 0, no data points are excluded, and the result is equivalent to AVERAGE(array).
- **Equal trimming:** The function trims data symmetrically from both ends

TRUE Function

Logical Functions

Introduction

The TRUE function returns the logical value TRUE. It is commonly used in logical operations and conditional expressions. In Excel, TRUE is equivalent to the number 1 in arithmetic operations.

- **Simple explanation:** Returns the logical value TRUE.
- **Common use cases:** Used in conditional formulas, logical comparisons, and as a constant in calculations or testing logical expressions.
- **When to use this function:** Use when you need a logical TRUE value explicitly in a formula or for comparison purposes.

Syntax

```
=TRUE()
```

- The function takes no arguments.

Worked Example

Challenge: Create a formula that checks if a number (15) is greater than 10 and returns TRUE if the condition is met.

Formula:

```
=A1>10
```

	A	B	C
1	15		**Example**
2			=A1>10
3			**Answer**
4			TRUE

Result: TRUE
Explanation: Since 15 is greater than 10, the formula returns TRUE.

Explore Further with GPT

Ask GPT how to use TRUE with functions like AND, OR, or IF to build advanced logical formulas.

Tips for Using TRUE

- **Logical equivalence:** In Excel, TRUE is equivalent to 1 in arithmetic operations:

  ```
  =TRUE() + 1
  ```

  This returns 2.

- **Using directly:** Instead of using =TRUE(), you can directly type TRUE in logical formulas:

  ```
  =IF(A1>10, TRUE, FALSE)
  ```

  This checks if the value in A1 is greater than 10 and returns TRUE or FALSE accordingly.

TRUNC Function

Math & Trigonometry

Introduction

The TRUNC function truncates a number by removing its fractional part or by reducing it to a specified number of decimal places. Unlike ROUND, it does not perform any rounding—values are simply cut off.

- **Simple explanation:** Removes the decimal part of a number or reduces it to a specified number of decimal places without rounding.
- **Common use cases:** Used in financial calculations, data formatting, and when integer values are needed without rounding.
- **When to use this function:** Use when you need to truncate decimal places without rounding.

Syntax

```
=TRUNC(number, [num_digits])
```

- **number**: The number to be truncated.
- **[num_digits]** *(optional)*: The number of decimal places to retain. If omitted, it defaults to 0 (truncating to an integer).

Worked Example

	A	B
1	**Example**	
2	=TRUNC(12.3456)	
3	**Answer**	
4	12	

Challenge: Truncate the number 12.3456 to an integer.

Formula:

```
=TRUNC(12.3456)
```

Result: 12
Explanation: The function removes the decimal part, returning only the integer portion.

Explore Further with GPT

Ask GPT how to combine TRUNC with functions like MOD, INT, or ROUND for advanced numerical operations.

Tips for Using TRUNC

- **Default behavior:** If num_digits is omitted, the function truncates to an integer.
- **Handling negative digits:** Use negative values for num_digits to truncate digits to the left of the decimal point:

  ```
  =TRUNC(98765, -2)
  ```

  This returns 98700.

T.TEST Function

Statistical Functions

Introduction

The T.TEST function returns the probability (p-value) associated with a Student's t-test. It is used to determine whether two data sets are significantly different from each other. The p-value helps assess whether the observed difference is likely to have occurred by chance.

- **Simple explanation:** Computes the p-value for a t-test comparing two data sets.
- **Common use cases:** Used in hypothesis testing to compare means of two samples, such as comparing test results, experimental data, or financial metrics.
- **When to use this function:** Use when performing a t-test to assess whether the means of two data sets are significantly different.

Syntax

```
=T.TEST(array1, array2, tails, type)
```

- **array1**: The first data set (sample 1).
- **array2**: The second data set (sample 2).
- **tails**: Specifies the number of tails for the test:
  - 1: One-tailed test.
  - 2: Two-tailed test.
- **type**: Specifies the type of t-test to perform:
  - 1: Paired t-test (used when data sets are paired).
  - 2: Two-sample equal variance (homoscedastic).
  - 3: Two-sample unequal variance (heteroscedastic).

Worked Example

Challenge: Perform a two-tailed, two-sample unequal variance t-test for the following data sets:

- **Sample 1**: {12, 14, 16, 18, 20}
- **Sample 2**: {22, 24, 26, 28, 30}

Formula:

```
=T.TEST(A1:A5, B1:B5, 2, 3)
```

	A	B	C	D	E	F
1	12	22		**Example**		
2	14	24		=T.TEST(A1:A5, B1:B5, 2, 3)		
3	16	26		**Answer**		
4	18	28		0.001053		
5	20	30				

Result: 0.001053
Explanation: The function returns 0.001053, which is the p-value for a two-tailed, two-sample t-test with unequal variances. Since the p-value is very small, it suggests a significant difference between the means of the two data sets.

TTEST Function

Compatibility Functions

Introduction

The TTEST function returns the probability (p-value) associated with a Student's t-test. It is used to determine whether two data sets have significantly different means. This function is maintained for compatibility with older versions of Excel.

Note: In newer versions of Excel, TTEST has been replaced by T.TEST, but it remains available for backward compatibility.

- **Simple explanation:** Computes the p-value for a t-test comparing two data sets.
- **Common use cases:** Used in hypothesis testing to assess whether two sample means are significantly different.
- **When to use this function:** Use when performing a t-test in older versions of Excel or when backward compatibility is needed.

Syntax

```
=TTEST(array1, array2, tails, type)
```

- **array1**: The first data set (sample 1).
- **array2**: The second data set (sample 2).
- **tails**: Specifies the number of tails for the test:
    - 1: One-tailed test.
    - 2: Two-tailed test.
- **type**: Specifies the type of t-test to perform:
    - 1: Paired t-test (used when data sets are paired).
    - 2: Two-sample equal variance (homoscedastic).
    - 3: Two-sample unequal variance (heteroscedastic)

Worked Example

Challenge: Perform a two-tailed, two-sample unequal variance t-test for the following data sets:

- **Sample 1**: {10, 12, 14, 16, 18}
- **Sample 2**: {20, 22, 24, 26, 28}

Formula:

```
=TTEST(A1:A5, B1:B5, 2, 3)
```

Result: 0.001053

Explanation: The function returns 0.001053, which is the p-value for a two-tailed, two-sample t-test with unequal variances. A small p-value suggests a significant difference between the means of the two data sets.

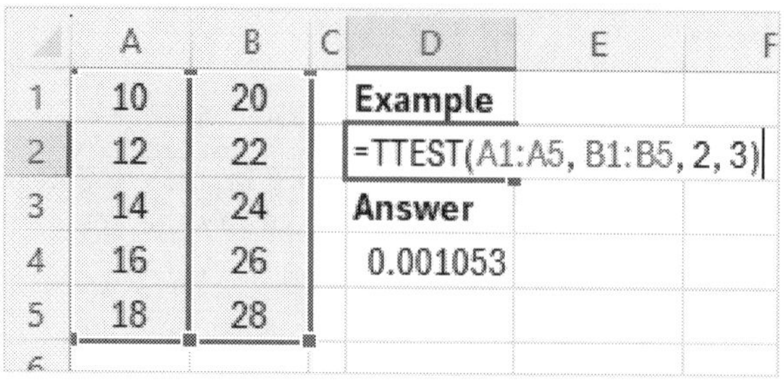

	A	B	C	D	E	F
1	10	20		**Example**		
2	12	22		=TTEST(A1:A5, B1:B5, 2, 3)		
3	14	24		**Answer**		
4	16	26		0.001053		
5	18	28				

TYPE Function

Information Functions

Introduction

The TYPE function returns a number representing the data type of a value. It helps identify whether a given input is a number, text, logical value, error, or array. This is useful for error handling, debugging formulas, and ensuring correct data types in calculations.

- **Simple explanation:** Returns a number that indicates the data type of a value.
- **Common use cases:** Used in data validation, error handling, and checking the type of data returned by a formula or function.
- **When to use this function:** Use when you need to determine the type of a value in a formula or cell.

Syntax

```
=TYPE(value)
```

- **value**: The value or reference to a cell whose data type you want to determine.

Returned Values

Return Value	Data Type
1	Number
2	Text
4	Logical value (TRUE or FALSE)
16	Error value (#DIV/0!, #N/A, etc.)
64	Array

Worked Example

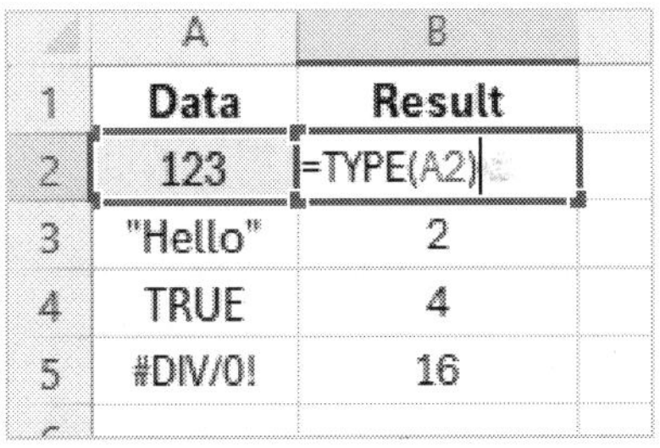

	A	B
1	Data	Result
2	123	=TYPE(A2)
3	"Hello"	2
4	TRUE	4
5	#DIV/0!	16

Challenge: Determine the data types of various values.

Formula: =TYPE(A2)

Explanation: The function returns 1 for numbers, 2 for text, 4 for logical values, and 16 for error values.

Explore Further with GPT

Ask GPT how to combine TYPE with functions like IF, ISNUMBER, or ERROR.TYPE for advanced data validation and error checking.

Tips for Using TYPE

- **Error handling:** Use TYPE to check for errors before performing operations:

  ```
  =IF(TYPE(A1)=16, "Error in cell", A1*2)
  ```

  This returns "Error in cell" if the value in A1 is an error.

- **Logical operations:** When checking for logical values, note that TRUE and FALSE return 4.
- **Arrays:** If the value argument is an array, the function returns 64, which can be useful when working with dynamic arrays in Excel 365 or Excel 2021.

UNICHAR Function

Text Functions

Introduction

The UNICHAR function returns the Unicode character corresponding to a given numeric code. It supports a wide range of characters, including symbols, emojis, and special characters, making it useful for working with international text and symbols.

- **Simple explanation:** Converts a Unicode number to its corresponding character.
- **Common use cases:** Used for displaying special symbols, creating dynamic text with symbols, and handling multilingual text.
- **When to use this function:** Use when you need to display a character based on its Unicode code.

Syntax

```
=UNICHAR(number)
```

- **number**: The Unicode number (integer) representing the character to be returned.

Worked Example

Challenge: Display the Unicode character for the number 9731 (a snowman symbol).

Formula:

```
=UNICHAR(9731)
```

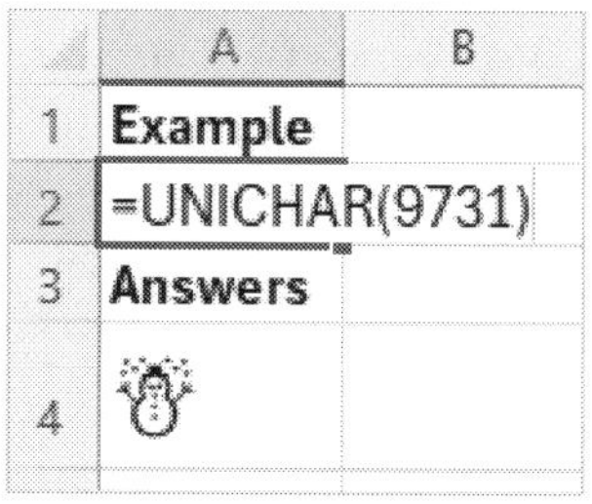

	A	B
1	**Example**	
2	=UNICHAR(9731)	
3	**Answers**	
4	☃	

Result: ☃

Explanation: The function returns the snowman symbol (☃) corresponding to the Unicode code 9731.

Explore Further with GPT

Ask GPT how to combine UNICHAR with functions like SEQUENCE, TEXTJOIN, or CHAR to create dynamic text and symbol lists.

Tips for Using UNICHAR

- **Valid Unicode range:** The number argument must be a valid Unicode code point. If the number is outside the valid range (1 to 1114111), the function returns a #VALUE! error.
- **Combining with other functions:** Use TEXTJOIN to create strings with multiple Unicode characters:

  ```
  =TEXTJOIN("", TRUE, UNICHAR(9731), UNICHAR(128515), UNICHAR(10084))
  ```

  This combines a snowman, smiling face emoji, and heart symbol into a single string (☃😃❤).
- **Dynamic symbols:** Use SEQUENCE with UNICHAR to generate lists of Unicode characters:

  ```
  =UNICHAR(SEQUENCE(10, 1, 65))
  ```

  This generates the first 10 capital letters (A–J) based on their Unicode codes.

UNICODE Function

Text Functions

Introduction

The UNICODE function returns the numeric Unicode code point of the first character in a text string. It is useful for identifying characters, working with special symbols, and handling multilingual text in different languages.

- **Simple explanation:** Returns the Unicode number of the first character in a text string.
- **Common use cases:** Used for identifying characters, working with encoding systems, and transforming text data.
- **When to use this function:** Use when you need to determine the Unicode code of a character for processing or converting text.

Syntax

```
=UNICODE(text)
```

- **text**: A text string or cell reference. The function returns the Unicode code of the first character in the string.

Worked Example

Challenge: Find the Unicode code for the character "A".

Formula:

```
=UNICODE("A")
```

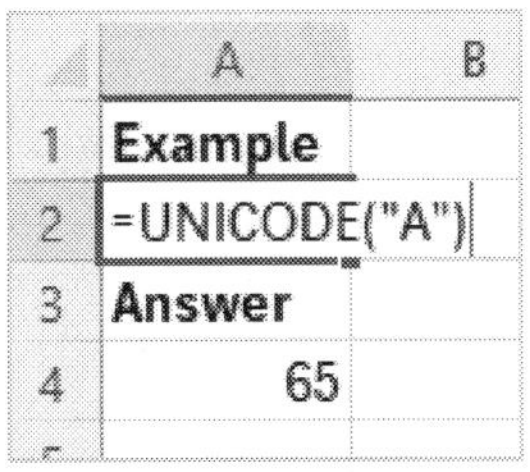

Result: 65
Explanation: The function returns 65, which is the Unicode code point for the uppercase letter "A".

Explore Further with GPT

Ask GPT how to combine UNICODE with functions like UNICHAR, TEXT, or SEQUENCE to create advanced character manipulation solutions.

Tips for Using UNICODE

- **First character only:** The function only returns the Unicode code for the first character in the string. To get codes for multiple characters, use MID or LEFT:

  ```
  =UNICODE(LEFT(A1, 1))
  ```

  This returns the Unicode code for the first character in A1.

- **Combining with UNICHAR:** Use UNICODE with UNICHAR to verify character encoding:

  ```
  =UNICHAR(UNICODE("A"))
  ```

  This returns the original character "A".

UNIQUE Function

Lookup & Reference Functions

Introduction

The UNIQUE function returns a list of unique values from a specified range or array. It can be used to extract distinct values, remove duplicates, and generate lists of unique items dynamically.

- **Simple explanation:** Extracts unique values from a range or array, removing duplicates.
- **Common use cases:** Used for data analysis, filtering unique entries, and generating lists without duplicates.
- **When to use this function:** Use when you need to remove duplicates or generate lists of distinct values.

Syntax

```
=UNIQUE(array, [by_col], [exactly_once])
```

- **array**: The range or array from which to extract unique values.
- **[by_col]** *(optional)*: A logical value indicating whether to compare values by row or by column:
  - FALSE or omitted: Compares values by row (default).
  - TRUE: Compares values by column.
- **[exactly_once]** *(optional)*: A logical value specifying whether to return values that appear exactly once:
  - FALSE or omitted: Returns all unique values (default).
  - TRUE: Returns values that appear exactly once in the array.

Worked Example

Challenge: Extract unique values from a list of fruits.

Formula:

`=UNIQUE(A1:A5)`

Result: Apple, Banana, Cherry

Explanation: The function removes duplicates and returns a list of unique values.

	A	B	C	D
1	Apple		**Example**	
2	Banana		=UNIQUE(A1:A5)	
3	Apple		**Answer**	
4	Cherry		Apple	
5	Banana		Banana	
6			Cherry	

Explore Further with GPT

Ask GPT how to combine UNIQUE with functions like SORT, FILTER, or TEXTJOIN to create dynamic lists and reports.

Tips for Using UNIQUE

- **Dynamic arrays:** In Excel 365 and Excel 2021, UNIQUE automatically spills results into adjacent cells. Ensure there's enough space for the output.
- **Excel compatibility:** The UNIQUE function is available in Excel 365 and Excel 2021.

UPPER Function

Text Functions

Introduction

The UPPER function converts all lowercase letters in a text string to uppercase. It leaves non-text characters, such as numbers and symbols, unchanged.

- **Simple explanation:** Converts a text string to all uppercase letters.
- **Common use cases:** Used for standardizing text data, ensuring consistent formatting, and preparing data for case-insensitive comparisons.
- **When to use this function:** Use when you need to convert text to uppercase for formatting or comparison purposes.

Syntax

```
=UPPER(text)
```

- **text**: The text string or cell reference to be converted to uppercase.

Worked Example

Challenge: Convert the text "hello world" to uppercase.

Formula:

```
=UPPER("hello world")
```

Result: "HELLO WORLD"
Explanation: The function converts all lowercase letters in "hello world" to uppercase.

	A	B
1	**Example**	
2	=UPPER("hello world")	
3	**Answer**	
4	HELLO WORLD	
5		

Explore Further with GPT

Ask GPT how to use UPPER with functions like LOWER, PROPER, or TEXTJOIN for advanced text formatting and manipulation.

Tips for Using UPPER

- **Combining with other functions:** Use UPPER with CONCAT or TEXTJOIN to create standardized uppercase strings:

  ```
  =UPPER(CONCAT(A1:A3))
  ```

  This converts the concatenated string to uppercase.

- **Case-insensitive comparisons:** Use UPPER in combination with IF to perform case-insensitive comparisons:

  ```
  =IF(UPPER(A1)=UPPER(B1), "Match", "No Match")
  ```

  This checks if the text in A1 and B1 are the same, regardless of case.

VALUE Function

Text Functions

Introduction

The VALUE function converts a text string that represents a number into an actual numeric value. It is useful for converting text representations of dates, times, and numbers into a format that Excel can recognize and use in calculations.

- **Simple explanation:** Converts a number stored as text into a numeric value.
- **Common use cases:** Used when importing data where numbers are stored as text, converting text-based dates or times into proper numeric values, and ensuring consistent data formatting.
- **When to use this function:** Use when you need to transform text that looks like a number into an actual number for calculations.

Syntax

```
=VALUE(text)
```

- **text**: A text string that represents a number, date, or time.

Worked Example

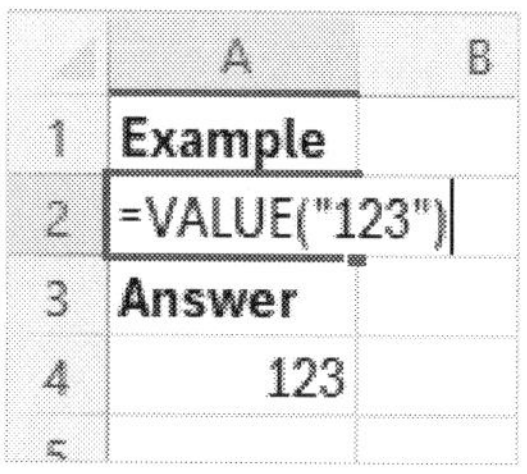

Challenge: Convert the text "123" into a numeric value.

Formula:

```
=VALUE("123")
```

Result: 123

Explanation: The function converts the text string "123" into the numeric value 123, which can now be used in arithmetic operations.

Explore Further with GPT

Ask GPT how to use VALUE with functions like TEXT, DATEVALUE, or TIMEVALUE to perform advanced text-to-number transformations.

Tips for Using VALUE

- **Automatic conversion:** In many cases, Excel automatically converts text to numbers when needed, so using VALUE may not be necessary. However, it's useful for explicitly converting text when automatic conversion doesn't occur.
- **Combining with TRIM and CLEAN:** Use VALUE with TRIM or CLEAN to handle text that may contain extra spaces or non-printable characters:

  ```
  =VALUE(TRIM(A1))
  ```

  This ensures that any extra spaces in A1 are removed before converting to a number.

VALUETOTEXT Function

Text Functions

Introduction

The VALUETOTEXT function converts a value (number, text, or array) into a text string. It is particularly useful when you need to display values as text or ensure consistency in formatting. This function can handle both single values and arrays.

- **Simple explanation:** Converts a value or array into text, preserving its display as a string.
- **Common use cases:** Used for formatting values as text, creating dynamic reports, and preparing data for export or display.
- **When to use this function:** Use when you need to display numbers, dates, or arrays as text without performing calculations on them.

Syntax

```
=VALUETOTEXT(value, [format])
```

- **value**: The value or array to convert to text.
- **[format]** *(optional)*: Specifies the output format:
    - 0 or omitted: Returns a single text string.
    - 1: Returns a structured array text format (used for arrays).

Worked Example

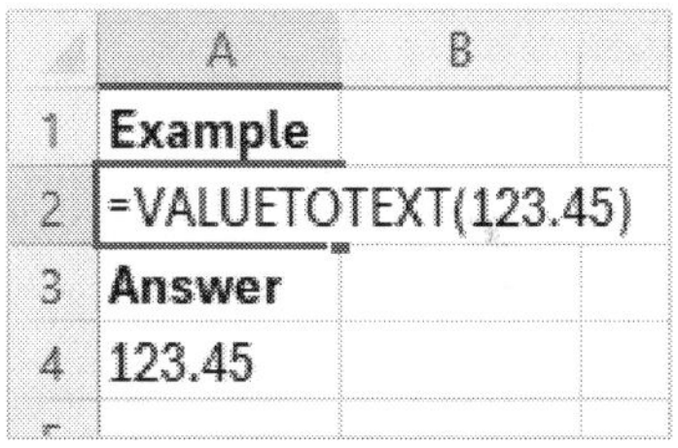

Challenge: Convert the number 123.45 into text.

Formula:

```
=VALUETOTEXT(123.45)
```

Result: "123.45"
Explanation: The function converts the numeric value 123.45 into the text string "123.45".

Explore Further with GPT

Ask GPT how to use VALUETOTEXT with functions like TEXT, TEXTJOIN, or ARRAYTOTEXT for advanced text formatting and data transformation

Tips for Using VALUETOTEXT

- **Combining with TEXT:** Use VALUETOTEXT with TEXT to apply specific number formatting before converting to text:

  ```
  =VALUETOTEXT(TEXT(A1, "0.00"))
  ```

  This formats the number in A1 to two decimal places before converting it to text.

- **Array handling:** When converting arrays, use format = 1 to display the array structure explicitly.

VAR Function

Compatibility Functions

Introduction

The VAR function calculates the variance of a sample data set. Variance measures how far each number in the data set is from the mean and is commonly used in statistics to assess data spread or dispersion.

- **Simple explanation:** Computes the variance for a sample data set, which indicates how much the data points deviate from the mean.
- **Common use cases:** Used in statistical analysis, hypothesis testing, and financial modeling to assess data variability.
- **When to use this function:** Use when you need to measure the spread of a sample data set.

Syntax

```
=VAR(number1, [number2], ...)
```

- **number1, [number2], ...**: Numeric values, cell references, or ranges representing the sample data set. You can provide up to 254 arguments.

Worked Example

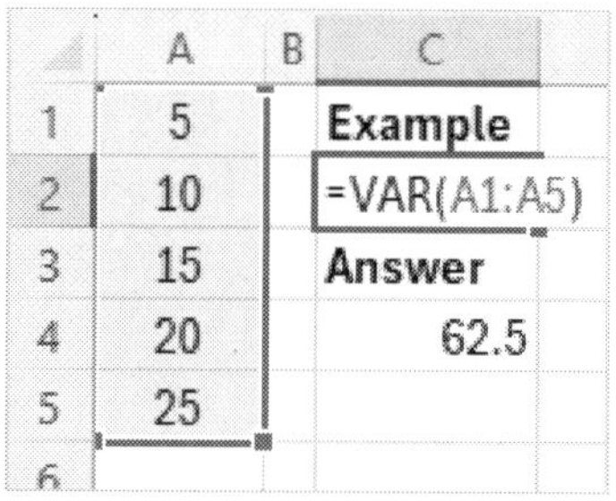

Challenge: Calculate the variance for the data set {5, 10, 15, 20, 25}.

Formula:

```
=VAR(A1:A5)
```

Result: 62.5
Explanation: The function computes the variance for the sample data set by calculating the average squared deviation of each value from the mean.

Explore Further with GPT

Ask GPT how to use VAR with functions like STDEV, VARP, or AVERAGE to perform advanced statistical analysis.

Tips for Using VAR

- **Sample vs. population:** The VAR function calculates the variance for a sample. For population variance, use VARP or VAR.P in newer Excel versions.
- **Modern equivalent:** In newer versions of Excel, VAR.S is used instead of VAR for sample variance.
- **Ignoring non-numeric values:** The function ignores non-numeric values in the input range.

VAR.P Function

Statistical Functions

Introduction

The VAR.P function calculates the variance of an entire population. Variance measures the spread of data points around the mean. Unlike VAR.S, which is used for sample data, VAR.P assumes the data represents the entire population.

- **Simple explanation:** Computes the variance for an entire population, indicating how much the data points deviate from the mean.
- **Common use cases:** Used in statistical analysis, financial modeling, and quality control when working with complete population data.
- **When to use this function:** Use when calculating the variance for a full data set (population) rather than a sample.

Syntax

```
=VAR.P(number1, [number2], ...)
```

- **number1, [number2], ...:** Numeric values, cell references, or ranges representing the population data set. You can provide up to 254 arguments

Worked Example

Challenge: Calculate the population variance for the data set {5, 10, 15, 20, 25}

Formula:

`=VAR.P(A1:A5)`

Result: 50
Explanation: The function computes the population variance by calculating the average squared deviation of each value from the mean.

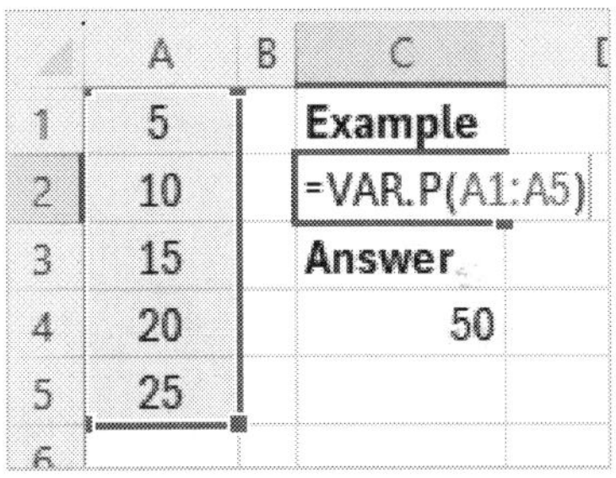

Explore Further with GPT

Ask GPT how to use VAR.P with functions like STDEV.P, VAR.S, or MEDIAN for comprehensive statistical analysis.

Tips for Using VAR.P

- **Sample vs. population:** Use VAR.P for population data. For sample data, use VAR.S.
- **Modern equivalent:** The VARP function in older versions of Excel has been replaced by VAR.P in Excel 2010 and later versions.
- **Ignoring non-numeric values:** The function ignores non-numeric values in the input range.

VAR.S Function

Statistical Functions

Introduction

The VAR.S function calculates the variance of a sample data set. Variance measures how spread out the data points are around the mean. This function is typically used in statistical analysis when the data represents a sample rather than the entire population.

- **Simple explanation:** Computes the variance for a sample, indicating how much the sample data points deviate from the mean.
- **Common use cases:** Used in statistical analysis, hypothesis testing, and financial modeling to measure variability in sample data.
- **When to use this function:** Use when calculating the variance for a sample of data, not the entire population.

Syntax

```
=VAR.S(number1, [number2], ...)
```

- **number1, [number2], ...:** Numeric values, cell references, or ranges representing the sample data set. You can provide up to 254 arguments.

Worked Example

Challenge: Calculate the sample variance for the data set {5, 10, 15, 20, 25}.

Formula:

```
=VAR.S(A1:A5)
```

Result: 62.5
Explanation: The function computes the sample variance by calculating the average squared deviation of each value from the mean, dividing by n - 1 (where n is the number of data points).

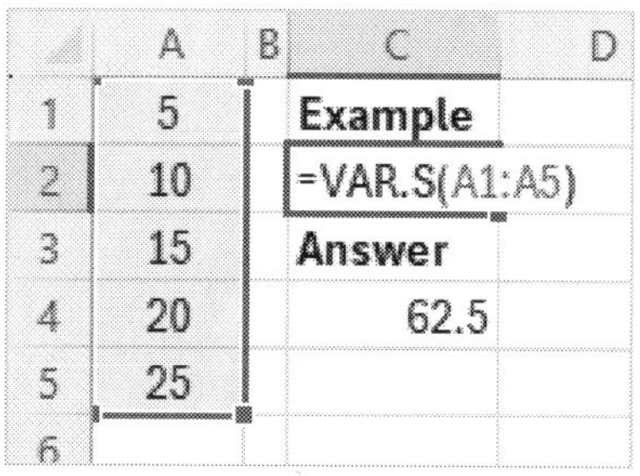

	A	B	C	D
1	5		**Example**	
2	10		=VAR.S(A1:A5)	
3	15		**Answer**	
4	20		62.5	
5	25			
6				

Explore Further with GPT

Ask GPT how to use VAR.S with functions like STDEV.S, AVERAGE, or COUNT for advanced statistical analysis.

Tips for Using VAR.S

- **Sample vs. population:** Use VAR.S for sample data. For population data, use VAR.P.
- **Modern equivalent:** In older versions of Excel, VAR was used for sample variance. VAR.S is the updated function in Excel 2010 and later versions.
- **Ignoring non-numeric values:** The function ignores non-numeric values in the input range.
- **Excel compatibility:** The VAR.S function is available in Excel 2010 and later versions.

VARA Function

Statistical Functions

Introduction

The VARA function calculates the variance of a sample data set, including both numeric and non-numeric values. Unlike VAR.S, which only considers numeric values, VARA treats logical values and text differently:

- Logical values TRUE and FALSE are treated as 1 and 0, respectively.
- Text values are treated as 0.
- **Simple explanation:** Computes the sample variance while treating logical and text values as part of the data set.
- **Common use cases:** Used in statistical analysis when working with data sets that may include logical values or text data.
- **When to use this function:** Use when calculating the sample variance for data sets containing both numeric and non-numeric values.

Syntax

```
=VARA(number1, [number2], ...)
```

- **number1, [number2], ...:** Numeric values, logical values, text, or ranges representing the sample data set. You can provide up to 254 arguments.

Worked Example

Challenge: Calculate the sample variance for the data set {5, 10, TRUE, "Text", FALSE}.

Formula:

```
=VARA(A1:A5)
```

	A	B	C
1	5		**Example**
2	10		=VARA(A1:A5)
3	TRUE		**Answer**
4	Text		18.7
5	FALSE		

Result: 18.7

Explanation: The function computes the sample variance by treating TRUE as 1, "Text" and FALSE as 0, resulting in the data set {5, 10, 1, 0, 0}.

Explore Further with GPT

Ask GPT how to use VARA with functions like STDEVA, AVERAGEA, or COUNTIF for more advanced data analysis.

Tips for Using VARA

- **Handling text values:**
  - Text values, including empty strings (""), are treated as 0.
- **Comparing with VAR.S:** Use VARA when working with mixed data types. For purely numeric data, use VAR.S.

VARP Function

Compatibility Functions

Introduction

The VARP function calculates the variance of an entire population. It measures how far each data point in the population is from the mean. Unlike VAR, which is used for sample data, VARP assumes the data set represents the entire population.

Note: In newer versions of Excel, VARP has been replaced by VAR.P, but it remains available for backward compatibility.

- **Simple explanation:** Computes the variance for an entire population, indicating how much the data points deviate from the mean.
- **Common use cases:** Used in statistical analysis and financial modeling when working with complete population data.
- **When to use this function:** Use when calculating the variance for a full data set (population) rather than a sample.

Syntax

```
=VARP(number1, [number2], ...)
```

- **number1, [number2], ...:** Numeric values, cell references, or ranges representing the population data set. You can provide up to 254 arguments.

Worked Example

Challenge: Calculate the population variance for the data set {4, 8, 12, 16, 20}

Formula:

```
=VARP(A1:A5)
```

Result: 32

Explanation: The function computes the population variance by calculating the average squared deviation of each value from the mean.

	A	B	C
1	4		**Example**
2	8		=VARP(A1:A5)
3	12		**Answer**
4	16		32
5	20		

Explore Further with GPT

Ask GPT how to replace VARP with VAR.P in newer Excel versions for improved statistical analysis

Tips for Using VARP

- **Sample vs. population:** Use VARP for population data. For sample data, use VAR.
- **Modern equivalent:** In newer versions of Excel, VAR.P replaces VARP.
- **Ignoring non-numeric values:** The function ignores non-numeric values in the input range.

VARPA Function

Statistical Functions

Introduction

The VARPA function calculates the variance for an entire population, including both numeric and non-numeric values. Unlike VAR.P, which only considers numeric values, VARPA treats logical values and text differently:

- Logical values TRUE and FALSE are treated as 1 and 0, respectively.
- Text values are treated as 0.
- **Simple explanation:** Computes the population variance, including logical and text values as part of the data set.
- **Common use cases:** Used in statistical analysis and modeling when working with complete data sets that include logical values or text.
- **When to use this function:** Use when calculating the population variance for data sets containing both numeric and non-numeric values.

Syntax

```
=VARPA(number1, [number2], ...)
```

- **number1, [number2], ...:** Numeric values, logical values, text, or ranges representing the population data set. You can provide up to 254 arguments.

Worked Example

Challenge: Calculate the population variance for the data set {5, 10, TRUE, "Text", FALSE}.

Formula:

```
=VARPA(A1:A5)
```

Result: 14.96
Explanation: The function computes the population variance by treating TRUE as 1, "Text" and FALSE as 0, resulting in the data set {5, 10, 1, 0, 0}.

	A	B	C	D
1	5		**Example**	
2	10		=VARPA(A1:A5)	
3	TRUE		**Answer**	
4	Text		14.96	
5	FALSE			
6				

Explore Further with GPT

Ask GPT how to combine VARPA with functions like STDEVA, AVERAGEA, or COUNTIF to enhance statistical analysis.

Tips for Using VARPA

- **Handling logical values:** TRUE is counted as 1, and FALSE is counted as 0.
- **Handling text values:** All text values, including empty strings (""), are treated as 0.
- **Comparing with VAR.P:** Use VARPA when working with mixed data types. For purely numeric data, use VAR.P.

VDB Function

Financial Functions

Introduction

The VDB function calculates the depreciation of an asset for a specified period using the variable declining balance method. This method allows switching to straight-line depreciation when it results in greater depreciation than the declining balance method.

- **Simple explanation:** Computes depreciation using a variable declining balance method, switching to straight-line depreciation when it yields a higher deduction.
- **Common use cases:** Used in accounting and financial modeling to determine the depreciation of assets over time with flexibility in switching depreciation methods.
- **When to use this function:** Use when you need a flexible depreciation calculation that can switch between declining balance and straight-line methods.

Syntax

```
=VDB(cost, salvage, life, start_period, end_period, [factor], [no_switch])
```

- **cost**: The initial cost of the asset.
- **salvage**: The value of the asset at the end of its useful life (salvage value).
- **life**: The total useful life of the asset (in periods).
- **start_period**: The starting period for which to calculate depreciation.
- **end_period**: The ending period for which to calculate depreciation.
- **[factor]** *(optional)*: The rate at which the balance declines (default is 2 for double-declining balance).
- **[no_switch]** *(optional)*: A logical value specifying whether to switch to straight-line depreciation when it yields greater deductions:
    - FALSE or omitted: Allows switching to straight-line depreciation.
    - TRUE: Prevents switching to straight-line depreciation.

Worked Example

Challenge: Calculate the depreciation of an asset with the following details:

- Initial cost: $10,000; Salvage value: $1,000; Useful life: 5 years; Depreciation from year 1 to year 2

	A	B	C
1	**Example**		
2	=VDB(10000, 1000, 5, 1, 2)		
3	**Answer**		
4	2,400.00		
5			

Formula:

```
=VDB(10000, 1000, 5, 1, 2)
```

Result: 2400.00

Explanation: The function calculates the depreciation for the specified period using the double-declining balance method and switches to straight-line if it yields a higher depreciation.

VLOOKUP Function

Lookup & Reference Functions

Introduction

The VLOOKUP function searches for a value in the first column of a range and returns a value in the same row from a specified column. It is useful for retrieving data from structured tables.

- **Simple explanation:** Searches for a value in the first column of a range and returns a corresponding value from another column in the same row.
- **Common use cases:** Used for looking up prices, retrieving product details, matching data across tables, and generating reports.
- **When to use this function:** Use when you need to search vertically in a table and retrieve related data from a specific column.

Syntax

```
=VLOOKUP(lookup_value, table_array, col_index_num, [range_lookup])
```

- **lookup_value**: The value to search for in the first column of table_array.
- **table_array**: The range containing the data. The first column is where the lookup will occur.
- **col_index_num**: The column number (starting from 1) from which to return the value.
- **[range_lookup]** *(optional)*: A logical value specifying whether to find an exact match (FALSE) or an approximate match (TRUE or omitted):
  - FALSE: Finds an exact match.
  - TRUE: Finds an approximate match (useful for sorted data).

Worked Example

Challenge: Look up the price of "Apple" from a product table.

Formula:

```
=VLOOKUP("Apple", A1:B4, 2, FALSE)
```

Result: 1.50

Explanation: The function searches for "Apple" in column A, finds it in row 1, and returns the corresponding value from column B, which is 1.50.

	A	B	C	D	E	F
1	**Product**	**Price**		**Example**		
2	Apple	1.5		=VLOOKUP("Apple", A1:B4, 2, FALSE)		
3	Banana	0.75		**Answer**		
4	Cherry	2		1.5		

Tips for Using VLOOKUP

- **Exact match vs. approximate match:** Use FALSE for exact matches to avoid incorrect results:

  ```
  =VLOOKUP(100, A1:B10, 2, FALSE)
  ```

  This ensures only exact matches are returned.

- **Column index number:** Ensure col_index_num is within the range of the table array. If it exceeds the number of columns, Excel returns a #REF! error.

VSTACK Function

Lookup & Reference Functions

Introduction

The VSTACK function vertically stacks arrays or ranges into a single array. It combines multiple arrays by placing them one below the other. Empty cells in the input are preserved in the output.

- **Simple explanation:** Combines multiple arrays vertically into a single array by stacking them.
- **Common use cases:** Used for consolidating data, creating lists, and dynamically combining ranges.
- **When to use this function:** Use when you need to merge multiple arrays or ranges vertically into a single output array.

Syntax

```
=VSTACK(array1, [array2], ...)
```

- **array1, [array2], ...:** One or more arrays or ranges to stack vertically.

Worked Example

Challenge: Stack two ranges {1, 2, 3} and {4, 5, 6} vertically.

Formula:

Result: The function stacks the two arrays one below the other, creating a single array.

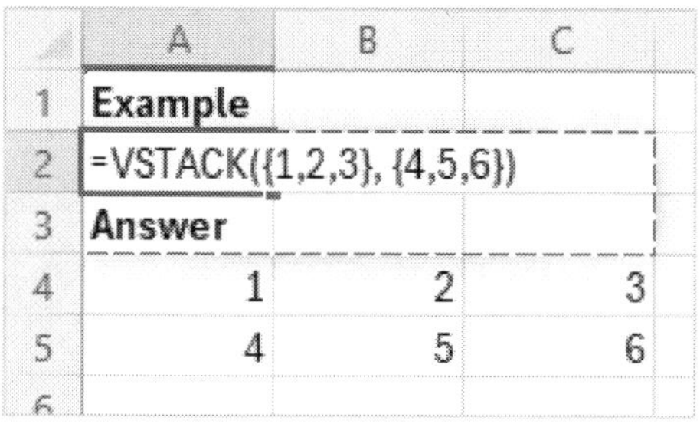

Explore Further with GPT

Ask GPT how to combine VSTACK with functions like HSTACK, SORT, or UNIQUE to create dynamic lists and tables.

Tips for Using VSTACK

- **Combining with UNIQUE:** Use VSTACK with UNIQUE to create a list of unique values from multiple ranges:

  ```
  =UNIQUE(VSTACK(A1:A10, B1:B10))
  ```

  This returns a unique list of values from both ranges.

- **Preserving empty cells:** VSTACK preserves empty cells in the output, which can be useful when working with sparse data.
- **Combining ranges dynamically:** Use VSTACK with FILTER to create dynamic lists based on conditions:

  ```
  =VSTACK(FILTER(A1:A10, B1:B10="Yes"))
  ```

  This stacks values from A1:A10 where corresponding cells in B1:B10 equal "Yes".

WEBSERVICE Function

Web Functions

Introduction

The WEBSERVICE function retrieves data from a specified URL by making a web request. It is useful for importing data from web APIs, online databases, or external web services directly into Excel.

- **Simple explanation:** Retrieves data from a web URL and displays the result in a cell.
- **Common use cases:** Used for importing real-time data, such as stock prices, weather information, or currency exchange rates from online sources.
- **When to use this function:** Use when you need to fetch data from a web service or API directly into Excel.

Syntax

```
=WEBSERVICE(url)
```

- **url**: The URL of the web service or API to retrieve data from. It must be a valid URL enclosed in quotes or referenced from a cell.

Worked Example

Challenge: Retrieve the current exchange rate from an online currency converter API.

URL Example: https://api.exchangerate-api.com/v4/latest/USD

Formula:

```
=WEBSERVICE("https://api.exchangerate-api.com/v4/latest/USD")
```

Result: A JSON string containing exchange rate data.
Explanation: The function retrieves real-time exchange rate data from the API and displays it as a string.

	A
1	**Example**
2	=WEBSERVICE("https://api.exchangerate-api.com/v4/latest/USD")
3	**Answer**
4	*{"provider":"https://www.exchangerate-api.com","WARNING_UPGRADE_TO_V6":"https://www.exchangerate-*
5	

Explore Further with GPT

Ask GPT how to parse the results of WEBSERVICE using FILTERXML or JSONPARSE (if supported by add-ins) for advanced data manipulation.

Tips for Using WEBSERVICE

- **Handling large data:** If the web service returns a large amount of data, consider using FILTERXML to extract specific parts of the response:

  ```
  =FILTERXML(WEBSERVICE("https://example.com/api"), "//desired_element")
  ```

- **API key management:** Some web services require an API key for access. Ensure your URL includes the necessary authentication details.
- **Excel compatibility:** The WEBSERVICE function is available in Excel 2013 and later versions for Windows.

WEEKDAY Function

Date & Time Functions

Introduction

The WEEKDAY function returns the day of the week as a number for a given date. It allows you to specify different numbering systems, making it flexible for different regional or business needs.

- **Simple explanation:** Returns a number representing the day of the week for a given date.
- **Common use cases:** Used for scheduling, calculating workdays, and determining specific days (e.g., weekends or weekdays).
- **When to use this function:** Use when you need to determine the day of the week for a given date.

Syntax

```
=WEEKDAY(serial_number, [return_type])
```

- **serial_number**: A valid Excel date for which to determine the day of the week.
- **[return_type]** *(optional)*: Specifies the numbering system for the days of the week:
    - 1 or omitted: Numbers from 1 (Sunday) to 7 (Saturday).
    - 2: Numbers from 1 (Monday) to 7 (Sunday).
    - 3: Numbers from 0 (Monday) to 6 (Sunday).
    - 11: Numbers from 1 (Monday) to 7 (Sunday).
    - 12: Numbers from 1 (Tuesday) to 7 (Monday).
    - 13: Numbers from 1 (Wednesday) to 7 (Tuesday).
    - 14: Numbers from 1 (Thursday) to 7 (Wednesday).
    - 15: Numbers from 1 (Friday) to 7 (Thursday).
    - 16: Numbers from 1 (Saturday) to 7 (Friday).
    - 17: Numbers from 1 (Sunday) to 7 (Saturday).

Worked Example

Challenge: Find the day of the week for 01-Jan-2024, assuming Sunday is day 1.

Formula:

```
=WEEKDAY(DATE(2024,1,1))
```

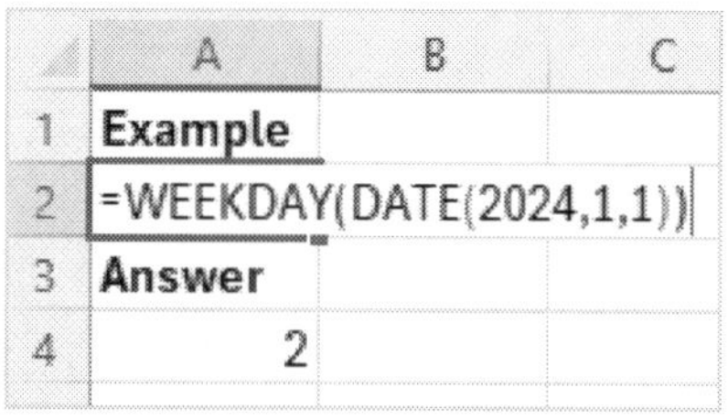

	A	B	C
1	Example		
2	=WEEKDAY(DATE(2024,1,1))		
3	Answer		
4	2		

Result: 2

Explanation: Since 01-Jan-2024 is a Monday, the function returns 2 because the default numbering system starts with Sunday as 1.

Tips for Using WEEKDAY

- **Custom numbering systems:** Use different return_type values to adapt to regional or organizational standards for the start of the week.

WEEKNUM Function

Date & Time Functions

Introduction

The WEEKNUM function returns the week number of the year for a given date. By default, it considers January 1 as part of week 1, but it also allows specifying different starting days of the week.

- **Simple explanation:** Returns the week number of the year for a specified date.
- **Common use cases:** Used for scheduling, reporting, and tracking weekly progress throughout the year.
- **When to use this function:** Use when you need to determine the week number for a given date or create weekly-based reports.

Syntax

```
=WEEKNUM(serial_number, [return_type])
```

- **serial_number**: A valid Excel date for which to find the week number.
- **[return_type]** *(optional)*: Specifies which day the week starts on:
  - 1 or omitted: Week starts on Sunday (default).
  - 2: Week starts on Monday.
  - 11: Week starts on Monday (ISO week numbering, week 1 is the first week with at least 4 days in January).

Return Types for WEEKNUM:

Return Type	Start of Week
1	Sunday
2	Monday
11	Monday (ISO 8601)
12	Tuesday
13	Wednesday
14	Thursday
15	Friday
16	Saturday
17	Sunday

Worked Example

Challenge: Find the week number of 01-Jan-2024, assuming the week starts on Sunday.

Formula:

```
=WEEKNUM(DATE(2024,1,1))
```

Result: 1
Explanation: Since 01-Jan-2024 is in the first week of the year and the default start day is Sunday, the function returns 1.

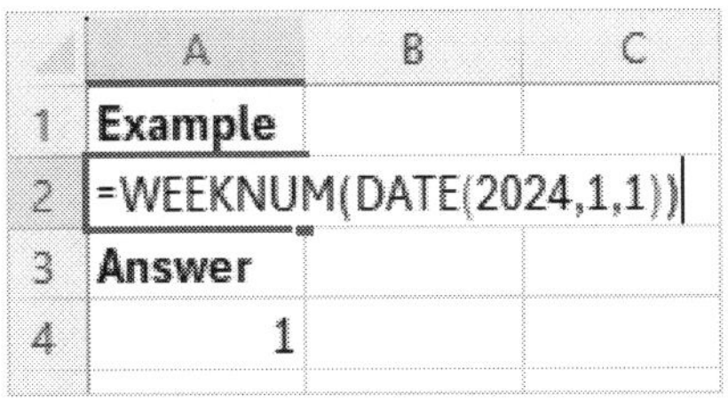

WEIBULL Function

Compatibility Functions

Introduction

The WEIBULL function returns the Weibull distribution, a continuous probability distribution commonly used in reliability analysis, life data analysis, and survival studies. It is maintained for compatibility with older versions of Excel.

Note: In newer versions of Excel, WEIBULL has been replaced by WEIBULL.DIST, but it remains available for backward compatibility.

- **Simple explanation:** Computes the Weibull distribution for a given value.
- **Common use cases:** Used in statistical modeling, reliability engineering, and quality control.
- **When to use this function:** Use when you need to model time-to-failure data or analyze the reliability of systems.

Syntax

```
=WEIBULL(x, alpha, beta, cumulative)
```

- **x**: The value at which to evaluate the function (must be ≥ 0).
- **alpha**: The shape parameter of the distribution (must be > 0).
- **beta**: The scale parameter of the distribution (must be > 0).
- **cumulative**: A logical value specifying the form of the function:
  - TRUE: Returns the cumulative distribution function (CDF).
  - FALSE: Returns the probability density function (PDF).

Worked Example

Challenge: Compute the cumulative Weibull distribution for x = 2, alpha = 3, and beta = 1.5.

Formula:

```
=WEIBULL(2, 3, 1.5, TRUE)
```

Result: 0.906554

Explanation: The function computes the cumulative probability for the specified value using the Weibull distribution formula.

	A	B	C
1	**Example**		
2	=WEIBULL(2, 3, 1.5, TRUE)		
3	**Answer**		
4	0.906554		

Explore Further with GPT

Ask GPT how to use WEIBULL with functions like NORM.DIST, EXPON.DIST, or GAMMA.DIST for advanced statistical analysis and modeling.

Tips for Using WEIBULL

- **Cumulative vs. probability density:** Use cumulative = TRUE for the cumulative distribution function and cumulative = FALSE for the probability density function.

WEIBULL.DIST Function

Statistical Functions

Introduction

The WEIBULL.DIST function returns the Weibull distribution, which is commonly used in reliability analysis, survival analysis, and failure time analysis. This function allows you to calculate both the cumulative distribution function (CDF) and the probability density function (PDF) for a given value.

- **Simple explanation:** Computes the Weibull distribution for a given value, either as a cumulative probability or as a probability density.
- **Common use cases:** Used in reliability engineering, life data analysis, and quality control to model time-to-failure data.
- **When to use this function:** Use when analyzing the reliability of systems or modeling survival data.

Syntax

```
=WEIBULL.DIST(x, alpha, beta, cumulative)
```

- **x**: The value at which to evaluate the function (must be ≥ 0).
- **alpha**: The shape parameter of the distribution (must be > 0).
- **beta**: The scale parameter of the distribution (must be > 0).
- **cumulative**: A logical value specifying the form of the function:
  - TRUE: Returns the cumulative distribution function (CDF).
  - FALSE: Returns the probability density function (PDF).

Worked Example

Challenge: Compute the cumulative Weibull distribution for x = 2, alpha = 3, and beta = 1.5.

Formula:

```
=WEIBULL.DIST(2, 3, 1.5, TRUE)
```

Result: 0.906554
Explanation: The function computes the cumulative probability for x = 2 using the Weibull distribution formula.

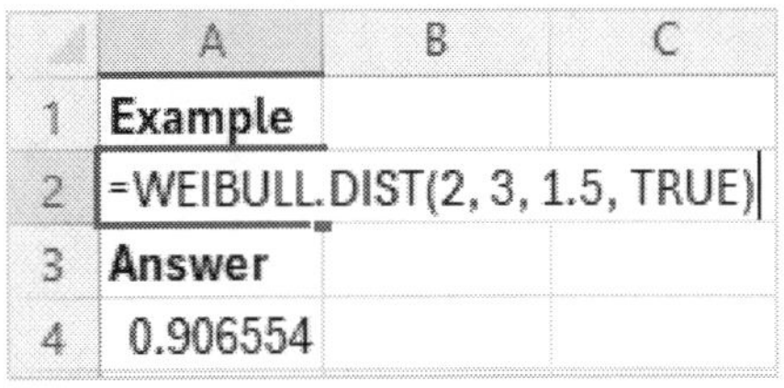

	A	B	C
1	**Example**		
2	=WEIBULL.DIST(2, 3, 1.5, TRUE)		
3	**Answer**		
4	0.906554		

Explore Further with GPT

Ask GPT how to combine WEIBULL.DIST with functions like EXP, NORM.DIST, or GAMMA.DIST to model complex reliability and survival scenarios.

Tips for Using WEIBULL.DIST

- **Cumulative vs. probability density:** Use cumulative = TRUE for cumulative probabilities and cumulative = FALSE for probability densities.
- **Handling errors:**
  - Ensure x is greater than or equal to 0. If x < 0, the function returns a #NUM! error.
  - Ensure alpha and beta are greater than 0; otherwise, the function returns a #NUM! error.

WORKDAY Function

Date & Time Functions

Introduction

The WORKDAY function returns the date that is a specified number of workdays before or after a given start date. It excludes weekends (Saturday and Sunday by default) and optionally excludes specified holidays.

- **Simple explanation:** Calculates a future or past date by adding or subtracting workdays, excluding weekends and optional holidays.
- **Common use cases:** Used for project planning, scheduling deadlines, and calculating delivery dates that fall on business days.
- **When to use this function:** Use when you need to determine a date based on a specific number of business days, excluding weekends and holidays.

Syntax

```
=WORKDAY(start_date, days, [holidays])
```

- **start_date**: The starting date from which to count workdays.
- **days**: The number of workdays to add (positive) or subtract (negative) from the start date.
- **[holidays]** *(optional)*: A range or array of dates to exclude from the calculation, representing non-working days.

Worked Example

Challenge: Calculate the delivery date that is 10 workdays after 01-Jan-2024, excluding weekends.

Formula:

```
=WORKDAY(DATE(2024,1,1), 10)
```

Result: 15-Jan-2024
Explanation: The function adds 10 workdays to 01-Jan-2024, skipping weekends to arrive at 15-Jan-2024.

	A	B
1	**Example**	
2	=WORKDAY(DATE(2024,1,1), 10)	
3	**Answer**	
4	January 15, 2024	

Explore Further with GPT

Ask GPT how to use WORKDAY with functions like NETWORKDAYS, EDATE, or TEXT to create advanced project timelines and schedules.

Tips for Using WORKDAY

- **Negative days:** Use a negative value for days to count backward:

  ```
  =WORKDAY(DATE(2024,1,15), -10)
  ```

  This returns the date 10 workdays before 15-Jan-2024.

- **Handling holidays:** Use a range of holiday dates to exclude multiple non-working days:

  ```
  =WORKDAY(A1, 20, B1:B5)
  ```

  This calculates 20 workdays after A1, excluding dates in B1:B5.

WORKDAY.INTL Function

Date & Time Functions

Introduction

The WORKDAY.INTL function returns the date that is a specified number of workdays before or after a given start date, allowing for custom definitions of weekends. It also optionally excludes specified holidays.

- **Simple explanation:** Calculates a future or past date by adding or subtracting workdays, with customizable weekends and optional holidays.
- **Common use cases:** Used in project management, scheduling, and business operations where weekends may not follow the standard Saturday-Sunday format.
- **When to use this function:** Use when you need to calculate workdays with non-standard weekends or account for region-specific work schedules.

Syntax

```
=WORKDAY.INTL(start_date, days, [weekend], [holidays])
```

- **start_date**: The starting date from which to count workdays.
- **days**: The number of workdays to add (positive) or subtract (negative) from the start date.
- **[weekend]** *(optional)*: A string or number representing which days of the week are weekends.
- **[holidays]** *(optional)*: A range or array of dates to exclude from the calculation, representing non-working days.

Weekend Codes: [Weekend Code: *Weekend Days*]

[1: *Saturday, Sunday (default)*]; [2: *Sunday, Monday*]; [3: *Monday, Tuesday*]; [4: *Tuesday, Wednesday*]; [5: *Wednesday, Thursday*]; [6: *Thursday, Friday*]; [7: *Friday, Saturday*]; [11: *Sunday only*]; [12: *Monday only*]; [13: *Tuesday only*]; [14: *Wednesday only*]; [15: *Thursday only*]; [16: *Friday only*]; [17: *Saturday only*]

Worked Example

Challenge: Calculate the date that is 10 workdays after 01-Jan-2024, with a weekend of Friday and Saturday.

Formula:

```
=WORKDAY.INTL(DATE(2024,1,1), 10, 7)
```

Result: 15-Jan-2024
Explanation: The function adds 10 workdays to 01-Jan-2024, skipping Fridays and Saturdays as weekends.

	A	B	C	D
1	**Example**			
2	=WORKDAY.INTL(DATE(2024,1,1), 10, 7)			
3	**Answer**			
4	15-Jan-24			

Tips for Using WORKDAY.INTL

- **Handling holidays:** Provide a range of holiday dates to exclude non-working days:

  ```
  =WORKDAY.INTL(A1, 15, 1, B1:B5)
  ```

  This calculates 15 workdays after A1, excluding holidays listed in B1:B5.

WRAPCOLS Function

Lookup & Reference Functions

Introduction

The WRAPCOLS function arranges values from a single row or column into multiple columns of a specified width. It is useful for transforming long lists of data into structured tables.

- **Simple explanation:** Rearranges a list of values into multiple columns with a specified number of elements per column.
- **Common use cases:** Used for reshaping data, creating dynamic tables, and converting long lists into more readable formats.
- **When to use this function:** Use when you need to organize data into a grid with a fixed number of values per column.

Syntax

```
=WRAPCOLS(vector, wrap_count, [pad_with])
```

- **vector**: The array or range of values to wrap into columns.
- **wrap_count**: The number of values to place in each column.
- **[pad_with]** *(optional)*: The value to use for padding if the total number of values is not evenly divisible by wrap_count. If omitted, the function leaves blank cells as padding.

Worked Example

Challenge: Arrange the list {1, 2, 3, 4, 5, 6, 7} into columns with 3 values per column.

Formula:

```
=WRAPCOLS({1, 2, 3, 4, 5, 6, 7}, 3)
```

	A	B	C
1	**Example**		
2	=WRAPCOLS({1,2,3,4,5,6,7}, 3)		
3	**Answer**		
4	1	4	7
5	2	5	#N/A
6	3	6	#N/A
7			

Result: The function arranges the values into 3 columns with up to 3 values per column. Since there aren't enough values to fill all columns completely, blank cells are used as padding.

Explore Further with GPT

Ask GPT how to use WRAPCOLS with functions like WRAPROWS, SEQUENCE, or SORT to dynamically transform and format data.

Tips for Using WRAPCOLS

- **Combining with SEQUENCE:** Use WRAPCOLS with SEQUENCE to generate structured arrays dynamically:

  ```
  =WRAPCOLS(SEQUENCE(10), 2)
  ```

  This generates a sequence of numbers from 1 to 10, arranged into columns with 2 values per column.

WRAPROWS Function

Lookup & Reference Functions

Introduction

The WRAPROWS function arranges values from a single row or column into multiple rows of a specified width. It is useful for transforming long lists of data into structured tables with a fixed number of values per row.

- **Simple explanation:** Rearranges a list of values into multiple rows, each with a specified number of elements.
- **Common use cases:** Used for reshaping data, creating dynamic tables, and organizing long lists into a more readable grid format.
- **When to use this function:** Use when you need to convert a list of values into rows with a fixed number of values per row.

Syntax

```
=WRAPROWS(vector, wrap_count, [pad_with])
```

- **vector**: The array or range of values to wrap into rows.
- **wrap_count**: The number of values to place in each row.
- **[pad_with]** *(optional)*: The value to use for padding if the total number of values is not evenly divisible by wrap_count. If omitted, the function leaves blank cells as padding.

Worked Example

Challenge: Arrange the list {1, 2, 3, 4, 5, 6, 7} into rows with 3 values per row.

Formula:

```
=WRAPROWS({1, 2, 3, 4, 5, 6, 7}, 3)
```

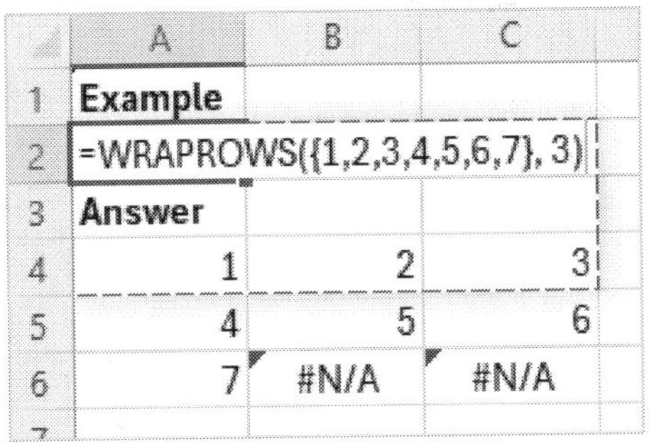

	A	B	C
1	**Example**		
2	=WRAPROWS({1,2,3,4,5,6,7}, 3)		
3	**Answer**		
4	1	2	3
5	4	5	6
6	7	#N/A	#N/A
7			

Result: The function arranges the values into rows with 3 values each. Since there aren't enough values to fill the last row completely, blank cells are used as padding.

Explore Further with GPT

Ask GPT how to use WRAPROWS with functions like WRAPCOLS, SEQUENCE, or SORT to dynamically reshape and transform data.

Tips for Using WRAPROWS

- **Combining with SEQUENCE:** Use WRAPROWS with SEQUENCE to create structured arrays dynamically:

  ```
  =WRAPROWS(SEQUENCE(10), 4)
  ```

  This generates a sequence of numbers from 1 to 10, arranged into rows with 4 values each.

XIRR Function

Financial Functions

Introduction

The XIRR function returns the internal rate of return (IRR) for a series of cash flows that occur at irregular intervals. It is commonly used in financial analysis to evaluate investment performance, where cash flows are not evenly spaced in time.

- **Simple explanation:** Computes the internal rate of return for a set of cash flows occurring at irregular dates.
- **Common use cases:** Used for calculating IRR in projects, investments, and loans with non-periodic cash flows.
- **When to use this function:** Use when evaluating investments or financial projects where cash inflows and outflows occur on different dates.

Syntax

```
=XIRR(values, dates, [guess])
```

- **values**: A range or array of cash flows corresponding to the specified dates. The first value typically represents the initial investment and should be negative.
- **dates**: A range or array of dates corresponding to the cash flows. These dates must be in chronological order.
- **[guess]** *(optional)*: An initial guess for the IRR (default is 0.1 or 10%)

Worked Example

Challenge: Calculate the IRR for the set of cash flows occurring on irregular dates:

Formula:

```
=XIRR(B1:B4, A1:A4)
```

Result: 0.39661 (or 39.66%)
Explanation: The function computes an IRR of 39.66% based on the irregular cash flows and their corresponding dates.

	A	B	C	D	E
1	Date	Cash Flow		Example	
2	01-Jan-24	-1000		=XIRR(B2:B5, A2:A5)	
3	01-Mar-24	300		Answer	
4	01-Jun-24	400		0.39661	
5	01-Dec-24	500			
6					

Explore Further with GPT

Ask GPT how to combine XIRR with functions like NPV, XNPV, or IRR for more comprehensive financial analysis and investment evaluations.

Tips for Using XIRR

- **Cash flow order:** Ensure that the dates are in chronological order and match the corresponding values.
- **Initial investment:** The first cash flow (initial investment) is typically negative, representing an outflow.

XLOOKUP Function

Lookup & Reference Functions

Introduction

The XLOOKUP function searches a range or array for a specified value and returns a corresponding value from another range or array. It is more flexible and powerful than VLOOKUP and HLOOKUP, supporting exact matches, approximate matches, and reverse searches.

- **Simple explanation:** Searches for a value in a range and returns a corresponding value from another range.
- **Common use cases:** Used for looking up values in tables, dynamic reporting, and replacing older lookup functions like VLOOKUP, HLOOKUP, and INDEX-MATCH.
- **When to use this function:** Use when you need a flexible and efficient way to retrieve data based on a search criterion.

Syntax

```
=XLOOKUP(lookup_value, lookup_array, return_array, [if_not_found], [match_mode], [search_mode])
```

- **lookup_value**: The value to search for.
- **lookup_array**: The range or array to search within.
- **return_array**: The range or array containing the values to return.
- **[if_not_found]** *(optional)*: The value to return if lookup_value is not found. If omitted, the function returns an error (#N/A).
- **[match_mode]** *(optional)*: Specifies the type of match:
  - 0: Exact match (default); -1: Exact match or next smaller item; 1: Exact match or next larger item; 2: Wildcard match (supports ? for single characters and * for multiple characters).
- **[search_mode]** *(optional)*: Specifies the search direction:
  - 1: Search from first to last (default); -1: Search from last to first; 2: Binary search (ascending order); 2: Binary search (descending order).

Worked Example

Challenge: Look up the price of "Apple" from a product table.

Formula:

```
=XLOOKUP("Apple", A2:A4, B2:B4)
```

	A	B	C	D	E	F
1	**Product**	**Price**		**Example**		
2	Apple	1.5		=XLOOKUP("Apple", A2:A4, B2:B4)		
3	Banana	0.75		**Answer**		
4	Cherry	2		1.5		
5						

Result: 1.50

Explanation: The function searches for "Apple" in A1:A3 and returns the corresponding value from B1:B3.

Tips for Using XLOOKUP

- **Replacing VLOOKUP and HLOOKUP:** Unlike VLOOKUP, XLOOKUP can search both horizontally and vertically without requiring sorted data or specifying column numbers.

XMATCH Function

Lookup & Reference Functions

Introduction

The XMATCH function searches for a specified item in an array or range and returns its relative position. It is a more powerful and flexible replacement for the older MATCH function, supporting exact matches, approximate matches, and reverse searches.

- **Simple explanation:** Returns the position of a value in a range or array, with advanced options for matching and searching.
- **Common use cases:** Used for finding the position of values in lists or tables, performing dynamic lookups, and replacing MATCH in advanced lookup formulas.
- **When to use this function:** Use when you need to find the relative position of an item in an array or range with greater flexibility than MATCH.

Syntax

```
=XMATCH(lookup_value, lookup_array, [match_mode], [search_mode])
```

- **lookup_value**: The value to search for.
- **lookup_array**: The range or array to search within.
- **[match_mode]** *(optional)*: Specifies the type of match:
  - 0: Exact match (default); -1: Exact match or next smaller item; 1: Exact match or next larger item; 2: Wildcard match (supports ? for single characters and * for multiple characters).
- **[search_mode]** *(optional)*: Specifies the search direction:
  - 1: Search from first to last (default); -1: Search from last to first; 2: Binary search (ascending order); -2: Binary search (descending order).

Worked Example

Challenge: Find the position of "Banana" in a list of products.

Formula:

```
=XMATCH("Banana", A1:A3)
```

Result: 2
Explanation: The function searches for "Banana" in the range A1:A3 and returns its position, which is 2.

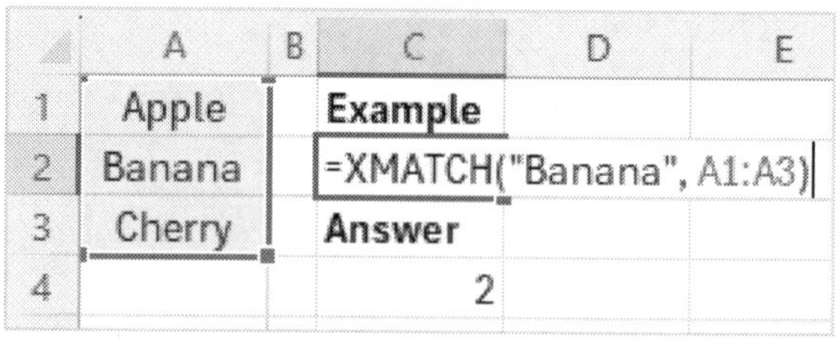

Tips for Using XMATCH

- **Wildcard matching:** Use match_mode = 2 to enable wildcard searches:

  ```
  =XMATCH("A*", A1:A10, 2)
  ```

  This returns the position of the first value that starts with "A".

- **Binary search:** Use search_mode = 2 or -2 for binary search when the data is sorted in ascending or descending order. Binary search improves performance for large data sets.

XNPV Function

Financial Functions

Introduction

The XNPV function returns the net present value (NPV) for a series of cash flows occurring at irregular intervals. It discounts each cash flow based on the exact date it occurs, providing a more accurate calculation than the regular NPV function, which assumes evenly spaced periods.

- **Simple explanation:** Computes the net present value of a series of cash flows with specific dates, using a given discount rate.
- **Common use cases:** Used in financial analysis to evaluate investments, cash flow projections, and project profitability when cash flows occur at irregular intervals.
- **When to use this function:** Use when calculating the NPV for cash flows with irregular dates or non-periodic intervals.

Syntax

```
=XNPV(rate, values, dates)
```

- **rate**: The discount rate to apply to the cash flows.
- **values**: A range or array of cash flows. The first value represents the initial investment and should typically be negative.
- **dates**: A range or array of dates corresponding to the cash flows. These dates must be in chronological order.

Worked Example

Challenge: Calculate the net present value of a set of cash flows at a discount rate of 10% per year.

Formula:

```
=XNPV(0.1, B1:B4, A1:A4)
```

Result: 137.89
Explanation: The function discounts each cash flow based on its date and sums them to calculate the net present value, resulting in an NPV of 137.89.

	A	B	C	D	E
1	Date	Cash Flow		Example	
2	01-Jan-24	-1000		=XNPV(0.1, B2:B5, A2:A5)	
3	01-Mar-24	300		Answer	
4	01-Jun-24	400		137.89	
5	01-Dec-24	500			

Tips for Using XNPV

- **Chronological order:** Ensure that the dates array is in chronological order. If the dates are not properly ordered, the function returns a #NUM! error.
- **Units of rate:** The rate should match the units of time between dates. For example, if the cash flows are annual, use an annual discount rate. If they are monthly, convert the annual rate to a monthly rate.

XOR Function

Logical Functions

Introduction

The XOR function returns a logical TRUE or FALSE based on exclusive logical operations. It performs an "exclusive OR" operation, meaning it returns TRUE if an odd number of logical expressions evaluate to TRUE, and FALSE if an even number of them are TRUE.

- **Simple explanation:** Returns TRUE if an odd number of arguments are TRUE, otherwise returns FALSE.
- **Common use cases:** Used in conditional logic, data validation, and decision-making models where exclusive conditions must be met.
- **When to use this function:** Use when you need to evaluate multiple conditions and ensure only an odd number of them are true for a TRUE result.

Syntax

```
=XOR(logical1, [logical2], ...)
```

- **logical1, [logical2], ...:** One or more logical expressions that evaluate to TRUE or FALSE. You can provide up to 254 logical arguments.

Worked Example

Challenge: Check if exactly one of two given conditions is true.

Formula:

```
=XOR(A1, B1)
```

Result: TRUE
Explanation: Since only one of the two conditions is TRUE, the function returns TRUE.

	A	B	C	D
1	TRUE	FALSE		**Example**
2				=XOR(A1, B1)
3				**Answer**
4				TRUE

Explore Further with GPT

Ask GPT how to use XOR with functions like AND, OR, or NOT to build complex logical expressions and data validation rules.

Tips for Using XOR

- **Odd/even logic:** The XOR function returns TRUE when the number of TRUE values in the arguments is odd and FALSE when the number is even.
- **Combining with IF:** Use XOR within an IF statement to return custom results:

  ```
  =IF(XOR(A1, B1), "Exclusive TRUE", "Exclusive FALSE")
  ```

  This returns "Exclusive TRUE" if an odd number of arguments are TRUE.
- **Error handling:** Ensure that all arguments are logical expressions or values that can be coerced into logical values (TRUE/FALSE). Non-logical inputs may cause errors.

YEAR Function

Date & Time Functions

Introduction

The YEAR function returns the year from a given date as a four-digit number. It is useful for extracting the year component from a date value for reporting, filtering, or analysis.

- **Simple explanation:** Extracts the year from a date.
- **Common use cases:** Used in financial analysis, reporting, and organizing data by year.
- **When to use this function:** Use when you need to isolate the year from a date or calculate year-based metrics.

Syntax

```
=YEAR(serial_number)
```

- **serial_number**: A valid Excel date from which to extract the year. This can be a date entered directly, a cell reference, or a formula that returns a date.

Worked Example

Challenge: Extract the year from the date 15-Mar-2024.

Formula:

```
=YEAR(DATE(2024, 3, 15))
```

Result: 2024
Explanation: The function extracts 2024 as the year from the specified date.

	A	B	C
1	**Example**		
2	=YEAR(DATE(2024, 3, 15))		
3	**Answer**		
4	2024		

Explore Further with GPT

Ask GPT how to combine YEAR with functions like DATE, MONTH, TEXT, or EOMONTH for advanced date manipulation and dynamic reporting.

Tips for Using YEAR

- **Combining with DATE:** Use YEAR with DATE to reconstruct a date with a modified year:

  ```
  =DATE(YEAR(A1) + 1, MONTH(A1), DAY(A1))
  ```

  This adds one year to the date in A1.

- **Text-based dates:** If dates are stored as text, use DATEVALUE to convert them to proper Excel dates before applying YEAR:

  ```
  =YEAR(DATEVALUE(A1))
  ```

YEARFRAC Function

Date & Time Functions

Introduction

The YEARFRAC function returns the fraction of the year between two dates. It is useful for calculating the proportion of a year between two dates, commonly used in financial calculations such as interest accrual and bond yields.

- **Simple explanation:** Computes the fraction of the year between two dates.
- **Common use cases:** Used in financial modeling, loan amortization schedules, and accrual calculations.
- **When to use this function:** Use when calculating time-based metrics that require a fractional year representation.

Syntax

```
=YEARFRAC(start_date, end_date, [basis])
```

- **start_date**: The starting date of the period.
- **end_date**: The ending date of the period.
- **[basis]** *(optional)*: Specifies the day count basis to use:
  - 0 or omitted: US (NASD) 30/360 (assumes 30-day months and 360-day years).
  - 1: Actual/actual (uses actual days between dates).
  - 2: Actual/360 (uses actual days but assumes a 360-day year).
  - 3: Actual/365 (uses actual days but assumes a 365-day year).
  - 4: European 30/360 (assumes 30-day months and 360-day years, European method).

Worked Example

Challenge: Calculate the fraction of the year between 01-Jan-2024 and 30-Jun-2024 using the actual/actual basis.

Formula:

```
=YEARFRAC(DATE(2024,1,1), DATE(2024,6,30), 1)
```

Result: 0.4945

	A	B	C	D	E
1	**Example**				
2	=YEARFRAC(DATE(2024,1,1), DATE(2024,6,30), 1)				
3	**Answer**				
4	0.4945				
5					

Explanation: The function calculates the exact fraction of the year between the two dates using the actual number of days.

Tips for Using YEARFRAC

- **Selecting the correct basis:** Choose the appropriate basis based on your financial or business requirements: Use 0 or 4 for bond and securities calculations, use 1 for precise day counts (e.g., loan interest), use 2 or 3 for accounting purposes.

YIELD Function

Financial Functions

Introduction

The YIELD function calculates the annual yield of a security that pays periodic interest, such as a bond. The yield represents the return an investor can expect based on the bond's price, coupon rate, and time to maturity.

- **Simple explanation:** Computes the annual yield of a bond that pays interest periodically.
- **Common use cases:** Used in bond valuation, investment analysis, and financial modeling to determine the effective return on fixed-income securities.
- **When to use this function:** Use when evaluating bonds or other securities with periodic coupon payments to find the annual yield.

Syntax

```
=YIELD(settlement, maturity, rate, pr, redemption, frequency, [basis])
```

- **settlement**: The settlement date of the bond (the date the investor buys the bond).
- **maturity**: The maturity date of the bond (the date when the bond expires and the principal is repaid).
- **rate**: The annual coupon rate of the bond.
- **pr**: The price of the bond per $100 face value.
- **redemption**: The redemption value per $100 face value (typically 100).
- **frequency**: The number of coupon payments per year:
  - 1: Annual; 2: Semiannual; 4: Quarterly
- **[basis]** *(optional)*: Specifies the day count basis:
  - 0 or omitted: US (NASD) 30/360; 1: Actual/actual; 2: Actual/360; 3: Actual/365; 4: European 30/360

Worked Example

Challenge: Calculate the annual yield of a bond with the following details:

- Settlement date: 01-Jan-2024; Maturity date: 01-Jan-2029; Annual coupon rate: 5%; Price: 95; Redemption value: 100; Semiannual payments

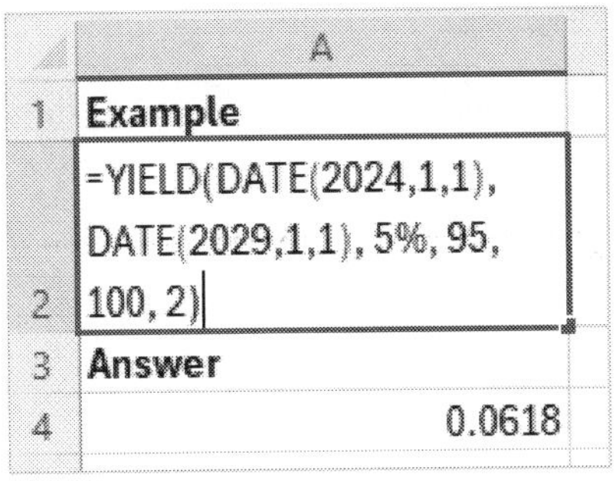

Formula:

```
=YIELD(DATE(2024,1,1), DATE(2029,1,1), 5%, 95, 100, 2)
```

Result: 0.0618 (or 6.18%)

Explore Further with GPT

Ask GPT how to use YIELD with functions like PRICE, DURATION, or YIELDDISC to build comprehensive bond valuation models.

YIELDDISC Function

Financial Functions

Introduction

The YIELDDISC function returns the annual yield of a discounted (zero-coupon) security. Unlike bonds that pay periodic interest, a discounted security is purchased at a price lower than its face value and pays no periodic interest. The yield is calculated based on the difference between the purchase price and the redemption value.

- **Simple explanation:** Computes the annual yield of a zero-coupon (discounted) security.
- **Common use cases:** Used in financial analysis to evaluate treasury bills, zero-coupon bonds, and other discounted securities.
- **When to use this function:** Use when determining the yield of a security purchased at a discount that does not pay periodic interest.

Syntax

```
=YIELDDISC(settlement, maturity, pr, redemption, [basis])
```

- **settlement**: The settlement date of the security (the date the investor buys the security).
- **maturity**: The maturity date of the security (the date when the security matures and the face value is repaid).
- **pr**: The price of the security per $100 face value.
- **redemption**: The redemption value per $100 face value (typically 100).
- **[basis]** *(optional)*: Specifies the day count basis:
  - 0 or omitted: US (NASD) 30/360; 1: Actual/actual; 2: Actual/360; 3: Actual/365; 4: European 30/360

Worked Example

Challenge: Calculate the yield of a discounted security with the following details:

- Settlement date: 01-Jan-2024; Maturity date: 01-Jun-2024; Price: 95; Redemption value: 100

Formula:

```
=YIELDDISC(DATE(2024,1,1), DATE(2024,6,1), 95, 100)
```

Result: 0.1263 (or 12.63%)

Explanation: The function computes an annual yield of 12.63%, accounting for the difference between the purchase price (95) and the redemption value (100).

	A	B	C	D	E
1	**Example**				
2	=YIELDDISC(DATE(2024,1,1), DATE(2024,6,1), 95, 100)				
3	**Answer**				
4	0.1263				

Tips for Using YIELDDISC

- **Settlement and maturity dates:** Ensure that settlement is before maturity and both are valid Excel dates.
- **Price and redemption:** Both should be expressed as values per $100 face value.

YIELDMAT Function

Financial Functions

Introduction

The YIELDMAT function returns the annual yield of a security that pays interest at maturity. Unlike securities that pay periodic interest (like bonds), this function calculates the yield for securities where interest is paid in a lump sum on the maturity date.

- **Simple explanation:** Computes the annual yield for a security that pays interest only at maturity.
- **Common use cases:** Used for evaluating treasury bills, zero-coupon bonds, and other lump-sum interest-paying securities.
- **When to use this function:** Use when calculating the yield for securities that do not have periodic interest payments and pay interest in a single payment at maturity.

Syntax

```
=YIELDMAT(settlement, maturity, issue, rate, pr, [basis])
```

- **settlement**: The settlement date of the security (the date the investor buys the security).
- **maturity**: The maturity date of the security (the date when the security matures and the principal is repaid).
- **issue**: The issue date of the security (the date the security was originally issued).
- **rate**: The annual coupon rate of the security.
- **pr**: The price of the security per $100 face value.
- **[basis]** *(optional)*: Specifies the day count basis:
    - 0 or omitted: US (NASD) 30/360; 1: Actual/actual; 2: Actual/360; 3: Actual/365; 4: European 30/360

Worked Example

Challenge: Calculate the yield of a security with the following details:

- Issue date: 01-Jan-2024; Settlement date: 01-Mar-2024; Maturity date: 01-Jan-2025; Annual coupon rate: 5%; Price: 95

Formula:

```
=YIELDMAT(DATE(2024,3,1), DATE(2025,1,1),
DATE(2024,1,1), 5%, 95)
```

	A
1	**Example**
2	=YIELDMAT(DATE(2024,3,1), DATE(2025,1,1), DATE(2024,1,1), 5%, 95)
3	**Answer**
4	0.1148
5	

Result: 0.1148 (or 11.48%)
Explanation: The function computes an annual yield of 11.48%, considering the lump-sum interest payment at maturity and the purchase price of 95.

Tips for Using YIELDMAT

- **Dates:** Ensure that settlement, maturity, and issue are valid Excel dates. The function returns a #NUM! error if settlement is not between issue and maturity.

Z.TEST Function

Statistical Functions

Introduction

The Z.TEST function returns the one-tailed probability value of a z-test, which is used to test the hypothesis that a sample mean is equal to a population mean. It is commonly used in hypothesis testing to determine how likely it is that an observed sample mean comes from a population with a specified mean.

- **Simple explanation:** Computes the p-value for a z-test, which helps determine whether a sample mean is significantly different from a hypothesized population mean.
- **Common use cases:** Used in hypothesis testing, quality control, and statistical analysis to assess deviations from expected values.
- **When to use this function:** Use when performing a z-test for a sample with a known or hypothesized population mean.

Syntax

```
=Z.TEST(array, x, [sigma])
```

- **array**: The range or array of sample data.
- **x**: The hypothesized population mean.
- **[sigma]** *(optional)*: The population standard deviation. If omitted, Excel uses the sample standard deviation.

Worked Example

Challenge: Perform a z-test to determine if the sample {10, 12, 14, 16, 18} has a mean significantly different from 15, assuming a population standard deviation of 3.

Formula:

```
=Z.TEST(A1:A5, 15, 3)
```

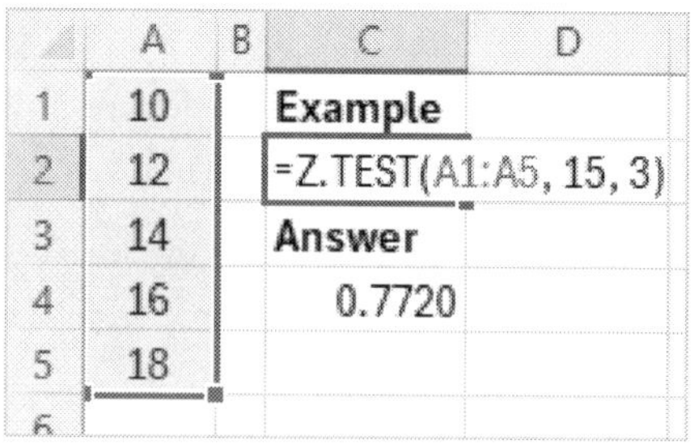

	A	B	C	D
1	10		Example	
2	12		=Z.TEST(A1:A5, 15, 3)	
3	14		Answer	
4	16		0.7720	
5	18			
6				

Result: 0.7720
Explanation: The function returns a p-value of 0.7720. Since the p-value is greater than the common significance level of 0.05, we fail to reject the null hypothesis, meaning there is no significant difference between the sample mean and 15.

Explore Further with GPT

Ask GPT how to combine Z.TEST with functions like NORM.DIST, AVERAGE, or STDEV for advanced hypothesis testing and statistical modeling.

Tips for Using Z.TEST

- **One-tailed vs. two-tailed:** The Z.TEST function returns a one-tailed p-value. To obtain a two-tailed p-value, multiply the result by 2:

  ```
  =2 * Z.TEST(A1:A5, 15, 3)
  ```

ZTEST Function

Compatibility Functions

Introduction

The ZTEST function returns the one-tailed probability value of a z-test, similar to Z.TEST. It is maintained for compatibility with older versions of Excel. This function helps assess whether a sample mean is significantly different from a specified population mean.

Note: In newer versions of Excel, ZTEST has been replaced by Z.TEST, but it remains available for backward compatibility.

- **Simple explanation:** Computes the p-value for a one-tailed z-test to determine how likely it is that the observed sample mean comes from a population with a specified mean.
- **Common use cases:** Used in hypothesis testing and quality control to evaluate deviations from expected values.
- **When to use this function:** Use when performing a z-test in older versions of Excel or for backward compatibility.

Syntax

```
=ZTEST(array, x, [sigma])
```

- **array**: The range or array of sample data.
- **x**: The hypothesized population mean.
- **[sigma]** *(optional)*: The population standard deviation. If omitted, Excel uses the sample standard deviation.

Worked Example

Challenge: Perform a z-test to determine if the sample {10, 12, 14, 16, 18} has a mean significantly different from 15, assuming a population standard deviation of 3.

Formula:

```
=ZTEST(A1:A5, 15, 3)
```

Result: 0.7720

Explanation: The function returns a p-value of 0.7720. Since the p-value is greater than 0.05, we fail to reject the null hypothesis, meaning there is no significant difference between the sample mean and the hypothesized mean of 15.

	A	B	C	D
1	10		**Example**	
2	12		=ZTEST(A1:A5, 15, 3)	
3	14		**Answer**	
4	16		0.7720	
5	18			
6				

Tips for Using ZTEST

- **Backward compatibility:** Use ZTEST in older Excel versions where Z.TEST is not available. In newer versions, Z.TEST is preferred for clarity and consistency.
- **Error handling:** Ensure that the array contains only numeric values. If it contains non-numeric values, the function returns a #VALUE! error.

Section 4: Appendices

Appendix 1: Advanced Tips & Tricks Using an AI Companion

Excel's advanced features are most powerful when paired with the dynamic assistance of your AI Companion. This section provides a series of prompts to guide your exploration of advanced Excel techniques. Use these examples to enhance your workflows, troubleshoot complex scenarios, or discover new ways to leverage formulas.

Combining/Nesting Multiple Formulas

ChatGPT can help you create powerful combinations of formulas for complex tasks. Try these prompts:

- "How can I combine IF, AND, and SUMIF to analyze sales data?"
- "Can you show me how to nest INDEX and MATCH for a dynamic lookup?"
- "What's the best way to combine TEXT, TRIM, and CONCAT for formatting names?"

Integrating Formulas with Other Tools

Enhance your Excel work by integrating formulas with Power Query, VBA, or external tools:

- **Power Query Integration:**
    - "How do I combine Power Query transformations with XLOOKUP in Excel?"
    - "Can you explain how to clean data in Power Query and summarize it with formulas?"
- **VBA Automation:**
    - "Write a VBA macro that applies a formula to an entire column in Excel."
    - "How can I use VBA to automate conditional formatting based on a formula?"
- **External Data Connections:**
    - "How can I use WEBSERVICE to retrieve data from an API and process it with Excel formulas?"

Exploring Dynamic Arrays and Advanced Use Cases

Dynamic arrays open the door to adaptable and efficient models. Use these prompts to explore their potential:

- "What are the best use cases for FILTER, UNIQUE, and SORT together?"
- "Can you build a dynamic model using SEQUENCE to create a calendar layout?"
- "How can I use ARRAYFORMULA concepts in Excel for automatic updates?"

Custom Dashboards and Visualization

Integrate formulas into dashboards for real-time insights:

- "How can I use TEXT and IF functions to create dynamic chart labels?"
- "What's the best way to combine slicers and FILTER for a dashboard?"
- "Can you suggest formulas for creating progress bars in Excel using conditional formatting?"

Formulating New Approaches

Experiment with creative uses of Excel:

- "What are some unconventional ways to use RANDARRAY in Excel models?"
- "Can you generate a dataset of random but realistic sales figures using Excel formulas?"
- "How do I design a scoring system for a survey using nested formulas?"

How to Use These Prompts

Simply enter these or similar questions into your AI Companion and watch it generate tailored examples, explanations, and even step-by-step guides to meet your needs. The more specific your query, the more targeted the solution will be.

Appendix 2: Troubleshooting Guide with an AI Companion

Excel errors can be frustrating, but they are often opportunities to learn and refine your formulas. This troubleshooting guide equips you with strategies to handle common errors while encouraging you to leverage your AI Companion for personalized, step-by-step assistance.

Common Errors and Solutions

While many errors are addressed in the formula pages, here are some common challenges and how your AI Companion can help resolve them:

- **#DIV/0!: Division by Zero**
  - **Cause:** A formula attempts to divide by zero or an empty cell.
  - **Solution:** Use IF or IFERROR to handle cases where the denominator is zero.
    - Example: =IF(B1=0, "N/A", A1/B1)
  - **Ask AI:**
    - "How do I create a formula to avoid #DIV/0! errors while dividing two columns?"
- **#VALUE!: Incorrect Data Type**
  - **Cause:** The formula references incompatible data types, such as adding text to numbers.
  - **Solution:** Use ISNUMBER or ISTEXT to validate inputs before performing calculations.
    - Example: =IF(ISNUMBER(A1), A1*2, "Invalid Input")
  - **Ask AI:**
    - "How can I troubleshoot a #VALUE! error in a formula with mixed data types?"
- **#N/A: No Match Found**
  - **Cause:** Lookup functions like VLOOKUP or XLOOKUP fail to find a match.
  - **Solution:** Ensure lookup values and ranges are correct. Use IFERROR to return custom messages.
    - Example: =IFERROR(VLOOKUP(A1, B1:C10, 2, FALSE), "Not Found")
  - **Ask AI:**
    - "What are the best practices to troubleshoot #N/A errors in lookup formulas?"
- **#REF!: Invalid Reference**
  - **Cause:** A formula references a deleted or invalid cell/range.
  - **Solution:** Check formulas for broken links and restore missing references where possible.
  - **Ask AI:**
    - "How do I fix a #REF! error caused by deleted rows or columns?"

Error-Handling Techniques for Advanced Scenarios

Advanced workflows often involve dynamic or complex formulas, increasing the potential for errors. Here's how to handle them effectively:

- **Dynamic Arrays and Spill Errors (#SPILL!):**
  - **Cause:** A formula's output overlaps with existing data.
  - **Solution:** Clear cells in the spill range or adjust the formula to avoid conflicts.
  - **Ask AI:**
    - "How can I troubleshoot #SPILL! errors in Excel formulas?"
- **Circular References:**
  - **Cause:** A formula refers back to its own cell, creating an infinite loop.
  - **Solution:** Use iterative calculations or rework your formula logic.
  - **Ask AI:**
    - "What strategies can I use to resolve circular references in complex Excel models?"
- **Error Checking in Nested Formulas:**
  - Use IFERROR or ISERROR to handle potential errors gracefully.
    - Example: =IFERROR(A1/B1, "Error: Division Issue")
  - **Ask AI:**
    - "How do I nest error-checking functions into a larger formula?"
- **Custom Error Messages for Dashboards:**
  - Use conditional logic to display user-friendly error messages.
  - Example: =IF(A1>100, "Valid", "Error: Value Exceeds Limit")
  - **Ask AI:**
    - "Can you help me create dynamic error messages for an Excel dashboard?"

How to Use This Guide

This troubleshooting guide provides foundational solutions for common errors, but your AI Companion offers dynamic support tailored to your specific challenges. When you encounter a problem:

1. Describe your issue in detail, including the formula and data structure.
2. Ask targeted questions, such as:
   - "Why does my formula return #VALUE! when referencing multiple columns?"
   - "How can I fix a lookup formula that isn't finding matches?"

The combination of this guide and your AI Companion ensures you have the tools to resolve any Excel issue efficiently and effectively.

Appendix 3: Shortcut Keys for Windows and Mac

Mastering shortcut keys in Excel can significantly boost your productivity. This cheat sheet highlights essential keyboard shortcuts for both Windows and Mac, helping you navigate, format, and analyze data with speed and efficiency.

General Shortcuts

Action	Windows Shortcut	Mac Shortcut
Save Workbook	**Ctrl + S**	**Command + S**
Open Workbook	**Ctrl + O**	**Command + O**
Close Workbook	**Ctrl + W**	**Command + W**
Undo	**Ctrl + Z**	**Command + Z**
Redo	**Ctrl + Y**	**Command + Y**
Copy	**Ctrl + C**	**Command + C**
Cut	**Ctrl + X**	**Command + X**
Paste	**Ctrl + V**	**Command + V**
Select All	**Ctrl + A**	**Command + A**
Find	**Ctrl + F**	**Command + F**
Replace	**Ctrl + H**	**Command + H**

Navigation Shortcuts

Action	Windows Shortcut	Mac Shortcut
Move to Next Cell	**Tab**	**Tab**
Move to Previous Cell	**Shift + Tab**	**Shift + Tab**
Go to Beginning of Row	**Home**	**Fn + Left Arrow**
Go to End of Row	**End**	**Fn + Right Arrow**
Move to Beginning of Worksheet	**Ctrl + Home**	**Command + Up Arrow**
Move to End of Worksheet	**Ctrl + End**	**Command + Down Arrow**

Formatting Shortcuts

Action	Windows Shortcut	Mac Shortcut
Bold	**Ctrl + B**	**Command + B**
Italic	**Ctrl + I**	**Command + I**
Underline	**Ctrl + U**	**Command + U**
Open Format Cells Dialog	**Ctrl + 1**	**Command + 1**
Apply Currency Format	**Ctrl + Shift + $**	**Command + Shift + $**
Apply Percent Format	**Ctrl + Shift + %**	**Command + Shift + %**
Apply General Format	**Ctrl + Shift + ~**	**Command + Shift + ~**

Data and Formula Shortcuts

Action	Windows Shortcut	Mac Shortcut
Enter Current Date	**Ctrl + ;**	**Command + ;**
Enter Current Time	**Ctrl + Shift + :**	**Command + Shift + :**
Show Formulas	**Ctrl + `**	**Command + `**
Calculate Workbook	**F9**	**Fn + F9**
Toggle Absolute/Relative Reference	**F4**	**Command + T**
Insert Function	**Shift + F3**	**Shift + F3**

How to Use This Cheat Sheet

Print or bookmark this cheat sheet for quick reference while working in Excel. To further personalize your workflow, ask your AI Companion:

- "Can you recommend shortcuts for navigating large datasets in Excel?"
- "What are the best shortcuts for applying conditional formatting quickly?"
- "How can I create custom keyboard shortcuts for Excel actions?"
- "What are the best shortcuts for quickly jumping between worksheets?"
- "How can I navigate to the last used cell in a worksheet with a shortcut?"
- "Is there a shortcut to instantly format a table as a predefined style?"

With these shortcuts and AI support, you'll master Excel's interface in no time!

Glossary

This glossary serves as a quick reference for key Excel concepts and terms. For more specific explanations or personalized examples, consult your AI Companion to dive deeper into any term or topic.

Glossary of Terms

A

- **Absolute Reference:** A cell reference that remains constant when copied, denoted with dollar signs (e.g., $A$1).
- **Active Cell:** The currently selected cell in a worksheet, highlighted with a border.
- **Array:** A collection of values arranged in rows and columns, used in calculations or returned by array formulas.
- **Array Formula:** A formula that performs multiple calculations on a range or array of values.
- **AutoFill:** A feature to automatically fill cells with data based on a pattern or adjacent values.
- **AutoFilter:** A tool to filter data in a range or table based on criteria.

B

- **Bar Chart:** A chart that uses rectangular bars to represent data values.
- **Binary Number System:** A base-2 numeral system used in Excel functions like BIN2DEC.
- **Book:** Another term for an Excel workbook.

C

- **Cell:** The intersection of a row and column where data or formulas are entered, identified by a unique address (e.g., A1).
- **Cell Reference:** The identification of a cell or range in a formula (e.g., A1:A10).
- **Chart:** A visual representation of data, including line, bar, and pie charts.
- **Circular Reference:** A formula that refers to its own cell, directly or indirectly.
- **Column:** A vertical group of cells in a worksheet, labeled with letters (A, B, C, etc.).

D

- **Data Validation:** A feature to restrict or control the type of data entered into a cell.
- **Delimiter:** A character, such as a comma or tab, used to separate data elements.
- **Dynamic Array:** An array that automatically expands or contracts based on the source data.

E

- **Error Bars:** Visual indicators in charts that show variability or uncertainty in data points.
- **Error Code:** A message returned when Excel encounters an issue, such as #VALUE! or #DIV/0!.
- **External Data Source:** Data imported from an external system, such as an SQL database or API.

F

- **Fill Handle:** A small square at the bottom-right corner of a cell, used to copy or extend data.
- **Flash Fill:** A tool that automatically completes data patterns based on examples.
- **Formula:** An expression that performs calculations or operations, starting with = (e.g., =A1+B1).
- **Formula Auditing:** Tools to trace and evaluate formulas for errors or relationships.
- **Freeze Panes:** A feature to lock rows or columns in place while scrolling.

G

- **Goal Seek:** A tool to find the input value needed to achieve a specific result in a formula.
- **Gridlines:** Light lines that separate cells, which can be toggled on or off for printing or display.

H

- **Header Row:** The first row of a table containing column titles.
- **Histogram:** A chart that shows the frequency distribution of a dataset.

I

- **Indentation:** Adjusting text alignment within a cell for hierarchy or emphasis.
- **Index/Match:** A powerful combination of functions used for flexible lookups in Excel.
- **Iterative Calculation:** A method Excel uses to repeatedly calculate a formula until a specific condition is met.

K

- **Keyboard Shortcuts:** Key combinations to perform actions quickly without using the mouse.

L

- **Line Chart:** A chart type that connects data points with lines to show trends.
- **Linked Workbook:** A workbook that references data from another workbook.

M

- **Macro:** A sequence of commands or code to automate repetitive tasks in Excel.
- **Mixed Reference:** A cell reference that is partially absolute and partially relative (e.g., $A1 or A$1).

N

- **Named Range:** A user-defined name for a cell or range to simplify references in formulas.
- **Normalization:** Adjusting values to a common scale for comparison or analysis.

P

- **Pivot Chart:** A dynamic chart linked to a PivotTable, enabling interactive data exploration.
- **PivotTable:** A tool for summarizing, analyzing, and presenting large datasets in a dynamic format.
- **Protect Workbook:** A feature to restrict editing or access to a workbook.

R

- **Relative Reference:** A cell reference that adjusts based on the position of the formula when copied.
- **Ribbon:** The toolbar at the top of Excel containing commands organized into tabs.
- **Row:** A horizontal group of cells in a worksheet, labeled with numbers.

S

- **Scatter Plot:** A chart that uses points to represent data relationships between two variables.
- **Solver:** An advanced tool for optimization problems, finding solutions based on constraints.
- **Spill Range:** The range of cells automatically populated by a dynamic array formula.

T

- **Table:** A structured range of data with built-in formatting, sorting, and filtering options.
- **Template:** A pre-designed workbook used as a starting point for new workbooks.
- **Transpose:** A function or feature that switches rows and columns in a dataset.

U

- **Undo/Redo:** Commands to reverse or repeat recent actions.
- **User-Defined Function (UDF):** A custom formula created using VBA.

V

- **Validation List:** A drop-down list created with data validation to restrict inputs.
- **Visual Basic for Applications (VBA):** A programming language for automating Excel tasks.

W

- **Workbook:** An Excel file containing one or more worksheets.
- **Worksheet:** A single spreadsheet within a workbook.

X

- **XML (eXtensible Markup Language):** A structured data format often used for importing or exporting data in Excel.

Z

- **Zoom:** A feature to adjust the magnification of a worksheet for easier viewing.

Formula Category Index

This index presents the page numbers for each formula reference page by category to help you find what you are looking for.

Logical Functions	
AND Function	64
BYCOL Function	101
BYROW Function	102
FALSE Function	215
IF Function	267
IFERROR Function	268
IFNA Function	269
IFS Function	270
LAMBDA Function	322
LET Function	327
MAKEARRAY Function	339
MAP Function	340
NOT Function	379
OR Function	393
REDUCE Function	431
SCAN Function	445
SWITCH Function	485
TRUE Function	515
XOR Function	548
Lookup & Reference Functions	
ADDRESS Function	61
AREAS Function	66
CHOOSE Function	117
CHOOSECOLS Function	118
CHOOSEROWS Function	119
COLUMN Function	122
COLUMNS Function	123
DROP Function	191

EXPAND Function	210
FILTER Function	219
FORMULATEXT Function	238
GETPIVOTDATA Function	255
HLOOKUP Function	261
HSTACK Function	263
HYPERLINK Function	264
IMAGE Function	272
INDEX Function	297
INDIRECT Function	298
LOOKUP Function	337
MATCH Function	341
OFFSET Function	392
ROW Function	440
ROWS Function	441
RTD Function	444
SORT Function	462
SORTBY Function	463
TAKE Function	490
TOCOL Function	508
TOROW Function	509
TRANSPOSE Function	511
UNIQUE Function	522
VLOOKUP Function	533
VSTACK Function	534
WRAPCOLS Function	542
WRAPROWS Function	543
XLOOKUP Function	545
XMATCH Function	546
Text Functions	
ARRAYTOTEXT Function	67
ASC Function	68
BAHTTEXT Function	79
CHAR Function	108
CLEAN Function	120
CODE Function	121

CONCAT Function	127
DBCS Function	172
DOLLAR Function	187
EXACT Function	208
FIND Function	221
FINDB Function	222
FIXED Function	228
LEFT Function	325
LEN Function	326
LOWER Function	338
MID Function	348
NUMBERVALUE Function	383
PROPER Function	416
REPLACE Function	433
REPT Function	434
RIGHT Function	435
SEARCH Function	446
SUBSTITUTE Function	475
T Function	487
TEXT Function	498
TEXTAFTER Function	499
TEXTBEFORE Function	500
TEXTJOIN Function	501
TEXTSPLIT Function	502
TRIM Function	513
UNICHAR Function	520
UNICODE Function	521
UPPER Function	523
VALUE Function	524
VALUETOTEXT Function	525
CONCATENATE Function	128
Math & Trigonometry Functions	
ABS Function	53
ACOS Function	56
ACOSH Function	57
ACOT Function	58

ACOTH Function	59
AGGREGATE Function	60
ARABIC Function	65
ASIN Function	69
ASINH Function	70
ATAN Function	71
ATAN2 Function	72
ATANH Function	73
BASE Function	80
CEILING.MATH Function	105
CEILING.PRECISE Function	106
COMBIN Function	124
COMBINA Function	125
COS Function	134
COSH Function	135
COT Function	136
COTH Function	137
CSC Function	153
CSCH Function	154
DECIMAL Function	179
DEGREES Function	180
EVEN Function	207
EXP Function	209
FACT Function	213
FACTDOUBLE Function	214
FLOOR.MATH Function	230
FLOOR.PRECISE Function	231
GCD Function	252
INT Function	300
ISO.CEILING Function	318
LCM Function	324
LN Function	329
LOG Function	330
LOG10 Function	331
MDETERM Function	345
MINVERSE Function	353

MMULT Function	355
MOD Function	356
MROUND Function	361
MULTINOMIAL Function	362
MUNIT Function	363
ODD Function	387
PI Function	405
POWER Function	409
PRODUCT Function	415
QUOTIENT Function	421
RADIANS Function	422
RAND Function	423
RANDARRAY Function	424
RANDBETWEEN Function	425
ROMAN Function	436
ROUND Function	437
ROUNDDOWN Function	438
SEC Function	447
SECH Function	448
SEQUENCE Function	450
SERIESSUM Function	451
SIGN Function	454
SIN Function	455
SINH Function	456
SQRT Function	464
SQRTPI Function	465
SUBTOTAL Function	476
SUM Function	477
SUMIF Function	478
SUMIFS Function	479
SUMPRODUCT Function	480
SUMSQ Function	481
SUMX2MY2 Function	482
SUMX2PY2 Function	483
SUMXMY2 Function	484
TAN Function	488

TRUNC Function	516
ROUNDUP Function	439
TANH Function	489
Date & Time Functions	
DATE Function	164
DATEDIF Function	165
DATEVALUE Function	166
DAY Function	168
DAYS Function	169
DAYS360 Function	170
EDATE Function	198
EOMONTH Function	201
HOUR Function	262
ISOWEEKNUM Function	319
MINUTE Function	352
MONTH Function	360
NETWORKDAYS Function	368
NETWORKDAYS.INTL Function	369
NOW Function	380
SECOND Function	449
TIME Function	503
TIMEVALUE Function	504
TODAY Function	510
WEEKDAY Function	536
WEEKNUM Function	537
WORKDAY Function	540
WORKDAY.INTL Function	541
YEAR Function	549
YEARFRAC Function	550
Financial Functions	
ACCRINT Function	54
ACCRINTM Function	55
AMORDEGRC Function	62
AMORLINC Function	63
COUPDAYBS Function	143
COUPDAYS Function	144

COUPDAYSNC Function	145
COUPNCD Function	146
COUPNUM Function	147
COUPPCD Function	148
CUMIPMT Function	162
CUMPRINC Function	163
DB Function	171
DDB Function	175
DISC Function	184
DOLLARDE Function	188
DOLLARFR Function	189
DURATION Function	195
EFFECT Function	199
FV Function	242
FVSCHEDULE Function	243
INTRATE Function	302
IPMT Function	303
IRR Function	304
ISPMT Function	320
MDURATION Function	346
MIRR Function	354
NOMINAL Function	370
NPER Function	381
NPV Function	382
ODDFPRICE Function	388
ODDFYIELD Function	389
ODDLPRICE Function	390
ODDLYIELD Function	391
PDURATION Function	394
PMT Function	406
PPMT Function	410
PRICE Function	411
PRICEDISC Function	412
PRICEMAT Function	413
PV Function	417
RATE Function	429

RECEIVED Function	430
RRI Function	442
SLN Function	459
STOCKHISTORY Function	467
SYD Function	486
TBILLEQ Function	491
TBILLPRICE Function	492
TBILLYIELD Function	493
VDB Function	532
XIRR Function	544
XNPV Function	547
YIELD Function	551
YIELDDISC Function	552
YIELDMAT Function	553
Statistical Functions	
AVEDEV Function	74
AVERAGE Function	75
AVERAGEA Function	76
AVERAGEIF Function	77
AVERAGEIFS Function	78
BETA.DIST Function	86
BETA.INV Function	88
BINOM.DIST Function	93
BINOM.DIST.RANGE Function	94
BINOM.INV Function	95
CHISQ.DIST Function	112
CHISQ.DIST.RT Function	113
CHISQ.INV Function	114
CHISQ.INV.RT Function	115
CHISQ.TEST Function	116
CONFIDENCE.NORM Function	130
CONFIDENCE.T Function	131
CORREL Function	133
COUNT Function	138
COUNTA Function	139
COUNTBLANK Function	140

COUNTIF Function	141
COUNTIFS Function	142
COVARIANCE.P Function	150
COVARIANCE.S Function	151
DEVSQ Function	182
EXPON.DIST Function	211
F.DIST Function	216
F.DIST.RT Function	218
F.INV Function	223
F.INV.RT Function	224
F.TEST Function	240
FISHER Function	226
FISHERINV Function	227
FORECAST Function	232
FORECAST.ETS Function	233
FORECAST.ETS.CONFINT Function	234
FORECAST.ETS.SEASONALITY Function	235
FORECAST.ETS.STAT Function	236
FORECAST.LINEAR Function	237
FREQUENCY Function	239
GAMMA Function	244
GAMMA.DIST Function	245
GAMMA.INV Function	247
GAMMALN Function	249
GAMMALN.PRECISE Function	250
GAUSS Function	251
GEOMEAN Function	253
GROWTH Function	256
HARMEAN Function	257
HYPGEOM.DIST Function	265
INTERCEPT Function	301
KURT Function	321
LARGE Function	323
LINEST Function	328
LOGEST Function	332
LOGNORM.DIST Function	334

LOGNORM.INV Function	336
MAX Function	342
MAXA Function	343
MAXIFS Function	344
MEDIAN Function	347
MIN Function	349
MINA Function	351
MINIFS Function	350
MODE.MULT Function	358
MODE.SNGL Function	359
NEGBINOM.DIST Function	366
NORM.DIST Function	371
NORM.S.DIST Function	375
NORM.S.INV Function	377
NORMINV Function	373
PEARSON Function	395
PERCENTILE.EXC Function	396
PERCENTRANK.EXC Function	399
PERCENTRANK.INC Function	400
PERMUT Function	402
PERMUTATIONA Function	403
PHI Function	404
POISSON.DIST Function	407
PROB Function	414
QUARTILE.EXC Function	419
QUARTILE.INC Function	420
RANK.AVG Function	426
RANK.EQ Function	427
RSQ Function	443
SKEW Function	457
SKEW.P Function	458
SLOPE Function	460
SMALL Function	461
STANDARDIZE Function	466
STDEV.P Function	469
STDEV.S Function	470

STDEVA Function	471
STDEVPA Function	473
STEYX Function	474
T.DIST Function	494
T.DIST.2T Function	495
T.DIST.RT Function	496
T.INV Function	505
T.INV.2T Function	506
T.TEST Function	517
TREND Function	512
TRIMMEAN Function	514
VAR.P Function	527
VAR.S Function	528
VARA Function	529
VARPA Function	531
WEIBULL.DIST Function	539
Z.TEST Function	554
PERCENTILE.INC Function	397
Information Functions	
CELL Function	107
ERROR.TYPE Function	206
INFO Function	299
ISBLANK Function	305
ISERR Function	306
ISERROR Function	307
ISEVEN Function	308
ISFORMULA Function	309
ISLOGICAL Function	310
ISNA Function	311
ISNONTEXT Function	312
ISNUMBER Function	313
ISODD Function	314
ISOMITTED Function	315
ISREF Function	316
ISTEXT Function	317
N Function	364

NA Function	365
SHEET Function	452
SHEETS Function	453
TYPE Function	519
Database Functions	
DAVERAGE Function	167
DCOUNT Function	173
DCOUNTA Function	174
DGET Function	183
DMAX Function	185
DMIN Function	186
DPRODUCT Function	190
DSTDEV Function	192
DSTDEVP Function	193
DSUM Function	194
DVAR Function	196
DVARP Function	197
Cube Functions	
CUBEKPIMEMBER Function	155
CUBEMEMBER Function	156
CUBEMEMBERPROPERTY Function	157
CUBERANKEDMEMBER Function	158
CUBESET Function	159
CUBESETCOUNT Function	160
CUBEVALUE Function	161
Engineering Functions	
BESSELI Function	81
BESSELJ Function	82
BESSELK Function	83
BESSELY Function	84
BIN2DEC Function	89
BIN2HEX Function	90
BIN2OCT Function	91
BITAND Function	96
BITLSHIFT Function	97
BITOR Function	98

BITRSHIFT Function	99
BITXOR Function	100
COMPLEX Function	126
CONVERT Function	132
DEC2BIN Function	176
DEC2HEX Function	177
DEC2OCT Function	178
DELTA Function	181
ERF Function	202
ERF.PRECISE Function	203
ERFC Function	204
ERFC.PRECISE Function	205
GESTEP Function	254
HEX2BIN Function	258
HEX2DEC Function	259
HEX2OCT Function	260
IMABS Function	271
IMAGINARY Function	273
IMARGUMENT Function	274
IMCONJUGATE Function	275
IMCOS Function	276
IMCOSH Function	277
IMCOT Function	278
IMCSC Function	279
IMCSCH Function	280
IMDIV Function	281
IMEXP Function	282
IMLN Function	283
IMLOG10 Function	284
IMLOG2 Function	285
IMPOWER Function	286
IMPRODUCT Function	287
IMREAL Function	288
IMSEC Function	289
IMSECH Function	290
IMSIN Function	291

IMSINH Function	292
IMSQRT Function	293
IMSUB Function	294
IMSUM Function	295
IMTAN Function	296
OCT2BIN Function	384
OCT2DEC Function	385
OCT2HEX Function	386
Compatibility Functions	
BETADIST Function	85
BETAINV Function	87
BINOMDIST Function	92
CEILING Function	104
CHIDIST Function	109
CHIINV Function	110
CHITEST Function	111
CONFIDENCE Function	129
COVAR Function	149
CRITBINOM Function	152
EXPONDIST Function	212
FDIST Function	217
FINV Function	225
FLOOR Function	229
FTEST Function	241
GAMMADIST Function	246
GAMMAINV Function	248
HYPGEOMDIST Function	266
LOGINV Function	333
LOGNORMDIST Function	335
MODE Function	357
NEGBINOMDIST Function	367
NORM.INV Function	374
NORMDIST Function	372
NORMSDIST Function	376
NORMSINV Function	378
PERCENTILE Function	398

PERCENTRANK Function	401
POISSON Function	408
QUARTILE Function	418
RANK Function	428
STDEV Function	468
STDEVP Function	472
TDIST Function	497
TINV Function	507
TTEST Function	518
VAR Function	526
VARP Function	530
WEIBULL Function	538
ZTEST Function	555
Web Functions	
ENCODEURL Function	200
FILTERXML Function	220
WEBSERVICE Function	535
Add-in & Automation Functions	
CALL Function	103
REGISTER.ID Function	432

Made in United States
Orlando, FL
11 November 2026

90590422R00317